Roots of
Chicano Politics,
1600–1940

Roots of Chicano Politics, 1600-1940

JUAN GÓMEZ-QUIÑONES

UNIVERSITY OF NEW MEXICO PRESS
Albuquerque

Library of Congress Cataloging-in-Publication Data
Gómez-Quiñones, Juan.
   Roots of Chicano politics, 1600–1940 / Juan Gómez-Quiñones. — 1st ed.
      p.   cm.
   Includes bibliographical references and index.
   ISBN 0-8263-1471-6. — ISBN 0-8263-1431-7 (pbk.)
   1. Mexican Americans—Southwest, New—Politics and government.
   2. Mexican Americans—Southwest, New—Intellectual life.   I. Title.
F790.M5G65   1994
979'.0046872073—dc20   93-31940
                                                                                        CIP

First edition

Contents

Introduction

Continuously, from the nineteenth century to the end of the twentieth century, Mexican communities within the United States have presented a vivid illustration of one ethnic group's irreducible condition in the contemporary world.[1] In the United States today, the Mexican community, numbering several million, is a charter as well as an immigrant group, concentrated within a region and possessing a past as long and as rich as any ethnic population in the U.S.

This study emphasizes one aspect of that past—the political experience shaped by social change from the seventeenth-century origins of these people to the period of national and international change occasioned by World War II. The sources of this study include the voice of the participant in that history, with its insider perspective tempered by extensive familiarity with the historiography of the region as well as by the objectivity afforded by distance in time. Politics here interacts with social homage; transformation of the economy drives social change, with alterations in social relations as the result. Politics, then, is a response to such alterations. Specific concepts orient the narrative and the interpretation of politics: class, gender, ethnicity, governance, leadership role/status, ideology, force, and repression—all ideological devices useful in interpreting the expression of social change as politics and providing thematic threads running through the narrative.

The primary focus here is devoted to a reconstruction of the political history of the Mexican people in what is today the southwestern United States; like any political history, this one is also the result of an interpretation,[2] which in itself evolves from an interest in contributing to a more complex understanding of U.S. history as well as strengthen-ing the political memory of the Mexican American community. In effect, this study is a record related to the histories of both Mexico and the United States, for neither of these two "national histories" have provided the space in which to tell the story of this population. Such an enterprise requires maintaining a tenuous balance between appropriate detail, a logically salient pattern, and informative generalization. It is hoped the result is a reconstruction of history, both thematic and chronologically, wherein continuity and change will both be more clearly perceived.

A secondary intention here is to look at heterogenity or diversity among Mexicans as they relate to politics.[3] Certainly, Mexicans in the United States have experienced sentiments of pleasure or grief similar to those in other groups, with whom they probably will share a com-mon end in a distant future; but Mexican Americans have been and are distinct in history and in their social being. Mexicans in the U.S. are unique in several ways among all of the country's other ethnic groups, and within these "ways" are multiple diversities. Mexicans are native to the Americas; they originated in North America, not elsewhere. From its origins, this ethnicity was internally diverse; the "modern" Mexican American of today was forged in the crucible of the economic and social transformation of nations in the postfeudal, capitalist period of world development. Mexican Americans derive from one such multi-class, multiethnic nation in North America, Mexico—not from the Anglo-Germanic, European mix of the origins of dominant United States society or from East European, Asian, or African importations. The geographical spread of this social development is so wide it allows for regional and subregional developments within the broader com-monalities. Moreover, though they have not always been understood by outside observers, class distinctions have existed in practice and been understood within the Mexican American community for genera-tions. Moreover, the Mexican community has considerable variety in its sequential organizational and leadership expressions. The commu-nity is linked, in particular, to its transborder-lands origin. For a variety of reasons, relations with central Mexico are a significant part of the ongoing history.

To be sure, since the midnineteenth century the ethnic politics of Mexican Americans have been very distinguishable from those events and players in central Mexico; and the political programs emanating from and centering upon Mexico, particularly the insurgencies of the Mexican political process are distinct from the political priorities of Mexican Americans. The political ethnicity of the offshoot and the nationalist programs of the core country are quite different. For Mexican Americans the questions of appearance, language, religion, and other ethnic identifiers can be answered in general terms, but what is also notable is the insufficiency of such answers as single identifiers. What gives the Mexican American community cohesion is indeed its continuing historical development and its commitment to group survival, which is achieved in a broad panorama whose design is comprised of the commonalities of many particular parts, each with its own hue, its particular economy, government, and society.

A tertiary intention of this study is to look at ethnicity vis-à-vis Mexicans over a long historical period and to discern its relation to politics. For generations, Mexican American ethnicity was singular as well as part of a larger amalgam which, in turn, contains American identity.[4] Ethnicity and its maintenance are elusive but very real social phenomena. As a general sense of peoplehood, ethnicity develops over time through a conglomeration of experiences and rhythms expressing its ongoing synthesis. The historical, the structural, and the cultural are the woof and web in this process; power, wealth, and prestige affect the dye and cut. Consciousness and choice assume greater importance when there is more interaction across ethnic boundaries. Consciousness of identity and of membership in an ethnic community may be integral characteristics of ethnicity, but they also are private and public strategies and resources. When more consciously elaborated, they comprise an ideology, a point of view, a program for living or acting vis-à-vis the world, and a catalyst to shape the world's future. Ethnicity and ethnic relations are shaped predominantly by economics and politics, not by the ideas or sentiments that rationalize their existence.

Force, violence, and repression had much to do with the making of colonial Mexico, including its far northern communities; but so did the less dramatic means for ensuring production and order. The Indian and the mestizo were viewed in particular ways because of their lack of property; hence, their lack of political influence. But they also responded within this context. The Mexican was defined by North Americans as an enemy; then, to the extent possible, they were despoiled and categorized pejoratively, generating, in turn, the Mexican response. Since the civil rights movement, there has been a consider-

able interest in the history and social characteristics of ethnic groups in
the United States. Many of the identified ethnic groups do not possess
over time the cohesion or consistency that would encourage their study
beyond patterns of immigration and second-generation integration. In
any case, the study of ethnicity in the United States is markedly
incomplete without an appreciation of Mexican Americans.

Ethnicity has a variety of contextual origins, perceptions, and
resolutions.[5] To delineate its emergence in a particular ethnic experience entails not only making interpretive generalizations but establishing a sequential narration based on the empirical record available and
the general consistency extant in references. Pluralist societies, such as
colonial Mexico and the United States, are the result of multiple forms
of expansion and exploitation, to be sure, but they also represent
variant forms of synthesis. Political mechanisms and mechanisms of
repression are important in the evolution of a society.

When viewed with benign tolerance, ethnicity is an understandable historical and social expression, one with rituals that are supported
and applauded and with political claims that are permissible within
certain boundaries for certain satisfactions. Worldwide, ethnic groups
often have faced discrimination and repression that threaten their
survival. Survival is possible for a group when it is needed and when it
develops strategies for survival. Such a group expresses a belief in itself
and for itself, which grows out of the understanding of a common past,
present, and future.

Often proferred by students of ethnicity are certain sociological
phases to be observed in the tides of some minority groups associated
with larger societies.[6] One phase is the foundational one of early
beginnings, a terrain that many social scientists avoid. This phase
is gaining increasing importance among students of ethnicity, even
though any knowledge of such origins is empirically hazy for nearly all
ethnic groups. Next is the formative phase of a colonial or an intense
assault period when the group forms while it is in captivity and/or exists
in a state of subordination. Then comes the attempt to make an
autonomous political expression, to create, indeed, an exercise in
modern sovereignty, and possibly witnessing its interruption in the
group's annexation by another state, society, economy, and body poli-
tic. Eventually, what succeeds is either a process of gradual integration
into the larger society or insurgency. There is, of course, a range of
possible conclusions beyond the contrasting extremes of annihilation,

assimilation, or endemic violence; and such "outcomes" are not stable or permanent. In fact, Mexican American history can be matched only very broadly with these sociological phases.

Just as Mexicans are viewed through a schema derived from sociology, so is there a historical typology derived from an uninformed political economy which is specific to Mexicans.[7] This typology reads roughly as follows: Spain and New Spain were "feudal," and so was the frontier—perhaps more so rather than less. This meant that a European elite controlled all agriculture and mining, exploiting an enslaved and undifferentiated Indian work force, and giving a share of the profit to the overlord, the king; for on the frontier there were great estates with serfs. There is no explanation for such a society's internal social dynamics, its changing economy, or its eventual political independence. In contrast to this picture of stagnation is one of a vibrant, progressive United States whose entrepreneurs move into the frontier, annex the territory, and make it prosper through the use of Mexicans who are an indentured work force somewhat similar to Blacks in the slave South. In this scenario, the heroism and enterprise of U.S. entrepreneurs result in a developed economy, with Mexicans integral to its secondary sectors. Thus, change is seen as vital to the ever greater sophistication of the directors of capital, and Mexicans are viewed not only as victims, but as unconscious and passive victims. This schema is even less elegant than the sociological one, for it contradicts history itself.

There are no simple polarities or absolutes in the historical development of the Mexican people in what is now the United States Southwest. The following chapters delineate the roots and trunk of the Mexican American political tree with its several branches. The rings that form the trunk of this tree are major economic transformational events: the European annexation of Mesoamerica; the expansion of the cattle, farming, and mining frontiers of the colonial state of New Spain; the increase in production and trade on the frontier; the contradictions leading to independence; the increase in trade and commerce with a weak central government and economy; the transnational economic impulses leading to the war between Mexico and the United States; the accelerating development of the production of raw materials in the Southwest; the transformation of the United States into a major industrial and commercial power; and the economic need for and integration of a multiethnic wage-labor force. The chronological sequence of these events and their consequences spans four hundred years.

The first chapter takes note of the antecedents of a colonial governance, relating the development of governing practices and mispractices in relation to social groups as well as the advance of the frontier socially and economically. Analytically central here is the notion of an economically motivated frontier process moving from south to north and the contradictions that serve as a harbinger of the movement for independence. This is the most problematic chapter because in attempting to outline the origins of the people, a range of elements must be covered. The second chapter analyzes the political practices and frustrations of Mexican independence in the far northern territories as well as providing attention to questions and players important in the period after the decade 1836–1846. Central here are notions of political assault and of coping with hostile intervention. The first chapter, then, deals with early roots as the second discusses later roots, if you will.

The third chapter covers political developments in the initial decades of United States rule and presents early elements of choices and practices that continue into the twentieth century. Important to understanding the events here are notions of subordinate incorporation and integration concurrent with varied ethnic responses. The fourth chapter covers the persistence of Mexican American politics through decades of great change within the United States. Facilitating the understanding of this period are notions of economic transformation and of crisis that impacts upon a vigorous ethnic community. This narrative breaks at World War II; but the story, of course, continues. An interpretive historical narrative must be selective. Here, selected for commentary within the various periods of history are issues, patterns, collective practices, or leadership efforts, and interethnic relations related to class and resource priorities that are assessed with regard to their positive or negative political resolutions. An interpretive history connects the past to the present, to be sure, but it also relates the past itself to its own particular, internal histories.

The Mexican in the Southwest went from a frontier experience to one in which sovereignty and statehood were shared as an integral part of a larger developing national society; a subordinate minority was incorporated within a foreign society and augmented by a continuous stream from the previous, core society. From the midnineteenth century to the present day, Mexican ethnicity has been not only a condition of social being; it was a political equity to be avoided, demanded, and exercised, and these choices were resulted in political conflict, both internally and externally. In general, being Mexican and demanding or maneuvering for political participation resulted in the expression of economic, social, and cultural realities and grievances. At times, the economic, cultural, or social aspects were more visible within the different political ways and means—from the business contract to the electoral franchise, and from the terrorist reprisal to the celebratory song; for ethnic content in an aggrieved context of dominant-subordinate relations made these phenomena political. Ethnicity is sometimes seen only as the personal and the social, a succor or a fact; however, within a dominant arena that subordinates ethnicity, it is often a resource and therefore a political one as well. It is the political which gives birth to equity, the full bestowal of human rights in a struggle whose resolution is sought collectively; hence, the birth of the political history whose heirs are the Mexican American people.

1

The Septentrion: Political Culture
of the North, 1600–1822

Legacies and Pathologies of a Colonial State

The political traditions of Mexico's far north were linked, along with its values and institutions, to those of central Mexico, where the fusion of the European and Indian forged a new synthesis.[1] Western European politics was therefore part of the historical formation of the native people of Mesoamerica, a new dispensation introduced with the initial conquest of central Mexico.

Western Europe was in Mesoamerica from the first. International and domestic politics were aspects of Castilian expansion.[2] The conquest of Mexico was the result of international relations and of economic and political forces; and in turn, it impinged upon these forces. The result was the colonial state that had begun in 1522 with the European imposition upon the native. The motivation underlying the encounter between Indian and European was wealth, with its extension of power and control over specific resources justified by a rationalized ideology. The political sphere of the colonial regime was centered most often on resources, labor, and prerogatives pertinent to individuals, institutions, and corporate entities. Such politics grew out of a specific social and economic context where power and wealth were the motor and force and manipulation the means, with monarchism and Catholicism providing ideological rationales. This hegemonic imperative was met by resistance from the local peoples, but the parties of resistance could not break the domination[3] because they could not

provide effective ideological or technological weapons. Th
forces were significantly altered by their own internal evoli
as by the continuing tradition of resistance and its owr
which produced new forces of resistance over time. Thr
three hundred years of the colonial regime there occurred
reported rebellions, riots, work stoppages, and destruct
within a sphere of politics that lay beyond the formalities o
The colonial order was a European superimposition on
native order, but the native survived not only literal
inspirational symbol.

The Native Heritage

Indian societies range from the developing state of the *Mexica-
Tenochca*, a complex and stratified society numbering in the millions
and ruled according to precepts, deploying a disciplined large-scale
force to small bands dependent on gathering and hunting and led by
the strongest members, and knitted together by kinship.[4] Sooner or
later, all Indian groups were subjected to European authority and
therefore were impacted significantly by Europe. Within the vast,
lengthy, and diverse process of colonization, the measures of domination—ethnicity, culture, language, ideology, and comportment—also
comprised the commonalities of resistance. In the diversity of the
colonial experiment, a geographical, sociological, and historical center, the Central Valley of Mexico, or Anahuac, contained a predominant people, the *Mexica*, who joined community and land into *Mexi-
coytl*, an abstraction that commanded supreme value, linking people
together both socially and economically.

Mexica society was organizationally complex and socially diverse,
and in the course of this society's development women experienced
both continuity and change in the areas encompassing their economic,
religious, familial, and social roles. When the Europeans truncated the
autochthonous development of Mesoamerica—an emerging historical
synthesis with a particular historical and gender ascription—in the
years that followed a new social synthesis was created from an amalgam
of ethnic groups, economic practices, and local cultures; this synthesis,
however, also included specific gender roles and class and ethnic differences. Politics and economics were correlated both to perpetuate and
initiate the transitions in women's roles, and, immersed in such ten-

sion, they redefined the place of women in the political arena and, of course, in the family and the society.

The society of the Mexica provided the most important pre-Columbian social and cultural basis for the future of Mexico. Fortunately, concise documentation survives from Mexica civilization which describes and proscribes both the governance and the female aspects of the culture. Obviously, the Mexica were one among many societies of Mesoamerica, including some with distinctly matriarchal features.

Mexica society was politically an emerging state with both elective and hereditary aspects governed by codes of law that were applicable to all and interpreted by courts. Women were part of these arrangements. Labor, distribution, and ownership of property were generally communal, providing a base for egalitarian practices and recognizing equities. Mexica society was disciplined and authoritarian. All members were expected to adhere to a strict moral code that was finely documented in the Aztec codices. Every member of society had a prescribed position and manner of conduct. Dishonor could lead to a grave punishment, while honor was gained by service and had to be earned again within each generation.

Mexica society, dominated by its men, was divisible into receivers and providers of tribute. It had strong collective and communal aspects in its economic and political organization, and it exacted a high degree of conformity and civic devotion from its citizens. It was divided along status and wealth lines, but property rights were delimited for all. Women were participants in diverse activities, and they voiced their needs. They had limited access to power through the *calpulli*, the basic political, economic, and social unit of the society. Women were a part of the privileged sectors as well as being among those who worked the hardest and were the poorest. In the key areas of the society, power-legitimacy and religious cosmology, a female stamp was clearly visible. Arguably, women shared power in ancient times, as is suggested by the evidence of matriarchal societies and matrilineage, including among the Mexica. As time went by, and a shift occurred from hunting and gathering to agriculture, and then to conquest and trade, female equities allegedly were decreased by the male population. In the beginning, the ruling dynasty was initiated through the female side; the woman Ilancueitl, who brought the Toltec lineage of *Colhuacán* to Tenochtitlán, claimed status for the Mexica dynasty through her descent from the lineage of Quetzalcóatl. The position designated as the "snake woman," and identified as perhaps second only to, if not equal with, the Huey Tlatoani, or great speaker, was held by men in later times and is protean with suggestions of female origins. Cosmological and theological speculations at the time of the conquest had led to the view of a single, all-encompassing creative force diffused and expressed throughout the universe. This force was represented in a multiplicity of opposite forms. There were both male and female expressions specified in the religious calendar of festivities, which referred to far more ancient beliefs concerning the forces of the hearth—fire and earth. In total recognition of universal female expressions, women celebrated female deities and festivities.

The main sphere of women's lives, however, was in agricultural production; in the bearing and raising of children; and in cooking, weaving, and other duties that were part of the household economy. To a great degree, the structure of Aztec society was based on family ties, and marriages played an important role in economic and political alliances.

Mexican women participated in the priesthood and in medicine, with these two areas often overlapping. The *ciuatlamacazqui* were usually in the company of older women, who guarded and instructed them. These young women were taught dignified speech and appearance, and instructed in the development of reflection. Daughters of the elite were sent to a gender-segregated school to learn poetry, history, art, painting, music, and rhetoric. The object of education was to prepare them to devote themselves to the community and to excel in crafts or in arts.

Marriage marked the full transition into adulthood. Parents arranged the marriages, with the male's family proposing the marriage. Significantly, divorce could be initiated and obtained if the woman proved that her husband did not provide for her and the family. In turn, a man would be granted a divorce if his wife were sterile, failed to perform her domestic duties, or abandoned the household. Divorce was generally, however, a rare occurrence. Monogamy was the common rule, although polygamy was permitted. A distinction was made between the principal wife and the secondary wives; only children from the principal marriage were legitimate. Divorced women retained rights and may have gained additional ones which were similar to those of widows.

Archetypal figures from the society reflect its gendered past and the conditions of historical transition. Some of the ancient power deities—

Coatlicue (Earth) and Tonantzin (Fertility)—were telluric, populist, and female; and their features found their way into what became Mexican Catholicism. Significantly, their ethnic partisanship and their nurturing qualities were transferred, but the new "goddess" Guadalupe was more passive than the ancient figures, who were active, multi-faceted, and independent sources of power. Coatlicue was described as acting out "promiscuous maternity"—quite the opposite of the concept of the Virgin Mary, whose power derives from serving as a vessel for the Holy Spirit and is visualized theologically and simplistically. Indisputedly, the figure of Coatlicue–Tonantzin became a major cultural component and significantly represents a projected idealization. As an example to all Mexica and specifically to women, a mythical figure known as La Llorona demonstrated the serious obligation of one's role in life. According to the common interpretation, the woman La Llorona supposedly strayed from her proper role as wife and mother—hence, patriot—came to regret her transgression, and eternally lamented her fate. Another more provocative interpretation places the figure at the time of the conquest and as a symbol of the nation-to-be, lamenting subjugation and calling for revolt, and thus making the figure emancipatory and political. With the arrival of the Spaniards and the conquest, another woman, La Malinche—both historical figure and archetypal myth—played a major role. In the traditional interpretation, this Indian woman of status was a traitor in becoming the mistress, interpreter, and political facilitator of the Europeans, thus symbolizing the invaders' physical, spiritual, and moral domination of her own people, the indigenous society. Thus Malinche embodied the "bad woman," and as the one who makes an end to innocence, she shares somewhat the role of Eve in Christian mythology. A contrasting interpretation views her as a skillful and pragmatic political actress, coping in a positive way with a negative crisis and, in any case, not bound to Mexica precepts. This revisionist interpretation suggests that she was held in high esteem by both her Indian and European contemporaries for her intelligence and skills, and that she was a survivor who made choices and used diplomacy and intelligence to save the indigenous communities. In both interpretations, she transcends historical specificity, becoming symbolically the mother of the *mestizo,* and thus a symbol for the rise of the Mexican people, but she also provides a social contrast to the idealization of Indian resistance or conquest as annihilation.

The historical role of the woman in Mexico and its far north begins with its roots in Mesoamerican culture and civilization, the social and economic base for the evolving new and Mexican society and culture. In pre-Columbian society, myths refer to former times, when women held power and there were venerable female figures. Equally, women had legal status, retained property, could do business, exercise certain specialties, and experience a measure of independence in these professions as well as enjoy, significantly, legal protection. Although priestesses and the women of the ruling class had a share of power, few women apparently were present in councils and the government, even though they did participate in the calpulli. There was a close interrelationship between the private and public spheres.

In general, the Mexica woman was taught to be stoic and to possess endurance in facing the demands of life. Most importantly, every member of society was expected to fulfill his or her role without deviating from specified behavior, and the end sought was a strong and united community. Women's role in society was clearly defined, with strongholds in religion and health care, and with moral codices for appropriate behavior as well as an elaborated legal structure that provided the framework for the role. Considering their legal and religious standing, women in Aztec society possessed a few claims for equality with men in the modern sense, and they were "by no means perpetual minors." Arguably, their status in Mexica society was stronger than that of women in Europe.

Mexicas provided an important formative base to colonial society, and in time they acquired a symbolic significance for future generations. A complex and efficient Mexica political organization was based on an extensively developed economy whose ethos was service and responsibility for enhancement of the total collective. A formal, defined, and legitimate organization which had evolved historically among the Mexica rested on force and consensus. The exercise of power combined elective and hereditary features; leadership could be exercised in single, dual, triple, and quadruple forms, and there were also different levels of councils or representative assembly bodies as well as small, medium, and large administrative political units. The individual was subject to impartial law, codified and administered by the state through a system of local, intermediary, and general courts. The common language was classical Nahua, and the political center Tenochtitlán. Principal authorities were the Huey Tlatoani (the great speaker, the major civil and

military leader), *ciuacoatl* (the head of the religious–educational structure), the four electors (the supreme inner council), the general supreme council (all representatives of *calpullis*, plus major office holders, the elite of service—military commanders, fiscal administrators,
judges, provincial governors). A large and select administrative sector
was required to maintain the Mexica system. The Mexica hegemony
was exercised through a loose confederation of city-states aligning
themselves voluntarily or by force with the surrounding countryside.
Local governances and customs were generally respected, and the
union was based on mutually specific duties and responsibilities; tribute
was exacted, and governors and garrisons were maintained. Education
was institutionalized, publicly supported, imparted by specialists, and
organized according to gender, social rank, and specialization; but it
was based on a core curriculum of ethics, religion, and history. The
military, like the economy, was an indication of organization. In a
literal sense, the Mexica were a people in arms, all of whom were part
of the military apparatus. To future generations, *lamentos* (lamen-
tations), *anales* (yearly records), and *crónicas* (historical chronicles)
transmitted aspects of the culture and pride of the Mexica. In the
aftermath of Cortés's success, Mexica's institutions, its formal culture,
and its social organizations for the most part were deliberately and
systematically erased; but the people survived, as did their mutual self-
identification, their folk traditions, vestiges of their economy, and their
ideals, particularly the notion of an egalitarian society.

Colonial Practices

Several pathologies—betrayal, violence, and rationalization—
stand out in the establishment of colonial governance. Particularly
troublesome on occasion to civil and religious authorities were covert
leaders or spokespersons who combined claims to special traditional
knowledge with Western education in agitating among the indigenous
people. In the early 1530s, for example, the cacique of Texcoco, Don
Carlos, was reputedly a wizard who not only claimed special powers but
propagandized to youth the end of European rule. With the completion
of the initial conquest, accomplished by fire and the murder of the
senior native male elite, the Spanish crown moved quickly to assert
through the Council of the Indies royal control over both the conquistadores and the newly conquered peoples. Immediately following

the conquest, the colony had been governed by Cortés and his fellow conquistadores.

To initiate his expedition, Cortés betrayed the governor of Cuba, who he had persuaded of his loyalty in order to secure the appointment of command. After his betrayal of the governor, Cortés astutely established a *cabildo* to provide legitimacy for his actions. This cabildo was an entity of local government whose prerogatives and aspects of collective participation allowed Cortés to argue the validity of his actions. However, royal officials soon arrived to check the power and limit the ambitions of the conquistadores, for it was believed that they might attempt to establish an autonomous kingdom. A colony entailed not only wealth but the possibility of subversion, and such plots were reported every generation.

The far north of Mexico was part of an evolving economic and governing entity; in effect, what was established in Mesoamerica was a colonial substate with several features of an evolving state.[5] Preeminent loyalties were devoted to crown and church. Through the Council of the Indies, Spanish colonial authorities organized a kingdom according to, ostensibly, the monarchical European model with its corporate and estate structures, a system in which the Spanish ruler was "king" of this newly created and separate "kingdom."

Senior officials were appointed mainly from Spain, and they were expected to support themselves through their offices. Initially, the military was organized on the basis of a "nobility"; all *hidalgo* Spaniards except the religious were knights who could be called upon to defend the colony. A judicial system was established, and in Mexico the judiciary enjoyed considerable administrative power. From the first, the church played a major role in the Spanish colonial government, with its dual religious and political character. The secular as well as religious population was subject to the courts of the church, as the Inquisition attested. The church, particularly in the earlier colonial period, enjoyed governmental authority by collecting church taxes from the indigenous population.

The administrative structure of the colony was complex, with much overlapping authority. The entire country came to be divided into administrative districts, known by various names. Appointed administrators, like other officials, were expected to take their livelihood from their offices, a practice that not only involved the manipulation of power but led to an administration devoted to the interests of the larger and wealthiest landowners and mine owners as well as the church. Though they had several duties and possessed certain legal rights based on their places in the caste system, the people had few political rights. Reforms, however, did occur periodically and often were preceded by major policy debates. Still, administration meant legal rather than legislative discourse. Social control and ideological homogenization were ends consciously and actively pursued by the state.

Beginning with Antonio de Mendoza in 1529, European viceroys ruled Mexico for three hundred years. The viceroy was the direct representative of the Hapsburg king and received extraordinary deference, but it was well understood that the viceroy's tenure was limited. The scope of his considerable power was both military and administrative, although it was partially counterbalanced by the power of other independent royal officials, such as the Treasurer of the Real Hacienda, who administered mining regulations and the export and minting of all bullion. In addition to the viceroy, the colony was also administered by the Audiencias or Royal Courts of Nueva España and Nueva Galicia, which had both judicial and regulatory authority. Authority in the towns was exercised by the *ayuntamientos*, or by the royal officers or the local *hacendados*, or mine owners, who functioned as such. Although all hidalgos could be called to serve in the military, there was no standing army in the first years of the colony, only small regular detachments of the viceroy, the *audiencias*, and a few regular garrisons stationed at the frontier and at the ports where bullion was exported. This militia provided an avenue of mobility for those of modest means and the poor, as well as mestizos and colonists of European descent. In 1789, the new Bourbon regime succeeded the Hapsburg dynasty, redividing the country on the basis of *intendencias*, which were headed by *intendentes*, officials who were paid a salary. The Bourbons reorganized the military forces by establishing a standing army supported by a larger militia which came to supersede the church as the institution of status and proved to be one with political power.

Following the *reconquista*, its own lengthy period of opposition to foreign domination, the Iberian colonial state imposed its rule by force and by cooptation through a labyrinth of laws and an authoritarian bureaucracy. Their historical experience had made Castilians defensive and suspicious, and despite their eminent position as a world power, the Iberians were ever watchful of a loyalty to crown and church that was judged by the outward expression of behavior and beliefs; they were also suspicious of foreign enemies, the most prominent of whom were the English. Status was determined among Iberians by family background, earned credentials, and service as well as through favors dispensed by those in a higher echelon than the petitioner. For the junior elite, practicing politics meant being a supplicant and time-server. However, in an uneasy land with uneasy people the forceful personality was useful to others who were, within limits and under specific circumstances, more powerful, especially on the frontier. The bureaucratic state also required knowledge of its rules and customs and the art of dispensing and seeking favors. Thus, politics required specialists who were skilled in writing and argumentation, as well as learned in regulations and precedents. Force, skills, and manipulation provided the individual with opportunity, but it was the chance to serve the state only.

Also at the core of colonial politics was ethnicity. The state involved rule by one people, Europeans, over the other, Indians. Not readily foreseen was the mass evolution of a third group, *mestizos*, who numerically would become the majority and continually absorb the original two peoples. But as amalgamation occurred, status, wealth, and ethnicity remained near obsessions in a society comprised of five major ethnic groups, a spectrum of institutional stations, and classes, and a diversity of labor and property forms, and rigid, even pathological, forms of social control.

A General Community Is Forged

During the colonial period, several aspects combined to integrate the rudimentary foundation of a modern nation. If, from one perspective, these aspects may be seen as an amalgamation, they also may be differentiated: they set off New Spain from Mesoamerican societies established prior to 1519, and the Mexican colony from Spain as well as from other Spanish-American colonies. Certainly, during any one period, elements of disharmony and discontinuity can be identified; yet unity and continuity also prevailed, not only in colonial times but through the nineteenth century, and these elements can be seen as commonalities or as gains resulting from the European impact.

Apart from the general ecological environment and the preliminary unification under the Mexica, the outstanding unifying phenomenon of the colonial period was the experience of the conquest itself and the "colonial situation" it created. The colonial experience was unifying for both the conquered and their conquerors, or rather for their respective descendants. In social, economic, and political spheres, the peoples of New Spain were being integrated, albeit rudimentarily, into a common community of local attachments, ethnicities, and identities. Tremendous differences were partially bridged. Most significant socially was the process of *mestizaje* (miscegenation) which moved from Central America to New Mexico, destroying undermining racial prejudice in its wake. Regardless of the attitude of the *criollo* (a person born in America of European parents), it was the mestizo's consciousness and his numbers that were to prove decisive in the future. The criollo, mestizo, and *indio* were prejudiced against one another, and they all suffered prejudice from a common source—the European—and for a common reason—because they were natives. Also developing at that time was the social kinship that resulted from sharing a common situation, customs, religious beliefs, and language; and among some sectors of the population, this last commonality grew in importance and attachment. Among the principal unifying agents were religious cosmology and theology, religious practices, public ceremonials, and religious symbols. But more than these, common necessities of survival and defense, and, above all, work united people. Economic changes partially welded New Spain into a unit. Despite difficulties, the building of a rough communication system made travel, shipping, and correspondence possible. Although there were rigid features in the economy, there were also dynamic elements such as mining in the north, commercial crops, textile mills in the south, and the money-lending, trade, and manufacturing in the cities.

Political focus and administration helped to forge New Spain. The distant crown provided through the viceroy a focus of loyalty for all regions and peoples. Hence, this abstract yet common political loyalty as well as a common political administrative center were introduced before independence, and both were reinforced by a body of common law administered by specialists. The system of administration was felt in all spheres of life, although the particulars of application might differ. Administration was also an avenue for political experience, even if only a limited one for certain sectors of the population; it was, in a sense, also an incentive toward greater aspirations. The European bureaucracy was another focus of resentment common to all groups, albeit for different reasons. Widespread grievances often arose over clerical privileges, appointments, personal prerogatives, land rights, discrimination, and unfair administration. On the surface, these grievances could be viewed solely as a reflection of misadjustments; but more to the point, they were based on fundamental notions of justice, shared responsibilities, and the general ideal of a common, productive, and harmonious community. Among the Indian population one attempt was made to organize a planned equitably functioning enlightened community between 1530 and 1580 by a Franciscan Bishop, Vasco de Quiroga, among the Tarascans.

Among a reflective few, apart from the general ideological orthodoxies of the system and covert messages from the indigenous past, some particular sets of ideas were emerging in colonial Mexico as distinctive to this society. These ideas and reflections had to do with local nature, history, religion, social responsibility, and refashioning of Indian beliefs. Pride in being "native" is an attitude noticeable early among some writers born in New Spain during the generations following 1520.[6] *Criollismo* was the earliest of Europeanized general attitudes emphasizing history, lineage, rights, and religion. The process of differentiation that operated to set off the Mexican born *criollo* from the European born *peninsular* encouraged a manifest distinctive pride on the part of the *criollo* in his family, place of birth, and idealized character, manners, and customs. A major source was the land and its wealth; *criollos* also took pride in the cities, the learning, and literature to be found in New Spain. To counter the biases of Europeans there was argued a sense of superiority of America over Europe. Some high status mestizos shared criollismo convictions. Criollo and Europeanized mestizos writers first began to discuss and argue name and identity. Across the centuries a gradual change occurred in self-denotation from *español, criollo, americano, español-mexicano* to, finally, *mexicano.*

Perhaps because their world was so permeated with religion, the people's sense of pride focused early on religious symbols, particularly on the Virgen de Guadalupe. The phenomenon of *guadalupanismo* is truly interesting for the motivation and the factors that explain its rapid acceptance by the peoples of New Spain.[7] It quickly became an indigenous symbol for the Indians, mestizos, and criollos. Although the apparitions are dated from the sixteenth century, its popular magnetism began to flourish in the mid-seventeenth century when New Spain was crystallizing into something neither Spanish nor Indian, but a unique combination of both.

Certainly, guadalupanismo was present in the far north in the seventeenth century, when a literature on Guadalupe, written by creole clerical intellectuals, appeared in Spanish and in Nahua. These writings emphasized nativist self-assertion and pride more than religion. By the late eighteenth century, as today, guadalupanismo was a conglomeration of ideals, values, and sentiments which were far more secular than theological, as even the most cursory knowledge of Mexico would attest. The cult of Guadalupe was of singular importance in forging a sense of community. The prominent role of intellectuals in giving meaning and substance to Guadalupe presaged their later activity in creating a sense of community.

Among the savants of the seventeenth century were several noted for their sense of regional pride as well as for their anxieties and ambiguities.[8] The writings of Fernando de Alba Ixtlilxochitl (1580–1648) represent the work of the *indio-mestizo* driven by the urge to inform the world of the glories of ancient Mexico, with which he identified. Yet his writings also bear an apologetic tone, as well as a split perspective: a militant, "new" Catholic upholding Catholicism by describing a religious world that he admired even though he also condemned it as "pagan." But he was also at war with himself in empathizing with the Indian past while simultaneously claiming credit for the conquest by highlighting the Indian contributions to it. Another transitional writer was Carlos de Sigüenza y Góngora (1654–1700), whose concern for Mexico does not have the driving anxiety of Ixtlilxochitl, but is more studied and more political. Sigüenza had a country—New Spain—and a community—other criollos. Nonetheless, his writings heralded what was American and defended the Indian past. Sor Juana Inés de la Cruz, the most gifted though deeply religious and introspective writer, was more pointed politically in her references to ethnicity and the Mexican eagle, her use of nahua, and in her conscious linkage of Tonantzin and Guadalupe.

By the late seventeenth and through the eighteenth century, prideful identification with New Spain among an educated few led to a consideration of how best to serve the colony in and of itself, a rudimentary expression of conscious concern for public welfare. Such service meant knowing and defending the historical legacy of New Spain, perceiving the reality of Mexico, and arguing for the colony's improvement in a general sense—all reflections of the changes in colonial discourse associated with the impact of Cartesian thought.

The "new thought" was relatively rational and experimental: it represented the breaking of the scholastic mode which dealt with abstract universal categories and whose emphasis was on particulars; and while it was a step toward modernity, it was even more a movement toward reshaping New Spain and its inhabitants through ideologically guided action. The Cartesian influence forced colonials to reckon with and speculate about their own physical and social reality; it reinforced self-consciousness as a mode of thought and as a reaction to European readings.

In the European writings expounding Cartesian thought a clear prejudice was expressed. Reading misinformed European writers who mentioned New Spain, or Americans, often aroused dismay in colonial intellectuals. Colonial writers were stirred to defend Mexico by European writers' pejorative judgments as well as by their own speculations. Most often the male intellectual creole not only had to defend himself, his society, and his natural environment, but also the Indian and the precolonial past. He also needed to be more inclusive in his social considerations because the geography of the country and the range of its peoples were indeed expanding. Those who traveled north took with them the historical and contemporary political cultures of the larger society of which they were part.

Expansion to the North

Over time, the region of Mesoamerica evolved economically from communalism to a Western precapitalist and class society under the initiative of leadership in Europe and Mexico City while expanding territorially and demographically.[9]

The Mexican or mestizo as a social type in the context of a particular social complex may have appeared first on the northern frontier as a result of an economy and its demands as well as the sparsity of sedentary populations; all of these features contributed to a particularly dynamic characteristic of northern settlements. As a result, the indio, mestizo, and criollo developed common bonds.

From the beginning of colonial society, people moved to the greater Mexican north, where the initial major northern area was the Bajió, followed by the large region between this area and the Bravo, and, next, the even larger area north of this river. Hispano-Mexican expansion into the northern frontier continued from the seventeenth to the nineteenth centuries.[10] Guanajuato, San Luis Potosí, Querétaro, Aguascalientes, and Zacatecas marked the expansion. In the far north New Mexico was the first area to be settled, in approximately 1598, with Santa Fe founded in 1609–10. From 1716 to 1721 the northeastern region known as Tejas was settled, and such towns as San Antonio, Nacogdoches, and La Bahía were established. At the beginning of the eighteenth century, Arizona was explored and a base established by the Jesuits, led by Father Eusebio Francisco Kino. These missions marked the northwesternmost settlements of New Spain until the colonization of Alta, or upper, California. Since the sixteenth century Baja and Alta California had been discussed for colonization, which was accomplished during the next two centuries. Later, expansion spread into Colorado and other places.

Usually migrating in family units, the pioneers were predominantly mestizos, a mixture of Indian and Spanish. There were also many mulattoes and a few Europeans—some born in Spain, others in Mexico—as well as Hispanicized Indians from the interior of Mexico, and later, Indians from the north, who themselves were pioneers. The culture, with variant regional adaptations, corresponded to that of central Mexico. Indians in the far north had shared partially in the culture and trade relations of central Mexico prior to the arrival of the Europeans, and they continued to do so after the imposition of colonial authority. There was mixed acceptance of the settlers by the Indians. Though there was peace at times, there were often conflicts between the settlers and Indian groups. The socioeconomic process of development was parallel to that of the central region, and it was part of the process of formation of the Mexican nation. The north was an area characterized by a particular combination of geographic and demographic factors, as well as by unexploited natural resources. The expansion from central Mexico to the north was a socioeconomic political process. Settlers brought skills, livestock, farming implements, smelting and forging, carpentry and building, crafts, and the mining knowledge necessary to develop the wealth of the expanding homeland. They also brought institutions, values, and practices.

The period 1600–1810, the time of the formation of the Mexican nation, had visible basic patterns in the far north, although they varied depending on locality. Because of preference and initiative, the expansion of the cattle and mining frontier, and religious and state encouragement, settlers from the middle and lower sectors of the northern frontiers of New Spain established ranchos and pueblos further north, across the Bravo into Tejas, Nuevo México, Arizona, Colorado, and Alta California. Survival involved intense hardship and work, an effort demanding a test of endurance and courage, and particularly of the local leadership. During this time, acclimatization and refinement of suitable technology, social practices, and institutions expressed organizational creativity. Throughout the period, the population grew, the area of settlement expanded, and class stratification developed according to fortune and foresight. Contact with central Mexico and the separate subregions was maintained through local communication networks which helped to spur the shared commonalities determined by culture and by time. The scattered indigenous tribes underwent a process of transculturation and amalgamation that contributed to the economy and society. In customs, values, technology, and economy, the area north of the Río Bravo was most closely related to what is now northern Mexico; both areas comprised the greater Mexican north. Expansion north of the Río Bravo was a part of the general social expansion beyond the central area.

Mining, stock-raising, agriculture, trade, and, in effect, profit drove the frontier northward socially. In spite of occasional dislocations, the northern Mexican settlement grew in numbers and spread over a larger geographical area during every generation, an important trend that continued into the nineteenth century. Mining stimulated economic development that proved to be particularly important in expanding the frontier. The mining industry employed a relatively large work force which required great quantities of food, thus encouraging the establishment of ranchos and the development of agriculture. The mining industry also stimulated trade in the tools and minerals needed for the mine itself, as well as in clothing and other personal articles and necessities required by the miners. Agriculture and livestock-raising also expanded, either because of the needs of mining or because of its own momentum. Ranchos and haciendas meant the emergence of the Mexican *vaquero*, both as a skilled laborer and as a member of the mobile social strata alongside the *minero*. Vaqueros and mineros gravitated to forceful local leaders from their own ranks. In the north, some economic activities offered relatively better compensation and working conditions to attract the skilled labor force which was required. The scarcity of a labor force in the north meant that many occupations were open to persons of the *castas*, with the ultimate condition being the ability to perform the work. These economic forces attracted and engendered a diverse labor force and gave rise to what can be considered a Mexican cultural network which was neither Indian, Spanish, nor African, but a combination of diverse cultural influences.

In principle, the process of expansion, or conquest, was tightly controlled by strict regulations pertaining to the organization of *entradas* (expeditions) and the founding of *pueblos* according to state sanction and needs.[11] In actuality, expansion to the north combined both the government-sanctioned aspect of formal conquest and occupation and the informal, and perhaps more important, nonformalized expansion of the frontier through the migration of large numbers of people—indios, mestizos, mulattoes, criollos, and poor Spaniards—to the northern settlement. The primary attractions for these settlers were economic: the availability of land and the possibility of mining strikes. The expanding frontier represented both freedom from the more established and coercive authority of the European colonial regime in the central regions and the opportunity to establish ranchos, to own individual or family herds of livestock, to engage in contraband, and more. People migrated to avoid the special taxes and other obligations to which members of the castas were subject. Most were predominantly mestizos or Hispanicized Indians who perhaps were more interested in ranching and mining than in farming, although farming was basic.

These northern settlements were extensions of the social relations of north-central Mexican culture, upon whom their social and cultural life was modeled and from whom, in large measure, their inhabitants derived. The most immediate influences came from the people of the regions to the south with whom there was the most immediate contact: Texas with Coahuila, Nuevo León and Tamaulipas; Nuevo México with Chihuahua, and the Californias with Sonora, Sinaloa, and Jalisco. The strong influence of the local indigenous populations, with whom the overwhelmingly indio-mestizo-mulatto *pobladores* (settlers) mixed, interlinked and interpenetrated these major north-central Mexican influences in an uneven and unequal process of amalgamation. The growing mexicano culture and identity, with particular regional variations, was dominant over the local indigenous peoples, who were largely amalgamated through forced Mexicanization as part of the continuing process of mestizaje.

Governance, Institutions, and Settlement on the Northern Frontier

With the informal process of expansion came the extension of formal authority, which either preceded or followed depending on a particular region's specific geographic and economic conditions, which interpenetrated each other. On the policy level, the Spanish colonial administration sought to create an ordered process of expansion and settlement that was controlled by the central government and its military, civil, and religious representatives in the north. In specific instances, settlement stemmed from the ideological responsibility of Christianization to expand missionary efforts, which were usually a result of intense lobbying by religious. In other cases, settlement resulted from the major policy question of a defense perimeter erected against encroachment by international competitors. But in either case, what was important for future consequences was the social reality of settlement and the initiation of a particular sense of community among specific peoples and families linked to particular places.

The fundamental authority governing settlement in the north and throughout New Spain were the codes of royal law, *La Recopilación de las Leyes de las Indias* of 1680, reissued with changes in 1774, and the reorganized and revised *La Nueva Recopilación* of 1791. These codes were supplemented by instructions to the governor from the viceroy in Mexico City. In this carefully elaborated and "planned" document, the sections of these codes governing the granting of land and the founding of towns were detailed and included the physical layout of the settlements, the authority and powers of municipal authorities, and even the occupations and equipment of the settlers.

Aspects of settlement to the north of the Valley of Anahuac were deeply influenced by decades of relatively fast frontier expansion within circumstances of war and dislocation affecting large numbers of people. [12] From the viceregencies of Mendoza through those of Martín Enríquez de Almanza (1568–1580), Alvaro Manrique de Zúñiga (1585–1590), and Luis de Velasco (1590–1598), the vast region of New Spain underwent major change. In the late 1520s and during the 1530s violence had been widespread in the areas that would be known as Jalisco and Michoacán, where Europeans and thousands of Nahua-speaking peoples fought the Tarascans. Next came the region known as the Gran Chichimeca, which for three generations witnessed extensive violence and reorganization, punctuated by the Mixton War of 1541–

42 and the long Chichimeca War, extending from 1550 to 1590, in which the Europeans and Nahuas were joined by over thirty thousand mestizos, mulattoes, and Tarascans against the local Zacatecos, Guachichiles, Cazcanes, and Chichimecs. Major silver finds at Zacatecas and San Luis Potosí speeded the process. Entire populations were uprooted and set into new economic and civil patterns as the so-called Chichimeca Peace followed the Chichimeca War. Yet, in July 1599, Captain Gabriel Ortiz de Fuenmayor had hung a Chichimeca woman, an accused *hechicera*, for profaning two churches and rousing the Chichimecas into rebellion. Much prior to this event came the ferment of European individual activity which would affect the north. By coincidence, they were Basques, not Castilians, and frontier captains, not administrators. Cristobal de Oñate, father of Juan de Oñate, contributed to the development of Zacatecas, which, in turn, served as a base for developments in the north, northwest, and northeast.

At great risk and with sheer good fortune, Francisco Miguel and Diego de Ibarra engaged in activity in Sonora, Sinaloa, Zacatecas, Durango, and Chihuahua. Francisco de Urdiñola contributed to the advance into New Mexico and to the organization of Nueva Vizcaya from the areas of Chihuahua and Durango; and he laid the basis for the fortune the Marqués de Aguayo of Nuevo León would have a hundred years later when he entered the Tejas plains. A Castilian, Pedro Caldera, did not achieve the renown or wealth of the others, all of whom he met at one time or another, but he was among the indefatigable soldiers of fortune who were often in dire straits and often among the Indians. He had a son with a Chichimeca woman and placed him in the Franciscan house at the recently established mining center of Zacatecas—a house, incidentally, which remained part of the center of Franciscan activity two hundred years later, when Junípero Serra served his apprenticeship in the nearby Sierra Gorda country.

During the late sixteenth century, a major figure active in pushing the frontier into the Chichimeca and establishing settlements there was Miguel de Caldera, a mestizo and alcalde of Jerez, who was respected by both settlers and Indians. Possessed with a strong character and experienced in the use of arms, Caldera was an early example of frontier leadership. He described his activities:

Here I, Captain Miguel de Caldera, grant a title in this town of Santa María de Meca Tabasco, jurisdiction of Juchipila, Kingdom of New Galicia. At the time when the Guachichiles-Chichimecas were in rebellion, I came here gathering people to serve as soldiers. When I arrived at this town of Meca Tabasco, in the year 1583, I enlisted and took with me foot soldiers with bow and arrow, under command of Captain Martín García. These soldiers remained with me during five or more years of war, until they were victorious over the Guachichiles of San Luis and Tequizquiapan. I then asked them to go to the town of Huejotitlan, Tabasco. Accordingly, they embraced in Juchipila, and that jurisdiction remained in peace. After arrangement of this friendship between the Guachichiles and those of Meca Tabasco, I, the said Caldera, took the Guachichiles and left them in their settlement, which is in San Luis and Tequizquiapan.

After this, I went to Mexico City, to talk with His Excellency, Viceroy Don Luis de Velasco, and ask him for four hundred Tlaxcalans to serve as colonists on the existing frontiers. The viceroy granted them to me, and I made distribution of them at the hot springs called Cuisilique [Cuicillo]. Some of the Tlaxcalans I left in Tequizquiapan, and some in Mezquitic; others in Las Charcas; others in Castillo [Saltillo]; some in San Andres Chalchihuites; and those remaining, I settled on the San Luis Colotlan frontier, in the year 1592.

Later, I and my soldiers accompanied those of Meca Tabasco back to their town, where they could live and rest in peace and quiet in their lands, pastures, and woodlands, along the road of Santicatiche and San Sebastián de Teochicacan in the east. I now request and implore that all of His Majesty's justices, viceroys, and oidores protect these poor people in their work and necessities, for they have done very well in my campaigning, serving His Majesty bravely in the war. I hereby attest this, as their captain. Done on 20 January 1593. *Miguel Caldera.*

As chief justice, *justicia mayor,* he implemented policy on the frontier and was particularly charged with effectuating laws that protected settled natives.

Generally, settlement proceeded according to a plan and a set of explicit regulations. Officials in Mexico or in Madrid made the initial major decisions, and local authorities carried them out. In political life, regulations covered political, social, and economic rights; the town layouts; land tenure; irrigation; Indian relations; trade and military organizations; and individual or group rights. Correspondence and communication were conducted with central Mexico. Yet defense and irrigation, as well as many aspects of subsistence on a frontier, required cooperation and adaptation to circumstances. Decisions could not be feasibly postponed until a Mexico City decision was received. There were both local despotism and leaders elected by local consent.

The major institutional components were modeled on those Spanish colonial institutions which arose during the reconquest of southern Spain, though they were now modified by both general conditions in Mexico and particular conditions in the north.[13] Here, institutional forms tended to be simplified and standardized in an attempt to adapt them to northern conditions; but the indio and mestizo clashed, and both shared an antagonism to the European. Nevertheless, frontier expansion was relatively planned and specifically organized and supervised. Periodically, throughout the era, changes were instituted which also followed an orderly process of reports, criticism, and recommendations.

Among the major institutional forms appearing throughout the north, in more or less developed expression given local and regional conditions, were the entrada, the initiating military expedition that followed a stated plan; the *presidio,* or military outpost; the *misiones,* combined religious and ideological centers; and the pueblos and villas, or civilian settlements. During the three-hundred-year process of expansion and colonization, these institutions experienced many changes and modifications as the socioeconomic, cultural, and ideological structures of colonial society. They continued to exist until the end of the colonial era and persisted in modified form during the postindependence period of national development. In the earliest period of northward expansion, military forces were composed primarily of irregular mestizo levies or militia locally organized by powerful administrators, mineowners, or ranchers. Increasingly, these militia were supplemented, although never replaced, by regional and local garrisons located at central points along the frontier in fortified posts. Presidios were important as well as expensive and diverse. The mission was a triple ideological, labor, and administrative institution of particular importance in the far north. But presidios and misiones north of the Bravo were modified, short-lived, and not as widespread as civilian towns. On the frontier, a minimum of private married males—usually not less than ten—could petition to form a town with a four-league boundary and were allowed to form a town council, or cabildo. Lands were assigned according to prescribed limits, and possession also was required to be petitioned and certified. Municipal officers were to be chosen from the residents and could be elected; in practice, they were married and older, and selected from families who had the trust of governors. In effect, towns were civilian, structured, more participatory in governance and economy than either the presidio or the mission, and had a greater potential for growth. Towns, of course, varied in size and wealth from Zacatecas to New Mexico and from Goliad on the Gulf of Mexico to San Francisco on the Pacific. The three major institutions provided control, labor, and distribution of surplus goods and were vehicles for acculturation and transculturation.

Exposed, ambiguous, and amorphous, the location of the frontier shifted many times in the course of more than three centuries of expansion. During the late sixteenth century, it was located along the southern edge of the Gran Chichimeca, in the areas of Aguascalientes, Guanajuato, and southern San Luis Potosí. By the end of the colonial period, the northernmost outposts reached to Alta California, what is now southern Colorado, southern Arizona, and east Texas, which included what was then the Spanish province of Louisiana. More accurately, there were several frontiers of settlements. Missionary and military activity varied widely in their degree of effectiveness. Geography, type of settlement, and the existence of autonomous or independent peoples who did not recognize domination affected the occupational hold of the settlers and of Spanish authority. In reality, the territories were jointly occupied by mexicano and independent indigenous populations.

The establishment of permanent settlements was not easy and depended on available resources. Lines of communication were not only difficult to maintain, but hazardous. Groups of Christianized Indians from the south were brought to the lower Rio Grande, in what is now southern Texas and in New Mexico. Though the skills necessary for the formation of settlements were important, more significant were the social and political institutions and practices based on class division, wealth, and contemporary forms of property holding.

Because the basis of wealth in the far north was agrarian, land and water rights were primary concerns. Trade, crafts, primitive manufacturing, and mining were of lesser importance for survival, but they did exist and eventually were important in social and political development and in other matters concerning governance. While land was the major political concern, its acquisition and safeguarding were concerns of governance. Property was held by individuals, though there were collective ownership forms such as Indian and mestizo communal grants or land held by the church. Laws provided some protection and recognition of agricultural Indian property rights. Property extension varied from small to medium to large. One immediate measure of success for the settlement enterprise was self-sufficiency; but there was also the less material, more social goal which declared that frontier communities should be comprised of commendable persons—civilians, soldiers, priests. By working in concert, they would bring about what the Puritan John Winthrop had called a "city on a hill," but theirs would not only be prosperous, but harmonious and sharing. This notion characterized even mundane grievances.

The Issues, Difficulties, and Instruments of Governing

Politics during the seventeenth, eighteenth, and nineteenth centuries revolved around the acquisition of land, the allocation of labor resources, the securing of appointed offices, and lobbying before the authorities in central Mexico on behalf of local rights or privileges. The groups involved were the wealthier landowners, the clergy, military officers, spokesmen for the small landholders, artisans, and sometimes important local Indian leaders. The poor, landless women and most Indians were generally excluded. The power stratification produced tensions between the groups, which were exacerbated by the continual increase in the "mixed" populations and by complications within the castelike social order.

Correspondence and reports were integral to administration. Complaints and calamities were the most common items: disputes between officials, colonists, and clergy, as well as appeals for funds, soldiers, settler families, priests, arms, tools, and animals. Officials at the end of their terms underwent a *residencia,* an administrative review of their tenure in office. Governors often did not find their tenure rewarding, as one noted in 1636:

> governors desire to quit this office as soon as they enter it, for it is
> of no benefit to them but rather an expense, as the land is so poor
> and they cannot serve his Majesty as they would wish because of
> the small force of soldiers and arms (as has been said). There is
> nothing but quarrels and more quarrels with the religious, and the
> governors have to resist vituperations and depositions.[14]

Governors were supported in some cases and criticized in others. Complaints against officials were acted upon if there was evidence. Conflicts between clergy and secular officials were particularly sharp in the far north, and were explainable, in part, because resources were limited and the priorities of the two groups often different.

Conflicts between Franciscan, Jesuit, and Dominican missionaries and military and civil authorities (as well as settlers) were a regular, typical feature of the expanding *frontera* during its various stages. Missionaries, of course, appealed to religion and to their own presumed integrity for justification. One missionary put his case this way:

> *Very Reverend Father and our Minister Provincial:* I, Fray Carlos José Delgado, preacher general, commissary, notary, and censor of the Holy Office, apostolic notary, and missionary in the *custodia* of the conversion of San Pablo of this province of El Santo Evangelio in the kingdom of New Mexico, appear before your reverence only for the purpose of lamenting before your paternal love the grave extortions that we, the ministers of these missions, are suffering at the hands of the governors and *alcaldes* of that kingdom. I declare, that of the eleven governors and many *alcaldes mayores* whom I have known in the long period of forty years that I have served at the mission called San Agustín de la Isleta, most of them have hated, and do hate to the death, and insult and persecute the missionary religious, causing them all the trouble and annoyances that their passion dictates, without any other reason or fault than the opposition of the religious to the very serious injustices which the said governors and *alcaldes* inflict upon the helpless Indians.[15]

Conflicts of these types followed patterns long familiar in other earlier frontier areas of the *Tierra Adentro* (northern borderlands).

The major unit of government was that of the *provincia* or *reino* headed by a governor, with several assistants including a notary and individuals who adjudicated matters.[16] North of the Bravo, where Santa Fe (established in 1609) was the oldest continuous government, the most immediate local unit was the cabildo or ayuntamiento, comprised of nine to eleven or more officials, headed by an *alcalde mayor*, and including *alcaldes ordinarios*, council members, and *regidores*, who were representatives of the *vecinos*, or settlers; officers were *aguaciles* and *escribanos*, deputies and clerks. Underpinning this structure were the concepts of representation and participation in governance, responsibility for local justice, and the need for local revenues. At the same time, there existed the tradition of the *consejo*, a public assembly, to deal with major crises. In broad terms, cabildos dealt with buildings; town layout and plots; public health; roads and bridges; local licenses; public order and civil disputes; support for education, when viable; and general development of agriculture and industry. Mundane public business, other than land and water claims, revolved around debts, theft, physical abuse, other types of violence, or acts giving rise to public scandal. Cabildos also dealt with accused Indians and aggrieved widows. Areas of authority were proscribed by the higher authorities, and local officials were subordinate to the alcalde, who had both executive and judicial powers. Although governing could be accomplished by decree, harsh frontier conditions created the necessity for collective agreement; thus, the means for reaching a local consensus were developed and practiced. In the beginning of the settlement of any given area, leadership was primarily formal, but it became both formal and informal as the society of the settlement evolved. Leaders were generally strong and experienced individuals who had to be knowledgeable about regulations and capable of dealing with a range of people.

Indian relations, a major problem for administrators and one whose negotiation required policy strategy and tactics, were considered broadly in terms of *indios de pueblo*, sedentary and agriculturalists, and of *indios barbaros*, nomads. Large areas of only loosely held frontier were subject to active resistance by indigenous populations, particularly nomadic peoples such as the Apache and Comanche, who often raided as far south as Durango, lying far below the northernmost New Mexico settlements and garrisons. With the exception of the Pueblos, Indians in the far north were not concentrated into permanent settlements, but were small groups, intermittently violent or cooperative and with no tradition of paying tribute or doing forced labor.

Beginning as early as the establishment of European rule, control over Indians was facilitated by their concentration; or as one decree stated:

> The King. To our *oidores, alcaldes mayores* [judges and magistrates]
> of the Audiencia of the province of Nueva Galicia: Juan de la
> Peña, in the name of the council of justice and government of the
> city of Guadalajara, has made a report to me saying that because
> the Indian inhabitants of the province are not gathered into towns
> where they may have political government, much harm is done
> and many difficulties arise in their conversion and indoctrination,

and they are not taught to live under the control and ordered system conducive to their salvation and welfare. For, scattered as they
are over the mountains and deserts, the religious are unable to go
everywhere to visit them; moreover, the Indians began to flee for
the purpose of preventing interference with their manner and
custom of life, and of securing better opportunities to assault, rob,
and kill both Spaniards and peaceful Indians on the highways as
they had repeatedly done. . . . I have therefore approved it, and do
now command you to issue orders and instructions for gathering
the Indians of that province who are wandering in the mountains
into towns where they may live in a civilized manner and have
their organized government, that they may better communicate
with each other, have order and system in their living, be more advantageously converted and indoctrinated, and escape the dangers
and difficulties which may attend the opposite mode of living in
the mountains and deserts. Whatever you may do in this matter
above your ordinary obligation we shall accept as service to us, and
you will report to us how this order is complied with and executed.
Dated at El Carpio, May 26, 1570
I the *King*.[17]

In Nueva Galicia and Nueva Vizcaya, when an Indian "threat" carried
with it sufficient portent, a major campaign of extermination was
considered and either approved or rejected. Hostile relations could
occur even as trade and social exchange continued, and miscegenation
as well as intermarriage were not only tolerated but particularly common among the popular classes. A special office, *protector de indios*,
represented the legal rights and privileges of Indians. Though non-
Hispanicized Indians were classified as minors, they were granted access
to legal protection and to courts, both of which they frequently used.

The Administration and Politics of the Frontera: From Cibola to the Provincias Internas

The development of the Septentrion's political dimension was
marked by both continuities and differences that reflected the period of
settlement; geographical and climatic conditions; the presence or absence of water as well as exploitable deposits of precious minerals; and
the type of social organization utilized by the indigenous peoples. In

reality, there was not simply a *frontera*, but a series of overlapping frontiers that included varieties of mining, agriculture, grazing, evangelism, and strategic defense. In addition, political and cultural dimensions connected all of these types of frontiers with larger geographical and provincial units.

The major provinces comprising the colonial Septentrion were organized at different time periods and developed at different rates according to their particular characteristics. Within the area of the far north ceded to the United States (in 1848 and 1854) were three major regions settled in the following chronological order: Nuevo México; Tejas, or Nuevas Filipinas; and Alta California. The Mexican settlements in what is today Arizona did not make up a separate province but, rather, formed the northern frontier of Sonora and dated from the founding of San Javier del Bac (Tucson) in 1700. The vast territories of Louisiana and La Florida were also at various periods under jurisdiction of the Viceroyalty of Nueva España or administered from Havana. The major settlement established at San Augustín in 1565 and the efforts in the Carolinas during 1561 were abandoned, but fifteen hundred descendants of *isleños* who had settled in Louisiana during the 1770s survived through the nineteenth century.

Nuevo México

Nuevo México was not only the first region to be occupied, in 1598; it was also historically the largest, most populated, and most developed province within the far northern frontier, and its political patterns were partially shaped by this density.[18] It was characterized by a greater degree of economic stratification and a more sophisticated as well as sedentary indigenous culture, that of the Pueblo Indians. These factors gave the political process of Nuevo México a much more complex dimension than politics in Tejas and Alta California, which were settled later and were less complex socially. In contrast to the defensive motives initiating the settlement of Tejas and Alta California, New Mexico's settlement conformed to the expansionist motor of the initial conquest and to the colonial power's wealth and religion. New Mexico, organized at the early date of 1598, was first a *reino* (kingdom) and later a *gobierno* (province) under the Viceroyalty of Nueva España and the Audiencia of Guadalajara.

After considerable lobbying and competition, the wealthy Juan de

Oñate, whose wife was descended from the family of Moctezuma, was awarded the right to enter and colonize New Mexico:

> Don Luis de Velasco, my viceroy, had made a contract with you, the said Don Juan de Oñate, for this project and you have accepted it on the conditions and stipulations which will be delivered to you, signed and attested by notary. . . . I name you as my governor and captain general, chief, discoverer, and pacifier of the said provinces of New Mexico and its immediate environs so that, as such, in my royal name, you may enter them with the colonists and soldiers, baggage, belongings, munitions, and other necessary things that you would bring for this purpose, in all peace, friendship, and good treatment, which is what I particularly charge you. . . . You shall take care that the people who might go in your company shall proceed quietly and peacefully, without committing any excesses or setting a bad example or causing those you wish to draw to you to be angered or feel differently than is just.
>
> You shall order everything for the best and principal end, as stated, for you see it is a matter of importance. You shall arrange all things regarding it wisely and harmoniously, always ordering everything for the glory of God and the increase of our holy Catholic faith. You shall prepare with prudence for the events that may arise, so that neither by carelessness, neglect, nor remissness the Indians lose their zeal and enthusiasm, keeping but not overstepping the instructions of my viceroy that shall be committed to you with this. I order the soldiers, colonists, and servants who may go and remain with you that they shall consider you as their governor and captain general and keep and fulfill whatever you command them and respect your authority under the penalties that you may mete out to them. You shall be prepared to punish any rebels and proceed against those who overstep the bounds of authority, punishing them according to the usages of war, and do anything which may be appropriate in this regard and use the said charges and offices of governor and captain general, chief, discoverer, and pacifier of the said provinces and their immediate environs, conduct and enlist people and name and summon captains and other offices necessary for it and remove and re-appoint as may seem fitting to you. I give you the full power which may rightfully be required in such cases and order my governors, *alcaldes mayores, corregidores,* and other justices in whatever places they may be in order that for the above they give and do you the favor and aid that you might ask of them and that may be necessary . . .

Given in Mexico, October 21, 1595. Don Luis de Velasco. I,
Martin López de Gaona, chief notary of New Spain for the king,
our lord, transcribed the above at the command of the viceroy in
his name. Corrected. Juan Serrano (rubric).[19]

Oñate established headquarters in 1598, first at San Juan, near the
confluence of the Chama and Rio Grande rivers, and later at San
Gabriel. The founding of the colony was accompanied by celebrations
written and performed evidently with a conscious intent to underscore
historical importance and pride of achievement. Captain Farrar and
others staged a play near Socorro in 1598 to celebrate their efforts, and
Gaspar Pérez de Villagra wrote an epic that was, in effect, an early
history. Later, in 1609–1610, Pedro de Peralta, the first regular governor, founded Santa Fe as the permanent capital and established there
Analco, a Nahua barrio.

During the first period of colonization, 1591–1680, the population
of Spanish mestizo settlers was widely dispersed throughout the major
areas of Pueblo Indian habitation, in the areas around north Santa Fe
and along the Río Bravo Valley. The settlement pattern consisted of
isolated ranches and farms located in proximity to sources of coerced
Pueblo Indian labor. For several generations Santa Fe was the only
Spanish mestizo town in the entire province, with the exception of the
concentrated Christianized Indians of El Paso del Norte (Juárez), which
was actually a mission called Nuestra Señora de Guadalupe (established
in 1659). Mestizo communities were dispersed among Indian areas, and
both peoples thus were forced to confront each other.

Though weak and unstable in New Mexico, the development of
this type of settlement pattern was encouraged by the attempt to
introduce a partial *encomienda* practice, granting to selected settlers
some of the Indian population at specific intervals to provide goods and
work for them. Civil and religious disputes soon erupted. In 1639, the
cabildo of Santa Fe made an extensive complaint.

> *Most Excellent Sir:* In the past year of 1637 and in that of 1638,
> in the month of October, this *cabildo* gave account to your Excel-
> lency of the affairs of these provinces, transmitting some papers in
> which are set forth to your Excellency the justification and neces-
> sity with which this *cabildo* asks for their remedy made necessary by
> the excessive annoyance and disturbances against the royal juris-
> diction from which this commonwealth and the governors and
> other magistrates are suffering, a thing not to be remedied with the

power and forces of this land, for they are so few and so poor that
no remedy is to be had except from the powerful hand of his Majesty and that of your Excellency in his royal name . . . it is not
possible to express in writing what we are suffering or to give account of all that happens, although it is a consolation to know that
your Excellency, with your Christian zeal, will learn of it from the
despatches that have been sent to your Excellency and from that
which is now drawn up by our captain-general and this *cabildo*.
   The cause, Sir, is that the inhabitants are few, poor, and have
little knowledge of business affairs or of anything except arms,
while the religious are many and enjoy rich profits, acquired from
the labor of the natives and the poverty of the Spaniards. These
profits were neither asked for nor given as alms but [acquired] from
private dealings and contracts, and since these [ecclesiastics] are all
of the same religious Order they are all-powerful, which only serves
to produce more disturbances. . . .[20]

By the late seventeenth century, the settler population of Nuevo México consisted of approximately twenty-five hundred persons, of whom
no more than three hundred were European or criollos, Spaniards born
in Mexico. The majority of the pobladores, including some of the more
prominent, were mestizos of mixed caste, or *españoles mexicanos*, as well
as local Hispanicized Indians and Nahuas of central Mexican Indian
descent who had accompanied the criollos as settlers and as auxiliary
troops and servants. Settlers intermarried extensively with local Indians and had children. In addition to the pobladores, there were small
numbers of officials and Franciscan missionaries, with the latter scattered among the Pueblo towns at mission churches that were established for the conversion and social control of the Pueblo peoples.
   The majority of the Pueblo Indian population was comprised of the
Tiwa, Towa, Keresan, and Piro peoples, who numbered about sixteen
thousand. This marked a decline in population from about forty thousand in 1542, caused mainly by the introduction of European diseases
through the mestizo settlers and foreign visitors. Depopulation had
resulted in the abandonment of over half of the Pueblo settlements,
even prior to settlement in the 1590s. In the area that was to comprise
the *alcaldía* of Albuquerque, the major Pueblo settlements were those of
the southern Tiwa at Isleta Pueblo, on the Río Bravo, and several
pueblos of the Piros. These Piro towns were located east of the river, in
the Manzano Mountains, and included Chilili, Quarai, Abo, and Gran

Quivira, all of which were subsequently abandoned during the Pueblo revolt.

A major ongoing dispute pitted clergy, civil authority, settlers, and Indians against one another. Bernardo López de Mendizábal (governor, 1659–61) faced extensive complaints in an acrimonious review, particularly from Antonio González, *escribano* of the *cabildo*, who focused on Indian matters. Juan de Miranda (governor, 1664–65 and 1671–75) also had to answer to those of Francisco Gómez Robledo.

Political, economic, personal, racial, and class tensions on the early frontier were evident in the Pueblo revolt of August 10, 1680.[21] The revolt was preceded by increased economic abuse from both civil and religious authorities, including a renewed assault upon Indian religious practices. Governor Juan Francisco Treviño captured forty-seven *hechiceros*, executed three, and ordered the rest to be flogged. Following this action, the revolt was organized by recognized Pueblo leaders and based on specific grievances, but overall it was a rejection of Spanish domination. One leader was Popé of San Juan, a mestizo and religious practitioner. Another was Domingo Naranjo of Santa Cruz, son of a mulatto father and a Tlascaltecan mother, and also suspected to be a religious practitioner. Immediately prior to the revolt, Indian rituals were practiced again and hidden knowledge preached; or so Governor Antonio de Otermín reported:

> I received information that a plot for a general uprising of the Christian Indians was being formed and was spreading rapidly. This was wholly contrary to the existing peace and tranquillity in this miserable kingdom, not only among the Spaniards and natives, but even on the part of the heathen enemy, for it had been a long time since they had done us any considerable damage. It was my misfortune that I learned of it on the eve of the day set for the beginning of the said uprising, and though I immediately, at that instant, notified the lieutenant-general on the lower river and all the other *alcaldes mayores*—so that they could take every care and precaution against whatever might occur, and so that they could make every effort to guard and protect the religious ministers and the temples—the cunning and cleverness of the rebels were such, and so great, that my efforts were of little avail. To this was added a certain degree of negligence by reason of the [report of the] uprising not having been given entire credence, as is apparent from the case with which they captured and killed both those who were escorting some of the religious as well as some citizens in their

houses, and particularly, in the efforts that they made to prevent
my orders to the lieutenant-general passing through.[22]

The dispute exploded into the Pueblo revolt of 1680, which saw the
overthrow of Spanish colonial rule in New Mexico for over a decade
and the destruction of Spanish-mestizo ranchos, farms, and missions,
and the evacuation of the capital, Santa Fe. Both Pueblo and settlers
abandoned these areas; some Indians and mestizos joined the rebellion,
while others remained loyal to the colonial authorities. The inhabitants of the areas affected were forced to either accompany the fleeing
authorities south to El Paso del Norte or join the Pueblo peoples and
remain.

After the initial rebel victory, mestizo and Nahua settlers were
given the choice of joining the rebellious sector voluntarily or aban-
doning the area. In effect, agreement and coexistence was not out of
the question and not strictly to be decided by ethnicity.

Santa Fe was occupied by rebels, and settlers loyal to the authorities
were driven back to El Paso del Norte—one of the few instances in the
seventeenth and eighteenth centuries when Spanish colonial authority
was repelled. As noted, two days before the revolt Governor Otermín
had learned of the conspiracy when two of the rebels' messengers
were captured. Otermín and the Maestro de Campo Francisco Gómez
Robledo sought to organize resistance in advance. A council was called
to discuss and decide on a course of action, but eventually retreat was
forced. Lieutenant Governor Alonso García, Captain General of Rió
Abajo, also called a council; and from the discussions he reported what
is perhaps the most succinct statement on the events and composition
of the historic rebellion:

> As I learned that one of the Indians who was leading them was
> from the *villa* and had gone to join them shortly before, I sent some
> soldiers to summon him and tell him on my behalf that he could
> come to see me in entire safety, so that I might ascertain from him
> the purpose for which they were coming. Upon receiving this mes-
> sage he came to where I was, and, since he was known, as I say, I
> asked him how it was that he had gone crazy too—being an Indian
> who spoke our language, was so intelligent, and had lived all his
> life in the *villa* among the Spaniards, where I had placed such con-
> fidence in him—and was now coming as a leader of the Indian reb-
> els. He replied to me that they had elected him as their captain,
> and that they were carrying two banners, one white and the other

red, and that the white one signified peace and the red one war. Thus if we wished to choose the white it must be [upon our agreeing] to leave the country, and if we chose the red, we must perish, because the rebels were numerous and we were very few; there was no alternative, inasmuch as they had killed so many religious and Spaniards . . . to his people and tell them in my name all that had been said to him, and persuade them to [agree to] it and to withdraw from where they were; and that he was to advise me of what they might reply. He came back from there after a short time, saying that his people asked that all classes of Indians who were in our power be given up to them, both those in the service of the Spaniards and those of the Mexican nation of that suburb of Analco. He demanded also that his wife and children be given up to him, and likewise that all the Apache men and women whom the Spaniards had captured in war [be turned over to them], inasmuch as some Apaches who were among them were asking for them. If these things were not done they would declare war immediately and they were unwilling to leave the place where they were because they were awaiting the Taos, Pecuries, and Theguas nations, with whose aid they would destroy us.[23]

The instigators of the revolt were soon facing problems of their own that were often brought on by their inability to govern their disparate coalition as well as by their arbitrary methods. The loyalists were safeguarded by the *presidio* built at El Paso del Norte in 1682.

Through the efforts of Domingo Jironza Petriz de Cruzate, Pedro Reneros de Posada, and Diego de Vargas, authority was reestablished after twelve years. Luis Granillo was second in command under Vargas and Roque de Madrid in charge of troops. Preceded by armed sallies as well as by negotiation, in 1691 Governor Diego de Vargas led a successful *entrada* to reestablish Spanish authority, and Santa Fe was recaptured in December 1693. Following the reoccupation, new settlements were established: Villa Nueva de Santa Cruz de Españoles Mejicanos del Rey Nuestro Señor Carlos Segundo (in 1695) and Bernalillo (in 1695). The significance of the Pueblo revolt lay in its expression of ethnic tensions and in its class aspects.

New settlement patterns and population distribution differed significantly from those of the seventeenth-century colony. Now clergy were less prominent in exercising authority over Indians. During the first decade of the reconquest period the settler population was concentrated in the reestablished capital of Santa Fe for defense purposes; but thereafter new mestizo settlements expanded steadily throughout the province. The first such settlement was established in 1695 at Santa Cruz de la Cañada de los Españoles Mexicanos, with settlers from Zacatecas and Chihuahua. In 1706, Francisco Cuervo y Valdéz established thirty families at a villa to be called San Felipe Albuquerque.

Though force was paramount, certain rights were retained by the rebels. Significant differences between the first and second periods of colonization included respect for Pueblo distinctiveness, greater caution by missionaries, and the material absence of the enforced labor practices that had been tried earlier. The process of resettlement was characterized by formal and informal dimensions. The formal dimension consisted of the implementation of colonial laws and viceregal instructions governing settlement and the granting of land to settlers. Following the reconquest, official policy was dominated by the pacification of the Pueblos and then by gradual and strictly regulated resettlement of the province. The informal dimensions consisted of the settlers' interest in occupying the most fertile land and using it in any way that would strengthen their private or collective interests. This attempt was limited by the resistance of the Pueblo peoples, the threat of attack by nomadic Indians, and the coercive abilities of the governor. Throughout the eighteenth century, the actual process of settlement proceeded, oscillating between both settler and Pueblo interests and generally characterized by an accommodation between the two.

Relations between civil authorities and the religious continued to be contentious, although the civil sector was more predominant. Church persons spoke in a polemical and accusatory manner. One priest, for example, declared that

> only the said *alcaldes* and governors . . . ill-treat the Indians in the manner described, but even the judges who enter to conduct the *residencias* of the *alcaldes* and governors who have completed their terms of office, inflict upon the Indians as much injury and hardship as may conduce to the advancement of their own interests and the success of their ambitious desires. It is public knowledge throughout the kingdom that such persons seek to conduct these *residencias* more for what they gain by unjust and violent spoliation of the Indians than for what they receive from the office that they exercise . . .
>
> The second oppression that the Indians frequently suffer at the hands of the governors is being compelled arbitrarily and by force, for the small price of an awl or other similar trifle, to work on the

buildings that they need, whatever they may be and whether they require little or much time. The Indians also are required to drive cattle as far as the *villa* of Chihuahua, which is more than two hundred leagues distant from the place where the governors live. They receive in payment for this service only a little ground corn, which they call *pinole,* and the Indian cattle drivers are compelled to pay for those [animals] that are lost or die for want of care or by any other accident. A pernicious evil arises from this cattle driving, for the Indians must abandon their families and leave their lands uncultivated, and, as a consequence, be dying of hunger during the greater part of the year.

The third oppression, and the most grievous and pernicious, from which originate innumerable evils and sins against God, and manifest injuries against the missionaries and Indians, is the wicked dissimulation of the governors in regard to the acts of the *alcaldes mayores,* for it is publicly known throughout the realm that when they give them their *varas,* or wands of office, they tell and advise them to make the Indians work without pity.

With such express license, your reverence can imagine how many disturbances will be caused by men who usually take the employment of *alcaldes mayores* solely for the purpose of advancing their own interests and acquiring property with which to make presents to the governors, so that the latter will countenance their unjust proceedings, even though they be denounced before them, and perhaps will even promote them in office.[24]

Though the language and particulars varied, this and other disputes grew out of the battle over resources.

Land distribution and settlement patterns would mark deeply the politics and leadership of New Mexican society. Fortuitous land recipients and graziers established families that would be prominent in politics for many generations. Three categories of royal grants and *mercedes reales* were authorized: community grants to an individual *poblador principal* or group of settlers; individual private grants to ranchers and farmers; and grants that guaranteed Pueblo Indians possession of all lands in their use or occupied by them.[25] Otherwise, no settlement or occupation of land had any recognized legal status; nor could title generally be acquired except through regulation in one of the three categories. Communal grants were of the greatest political consequence from the nineteenth through the twentieth centuries. The origin of one such grant was rather clear:

I, Lorenzo Marquis, resident of this town of Santa Fe, for myself and in the name of 51 men accompanying me, appear before your excellency and state that, in consideration of having a very large family, as well myself as those accompanying me, though we have some land in this town it is not sufficient for our support, on account of its smallness and the great scarcity of water, which owing to the great number of people we cannot all enjoy, wherefore we have entered a tract of land on the Río Pecos, vacant and unsettled, at the place commonly called El Vado, and where there is room enough, not only for us, the 51 who ask it, but also for everyone in the province not supplied. Its boundaries are on the north the Río de la Baca from the place called the *ranchería* to the Agua Caliente, on the south the Cañón Blanco, the east the Cuesta with the little hills of Bernal, and on the west the place commonly called the Gusano—which tract we ask to be granted us in the name of our Sovereign, whom may God preserve, and among these 51 men petitioning and 13 Indians, and among them all there are 25 firearms, and they are the same persons who appear on the subjoined list, which I present in due form, and we unanimously and harmoniously as one person do promise to enclose ourselves in a *plaza* well fortified with bulwarks and towers, and to exert ourselves to supply all the firearms and ammunition that it may be possible for us to procure. And as we trust in compliance with our petition we request and pray that your Excellency be pleased to direct that we be placed in possession, in the Name of his Royal Majesty our Sovereign, whom may God preserve, and we declare in full legal form that we do not act with dissimulation.

Lorenzo Marquis
For himself and the Petitioners

Marquis received the following reply from Antonio José Ortiz:

On the 26th of the month of November, One Thousand Seven Hundred and Ninety-Four, I, Antonio José Ortiz, Captain in the militia and principal *alcalde* of the town of Santa Fe, . . . in company with two witnesses who were Xavier Ortiz and Domingo Santiestevan, the 52 petitioners being present, caused them to comprehend the petition they had made and informed them that to receive the grant they would have to observe and fulfill in full form of law the following conditions:

First—That the tract aforesaid has to be in common, not only in regard to themselves but also to all settlers who may join them in the future.

Second—That with respect to the dangers of the place they shall have to keep themselves equipped with firearms and bows and arrows in which they shall be inspected as well at the time of settling as at any time the *alcalde* in office may deem proper, provided that after two years settlement all the arms they have must be firearms, under the penalty that all who do not comply with the requirement shall be sent out of the settlement.

Third—That the *plaza* they may construct shall be according as expressed in their petition, and in the meantime they shall reside in the Pueblo of Pecos where there are sufficient accommodations for the aforesaid 52 families.

Fourth—That to the *alcalde* in office in said *pueblo* they shall set apart a small separate piece of land for him to cultivate for himself at his will, without their children or successors making any objection thereto, and the same for his successor in office.

Fifth—That the construction of their *plaza* as well as the opening of ditches, and all other work that may be deemed proper for the common welfare shall be performed by the community with that union which in their government they must preserve.[26]

Notable in this instance was both the collective access to land and the relative simplicity with which it was secured, as well as the ambiguity of boundaries and the specific rights of participation.

The general pattern of settlement during the eighteenth century was characterized by settlements that consisted of dispersed plazas or ranchos, groupings of small farms.[27] This development occurred by necessity and choice as well as by official requirement, with the latter involving conflict between officials and settlers. Another area of conflict between the interests of official authorities and settlers involved the policy of requiring pobladores to live in compact settlements for protection against nomadic attack, a policy that was opposed to their frequent desire to live on their farms and ranches as a way of better developing and protecting crops and herds. Generally, the policy of concentrated settlement was successful only when and where the threat of attack was immediate and acute. In some cases the danger was so great that new settlements had to be abandoned, while older settlements were restrained from further expansion or suffered great damage and loss of life. This historical pattern left a legacy of intense local loyalties. Towns were modest; even the capital of Santa Fe was described by Bishop Tamarón in 1769 as having one principal street. Their populations were a mixture of peoples. El Paso was described, by

Nicolás de Lafora, as inhabited by Spaniards, mestizos, mulattoes, genizaros, captive Indian slaves, and Tigua and Piro Indians; the Spanish-speaking families outnumbered, notably, the Indian speaking, and the captain served as alcalde.

Smaller settlements were politically, juridically, and militarily dependent upon higher authorities, namely, the alcalde mayor and *teniente comandante* located at the larger economic center, who were, in turn, dependent upon the governor and *comandante* of the province.[28] In the religious sphere, these smaller, dependent settlements usually possessed only a chapel without a resident priest. The priest resided in the parish center and occasionally visited these settlements to perform Mass and offer sacraments. The twenty-eight missions established in the New Mexico area differed from those in Texas and California, consisting entirely of a modest chapel and house for the cleric rather than being extensive productive units; also, in New Mexico the religious attended the mestizos more than the Indians. In 1767 the four major mission sites of Santa Fe, Albuquerque, Santa Cruz, and La Cañada were secularized.

Settlers engaged in extensive relations with the Pueblos. The Indian pueblo encompassed native and mestizo economic and social practices, characterized by the persistence of traditional forms of economic organization and distribution and consumption patterns.[29] Also present was the influence of the mestizo and of European technology, production for exchange, trade, and the administrative, military, cultural, and religious penetration of Pueblo culture and social relations. Administratively, the settlements of the Pueblo Indians were administered by an Indian governor who was appointed by the colonial governor. In reality, the Pueblos had two sets of officials, one for conducting external relations with colonial officials, and the other comprised of the actual leaders of the community who were headed usually by the *capitán de guerra*. In practice, the appointed governor acted as an intermediary between the real leaders and the colonizers. In general, the formal and informal policy of accommodation adopted by both the mestizo and Pueblo peoples guaranteed to the Pueblos the preservation of the core of their economic basis as well as relative autonomy within a subordinate relationship. This unequal relationship was recognized as such by the Pueblos; however, they were conscious of rights guaranteed to them and active in the defense of rights that were violated.

Generally, the trend was toward an unequal but understood interdependence between the Pueblos and the Spanish–mestizo settlements. This trend was reflected in the extensive use of Pueblo auxiliaries to repel raids and in military campaigns against the nomadic peoples surrounding New Mexico. The Pueblo troops, who fought under their own capitanes de guerra and used horses, swords, and *escopetas* (blunderbusses), more than once prevented the destruction of mestizo plazas. Interdependence was also reflected in many formal and informal economic and social relationships between Pueblo Indians and mestizo and Spanish pobladores, including marriage, *compadrazgo*, and trading activities that were often in violation of prohibitions against trade with nomadic Indians. Conversely, inequality and resistance to inequality were reflected in relatively persistent encroachments by settlers on Pueblo lands; and these, in turn, were vigorously contested through lawsuits and appeals to the colonial governor.

Under harsh conditions several organizational modes emerged, among them the *acequia* system and the Penitente structure and rituals.[30] The most notable groups of this type were the Penitentes, lay brotherhoods in northern New Mexico and southern Colorado, where large numbers of rural Catholics organized at local parish levels beginning sometime in the middle or late eighteenth century. Formally, the brotherhoods were known as La Fraternidad Piadosa de Nuestro Jesús Nazareno. Members performed acts of charity and good deeds. Penitent rituals demonstrated discipline and atonement. More importantly, service performed by local Penitentes included caring for the sick of the village, making funeral and burial arrangements for members as well as for others upon request, assisting widows and orphaned children, and arbitrating individual or group disputes. At a certain point in time, to care for the sick the Brothers began to appoint from among the membership an *Enfermero* (nurse) and an *Auxiliadora* (a woman auxiliary member). These selected representatives were charged with visiting the sick, reporting on family needs, and providing both spiritual and material assistance. In the event of death, the Brothers would prepare the deceased, organize a *velorio* (wake) and funeral procession, and perform the burial ceremonies. These groups became extensively structured in the nineteenth century.

Other organized groups active in the mestizo villages during the late eighteenth and early nineteenth centuries included the church-sponsored *cofradías* or *confraternidades*. These organizations were also lay and religious centered, but they limited their activities to the more conventional, service needs of the church and the local congregations. In places without a permanent priest, these religious groups, such as the Poor Souls founded in 1718 in Albuquerque, cared for the parish building and fixtures, conducted prayer services, and collected donations for charitable purposes. Other examples included, by 1776, the confraternities of Our Lady of Light, the Blessed Sacrament, the Rosary, and the Third Order of Saint Francis. The primary purposes of these organizations were to maintain the church and the statues of saints and to provide mutual aid during times of crisis for the members.

Still extant and quite common during the colonial period were local ditch associations charged with the development, upkeep, maintenance, and administration of irrigation waters that were essential to the agricultural economies of each and every village. Farmers belonged to an acequia (ditch) association, contributed annual assessments with in-kind labor or cash, and cooperated in ditch cleaning and maintenance chores. There were elected representatives, a commission, and *mayordomo* ("supervisor") who would administer the flow and usage of irrigation water on an equitable basis. The mayordomo inspected and organized repairs of the acequia, regulated the number of days of labor required of each farmer, distributed and apportioned water, adjudicated disputes, and searched for infractions of agreed-upon rules. The duty of the commissioners was to adopt rules, assess contributions to cover ditch maintenance, review reports submitted by the mayordomo and treasurer, keep and approve any written records of association proceedings, and direct the community work on the annual cleaning of the acequia in the spring. Major work tasks were performed collectively by all members. The acequia was a key developmental and supportive institution involved in the economic means for survival, linking farms and communities over a watershed and implicitly involving mobilization. Lay brotherhoods and acequia arrangements existed outside New Mexico, but they were not as extensive or continuous.

There were other organizations that had judicial standing—the militia foremost, but also volunteer participation and groups for public order. Occasionally self-appointed and covert groups operated to settle disputes. To the extent that they functioned in the far north, they provided protection in desolate areas against criminals and marauders; they possessed tribunal powers and their members were armed. In any case, the militia had greater sanction and participation. Defense required organization, as can be seen in Don Pedro Pino's complaint:

> In order to maintain this glory it has been necessary to keep constantly 1,500 men under arms. As the public treasury has disregarded their payment it was necessary to reduce the service to payment by corporation. These neighbors, then, work by turns in their military tasks with the same punctuality as if they were veterans. They have to present themselves with a change of horses, firelocks, pistols, bows, arrows and shields. They assume well the obligation of paying for the ammunitions and the provisions necessary during the time they are kept under arms which is wont to be regularly 45 days, and sometimes two or three months of continuous, cruel war with savage nations who are already armed and skilled in the use of the guns.
>
> This most hard and unsupportable burden, which has no like in any other province, causes New Mexico certain evils more easily conceived than explained; suffice it to say, that many of those unfortunates are ruined by a single campaign, for they have to sell their own clothing and their families' to provide themselves with ammunitions and provisions. [31]

The benefits—personal and family security—were plain but the costs were exacting.

As the oldest settlement area, New Mexico had the most extensive political experience, which was punctuated by a long list of governors, officials, and members of the cabildo. Beginning with De Vargas and extending to the period of Mexican sovereignty, the names of its competent governors included Juan Bautista de Anza, Fernando Chacón, and Pedro Fermín de Mendinueta; and they and others found administration more feasible when they had beneficial relations with prominent locals. For ten years, Governor Bautista de Anza was as energetic and capable in New Mexico and Arizona as he had been in California and Sonora. New Mexico was also an area that impelled settlement and trade into other areas. It extended northward into what became the San Luis Valley of Colorado, and periodically it made trade and travel arrangements with Tejas and California as well as with Chihuahua. It shared with other provinces the El Paso–Mesilla region and what later came to be southern Arizona, referred to as Pimería Alta or Alta Sonora.

Arizona

The pivot to the settlement of Arizona was a mission, San Xavier; a presidio, San Ignacio de Tubac; farming; and some mining.[32] Jesuit Father Kino's activity occurred in the area as early as the 1690s. Jesuits found missionizing here to be unusually difficult and slow. After their order's expulsion in 1767, the Franciscans came, but they were few in number. After the work of the missionaries had begun, there was a mining boom in Arizona in 1736, and one may have occurred as early as 1735, at a ranchería along the Santa Cruz River.

Indian relations were volatile. A tough soldier and diligent official, Juan Bautista de Anza worked to establish a stable settlement in the Tubac area by securing acceptable relations with the Comanches and Apaches. In 1776, on the Santa Cruz River, a presidio was built according to the plan of the *Reglamento* of 1772 to protect missionaries and travelers on overland routes. Here, at San Agustín de Tucson—as was the case at Tubac—there were eventually soldiers and families and civic life.

In addition to social life, the economy and government found their center in Tubac and Tucson, where there were, at most, two thousand residents, including ranchers, farmers, laborers, soldiers, priests, and partially Hispanicized Indians. An overwhelming number were mestizos, although several claimed to be Spaniards. Authority was concentrated in the commanding officers, and trade was conducted principally with the military, local Indians, and Indians living in the interior of Sonora. Families who emerged as the most prominent during the eighteenth century were associated with the military.

Although there was trade with the Indians, the area was continually affected by conflict. Tubac and Tucson were heroic survival stations of the frontier. Only the tenacity and skill of the residents enabled them to survive. Soldiers and priests were under orders, but the civilians remained at their own bidding. Sheer human will and love of the land must explain their persistence, for material incentives proved to be too costly on this frontier.

Tejas, or Nuevas Filipinas: Strategic Defense, Indian Raiders, Ranching and Contraband

After an earlier attempt ending in failure in 1693, and the initial settlements at San Juan Bautista near present-day Eagle Pass in 1700,

Tejas, or Nuevas Filipinas, was successfully colonized during the period 1716–21 as a gobierno, or province, of the Viceroyalty of Nueva España. Tejas was occupied for strategic defense against French expansion from Louisiana, which had been prompted by French attempts at colonization such as the unsuccessful effort by the Sieur de la Salle at Matagorda Bay in 1685 and the presence of French fur traders among Tejas Indians. The raiding Comanches were a continuous threat on the Llano Estacado and Texas plains.

Texas preeminently has been a borderland, with shifting boundaries comprising a basic aspect of Texas social and political history.[33] The boundaries of the colonial province of Texas differed significantly from those of both Tejas in the period of the Mexican republic and the present-day boundaries of Texas. The province's southwestern boundary was defined as the Río Medina (a small river north of the Río Bravo and the Río Nueces), located just south of present-day San Antonio. The eastern boundary was roughly the Río Colorado, or Rojo, found within the present state of Louisiana (the present-day Red River that is shared by the states of Louisiana, Texas, and Oklahoma, but not what is now known as the Colorado River). The northern boundary ran along the Río Colorado, or Rojo (between present-day Texas and Oklahoma); while the western boundary was a line within the Llano Estacado running roughly from the sources of the Río Medina to a point on the Río Colorado (Red River). The Río Bravo Valley (present-day south Texas) was within the neighboring colony of Nuevo Santander, while what is now the western part of the state of Texas was part of the provinces of Nuevo México, Chihuahua, and Coahuila. Colonial Tejas thus roughly included the areas from San Antonio north and eastward and excluded two major areas of Mexican settlement that were prominent in the enlarged Texas of the nineteenth century—West Texas, the El Paso area, and South Texas, the lower Río Grande Valley, where by 1750 there were over twenty settlements.

During the last decades of the seventeenth century, frontier expansion extended into Nuevo León and Coahuila. Querétaro and Zacatecas became the important staging areas, followed by Saltillo and Monclova. To fortify the area, Francisco de Urdiñola required a colony of several hundred Nahua Tlaxcalans at Saltillo. In the 1680s several problem-ridden expeditions went north.[34]

In 1690 two missions were established on the Neches River, a point of contact for settlers and, later, traders. Tejas was designated as a frontier province in 1691, and Domingo de Terán named the responsible governor, among whose first priorities was a thorough reconnoitering of the Red River area where civil and religious quarrels were epidemic. Father Damián Mazanet wrote his appraisal in a letter to the viceroy:

> Miro también el que todo cuanto se ha hecho ha sido hechura y disposición de Vuestra Excelencia; si salimos todos no queda bien, que aunque sea mal logrado el ver y registrar el rio, es culpa de don Domingo Terán por su mal gobierno y peor disposicion. De quedar aunque sea yo solo con dos soldados, porque hay algunas esperanzas. Hablo para el vulgo, que ya sé que para los creditos de Vuestra Excelencia es nada todo esto.[35]
> [I look also to the fact that everything that has been done has been the work and arrangement of your excellency. It will come out badly if we all leave. Although seeing and surveying the river may be unsuccessful, it is don Domingo Terán's fault for his bad governance and worse ability. If I stay, although alone with just two soldiers, it is because there is some hope. I speak for the common people, since I know that all this is nothing to your excellency's reputation.]

Mazanet left no doubt about the governor's responsibility for the expedition's incomplete success, but he admitted that conditions had been difficult.

Tejas Mexican settlements were embattled from the first, and this affected society and political patterns.[36] Founded to provide strategic international defense against French expansion, Tejas also faced a military threat from numerous groups of hostile indigenous tribes, such as the coastal Karankawa. An even greater threat was posed by the arrival of two groups of highly mobile and warlike raiders, the Apaches and the Comanches. Driven south into Tejas and New Mexico by the more numerous Comanches, the Apaches collided with incoming Mexican settlers at the beginning of the eighteenth century. By mid-century the Comanches entered Tejas, driving the Apaches westward into Nuevo México and the present state of Arizona. Both groups posed a serious and continuing threat that restricted the growth of Mexican population and settlements in Tejas. The impact of the Comanches was further magnified as the tribe gained firearms and other weapons through a contraband trade with mestizo settlers and the French in Louisiana.

Given these circumstances, the administration of Tejas was placed primarily in the hands of the military; as later in the Californias, all of the colonial governors were military officers who often faced campaigns during their terms in office. The governor was both principal administrator and *capitán general,* combining military and civil governmental authority. Prior to the creation in 1776 of the Provincias Internas (the internal or northern frontier provinces), the governor was directly subordinate to the viceroy and the audiencia in Mexico City. After 1776 the governor was subordinate to the capitán general of the Internal Provinces, and later, when the eastern region formed a separate jurisdiction, to the captain general of the eastern Internal Provinces. Because of Tejas's exposed situation, administrators and local leaders continually faced, more than elsewhere, problems created by the consequences of population density as well as the need for supplies or trade.

There were three major areas of Mexican settlement in colonial Tejas: the San Antonio de Bexar central area; the La Bahía coastal area; and the Los Adaes/Nacogdoches area of east Tejas, near Louisiana. The first continuing settlements were established in east Tejas in 1716 by an expedition led by Coahuila's Governor Capitán Domingo Ramón and Juchereau Saint-Denis, a Frenchman in the service of Spain. In 1721 the east Tejas settlements were reorganized, and the Presidio Nuestra Señora del Pilar de los Adaes was founded as the capital of Tejas. In 1772, Los Adaes and east Tejas were ordered abandoned and the inhabitants removed to San Antonio, but the area was resettled in 1774, with Nacogdoches founded in 1779.

The advance of mestizaje and the breakdown of the old caste hierarchy was implicit in the important role played in east Tejas by Don Antonio Gil y Barbo, a man of mulatto descent who was lieutenant governor of Tejas and the resettler in 1779 of the presidio of Nacogdoches.[36] While Gil y Barbo's official position required him to be formally an español, his ethnicity was well known and he was distinctive, in comparison with many other frontier officials, because his leadership was based on the support of his local community. In exercising personal initiative, the settlers sent petitions to the viceroy and within four years they received permission to return to east Tejas. In resettling there, Gil y Barbo realized a heroic achievement, for others in this area had failed. The economy of east Tejas included substantial trade with Indians for furs, as well as an extensive contraband trade in which the French and other European aliens were involved.

More fortuitous than other Tejas settlements were San Antonio and

La Bahía. The San Antonio de Bexar area, destined to become the capital of the most important Mexican settlement in Tejas, was established in May 1718 when the Mission of San Antonio de Valero (later known as the "Alamo") and the Presidio of San Antonio de Bexar were founded near the banks of the San Antonio River. Both sites involved Hispanicized Indians from Coahuila and were established at the orders of the Viceroy Marqués de Valero. Later, in 1731, a civilian town, the Villa de San Fernando de Bexar, was established. Earlier, civilian settlers were combined with a group of fifty-five isleños, or Canary Islanders, ten families recruited as pobladores for the new villa. The Villa de San Fernando de Bexar would remain the only municipality in Tejas, with a civilian governmental body, the cabildo, in operation to the end of the colonial period. The third area of settlement was at La Bahía (later to be known as Goliad), located southeast of the San Antonio. La Bahía was established as the site of a presidio and a mission in 1722 by the Marqués de San Miguel de Aguayo, who was then governor of Tejas. Several other missions also existed in the three major areas at various times. In 1722, the San Antonio area was incorporated with the province of Coahuila.

Throughout the colonial period, the province of Tejas was too economically dependent upon the presidios and military activities, as well as trade with foreigners. Its population fluctuated as the people suffered from epidemics.[37] While farming and ranching provided locally produced supplies, these were inadequate to feed the inhabitants; food and other supplies were delivered from Coahuila and Nuevo Santander to sustain the inhabitants. The population of the province increased, but it was subject to considerable fluctuations related to problems of supply, the intensity of Indian hostilities, the occurrence of epidemics and droughts, and other circumstances. In 1777, according to the census conducted by the governor, Colonel Baron Juan Vicencio María de Riperda, there were 3,103 inhabitants including settlers, soldiers, and peacefully settled Indians. The census of 1792 enumerated a total of 2,992 people in colonial Texas, a slight decrease from 1777.

An event of major consequence was the settlement of the present-day lower Rio Grande Valley, which would soon be the strongest settled area.[38] In 1746, Colonel José de Escandón was commissioned to recruit settlers and to establish settlements in the lower Río Grande Valley Nuevo Santander. Over three thousand settlers and soldiers started from Querétaro. Reynosa and Camargo were founded in 1748. The entire effort involved several capable leaders—Carlos Cantú, José Vásquez Borrego, José Fernando Vidaurri, José Baez Benavides, Tomás Sánchez de la Barrera, Vicente Guerra, Bernabé Gutiérrez de Lara, and Blas María de la Garza Falcón—whose families would long be active in local politics. Mexican longhorn cattle were introduced to the area and Revillas (Guerrero), Mier, and Laredo were founded in the early 1750s. Grants of land, mercedes, were made to settlers living at geographical right angles to the Bravo, north and south, with José de Escandon receiving the largest. The grantees established cattle ranchos that soon characterized the area from the Bravo to the Nueces and from Corpus Christi Bay to Laredo. Comanche and Apache raiders were the most immediate local problem.

Like the other areas of the far northern frontier during the late colonial period, Tejas experienced a mix of progress and problems. The population of Tejas reflected a high degree of mestizaje, which was steadily amalgamating criollos, españoles mexicanos, Tlaxcalan Indian allies, Texas Indians, a few mulattoes, and Europeans (including both peninsulares and a scattering of Frenchmen and others).[39] In August 1731, the first town council of San Antonio was seated, and included two alcaldes, six councilmen, one aguacil, and a secretary.[40] As first settlers, the inhabitants were entitled to be recognized as hidalgos, and they insisted on their rights in preference to those of the religious and the Indians. The command was initially dominated by the leading families among the first settlers, including Canary Islanders; the latter, however, experienced differences among themselves and were challenged by later arrivals. The council was often lively and contentious, and the influence of its members waxed and waned. Kinship and economic ties were important in alliances, and as in other places, land, water, labor, and trade were central issues.

The most urgent problem was how to survive through agriculture and stock-raising and in the face of raiding nomads. The best, most immediate lands were held by the missions, and soon the civilians were writing letters of complaint to the viceroy, asking for consolidation of the missions to reduce their number, for Indian labor to help them in raising their crops, and for the curtailment of mission sales to the military which deprived them of their closest market. In August 1749, when peace was negotiated with the local Apaches, they received meat rations that reduced the number of stock intended for the settlers.

Next, the Comanches raided in retaliation for the protection of the Apaches, and a major Comanche campaign was conducted in 1759. The agreement with the Apaches was set aside, and one was made in 1785 with the Comanche which incensed the Apaches.

Tejas indeed survived. Father Agustín Morfi, Franciscan prelate, and Tedoro de Croix, soon to be the comandante general of the Interior Provinces, visited in 1778 and judged the inhabitants to be in desperate straits, although they also declared that the area possessed great potential. In 1793, missions were secularized and lands distributed. Zebulon Pike, usually a biased observer, had a more positive impression years later, perceiving a prosperity that he believed was due to "the examples and encouragement given to industry, politeness and civilization by the excellent Governor Cordero and his colleague Herrera." In January 1811, a local Juan Bautista de las Casas rose in a revolt that favored the movement of Hidalgo for independence and paid with his life, with his head displayed at the central plaza. Two years later in 1813, the patriots, in retaliation, killed an official once met by Pike, Simón de Herrera. By the second decade the town council was dominated by the Ruiz, Navarro, and Seguin families, who aggressively emphasized their economic interests but also competed with other families. The Navarros had emigrated from Saltillo, but the head of the family, Angel Navarro, a Corsican, had served in the Spanish army before immigrating to New Spain. Like others, the Navarros sought land grants, but they also dealt in trade with the eastern border and experienced profitable relations there. Angel Navarro was alcalde for a time. The eldest son, José Antonio Navarro, received his education in Saltillo, but he also worked for a firm in New Orleans and studied law on his own.

The heads of families in towns in the southern Río Bravo comprised an elite (among them, persons with officer rank) which had received *porciones* of land, and civic activity in these towns was the result of a combination of enforcing decrees and solving local problems. Horses and weapons were indispensable accoutrements to survival. The building of a church, the laying out of town lots, and, in the case of Laredo, the building of a jail were priorities that were accomplished collectively. Civic concerns focused on morals, contraband, the sale of liquor, and the tobacco trade. Decrees were read at assemblies in the plaza, and strangers were to be reported. There were frequent disputes concerning land, inheritance, and marriage. After 1810 gatherings of more than six persons were prohibited and permits were required to leave town as a way of inhibiting civil disorder. By the late eighteenth century Laredo had a school, which was made possible by cooperation between the clerical and civic authorities and was supported by tuition.

Until the end of the colonial period, the province of Tejas was subject to extreme fluctuations in economic, political, and population conditions, all of which required major administrative decisions.[41] While the province was under military rule, the vast distances allowed some groups of settlers to evade formal regulations and official scrutiny. The temporary abandonment of east Tejas in 1772 resulted from recommendations that were made following an inspection tour by the Marqués de Rubi in 1767. Because of the tenuous nature of colonial authority in east Tejas, de Rubi felt that the settlements were more of a liability in promoting illicit trade, and that concentration in the San Antonio area would make for more efficient military control. While the authorities were able to compel most east Tejas settlers to leave the settlements, they were unable to keep them very long in the San Antonio area. Thus, if they persisted, determined individuals and groups often were able to find ways around, or to gain exemptions from, the rules. Opposition to colonial authority would soon find more dramatic expression before the end of colonial rule in all of Mexico, including Tejas. By the 1790s Governor Manuel Muñoz had five major problems: foreign incursions, illegal trade, indomitable nomadic Indians, land allocations, and local governance.

Alta California: Ranchos Pueblos, Presidios, Missions

California settlement was made possible by the earlier pioneering and mission activity in Sinaloa, Sonora, and Baja California. In the case of Nueva, or Alta, California, the initial and major motivation for colonization was to provide strategic international defense along the Pacific Ocean to counter the expansion of Czarist Russia from Alaska and to compete with Britain in the Pacific Northwest. While actual occupation did not begin until 1769, Spanish officials had considered the need for settlements in Alta California as early as the sixteenth century.[42] The colonization of Alta California was undertaken in the period 1765–71, with the visitation and administrative inspection of the Viceroyalty of Nueva España by Vistador General José de Gálvez, who initiated a new program for administrative reorganization. Within this extensively considered program, known as part of the "Bourbon reforms," there occurred the creation of the Comandancia General of the Provincias Internas, as well as a reorganization and systematization of frontier military defense under a single unified command. This command included a new line of continuous presidial defense whose Pacific Northwest end was provided by the colonization of Alta California. The ambitious program of northern expansion was rationalized by Gálvez as a long-range investment designed to increase revenues from the Viceroyalty of Nueva España. Though foreign presence in Alaska and the Pacific Northwest gave a more immediate impetus to royal approval for the colonization of Alta California, Gálvez's motivation was apparently the more long-term strategic-defense value of the region for the protection of the colonial empire in North America as a whole. Another long-term motivation was Alta California's potential value for increasing future trade with Asia. Less significant to Gálvez as a reason for occupation, but of value as an ideological justification, was the desire of the Franciscan order to open a new missionary province in Alta California. Eventually, the colonists came for individual economic reasons.

Settlers were the key to establishing a society and an economy that would supersede both military and missionary outposts. As in other frontier areas, mestizos and Hispanicized Indians were the bulk of the settler contingent. As planned by Gálvez, the occupation of Alta California would be carried out by a joint land–sea expedition consisting of two land and two sea components.[43] The primary objective of the 1769 expedition was to rediscover and occupy the port of Monterey, which had been noted by Sebastián Vizcaíno in 1602, and secondarily to found missions and presidios there and at San Diego. Gálvez selected as the leaders of this military–missionary enterprise the newly appointed governor of Baja California, the veteran frontiersman Lieutenant Colonel Gaspar de Portola, and the recently arrived Franciscan head of the missions of Vieja (Baja) California, Father Junípero Serra. They proved to be fortuitous choices. Portola was to be the military commander and civil governor of the Californias, while Serra would be Father President of all new missions to be founded in Alta California. The makeup of the expedition and its dynamics presaged later aspects of California. Supporting Portola and Serra were several veteran military and naval officers. Among the ships and their crews were the *San Carlos* and *San Antonio,* commanded, respectively, by the experienced Pacific Ocean captains Vicente Vila and Juan Pérez. A ten-year veteran of the Baja California frontier presidios, Mexican-born Captain Fernando de Rivera y Moncada (later to be promoted) would command the advance land column of presidial troops known as *soldados de cuera*, or "leather-jacket soldiers," named after the thick leather outfits they wore for protection against arrows. Also part of the expedition were twenty-five soldiers from the Voluntarios de Cataluña, a newly formed regiment under the command of Lieutenant Pedro Fages, who later became governor. Participating in the expedition were a small contingent of Franciscan missionaries, a dozen artisans, and about eighty Christianized Baja California Indians, both men and women.

After many difficulties, including strong disputes between Portola, the officer, and Serra, the priest, over route choices and Indian relations, the expedition accomplished its primary objectives. During the course of long marches from San Diego to the vicinity of Monterey, promising sites were identified for future missions and ultimately for major towns.

The entire project depended on a social and economic anchoring, and a viable route of land communication between 1773 and 1776 resulted from the heroic efforts of Captain Juan Bautista de Anza, who (in 1776) twice crossed from Sonora–Arizona to San Francisco by land. The first journey was made with 34 men and the second with 240 men, women, and children.

During the years 1769–70, while the presidios of Monterey and San Diego, and the missions of San Diego de Alcalá and San Carlos de Borromeo de Carmelo were being founded, civil and religious authorities planned for the establishment of a chain of missions along the coast of Alta California. By this time, the mission had long been a reliable institution in New Spain and was viewed by officials as an important component of the colonization of frontier areas. While the primary rationale for the mission system was the salvation of souls, it also served a much more material objective, the development of resources and labor. Missions also comprised a system of extensive ideological and economic communication that was, in large measure, planned. In addition, they were a systematic effort to promote change, including, of course, an effort to train and control a labor force.

In contrast to Nuevo México and Tejas, where Indians resisted more effectively, California's Native American peoples underwent intense indoctrination and acculturation. Thus, they were trained as a labor force to produce foodstuffs, materials, and unfinished products available for official purposes.[44] Indians were attracted to the missions by the opportunity to acquire new commodities, technology, and skills such as iron tools and agricultural techniques; by regular meals and mission foods; by their curiosity about the religious ceremonies and activities; and perhaps by their belief in the promises of the missionaries that Christianity would confer a special grace, everlasting life. When priestly persuasion and material goods failed to attract new converts, the threat or actual use of military force coerced villages to relocate to the mission. Following the policy of *congregación y reducción*, which was more feasible in California than elsewhere, by the end of the decade the missionaries with soldiers had succeeded through a combination of persuasion and coercion in concentrating a population of several hundred Indian workers and their families at the two main missions. The *neophytes,* or converts—as Indians living at the mission were known, to distinguish them from the *gentiles,* or unconverted Indians—followed a strict schedule of work and religious indoctrination under the direction of the Franciscan missionaries. They also were taught a wide range of skills and crafts. Thus, the missions may be viewed as the first schools. The missionaries were writers as well as teachers. Francisco Palou wrote the first book on California, *Noticias de la Nueva California,* and the first biography, *Vida de Junípero Serra,* which primarily dealt with mission activity. As a result of this notable productivity, the missions were able to provide a base of support for the foundation of pueblos.

Settlements in this region had an expected role related to the aim of the colony. The first civilian pueblo, San José, was founded on November 29, 1777, on the banks of the Guadalupe River in present-day Santa Clara County, by fourteen families totaling sixty-six persons. By the end of the first decade, 1769–79, there were three presidios, one pueblo, and eight established missions in Alta California, with a total Mexican and Spanish population of five hundred.[45] A limited number of Spanish-speaking Christianized people, of whatever ethnic background, were included among a larger coastal Native American population from San Diego to San Francisco. The purpose of the civil pueblos was threefold: to create agricultural settlements producing a surplus that would supply the presidios, thus reducing their dependence on costly shipments of supplies from San Blas; to create a permanently increasing population of *gente de razón* to settle Alta California; and to provide a source for a population of military-age youths who could be recruited from among the families of retired soldiers and pobladores to fill the ranks of the presidial garrisons.

Eventually, several small settlements came into existence. From the first years, Alta California was governed jointly with Baja California, and the capital for both was located at Loreto in Baja. Pedro Fages, who succeeded Portola, experienced many problems with the clergy. Conflicts between religious and civil authorities in California followed patterns that were roughly similar to those experienced in other frontier areas of Nuevo México and Tejas. In 1777, at the order of the viceroy, Felipe de Neve exchanged places with his lieutenant governor, the veteran Fernando de Rivera y Moncada, who moved from Monterey to Loreto, Baja California. De Neve had proposed to the viceroy the founding of a new agricultural settlement in northern Baja California to provide an additional source of supplies for Alta California. After de Neve's transfer to Monterey, Viceroy Bucareli ordered him to identify possible sites for agricultural settlements in Alta California. Plans for the founding of San José and Los Angeles, two pueblos, and Santa Bárbara, a presidio, including the selection of their sites, were accelerated in November 1777 by de Neve, who became a vigorous governor of the Californias and a colonel in the colonial army. A European Spaniard, de Neve was the third governor of both Baja and Alta California and the first to reside at Monterey, in Alta California. De Neve was highly regarded as a skilled administrator by his superiors, Viceroy Antonio María de Bucareli and the Commandant General of the Provincias Internas, Teodoro de la Croix. In planning the new settlement, de Neve had the example of two centuries of colonial experience in the founding of new towns as well as a large existing body of colonial law. Later, de Neve was promoted to inspector general with responsibility for the Provincias Internas as a whole.

As a result of the confidence of his superiors in his ability, de Neve was asked to write the specific regulations governing settlement in Alta California.[46] In 1777, the viceroy ordered him to draft suggestions for a new set of regulations to govern the Californias. With some slight modifications and additions, his draft, premised on the Laws of the Indies, was adopted as the new "Reglamento e instrucción para el gobierno de la provincia de Californias" in October 1781. This draft was to be significant in outlining the specific regulations and conditions for the establishment and operation of the pueblos and the granting of lots and allowances to the founding pobladores in Alta California, as well as in defining their responsibilities. Thus, the *reglamento* is one of the documents concerning initial governance that is pertinent to California.

The founding of towns involved problems of governance and other political issues for some of their inhabitants, but they also involved the creation of a sense of community and the practice of civic virtues. Initially, the alcalde and regidores of the ayuntamiento were appointed, but eventually they would stand for election. They received petitions and complaints, and passed ordinances. The expectation was that sound colonists would result in a sound colony. A few years later, in 1796, Fray José Senan wrote to expound grievances but also to express normative views concerning "community":

My Lord, the means which would best facilitate the colonization of New California and foment its material progress are, it seems to me, as follows:

First: Those who are to establish themselves there and erect towns must be persons of honest Christian character. . . .

It is equally necessary that new settlers be energetic workers; . . .

Second: It is my opinion that the information of settlements and their prosperity would be greatly enhanced if the inhabitants were permitted, through certain advantages and privileges, to enjoy the fruits of their own labor and make some profit therefrom. . . .

The third measure to facilitate the founding of settlements and to further their material progress, it seems to me, would be to appoint in each town a person to exercise authority over its residents and to act as their representative. His authority should derive not only from the prestige of his office, but also (as far as possible) from his own distinction and honesty, and his judicious conduct of affairs. He should be an enlightened and understanding person, one who would faithfully execute the instructions of the Governor of the Province. He would also be expected to discourage bad conduct among the colonists. . . .

Finally: Towns cannot exist without people; as the number of inhabitants increases, so do the opportunities for their well-being. I therefore believe that under no circumstances should retired soldiers or others with special credentials who wish to settle in the Province be permitted to establish themselves separately in remote areas or in villages outside the towns, a practice that I have seen tolerated these past few years. Such persons should rather be required to reside in the towns, as lands and adequate water supplies become available for their maintenance; otherwise we shall never have towns.[47]

The priest was an insightful observer as well as a special pleader in a partisan dispute; yet he also had a vision of the ideal community as a place of kinship, work, relationships, values, discourse, sacrifice, and commitment to a shared future. Such a community would also emphasize the predominance of the group over the individual.

The emerging local leadership reflected the influence of both the presidio society and the social structure of the Indian communities.[48] The most prominent families in the pueblo tended to be those of former sergeants and corporals, who constituted a developing local elite since there were few officers. A pronounced nexus existed between town and fort. Northern California and the San José area were responsibilities based in both Monterey and San Francisco. Southern California and the Los Angeles area were divided administratively between the jurisdictions of the commandants of the presidios of Santa Bárbara and San Diego. Los Angeles, at this time, was under the administrative jurisdiction of Santa Bárbara; and the first local representative of the commander at Santa Bárbara, an acting corporal named Vicente Feliz, established a notable family. Economic relationships between the pueblos and the presidios were also strengthened by the sale of surplus crops to the garrisons.

Local citizens and their spokespersons from the pueblos also experienced close, if occasionally less amicable, ties with nearby missions.[49] In the Los Angeles area, for example, Mission San Gabriel was under the jurisdiction of the San Diego presidio, while Mission San Fernando was, like the *pueblo*, under the jurisdiction of the Santa Bárbara presidio. Lesser ties existed with Mission San Juan Capistrano, which later marked the boundary between the Los Angeles and San Diego districts during the Mexican national period. While San Gabriel was established before Los Angeles, San Fernando was founded sixteen years after the pueblo, in 1797. Relations between the settlers and the missionaries were often ambivalent and sometimes antagonistic. The missionaries felt threatened by the influence of the pueblo's secular life on the surrounding Indians, many of whom were more attracted to the town than to the missions. Conflicts also developed between *pobla-*

dores and missionaries over land and the use of limited natural resources like water. The missionaries claimed priority on the basis of
their religious mission of conversion and their role as guardians of the
property interests of the original Native American inhabitants.

Conflicts between religious and secular interests in the north ran
much deeper than those between the people of Los Angeles and the
clergy at Mission San Gabriel. Franciscan authorities were even more
critical of governors and lieutenant governors such as Rivera y Moncada, de Neve, and Fages than of ordinary settlers. These conflicts
stemmed from two different sets of priorities. For the missionaries,
quite logically, the primary purpose of colonization was the religious
conversion of the California Indians. For the secular administrators,
the missions provided a means toward a larger strategic end and were
secondary in importance to the presidios and pueblos. Colonial officials viewed missions as transitional institutions that eventually would
be converted to civil towns and secular parishes as Indians were absorbed into the Spanish-speaking mestizo society. The missionaries,
conversely, had a vested interest in prolonging the neophytes' period of
dependency. Settlers wanted to prosper, and they expected the missions to serve their needs for products and labor.

From the first, Alta California pobladores developed interactive
relationships with the California Indian peoples.[50] While some aspects
of Mexican–Indian relations have received attention, such as the
pobladores' use of Indian labor, equally significant aspects such as
Mexican–Indian intermarriage and cultural exchange have been less
explored. For the Indians who were accustomed to trading among
themselves, between the interior and the coast, trade with the settlements provided an extension of their previous experience. Another
incentive for the Indians to contact the settlers was the acquisition of
trade goods, technology, and foodstuffs without the risk of making
themselves vulnerable to control by the Franciscan missionaries. The
settlers themselves welcomed trade, labor, and other relationships with
the surrounding Indian peoples. Trade with the gentiles brought into
the pueblo assorted raw materials such as deer skins, herbs, and fresh
game meat. Indian labor was also sought early by small, struggling
communities that required extensive hard work to bring the land under
cultivation.

The California process of transculturation also had political and
economic dimensions which were influenced by the inequality of power

among the groups in the process of being merged.[51] Mestizo culture and the Spanish language were institutionalized as dominant, reflecting the exercise of political, economic, and coercive authority. Especially significant here was the economic dimension of mestizaje, as expressed in the socializing function of work. Labor was one of the most important means of contact that brought together Indians, Africans, Europeans, and persons of mixed origins, exposing them to each other's cultures. Thus, largely through work, social communication and relationships developed among persons of different ethnic groups but of relatively similar class status. The pobladores, who were themselves racially mixed persons of mainly Indian and African descent, imposed a few color barriers to social relationships with Indians, although there were status distinctions. Mexican children were raised with Indian children and mestizo adults socialized with Indian adults. Indeed, so extensive was the contact that Governor Fages issued an order regulating the number of Indians allowed in the village of Los Angeles at a single time and prohibiting Indians from staying in the pobladores' homes overnight for reasons of security, although he himself apparently did not abide by the order. An important aspect of the relations between the pobladores and Alta California Indians was the racial–cultural intermixture—mestizaje—resulting from both marriage and casual relationships. The children of the marriages and of many of the casual relationships were incorporated into the growing population of gente de razón.

However, there was also real conflict and the apprehension of more to come.[52] Indian relations deteriorated into raids or uprisings that occasionally threatened the missions and pueblos. Two instances, for example, significantly involved Christianized Indians. In 1785 a planned revolt against Mission San Gabriel was discovered and suppressed; the plan included the participation of several nearby *rancherías* (villages). Encouraged by a seventeen-year-old maiden, an alleged witch named Toypurina, the plan of the rebels was to seize the mission and kill its priests and soldiers. A neophyte betrayed the plan to the corporal of the guard, José María Verdugo, who surprised the rebels as they prepared to ambush the soldiers. If the plan had been executed, it might have led to a successful attack on Los Angeles. The suppressed revolt, however, gave rise to a fear that increased the vigilance of the authorities, who sent a supply of guns, powder, and ammunition to Los Angeles from the presidio at Santa Bárbara. Toypurina, who may have been the daughter

of parents deeply committed to Indian religious culture, was an exceptionally intelligent woman who deeply resented mestizo occupation.
Announcing that she had visions of a mestizo defeat and Indian restoration, Toypurina inspired and participated in the major uprising at San
Gabriel, California. Following the defeat of the Indians, she was exiled
to northern California where, paradoxically, she married a mestizo
soldier and gave birth to descendants who became prominent pioneers.
In November 1810, plans for a neophyte uprising at Mission San
Gabriel, simultaneous with an attack by Mojave Indians, were exposed
before they could be executed. The Mojaves had conducted intermittent hostilities against the settlers and missionaries, and periodically,
had raided the fringes of the Los Angeles Basin for livestock and other
goods. The plans revealed to Verdugo by the neophyte indicated that
the Mojaves and the rebellious neophytes intended to attack and
destroy not only the mission but Los Angeles as well. Over four
hundred rebels were mobilized. Troops were ordered to San Gabriel
from the north, under Alferez Gabriel Moraga, and from the San Diego
presidio, under Sergeant José María Pico, the father of the later governor Pío Pico. These forces were joined at the mission by a company of
militia from the Los Angeles pobladores, and under the command of
the comisionado, Sergeant Guillermo Cota. By December 31, 1810,
the troops had captured twenty-one rebel neophytes and twelve gentiles and charged them with complicity in the planned revolt. Most
captured rebels were imprisoned at the Santa Bárbara presidio, where
the men were sentenced to hard labor and the implicated women were
assigned to households.

Settlement and land allocation were nearly concurrent.[53] Early
settlers included many retiring presidial veterans, and among the best
known and most successful of these veterans were those who received
grazing permits to establish what became the first private ranchos in the
Los Angeles area. These permits granted the holder the right to use the
land conferred for grazing purposes, but they did not give title. Legal
title had to be petitioned for, and only after the land had been improved and occupied for several years. The first grazing permit in Alta
California was issued in 1775 to soldier Manuel Butron, married to
Margarita, an Indian woman of Mission Carmel near Monterey. This
permit was for 140 *varas* of land in the Carmel Valley. The next permits
were issued in 1784, for land in the Los Angeles area, to three retiring
veterans of the San Diego presidial company. During the entire colo-

nial period only thirty grazing permits were made, compared to nearly eight hundred in the Mexican national period. Prior to secularization, the only properties in Alta California approaching the scale and wealth of the north central Mexican *hacienda* were, as Governor Figueroa said, the wealthiest and largest of the missions, such as San Gabriel and San Luis Rey.

But, as elsewhere, in California land and elite were joined. Up to the 1820s, the Alta California ranchos were developing. A rancho required livestock that needed several years to reproduce themselves; a labor force; a surplus to sell; and a market. Development of a labor force became possible, though not immediately so. Most coastal Indians were forced to live in the missions as neophytes, and the Indian population declined to half as a result of contagious diseases. Eventually, gentiles and vaqueros available to become laborers were relatively few; and competition for workers, for the services of those who were available, increased among the growing number of farmers and *rancheros*. But the mission had a potential labor force. Apart from sale to the presidios, prior to independence the trade of hides and tallow with ships from South America, and with privateers as well as ships from Mexico, was an incentive. Despite the limited wealth of their still developing properties, the rancheros of the colonial period were members of a rising local elite. This incipient sector was composed of a small number of officers and a larger number of noncommissioned officers and the senior privates who had retired from presidial service.

The final years of the colonial period in Alta California were characterized by some economic hardship resulting from a series of poor harvests caused by drought and from problems with commerce because of unrest in the Americas. [54] Conditions became even more harsh when the war of independence against Spain made it difficult for colonial officials to send supplies from San Blas. Officials in Alta California were instructed by the viceroy to take rigorous measures to prevent information regarding the revolution from being disseminated to the soldiers, settlers, and Indians. Concurrently, the governor and other officials were encouraged by the population to attempt to practice a more prudent administrative behavior; nevertheless, the atmosphere in the province was optimistic. In the last twenty years there were several competent governors and a more routinized administration. Diego de Borica, the governor between 1794 and 1800, was fairly popular and noted not only for his common sense and his belief in the developmental potential of ranchos and towns, but also for his good relations with the clergy. A thirty-six-year veteran of the frontier, he died in Durango while on leave. In contrast, José Joaquín de Arrillaga was more pessimistic about the province and less affable, but his competence and responsibility were notable. After a brief interim, with Captain José Darío Arguello, commandant of Santa Bárbara, in charge, Pablo Vicente de Sola, a lieutenant colonel previously at Guadalajara, arrived in December 1814; he proved to be a hard-working individual whose major document was an extensive report on the defense needs of California and whose most memorable actions were related not only to defense but also to the change in sovereignty.

Without much defense, California in the last years was visited by several incursions that included many with clearly hostile intent; among them, the French pirate Hipólito Bouchard, and the annexationist William Shaler who had been in Tejas. Russian traders as well as Englishmen also presented problems, and occasionally goods and even money were confiscated. The garrison of California included 412 men, 1 lieutenant colonel, 2 captains, 8 lieutenants, 9 sergeants, and 31 corporals, among others. In 1818, they were supplemented by an infantry company from San Blas and a dragoon company from Mazatlán, both constituted by mestizo soldiers recruited in Mexico. These forces were meager militarily, but they added to the political life of the province.

Socialization in the Far North

Mexican settlement in the far north involved transitions within the society that developed in several ways.[55] Local rule allowed more latitude, and there was more cooperation among settlers across status lines. The distance of the settlements from central Mexican society, coupled with frontier conditions, made the maintenance of traditional colonial institutions and customs uneven. Rather than inherited family status, honor on the frontier more commonly meant the qualities of courage, steadfastness, and loyalty. Miguel Ramos de Arizpe explained:

> The salubrious air, the agreeable climate, the exceedingly rich
> soil—all nature invites man to reap the benefit of the easiest and
> most solid prosperity by means of agriculture, the source of the true
> wealth of nations. This is, Sir, the most common occupation of the
> inhabitants of these vast and rich provinces. Agriculture has in

general formed their character; and as they have been employed day and night in the honest and systematic cultivation of the soil, from which alone they derive their sustenance, they are truly inflexible to intrigue, virtuously steadfast, haters of tyranny and disorder, justly devoted to true liberty, and naturally the most inclined toward all the moral and political virtues. They are very much devoted also to the liberal and mechanical arts.

These provinces, being by their location the natural bulwark of all the kingdom of Mexico, are in consequence on a frontier exposed to the barbarous Indian nations. Their inhabitants, therefore, are obliged to serve not only as militiamen but even as common soldiers. They are all soldiers; and in Coahuila and Texas, each month they are required to present their arms for inspection. This necessity, otherwise deplorable, has formed in them an extremely commendable character of integrity, honor, and subordination. They are extraordinarily long-suffering under the severest labor and much accustomed to the greatest privations. At times they even live upon the leather of their saddles and knapsacks without deserting nor as much murmuring. With this combination of such excellent qualities, which result from the celestial climate and are cultivated by such honest occupations, each citizen becomes a worker, each worker a soldier, and each soldier a hero that is worth a hundred ordinary soldiers.[55]

Honor and *Nobleza* referred to strength of character. These qualities were obviously more useful than ascribed status; and in the north, women also could be described as *honorable y noble*.

In addition to Toypurina several women were recognized as remarkable in character on the California frontier.[57] Among them was María Feliciana Arballo y Gutiérrez, a privileged widow of a regular soldier who died during preparations for the Juan de Anza expedition to San Francisco in 1775. When she persisted, continuing on the expedition with her two young daughters, her actions shocked those who believed a woman should not travel unaccompanied by a man because of the danger and duress she might encounter. During the trip she remarried and settled in San Gabriel, where she devoted herself to domestic duties and instructed mission Indian girls. Her descendants became prominent californios, holding high posts in the government and militia. Another woman, Doña Concepción Argüello, who was known as "la beata," or the blessed one, represented one type of feminine virtue for Alta California. She came from a prominent family and married a

Russian emissary who later died while traveling across Siberia. After his death, she remained a widow and refused marriage. Ostensibly devoted to embroidery and prayers as befitted her assigned station, late in life, at the age of sixty, she took religious vows, becoming California's first nun. Obviously, neither María Feliciana nor other women like her were exceptions economically or politically, but socially they were seen as influencing society positively, at least within the limitations that society imposed upon women. Yet another woman is called the "first lady of the Californias"—Doña Eulalia Fages, wife of an early governor of California, who was characterized by some as a self-absorbed and spoiled wealthy woman, and by others as tirelessly charitable. Though her husband built her an impressive home on the frontier, it was not a palace, and life proved to be a series of disenchantments for her. After endless arguments, she seemingly convinced her husband to resign finally from the governorship and return south. In the middle of this contentious relationship was the Indian woman Indizuela, who was accused of being Don Pedro's mistress and supposedly somewhat a contrast to the capricious and elitist Doña Eulalia. In protest of her situation, Doña Eulalia refused marital relations with her husband. Later, she asked the church to allow her to be separated from her husband because she was reportedly infatuated with the beautiful Indian woman; still later, however, she admitted this had been only a ruse. Next, to obtain relief, Doña Eulalia tried to get her husband discharged from his position as governor; but the letter was intercepted. Eventually, she and her husband both left for Mexico City. Doña Eulalia was admired for her generosity and character while reproached for her shortcomings by later californios.

Frontier transitions and socialization contributed in some as yet unspecified ways to the formation of political beliefs and practices as part of a total culture in which women as well as men were protagonists. Women, in addition to being integral to expeditions, spearheaded settlement and participated in all of the work connected with it. A strict division of labor, a subordinate and protected status for women, and the exclusive male direction of economic production would not fully apply in the frontier society.[58] Women who were part of the migrant bands characteristically involved in the expansion of the mining, cattle, and agricultural frontiers comprised the most unconventional pioneers. Contrary to alleged gender proscriptions or inhibitions, many women used weapons, rode horses, rounded up cattle, and worked the lariat. Occasionally, women defended the Mexican settlements. In a few instances, they also sought to force the males from their role as the sole authorities on the frontier, a role they had enjoyed in central Mexico. By being small producers on the frontier, it was possible for women and their families to survive with greater independence. Slowly, there came into being a modest tradition of less inequality with the male population.

Frontier social changes affected contemporary views as well as traditions, lifestyles and values. The frontier economy required women to be actively involved in all farming and stock-raising activities outside the home, including plowing and tending herds. A few women held sole ownership of herds of cattle or sheep. Occasionally, women settlers received animals, tools, and plots; and many developed multiple skills, including, obviously, the practice of midwifery and plant medicine.

In practice, the main political unit was the family,[59] where primary social formation took place. The family was the chief social institution for security and education as well as constraint, shaping beliefs and identity, enforcing values, and providing individual and group resiliency; it was also central to gender, class, and cultural behavior. As in central Mexico, women handled household affairs, maintaining and reproducing the family, and teaching and caring for the children, the elderly, and the male workers. Marriage, which was usually negotiated, was expected of everyone living within a nuclear and/or extended family; it also remained a vehicle for advancement and a means for economic security, and people sought it or avoided it with such ends in mind, but widows were common. Nevertheless, female heads of family were not unusual, and some women headed households during the eighteenth and nineteenth centuries.

Women made use of government and, in a few cases, participated in it.[60] They actively sought the courts' protection of their social and economic rights as well as those of their sons and daughters. They initialed complaints and acted as witnesses, and courts recognized their standing and secured satisfaction for them. Marital disputes were taken to courts, as were instances of violence and the usurpation of inheritance. A few women exercised sanctioned authority. Doña Ana Robledo was famous not only for her hospitality and kindness, but was the acknowledged leader in the Las Cruces area. The widow or wife of the *patrón,* the boss or overseer of a ranch, occupied an important place in the local social structure. Propertied women were often responsible for watching over the deportment and welfare of the employees, and for exerting social force in the community. When a man died or was absent for a period of time, the woman assumed responsibility for managing the family and business affairs. For example, Doña Josefa Herrera, the wife of Spanish Governor Cordero, dealt with members of the local government and drilled the troops stationed in San Antonio. During the 1820s, Josefa Seguin contested local authorities over water rights while her husband dealt with judicial matters in Mexico City. Women's assumption of such responsibilities on a temporary basis was perhaps a precedent, but not a major change; its practice did demonstrate the artificial nature of restraints.

Frontier conditions forced some modifications in traditional sex roles for colonial society, but northern practices continued to follow the customs in central Mexico. Some men of means looked upon seduction as a demonstration of, or an avenue to, power. Abduction, rape, or suspected rape was an unorthodox means that men used occasionally to intimidate a wealthy family into giving their daughter in marriage to avoid accusations that she was not a virgin. A quick marriage usually protected the reputation of both the daughter and the family. Such, however, was not always the case. In New Mexico, in 1767, Doña María Manuela de la Luz Romero filed a civil suit against Mariano Baca. Baca, a mestizo man of lower status, claimed that he had seduced the wealthier Doña María and wanted to marry her. She charged Baca with slander. Resolutely, she went to the home of the ecclesiastical notary of Albuquerque and asked him to witness a physical examination to determine her virginity. The notary attested to her claim and sentenced Baca to one hundred lashes and a year in jail to discourage other *coyotes* from slandering the reputation of wealthy women. If a woman lost her virginity the family was forced to offer a large dowry, which was consistent with the acceptance of an allegedly less than desirable woman. Lacking a large dowry, the family often had to accept a marriage partner of less status and wealth, a situation that upheld the family's reputation and one from which the male gained. Once gossip of known or suspected indiscretion had circulated through the community, it damaged a woman's reputation and her family lost public standing. Often, the object of the slander was to demean the woman and her family, thus weakening their status or influence.

Mestizo and Indian women were central participants in the advance of Mexican colonial society northward from the time of the establishment of missions, garrisons, and towns and through the period of Mexican independence. Some evidence indicates slightly greater fluidity and participation for women within the parameters of a continuous culture and the frontier's rudimentary class distinctions. Survival needs, the lesser pervasiveness of the church, and the absence of a traditional upper class were important considerations in the development of a more egalitarian society; this situation, to some extent, was similar to other frontier experiences.

The Anglo-English Intruders

Mexican–Anglo relations are rooted in the colonial period. Whether they took the form of actual contacts or of speculative plans, these ethnic "encounters" were riddled with conflict from the first. They were partly the result of Spanish–English relations and partly the more direct result of frontier invasion. During the two centuries that elapsed between the founding in 1607 of Jamestown, Virginia, and the Anglo-European penetration of Mexico's far north in the 1790s, there was continual conflict in the Americas between Spain and England. There was no lack of attention to these territories. Oliver Cromwell had a grand vision for the dismemberment of the Spanish monarchy's possessions in the New World; in the thirteen colonies, Cotton Mather had depression deliriums that Mexico, not New England, was the new Jerusalem; and Thomas Jefferson, when he looked westward from his plantation, postulated an Anglo-European empire, not a farmers' republic. Anglo-European excursions into the far north came late in the colonial era.[61] England had been more interested in other areas; the French territory stood between the English colonies and settlements in New Spain; and in any case, Anglo adventurers still possessed insufficient economic motive. But soon they sought a foothold in the Mississippi area and its trade. Spaniards, through the leadership of Bernardo de Gálvez, used Mexican resources as major support that contributed significantly to the possibility of encroachment on New Spain by the thirteen colonies in their movement for independence. The colonies' independence and the purchase of Louisiana from the French emperor Napoleon I changed the situation. There were several types of encounters on the frontier, ranging from those arising from individual initiative to others that involved organized groups for purposes beyond individual profit. Although both types were initially peaceful, they soon became hostile, with some emanating from conspiracies among marauders.

Sizable Anglo migration into eastern Tejas began in the first decades of the nineteenth century. The first Anglo-Europeans entering the area were most often marauders seeking profit. In 1791, Eduard Murphy of Pennsylvania acquired a land grant on the Arroyo Hondo, near the present-day Texas–Louisiana boundary, in what was recognized as Spanish colonial territory. Three other Anglos had settled in the same area by 1798: Luther Smith, William Barr, and Samuel Davenport. Their activities frequently carried them into the interior of Texas to trade with Mexicans and Indians. These men combined trading in weapons, liquor, goods, and wild horses. Philip Nolan, who was in the horse trade, may have been the first Anglo to travel beyond the Louisiana border and to be in communication with the Washington leadership; with Thomas Jefferson, for example. In October 1800, Nolan and twenty companions set out, without proper permits, for settlements in the vicinity of San Antonio, and they immediately caused conflict. On the Brazos River, not far from modern Waco, the marauders built a stockade and soon corralled three hundred mustangs. During the following spring, the fort was attacked by a force of Mexican settlers who killed Nolan and several of his followers. The others were initially taken to San Luis Potosí and later to Chihuahua. One survivor was Ellis P. Bean, ancestor of Judge Roy Bean.

Among the early privateering Anglos who followed Nolan and Bean, none was more publicized than Zebulon Montgomery Pike, an agent of a disreputable U.S. general, James Wilkinson, military governor of Upper Louisiana who conspired against the United States. The "explorer" Pike, a confirmed mestizo-hater, arrived in Santa Fe in 1806 as a prisoner of the authorities, and eventually he was sent to Chihuahua, charged with trespassing and illicit trade. During the year he spent in the north, he talked extensively with local officials and collected voluminous notes on the geography, soil, climate, resources, people, and military strength of New Spain. Pike was perhaps the first Anglo traveler to enter the vast territory beyond Louisiana and return to the United States with extensive knowledge about the previously unknown country. The official report of his expedition was published in 1810, and for more than a decade it remained a unique printed source of information about the Louisiana territory. General James Wilkinson, who was involved in the Aaron Burr conspiracy to seize territory and power from the U.S. government, sent his son Lieutenant James B. Wilkinson (in 1806), to the present-day area of Oklahoma and northeastern Texas, and out of this journey came a report to supplement Pike's.

Before and after Bean and Pike, Anglos conducted several official explorations into the far north territory. Thomas Jefferson and others in his circle made some rather exaggerated claims about the extent of the Louisiana Purchase. After Jefferson launched the Lewis and Clark expedition in 1804, he made plans for another party to ascend the Red and Arkansas rivers. Jefferson also chose Sir William Dunbar (a scientist) and Dr. George Hunter (a chemist) to direct the examination of the southwestern frontier. This expedition was stopped by colonial officials in 1806, and another led by Thomas Freeman in 1806 did not proceed beyond Louisiana. Further expeditions were primarily military in character, such as those of Major Stephen H. Long (1817–19) and of Colonel David Atkinson (1819).

Annexationist efforts date from approximately 1800, when the United States' unique trait of acquisitiveness became more pronounced following the Louisiana Purchase. In lower Louisiana and along the Tejas border, men gathered to plot in the midst of rumors concerning available capital and high connections in Washington, D.C. Some of these conspiring groups saw opportunities in the course of the prolonged struggle for independence. Anglo marauders made numerous filibustering attempts between 1813 and 1819. One of the more dangerous efforts occurred during 1819, led by a Dr. James Long, backed by several prominent citizens who were southern slave owners. Long, who knew a few men in high positions, including Senator Thomas Hart Benton, organized a government, solicited an army and proclaimed Texas an independent republic, and named himself both general and president. He asked the American pirate Jean Laffite to join him in the "glorious" enterprise, but he was refused. After his force was defeated at San Antonio and later at La Bahía, President and General Long was captured along with his followers. Unfortunately for Long, Senator Benton did not possess much influence in Mexico City, where Long was executed. Even so, foreign incursions continued to concern administrators, and Anglo marauders preceded Mexican independence.

The "Late Colonial" Years: Final Reorganization and Dissident Turmoil

Paradoxically, with the frontier invasion and discontent rumored among colonial subjects, the authorities planned a major reorganization which would affect New Mexico, Tejas, and California. José de Gálvez's recommendation of administrative reorganization in Alta California resulted in an outbreak of reorganizational zeal. While the Marqués de Cruillas was viceroy, the Marqués de Rubi was ordered to inspect the northern frontier in 1766; as Nicolás de Lafora, captain of engineers, explains:

> La parte de la América Septentrional. . . . Enterado el Rey de los continuos clamores de aquellos infelices vasallos fronterizos, representados por la Superioridad, ansioso de su remedio, envió al Mariscal de Campo Marqués de Rubi (1) a la inspección de todos los presidios internos y discurriendo el Exmo. Sr. Marques de Cruillas, (2) pudiera ser útil el que le acompañase un ingeniero que se dedicase a formar un mapa para el conocimiento de aquellas inmensas tierras, hasta ahora mal registradas y peor descritas, me hizo el honor de elegirme para esta comisión, en que he puesto el mayor esmero y trabajo personal para llenar el objeto de ella.[62]
> [The part of North America. . . . When the king was informed of the continuous clamoring of those unhappy vassals on the frontier, which you represented to him, eager to remedy the situation, he sent the field marshal, the Marqués de Rubí, to inspect all the internal presidios. Thinking about it, it occurred to the most excellent lord, the Marqués de Cruillas, that it might be useful to have an engineer accompany him, dedicated to making a map in order to know those immense lands, until now poorly surveyed and even more poorly described, and he gave me the honor of choosing me for this commission, in the fulfillment of which I have taken the greatest, most painstaking attention and personal effort.]

Recommendations followed this review. The long-range intention was to strengthen the far north militarily, economically, and demographically, creating an arch connecting present-day Galveston with San Francisco. In 1772, a new administrative jurisdiction, the Comandancia General de las Provincias Internas, included Alta California, Nuevo México, and Tejas, as well as Sonora, Sinaloa, Chihuahua, Durango, Coahuila, and Nuevo Santander (Nuevo León, Tamaulipas).

The Provincias Internas were headed by a comandante general with headquarters located at Arizpe, Sonora. The ambitious effort was to accomplish several ends, to unify frontier defense more efficiently; to enhance communications; to control Indian peoples; to improve provincial government administratively; and to cut administrative costs and stimulate economic development. Civil and military authority were combined in the comandante general. Bernardo de Gálvez spurred on the work of his uncle, which was implemented by commanders like Juan Bautista de Anza. Between 1772 and 1821, the provincias of the West and the East existed either as a single overall unit or were split into two subdivisions. The dividing line between the provincias of the West and these of the East run along the eastern borders of Nuevo México, Chihuahua and Durango, with Coahuila in the eastern division. As noted, each provincia reflected a distinct chronological sequence, and many specifically regional differences influenced political developments significantly.

The colonial rule established in 1598 in the far north, at Santa Fe, Nuevo México, moved into its final two decades in 1800. Most significant, however, was the development and growth of a *norteño* Mexican society in Nuevo México, Alta California, and Tejas, which was linked to the societies of Sonora and Sinaloa, Durango, Chihuahua, and Nuevo Santander, and through them, to Mexican society in general. Thus, by 1800 the frontier society was Mexican culturally, and by 1822 it was Mexican in its political organization and sovereignty.[63]

Dissidence and Loyalties Refashioned

Economic growth in central Mexico was concurrent with episodes of social discontent and a rising critical discourse on society throughout New Spain. By the eighteenth century, certain key phrases and concepts with a definitely modern cast were apparent in the writings of intellectuals throughout colonial Mexico.[64] Arguments and polemics rotated around *bien común, la felicidad pública,* and *la patria,* in an effort to define, respectively, the "general good," the "common welfare," and the general community of "New Spain." These writings focused on history as well as scientific solutions to colonial problems in agriculture and mining. In effect, a critical spirit was noticeable among an educated minority. Writers of the last half of the eighteenth century reflected a unique consciousness and contributed to the awakening of a similar consciousness in others. A number were college instructors interested in philosophy, science, and history, and many exhibited an activist strain by forming or participating in the discussion clubs of the day.

These writers—and particularly the Mexican-born Jesuits—focused their studies on New Spain, for which they professed a great commitment. Although they shared a strong interest in the glories of the past civilization, they were no less proud of the achievement of the creoles. Significantly, they viewed miscegenation positively, as a basis for social unity. Perhaps as a result of their humanism, their intellectual restlessness touched on matters that eventually became political. Valuing humanity in and for itself, they were concerned with human rights and freedom, and with temporal happiness. They criticized slavery and posited that the ultimate basis of authority was the people. These Jesuit writers and their students philosophically scrutinized the fabric of colonial society, touching on the concepts of liberty and progress, and motivated at least partially by their concern for Mexico. Fundamental to them were faith, experience, reason, and a commitment to the general welfare. Their faith was not only theological; it was a secular faith founded in their land and its people, and their writings both contributed to and exemplified developing sentiments. By the beginning of the nineteenth century there existed a sense of nationality, pride, and history, as well as a set of ideas and ideals for the future.

In the process of independence and, as a consequence, partisanship during the early nineteenth century, two ideological elements stand out.[65] One was an enlightened minority who advanced the ideas that influenced independence, ideas with both orthodox literature and newer liberal sources. The other was a group of polemicists who contributed to the development of Mexican liberalism and conservatism during the political debate from the 1820s to the 1850s. Unlike the writings of the midcolonial period, theoretical speculations in the early nineteenth century were joined with action. Conceptualizations of human nature and ideal forms of government, as well as explorations of Mexican character, were all eventually programmatic to political efforts leading in the direction of an independent state and a more integral civic society.

The writers of the independence period were influenced primarily by much earlier writers on New Spain's history, the Spanish Jesuits and their views of rational natural law, and by the French writers of the

Enlightenment who expounded on the rights of man and the social contract. From the premises provided by these historians and theoreticians, Mexican intellectuals such as the lawyer Francisco Primo de Verdad y Ramos and the priest Melchor de Talamantes argued that sovereignty was rooted in the people. Mexico was a national realm, coequal to others, and free to decide its form of government via the expression of the people acting through their own representative assembly of the incipient nation's constituent elements. The vassalage of the nation to the crown was viewed as stemming from an agreement, a contract, which involved two parties—in addition to the crown itself, the constituent elements of the nation-realm: the conquistadores, the Indian lords, and by extension, the liberated Blacks. Conceivably, the descendants of these three could claim sovereignty as a right that had always been theirs.

In effect, these early theorists had rationalized the existence of a nation, justified its freedom, and developed a theoretical and inclusive definition of the national community. One major current addressed the inevitable questions of church and state. Two particularly aggressive intellectuals, Servando Teresa de Mier and Carlos María Bustamante, were notable for their fervent commitment to propaganda and activism. Both emphasized republicanism and the veneration of Guadalupe, whom they identified with Tonantzin; and in claiming that Quetzalcóatl was Saint Thomas, they avowed that the Castilians had not brought Catholicism and thus could not claim rights to Mexico. They exalted the glories of the ancient Mexicans, saw independence as a continuation of historical resistance, and called for a strong government. Both of them, however, were contradictory in their thought and erratic in their political participation. Several conspiracies to initiate independence were frustrated between the 1790s and 1809.

The War of Independence

As had happened repeatedly during the colonial regime, European events once again impacted on New Spain at the beginning of the nineteenth century. The French occupation of Spain and Napoleon Bonaparte's deposition of the Spanish king, Fernando VIII, replacing him with his brother Joseph Bonaparte, in 1808, created an ideological and political crisis of authority and legitimacy in Spain and throughout the Spanish colonial empire. This crisis was to become the catalyst for the multitude of incipient and developed interests that separated the inhabitants of the colony from the interests of Spain and its Spanish rulers. Mexican intellectuals were quick to recognize and publicize the fact that dethronement of the Spanish monarchy created a legal question concerning the validity of the colonial administration in exercising political military and judicial authority over the colony and its people. The legal basis of Spanish rule in Mexico stemmed not from an organic political union of Mexico with the Spanish state; rather, it stemmed from Spanish law, from the political and juridical fact that the Spanish monarch was also the monarch of Nueva España. Thus, in a legal sense, the viceregal administration derived its legitimacy and authority only by virtue of its appointment by the king of Nueva España, and when the crown was relinquished, sovereignty would revert in a legal sense to the colony, kingdom, or nation. This ideological argument, while mainly expressed by the small and enlightened sector of the literate elite, nevertheless had wide ramifications for larger sectors of the population and ultimately for the colony as a whole. It allowed for ideological questioning of the legitimacy of the colonial regime. This legal weakness in the foundation of the authority of the colonial administration, as well as the very real political crisis of authority within the empire, increased the already existing polarization within the colonial elite between the *españoles americanos* (Mexican criollos) and the peninsulares.

A simmering ideological and political crisis erupted when Viceroy Iturrigaray proclaimed in 1808 that the colonial administration would operate autonomously in the absence of recognized central authority in Spain. Then Iturrigaray was deposed by the peninsular elite who feared that his proclamation would result in the españoles americanos gaining a predominant influence in the civil and military administration of Mexico. This political coup d'etat resulted in the centralization of power in the hands of Europeans who moved systematically to eliminate or weaken colonial power and authority. The European elite in control of the viceregal government recognized the newly formed *cortés* at Cádiz as the legitimate government of Spain; they acted as a regency for the imprisoned king, systematically seeking to devote Mexico's fiscal and material resources to the Spanish war against the French. The peninsular elite and viceregal administration took a strict attitude toward the anti-Spanish proponents of Mexican autonomy, whose ideas and interests were deemed to be treasonable. In practical terms, any colonial interest which did not contribute to Spain became questionable; included here were the interests of individual Mexicans that came into conflict with those of individual Spaniards. This anti-Mexican policy, combined with the fact that the new administration had come to power through questionable or illegal means, caused resentment among increasingly large sectors of the population, from the criollo elite, whose economic and political interests were viewed as having been usurped by the Spaniards, to the large mestizo, Indian sectors, who had always felt a popular hatred and resentment toward the Spaniards in general. In centers of population which were the most developed economically, and where the colonial elite was more exposed to enlightened ideas, discontent crystalized among intellectuals, priests, colonial militia, officers, and elements of the civil administration. One circle took the name *Guadalupes,* thus linking their convictions with the most indigenous symbol available.

In 1809, political crisis coincided with the formation of clandestine political groups in several of the major urban centers, which eventually reached the frontier.[66] These groups became public with the exposure and suppression of one of the most advanced groups at Valladolid (Morelia). In September 1810, this movement initiated an open revolt against the repressive administration, announced by Miguel Hidalgo's proclamation of the *Grito de Dolores* and by the *junta* of patriots in the Bajío. Almost immediately, the colonial elite's separatist movement was enveloped by a mass popular revolt, whose symbol was the Virgín of Guadalupe, its cry "Death to the *gachupín,*" and its demand for the land to be theirs once more.

When Miguel Hidalgo y Costilla called for revolt in 1810, a dynamic movement of popular participation rapidly became more explicitly radical and more under José María Morelos y Pavón. In effect, the movement for independence was shaped ideologically by two sets of ideas: the juridical theories already mentioned, and the agrarian, egalitarian, and indigenous tendencies that the people injected. Both Hidalgo and Morelos were well-educated priests and mestizo leaders in the movement for independence; and their followers articulated demands for the abolition of slavery, taxes, and the caste system, as well as advocating the redefinition of land tenure. In short, the colonial system was denounced as illegitimate. Between 1808 and 1810, when Hidalgo, the priest, and Ignacio Allende, the officer, were interested in calling a representative assembly, or congress, they had thought in terms of delegates of all of the cabildos. When Morelos convened the Congress of Chilpancingo in 1813, its authority theoretically stemmed from a sovereignty that resided in all of the people and was the expression of their general will through the representatives of the congress.[67] These points were described in detail in Morelos's "Sentimientos de la Nación," and the *Acta de la Independencia* further specified the rationale for insurgency. Both documents asserted that sovereignty had been usurped by Europeans and was now claimed by the people. Morelos, as Hidalgo before him, died in the struggle for independence.

With respect to program, ideological propaganda, and military strategy, this movement was headed by an elite that established an insurgent junta to direct strategy and coordinate regional activity; and its efforts spread rapidly throughout the central, north central, and southern provinces. The conflict itself, however, increasingly came under the direction of popular leaders, who, once they had risen through their political and military ability, assumed in the next phase the leadership of what became, in some instances—ideological, theoretical, political, military, and social—a radical populist movement for Mexican national independence and the establishment of an independent Mexican state that would not be subordinate to foreign interests.

Independence and the Northern Provinces

The news of the revolution eventually spread throughout the country, through both official and popular means of communication. On the official level, directives to the provincial military and civil authorities were intended to suppress any news of the revolt and to send financial, military, and material assistance to the central authorities to combat the revolution. They were commanded to take steps in strengthening the local authority to prevent any outbreak. On the popular level, merchants and muleteers carried the news to even the most remote provincial *mesón* and marketplace. In distant provinces such as Alta California, foreign smugglers brought the forbidden news of the great events convulsing the colony.

The impact of the crisis on the far north was uneven, but felt nevertheless. The revolution spread to the nearest northern province, arriving there in many cases, through appeals to support the colonial government or by the eruption of locally organized revolts and, later, with retreating troops and leaders of either insurgents or royalists. In the Arizona-Sonora area, news of the insurgency mobilized both the rebels and the colonial loyalists.[68] Both elements raised participants, but the loyalists were successful in ending the insurgent potential. Because of problems of distance and communication, and the suppression of information by provincial authorities, participation in the revolution in Alta California and Nuevo México was limited apparently to clandestine literature, hidden sympathetic discussion, and an aborted plan for revolt at San Diego, Alta California, in 1811. In his memoirs, Don Pío Pico reports the attempted revolt in which his father, a sergeant, was a participant along wtih some sixty men and officers who plotted to seize the barracks and were promptly arrested:

> I remember that in 1811, my father [Jose Pico] was put in prison on account of the talk in the company of which he was a sergeant, of Mexican independence, a question which was, even then much agitated through Mexico. He was released, after a few days, through the influence of the missionary fathers, but the soldiers, Ramón Rubio, José M. López, and one Candeo, and an artilleryman, Ygnacio Zúñiga, were kept in confinement, each with two pairs of irons (*grillos*), the first named dying in prison and Zúñiga remaining there until Mexican independence was established in 1821.[69]

During the 1800s Nuevo México was affected indirectly by the Mexican revolution against Spain, and there is no reported public action, as in Tejas, or suppressed revolts, such as those in Alta California. However, the *conspiración de Trespalacios* of 1814, centered in Chihuahua, envisioned action to the north.[70] Antonio Armijo and Dionisio Valdés were arrested for attempting to interest locals in the surviving northern insurgent groups. Spanish colonial authorities were concerned that revolutionary pamphlets and verbal accounts might be circulating in the province. Events were indeed known. Years later, the politically active priest Antonio José Martínez, who grew to manhood during the tumultuous era, delivered a sermon evoking the Virgin of Guadalupe in referring to the heroic support of independence and calling Hidalgo a liberator whose "eminent legacy endures in his worthy companions, apostles of our freedom." Like Tejas and Alta California, Nuevo México was affected in a limited manner by the liberal reform in Spain. Unlike Alta California or Tejas, the province had a large enough population to send a delegate to the meeting of the Spanish cortés in Cádiz. As a consequence, local politics were stimulated and an early document of local needs was written.

In 1810, Don Pedro Bautista Pino, a prominent landowner, was selected to represent Nuevo México after a contentious competition for the designation. Because of the distance, Pino arrived late in Cádiz and after the adoption of the Constitution of 1812. Nevertheless, he made several interventions and had the sense to understand the need for information on his region and his constituency in order to gain some support and sympathy. Thus, he declared that,

> in conformity with my instructions, it becomes indispensable that Your Majesty condescend to accede to the following petitions: 1st. The establishment of an Espiscopate in its Capital, Santa Fe, New Mexico; 2nd. The establishment of a seminary college of higher studies and of public schools for the teaching of the youth; 3rd. The uniformity in military service, enlarging the four garrisons that have been mentioned, and paying all the neighbors who are ordered to be placed under arms (including the three militia companies already referred to) as it is done in Durango, Sonora, Tejas and the other adjoining provinces; 4th. The establishment of civil and criminal courts in Chihuahua.[71]

In *Noticias históricas y estadísticas de la Antigua provincia del Nuevo México,* a pamphlet describing Nuevo México, Pino called for the establishment of a bishopric and of schools and courts; the payment and enlargement of the militia; and the establishment of presidios for the province. These proposals received, however, no immediate response. The major significance of the work was its contemporary description of the province and its list of some of the major administrative needs as viewed by various people. Pino returned to Nuevo México, and in 1820 he was again elected, with contention, as a delegate to the cortés; because of lack of funds, however, he could not travel beyond Veracruz and had to return while independence was being contested.

As it had throughout the colony, when news of the Grito de Dolores reached the northeast it found receptive listeners among the oppressed and their local leaders. The northeast was particularly favorable to independence, often because of the efforts of Rafael Iriarte, an insurgent leader who succeeded in raising resources and maintaining control over entire areas. In Nuevo Santander, or modern Tamaulipas, groups of patriots began to organize clandestinely. Among the insurgent leaders in Nuevo Santander were the brothers Gutiérrez, José Bernardo Gutiérrez de Lara and José Antonio Gutiérrez de Lara, descendants of a settler family. By the spring of 1811 notices of a reward for the head of Father Hidalgo were posted in Laredo.

In November 1810, when a revolutionary army under the command of General Mariano Jiménez liberated San Luis Potosí, Bernardo Gutiérrez de Lara, who had been distributing propaganda, raised the flag of insurrection in Tamaulipas.[72] A countereffort in support of the loyalists was mobilized by José Antonio Benavides of Laredo, also from a settler family; while Gutiérrez de Lara met with Jiménez, Hidalgo, Allende, and others. He was joined later by Miguel and José Menchaca. The insurgents then began to spread the revolution to the Río Bravo and to Coahuila, Nuevo León, and Tejas. Father José Antonio Gutiérrez de Lara, Bernardo's brother, was dispatched to the Valle del Río Bravo to revolutionize the towns of Laredo, Camargo, Reynosa, and Mier, as well as his hometown of Revilla (modern Guerrero in Tamaulipas). In a short time, Spanish authority was shaken throughout much of the valley. As a member of a respected and long-standing family, Gutiérrez de Lara had extensive support, and for the next fifteen years he was tireless in his support of independence and would become a notable regional leader.

The easternmost internal province, Tejas, which was then administratively a part of Nuevo Santander, had closer communication with the central region than with other parts of the far north. Here, the movement assumed a more fully developed form which involved or affected a majority of the population of that province, including many families who would be prominent in politics throughout the next generation. In the first phase, the revolution in Tejas took the form of a locally initiated revolt led by Captain Juan Bautista Casas of the San Antonio de Béxar militia against Lieutenant Colonel Manuel de Salcedo, the Spanish governor who had ordered the troops stationed in Tejas to be prepared to march against the insurgents in the valley.[73] This news caused widespread discontent among the soldiers and the civilian population of San Antonio de Béxar. A clandestine plan was organized to overthrow the governor when marching orders were given. In January 1811, Salcedo gave orders for field maneuvers and the plan went into motion.

In January 1811, Casas, at the head of the local forces, seized the Spanish governor and officials at San Antonio de Béxar, proclaiming support for the revolution and constituting himself as the Mexican governor of Tejas. Shortly afterward, Juan Aldama of the insurgent junta arrived in San Antonio on his way to the United States as an envoy, carrying a large amount of money from the independence movement. At the same time, the Spanish priest Juan Manuel Sambrano took advantage of the situation to organize a royalist countergroup from proroyalist elements, doing so under the deceptive pretext that the purpose of the coup was to replace Casas with another *independista* governor. Taking advantage of the confusion, the priest spread the word that Aldama was a French agent of Napoleon. This act angered many people because of the history of conflicts in Tejas with the French from Louisiana. On March 1, the royalists seized control of the town, imprisoned Casas and Aldama, and released the imprisoned Spanish governor and officials, who quickly armed and organized a royalist force of five hundred men. Aldama and, probably, Casas were sent to Monclova and executed by the Spaniards. A self-congratulatory communique summarized matters in the following way:

> The morning of January 22, just passed, as when Captain of Militia Juan Bautista Casas, accompanying the auxiliary troops of Nuevo Santander, took the command from our governor, Lt. Col. Manuel de Salcedo, also taking prisoners, the commander of said bodies, Lt. Col. Simon de Herrera; and Captains Geronimo de Herrera, Martin Echavarria, Jose Goceascoechea, Miguel de Arcos, Juan Ignacio Arrambide, Jose Joaquin Ugarte, Lieutenants Juan Jose Elguezabal, Bernardino Montero and Gregorio Amador, and other Europeans who had their residence in Bexar, generally confiscating all their properties and treating them as prisoners in the most execrable manner, and abrogating the authority of the government of the province, submitting it to the Captain General of the insurgents in Saltillo, Mariano Ximenez, taking all the arms, munitions, and artillery.
>
> Thus, they prevented the loyalists from taking any action; but with their combinations, they decided on the night of March 1, to address themselves to Subdeacon Juan Manual Sambrano, Ignacio Perez, Jose Antonio Saucedo, Erasmo Seguin, Martin Beramendi, Francisco Ruiz, Lt. Miguel Muzquiz, Luis Galan, Jose Maria Sambrano, Jose Angel Navarro, Gabino Delgado, and others, who in greatest secrecy, proceeded to the headquarters of the militia, where all the forces of the troop and artillery were deposited and immediately took possession of them, arresting the principal followers of the insurrection, persuading them with the most lively

and efficacious reasons to desert the iniquitous party which they had embraced. Finally, in one way or another, we managed to install a governing *junta*, as reported under separate cover. As soon as we entered the Capital of Béxar, we let it be known that the president of the governing *junta* was now the subdeacon Juan Manuel Sambrano; presenting the names of the members of the Junta by seniority, the undersigners, with the exception of two [Capt. Luciano Garcia, and Juan Jose Sambrano, who took oath on March 11 and 22, respectively] who were absent. Their secretary was Antonio Saucedo.

In this way winning the confidence of the majority of voters, who were submerged in the inky darkness of the insurrection, they authorized us to arrest them, unwittingly thinking perhaps that the purpose of the movement was directed to extinguish forever the legitimate authorities. Under this erroneous impression they continued for some time as did some members of the *junta*.

After each had voted, oath was taken, with greatest formality, to remain faithful to Religion and Patriotism, and to put into effective and immediate effect the measures dictated by the said *junta*, the president of it, in the presence of the troop, and the same was done from the first member to the secretary, and at daybreak, at the head of about four hundred armed troops, the inhabitants gathered, and all went to the Government House to take the command from the said Casas, keeping his person under good custody, and sure imprisonment. From that moment on, steps were taken for good government, tranquility and public peace, and for the reestablishing of the old order. Great changes had taken place, a continued movement and agitation, into which we had all been thrown.[74]

In March 1811, the local Juan Bautista de las Casas, who favored the Hidalgo independence movement, paid with his life and his head was ordered to be displayed at the central plaza. Two years later, the patriots killed one official responsible, Simón de Herrera. Thus ended, through confusion or misinformation apparently, the first phase of the independence movement in Texas, the first area in the far north to directly witness insurgent actions; but contrary to royalist wishes, there was no permanent return to the "old order," and Iriarte and Gutiérrez did not cease their actions.

Shortly after the March 1811 counterrevolutionary coup in Texas, of which the central insurgent junta was unaware, it was decided that the members of the junta should go north to reorganize, to purchase arms, to enroll volunteers, to secure the active assistance of the northern communities, and to establish contact with the United States government. Ignacio Allende, Mariano Jiménez, Miguel Hidalgo, and Mariano Abasolo were chosen to go; and Ignacio López Rayón, newly appointed commander of the Army of America, and Pedro de Oranda of Coahuila would remain in command until their return. At this point, Bernardo Gutiérrez arrived at the insurgent stronghold of Saltillo. Gutiérrez was appointed lieutenant colonel by the junta and given the special mission of raising troops in Tamaulipas which were to join the main army in Saltillo. Before leaving, junta members Ignacio Allende and Mariano Jiménez gave Gutiérrez the additional assignment of carrying out Aldama's mission as envoy to the United States if Aldama were captured; and unbeknownst to the junta, he already had been. Gutiérrez was to receive a formal written commission, but on March 21, 1811, the insurgent junta, including Allende, Jiménez, Hidalgo, and Abasolo, was captured by the royalists at Acatita Bajan en route to Monclova, after its betrayal by Captain Ignacio Elizondo, who had been an officer in the insurgent forces of Coahuila. In addition to Rafael Iriarte, Gutiérrez de Lara survived, and with a group of fifteen insurgents and the assistance of Captain Miguel Menchaca, he went north and managed to escape capture by royalist troops.

The next active military phase of the revolution in Tejas occurred in 1812 as a result of plans set in motion by the central junta. Bernardo Gutiérrez de Lara, a leader of the revolution in the northeast and a Mexican diplomatic agent, was appointed by Allende to seek assistance in the United States.[75] He arrived at Natchitoches and Natchez, aided by a Spanish officer, Juan Cortés; here, he wrote to James Monroe, asking for aid and suggesting a future treaty. Eventually, he reached Washington, D.C., where he became the first native representative of the movement for independence. He was refused aid, but the secretary of war offered to occupy Tejas—an offer Gutiérrez also rejected. While he was in the city, to help his cause Gutiérrez wrote a ten-page memorandum on the causes and progress of the independence movement. He then met with Monroe, who insisted upon discussing the possibility of Tejas's availability for annexation; and later he was introduced to President James Madison and representatives of several countries, including a Spaniard, Alvárez de Toledo, who called himself a liberal. When he returned to Natchitoches, he remained in contact with

United States and French representatives while he began to organize a force, to distribute propaganda, and to recruit Mexicans and foreigners. With Gutiérrez as the overall commander, Augustus Magee was field commander, Miguel Menchaca was second in command, and several Anglos were officers. Captain William Shaler, previously marauding at California, served as an advisor. On September 1, 1812, he issued four proclamations from Nacogdoches, the first such documents released north of the Río Bravo. These proclamations stressed the provision of electoral government for provinces and towns; guaranteed freedom for business and exportation transactions; the development of agriculture, crafts, and education; protection for religion and the ideal of "happiness of families"; all of the documents called for mass uprising. One of the proclamations was addressed to the Anglo Americans and offered them citizenship and economic prerogatives.

From the Mexican point of view, the revolutionary activities of Bernardo Gutiérrez de Lara in Tejas were controversial. Unwisely, large numbers of Anglo mercenaries participated in his forces and played questionable roles in the events of 1812. This problem was underscored by the recurring Anglo *filibusterismo* in Tejas. Subsequently, some Anglo participants in the Gutiérrez de Lara movement of 1812 displayed interests contrary to those of the Mexican people of Tejas and the independence movement. However, in assessing the events of 1812 and the large participation of *tejanos mexicanos* in the Gutiérrez campaign against the Spaniards, the vulnerable frontier position of Texas in the events of 1836 and 1848 must be noted. The convergence of filibustering motives and the independence struggle unavoidably complicated events in Texas.

The leadership of Gutiérrez was fraught with difficulties. Though he was erratic at times, his overall conduct in the United States, in Texas, and in his subsequent life in Mexico demonstrated his personal integrity and his patriotism. In particular, he resisted all offers of aid in exchange for the cession of national territories in Texas.[76] While in the United States, he tried unsuccessfully to gain the support of the American government. Gutiérrez de Lara then tried to gain private support and to recruit men and arms to fight the Spaniards.

At this time, the Mexican cause experiencing one of its lowest ebbs, with the capture and execution of Hidalgo, Allende, Jiménez, and many of the other insurgent leaders at Chihuahua and Monclova, and the dispersal of the Army of America. The immediate conflict

facing the Mexican leadership and the independence movement was
between Mexico and Spain; and more specifically, between the independence forces and the Spanish royalists throughout Mexico. Mexican patriots marshaled all available support to attack the Spanish
forces; for Gutiérrez this apparently meant the recruitment of any forces
and arms he could get in order to enter Tejas and engage the royalists.
In June 1812, Gutiérrez de Lara entered Tejas with 158 men, including
Anglo mercenaries, and took the towns of Nacogdoches and Salcedo
from the royalist garrison. In both places, many of the enemy soldiers
and the locals simply went over to the liberating forces. Though Anglo
mercenaries increased to several hundred, he was joined by many more
Mexican Texanos. Gutiérrez also sent several agents with revolutionary
propaganda to other parts of Tejas and the Valle del Río Bravo. Despite
the efforts of the royalists to suppress revolutionary information, the
message spread to all sectors of the population was as it is described by
the historian Carlos E. Castañeda:

> The Indians were not just silent spectators. Their attitude along
> the northern frontier has been noted. Disregard for Spanish author-
> ity was becoming widespread and developing into insolence. By the
> summer of 1812 the changed attitude was apparent even along the
> Rio Grande. Unmistakable signs were the indications of propa-
> ganda activity. Governor Salcedo was both puzzled and perturbed
> by a letter from Captain Bustamante. The veteran Indian fighter
> reported that the natives along the Rio Grande displayed an un-
> common knowledge of insurgent doctrines. It was strange, he de-
> clared, to hear the Indians questioning the right of the King over
> the people, and asserting the right of self-government, and protest-
> ing love of liberty and freedom. Bustamante noted that they were
> becoming more hostile and daring in their raids against un-
> protected settlers, and brazenly friendly with the leaders of the
> Revolution. This was particularly true in the vicinity of Revilla
> and Camargo, where it was generally asserted that Gutiérrez was on
> his way with fifteen thousand men and eight thousand Indians.[77]

As Castañeda suggests, the message not only was spread, but support
was aroused.

Benefiting from unintended support, provided by the mistakes of
the royalists, some success was achieved. Marching further into Texas,
Gutiérrez took La Bahía, and after its occupation, on March 2, his
besieged forces engaged and defeated fifteen hundred royalists under

Governor Manuel Salcedo and Governor Simón Herrera. Next, on March 29, 1813, Gutiérrez's force of nine hundred engaged twelve hundred royalist troops under Salcedo at the Battle of Rosillo, on the Guadalupe River near San Antonio. Spanish officers surrendered, with losses numbering a thousand. However, differences were now recurrent between Anglos and Mexicans, among the independent forces. Magee, who had wanted to betray Gutiérrez, had died, and his place was taken by Samuel Kemper.

Efforts at stabilizing success were undermined by petty conspiracies. With the capture of San Antonio, a provisional government of the Mexican state of Texas was organized, with Gutiérrez appointed as general and governor. A junta of thirteen members, of whom two were Anglo, was elected. A declaration of independence was issued, emphasizing universal rights and the larger struggle. At this point, Anglo mercenaries began to act autonomously, demanding compensation and objecting to their exclusion. Ostensibly, they objected to the execution on April 5th by Mexicanos and some Anglos of the Spanish governors Manuel Salcedo and Simón Herrera. A major factor motivating these executions was the active part played by Salcedo and Herrera in the capture and execution of Hidalgo and other independista leaders, which was a grave matter for the patriots; more to the point, however, was the execution of the elder head of the Delgado family of San Antonio whose son, a republican soldier, demanded their death, as did Miguel Menchaca with regard to the execution of his relative José. As the prospects for independence grew, two of Gutiérrez's former allies, Shaler and Toledo, turned on him. Toledo, a practiced propagandist, established the *Gaceta de Tejas* in May 1833 to criticize the movement; this was the first newspaper in Tejas, even though it ran only one issue, and it was followed by *El Mejicano*, which also published one issue— both papers were products of the political tumult. At any rate, the Anglos, who were well armed, seized Gutiérrez and put him on trial for his supposed complicity in the "murders." Next, his proposals at the junta were blocked. While all this was occurring, a royalist army of fifteen hundred men under Colonel Ignacio Elizondo, the betrayer of Hidalgo and now a royalist officer, approached San Antonio.

The serious internal conflict boded ill, despite successes. Due to impending battles, the Anglos decided to restore Gutiérrez to his overall position as governor and general, because the Bexar people were divided in their opinion concerning the issue of Gutiérrez's "trial," which was debilitating the defense of the town. On June 19, 1813, a battle was fought at the Rio Alazán, in which seven hundred Mexicanos and Anglo mercenaries fought the royalists, led by Miguel Menchaca of Bexar, who possessed a great influence with local residents. Bancroft describes Menchaca as "a man of vigor, bold and resolute, but rude and uneducated."[78] After the royalists were defeated, the Anglos deposed Gutiérrez on August 4, 1813, and sought to appoint in his place the mendacious Spaniard Toledo who, surprisingly, was now tentatively supported by Menchaca, whose influence with local Mexicans was decisive. Gutiérrez left for Natchitoches, now understanding perhaps that past support by some Anglos was part of a conspiracy to use his movement and its legitimacy to occupy Tejas. The exact situation was unclear, although the *bexareños* clearly were more antagonistic toward the royalists than toward the Anglos or Toledo. Perhaps they felt that whatever the motives of the Anglos, it would be advantageous to let them fight against the royalists. Subsequent events indicated that large numbers of the population willingly fought against the royalists under Gutiérrez de Lara and Miguel Menchaca, their own local leaders.

Tenacity did not compensate for lost momentum.[79] The royalists reorganized, assembling a large force of 1,930 men, who were placed under the command of General Joaquín Arredondo. Antonio López de Santa Anna was an ensign in Arredondo's royalist army. On August 18, 1813, a major battle was fought at the Río Medina near San Antonio. The royalists were opposed by a combined force of 3,000 men, composed of 1,700 mexicanos, 850 Anglos, and 60 Indian allies under the overall command of Toledo. The mexicanos again were directly commanded by Menchaca. The Spaniards emerged victorious from the battle in which most Mexicans and Indians and all but 90 Anglos were killed. Worse, Menchaca was killed during the battle. According to Bancroft, "In the pursuit every fugitive overtaken was ruthlessly sabred or lanced, the captured were immediately shot (among them 100 Anglos) and for weeks an exterminating persecution was carried on."[80] Meanwhile, Gutiérrez de Lara survived and continued in the independence movement, while Toledo eventually returned his loyalties to Spain and later was made ambassador to Naples.

Setbacks did not end the movement. Immediately following the defeat of the independistas, many insurgent Tejanos went to the United States border to escape from the royalists; among the insurgents was Francisco Ruiz, who, after the death of Menchaca, became a major San

Antonio political leader for decades to come. Gutiérrez began organizing again, cooperating with José Manuel de Herrera and Javier Mina, who had credentials from the movement leaders in the interior of Mexico. Subsequently, in 1815 and 1816, other expeditions were organized from the United States; they consisted mainly of Anglo adventurers whose activities were centered mainly in East Texas, but who were also interested in Florida. In 1816, José Manuel de Herrera, who had been appointed by Morelos as minister to the United States, cooperated with some of these elements, including Toledo, in establishing a privateering base in Galveston. On September 12, 1816, Herrera formed a proindependent junta at Galveston, which was declared to be an established port of the Mexican republic. He appointed a French privateer, Luis de Auryl, as independista civil and military agent of the Mexican province of Tejas. At the same time, Bernardo Gutiérrez de Lara, now a general in the independista Mexican army, was appointed agent at Nacogdoches. The major focus of these activities seems to have been privateering against Spanish commerce and raids against the Spanish military; to the extent that these activities affected Spanish shipping, they can be said to have aided the Mexican cause.

While his brother was a member of the constituent congress of 1824 for Tamaulipas, Gutiérrez eventually returned to his home in Tamaulipas, Mexico, where he served in office until his death in the late 1830s. He was governor and concurrently military commander of Tamaulipas in 1824. His last mobilization was against the separatist movement of 1837–39, led by filibusterers and traitors seeking to detach Tamaulipas from Mexico.

As the events of 1812–13 demonstrated, there was a significant proindependence and antiroyalist sentiment among the Tejanos who fought against the royalists; yet there was also royalist sympathy. Such conscious participation, finally, stands in contrast to the *filibusterismo* among the Anglo adventurers and privateers. The dislocations and animosities created during the decade from 1812 to 1822 were consequences that would extend into the future.

Independence: Looking Forward, Looking Back

Independence was a major political event whose social and political expression had been several hundred years in the making. Generally speaking, after 1820 the task for Mexican political leaders lay in deciding the purpose and benefits of independence and in cementing and enlarging the elements that made nationhood possible. Eventually, after twelve years of struggle, independence was consummated by the creoles who held some political and economic power.[81] Their achievement was the result of self-interest capitalizing on the support for the idea of independence, expressed in the insurgents' mestizo–indio movement of 1810. Paradoxically, the decision to secure independence stemmed from conservative reaction in Mexico, which was due, in turn, to apprehension on the part of the creoles toward liberal policies instituted in Spain and toward a resurgence of militancy by the survivors of the Hidalgo–Morelos effort. Henceforth, national politics revolved around interpretations of the mandate that developed from the gestation of 1810–21. The *Plan de Iguala* of 1821 bore the semblance of statesmanship in its offer of a unifying consensus: an independent government under a constitutional monarchy, equality for criollos and mestizos, and respect for the preeminence of the church as a social and religious institution.

After independence, achieved in 1821, the major political issue was the form of government—which sector of the elite was now empowered and how benefits were to be distributed. Some held to the dream of a Mexican monarchy, others to the ideal of a republic, and within each of these camps there was diversity of opinion as to the policy of the preferred government.

Rooted in the political process of independence, partisan activity was initiated after independence; the poles were "Liberals" and "Conservatives."[82] Although the Liberals and Conservatives called themselves "parties," they were, in fact, tendencies and movements within which personal followings and circles of affinity operated. Between the two camps there was some convergence, and within each camp a divergence, of opinion. The Conservatives favored a monarchy, a centralized state, and a hierarchically exclusive social order; and they favored, for the church, a preeminent position within the state and society. For the most part, they were from the upper bourgeoisie and drew their strength from property, the army, the church, and the social values inherited from the colony. Furthermore, the Conservatives held specific ideas about economic development and the strengthening of national unity. In contrast to the Conservatives, the Liberals were identified with aspirations of middle sectors of the society, composed of professionals, small merchants, manufacturers, and small farmers. Since they could not base their strength on economic power or institutions, they sought popular support. The ideological structure of liberalism was not free of contradictions, as has been observed. In brief, Liberals were republicans favoring federalism, juridical equality, subordination of clerical–military institutions to the state, popular sovereignty, and economic entrepreneurship; they were opposed to specially privileged sectors. One wing, the *puros*, was intransigent; while another, the *moderados*, was willing to compromise. In effect, the Liberals contributed the type and framework of government and the political ethos accepted by subsequent generations.

Summary

A range of elements and forces contributed to the development of Spanish-speaking mestizo communities in what is now the United States Southwest. A few of these factors are more immediate and open to view, while others are removed and more disparate in their consequences. The clearest development was the establishment of areas of settlement involving land, production, and organizational arrangements among the settlers; these places provided the basis for later developments.

In the far north, as in other parts of Mexico, a national character emerged and became defined between 1590 and 1821. From 1700 through the 1800s, the Mexican cultural influence became a stronger integral part of the economic and social life of the communities. These communities—the specific families, the cultural practices they transmitted, and their conscious identification with the land—were the significant achievement of the early centuries. As in the case of the initial colonial conquest, international events and forces were important to independence and to its loss in the far north; but in spite of shifting fortunes and interests, independence was gained and maintained through the people's support. The struggle for independence and successive disorders caused economic dislocation and recession, which generally affected all classes; and yet, political and economic instability also created a degree of social and economic fluidity. The population grew slowly, and the growth increased the process of *mestizaje*. Socially, culturally, and politically a core of nationhood emerged.

2

Mexican Republicanism
on the Frontera, 1822–1848

The New Republic, the Nation, and the North:
Accomplishments and Problems

Mexicans in the far north* were part of the revolts ending Spanish colonial rule that swept across Latin America during the first two decades of the nineteenth century. At the same time, a capitalist economy was developing, and the new economic order drew support from emerging liberal republican institutions, which supplanted colonial rule.[1] During the late eighteenth and early nineteenth centuries, Mexico and all of Latin America experienced an accelerated growth both economically and demographically. The Americas, with the exception of Cuba, Brazil, and Puerto Rico, gained their independence from Spain and Portugal. Early moves for independence in Mexico had occurred in north-central areas where the people shared economic circumstances which were similar to those in the northernmost provinces of California, Texas, and New Mexico.

The movement for Mexican independence was the first modern, consciously directed political effort to create institutional and social change. In favoring independence from Spain, the people of northern areas hoped for a freer trade policy, one which would result in more economic growth and more social and political latitude for criollos and mestizos. Although independence was supported and endorsed in the

---

*Which included what is today California, New Mexico, Texas, and Arizona, and parts of the states of Nevada, Utah, Wyoming, Colorado, Kansas, and Oklahoma.

north, there were also loyalists to the colonial regime. Immediately after independence in 1822, representatives of presidios, pueblos, and misiones across Mexico swore allegiance to the sovereign Mexican government. The Plan of Iguala, announced on February 24, 1821, proclaimed Mexican independence from Spain; and the Manifesto of Iguala, of August 24, 1821, established the regency of the former royalist colonel Agustín de Iturbide. The strongest supporters of this arrangement were *monarquistas*, who had backed the Spanish monarchy, and whose opponents or critics referred to themselves as *repúblicanos*. Eventually, a constitutional monarchy was rejected and the Mexican republic established in 1824. The major national figures were, on the one hand, liberals such as Guadalupe Victoria, Vicente Guerrero, and the outstanding Valentín Gómez-Farias, and among the conservatives, Anastasio Bustamante, Lucas Alamán, and the erratic Antonio López de Santa Ana.

For those who were politically informed, and more so for those who were active politically, a clear recognition prevailed that territory and people were integral to both nation and state and that the far north was Mexican. In the far north, as in the center, optimism about the bountiful territory and the people's self-confidence was commonplace, though there were those who disagreed.

Governance and Economy

Clearly, the struggle for independence had a political impact on the northernmost provinces. Throughout Mexico, a republican government was established at the provincial, state, and municipal levels. The tenor and form of administration depended on whether there was an emphasis on states rights, local rights, or the chief executive. People from the northern areas of California, Tejas, and New Mexico served in the Mexican congress, and at least two delegates signed the constitution. As a result of independence, greater numbers of officials arrived in the northern provinces and increased official communication with central Mexico. Although political change was as authentic and as dramatic as the change in sovereignty and form of government from a monarchy to a republic, the persistence of individuals in moving from one regime to the other as well as the persistence of some general institutional practices and values were also notable. Many of the same individuals or families involved in politics in the 1820s and 1830s were active in the post 1848 period. Certain individuals benefited by independence, but economic and social inequalities remained present between those who held land and those who were landless.

Factionalism and changes in local government were as common in the far north as in other parts of Mexico.[2] Property interests as well as class and ideological differences resulted in the rise of liberal or conservative partisan groups, which were roughly analogous to their counterparts throughout the rest of Mexico. Control of land and access to labor hastened the secularization of mission lands. Importantly, the interest in trade was strengthened among both officials and the wealthy.

During the early national period, the northern territories generally increased in population and grew economically.[3] Particularly important here was the expansion of cattle and sheep grazing, as well as the growth of ranchos. Prior to 1821, Spanish colonial authorities in the far north simultaneously allocated communal grants and a limited number of individual land grants. Following independence, the Mexican authorities of the territories made scores of individual grants, both major and small, and the number and value of these grants would increase with the secularization of the missions in the 1830s. The caste system was abolished *de jure* thus guaranteeing that Mexican citizenship for indigenous peoples was equal, in form, to the credentials of any other citizen. Yet the actual result was to accelerate the incorporation of indigenous citizens at the bottom of the socioeconomic hierarchy, where they functioned as a labor force.

In the more developed localities of the Mexican north, class divisions, interests, and consciousness reflected general patterns that were current in Mexico at the time. Class relations, however, were not yet stratified or demarcated by great extremes of wealth and social position between the owners of the means of production and the mestizo laborers. To the extent that owners of production in the far north were conscious of their interests and objectives, they aspired to the patterns and social relations prevailing in the south. In general, society in Mexico's far north developed with increasing socioeconomic stratification and the monopolization of wealth by the rising elite.

To the social elite, the process and control of political institutions, both civil and military, were matters of major significance. Departmental, district, and municipal governments represented the control of large and regionally significant financial resources derived from the collection of customs, the sale of tobacco (a government monopoly), the sale of official paper and stamps, the sale of permits, the awarding of contracts, the sale of land, and fines. Judicious administration was a widespread goal, and there were many conscientious officials; in contrast, embezzlement and misappropriation of government funds was occasionally a practice at the time, and indeed one that implicated most governments. People holding official posts often were paid a salary, but usually they were offered greater remuneration in the form of gifts and the appropriation of public resources. Especially significant to regional elites was the control of the allocation and grant or sale of public lands and/or use of mineral bearing lands, which were the major productive or potentially productive resources in these regions.

The political process included both formal and informal dimensions. Informally significant were the dynamics of interrelationships between competing circles of the elite and their followings. The formal aspect was represented by changes in the institutional organization of government. Under Spanish rule, the formal political process in the far north's Internal Provinces often had been limited to implementation of orders from the comandante general by the colonial governor and his subordinate military officers. Local residents were included in the formal regional political process at the level of the ayuntamientos. As a result of independence, Mexicans in the far north were able to propose major policy for the regions and to hold major posts in the civil and military administration.

The political life of the frontier existed within the context of the Mexican republic during the first half of the nineteenth century, all of which was distinct from an idealized version of the political process in the nineteenth-century United States. Politics on the Mexican frontier was thus neither better nor worse than the politics practiced in the Jacksonian United States; Mexico's politics were simply the moderate, alternative response of another society. Yet there were also very general commonalities. That Mexican frontier politicians often acted in their personal, familial, or factional interests should cause no surprise, for such has been true in nearly all societies. At the time, they also acted upon what they believed or claimed to be the best interests of town, territory, and country—and sometimes at great personal sacrifice. Political activity on the Mexican frontier involved not only maneuvering, but was also focused upon a set of immediate issues and principles.

This experiment in the operation of a republic provided for a representative government based upon the ideals of the equality of citizens before the law, the election of public officials, and the promotion of public good through a specified deliberative process. Within this framework, one major political issue was the desirability of a centralized form of government, with the states or departments placed under a uniform system of laws and administration overseen by the national government or a federal system providing greater autonomy to the states. From 1824 until 1836, then, the United States of Mexico were organized as a federal republic, or federation, in which the states enjoyed, in principle, considerable administrative autonomy; and in California greater stress was placed on local mechanisms, even though it remained a territory.

Regional Administration

Nuevo México and the Californias (Alta and Baja) were territories under the *Acta Constitutiva* and the Constitution of 1824, which established Mexico as a federal republic of states and territories.[4] Territorial government fell under the authority of the federal government, which appointed the major officers: the governor, who was responsible to the minister of interior and foreign relations; the comandante general, who was responsible to the minister of war and the navy; and the *comisario subalterno,* who was in charge of customs and internal taxes and was responsible to the minister of finance through the *comisario general de hacienda* at Chihuahua and Guadalajara. In practice, the offices of governor and comandante general were combined in the same person, who, during most of the period, was usually a military officer.

Each territory had a territorial legislature, or *diputación territorial,* composed of full members and alternates selected from the districts into which the territory was divided for administrative purposes. The diputación functioned as an advisory council to the governor, and its members were chosen by electors selected from each of the *distritos.* In theory, the electors, for whom there were property requirements, were elected by citizen voters, qualified adult males. In practice, participation in elections was limited to the propertied residents, as was true in other republics, but gradually the number of voters increased.

The administrative arrangement in Tejas was distinct from those in Nuevo México and California. Under the federal constitution, Tejas was attached to the state of Coahuila y Tejas, under whose constitution the state was divided into a series of subdivisions known as departments, of which Tejas was one. The chief administrative officer was known as the *jefe del departamento;* otherwise, the organization of the departamentos was similar to that of the distritos of the territorial system, already described. A major difference lay in the fact that Tejas as a departamento, rather than being directly under the federal government, was under the authority of the governor and legislature of the state of Coahuila y Tejas in most matters that were not reserved for the national government. The department of Tejas was later divided into three municipal districts: San Antonio de Bejar, Brazos, and Nacogdoches.

Tucson and Tubac were in the Arizpe district of Sonora. Once a part of the Provinces Internas, the towns were joined to Sonora as a single state, called Occidente, and then it was separated again. Tucson and Tubac were delayed in having town councils, but they did elect individual officials. Since Indian conflict continued, the military continued to be influential in local affairs. In this military–civilian arrangement on the frontier, civilian positions were generally held by members of pioneer families with past or current familial relations with the military.

In the far north, the major officials at the local or district level consisted of an alcalde, the chief administrative officer of the district; a *procurador síndico,* a judicial officer; and several regidores, or councilmen. Together, they comprised the district's ayuntamiento, or council. In addition to all of these offices were other offices within the various branches and levels of administration.

Apart from the broad commonalities of governance, a major common enterprise was the local militia, which was necessary for both regional defense matters and for local requirements. This militia required organization, mobilization, and, not least, a hierarchical leadership that would focus on working toward a common purpose involving numbers greater than those within the immediate rancho or pueblo. Militia service, particularly for the officers and political participation, was interrelated.

The External and the Internal

The early national period can be characterized, then, as a time of challenge and expansion for those who could take advantage of new opportunities. Social and economic life followed regional variants of national patterns, with politics and ideology reflecting the nation's general development. Cultural evolution also followed trends in the more developed intermediate north, which, in turn, was strongly influenced by occurrences in the central core.

There were also a number of significant contradictions within policies that otherwise appeared to be beneficial for the development of the frontier and of the republic as a whole.[5] Most serious was the foreign economic relation with northern settlements. Given the severe internal contradictions of the nation and its weakness in relation to the increasing strength of foreign powers, particularly of the neighboring United States, such a policy risked the possible loss of national territory. Debated colonization measures were part of a tentative defensive policy; they sought to exert regulative control over a phenomenon that was already occurring, and they also were intended to bring about regional economic development which would strengthen the country's economy. With large tracts of land in Tejas granted to Anglo-Americans and other outsiders, conflicts with foreign settlers steadily increased from 1821 on. During the 1820s, however, these dangers were not yet generally apprehended by the central government or the Mexican elite. Much more widespread was the view that foreigners would appreciate the Mexican government's generous settlement policy; it was felt that they would make significant contributions to the nation's development. Similarly, official members of the social strata who benefited from Mexico's economic dependence on foreign trade did not fully perceive the liabilities of allowing foreigners to increase their role in the nation's trading arrangements. Notably, in the far north and elsewhere, those who emulated and associated with foreigners—particularly those in contact with Anglo-Americans—were recognized and stigmatized by others in the population. Tellingly, economic interests invariably were at stake in such foreign relations.

The benefits of foreign trade were considerable in the far north, particularly for the elite and for Nuevo México and Alta California. Prior to independence, foreign smugglers occasionally traded with the inhabitants of Alta California; and soon after independence, a regular trade route was established between Alta California and New England.[6] Several ships with headquarters in Boston traded manufactured commodities for hides, tallow, and other raw materials. To an even greater extent, the United States interests traded with the more developed states of the Mexican Pacific Coast, with ships regularly visiting such major ports as Acapulco, Mazatlán and Guaymas, as well as parts of Alta and Baja California and Asia. Indeed, the major currency used in the China trade throughout the nineteenth century was the Mexican silver peso, greatly valued in the Far East where silver was in demand. Similarly, following independence, a major trade route, the Santa Fe Trail, was opened between Independence, Missouri, and north-central Mexico.[7] Though Nuevo México was not the terminus of the Santa Fe Trail, it had a major impact on the province. The stimulus of the trade came from the silver-mining states of Chihuahua, Durango, and Zacatecas. Once again, foreign manufactured goods were exchanged for a Mexican resource, silver. Annual trade fairs were held in major Mexican cities, from which imported goods were redistributed to most of the north-central portion of the country. Immediately but briefly, and despite the drain of currency, such commerce spurred economic development in the northern region. In the long run, however, it was injurious to national development and sovereignty.

During the period 1830–48, increasing conflict and turmoil resulted from both domestic and international causes. Important issues concerning the structure and ethos of the state's formal organization were debated throughout Mexico. At the same time, acute problems were created by the changeover from colonial to independent administration. Partisan debate about these issues and problems intensified in the far northern communities. At the same time, Spain, France, England, and the United States harassed Mexico. In the far north, internal matters became entangled with problems in foreign relations.

Internationally, this era of expanding industrial capitalism was marked by an increase in the competition for both domestic and international markets. The period also marked the beginning of a new era of intercolonial rivalry, which was reflected on a world scale by commercial, territorial, and strategic rivalry between Britain and France, the major European powers. In the Americas, and particularly in Mexico, a third rival, the United States, joined this battle for trade, territory, and strategic hegemony. Competition among foreigners for Mexico's foreign trade increased. But there were other aspects of foreign interest already in Mexico, including loans made by foreign bankers to the Mexican government, investments in mining, and strategic and territorial considerations. As a matter of policy, those in power sought to prevent rivals from getting the upper hand over their own nationals in any of these areas, while, at the same time, attempting to gain special concessions for themselves.[8]

Because of geographical proximity, the United States posed the greatest external threat to Mexico. Following its own revolution against the restrictions of British mercantilism—during which it received aid from other countries, among them Spain and the Spanish colonies, including Mexico—the United States began a process of economic and territorial expansion. After the purchase of Louisiana in 1803, the new Anglo nation continually expressed an active interest in acquiring Mexican territory, particularly in Tejas. Although the United States had pledged to respect the boundaries of New Spain through the Adams–Onís Treaty of 1819, this treaty also was used to argue the extension of U.S. boundaries. United States diplomatic representatives in Mexico City had made attempts during the 1820s to persuade the government to sell either Tejas or some other territory. Throughout this period, the influence of Anglo-Americans and other foreigners was steadily increasing within northern Mexico. By the end of the 1820s, the number of Anglos equaled or surpassed the Mexican population in eastern and central Tejas; and Tejas rapidly became the earliest and most intense scene of conflict between Mexican settlers and Anglo-American filibusters.

The United States was growing commercially and industrially at this time, and sought to expand even more. Many U.S. politicians believed that the best opportunity to expand the wealth of their country was to annex parts of Canada or Mexico. Anglos were extending their control throughout northern Mexico, just as other foreign countries were penetrating the entire Mexican republic. Many Anglo trappers, merchants, settlers, and military officers were entering Alta California and Nuevo México in the guise of "scientific explorers." Even though official observers had warned of the impending dangers, it was only after the actual loss of Tejas that the Mexican government understood the consequences of its economic weakness in the north.

Popular during this period was the idea that the United States had a preordained "right" to control all the land from the Atlantic to the Pacific, and from the North to the South Pole.[9] This expansionist doctrine of Manifest Destiny, as well as the ideology of ethnic chauvinism, were espoused by Anglo-Americans as the justification for their aggressive actions. Yet U.S. desires were both concrete—the quest for land, resources, and ports—and strategic, seeking an advantageous position for further domination. Apostles of these so-called ideals clamored for war with Mexico. The economic motives of the warmongers were concealed beneath the subterfuge of idealism intended to elicit support for a war from an often gullible United States electorate.

Mexico was not in a position to cope with external threats.[10] The country was weakened by severe internal problems, most basically by the dependent state of the economy, one aspect of which was the Catholic church. The church owned from one-half to two-thirds of all real property in the nation; and with the exception of the government itself, it was undoubtedly the largest landowner. Total church revenues were estimated to be five times the size of those of the national government. In addition, the church generally was a retrogressive influence on the nation's sociopolitical development. Repeatedly, it endorsed the more reactionary leadership through its ideological hold over the majority of the population; and from one generation to the next, it reinforced negative values through its institutions of formal education.

Social relations arising from relations of production reflected the severe imbalance in the distribution of national wealth. In spite of social and occupational diversity, extreme class divisions existed within the nation. While independence had abolished the fading caste system in principle, the criollos, or "Mexican Spaniards," were generally Mexico's dominant social and economic elite. The class stratification continued to reflect ethnic aspects. Although a tiny elite enjoyed tremendous wealth, the masses of the population were undereducated and excluded from the nation's formal political life. A definite weakness lay in the ineffective and unstable leadership that stemmed from the landed elite.

Below the small ruling elite, composed of the largest landowners, the Catholic hierarchy, the mine owners, and wealthy merchants, came a larger medium strata of smaller hacendados, senior military officers, merchants, and middle clergy; below them was a larger group composed of rancheros, small merchants, clergy, artisans, and the lower ranks of the military. Between these groups and others were mineros, vaqueros, transporters, and common artisans. The majority of Mexicans were members of the large sector composed of both urban and rural laborers. At the margins were the unemployed and the nonassimilated indigenous peoples. Governmental efficiency suffered from insufficient resources, and the political sphere was amorphous. The national government was poorly administered, weakened by malfeasance and the maldistribution of funds, and partisan politics rather than national interests were predominant. While as much as 90 percent of the national budget was allocated for military expenses, the army was poorly equipped, its payrolls padded, and the troops rarely paid on time or adequately cared for. Taxes were limited to customs revenues, but since these were insufficient, the government was re-duced to foreign or domestic private loans at extremely high rates of interest, which created, in turn, a national debt that outstripped revenues. The political norm was conspiracy rather than civil election, and one coup d'état followed another in continually destabilizing the state. Nevertheless, civilian leaders occasionally rallied against the political deterioration. Here and there, patriotic voices decried the tragic weakness of the Mexican state and proposed and demanded alternative solutions. Thus, Mexico's government was hindered in attempting to cope with the needs, problems, threats, and steadily escalating aggressions of foreign powers.

The Developing Political Culture in the Far North, 1821–1837

The achievement of Mexican independence in 1821 initiated an era of political change in the far north.[11] Underpinning these changes was a deep conviction concerning the potential wealth in each of the far north's major areas and the virtues of its inhabitants. When the northern provinces of Tejas, Nuevo México, and Alta California still formed part of the Captaincy General of the Provincias Internas, political authority resided primarily in the hands of governors, with the partial exception of the ayuntamientos and cabildos located in the larger settlements. Pobladores were legally subjects, not citizens; and they possessed only those privileges, not rights, that were guaranteed by the law, as it was interpreted by the governor. Often, municipal bodies were under the influence of the governor and military authori-ties, administered according to the governor's priorities, and were subservient to existing codes when dealing with local matters. In contrast, Mexican independence initiated a process of change in politi-cal discourse that seems dramatic when compared to the authoritarian orthodoxy of colonial domination. Republicanism introduced the con-cepts of citizenship, civil rights, representation by deputies, equality under the law, and legitimacy by popular acclaim. Regardless of the government's actual effectiveness, the new republican liberal ideology fostered a new political culture and ambience. There was also incremental yet relatively wide popular support not only for the republicans and their factions, but for issues such as statehood, autonomy within the federation, effective representation, increased colonization and immigration, the secularization of missions, the fair conduct of courts of law, the appropriate location of the provincial capital, curbs on the military, Indian integration, and control of governmental revenues.

The popular political ideology of the early independence period was transmitted from the central regions of Mexico. New political concepts, terms, and practices engaged the attention of the politically oriented and affected many others as well. For the politically active, many issues were synthesized in choices favoring either decentralized or centralized government, and a person could favor one or the other as a republican.

Norteños held that concepts such as "municipio libre" and "soberanía estatal" were encompassed by the meaning of the word *federalismo,* or federalism. Independent Mexico was a federal republic in which the states and *municipios* were guaranteed a degree of autonomy, or self-government, by the Constitution of 1824. Separate state status was sought by Alta California and Nuevo México, as territories of the Mexican federation, and by Tejas, a province joined to Coahuila. This federalist precept appealed to many norteños because it implied that Alta California, Nuevo México, and Tejas were entitled to eventual statehood, and thus appropriate autonomy within the federation. It was believed that state autonomy made for better economics because it implied that the local election of the governor and other officials promised benign rule rather than the exception. The territorial rule resulted from their appointment by Mexico City authorities—whether the president, the ministers, or the congress of the federation, and it subordinated local development.

The precept of governance opposed to federalism was *centralismo,* or centralism, which implied a strong centralized national government that would supervise the states directly and rule the territories through appointed officials known as *jefes políticos,* or political chiefs, in contradistinction to the rule of the governor under federalism. Many former monarchists were centralists. Few *tejanos, nuevo mexicanos* or *californios* advocated centralism, although under the centralist regime (of 1835–44), many local políticos declared themselves centralists, employing a political stratagem necessary to gain recognition from the national government. As often happens with political terminology, *centralism* and *federalism* were often interpreted to suit the immediate interests of those concerned.

Associated with federalism and centralism were the ideological concepts of *liberalismo* (liberalism) and *conservatismo* (conservatism).[12] Liberalism implied support for a federal form of government and encompassed a range of social and economic measures, including support for low tariffs, free trade, secularism, civilian control of the military, and a system of public education; and, incidentally, among some liberal intellectuals an identification with a romanticized Aztec past. Conversely, conservatism advocated a centralized government, support for the hierarchy and the institutional church, the protection of selected home industries, a religiously based education, and an alliance with military leaders to maintain the status quo; and for some conservatives an identification with a romanticized colonial society. In reality, the situation was much more fluid, and at different times in different regions of Mexico these ideological terms reflected different emphases, varying according to local, regional, or national contexts. In the far northern context, both liberalism and conservatism reflected the general contention of liberalism and federalism vis-à-vis centralism and conservative rule as well as the diverse reality of contemporary events, and their meanings varied in changing and specifically regional and even local contexts.

The Mexican period, in comparison to the colonial regime, introduced a more inclusive as well as dynamic and representative political process. Though this process was far from perfect, it clearly represented an improvement over the authoritarianism of a colonial governor. Most dramatically, independence resulted in an incremental change in the participation of somewhat larger numbers of people in the political process as well as in other kinds of public events. Again in contrast to the colonial period, *el pueblo,* when it acted in disconformity, argued for rights as *ciudadanos,* or citizens, rather than concentrating on their privileges as subjects. Yet political life was mainly the province of a growing elite, which was somewhat the case in other American republics, including the United States. Political participants eventually had to deal with and grudgingly and imperfectly develop the extension of political access.

A specific foreign enemy became the concern not of distant policy planners, but of both national and local leaderships. Upon attaining independence in 1821, Mexico inherited the strategic geopolitical situation of Tejas, Nuevo México, and Alta California. The latest grand decisions had been arranged between the U.S. and Spain in the Adams–Onís Treaty of 1819, which declared the northern boundaries of the Viceroyalty of New Spain with the U.S. As already mentioned, a retreating monarchical Spain, represented in this agreement by its foreign minister, Don Luis de Onís, sought to safeguard its colonial possessions, bordering the expanding area of the U.S. At best, the Spanish court's concessions marked a territorial consolidation of the frontier in face of the looming Anglo-American advance. An independent Mexico and the U.S. recognized the Adams–Onís arrangement by treaty in 1829; without such, a retrospective view suggests that an earlier collision with the U.S. might have occurred, and thus Mexico would have been forced to confront the challenge much earlier than it actually did. There was no lack of concern, but the problem was one of effectiveness in defending the far north.

Alta California

After independence, the northernmost territory of Mexico was Alta California, settled since the 1770s and for the most part by people drawn from the western coastal areas of Sonora, Sinaloa, and Jalisco.[13] On contemporary maps, Alta California comprised a vast territory expanding north and northeast of the Colorado River, including what are now Nevada, Utah, and part of Wyoming. However, the actual settlement effectively under the control of territorial authorities extended approximately a hundred miles inland along the coast from San Diego to Sonoma, just north of San Francisco Bay. The population of the coastal zone in 1820 has been estimated, at a minimum, as 23,770 inhabitants, of whom 3,270 were described as gente de razón, or Spanish-speaking mestizos and criollos, and 20,500 as neophytes, or missionized Indians. While Alta California had been settled primarily to protect the northern boundaries by preventing foreign expansion into the south, it was increasingly recognized that the territory possessed tremendous potential resources and was strategically located for Pacific Ocean trade. In the last decade of colonial rule, and during the Mexican wars of independence, the province increased its trade and production despite intermittent communication with the south. Undoubtedly, there was awareness of the independence struggle among all sectors of the population, but the monarchist authorities maintained control. Colonial officials and missionaries had received special in-structions and took particular care to prevent news of the war of independence from circulating among the people. Mexican indepen-dence was greeted with considerable enthusiasm by the people of Alta California, except for the tiny elite of military officers and missionaries who, until then, had exercised major control over the province.

In March 1822, dispatches were received by Governor Joaquín Sola of Alta California, officially informing him of the establishment of the independent Mexican monarchy and calling on the authorities of Alta California to recognize independence and California's status as a terri-tory of the new nation.[14] In April 1822, a junta composed of the governor, the presidial commanders, and the president of the Francis-can missions met at Monterey and agreed to acknowledge Alta Califor-nia's acceptance of Mexican independence. Public ceremonies and celebrations, including the taking of an oath of allegiance, were held in Monterey and the district centers from April 9 through April 20, 1822. At about the same time public festivities were held in all other pueblos, presidios, and misiones. The news of Alta California's acceptance of Mexican independence was delayed in reaching Mexico City, resulting in the fear that officers and missionaries loyal to Spain had prevented its acceptance. The Mexican congress therefore sent a special commis-sioner a *canónigo* (canon) of the Durango cathedral, Father Agustín Fernández, to facilitate California's integration into an independent Mexico.

When Commissioner Agustín Fernández de San Vicente arrived at Monterey on September 26, 1822, he was welcomed by public cere-monies. Soon afterward, additional ceremonies were held throughout Alta California, replacing the Spanish royal colors with the flag of the Mexican empire and swearing allegiance to the government of Agustín Iturbide.

Independent Mexican authority introduced some significant changes and innovations in Alta California politics and social life. Mexican californios, for the first time, formulated local policies for the territorial, district, and municipal governments, and held major civil and military positions of authority. Church prerogatives were weak-ened, and church personnel now became sensitive to partisan shifts in Mexico City, as well as developing a more interactive relationship with local authorities.

Mexican independence thus stimulated the growth of a local territorial elite of second-generation californios who, together with officials sent by the national government, dominated the political life of Alta California until its annexation by the United States in 1848. Concurrent with and underlying political change was the economic transformation of the territory during the republican period. Independence ended the colonial limitations on trade with foreigners, thus greatly stimulating grazing and agricultural production for export. At that point in time, the mission system and its monopoly of the most productive coastal lands became a major stumbling block to the realization of the territory's potential economic development. The politics of Alta California during the period 1821–48 can be characterized as reflecting not only a struggle among competing elite groups for the control of productive resources, but also the economic politics representing their interests. Control of public institutions and revenues was the key to the ability of the elite groups to implement and legitimize policies favorable to themselves.

The Mexican national period, extending from 1822 to 1848, was an era of significant growth and development for Alta California. Members of the elite, and occasionally other vocal individuals, assumed control of the direction of affairs of the Indians and the regional government, which previously had been in the hands of the governor. In contrast to the colonial era, when the governor decided on significant matters, the Mexican period was one of experiment, innovation, and public debate. Patterns of life and events were more complex, moving more rapidly and involving the participation of larger numbers of people. While the political innovations of an essentially emergent form of government were often frustrated, a popular political culture developed in the far north.

By late 1822 reorganization of the government was under way, giving more administrative authority to local authorities, and in a system of representative territorial government established through a *diputación*, a territorial legislature, chosen by electors selected in regular local elections. The first assembly was constituted on May 21, 1823, and was comprised of José Cruz, Francisco Ortega, Francisco Castro, José Palomares, and José Antonio Carrillo. The members of the diputación, in turn, elected a *diputado* to the congress in Mexico City; chosen was Pablo Vicente de Sola and a governor, Captain Luis Argüello.

The establishment of the republic in 1823 resulted in a further broadening of interest and participation in government and politics by larger numbers of citizens. On January 7, 1825, Argüello met with the assembly and the major presidio commanders to discuss the question of federation and the effective forms of government for California. The "Plan de Gobierno Provisional," issued on January 17, contained four sections and twelve articles. It reaffirmed the need to combine political and military authority in the governor's office and advocated the establishment of a *junta general* to serve as the main body on taxes, land allocations, external relations, and public funds. In July 1827, Moctezuma as the name of the province was proposed and debated, but the possibility of California remained. Los Angeles was proposed as a villa and as the capital of the territory. Even though the proposals were forwarded, no action was taken. On January 31, 1825, Lieutenant Colonel José María Echeandia, former head of the college of engineers in Mexico City, was named administrative and military commander of both Baja and Alta California. In October, headquarters were established at San Diego. One of Echeandia's first decisions, this one was controversial, and he would continue to be a center of controversy through 1831.

During the Echeandia years, a rising figure was the very young Mariano Guadalupe Vallejo of Monterey. At sixteen he enlisted as a cadet; and by nineteen he was a lieutenant and nominated to the provincial assembly. His father, Ignacio Vicente Vallejo of Guadalajara, had only reached the modest rank of sergeant, but he had received grants of land. His son, active in Mexican politics, added so much to this patrimony that he was perhaps the largest and wealthiest landowner in the territory within the next fifteen years. Vallejo and his relatives and closest friends, Juan Alvarado and José Castro, who were also young and about to rise politically, all considered themselves liberals; and their criticism focused on the missions and local government.

Politics in Alta California was generally both a microcosm and reflection of the larger political process throughout the northern frontier and the republic as a whole. During the 1820s and 1830s, the competing elites included foreign and Mexican commercial interests, Franciscan missionaries, territorial officials, the growing landholding elites (*arribeños* and *abajeños,* respectively) in the northern and southern parts of the territory, and the various branches of the federal government concerned with the territory. Throughout the period, political struggles were ultimately related to the principal issues of colonization, including settlement and distribution of the land, secularization of the missions, tariffs and customs administration, military affairs, and the capital's location; the first three factors were the more basic issues, and the last two were important primarily as they were able to influence the first three. Subsequently, with the secularization of the missions and the initial consolidation of the propertied elites during the 1840s, the question of foreign settlement loomed as a major concern.

Apart from women, who were not fully represented in the formal political process, two other major interest groups comprised the majority of the territorial population: the small mestizo rancheros and *labradores*; and the majority Indian population, in turn, divided into an acculturated Mexican laboring class and a larger number of unincorporated peoples living a changing communal and indigenous life. At times, these large sectors of the population affected both the elites and the formal political process, exercising their influence in a variety of ways, including cooperation or noncompliance with authorities and laws; support for or opposition to authorities or factions during occasional *pronunciamientos*; Indian flight from the missions; and Indian protests. These issues involved contradictions not only among the elite and between the elite and its allies within other sectors of the population, but also among the poorer mestizos and Hispanicized Indians.

In addition to Mexican independence, major events and trends of the 1820s in Alta California included the growth of agriculture and cattle ranching; an increase in the Mexican population; the development of a regional California identity and cultural expression within the context of norteño, or northern, Mexican cultural development; the expansion of an active local political life frequently marked by conflict among individuals and factions; changes in church administration; neophyte unrest; and the increasing political prominence of Los Angeles in the affairs of Alta California.

Monterey, in the north, and Los Angeles, in the south, increased their political prominence in the affairs of Alta California. Lands were developed in and around San Francisco and in what became the Sonoma area. There were also extensive campaigns conducted against Indians, and as in other places, such campaigns provided opportunities for promotion and enrichment. By 1840 Mariano Vallejo was a colonel and doing well enough to secure at least two hundred thousand acres, to which he was to add more.

A political sector and leadership grew in concert with land-tenure practices. The number of ranchos increased slightly during the 1820s, when seven additional grants were made.[15] The largest number of grants and the real period of growth occurred in the 1830s and 1840s, especially after secularization of the missions in 1836.

Elite consolidation was related to the greater number of land grant-ees as well as to the size of the grants. Under Spanish colonial rule, from 1781 to 1822, and early Mexican administrations to 1833, only about two dozen land grants had been issued in the Los Angeles area. After secularization in 1833 and until the end of independence in 1847, approximately 50 additional grants were made. In all of Alta California, about 47 land grants were made prior to 1832 and over 470 after that date. In the Los Angeles area, for example, the majority of grants were made between 1833 and 1840, with only about a dozen after that. Owners and their families lived on the grants and were directly involved in their work. The reality was comprised largely of working mestizo rancheros of the colonial and Mexican periods, in contrast to notions of a supposedly European wealthy and leisurely elite.

Many of the existing grants experienced considerable growth in the number of livestock and inhabitants. Despite their increasing herds and the growth of a legal export trade of hides and tallow through the use of foreign vessels, the ranchos were eclipsed by the missions, which remained large commercial producers during the 1820s and early 1830s. Besides the much greater size of their lands, the missions' growth was due mainly to the missionaries' control of a large neophyte labor force that was many times the size available to private ranchos. The larger volume of mission production and trade, however, did not always mean great wealth, for it was essential to use profits for the support of the neophytes and the upkeep of the missions. Other surplus was absorbed by the territorial government in the form of loans for the support of the presidios, loans which were never repaid.

The decade of the 1830s was characterized by an economic growth that was reflected in an expansion of the cattle herds, the increased trade with foreigners transacted through several ports, and the multi-plication of ranchos.[16] Legal and illegal commerce also burgeoned as a result of Mexican laws that opened the California coast to foreign merchant ships, which nevertheless were required to pay customs duties at Monterey before being permitted to trade. Because of the greater profits to be made by evading the duties, large-scale smuggling continued throughout the Mexican period. However, foreign ships that declared their cargos and paid the customs duties at Monterey were legally permitted to trade in coastal towns. By the 1830s an increasing number of foreigners were participating in the economy, particularly entrepreneurs from the United States. Commerce quickened following a major turnover in church property and labor in the mid-thirties.

From the 1830s on, California politicians increasingly played a role in the formal institutional political life of the Mexican Territory/Department of Alta California.[17] Under the Mexican Federal Constitution of 1824, Alta California was a territory, and the governor was appointed or confirmed in office by the national government. A territorial diputación, or legislature, consisted of diputados who each represented the districts in the territory. The diputados were chosen in their districts by electors who had been selected in a general election in which all adult male citizens were eligible to vote. In addition to its legislative role, the diputacion also elected Alta California's representative to the congress in Mexico City. Several changes were also made in the organization of the ayuntamientos (town councils); a síndico (public attorney) and secretary were added to the alcalde and the regidores comprising pueblo governments such as those at Los Angeles and San José. The chief public official of the territory's districts was the alcalde, an office that combined the functions of a judge and an administrator. He was assisted by two regidores, or councilmen and also a public attorney; and a secretary and treasurer. Numerous individuals served in such other offices as *subalcalde, juez de campo, regidor, secretario,* or *tesorero* of the ayuntamiento during that period. The alcalde of Los Angeles, for example, frequently had several subalcaldes for the distant parts of the district. Many persons who held these and other offices also held appointments as electors, militia officers, receivers of customs, or administrator of former mission properties. Holders and would-be holders of elected and appointed offices were not the only participants in the political process. Occasionally, popular leaders became spokespersons voicing the grievances of the people on particular issues or principles. Presumably hundreds participated in the political process when they were aroused by particular injustices or needs, or by supporting particular leaders with whom they had economic or social relationships.

Political activity in the Mexico's California territory followed a logic based on national and local issues of public importance and divergent positions, which were, in turn, based upon both economic interest and political principles.[18] It was a game of "ins" versus "outs," accompanied by the "rhetoric" often common in local politics. In Alta California, a territory until 1836 and a department afterward, the issue of centralism versus federalism was primarily a question of whether the governor and other major officials would be locally elected natives of California or appointed by the president as outside officials from Mexico City and the central states. In practice, the positions of californio politicians on this question varied in relation to other issues such as secularization and north–south rivalries. Thus, at different times, leaders such as the Carrillos and Picos changed their positions on this issue, sometimes according to which faction the government in Mexico City recognized as the legitimate authority in Alta California.

A recurrent issue throughout the Mexican period was the rivalry between northern californios, the arribeños, and southern californios, the abajeños, for control of the governorship, the diputación, the customs house revenues, and military authority. Since two-thirds of the Mexican population lived in southern Alta California, the position that Los Angeles, the largest center of population, should be the capital rather than Monterey had both a logical and an emotional appeal. However, because Monterey had been the capital and the arribeños had control of the records, the governmental framework, and the major offices, they were able to effectively prevent the transfer of government to Los Angeles until 1845, when Pío Pico was confirmed as governor by the national government. Related to north–south rivalries was the tendency of northern leaders to seek greater autonomy from Mexico City vis-à-vis a stronger sense of national community among the Angelinos. Northern Alta California, with a smaller population and an elite political tradition stemming from the government's presence at Monterey during the colonial period, tended to maintain a looser attachment to Mexico than southern Alta California, which was in closer contact with the other northern Mexican regions, especially Sonora, Sinaloa, and the ports of Guaymas, Mazatlán, San Blas, and Acapulco. With a larger population and a stronger Mexican cultural identity, the south possessed stronger political loyalties.

The dramatic political question facing political leaders in California, as well as those in Nuevo México and Tejas, was the threat posed by the United States. With a few exceptions, the leaders and the people in both the north and the south opposed foreign efforts to acquire Alta California. Most of the people desired to remain a Mexican territory, living under the leadership of politicians selected from the territory itself. The pressure of increasing foreign immigration and filibustering, largely from the United States and its clear intention of acquiring the territory, created a political crisis for southern leaders such as the Picos, the Carrillos, and the de la Guerras, and northern leaders including the Vallejos, the Alvarados, and the Castros.

A major political issue in Alta California during the Mexican period was the changing relation of the society and the civil government to the church. This issue was overshadowed by the more polemical problem of secularizing the missions and the conditions under which it would occur. Although the twenty-one Franciscan missions included lands and labor, they were also social and cultural mainstays of the territory. Secularization meant a loss in revenue for church-related activity and a transition from regular to secular clergy, as well as a transfer from Spanish-born to Mexican-born clergy, among whom were clergy who had contacts within the government and were ready to work with it. The Franciscans sought negotiation in lieu of outright opposition to negative measures, and they realized two accomplishments: the Californias became a diocese, and a seminary was established which ordained its first priests in 1846.

Secularization Resolved

The central issue of this period, as stated previously, was the question of secularization of the missions.[19] Since the missions controlled the majority of the territory's productive resources and its major source of labor, their fate would generally determine the direction of economic and social development affecting all sectors of the population. Further complicating the issue was the fact that most Franciscan missionaries were Spaniards, many of whom preferred Mexico's previous dependence upon Spain. But the idea of secularization was not new; when it had been discussed prior to independence, one of its original premises had maintained that the missions would be converted into towns once the Indians had been sufficiently Hispanicized to form a free-standing laboring class. The liberal Spanish Constitution of 1812 had decreed the secularization of the missions, but this decree was not implemented in California, even though California officials had sworn to it in the last year of Spain's rule. In time, the issue was keenly debated in the Mexican federal congress, which had established the Comisión de Fomento de las Californias to study secularization, among other questions related to California's development, and to make policy recommendations to the government.

Ostensibly, the purpose of secularization was to convert the missions into regular parishes and civil pueblos and to transform the neophytes into regular Mexican citizens. The mission lands and property would be divided among the neophytes, with any excess to be made available for granting to other citizens. While the missions were involved in the process of transition, they would be run by administrators or commissioners appointed by the government. In reality, since the mission lands comprised the wealthiest and most developed properties in the territory, the control of secularization and the conditions under which it took place became a political prize among the various political factions. Similarly, when secularization actually occurred, appointments to administrative positions in the former missions became lucrative political resources. Through the administration of the mission's former lands and property, several dozen civil officials, military officers, and their friends and relatives were able to profit, and by the early 1840s an economic elite of some wealth emerged for the first time in the history of Alta California.

In Alta California, groups opposed to secularization included the Franciscans; civil and military authorities who feared the loss of large subsidies contributed by the missions; and most foreign merchants who felt that secularization might undermine the economy. Those favoring secularization included the majority of the California elite who sought mission lands, and the mission Indians who desired freedom from forced labor. While both groups based their arguments largely on the supposed welfare of the Indians, the actual, underlying concern was the control of land and labor.

Despite their limited ability to influence the political process, the Indians were not slow to state their own case. Echeandia and succeeding governors received petitions from Indians asking to be allowed to leave the missions or to receive a part of the land because the Mexican constitution guaranteed them full citizenship rights. Thousands of Indians simply left the missions during this period, indicating that the majority of mission Indians wanted to disband the missions, desiring the freedom to choose between returning to an indigenous way of life or adapting on their own terms to a Mexican–Californian society. They were not offered the first alternative, since what both proponents and opponents of secularization feared most was the loss of the indigenous labor force, which was a significant component of Alta California's economy.

Local and national politics were dramatically intertwined in California. At the end of 1829, as a result of the Plan de Jalapa, the administration of President Vicente Guerrero was terminated, and General Anatasio Bustamante became president. While claiming to uphold the federal constitution, the Bustamante regime marked a turn to authoritarian conservativism and clericalism. In late 1830, the new government appointed Lt. Col. Manuel Victoria, then *comandante principal* of Baja California, as jefe político of Alta California.[20] When the news of Victoria's appointment reached Alta California, Echeandia moved quickly to decree a plan to secularize the missions (issued on January 6, 1831), with the support of the diputación and influenced by *ayudante inspector* José María Padres, a liberal federalist who had been appointed prior to the Bustamante administration. Echeandia correctly believed that the new administration opposed unregulated secularization, which was what the locals wanted. With the encouragement of Padres, an ostensibly liberal group emerged, involving members of the Carrillo, Osio, Vallejo, Pico, Alvarado, and Bandini families, all of whom would be at the center of the struggles that followed.

When in 1831 jefe político Colonel Victoria arrived in Alta California, he moved forcefully to assert his authority, and as one of his first acts, he annulled Echeandia's decree of secularization. Mistakenly, Victoria quickly demonstrated that he intended to govern the territory without the assistance of the California elite and without consultation, and he refused to call the diputación into session. To buttress his authority, he began to arrest and harass potential or already known opponents among the officers of the Echeandia administration and the local elite. Victoria made himself unpopular and angered political leaders. In November 1831, a junta, led by abajeños Pío Pico and José Antonio Carrillo, and Juan Bandini, future California diputado to the congress, initiated a revolt at San Diego that was supported by ex-governor Echeandia.

Success and realignment followed. After issuing the *Pronunciamiento de San Diego* against Victoria's allegedly arbitrary rule, the anti-Victoria forces marched north to occupy Los Angeles on December 4,

1831, and to free some prisoners.[21] Governor Victoria, who had marched south with about 30 soldiers and some supporters, reached the Cahuenga Pass on December 5, 1831; and here, he fought a brief engagement with a force of about 120 volunteers and 30 soldiers led by José Antonio Carrillo. Two men were killed, and Governor Victoria was seriously injured. On December 8, at San Gabriel, the wounded Victoria resigned as governor and left for San Blas. Pío Pico, the senior *vocal*, or speaker, of the diputación, would have succeeded Victoria as governor, but the former governor Echeandia declared Pico's claims to be illegal and named himself as governor.

During late 1831, the struggle was between Pico, a ranchero; Echeandia, an administrator; and Agustín Zamorano, a former associate, printer, and entrepreneur. A brief power struggle ensued between Echeandia and Pío Pico, with Echeandia winning and proclaiming himself jefe político. At this point, Agustín Zamorano was supported by some of Victoria's officers, foreign merchants, and members of the arribeño elite; and he declared that Echeandia's assumption of the office of jefe político was illegal and a blow directed against the national government. Zamorano's supporters acted upon a variety of motivations. Officials who sought to remain in control of government institutions and customs revenues were members of a northern elite fearful that abajeños would gain control of the territory. There were also opponents of Echeandia's decree of secularization, as well as foreigners who sought to take advantage of the situation to gain land or who feared that secularization would ruin business opportunities. Another motivation for opposition lay in the fear that the Bustamante government would send troops to remove Echeandia, a possibility that made supporting the latter a poor prospect for personal gain. Active conflict between Echeandia and Zamorano was soon ended, however, by an ad hoc agreement that Zamorano would govern the northern part and Echeandia the southern sector of the territory. The revolt against Victoria was significant because it accelerated political coalitions, drew closer official attention to Alta California, and increased awareness of the need for secularization and a more effective colonization if Mexico were to retain effective control of the territory. It also underscored the weight the South carried in political conflict. However, major northern políticos like the Vallejos, Alvarados, and Castros may have encouraged Zamorano, but they did not support him strongly enough.

In late 1832, the government of President Anastasio Bustamante appointed General José Figueroa—a veteran of the independence wars; a former aide to Vicente Guerrero; a person close to Guadalupe Victoria; and former governor of the state of Sonora–Sinaloa—as jefe político and *jefe militar* of Alta California.[22] Figueroa was probably appointed to the post to remove him from the scene as a potential opponent of the Bustamante government. A moderate federalist, an insurgent hero, and a distinguished officer, Figueroa subsequently was acknowledged as the most capable Mexican governor of the territory. Arriving in the aftermath of the rebellion against Victoria, Figueroa began his administration with great difficulties. Not the least of these was the attempt to conciliate the californio elite, who ostensibly claimed to resent the insufficient attention of the national government, which, they argued, did little to develop the territory or to solve its many problems. Rather than merely attention, however, they preferred development.

Unlike Victoria, Figueroa was a more practiced politician and able to work with the diputación and local leaders in putting together a workable plan for secularization. The result minimized conflict among the major political factions by dividing the responsibilities of the administration of the former missions among the leaders and their major supporters. The key question that Figueroa faced was the secularization of the missions, which subsumed the issue of the future of the neophytes. The eventual policy concerning secularization would clearly determine future economic conditions and political events in the territory. Figueroa attentively investigated conditions in the missions and consulted extensively with the diputación, other officials, missionaries, and members of the elite. He also made a considerable effort to inform himself of the situation and attitudes of the Indians themselves, as well as the likelihood of their becoming economically and socially independent citizens. A fervent patriot and proud of his own Indian ancestry, Figueroa was the governor of Sonora–Sinaloa during the period of conflict with the Mayo and Opata Indians; and he had resisted demands for their extermination, championing a conciliatory policy of incorporation of the Indians.

Given the economic and political realities, Figueroa formulated a political and economic compromise, a plan for secularization that would convert the missions into self-governing pueblos and divide mission property among Indians who would become small farmers, with thirty-three acres granted to each adult male. Surplus mission properties would be available for distribution to Mexican californios. In principle, such a plan would have given the Indians the chance to become independent and hopefully successful Mexican small farmers. At the same time, the plan made available to Mexican californios large amounts of land for development and abolished the repressive regime of the missions. While Figueroa was formulating this plan, events accelerated in Mexico. The government of Bustamante was overthrown by Antonio López de Santa Anna, who became president; then, the radical liberal Valentín Gómez-Farías, the new vice president, gained control of the administration upon Santa Anna's temporary retirement. Although Gómez-Farías drew attention, and as a consequence, incited a clash of ostensibly well-intentioned purposes, more salient were the local pragmatics highlighted by Figueroa.

Gómez-Farías, a nationalist and an advocate of a strong federal colonization and development policy in the territories of the far north, initiated legislation for a government-financed colonization program for Alta California.[23] Eventually, the arrival of twenty-four teachers would make regular elementary schools in California possible. Overall, this project was complemented by the formation of a private corporation, *La Compañía Cosmopolitana*, which would establish enterprises to develop the territory economically. The Gómez-Farías supporters heading these ventures were the former ayudante inspector Padres and a prominent Guadalajara landowner and politician, José María Híjar. A fundamental aspect of the colonization plan, secularization, would have turned over the missions to the officers of the Padres–Híjar colony. Under this plan, the property of the missions would form the capital for colonization; lands would be available for division among settlers, Mexican Indians, californios, and others who were eligible. Persons with special skills were particularly desirable. To become a member of the colony, one was required to apply for land, and an applicant could not possess more than fifty acres. Population would increase, as would the sum of trades and skills; and small landholding would be strengthened. The instructions also appointed Híjar as jefe político of Alta California and Padres as jefe militar. One result was a major local political clash.

When news of the proposed colony reached Alta California, both Figueroa and California officials were incensed at what happened to be the allocation of the territory's most valuable resources to outsiders and políticos and their supporters. Since land would not be available to anyone who was not a member of the Padres–Híjar colony, or who owned more than the limit, the plan appeared to exclude most Indians and californios, particularly those with land; and arguably, local Indians would not have a first claim even if they joined.

In the interim, while the colony of farmers, artisans, mechanics, and a few professionals traveled by land to San Blas, and then by sea to Alta California, Santa Anna staged a coup that ousted the liberals and established a centralist dictatorship. As one of his first acts, Santa Anna genuflected in the direction of what he thought were clerical interests, hoping to gain by dispatching to Figueroa at Monterey a courier with orders voiding the appointments of Híjar and Padres— even though Santa Anna would have preferred to deal with someone other than Figueroa. When the colony arrived at Alta California, Híjar and Padres found that they had been removed from their official positions; nevertheless, they attempted to carry out the colonization plan. Acting in his capacity as director of colonization, Híjar demanded that Figueroa turn over the control of the missions to him. Figueroa and the diputación refused, and both carried out an acrimonious exchange of communications with Híjar and Padres. The end result was the dispersal of the colony of 239 farmers and artisans, although most of the colony remained as ordinary settlers on the same basis as other californios. Híjar, Padres, and their closest partisans were arrested and returned to central Mexico, where Figueroa charged them with being irresponsible and wholly interested in personal gain. He singled out the leaders José María de Híjar and José María Padres as culprits. The ensuing acrimony led Figueroa to issue the "Manifesto to the Mexican Republic" of 1835, a major political statement of the period.[24] Though it focused on the controversy of colonization, it included a miscellany of correspondence, and it addressed questions of ethics and priorities in governance. Figueroa defended his actions by arguing the patriotism of his protection of Indians whose right to mission lands he also upheld. In his words:

> I preserved the peace, order, and well-being of this California, of
> this important part of the Republic, which requires particular care
> and a highly sensitive guardian, so that the suggestions of the many
> native and foreign adventurers who, like flashes of lightning in a
> stormy night, criss-crossing amongst us on all sides, do not launch
> it on a career of disorder. From my childhood I have served in the
> ranks of those who fought for independence from its beginnings.

> With my slight talent and less instruction, with all my strength,
> with my blood and my health. I have contributed, so far as it has
> been possible for me, to the glories of the nation.

While secularization led to a greater empowerment of those who benefited from it, former mission Indians at least remained as members of
the community, and were given the choice of becoming workers or of
assimilating.

In summary, the whole episode of the Híjar–Padres colony high-
lights several of the major constrictions in Mexico's California society
and in the policies of the day. In one sense, the colony was a planned
but belated effort that was undermined by local pressures which were,
in turn, not sufficiently comprehended. Because of political instability
and an uneven system of public revenues and finance, administrations
could neither formulate a strong policy of colonization nor one of
frontier development; or when they were able to formulate an acceptable policy, either they could not finance it or were themselves removed before implementation could be carried through. Because resources were simply too small to allow for a more complex approach,
some groups inevitably were favored and some excluded. For example,
Indians who wished to retain their own culture and traditional economy found themselves in conflict with the desire of the Mexican elite
to assimilate them into the laboring strata of the Mexican population.
Subsequent events indicate one alternative to assimilation or remote
survival: Anglo conquest that resulted in the virtual extermination of
California Indians.

A strong, consistent, and balanced policy of colonization and development would have done much to reduce contradictions by providing increased opportunities for all parties. Such a policy, however,
could not have eliminated contradictions between the elites and the
laboring population; probably, its changing economic conditions would
have created new possibilities for conflict. Finally, in terms of the
conflict between Mexican and foreign interests, an energetic program
would not have eliminated conflict, but it would certainly have increased the possibilities of a favorable outcome for Mexican interests
(that is, the area remaining in Mexican hands).

Shortly after writing the *Manifesto to the Mexican Republic*, jefe
político José Figueroa died. Upon his death, members of the local
assembly declared:

Everyone commends and recognizes his exceptional merits and his long and distinguished services to his country. He always obeyed the laws and saw that they were obeyed, and sacrificed himself to fulfill his public duties. It was he who planted the olive of peace when he landed on the beaches of this coast; it was he who safe-guarded agriculture: it was he who watched over the establishment of education and schools for the young; it was he who enouraged all objectives for the welfare of the Territory.

This was an exceptionally respectful eulogy for a governor after his death, but it had been well earned. In May 1835, the Angelinos received public confirmation of their status as Alta California's largest town, when the Mexican congress passed a decree proclaiming the former pueblo to be a *ciudad* (city) and making it the official capital of the territory of Alta California. Public celebrations were held in Los Angeles, but because of the opposition of Monterey residents the government was not moved south for another decade. It was, however, moved in other ways; and California was viewed as a place to move to, even from New Mexico.

Nuevo México

The oldest and most populated territory of Mexico in the far north was Nuevo México, which geographically comprised in 1821 a huge territory bordered by Chihuahua on the south; by Tejas, including the area around present-day Amarillo, on the east; by the United States, along the Rio Arkansas, on the northeast; and by Sonora and Alta California on the west. Portions of this territory effectively under Mexican control centered primarily on the area along the Río Bravo del Norte, from Socorro in the south (Río Abajo) to Santa Fe, Santa Cruz de la Cañada, and Taos in the north (Río Arriba). To the west it included Laguna and Zuni, and to the east, in the Llano Estacado, the settlements around San Miguel del Bado.

The region, settled by Mexican settlers, criollos, mestizos, and allied Indians since the 1698 reoccupation, had continually developed its politics, economy, and areas of settlement. The settled population of Nuevo México in 1821 was approximately forty-two thousand people, of whom about thirty-two thousand were Mexicans, for the most part mestizo, and about ten thousand were Pueblo Indians.[25] The capital of Santa Fe was larger, and several towns had grown, including Santa

Cruz de la Cañada, Ranchos de Taos, and San Felipe de Albuquerque. The most important economic activities in the province were sheep grazing, the weaving and production of *jerga* (a rough woolen cloth) and other woolen articles, and the fur trade with Indian peoples. The basis of the economy was irrigated agriculture, sheep and cattle grazing, handicraft production, hunting, and trade with the Plains Indians for furs and hides. Other activities included the cultivation of wine grapes, the production of wine and *aguardiente,* subsistence agriculture, and seasonal buffalo hunting on the Llano Estacado and the plains to the east. There was also scattered mining activities for limited amounts of gold, silver, and copper. A significant amount of trade existed in sheep, woolen products, tobacco, dried foods, furs, and hides with Chihuahua and other points south. With Mexican independence, measures were taken to open trade with the United States. As always, agricultural production depended on water, and irrigation matters required regulation and consensus. These were articulated and organized, as were the penitentes' self-help and religious practices, which required responsibility and sacrifice.

Because it was more densely populated and had been settled longer than the other territories in the far north, New Mexican society was characterized by more marked socioeconomic sectors and tensions between social strata than either Alta California or Tejas. Concentration of landownership and other productive resources was increasing, and relations in the settled areas between owners and laborers were characterized by a more exact accounting of the laborer's compensation and increasing demands placed upon labor. These economic relations would condition and, at times, directly affect both the political process and events in the territory during the Mexican national period.

During the last half of the Spanish colonial period, Nuevo México was placed under a military governor, himself under the jurisdiction of the Comandante General de las Provincias Internas del Occidente at Arizpe, Sonora, and later, at Chihuahua.[26] The province was divided administratively into a number of alcaldías under the authority of alcaldes mayores appointed by and responsible to the governor. The provincial elite had direct influence on the administration only in their capacity as subordinate officers charged with implementation. Throughout the colonial period, policy questions centered around the settlement of new areas, problems with nomadic Indians, relations with the Pueblo Indians, and the regulation of trade with Chihuahua and points south. Also increasingly significant was the question of contraband as well as the presence of illegal traders arriving from Louisiana and the northeast.

During the 1800s Nuevo México was affected by the Mexican revolt against Spain, even though, except for an alleged conspiracy, there was no extensive involvement, as there was in Tejas. Vigilant colonial authorities were concerned that revolutionary pamphlets and verbal accounts were circulating in the province. Like Tejas and Alta California, Nuevo México was affected in a limited manner by Spain's liberal reform. Unlike Alta California or Tejas, the province's population was large enough to send a delegate, Pedro Bautista Pino, to the meeting of the Spanish Cortés in Cadiz. This combative and energetic representative wrote with pride as well as concern on the state of New Mexico; and after observing conflicts in Mexico's interior, he decided he preferred those in his own region. Probably, some revolutionary propaganda did circulate and there were some covert proindependence sympathizers. In September 1821, news of the Plan de Iguala, declaring independence from Spain, and the renewed effort for Mexican independence reached Santa Fe and other municipalities, all of which swore an oath of allegiance to the plan; and eventually an oath was taken to the new Mexican state. On January 6, 1822, a major local celebration of Mexican independence was proclaimed by Governor Facundo Melgares and the Santa Fe ayuntamiento.[27] This earliest known celebration in the far north was well organized and enthusiastically attended by members of all social groups. If there were any regrets for the overthrow of colonial rule, they were confined almost exclusively to a few Spanish officers and missionaries. Of more immediate concern were Indian relations, which continued to be of major importance—nothing less, in fact, than a matter of survival.

Significantly, authorities and Mexican settlers had readjusted relationships with Pueblo Indians who occupied a dozen villages in the valley of the Río Bravo. Even while they were dominated, the Pueblo peoples possessed greater internal autonomy as well as a dual structure of external and internal organization. Each pueblo had two sets of leaders, one whose offices were proscribed by colonial and, later, Mexican authorities, including the pueblo governor and regidores; a second internal set of traditional religious leaders functioned as the actual leadership. The investiture of officers was a notable public event in

Pueblo life. In principle, Indians like the Pueblos, who had recognized rights as well as formalized governance, gained with independence. The Pueblo Indians—a relatively dense, cohesive, and organized complex of non-Mexican communities—were now Mexican citizens, and Indian towns were considered civilian entities. However, the Pueblos, who numbered about ten thousand persons, stated no intention to further assimilate into the Mexican population; in practice, they continued the system of dual authority, with one set of officers and regulations for external contacts with Mexicans, while, at the same time, maintaining internally their traditions, which included their leadership. Pueblo Indian governors and officials exercised a limited influence on territorial government; they were actors in political relations because of the density of Indian communities, the need for their cooperation, and their legally recognized rights. As communities, the Pueblos periodically played an important role in the territory's affairs. Especially important was their continuing role in frontier defense, with each village maintaining a militia; together, these militias formed a major part of the defense of the territory. Aside from the militia, the Pueblo Indians' most consistent political involvement concerned continuing legal actions to protect community lands from encroachment by Mexican farmers.

After January 6, 1822, a meeting of forty electors from the alcaldías of Nuevo México was held at Santa Fe to elect a provincial diputación.[28] Seven diputados were elected as the members of the first diputación, and they, in turn, selected a representative to the national congress, Francisco Pérez Serrano y Aguirre. This election apparently was questioned because it occurred without authorization by the Mexican congress and may have been the only election of a provincial diputación to occur in Mexico without such authorization. Congress actually congratulated the province for its speedy attention to its elections. At this time, local government was divided administratively into eleven, and eventually, fourteen alcaldías, or municipalities. Each alcaldía was headed by an alcalde, a magistrate with the responsibility of a judge of the first instance as well as increasing administrative responsibilities. Ayuntamientos existed in several, but not all, of the alcaldías; they were found in the towns of Santa Fe, Santa Cruz de la Cañada, Albuquerque, and Taos, for example. El Paso del Norte, associated with Nuevo México, possessed an ayuntamiento, but it was part of Chihuahua in 1824. Much closer to larger numbers of people, ayuntamientos dealt with the civic deportment of individuals, grants of property, and the supervision of schooling.

On January 22, 1822, the first elections were held for governor, following those for the new diputación. Francisco Xavier Chávez was selected the first governor under Mexican administration. A noteworthy question at this time was whether Nuevo México was to be a part of the Estado Interno del Occidente, including Durango and Chihuahua, as outlined in the Acta Constitutiva de los Estados Unidos Mexicanos of 1824. Because of several disagreements, including the location of the capital, the proposed state never came into existence, and Nuevo México was formally made a territory by the Federal Constitution of 1824. Several municipios proposed in 1830 that the province be made a state, to be named Hidalgo; this proposal was met with objections from the local assembly and the current governor as well as a lack of support in congress. Nuevo México was a territory from 1824 to 1836, when it became a department under the centralist administration, as a result of the centralist coup and the Siete Leyes Constitucionales. In any case, because of the relatively large population, the territory was entitled to a diputado in the Mexican congress, unlike Alta California whose smaller population earned it no more than a nonvoting delegate. Territorial status brought with it the election of an assembly, while the governorship was appointed by the president and approved by the congress. The assembly was seen as a balance to the governor and as having a voice in the collection and expenditures of taxes, public works, schools, and some matters pertinent to church administration. In practice, the governorship was stronger, and the jefe político came to possess significant administrative authority.

With the inauguration and establishment of the republic, several appointments and initiatives were made. The first jefe político appointed by the new government of the federation was Bartolomé Baca, of El Paso del Norte and thus not a native of the densest part of New Mexico. [29] Father Agustín Fernández de San Vicente, previously in California, was appointed vicar general of the territory. Rather than secularizing missions and their property per se, which had occurred earlier, filling vacancies for parishes and collecting tithes were serious church problems. One of his accomplishments was to establish a school and propose a *colegio* in Santa Fe. Increasingly important to the New Mexican economy was the opening of economic relations with Missouri in the United States. Several small groups of Anglo traders had already reached Santa Fe with merchandise. Significantly, Baca's administration sent a trade expedition to Missouri to encourage the development and growth of the trade. Shortly thereafter, Baca assisted Manuel de Escudero of Chihuahua in his mission to the U.S. to discuss the trade as confidential representative of President Guadalupe Victoria.

Political issues in the early national period were to include the following: local government; frontier defense against nomadic Indians such as the Comanches, Apaches, Utes, and Navajos; the control of customs duties and government monopolies on the sale of tobacco and official sealed paper; the limitation of internal taxes; statehood and the regional autonomy of the province; regulation of foreigners and trading with foreigners; regulation of licenses for fur trapping and trading; and conflicts between civil and military authority. A sensitive issue was the collection of taxes; for the most part, government revenues in this region of the country were derived primarily from customs duties. These were collected irregularly and at rates below their authorization. Though occasionally the province sent out significant sums, it usually needed revenues from the federation or the state of Chihuahua. Another pressing problem involved regularizing and facilitating court proceedings. New Mexicans often had to travel as far as Chihuahua, Parral, or Mexico City to secure final judicial rulings.

The Santa Fe trade and the presence of foreign, primarily Anglo, merchants would be issues of increasing importance throughout the rest of the Mexican period. Other questions of significance included tariff duties, smugglers, foreign trappers, internal taxes, Indian warfare and defense, control of political institutions, and public revenues. Control of public policies concerning these matters and the formal political process itself was placed in the hands of a proactive elite drawn mainly from the ranks of wealthy property owners in the Río Abajo and Río Arriba, whose wealth stemmed from their hold on stock raising and trade. The political alignments of the period were characterized by shifting factions among this elite, which competed for the control of productive resources and public revenues. Other groups participating in or influencing the political process included officials appointed by the national government, commercial and political interests in Chihuahua, and foreign merchants.

Throughout the period, the majority population, composed of small

farmers, laborers, *pastores, ciboleros, comancheros,* and artisans, had limited direct participation in the formal political process, except in some
major events. Property qualifications limited those qualified to be electors and those eligible for elected positions, such as the members of the
diputación. In comparison to colonial rule, however, government officials and institutions were more accessible now to the population. Local
officials who were members of the elite shared with the laboring majority such general interests, as defense, maintenance of irrigation works,
provision of conditions for community subsistence, opposition to some
tariffs, and internal taxes. At the same time, these two groups also had
contradictory interests stemming from their ownership of productive
resources, which they would seek to monopolize to the exclusion of
competitors as well as the general public. Particularly important in a
still developing frontier zone was the ability to control a labor supply
and to maintain discipline. In the immediate term, independence benefited the small strata of the New Mexican elite who could hold major
offices and influence policy-making and administration.

While divided administratively into alcaldías, Nuevo México was
also characterized by an informal division into two subregions, with the
Río Arriba including the area from Santa Fe north, and the Río Abajo
the area from Santa Fe south along the Río Bravo del Norte.[30] The Río
Arriba was made up of about two-thirds of the population and characterized by diverse population of small farmers, artisans, hunters, traders, sheep grazers, and the inhabitants of Nuevo México's capital,
Santa Fe, and its largest town, Santa Cruz de La Cañada. The Río
Abajo, in contrast, seems to have possessed a more stratified social
structure, characterized by a greater concentration of landownership by
larger-scale rancheros and small-scale ranchos. Albuquerque was the
largest town within the Rio Abajo, and it was the hometown and
political base of several influential families. The increasing rivalry
between the two regions would continue to influence the politics of the
territory beyond the Mexican period and into the twentieth century.

The most important question after independence and the establishment of government was the opening of the land frontiers of the
territory to wider but regulated trade with the United States.[31] By the
mid-1820s the Santa Fe Trail, from Missouri to New Mexico, was a
well-traveled extension of the Chihuahua Trail. The Chihuahua Trail
had linked Nuevo México not only with Chihuahua, but with the trade
fairs of central Mexican cities such as Aguascalientes, Querétaro,

Guadalajara, and Mexico City; and a further extension of trade included New Orleans and Tejas. The Anglo American merchants from the United States exchanged manufactured goods such as weapons, cloth, tools, and furnishings for Mexican silver coins, livestock, furs, and other commodities. Some New Mexican merchants, who previously had acted primarily as agents for Chihuahua merchants, now took advantage of their geographical position as middlemen to become major traders. The Santa Fe trade stimulated some sections of New Mexico's economy by making the territory both a market and an important transit point. At the same time, imported foreign goods had a serious negative effect in the long term on artisan production in Nuevo México and the north-central Mexican states. Politically important New Mexican traders included the Chaves, Chávez, Artizes, Pino, and Otero families. Particularly notable was Manuel Armijo of Albuquerque, who not only competed with Anglo-American merchants, but later formed a partnership with the latter as they increased their dominance of the trade.

In 1827, former Albuquerque alcalde Manuel Armijo was appointed jefe político of Nuevo México, replacing former Governor Narbona, who continued as jefe militar. Armijo, a wealthy trader, grazier, and landowner, became the most prominent New Mexico politician of the period by serving three separate terms as jefe político.[32] Armijo's initial administration (1827–29) was characterized by conflicts that included nomadic hostilities. A major controversy erupted with Narbona over treatment of foreign trappers, with Armijo favoring exclusion. Later, Armijo clashed with alcalde Juan Bautista Vigil y Alarid of Santa Fe, who dissolved the city's ayuntamiento on the grounds that several of its members were not only Armijo supporters but related to him. Vigil y Alarid also attempted to challenge the legitimacy of the territorial diputación, thus reflecting a rivalry between the respective cliques with which Armijo and Vigil y Alarid were identified. At any rate, Armijo, as governor, had allied himself with one of several Santa Fe groups. The Armijo faction was stronger, and Vigil y Alarid's group temporarily was defeated in its maneuverings. This episode, which may have stemmed from Vigil y Alarid's personal grudge against Armijo, was typical of many conflicts during the period, and the rivalry between these two circles continued beyond the lifetimes of the two protagonists and into the period after 1848. Armijo's first administration was also characterized by conflicts with other officials over the allocation of revenues;

conflicts with incoming Anglo-American fur trappers over the licensing required to engage in the fur trade in Mexican territory; and as already mentioned, continuing hostilities with seminomadic Indians. These issues and conflicts, in variant forms, were to play a continuing role throughout the early period of the Mexican republic as well as later.

On both the territorial and district levels, control of public offices conferred important advantages on members of the elite who possessed them. Political and military authority allowed access to—and often the monopoly of—economic opportunities available to office holders, members of their families, and their friends. Many, if not most, profitable economic activities required licenses, the payment of fees, and often the protection of civil and military authorities; and access to these frequently required friendship, payment in gifts, or partnership with appropriate officials. At the territorial level, for example, governors, military comandantes, and comisarios contrived to gain control of the trade with the rest of Mexico and the United States as well as the profitable fur and hide trade with the Indians. Officials were frequently the quiet partners of both Mexican and foreign merchants, and these favored merchants often paid less than the legal amount charged for customs duties; their goods cleared customs inspection quickly and they maintained access to military protection more readily than their business rivals. Similarly, friends of the jefe político experienced easier access to obtaining grants of valuable lands, or if involved in a legal dispute, they received favorable rulings in record time.

Such informalities also applied to local government. Mexican politics at this time was characterized by frequent conflicts between government officials who were members of rival groups. This was frequently the case between the jefe político and the *comisario substitutivo de hacienda,* who controlled customs revenues and internal taxes such as the government tobacco monopoly. Elite competition was reflected in regional divisions; for example, in the divisions between the Río Abajo and Río Arriba, and regionally, between Santa Cruz de la Cañada and Santa Fe in the Río Arriba. At the same time, however, alliances also crossed regional lines when rival cliques were allied with enemies of their competitors in the capital or in other areas.

In other instances, members of the elite were concerned with policies that presumably would benefit the territory as a whole. For example, the respected Father Antonio José Martínez of Taos worked, as a member of several territorial diputaciones, for a reduction of internal taxes harming the poor, for better defense against nomadic attacks, for the creation of schools, and for famine relief and other reforms. While he was consistent, Father Martínez was not the only official concerned with the public good during this period; others included Judge Albino Chacón, and Diego Archuleta. Public resources, however, were inadequate; problems were in this frontier area rife, and consequently, progress in meeting public needs was limited. Often even modest innovations designed to promote the public welfare caused great controversy. For example, jefe político Santiago Abreu's attempt to initiate a limited, publicly financed program of compulsory primary education in 1831 was preempted by protest.

Educational reform was a recurring issue and involved both secular and religious authorities. Several civic leaders sought to improve its funding and availability. Bishop José Antonio Zubiria y Escalante of Durango recommended that each New Mexico parish include an annexed school. This concern for education, and particularly for literacy, resulted in Father Martínez's efforts to secure a printing press, and the publication of the first local newspaper, *El Crepúsculo de la Libertad* (1834), and several booklets, as well as the establishment of a school in Taos. Controversies over education during the period demonstrated how rival cliques among the elite were able to use this and other issues to manipulate popular sectors. Understandably, small farmers and laborers living on the margins of settlement could view education as a luxury that would contribute to the burdens of taxation and yet not benefit them. Only a small minority of children from the capital and major towns, and those from well-to-do strata, had access to instruction.

A poor harvest followed by famine had political consequences. During the first Armijo administration, reports of widespread hunger in the Río Arriba reached the federal government, and Armijo was ordered to investigate. One response requested increased supplies from the south. Periodic famine, especially in the Río Arriba, would be a feature of the republican period. One major circumstance contributing to famine was the land devoted to grazing, which limited cultivation. This situation also promoted popular unrest occasionally, for in certain cases of famine, some distribution of food apparently was necessary.

A significant political crisis of this period occurred in the administration of Santiago Abreu, who was appointed jefe político in April 1831.[33] Abreu had been a member of the diputación since its founding and was a recent diputado to the Mexican congress. Along with his brothers Ramón and Marcelino, he was an advocate of public primary education. Since no funds were available in the territorial treasury, Abreu secured the authorization of the federal government to transfer three thousand *pesos* of church funds to the school fund. This action provoked a major controversy that resulted in the New Mexican clergy allied with the enemies of Abreu. The clergy seized on this opportunity to attack Abreu by addressing a public petition to the Bishop of Durango and the federal government. Abreu's alleged "attack" on religion was used by his enemies to arouse widespread popular indignation. Threatened by public rejection, he was forced to resign and turned his power over to Francisco Sarracino. This incident underlined the constraints of territorial government in initiating reform measures.

Indian hostilities occurred at the same time that demands were being made on the militia. Throughout the 1830s and 1840s, hostilities erupted with one group or another of nomadic and seminomadic Indian peoples surrounding Nuevo México. The small number of presidial troops stationed at Santa Fe were inadequate to defend the territory. Local militia, including Mexicans and Pueblo Indians, had to be called up for several months of each year to fight either the Navajos, Apaches, Comanches, or Utes. Increasingly, the Navajos became the major enemy as they increased their population as well as the number of raids upon Mexican and Pueblo Indian towns. Since the members of the militia were required to furnish their own arms and supplies, military service increasingly became an economic burden upon the municipalities, the Pueblo Indians, and the poorer citizens, all of whom bore the burden of defense. These groups held steadily increasing resentments which would result in revolt during the 1830s, when a poor harvest resulted in famine conditions. Several efforts to reorganize and strengthen the militia as well as, ostensibly, the formal defense were proposed and attempted, but with uneven success. In any case, service in the militia provided experience beyond local economic and religious needs.

Despite these problems, New Mexico progressed. Antonio Barreiro, legal counselor to the territory and later its representative (like Pino before him), became convinced of the area's potential. For him (as for Pino), trade, the extension of farming, and an increased population were requirements for development, and they could be achieved through local initiative if it was supported by the federal government.

However, the instability of government was a hindrance; more darkly, he foresaw the threat posed by the influence of the United States. As a territory, Nuevo México was placed under the control of the federal government, which appointed its governor and approved important decisions and policies.[34] But such an arrangement also meant lower taxes and the federal subsidy of administration. As early as the 1820s New Mexico's diputación sought approval for the territory to be made a state, an act that would give it control over public lands as well as greater administrative, legislative, and judicial authority. Though the movement toward statehood was delayed, New Mexicans were appointed to the governorship of the territory from 1827 to 1835. Collection of the important customs duties was vested in a subcomisario, who was responsible to a comisario at Chihuahua. As the government of the territory increasingly relied upon a major portion of the customs revenues, a conflict between the governor, the diputación, other officials, and the subcomisario developed throughout the 1830s. The subcomisarios also controlled the funds derived from the government tobacco and official paper monopolies, all of which made the position of subcomisario politically sensitive. While New Mexico was evolving politically as it overcame problems, Tejas provided a study in contrast.

Tejas

As a part of the Provincias Internas del Oriente, Tejas above the Nueces, headquartered at Monterrey, was Mexico's easternmost territory in the far north and the area of the frontier most exposed to foreign aggression.[35] Settled in sporadic efforts since the 1680s, and intended primarily as a mission frontier and a buffer against French expansion from Louisiana, Tejas in 1811 had an estimated population of 7,000 settled inhabitants, of whom half were mestizo Mexicans, with some mulattoes and criollos, and settled Indians, as well as some Europeans. Nomadic Indians numbered approximately 14,000 at this time. In 1821, the Mexican mestizo population was estimated to be between 3,500 and 4,000. The major settlements included San Antonio de Bexar, the capital; La Bahía del Espíritu Santo; and later, Goliad Nacogdoches. Geographically, Mexican Tejas was bordered in the East by the Sabine River and in the north by the Arkansas River, thus connecting it to the United States; in the south by the Nueces River; and in the west by Nuevo México and Chihuahua. The major economic activities of the inhabitants were devoted to grazing cattle, horses, and mules; hunting or trading with the Indians for hides and furs; and developing some irrigated agriculture, primarily around San Antonio. Given the modest size of the Mexican population, there was a relatively considerable foreign presence, particularly in east Tejas around Nacogdoches where foreigners probably outnumbered Mexicans by the 1820s. A persistent and increasing problem was the smuggling of contraband goods by both foreigners and Mexicans; it was, in fact, a tradition in the area and one that would continue in spite of political consequences.

Tejas, because of its exposed geographical position on the Gulf of Mexico next to Louisiana, became the crucial test case of Mexico's strength and capability as an independent state. Events in Tejas during the 1820s and 1830s had their immediate roots in some of the previously mentioned final colonial dispositions.[36] During the War of Independence Tejas was the center of conflict in the far north, and in consequence, the province had suffered economic losses at the hands of two invaders—Spanish royalists, under General Arredondo, and Anglo marauders. The Adams–Onís Treaty, which established the Tejas–U.S. frontier while separating Tejas from Louisiana at the Sabine and Red rivers, transferred beyond the Sabine a strip of territory that had been part of colonial Tejas, and this area invited marauders. Foreign immigration concurrent with land allocations in Tejas was authorized during the last year of colonial authority.

Mexican politics in Tejas during the aftermath of independence, as elsewhere on the frontier, evolved from events of the last colonial decades. Those who had supported independence resented their previously royalist opponents, who now benefited from independence. Moreover, Tejas was affected in 1820 when the liberal revolution in Spain reinstated the Spanish Constitution of 1812, which provided for widespread reforms throughout the Spanish empire, including Nueva España and the Provincias Internas. The ramifications for Tejas included political representation in the Spanish cortés and a provincial diputación for the Provincias Internas del Oriente. The overt initial effects were limited, for only a few officials took part in the indirect elections that resulted in Tejas being represented by delegates from Coahuila and Nuevo León. Even so, there was competition among them; yet in the case of José Miguel Ramos de Arizpe, Tejas shared an excellent representative, but also one with royalist opponents who jailed him and left his friends with a lingering anger. Significantly, the cortés reforms encouraged settler colonization and the legalization of foreign immigration to the provinces. In September 1820, the cortés authorized foreign immigration, based upon the following conditions: respect for the Constitution of 1812, profession of the Roman Catholic religion, evidence of economic stability and the means for a livelihood, adherence to laws and regulations, and the taking of an oath of loyalty to the Spanish monarchy. Yet the proposals of the cortés stimulated discontent and avowals to avoid those found objectionable. In effect, issues from the late colonial period continued through the period of independence.

A relatively harmonious transition of authority from colonial status to independence contrasted with the earlier periods of conflict. During the War of Independence, some inhabitants of Texas had fought vigorously for the Mexican cause and had suffered from the severe treatment by the royalist authorities who had reconquered the province, which they had only barely dominated until 1821. On July 19, 1821, the province of Tejas, in the persons of Governor Antonio Martínez, the ayuntamiento of San Antonio de Béxar, and the people of San Antonio de Béxar, declared in favor of Mexican independence from Spain. This move was tacitly advised by even the former royalist military chief, the comandante general Arredondo. Thus, in contrast to the earlier conflict concerning independence, the transfer of authority was generally uneventful. The province was now part of the new Mexican state, but joined as part of the Estado Interno del Oriente; the previous governor, Antonio Martínez, acted as the first interim Mexican governor while awaiting his replacement. In August 1822 the province received a new governor, its first, José Félix Trespalacios, a citizen of Chihuahua and a veteran insurgent. In 1823, Tejas for the first and only time formed its own, separate provincial diputación and elected a delegate to the Mexican national congress. Erasmo Seguín, a member of the Béxar ayuntamiento and a wealthy landowner, was elected diputado to the national congress. The major issues included government organization, taxes, trade, Indian relations, land allocation, and, increasingly immigration; and church-related issues. These involved the maintenance of church property, the availability of services, the collection of tithes, and the appointment of clergy to fill vacancies. Secularization, declared for both Coahuila and Tejas in 1825, was not the potent issue it was in California because missions and their property were minor matters in Tejas.

As the republic was coming into being in late 1823 and early 1824 a major political question arose, namely, whether the province would be a state, part of a state, or a territory.[37] This issue affected the future of Tejas significantly. Statehood depended on meeting the population and revenue requirements for effective government. Earlier, with the fall of the short-lived monarchy under Iturbide, the Provincias Internas del Oriente had been made into a single large stage, the Estado Interno del Oriente. This arrangement, however, had been only temporary while each province sought separate statehood status. By January 1824 the provinces of Coahuila and Tejas were joined by the action of the Mexican congress to form the new state of Coahuila y Tejas, with its capital in Saltillo. This move had some support and made sense since it did not preempt future separate status.

The union of Coahuila y Tejas was largely the accomplishment of Coahuila's congressional deputy, the liberal Don José Miguel Ramos de Arizpe, previously mentioned, who argued that dual statehood with Coahuila was a means by which Tejanos could keep control of the vast public lands which would be under federal control if Tejas were reduced to territorial status. But elite opinion in Tejas was divided on the issue. In June 1824 the diputación of Tejas refused to recognize this union and protested to the congress by asking that the union with Coahuila be voided. For a time, violence loomed between the Tejas diputación and the Bexar ayuntamiento, until the military commander at Bexar took a position in support of the action of the federal congress. The members of the provincial diputación, the governor, and the Bexar ayuntamiento were polarized. While Tejano officials desired separate statehood, they feared the loss of control of the vast public lands that were the only major source of wealth in the province. The Béxar ayuntamiento, primarily representing landowners and merchants, was won over to union with Coahuila as a means of protecting their economic interests. Opposing the union were provincial officials, including the diputación and the governor, whose positions would be abolished with the end of separate political status. Tejas deputy Erasmo Seguín first made unsuccessful efforts to oppose the union with Coahuila and then changed his position in favor of it. At length the governor and the diputación resigned, and Tejas was united with Coahuila. A questionable choice, Felipe Enrique Neri, also known as the Baron de Bastrop, a Hollander and former Spanish royalist agent, was elected as Tejas delegate to the state legislature at Saltillo. Shortly, the legislature of Coahuila y Tejas voted to organize Tejas as a department of the state of Coahuila y Tejas, with an appointed jefe político as administrative officer, magistrate, and commander of the militia. The department of Tejas was first subdivided into two municipal districts, Béxar and the Brazos, with their municipal centers located, respectively, at San Antonio and San Felipe (Austin). Later in the 1830s Tejas would be divided into three departments—Béxar, Brazos, and Nacogdoches.

In the years 1822–1824, while more important political events were occurring, Stephen Austin had succeeded in obtaining approval first from the last colonial governor, then from the Iturbide government, and later from the federation for the establishment of a colony of Anglo-American settlers in central Tejas.[38]

The federal government was directly concerned with the public lands in territories such as Nuevo México and Alta California, while public-land policy in Tejas was primarily the concern of the new state of Coahuila y Tejas. The federal government set the policies on immigration, and public-land policy became the responsibility of the states. Both the Mexican congress and the state of Coahuila y Tejas adopted liberal immigration and land-colonization laws that encouraged foreign immigration offering highly favorable terms to immigrants who would be eligible for the lands.

On August 18, 1824, the congress of the Mexican federation passed a colonization decree inviting foreign colonization. The decree also declared that Mexican citizens should receive preferential treatment in the distribution of lands, but it undertook no concrete action to encourage the immigration of Mexicans to Tejas or to the other territories of the frontera. Furthermore, many foreigners, several of whom had changed citizenship several times, such as Stephen Austin and the Baron de Bastrop, were indeed naturalized citizens, and therefore entitled to preference. Erasmo Seguín was an active lobbyist for the measure. Officials of Coahuila y Tejas virtually allowed foreign *empresarios* to influence legislation and later gave them a free hand in developing their grants. Indeed, the Coahuila y Tejas colonization law of March 1825 was largely influenced by the Baron de Bastrop, the naturalized foreigner who was also appointed land commissioner. Immigrants were required to take an oath of allegiance to the state and to

Mexico, profess Roman Catholicism, prove sound moral character, and pay a fee in three installments over a six-year period. The fee for a square league of grazing land was set at thirty dollars, while a league of irrigatable land was valued at thirty-five dollars. By 1830 Stephen Austin had introduced 4,248 settlers and issued over one thousand titles in the Austin colony. By 1829 fifteen additional empresario grants had been made, primarily to individuals of foreign origin. The issue of slavery also emerged. The abolition of slavery in independent Mexico had affected relatively few because the number of slaves had declined for a variety of reasons; the largest number affected by emancipation were in Texas and held by Anglo immigrants, and three-quarters of the Anglos in Texas were southerners who were committed to slavery.

In Tejas, the political process centered around the local capital of San Antonio de Béxar and the state capital at Saltillo. Coahuilan politics were dominated by elite cliques of wealthy landowners, of whom the most prominent were the Sánchez Navarro family.[39] Generally speaking, Coahuilan políticos were interested in Tejas to the extent that its revenues could be diverted to serve their own ends. Tejas in the early 1820s was fiscally poor, however; and for this reason, politicians in Coahuila tended to view foreign colonization as a means of increasing the wealth of the area and hence, possibly, its own revenues. Continuing to be particularly active in the political maneuvering for favorable colonization in the state legislature was the Baron de Bastrop, the delegate from Tejas.

Local politics in San Antonio centered around the members of the few elite families living there, including the Seguíns, the Ruizes and their relatives the Navarros, the de la Garzas, and others. Some of them came to question Tejas's subordinate link in governmental status to Coahuila, though others had vacillated on this issue. An underlying major reason for the resentment was that the link limited the opportunities of the local elite to control local revenues and resources. Some members of the local elite found it expedient to ally themselves with the rapidly incoming foreign settlers, thus furthering their own financial interests and reopening the question. One of the elite, Erasmo Seguín, a former alcade of San Antonio who had held other offices, was the first colonization commissioner of Coahuila y Tejas in the Department of Tejas. He and members of his family continued to follow this pattern of foreign association, and eventually Seguín and his son supported the Anglo dissidents' declaration of rebellion. Another member of the elite, José Antonio Navarro, was particularly associated with Austin and the disreputable James Bowie, who married his niece. Both the Seguíns and Navarros increased their landholdings through grants from the Mexican republic. Navarro defied laws by using slave labor to raise cotton, but unlike others, he returned runaway slaves to their Anglo-American owners. Both Navarro and the Seguíns held offices under the Mexican republic and benefited from these positions.

The major questions that arose in Tejas politics, similar to those in California and New Mexico, revolved around filibusters, marauders, colonization policies and foreign immigration, and property.[40] In facing these issues, Mexicans were ambiguous in formulating policy and lacking in stable, experienced, and resolute leadership, whereas the foreigners had very clear objectives and increasingly experienced leadership. Even prior to independence, foreigners, Anglo-Americans in particular, conducted an expansion into Tejas. Indeed, the U.S. government for a while had tried to claim, without any justification, that Tejas was a part of Louisiana, which it had purchased from France in 1803. The U.S. and Spanish governments, and later the Mexican government, agreed to fix the boundary between Tejas and Louisiana at the Sabine and Red rivers, thus recognizing Tejas as Mexican territory. However, during the course of the Mexican independence movement against Spain, Anglo adventurers took advantage of the strife to enter the Tejas borderlands. These men ranged from outright marauders to a few who felt some solidarity with Mexicans who had enlisted with the insurgents against Spain. At the same time, the colonial administration considered various plans designed to strengthen its hold on the province. Except for those from Spain, the players continued their adventures after Mexico had won its independence. Bastrop was very active before and after independence in facilitating grants to Anglo and other foreign empresarios. In March and April 1825, the legislature of Coahuila y Texas enacted colonization legislation and simultaneously authorized grants to several foreigners, among them Green De Witt and Hayden Edwards. The grant to Edwards proved to be a foreshadowing of the dangers of Anglo colonists. His grant was invalidated for failure to meet contract stipulations; and later in December 1826, Edwards, after unsuccessfully trying to intimidate local officials in the Nacogdoches area and forcibly ejecting Mexicans, local Indians, and some Anglos, proclaimed the Republic of Fredonia in an attempt to separate the area from Mexico. This revolt, the so-called Fredonia rebellion, supported mainly by a few criminals, was settled relatively easily by local Mexicans, but it was to be the beginning of consistent trouble with foreigners. A powerful incentive attracting foreigners was the access to and ease in acquiring desirable land, a circumstance that was not common in the United States at the time. Land meant status, wealth, and security.

The attitude of the Anglo settlers varied as greatly as their comport-ment. Some were cordial, supportive, and cooperative with Mexican settlers and officials, while others were not. Generally, they had three convictions in common: their commitment to the United States, to the acquisition of land, and to the implantation of black slavery. The majority of settlers were Anglo-Americans from the southern United States, many of whom were slaveholders with ambitions to be planta-tion owners.[41] Some moved into Tejas with considerable capital and a retinue of slaves. Furthermore, cotton soon became the most lucrative export for foreign settlers along the central Gulf Coast and in East Tejas. Anglo-American developers evaded the law by introducing slaves from the United States under the guise of indentured servants contracted to their masters. Some local Mexican officials looked the other way, and some Mexican Tejanos, such as the Benavides family, even participated in the violation of Mexican laws by becoming slave-holders themselves. While many Anglo settlers were small farmers with few slaves at first, some large plantations were being developed by the end of the 1820s, especially in the Department of Nacogdoches and in the region around Brazoria on the Gulf of Mexico. Stephen Austin, unlike some of the other empresarios, seemed to publicly uphold his formal obligations as a Mexican citizen, and some of the Austin settlers were peaceable farmers or planters. However, some Austin colonists also came into conflict with Mexican laws such as those that dealt with slavery.

The other empresarios were generally much less efficient than Austin, and their settlers were less counseled and often possessed questionable ethics. Many foreigners intended to evade Mexican laws and conduct themselves as they pleased in sparsely populated Tejas. Among them were lawless and criminal individuals, some of whom were wanted for violations in neighboring Louisiana and in other states. For example, Sam Houston, former governor of the state of Tennessee, had killed a man and was wanted for murder in his home state. Because of their outspoken nature and their ready willingness to resort to violence, adventurers and criminals were able to exert an increasingly disproportionate influence among the foreign element. Poor whites were agitated negatively on the basis of ethnic and economic resentments. The key political motor of the Anglos was the Austin colony, which was numerous and financially productive and fortunate to have an experienced leadership. It was also a replica on a smaller scale of the U.S. South at the time. Social distances were created not only along nationality and racial lines, but between Anglo-American classes. The wealthy held the poor whites in contempt. Austin consciously adopted a premeditated hypocritical attitude toward Mexican authorities, as his correspondence reveals; his deception gained time in which his political and economic resources could be strengthened.

The Mexican Tejano and Coahuilan elites viewed Anglo-American colonization, for the most part, as economically beneficial for Tejas and for themselves. Members of the departmental government and ayuntamientos frequently acted as intermediaries for the empresarios and individual settlers. Erasmo Seguín, serving as Tejas deputy in the diputación of Coahuila y Tejas, and Coahuila's representatives in the Mexican congress sought and obtained a temporary exemption for Anglo slaveholders from antislavery provisions, although no new slaves could be sold or introduced. Officials in Coahuila viewed Tejas land sales as a valued source of revenue and Anglo-American developers as sources of much-needed funds.

By the late 1820s the federal government had become increasingly concerned about the expanding Anglo-American population in the department of Tejas, particularly as a result of Edwards's revolt.[42] At about the same time, Lieutenant José María Sánchez wrote observations commenting on the extent of Anglo-American influence in Tejas. A special commission headed by Colonel Manuel de Mier y Terán was named to investigate conditions in 1827. After traveling throughout Tejas in 1829, Colonel Mier y Terán, an esteemed liberal, became convinced that unless Mexico took immediate action Tejas would be lost to the republic.

> I tell myself that it could not be otherwise than that from such a
> state of affairs should arise an antagonism between the Mexicans
> and foreigners, which is not the least of the smoldering fires which
> I have discovered. Therefore, I am warning you to take timely
> measures. Tejas could throw the whole nation into revolution.[43]

In an extensive report, the skeptical Mier y Terán recommended that immigration from the United States be suspended; that a series of military colonies be established at strategic points to create Mexican settlements and ensure respect for Mexican law; that existing exemptions from customs duties be removed; that the laws against slavery be enforced; and that the federal government encourage colonization by Mexican civilians:

> The department of Tejas is contiguous to the most avid nation in the world. The North Americans have conquered whatever territory adjoins them. In less than half a century, they have become masters of extensive colonies which formerly belonged to Spain and France, and of even more spacious territories from which have disappeared the former owners, the Indian tribes.

In the aftermath of completing the report, the colonel exercised some administrative responsibilities and then committed suicide. Several years later, his efforts were followed by Juan N. Almonte's report on the need for defense.

In 1830 Mier y Terán inspired, at least in part, recommendations that were adopted by the Mexican federal government. Underpinning these plans was a belief in the need to strengthen the Mexican presence in Tejas, even to the point of providing Mexican place-names. The new settlement of Tenochtitlán, located at the Brazos crossing between San Antonio and Nacogdoches, bore a name that echoed the neo-Aztec current in the Mexican independence movement. Its garrison was envisioned as a hub for strengthening Tejas. Immigration was suspended; and Tadeo Ortiz de Ayala was commissioned to inaugurate a more carefully planned colonization effort, which envisioned a series of defensive militia colonies and customs houses in the interior and along the coast, including Anahuac near the present-day site of Houston. Mexican settlers welcomed officials initiating these reforms.

Several Mexican officers charged with implementation of reforms were themselves naturalized Mexican citizens of Anglo-American origin. Stephen Austin, for example, was for many years jefe político of the Department of the Brazos and a colonel in the militia. Other Anglo colonists held responsible official positions in the ayuntamientos and in the militia. The most notable such colonist was Colonel Juan Davis Bradburn, a native of Kentucky who had fought in the Mexican revolution against Spain and had advanced through the ranks. Unfortunately, the appointment of Bradburn and his counterparts did not help to conciliate subversive opinions among Anglo settlers. Bradburn was fairly responsible enforcing the collection of customs duties and laws against slavery, and he was viewed questionably by many propertied Anglo-American colonists.

Between 1830 and 1832 the situation rapidly deteriorated. A series of incidents occurred between Mexican officials and Anglo colonists. Given the rapid increase of the Anglo-American population in East Tejas by the 1830s, the large majority of the area's population was of foreign origin. Moreover, the flow of trade and income favored the propertied Anglos. The Anglo malcontents organized paramilitary bands and acquired more and better weapons; and Louisiana, their major base of support, was nearby. The Mexicans had become a minority; they were poorer, less united, and less prepared; and their bases of support were very distant from one another.

Mexican Tejano leaders seem to have enjoyed an extremely optimistic view of their ability to maintain their influence. Circumstances that contributed to the growth of a false sense of security among many leading Mexican Tejanos included the fact that a great number of Anglo-Americans were concentrated in areas of Tejas that were farthest from centers of Mexican population. Most of the propertied Anglo colonists lived in the districts of the Brazos and Nacogdoches, whose very small Mexican populations included few members of the Mexican Tejano elite. Also, most of the Anglo propertied settlers located closest to Mexican settlements, such as the members of the Austin colony, tended to be less conflictual. The majority of the illegal immigrants and the criminals tended to be concentrated closer to the United States, along the Louisiana border, and farthest from Mexican Tejanos. The supposed reasonableness of the so-called moderates, whose recognized spokesman was Stephen F. Austin, lulled some Mexican settlers and Mexican officials into complacency during the 1820s. The moderates were viewed basically as peaceable, law-abiding, and naturalized citizens who sought desired political changes through legal means, advocating reforms that were not too different from changes espoused by some Mexicans. Mexican officials relied on Austin and a handful of well-known moderates to represent the Anglo immigrants. Until 1832, Austin was probably viewed by most of the Tejano elite as speaking for all or most Anglo-American settlers, which was not, in fact, the case. Similarly, many elite Tejanos, such as the Seguíns, assumed that they shared a basic consensus on common economic and political interests with the moderate leaders and, by extension, with all of the colonists. These common concerns included desires expressed by both the Tejano elite and the colonists for the achievement of separate statehood status for Tejas and for measures promoting economic de-velopment. Austin and the other recognized leaders of the propertied colonists were viewed as men of wealth and property whose basic economic interests were fundamentally opposed to the secessionist plots of adventurers. Tejano leaders felt that they could work with Austin and the moderates, who, they believed, could maintain control over the Anglo colonists.

Stephen Austin and the moderates cultivated their moderate image by portraying themselves as loyal Mexican citizens who desired reason-able reforms, which meant equating such disparate aspirations as the legalization of slavery, statehood status for Tejas within the Mexican federation, and the reduction of customs duties. In fact, until 1832 this moderate perspective was relatively unexceptional. Many Anglo-American property owners, after all, were primarily interested in their economic activities, which were mainly agricultural. Thus, they pre-ferred to avoid potentially counterproductive political controversies, and in any case, they did not raise the bogus issues (to be proclaimed later) of religious "freedom" for public Protestant practices and political representation; the first would have demonstrated their hypocrisy when they agreed to convert to Catholicism, and in the second instance, they obviously had political representation since they made public appeals, lobbied, voted, and held office. This moderate posture, how-ever, was not held by all Anglo-Americans in Tejas. An increasingly vocal minority, soon to be called the "war party," arose from the ranks of malcontents and adventurers without property. With backing in the United States, the "war party" attracted steadily increasing support from marginal elements and began to advocate the separation of Tejas not merely from Coahuila, but from the Republic of Mexico; it also worked for annexation to the United States, and in particular, fought for slave interests or for a separate and independent state as its goal. In spite of the debate between the propertied members of the party and those who were economically resentful, the leadership of these factions communicated, cooperated, and shared many of the same sources of support in the U.S.

By 1832 some among the Tejano elite found themselves either

willingly committed to the Anglo settlers or de facto hostages of the larger group.[44] The Mexican Tejano intermediaries had become the pawns of Anglo leaders, but soon they would have to dance to their tune or face economic and personal ruin. While some Anglo settlers may have been sincere in their professed allegiance to Mexico, an increasingly large number ignored Mexican laws and showed their contempt for the Mexican inhabitants of Tejas. Constant problems arose over the illegal importation of black slaves and Anglos' large-scale smuggling of contraband to avoid customs duties; these were flash points of sensitivity, at least for Mexican officials who were charged with enforcing the customs laws. Mexican law prohibited slavery, and hundreds of slaves escaped, with each one representing a monetary loss to the Anglo owner. Furthermore, in customs Tejas already enjoyed special exemptions that lowered the duties to be paid on imported merchandise. During the early 1830s, the troops charged with collect-ing customs found themselves fighting skirmishes with Anglo and, sometimes, Mexican *contrabandistas* who were supplying the foreign colonies.

There also were conflicting political and economic interests among Anglo settlers during this period. The largest and most successful empresarios, such as Stephen Austin, benefited tremendously from their grants. Austin, in particular, acted as an economic and political middleman between the settlers and Mexican authorities. His special importation privileges and his revenue from land sales made him very wealthy, and he possessed even greater potential for future wealth. In acting as the spokesman for the Anglo colonists in their dealings with the national and state governments, Austin presented the image of a responsible man of property with a vested interest in maintaining order. Austin argued for special concessions to the propertied settlers as a means of controlling unrest and isolating the dissidents among them, and, at the same time, securing the strength of the generally aggressive Anglo position. Many Anglos were land poor and resentful and argued that their interests were different from Austin and others of his ilk. Austin and others successfully met the political challenge by proceed-ing to follow dual strategies, one vis-à-vis Mexico's government and Mexican residents, and the other vis-à-vis slavery interests and the poor whites.

In 1832 violence increased dramatically when Anglo dissenters attacked and captured the Mexican garrison at the town of Anahuac.[45]

Mexican settlers and some Anglos supported the Mexican commander at Anahuac, Colonel Juan Davis Bradburn, while some Anglo settlers particularly disliked Anahuac authority because it was the one most intrusive in their affairs. Soon afterward, another skirmish was fought at the settlement of Velasco. Both conflicts were waged ostensibly against the enforcement of customs duties and the liberation of slaves. Because of the military revolt against President Bustamante, the federal government was unable to counter these attacks immediately; and since the local officials were seen to be identified with the latest administration, the malcontents voiced their support for Bustamante's opposition.

Cleverly, Anglo dissident leaders took advantage of the internal strife to proclaim themselves partisans of General Santa Anna.[46] On October 1, 1832, a convention of malcontent settlers and others was called at San Felipe de Austin. A petition made to the new national Mexican government demanded the removal of the prohibition of further Anglo immigration, the creation of a separate state of Tejas, and the free importation of goods for three years. At the same time, United States adventurers, referring to themselves as the "war party," took advantage of the situation to continue their agitation of the settlers, imploring them to separate from Mexico and join the U.S. As tensions increased in 1832, the "war party," led by men like Sam Houston, William H. Wharton, and William Brett Travis, gained increasing popular influence at the same time that Mexico entered a national political crisis between the contending federalists and centralists. Anglo-led dissident action was successful, and irresponsibly, the Santa Anna regime rewarded its Anglo supporters by opening Tejas again to Anglo-American immigrants in 1833.

In 1832, while the Anglo dissidents held their convention, Mexican Tejano leaders in Béxar sought to return the situation to normal. The views of the Bexareños were expressed in a document dated December 21, 1832, and addressed to the government of the state of Coahuila y Tejas, "Representación dirijida por el Ilustre Ayuntamiento de la Ciudad de Béxar al honorable Congreso del estado . . ."[47] This document sought to incorporate the reforms proposed by the moderate Anglo settlers while ignoring or downplaying extreme demands, such as separation from Coahuila. Reflecting their position as middlemen, the Bexareños sought concessions for the colonists and portrayed them in a sympathetic light. This attempt to reduce tensions through concessions was to be preempted, and the Bexareños soon found themselves forced to choose between their country or their Anglo allies. In any case, the sentiment for statehood among some remained.

The Anglo dissident convention also set a date for a second convention on April 1, 1833. In this convention, the "war party" leaders were now in control and drafted a constitution for a state of Tejas, which they proposed to implement without waiting for approval from the Mexican congress, and which would, in turn, violate several constitutional precepts. This document would legalize slavery and reduce federal customs duties. Stephen F. Austin was selected to present the convention's demands to the Mexican national government in Mexico City, where Austin would receive an understandably cool reception. While in Mexico City, Austin sent a secret letter to the settlers and the Béxar ayuntamiento suggesting that they present the Mexican government with an accomplished fact by establishing the state of Tejas without Mexico's approval. When supporters of the liberal Valentín Gómez-Farías learned of this letter, Mexican authorities imprisoned Austin in Mexico City, where he would remain until July 1835.

During the same period, a civil dispute broke out in Coahuila between a clique desiring to keep the capital at Saltillo and another attempting to move it to Monclova. Anglo settlers took full advantage of the Coahuilan authorities' resulting difficulties. Santa Anna settled the situation for the moment by supporting the Monclova group. Meanwhile, Austin's mission in Mexico had reached a critical point; and after winning an agreement to remove the prohibition on U.S. immigration, he continued to press for further concessions, overtly threatening dire consequences if they were not granted.

Tensions increased steadily, reaching the point where the "war party" needed only an appropriate pretext to ignite an actual insurrection. As their spokesperson Austin languished in prison, the moderate Anglo settlers increasingly found themselves in an untenable middle position almost analogous to that of the Mexican Tejanos. The "war party" leaders found their justification in 1835, when Antonio López de Santa Anna led a centralist coup d'état, dissolving the federation and abolishing the Constitution of 1824, and replacing them with the Siete Leyes Constitucionales and a centralist dictatorship. Ironically and cynically, in a memorable turnabout the former Anglo Santannistas of 1832 now, in 1835, declared themselves against their benefactor and in favor of federalism and the Mexican Constitution of 1824. Through this maneuver, they were able to portray themselves as Mexican federalists while accomplishing their objective of Anglo rule over an independent Tejas. At the same time, the "war party" hypocritically claimed to be in step with federalist dissidents in the states of Coahuila, Zacatecas, Nuevo León, and Yucatán, who were against Santa Anna and the centralist coup.

In October 1835, while Anglo-settler delegates at the convention proclaimed themselves in support of the Constitution of 1824, Anglo-colonist militia clashed with Mexicans in capturing Gonzales and Goliad. Organized conflict prevailed. An Anglo "Texian" army was openly declared at Gonzales, with the returning Stephen Austin elected commander (though he was later relieved). Initially, the army's aim was San Antonio. Mexican residents rallied in attempting to defend themselves, but they had few weapons. At San Antonio de Béxar on October 27, "Texian" forces surrounded the small Mexican army under the command of General Martín Perfecto Cos, who was desperate for supplies. The Anglos formed a state government during November by using the cynical pretext of upholding the Constitution of 1824. Between December 5 and 11 the so-called Texians assaulted San Antonio, forced the surrender of General Cos, and secured his agreement to evacuate immediately. Mexican opinion was consolidated against the dissidents.

Feeling themselves to be in a position to dictate terms to the central government, the convention adjourned after forming a provisional government, electing as governor Henry Smith, a member of the "war party," and designating March 1, 1836, as the date for the convention to meet again at the town of Washington, on the Brazos. At about the same time, Sam Houston, the Tennessee adventurer, was appointed military commander of the "Texian" army. After the occupation of San Antonio, this "army" could find no opposing army to combat, and its mission became one of harrying and destroying Mexican residents and property. Eventually, after a tremendous effort, a first Mexican regular force reached Tejas.

The open rebellion of the Anglo dissidents and the Mexican military response during the events of 1835 set in motion the better-known events of 1836,[48] which would include the Mexican military expedition led by General Antonio López de Santa Anna; the siege and the Mexican assault of the Alamo in March 1836; the proclamation of an "Independent Texas Republic" on March 1, 1836; the Mexican victory at Goliad; and the successful defeat and capture of Santa Anna at San Jacinto on April 20, 1836. Santa Anna's capture was followed by the so-called Treaty of Velasco, a bogus agreement signed by Santa Anna under duress, ordering the Mexican army to withdraw across the Río Bravo and unconstitutionally recognizing the independence of the "Republic of Texas." These actions by Santa Anna were disavowed by the Mexican congress as well as by some commanders in the region.

By March 1836 the inhabitants of Tejas—Mexican Tejanos and moderate Anglo colonists—had largely lost control of a rapidly expanding military conflict, and they would have little influence upon decisions to be made by either Mexican military commanders or Anglo-American filibusterers.[49] Many among the Tejano Mexican elite had long since compromised themselves by becoming the intermediaries for the colonists; and most leading Tejanos, such as the Seguín, Ruiz, and Navarro families, now continued this alliance by joining the Texians. While the rebels' declarations against centralism at first provided a cloak of respectability for Tejano leaders, it was the preservation of home and property interests that dictated their adherence to the rebellious and bogus "Texas" republic. Similarly, the many Anglo colonists who would have been satisfied with statehood within Mexico and opposed a direct collision with Mexican authorities now saw their interests better served by the turn of events. Full-scale conflict would mean for many of them the destruction of their farms and plantations, burned, ironically, by a retreating "Texian" army as part of a scorched-earth policy. Later, however, large gains would indeed be realized.

By the time "Texas Independence" was declared on March 1, 1836, many of the Anglo-American colonists were engaged in the so-called running scrape, fleeing with their families toward the Louisiana border. Their places in combat were more than filled by a host of newly arrived volunteers, U.S. filibusterers who eagerly flocked to take advantage of the offer of eight hundred acres of free land for private soldiers and correspondingly larger rewards for the leaders. An increasingly large proportion of the Texian leadership came to consist of members of the "war party" and the leaders of these newly arrived adventurers interested in expanding the conflict with Mexico. In this context, political opinion and activity became an extension of war.

Individual Mexicans sided with the enemy and acted for them. As Seguín wrote:

I require your aid to carry off the cattle and place them where the enemy cannot make use of them. I have no doubt that you will assist cheerfully in this measure, thereby furnishing to the supreme government of Texas a proof of your attachment to the just cause, and the beloved liberty we are contending for. If, on the contrary, you fail to render this slight service, your disaffection will be manifest; and although a matter of regret to the said supreme government, yet it can then no longer treat you as Texians, but, perhaps, as enemies. Be not deceived with the idea that we have not forces wherewith to repel force—time will show to the contrary, and will convince you that Texas must be free. . . .

My ties of birth and the friendship I entertain towards you, cause me to desire your happiness, and I therefore address you in that spirit of truth which in me is characteristic.

TEXIANS! render every possible assistance, and soon shall you enjoy your liberty and your property, which is the wish of your countryman and friend,

John N. Seguín
Béxar, 21st June, 1836[50]

Mexicans understood that the "independence" claim was only a front for U.S. expansion. Juan Seguín, incidentally, was appointed captain by the "Texians" and eventually promoted to lieutenant colonel.

From 1836 forward, Tejas became increasingly Anglo demographically, and hostilities among nationalities became widespread. Bitterness arose as a result of the deception, the fighting, and the blatant greed for land. In consequence, the basis for Anglos' identity as Texans was, in large measure, negative—their apprehensiveness about their illegitimate claims to the land combined with their fanatical hatred of Mexicans. According to the Texas Constitution of 1836, persons who participated in the revolt or aided the enemy (that is, Mexico) forfeited both their property and their citizenship rights. Unless specifically vouchsafed, all Mexicans were assumed to fall under this stipulation; and nearly all did, but not all at once. Some Mexicans hurriedly sought to have their property rights protected under the new constitution; but, in any case, Mexicans were now to be "suspects," and concurrently even those the Mexicans who had assisted the "Texians" became the subjects of discriminatory actions.

Conflict in Tejas continued, with fortunes varying and involving much of the population on both sides. Loyal Mexican Tejanos fought often and well, and fought longer than has been acknowledged. At considerable effort, a second Mexican force was reorganized, and in 1842 forces under General Rafael Vásquez recaptured San Antonio. The land between the Nueces and Brazos rivers was also defended by Mexicans, often successfully. When Anglo raiders crossed the Nueces, their territorial ambitions were unmistakable. Laredo remained in Mexican control until 1846. The overwhelming majority of Mexican Tejanos remained loyal to Mexican sovereignty; hence, the bitter conflict for generations.

Lorenzo de Zavala, José Antonio Navarro, and José Francisco Ruiz signed the "Texas Declaration of Independence"; Juan Antonio Padilla had also intended to sign it, but he was unable to attend the convention. Between 1836 and 1845 four Mexicans, all from San Antonio, served in the Texian congress: Juan N. Seguín, José Antonio Navarro, and José Francisco Ruiz as senators; and Rafael de la Garza in the House. Members of the Esparza and Benavides families also served the Texas republic; Zavala, a Spaniard with Mexican citizenship, was interim vice president. All of these men, particularly Seguín and Navarro, received land grants from the "Texian" government; Navarro was now a particularly large landowner and a pro-South slave owner. Consistent with their chameleon political character, some of these men tried to return to the Mexican side when Santa Anna's fortunes were again on the rise.

During these years, formal Mexican political activities in Tejas, now the "Republic of Texas," were reduced for many to forced acceptance of the "Texian" government and active support in its behalf; such was the case of Juan Seguín, José Antonio Navarro, and Lorenzo de Zavala. Other Tejanos supported the Mexican government and armed resistance to the Anglo "Texian" rebels. As already mentioned, resistance in Texas continued for the next ten years, with Mexicans realizing several victories, including the retaking of San Antonio.

The political activities of traitors such as Juan Seguín, who was elected to the Texas Senate in 1838 and was twice mayor of San Antonio, steadily decreased as Anglo "Texians" severely limited Mexican political activity within the borders of the bogus republic. They were ineffectual in attempting to institute bilingual measures or to secure improvements in education. Seguín's terms in office were particularly bitter and difficult. He, Carlos de la Garza, and Vicente Cordova realized their ambiguous position in aiding the "Texians." By late 1842, under threat of indictment and even of lynching, Seguín had crossed with his family into Tamaulipas, seeking as refugees the safety of the only place, Mexico, that would offer him protection from his would-be Anglo friends. Rationalizing that he supported Texas "independence" but not annexation, and later pardoned by Mexican authorities, he sought to redeem himself during the Mexico–U.S. conflict by volunteering on the Mexican side. Before this, however, he and some of his associates would engage in one more filibustering secessionist attempt. The so-called Republic of the Rio Grande effort in 1838 targeted Tamaulipas, but was defeated by Mexican forces. On the Mexican side were old patriots such as Bernardo Gutiérrez de Lara and young ones like Juan N. Cortina. Navarro was captured in a Texian expedition to New Mexico and sentenced to death, and when this sentence was commuted, he served two and a half years in prison, returning to San Antonio where he avoided public activity for a while. While Seguín suffered financial losses, Navarro grew wealthier. Seguín, pardoned by Sam Houston in 1849, returned to claim his property, but as the antagonism toward Mexicans increased, he left for Laredo and then returned to Tamaulipas, Mexico, once more. Mexican politics in Texas indeed survived between 1836 and 1848, during the so-called Texas Republic, but momentous events were occurring elsewhere on the Mexican frontier.

The Far North, 1837–1847

While events in Texas occurred, the Liberal–Conservative debate continued over who should lead the country and what issues mattered. Liberals enjoyed a wider popular following, but they could not overcome the strengths of the Conservatives, who were rooted in the large landowners, the army, and the church. Since independence, three issues had reached dramatic importance on the frontier: the attempted centralization of government; the deterioration of relations with nomadic Indians; and the growth and consequences of foreign trade. Dealing with the first was believed to be the way to resolve the other two.

In 1836, as the result of a centralist coup d'état against the federalist reform program of Vice President Valentín Gómez-Farías, the federal constitution was suspended and the federation replaced with a centralist form of government,[51] in which the Siete Leyes Constitucionales (1836) became the fundamental law. According to the centralist constitution, the states became direct administrative subdivisions, or departamentos, of the central government. The territorios of Alta California and Nuevo México were also converted into departamentos; but since they were already under the central agreement in theory, the change in practice primarily affected the titles of the offices.

Under the departmental system, the position of jefe político became that of the governor; the comisario subalterno was renamed the subcomisario de hacienda, and the comandante general was now known as the jefe militar. The diputación territorial now became the junta departmental. The distritos were changed to *prefecturas;* the chief administrative officer was the *prefecto,* assisted by a *subprefecto;* the functions of alcalde were assigned to a *juez de paz;* and the ayuntamientos continued to function as before. Alta California was organized into two prefecturas, and Nuevo México into three. Tejas never came under the departmental system, since the successful revolt of Anglo dissidents (in 1836) had ended Mexican authority before the system could be implemented effectively. Reorganization varied in the far north. From 1836 to 1838, during the first part of the administration of Juan Bautista Alvarado, Alta California was under a virtually autonomous administration whose organization was a modified version of the federalist organization and its offices. In Nuevo México, the first government under centralism was briefly overthrown in the rebellion of 1837, but the centralist departmental organization was restored and remained in effect until 1848.

Mexican–Indian Relations

Apart from the Anglos, Indians remained the main outsider group with whom Mexicans continued to have political and economic relations during this period, which is so associated with foreign conflict.[52] Indian relations impacted on the ability of the Mexican frontier to survive, affecting the wider Anglo conflict now looming as well as its aftermath. Mexican–Indian relations continually required negotiation or force according to which one of two groups—the settled agriculturalists and the nomads—were involved. Significantly, relations with the agriculturalists were more positive, while relations with the nomads

usually resulted in conflict. Although Mexican–Indian relations affected all three provinces, relations in the New Mexico–Texas area
were the most prominent.

As conflicts occurred and administrative reorganization was attempted, the nature of relations with nomadic Indian groups loomed as
both important and troubled. Following the Spanish colonial example,
the Mexican government tried to use the policy combining negotiation
and defense to control marauding Indians, who were divided into
scores of small bands with no fixed place of settlement and no overall leadership, with leaders changing often within the bands. However,
no treaty or recruitment of volunteer Indian fighters could check
Apache depredations. Prior to Mexican independence, relations with
the Apaches had been relatively benign due to the colonial practice of
supplying rations to Indian groups on the frontier. After the Mexican
War of Independence, however, funds were no longer available to
sustain the rationing system in the military establishments. As a result,
Mexican colonies and Indian villages without military protection suffered renewed attacks by the Apaches. In the Arizona–Sonora area,
Apache raids prevented Mexican settlements from developing. By the
mid-1830s, five thousand Mexicans were reported as killed on the
northern frontier and four thousand others were known to have left
the area. With hardship, the colonies of Tucson and Tubac managed
to survive the onslaught. Marauding Indians murdered hundreds of
Mexicans and caused the widespread desertion of settlements, mines,
ranchos, and missions. In turn, state and local governments adopted
negative measures. In defiance of the constitution, slave trading was
employed in some areas to counteract the Indian threat, pitting one
tribe against another. On September 7, 1835, the Sonoran governor
Escalante y Arvizu initiated the payment of one-hundred-peso bounties
for the scalps of Apache males fourteen years and older. This bounty
practice eventually committed the states of Sonora, Chihuahua, and
Coahuila to a brutal policy that compounded the Indian problem.
Infuriated by the scalp trade, Apaches intensified their raiding between
1838 and 1845, with the death toll steadily mounting as Mexican
laborers and travelers were ambushed. The populace of northern Mexico was so harried that many settlements were abandoned. Chihuahua
and Sonora suffered the onslaught of Coyotero and Mogollon Apaches
who raided settlements, burned fields, and carried off women and
children.

In effect, the ostensibly positive policies adopted toward the Indians by the Mexican republic after its independence resulted in deepening rather than alleviating a serious threat to the viability of frontier Mexico, particularly from the Apaches.[53] Apart from the obvious disability of insufficient resources and the instability of functionaries, the difficulty lay not in the intentions of the measures that were adopted, but rather in their lack of realism. The Mexican republic's Indian policy involved full citizenship, for which the constitution insisted on no ethnic distinctions. No special status of *Indian* was recognized, nor was communal property. Persisting Indian communities were no longer recognized politically per se; what was recognized was the individual, formally constituted local government, and private property. For example, the people of the Yaqui and Mayo inner valleys in Sonora were required to set up municipal governments, with a roster of officials prescribed by law. To some extent, this requirement ran counter to the established governance of these groups, although as sedentaries they presumably were more likely to adopt such laws; in any case, however, they were obviously inapplicable to nomad raiders. The republican constitution stated a policy of equality and individual responsibility, which ran counter to kinship and group practices. Furthermore, land was to be privately owned, and lands belonging to inactive missions were to be divided as public property that would become available for distribution as soon as possible—all of which contradicted the practice of some Indian peoples and was totally irrelevant to others.

These measures lacked substantive economic meaning for northern groups such as the Mayos, Yaquis, Opatas, Pimas, Seris, Tarahumaras, Apaches, Comanches, and others; but they were particularly meaningless to the nomads. On the northern border of the frontier, these policies were only partially effectuated. Many Indians viewed them as a new form of intrusion and as a threat to an established way of life, which for some meant hunting and gathering, while for others it involved the practices introduced by missionaries, to which they now adhered and even considered "traditional," even though they had resisted them initially. The Mexican reaction to Indian refusal was often desultory, and, in any case, there were no resources. Under colonial rule Indians were granted some latitude regarding direct incorporation; under independence, incorporation became the premise. Economically, matters were clearer, centering on trade, which Indians opposed, abused, and supported. Officials knew that what the Indians

wanted was trade on their terms and for the items to which they had
become accustomed since European contact; and if necessary, they
would raid to acquire them. In fact, trade often increased raiding.

Mexican state ambiguity and irresoluteness toward the nomadic
tribes encouraged these Indians to become a formidable enemy. Conservatives were sure that previous methods of force and bribery were
effective, while Liberals believed in progressive measures, republican
practices, and private property. To the Liberals, it was important to
settle the frontier effectively and to bring the northern Indians into the
formal order of the national republic. When conflict with one group
grew worse, the consequences for other Indians and for the frontier as a
whole grew wider. Intensification of Apache raids, Mexican settlers
traveling on Indian land, poor working conditions, and the scarcity of
water prevented peaceful cooperation among the other Indians. Often,
their reaction was a determined violence, to which the Mexican reaction was frequently ineffective. Throughout the Mexican period, prior
to the U.S. war, no formal institution was established to provide a
framework of cooperative interaction in which Indian–mestizo relations could be equitably ameliorated; Indians and poor mestizos were
forced to work together.

United States intervention in the far north soon affected Mexican–
Indian relations to the detriment of both short- and long-term Mexican
interests. As large-scale trade entered the Santa Fe–Missouri and Chihuahua and south Rio Grande–Louisiana trade, village economies
soon changed from less acquisitive to more aggressive practices as
agents of trading ventures asserted their economic influence over local
agricultural producers. However, the increasing importance of the
trade and the arrival on the frontier of Mexican and Anglo settlers
further affected the economies of the neighboring nomadic Indians,
who were as committed to survival and economic gain as other peoples.
Their only recourse to securing trade and superseding the game deple-
tion, as well as to lessen land encroachments, was more raiding. Both
the Mexican and U.S. governments agreed to protect their merchants
from "Indian depredations," and on April 5, 1832, a very brief agreement was proclaimed. An article responding to Indian hostilities was
entered into the Treaty of Amity, Commerce, and Navigation:

> It is likewise agreed that the two contracting parties shall, by all
> the means in their power, maintain peace and harmony among the

several Indian nations who inhabit the lands adjacent to the lines
and rivers which form the boundaries of the two countries; and the
better to attain this object, both parties bind themselves expressly
to restrain, by force, all hostilities and incursions on the part of the
Indian nations living within their respective boundaries: so that
the United States of America will not suffer their Indians to attack
the citizens of the United Mexican States, nor the Indians inhabit-
ing their territory; nor will the United Mexican States permit the
Indians residing within their territories to commit hostilities
against the citizens of the United States of America, nor against
the Indians residing within the limits of the United States, in any
manner whatever.[54]

Indian relations were much more complex, however, than this article
acknowledged.

Indian–Mexican relations in the south Texas–Rio Grande area
were comparatively stable from 1820 to 1840; then, they changed for
the worse.[55] Lipan Apache, Kiowa, and Comanche groups periodically
inhabited the area between the Nueces River and the Rio Grande,
where they hunted unclaimed livestock, buffalo, and other wild game.
Mexican settlements had developed along the outer banks of both
rivers, and conflicts with Indians were relatively few as long as the two
peoples avoided each other and the food supply was not interrupted by
severe changes in the weather. Again, attempts to colonize the area
between the rivers were initiated, this time by the Mexican federal
government and the Mexican northern states in the 1830s. By 1842
this territory was the site for mounting hostilities; and it continued to
be an arena of conflict, even beyond the Mexican War. The various
small and indigenous groups were caught in a feud between two republics and their nationals. Mexicans favored migration to the area as a
means of forming a buffer against invading Anglos from the north,
while Anglos supported colonies to provide a buffer against their hostile neighbors to the south. Indians responded to the encroachments by
increasing their attacks on both Mexican and Anglo settlements; and
on occasion they would join one side or the other in the conflict when
it seemed likely to prove favorable to them.

Mexican economic development in southern New Mexico, Chihuahua, Coahuila, and West Texas deteriorated as Apache and Comanche groups responded to the contacts of commercial trade and
to retaliations against them.[56] Mimbreno, Chiricahua, and Tonto

Apaches known as Gilenos traveled great distances for booty, going far beyond their home areas and certainly not in self-defense. They attacked cities as far south as Chihuahua, and beyond, into Durango. Comanche and Lipan groups were the fiercest. Both Anglo and Mexican traders purchased the stolen goods as well as selling items obtained from the raiders; they also provided the Indians with weapons, all of which was viewed as part of the realm of commerce. For example, Apaches exchanged cattle, horses, sheep, mules, and goats for cloth, paints, rifles, lead, powder, knives, guns, and iron.

Indian policies adopted by the "Republic of Texas" added to the difficulties. Fueled by the land avarice that had already ignited conflict, Anglo Texas in the 1840s developed an aggressive policy toward all Indians, refusing to recognize any Indian rights and assuming that all lands belonged to the state. Texas Rangers conducted murderous campaigns against the Comanche, eventually removing the Lipan Apache from favorable geographical areas, although ranchers also used the Lipan against the Comanches and the Mexicans among others. Forcing the Comanches toward the Mexican border and into Apache territory created additional conflicts among the Indian groups and between the Comanches and Mexican citizens. As this displacement intensified, many members of all of these groups participated in the conflicts. At one point, the state government of Chihuahua offered supplies and a demilitarized safe ground. Apaches used this ground as a base from which to attack Sonora, whose officials, in turn, attacked the safe zone. In an effort to control nomadic Indian hostilities, Chihuahua and Coahuila governors offered bounties on Apache and Comanche scalps, which resulted in Anglo marauders joining Mexican scalping parties. Furthermore, agreements were also made with some Apache villages, calling for no incursions on Anglo property and Comanche scalps in return for rations. The immediate result was a fierce renewal of fighting among Mexicans, Anglos, and Indians.

Conflict with nomads in New Mexico ran along broad northern and southern lines, but the precipitators of the conflict and their ends were the same.[57] In their efforts to acquire scalps, Mexicans and Anglos raided peaceful Apache villages in southern New Mexico. The violation of these peaceful villages encouraged Apaches to retaliate, raiding copper mines, killing livestock, and burning large quantities of grain. Anglo scalpers killed Mexicans and peaceful Indians, and passed off their scalps as Apache. In some cases, both Indians and Anglos were accused of these actions, which led to bloody encounters between Anglo frontiersmen and enraged Mexicans, with both fighting the Indians.

Raiding in northern New Mexico was a livelihood for Navajos, Utes, and Apaches. During the Mexican republic, they evidently experienced no forced cultural assimilation, or at least none comparable to that attempted by colonial authorities; in fact, they were unrestrained by military and political control. Nevertheless, Indians were a ready source of labor for the construction and maintenance of irrigation projects and farms. Some Indians were captured, forced to do work, and even sold as slaves. Women and children of the roving tribes became the targets of slave raids. Indians also participated in their own slave raids, especially when the Santa Fe commercial activity increased the profits possible from the trade.

Sonoran Mexicans responded to the difficulties with nomads in two ways—economically by extracting labor and militarily by raising volunteers, comprised mostly of neighboring Indian groups, and offering them bounties.[58] Their campaigns experienced some success, but due to a lack of funds and an inadequate supply of arms, Apache raiding continued and extended further south into Sonora, where it affected Pimas, Papagos, and Opatas who provided labor to farmers, ranchers, and miners by working in seasonal harvests, in mines, and aiding Mexicans in raising cattle as well as in fighting Apaches. Because of economic difficulties, relations with these Indians deteriorated when Mexicans decreased their pay, encroached on Pima water supplies, and forced the Papagos to work more harshly. As a result, the neighboring Indians stopped fighting Apaches and entered into the conflicts on the Apache side. In southern Sonora, Yaqui resistance increased when the Mexican government attempted to parcel out their land into private landholdings. In northern Sonora, Yuman communities were affected by surrounding conflicts. Intertribal warfare along the Colorado River hindered and weakened the Mexican occupation. In this area, as in others, Mexican settlements faced local threats and a major foreign conflict as well as internal crises, such as those in New Mexico, with strong resolve.

New Mexico

Problems for New Mexicans followed the centralist coup d'état in 1836, when New Mexico became a department of the central government. [59] In effect, this change in status made Nuevo México similar to the states that had already been transformed into departments, for all departments were administered by governors who were appointed by the central government. The new status, however, was not altogether welcomed by some among the New Mexican elite. Like other norteños, many New Mexicans were federalists by preference, favoring regional control of regional offices and state autonomy. Immediately prior to the coup in early 1835, Lieutenant Colonel Albino Pérez, who had previously served in New Mexico, was appointed governor by the central government. A conscientious officer, Pérez soon alienated some of his constituency by his demeanor; furthermore, within a year of his appointment, he faced the task of implementing the changes required by the events of 1836.

Governmental change and Pérez's appointment came at a difficult time in the political and economic life of New Mexico. The new department found itself in the midst of serious hostilities with the nomadic Navajos, and, moreover, mestizo laborers were forced into the militia to supplement the small garrison. Poor harvests over a period of several years had resulted in famine conditions, especially in the Río Arriba, and conditions grew worse when people fled to seek safety in the larger towns. Conditions were such that some people moved to California. There was also acrimony among officials about the administration of government revenues. Governor Albino Pérez soon became embroiled in several matters. As an outsider and centralist, he was resented by many of the departmental elite. He aligned himself politically with one of the factions, the Abreus, instead of attempting to arbitrate between the various factions. Even worse, Perez introduced a series of reforms which included the right of the departmental government to introduce direct taxation. New Mexico previously had been exempt, due to the expense made in behalf of the frontier defense against nomadic Indians.

The change to the departmental system also engendered discontent because it meant the creation of a number of new offices as well as increased taxation. Furthermore, Nuevo México's exemption from internal duties on trade expired, thus heavily increasing the tax burden on the poorer classes. The establishment of new administrative divisions, the prefectures, under which were grouped the alcaldías, or districts, brought the alcaldes under tighter control and aroused their resentment; but the alcaldes at least had the support of those locals who had made their office possible. Such unrest was particularly strong in the northwestern area of the Río Arriba.

Albino Pérez's administration may be viewed in some respects as an attempt to reform and to make innovations in Nuevo México's government. Pérez, for example, established three public schools, decreed compulsory education for all children, and sought to ensure greater government revenue. One positive aspect was a clear statement on education:

> Ignorance, and idleness, have always been the cause of infinite evil among men in society, and to diminish them, the only remedy and the most efficacious adopted in all countries of the world, is the education of Youth. In this valuable and interesting province securing the good of the people being the principal object, the true lovers of the public weal should attend to this, and it is also the most sacred obligation of the local authorities.[60]

At the same time, Pérez and his supporters alienated many members of the elite who felt that they were excluded from office and/or were members of opposing factions such as the Pino and Armijo families. A few members of the elite gained under Pérez. Among the Nuevo Mexicanos holding high office were members of the Chacón family and the Abreu brothers, who were known for some innovative efforts; one Abreu brother held the new post of prefect of the Río Arriba area. The reaction to Pérez went beyond questions of support, speaking to social discontent and arguing for more inclusive mechanisms of local government among the elite. Colonel Pérez employed a no-longer-young sergeant who had joined the militia in 1822, Donaciano Vigil, from a propertied settler family. He had ties to Vigil y Alarid, but he had not yet advanced much, even though at that point he was an ardent supporter of his new benefactor Pérez, whom he eventually abandoned.

During the summer of 1837, unrest finally erupted into revolt when Prefect Ramón Abreu overruled the judgment of alcalde Juan José Esquibel of Santa Cruz de la Cañada, suspending him from office and jailing him. At the crux of this action was Abreu's order that a creditor, Victor Sánchez, be paid; Esquibel had sided with the debtors. When he was freed by a large and angry crowd, Esquibel, arguing legitimacy on the basis of his alcalde position, issued a pronunciamento attacking the departmental system and taxation, and then he gathered forces to occupy Santa Fe. Partially inspired by members of the Montoya and

Vigil families, a rebel junta was organized for the area of revolt calling itself a *cantón*. The plan was to have armed men capture Santa Fe and organize a new territorial government for Nuevo México. Numbering perhaps two thousand, the rebels were mainly composed of small farmers, laborers, artisans, Pueblo Indians, and the mestizo hunters known as ciboleros. At first, apparently, some anti-Pérez members of the elite encouraged the revolt and may even have initiated it in the belief that they could manipulate the poorer class and use them to gain greater influence. Donaciano Vigil was implicated, and Manuel Armijo was known to have met and held discussions with the rebel junta in what may have been an attempt to have them declare him governor; however, they did not do so. Donaciano Vigil then moved toward Armijo. The rebels, or *chimayeses*, as they were known, confronted Governor Pérez and his remaining supporters on the outskirts of Santa Fe. Most of Pérez's troops were Pueblo Indian militia whom he had mobilized together with the local garrison and officials. In a telling reflection of the degree of unrest, most of Pérez's troops went over to the rebels at the beginning of the fight, forcing the governor and a few loyal officers into a running retreat toward Santa Fe, where they were cut down.

The revolt of 1837, referred to in Nuevo México as "la guerra de los Chimayeses," was the most significant incident of popular unrest during the period. The victorious members of the cantón entered Santa Fe on August 9, 1837, where José Gonzáles, reputedly a half–Pueblo Indian cibolero from Taos, was selected as governor of the new territorial government, and Donaciano Vigil was named secretary. The departmental system was proclaimed to be abolished, and preparations were undertaken to spread the revolt to the people of the Río Abajo as well as to inform the national government of the rebels' fidelity to the republic as declared loyal Mexicans. At this point serious internal disagreements began to disintegrate the unity within the cantón. A moderate faction of small farmers and traders, including José Gonzáles, wished to end the conflict, restore normal conditions, and negotiate for recognition by the central government; while a more socially amorphous group of ciboleros, *arrieros*, and laborers sought to continue the conflict. As outsiders who were now insiders, the cantones acted in arbitrary ways that aroused apprehension. The cantón, as a protest movement directed against an officeholder, had achieved the major reason for its existence once the Pérez administration was eliminated.

The cantón may have been encouraged by members of the elite, such as Manuel Armijo, who used it as a tool to oust Pérez but were not interested in matters beyond his demise. Furthermore, Anglo Texian sympathizers among traders presumably welcomed discord in this Mexican province. The chimayeses, in turn, saw their opponents as violators of religious ethics and local loyalties, and as endorsers of arbitrary government that alienated the people.

A reaction followed the momentary success of the cantón and the subsequent turmoil. On September 8, 1837, members of the Río Abajo elite, led by Mariano Chávez, son of the first governor, and his cousin, Manuel Armijo, a former governor, issued the Plan de Tomé, which denounced the revolt, upheld patriotism, accused the cantón of plotting to separate Nuevo México from Mexico, and called for military assistance from the central government to crush the rebellion:

In the town of Tomé on the 8th day in the year 1837, the neighbors of said point, and those of Santa Maria of Belén, being assembled, with their respective *alcaldes,* the parish priest of Tomé, the lieutenant of the active militia, the honored citizen Don Manuel Armijo, from the jurisdiction of Albuquerque, fearing the disorders resulting from the anarchy, in which the Territory of New Mexico was plunged, by the deaths inflicted on the persons of the governor and other public officials, and being aware of the iniquitous measures which the so-called "Cantón of la Cañada" is taking for the destruction of the peace, harmony and good order of the citizens, and we being desirous to submit ourselves to the laws, and to keep within bounds the insults with which at every step we are threatened with as well as protecting our properties, and to make the supreme government know the good disposition and obedience which the District of Albuquerque professes it, they have agreed on the following articles:

1. Until the supreme government determines to execute what it may see fit in this Territory, no other authority is recognized but that of the Prefect of the District of Albuquerque, the only legal one remaining.

2. No one shall be attacked in his property, or rights.

3. An armed force will be placed under the command of the citizen Manuel Armijo, whom we have generally proclaimed as commandant, and as his second, the citizen Mariano Chávez, neighbor of los Padillas, and his secretary, the citizen Vicente Sánchez Vergara.

4. If, after all the forces are assembled, it is desired by the commanding officer to appoint another his will shall be obeyed in everything the same as it now is being done.

5. It being fit that the *pueblos* remain tranquil and not meddle in the difficulties of the Mexican citizens, they will be informed, that the war not being against them nor directed against any of them, not to take part in favor of either party, and that, until the supreme government appoints a governor, they must govern themselves, without obeying any authority which may not flow from themselves.[61]

This statement was backed by an armed militia joined by two hundred dragoon cavalry troops arriving from Chihuahua. An energetic campaign was mounted against the dissidents. The rebels, in the meantime, disbanded to return to cultivating their farms and herding animals, work upon which their families depended for a livelihood. The loyal militia and troops were able to defeat them before the rebels could consolidate their forces. Vigil had left González and aligned himself with Armijo. Many of the rebel leaders were executed, and control was restored throughout Nuevo México in the winter of 1838. Many who had participated in this event would become prominent in politics; among them, Donaciano Vigil, José Francisco Chaves, Albino Chacón, and Manuel Antonio Chaves. By the end of September the regular troops and militia commanded by Manuel Armijo defeated the remnants of the cantón in a short campaign in the Río Arriba. Pointedly, José Gonzáles was executed publicly, as were the Montoya brothers later, and the rebellion was crushed. Appointed governor was Manuel Armijo, who appeared as the patriot and restorer of order.

Equivocally, the events were recalled and judged negatively in one *décima*:

> Year one thousand and eight hundred
> Thirty seven, fateful year,
> Most unhappy Nuevo México,
> What has happened to us now?
> The judge of the district dead,
> And the prefect and the chief,
> And so let no one complain
> When he pays for his offense;
> And I cite them from this day
> When the innocent shall pay

All those augmented torments,
They will remember you sadly
Fateful year of eighteen hundred.
The departmental junta
Was established by rude force,
Who shall declare it was right,
This rebellious disobedience?
Who will walk into the presence
Of that court, Oh, woe is me,
To defend the territory
When he sees but hate and vengeance
For what has happened to us?
I wish I had never seen you,
Thirty seventh, fateful year.
Oh most unhappy territory,
What became of your submission,
Your gentleness and your patience,
Which adorned you as a treasure?
This is what I feel and weep for,
To see you in such misfortune,
Without defense you now stand,
Weep over your woes, oh weep,
Most unhappy Nuevo México.[62]

After the events, not many held positive views of the cantón, certainly not those acknowledged to be influential such as Father Antonio J. Martínez, Diego Archuleta, Rafael Chacón, or Manuel Chaves. Members of the elite were alarmed by the success of a movement composed of and led by members of the lower classes who evidently could control key parts of Nuevo México. They apparently realized that even if they had opposed the previous governor, if such people could defeat and kill the central governor and replace him with one of their own instead of a member of the elite, then the credibility and power of the elite, as a whole, was threatened.

Manuel Armijo was to serve a second time as governor of Nuevo México from 1837 to 1844, and later he served a third term from 1845 to 1846.[63] Armijo's second administration faced a major trauma successfully. The Texan Santa Fe expedition of 1841 was an attempt by the Republic of Texas, under Mirabeau Lamar, to invade Nuevo México and annex the department to Texas. After rebellion from Mexico, the so-called Texas Republic falsely claimed that its boundaries extended

the length of the Río Bravo del Norte, and as far as its source, encompassing half of the territory of Nuevo México, including Santa Fe and
Albuquerque. The would-be annexation effort claimed the guise of a
peaceful trading exchange, but it was organized and armed as a military
command led by General Hugh McLeod and Commissioners William
Cook and José Antonio Navarro. Misjudging either the circumstances
or the people, the organizers thought there would be support for annexation. Instead, the filibusterers were met resolutely by a locally organized militia backed by wide popular support, and they surrendered.
Manuel Chaves and Albino Chacón conducted the negotiations; Donaciano Vigil was an ardent enthusiast of the Armijo-led effort and was
promoted in quick succession, after years as a sergeant, to lieutenant
and then to captain. The filibusterers were sent as prisoners first to Chihuahua and later to Mexico City, charged with what were indeed
serious crimes. As recalled by a décima of the period:

> Cook into Mexico crossed
> With his Texan expedition,
> To recover from Santa Anna
> The lands he had sold to them.
> But Armijo made no payment,
> He met them with solid shot
> All these gentlemen from Texas.
> Let other collectors come
> for Armijo is dealing out.
> A constitution and laws
> They pretended to bring with them,
> But to plant slavery with us
> Was all they had in mind.[64]

Though they were defeated in their efforts, accounts of the travails of
these Texians aroused sympathy in the United States. On the other
hand, Armijo and Nuevo México were acclaimed by Mexico City, and
Armijo was promoted.

After 1837, local politics stabilized and included a few more participants. Armijo remained the major figure, except when he was suspended by the inspector general. Governors other than Armijo experienced short terms. For example, Mariano Martínez de la Jaraza, whose
wife saved him from death at the hands of complaining Indians (in
1844), was an interim governor; and José Chávez faced angry com-

plainants who felt discriminated against (in 1845). Electioneering was intense. In 1844, Father Martínez, backed by the vicar Juan Felipe Ortiz, competed for a congressional seat with Diego Archuleta, who won due to Armijo's support. Archuleta was followed by Tomás Chávez y Castillo. The departmental assembly elections were won by Father Martínez, Tómas Ortiz, Juan Perea, Juan Cristóbal Armijo, and Felipe Sena. Juan Bautista Vigil y Alarid was secretary of the department. In the somewhat irregular and unusual "senate" elections, major candidacies included those of Nepomuceno Urguides, N. Madrid, Marcelino Castañeda, Bonilla Arcillaga, and others. Taxes were a major issue, apart from defense and trade. Armijo was again appointed governor in July 1845 and took office in November.

As the province improved economically, so did some elite fortunes. Nearly two hundred additional land grants were made in Armijo's last term. Several mining deposits, such as the "Real de Dolores," were being developed. During the last years of the 1840s, the economic importance of the Santa Fe trade and the Chihuahua Trail continued to increase as did Mexican participation from New Mexico, bringing economic benefits to some Mexicans and Anglos alike and making possible other cooperation as well as strengthening travel with Chihuahua. There were, however, negative consequences as well. Anglo traders and marauders increased to the point of forming a colony. Mexican merchants such as Antonio Chávez were attacked, and arrieros and ciboleros complained of harassment. Difficulties with raiding Indians were increased by Anglo-American trade in weapons at fur trading posts such as Brent's Fort along the frontier. In addition, Anglo Texans drove the Comanches into the Llano Estacado, where other Indians and Mexican settlers were exposed to their raids. Father Antonio Martínez protested publicly against the ever greater North American presence and the lack of protection offered by the Mexican government. Donaciano Vigil, in contrast, increased his relations with Anglo traders and the circle at Bent's Fort, while criticizing the Mexican government. The major challenge facing Nuevo México as a Mexican territory would be invasion from the United States during the war of 1846–1848, which would exhibit a variety of aspects.[65] In 1846, when news of the outbreak of war reached Santa Fe, Governor Armijo called for the mobilization of the militia as the means available to resist the North Americans; the response was strong, with a few notable exceptions.

California

After 1836 a coup d'état begun by conservatives and military officers and led by Santa Anna abolished the federal constitution and initiated a centralized system of government under which the states and territories, including California, became departamentos that were administered under the central government, with their governors appointed or their selection confirmed by the president and congress. The Department of Alta California was then divided into two and later three prefecturas. The prefectura of Los Angeles, for example, included the area from Santa Bárbara to San Diego; both areas were *subprefecturas*, or *partidos*, of Los Angeles. The head of the prefecture was a prefect; the subprefectures, or partidos, were headed by subprefects. The alcalde replaced the two jueces de paz (justices of the peace); the regidores and other officers remained. Under the departmental system, the governor became the jefe político and the *diputación* was called the *junta departamental*. Under both systems, there were various other officials such as the jueces de campo, who held jurisdiction over disputes involving cattle and grazing rights. In 1840, the office of alcalde was abolished and replaced by two jueces de paz from 1841 to 1844. After 1845, the alcalde was restored and the jueces de paz abolished. None of these office changes fully dealt satisfactorily with the aspect of local governance, which caused understandable complaints. The territory of California had two distinct economic, social, and political hubs: one in the north and the other in the south. The members of one did not want to be secondary players in the eyes of the other, and the locations of the capital and the custom house were seen as vital matters.

The elite experienced difficulty in finding cooperation among its own members, on a territorial-wide basis, but it achieved subregional cooperation more readily. Concurrent with the instability in Mexico City and the Santa Anna coup of 1836, a brief period of factionalism ensued among californios following the death of José Figueroa in April 1835. In part, this factionalism was related to unacceptable choices for governor on the part of the central authorities, and in part it was related to the search for hegemony by the triumvirate of Castro, Alvarado, and Vallejo, who were both challenged by southerners and possessed with the desire for land grants and control of customs and its revenue. This period of jockeying for power lasted until December 1836.[66] During this year and a half, four interim governors held office.

First to serve, with local support, was José Castro; then came Nicolás Gutiérrez, who served as governor without local support. Following them, the central authorities appointed as governor Colonel Mariano Chico, a conservative who alienated the californios by his authoritarian enforcement of the laws and was deposed by a coup led by Castro. Nicolás Gutiérrez then briefly served again as governor until he was overthrown by a coup in Monterey led by the president of the diputación, Juan Bautista Alvarado. Both Chico and Gutiérrez were asked to leave the territory. On an interim basis, Alvarado was named as provisional governor, and Mariano Vallejo was appointed *comandante militar*, with Castro backing both of them. Monterey was the capital. Northern California federalist sentiment was ostensibly behind the proclamation in November 1836 that Alta California would be autonomous from the central government until the federal Constitution of 1824 was restored. The fact, however, was that the youthful liberalism of Vallejo, Castro, and Alvarado had hardened into a growing conservatism.

In December 1836, arribeño political leader Juan Bautista Alvarado succeeded in regularizing his service as governor and in creating some improvement in civil concerns.[67] Now there was more stability: lands were awarded, mission resources were administered, and some church matters were arranged. In July 1838, Alvarado was formally recognized by the Mexican government as jefe político of the Department of Alta California. A skillful politician, he had managed to prevent Carlos Carrillo from taking office as governor, despite the fact that Carrillo had briefly claimed an official appointment from the central Mexican government. Carrillo, the brother of Los Angeles's influential José Antonio Carrillo, seemingly enjoyed the majority support of both Los Angeles and San Diego. San Diego representatives demanded the customs house, and their inability to obtain it embittered Juan Bandini. After negotiations, Santa Bárbara políticos, including the de la Guerras, pledged their support to Alvarado; and Santa Bárbara tilted the balance between arribeños and abajeños. Through a policy of awarding land grants and appointing mission administrators who were sympathetic to rancheros, Alvarado was able to conciliate his opponents and reward his northern friends such as Castro and Vallejo as well as those who supported him in southern California, in particular the de la Guerras. In another arena, a potentially positive step lay in the creation of a bishopric for the Californias and the appointment of Francisco García Diego as the first bishop. These decisions were the result of a tentative but significant consensus between the central government, the Vatican, and the Franciscans. Alvarado had provided stability for several years, but one aspect of the support that made this possible weakened: he and Vallejo drew apart.

In 1842, Alta California accepted centralism by agreement; Alvarado's tenure ended; and appointed as the new governor from Mexico City was General Manuel Micheltorena,[68] who had served in Texas, an experience that may have moved him to do two things. First, he ensured himself of three hundred troops, and second, he actively sought to please major constituencies. He strengthened education, courted the disaffected church representatives, granted lands, and paid for expenses out of his own funds. Nevertheless, he was soon challenged by Alvarado. Unfortunately, both men accepted foreign supporters who made the dispute a bitter one. Before matters worsened, Micheltorena, to his credit, agreed to resign and leave California. With what influence remained to him, he inclined toward the southern group. At this time, the danger of foreign influence and territorial threats had greatly increased. Formal presence of the Americans came through representatives of the United States consulate. Influential Mariano Vallejo provided land to a colony of foreigners in the Sonoma area. Foreign settlers played a significant opportunist role as mercenaries in several political conflicts. Isaac Graham, a marauder, was arrested, deported, and allowed to return by authorities, whereupon he organized some forty Anglos to plot a revolt.

Perhaps the most notable, and certainly the most ominous, event of the Micheltorena administration was the seizure of Monterey by the U.S. Pacific squadron, which had received misinformation about hostilities between the two countries. It had sailed for California according to secret instructions from the secretary of the navy, which were to be followed if war was declared. This operation was planned six years before war actually occurred. On October 19 and 20, 1842, marines from the fleet commanded by Commodore Thomas Catesby Jones landed at Monterey, lowering the Mexican flag and raising that of the United States, and declaring that Alta California now belonged to the U.S. by right of conquest. Mexican officials protested. Commodore Jones, disappointed to learn from the U.S. consul that Mexico was not at war with the United States, understood that he had committed an act of unprovoked aggression. In apologizing to Governor Manuel Micheltorena, he expressed his regret for the mistake and withdrew.

The central government protested vigorously to the U.S. government for this outrage, but it only modestly strengthened the defenses of the department. The United States took the embarrassment in stride, and by 1843 Captain John C. Frémont, a regular officer, was ordered to advance and to map routes and defenses in California. Frémont was ousted by authorities, but he was back by 1845, building nothing less than a fort twenty-five miles from Monterey. In contrast, the Russians at the same time negotiated their withdrawal from California and sold their buildings and supplies, including military stores, to John Sutter.

Mexican governors faced troubling issues in the mid-1840s. The Micheltorena administration had been harried by differences between the governor and the northern departmental elite over land allocations and the prerogatives of local officials. One local official who prospered during both the Alvarado and Micheltorena years was Pablo de la Guerra, who at the age of twenty-one was appointed to the coveted post of customs collector. When Micheltorena, an outsider, left, he was replaced by a southern local, Pío Pico. He was immediately beset by the recurring quarrel between abajeños and arribeños over the location of the capital, which equated to political dominance, and the customs house, which meant revenue and jobs for the place selected. For awhile Governor Pío Pico controlled the administration of southern Alta California as far north as Santa Bárbara, and the north was controlled by comandante general José Castro from Monterey, where customs revenues were located. Castro continued to have the support of some— though not all—prominent northern families. In the south, key families consolidated their support around the Picos and the de la Guerras. During this time, too, danger remained present on two fronts: occasional Indian conflicts broke out in both northern and southern California and foreign conquest loomed ever more possible as increasing numbers of Anglo settlers entered the department without authorization or opposition. In the face of such challenges, the small regular Mexican military detachment became vulnerable through lack of finances and support.

The decade of the 1840s marked a period of increasing growth in population, economy, and political influence of the territory as well as greater contact with the interior. The Mexican government, because of its own internal economic, political, and social contradictions, was unable to take sufficient steps to protect or develop either its sovereignty or its territory. The territorial government and population, despite an ever-increasing awareness of the threat to its sovereignty, lacked the military manpower and resources to deter or prevent illegal settlement and trade by Anglos. The Texas revolt of 1836 against Mexico, Texan aggression, and U.S. attempts to purchase Mexican territory added to fears about the ambitions of foreign settlers. While the bulk of foreigners, especially U.S. settlers, were located in northern California, Los Angeles and southern California were no less aware of such dangers; this was especially the case after 1842. Moreover, there had been an increase in reports of discoveries of gold since the 1800s and 1820s.[69]

The intra-California north–south competition culminated in time for an even larger confrontation. After February 1845, the departmental junta had declared Pío Pico, the senior member of the junta, to be governor.[70] This appointment, tellingly, was recognized by the central government. Pico acted to move the capital from Monterey to Los Angeles, an act authorized by the Mexican congress in 1836. The northern californios refused to accept the move and attempted to support General José Castro, a northern military commander, as the governor. A fairly reasonable compromise was reached in which the governor and the legislature would be located in Los Angeles, but the customs house and military authority would remain in Monterey. Pico, however, now faced a graver issue. By late 1845 he called for unity, not as an abstract ideal but as a specific need, to oppose foreign aggression for the sake of the territory and nation. Inappropriately for all involved, a meeting was held by prominent Mexicans during late March 1847 at the house of Thomas O. Larkin, U.S. consul, to discuss the future. By his own admission, Mariano Vallejo alone called for annexation, while others argued for an English protectorate or independence as a means to thwart United States plans in case of the war voiced by Pablo de la Guerra. Even in this group hosted by the United States consul, the majority preferred to give their allegiance to Mexico.

The last two years of the Mexican republic in California, 1846–1848, were marked by the outbreak of war between the United States and Mexico. Major events included the invasion of Alta California by U.S. naval and military forces; the attempts of Governor Pío Pico to obtain military resources from the Mexican government; U.S. occupation of Los Angeles and other Alta California towns; the outbreak of widespread popular resistance throughout Alta California; a series of battles in southern California; and the capitulation of Mexican forces in an armistice agreement to await the outcome of the war between the two countries. Mexican Alta California, while accelerating its development in 1846, would face its ultimate rendezvous with Anglo American invasion and expansionism. War confronted californios with facing invasion while remaining within the limits of their material resources. Their responses indicate that californios considered themselves loyal Mexicans and did not desire independence or annexation to the United States. Nor did Alta California's leaders welcome the possible incorporation of the territory into the United States. Only a few californios with special ties to U.S. interests considered such a possibility desirable.[71]

The War in the Far North

The United States policy of aggression and annexation had resulted in a state of war between the United States and Mexico, as hostilities on the southern Río Bravo intensified. Immediate actions precipitating warfare included the entrance of the U.S. army under Zachary Taylor into Texas in 1845, followed by the annexation of this area, the U.S. army's advance across the Nueces, and its foray into the Río Grande with fighting in and around Laredo and Matamoros. Only then, and only after agreeing to recognize "Texas's" annexation with the Nueces as boundary, did the Mexican government order its troops to respond. Irregular warfare carried on by local citizens against the Anglos preceded and followed formal warfare. In all areas there was resistance, as well as negotiation, with the invaders.

The major challenge to Nuevo México and California and the Mexican territorial settlements between the Río Nueces and Bravo was the invasion from the United States, during the war of 1846–1848, which elicited many instances of political persistence and efforts toward accommodation.[72] Resistance was often a matter of local organization and leadership since there were no systematic garrisons nor even defense plans by the Mexican military, though the Anglos clearly had invasion plans. Partisan activity, raids, and counterraids had continued in Texas; and in 1846, when news of the outbreak of war reached Santa Fe, Governor Armijo called for the mobilization of the traditional standing militia, which was the means available to resist the North Americans, and for donations of silver to purchase arms. On August 16, 1846, the militia was assembled at Apache Canyon, an advantageous position on the route of advance by U.S. troops. A force of several thousand militia volunteers assembled at Armijo's orders, ready to resist the invasion. Though this constituted a notable response by the local citizenry, the volunteers were poorly armed, with more than half armed only with lances, lassos, or bows and arrows; and most did not possess firearms, only the expectation that arms would be available. One advisor to the governor, Captain Donaciano Vigil, cautioned that although the people were in favor of resistance, it would have negative results both militarily and economically. Governor Armijo, after consultation, ordered a withdrawal, explaining his reason in two self-rationalizing ways. He told locals that given the lack of arms, the untrained masses, and the superior armaments of the opposition, he would not order needless bloodshed. In a communiqué to Mexico City, he suggested that his volunteers were hesitant and that many of them had abandoned the site. For this reason and because of the poor armaments Governor Armijo decided that an effective resistance could not be waged, and he disbanded the militia, leaving the territory open to occupation. If he was attempting to avoid violence, his decision was surely difficult. However, members of the militia, including Lieutenant Governor Diego Archuleta, held a different view. According to them, the militia was ready to fight the invaders, even if they were poorly armed. For no apparent reason, Armijo ordered the troops to disband and to retreat. Behind Armijo's conduct, according to his enemies, lay a large bribe—the figure mentioned is 100,000 dollars—made by an Anglo-American merchant, James W. Magoffin, in return for Armijo's vow to cease resistance and to demoralize others. As acting governor, Juan Bautista Vigil y Alarid surrendered. A court-martial trial held by the Mexican government in Chihuahua acquitted Armijo of the charge of treason, and no direct evidence of a bribe was ever found.

Among Mexicans there was soon widespread discontent directed at the Anglo invaders.[73] However, the invading army commanded by General Kearny occupied Santa Fe and the other major towns by the end of September; an Anglo merchant, Charles Bent, was named governor, and Donaciano Vigil was named secretary and asked to devise a legal code. There followed only limited direct resistance. A rebellion was planned for December, but informants reported it to United States authorities, and among those arrested were Diego Archuleta and Manuel A. Chaves. On January 19, 1847, major resistance by Mexicans and Pueblo Indians began at Taos, where the U.S.-

appointed governor Charles Bent and his supporters were executed. Fighting rapidly spread to other points in the Río Arriba, especially at Santa Cruz de la Cañada, Mora, and Taos. United States authorities reacted quickly, and the town of Mora was partially leveled by artillery. At Taos the patriots were besieged in the church, where many were killed, and those captured were indicted in February 1847 for "treason" to the United States; some of the convicted men were hung, when, in fact, they had been patriots who dying for their homeland and thereafter called *los mártires*. Those imprisoned in December were jailed briefly and then released or not found guilty; if they held an officer's rank they could not be tried for treason.

California responses were various and, to an extent, commendably energetic. [74] Upon learning of the outbreak of war and assessing the immediate danger to Alta California, Governor Pío Pico, General Castro, and members of the departmental junta met at Santa Bárbara in May 1846 to consider defensive actions against a certain invasion. The principal concern was, of course, the preparation of a defense. Among the matters discussed at the Santa Bárbara meeting was the possibility of contacting the British or French consuls in Alta California to request temporary protectorate status for the territory as a means of avoiding occupation by the United States. Such a measure was considered only as an action of last resort to counter the United States, and even then if it were employed, it would presume with it the expectation that England would return Alta California to Mexico after the end of the war.

Events moved rapidly toward armed conflict in California. [75] In June 1846 a group of Anglo settlers in the Sacramento Valley rebelled in collaboration with a group of U.S. soldiers led by Captain Charles Frémont, who was allegedly conducting a scientific expedition, but whose real purpose was to map invasion routes to be used by the army in its attack on Mexican territory. The settlers occupied the small settlement of Sonoma, north of San Francisco Bay, and proclaimed a mock "California Republic," under the "Bear Flag," a "republic" which presumably could then appeal for U.S. support. Among the first to be arrested, mistreated, and despoiled was Mariano Vallejo, the erstwhile "friend of the Americans" who referred to himself as a general; even though he had no such appointment, Vallejo pledged allegiance to the United States. Contrary to the expectations that they would inspire defeatism among Mexican californios, the antics of the

Bear Flaggers, combined with the murder of civilians, solidified Mexican resistance even in thinly populated northern Alta California. Figures such as Castro, Alvarado, and de la Guerra opted for resistance. The flag of the filibusterers was popularly referred to as the "bandera de los marranos." The "Bear Flag" incident was soon followed by action at Monterey, where the ships of the U.S. Pacific naval squadron, under the command of Commodore John Sloat, seized the historic capital on July 7, 1846. On August 6, 1846, Commodore Robert F. Stockton anchored off San Pedro and landed several hundred sailors and marines, who proceeded to march on Los Angeles on August 11. Because of the element of surprise, the landing went unopposed at first. In contrast to the number of U.S. forces, the entire Mexican adult male population of the Los Angeles district was some 675 men; a few had military experience, and only a small local militia existed. One step of precaution was taken by a Mexican woman to hide a cannon.

Mexicans soon responded by exhibiting cohesion and organization. On August 10, the day prior to Stockton's landing, Governor Pico, together with Jefe Militar José Castro, issued the call:

> Prove to the nation and the whole world, that your difficult situation, and not your consent, make you bear the oppressive chain of the usurper. Conserve ever in your bosoms the sacred fire of liberty, and without shame the glorious name of good Mexicans.
>
> Californians all: Have confidence in the high National Government; it has sworn to perish or to save the Republic of all domination, and there is no doubt that this will be accomplished. Be persevering, and be not dismayed even in the face of torture. Let *Mexico* be your motto.[76]

To avoid capture, Pico, who was California's main legitimate authority, went to Sonora to appeal to the central Mexican government to send regular troops and weapons with which to fight the invaders. Pico was ordered to remain in Hermosillo and later in Guaymas, Sonora, to await reinforcements, but none came. In Los Angeles and elsewhere, however, there were responses to his call.

The Mexicans reacted to the overt hostility and brutality of U.S. occupation troops.[77] Resistance was countered heavily in northern California, and by November, leaders such as Pablo de la Guerra were arrested. In September 1846, the *angelinos* organized against their enemies under the leadership of Servulio Varela and Leonardo Cota. A patriot force, which soon increased to over three hundred men, surrounded troops commanded by Archibald Gillespie, who retreated. On September 24, a proclamation was issued expressing the sentiments of the people of Los Angeles; this "Pronunciamiento contra los Norte Americanos" declared their loyalty to Mexico and their resolution to drive the invaders from Mexican soil. Signed by three hundred persons, about half of the adult males in the Los Angeles district, the proclamation read as follows:

> Citizens: For a month and a half, by a lamentable fatality resulting from the cowardice and incompetence of the department's chief authorities, we see ourselves subjugated and oppressed by an insignificant force of adventurers of the U.S. of N. America, who, putting us in a condition worse than that of slaves, are dictating to us despotic and arbitrary laws by which, loading us with contributions and onerous taxes, they wish to destroy our industries and agriculture, and to compel us to abandon our property, to be taken and divided among themselves. And shall we be capable of permitting ourselves to be subjugated, and to accept in silence the heavy chain of slavery? Shall we lose the soil inherited from our fathers, which cost them so much blood? Shall we leave our families victims of the most barbarous servitude? Shall we wait to see our wives violated, our innocent children beaten by the American whip, our property sacked, our temples profaned, to drag out a life full of shame and disgrace? No! A thousand times no! Compatriots, death rather than that! Who of you does not feel his heart beat and his blood boil on contemplating our situation? Who will be the Mexican that will not be indignant, and rise in arms to destroy our oppressors? We believe there will be not one so vile and cowardly. Therefore, the majority of the inhabitants of this district, justly indignant at our tyrants, we raise the cry of war and with arms in our hands.

The document further stated:

> We, all the inhabitants of the department of California, as members of the great Mexican Nation, declare that it is and has been our wish to belong to her alone, free and independent.

It rejected U.S. authority, and called for punishment of traitors and Anglo residents who aided the enemy. Subsequent resistance by these and other *alta californios* indicate that this document expressed popular sentiments toward Mexico and toward the prospect of annexation to the United States.[78]

Following this resolve, further actions resulted in the forced retreat of foreign invaders.[79] Officers to lead the campaign against the invaders were elected from among the retired veterans of the army and the local militia. The leaders chosen were Captain José María Flores, as comandante general; José Antonio Carrillo, the second in command, as major general; and militia Captain Andrés Pico, as *comandante de escuadrón.* Servulio Varela was placed in command of fifty volunteers who were sent to Rancho Chino to arrest a garrison of twenty Anglo-Americans under the command of Isaac Williams. On September 26 and 27, 1846, volunteers under Varela and José del Carmen Lugo attacked and defeated the enemy at the Battle of Rancho Chino. On about September 29, 1846, Mexicans forced the surrender of Gillespie and the garrison that had been entrenched on the hill overlooking the plaza. On October 4, 1846, Gillespie and his men were allowed to march along the "Alameda" to San Pedro, where they boarded a merchant ship, the "Vandalia," and left the area. Following the recapture of Los Angeles, more volunteers joined the forces under José María Flores, and successful uprisings took place in Santa Bárbara and San Diego, with armed encounters reported in northern Alta California.

During these events, the women participated in resisting the invasion.[80] An old colonial cannon, capable of firing four-pound balls, had long stood in the *placita.* This old four-pounder had been used to fire salutes during fiestas and other occasions. When Commodore Sloat's force occupied the town, Francisca Reyes, a woman living near the placita, had the cannon buried in her yard to prevent it from falling into enemy hands. The cannon, now exhumed, was nicknamed *el pedrero de la vieja* ("the old woman's rock gun") in honor of Francisca Reyes's heroism. As a symbol of defiance and a warning to the foreigners, a group of women presented the departing Gillespie with the gift of a basket of peaches stuck with cactus needles. Other women provided information and supplies, attended the wounded, and arranged burials.

Despite the advantages of the invaders, southern Alta California reverted to Mexican control from San Luis Obispo to San Diego.[81] Yet the Mexican californios, civilian volunteers, were nearly without effective, up-to-date military weapons to oppose the enemy, who had more trained and well-armed sailors and marines in their ships at Monterey than the entire adult male population in that area of Mexican Alta California. In addition to more than three thousand men,

Commodore Sloat's forces had five heavily armed naval vessels, each one capable of bombarding the coastal settlements. In contrast, the californios had a volunteer force of perhaps seven hundred men, armed mainly with old flintlocks, swords, and lances, and the one small-caliber cannon for which they lacked sufficient gunpowder.

Several renewed Mexican encounters followed efforts by the invaders to regain the initiative in and around San Pedro.[82] On October 6, 1846, additional troops arrived at San Pedro aboard the warship Savannah, under United States Marine Captain William Mervine. The next day, Mervine began to march on Los Angeles with four hundred sailors and marines, occupying the main house of the Dominguez Ranch, where they spent the night. Militia from Los Angeles commanded by José Antonio Carrillo opposed their advance on October 8, with the Mexican force composed of vaqueros with lances charging U.S. troops who had formed a square formation from which they could fire effective volleys. Carrillo divided the angelinos into three groups of horsemen, with each one periodically charging and stopping short of rifle range. In the center of the californios, guarded by ten men, was the "old woman's rock gun" fired by Ignacio Aguilar. Strapped to a *carreta,* the old cannon was loaded with heavy rocks and metal scrap because the Mexicans had no regular ammunition for it.

The Battle of Dominguez Ranch was a victory for the californios, who succeeded in killing six and wounding another six U.S. troops with the old cannon. There were no Mexican casualties and United States Marine Captain Mervine was forced to retreat to the safety of his ships. In sum, one hundred vaqueros had defeated four hundred sailors and marines armed with modern weapons, again delaying the advance on Los Angeles. On October 23, Commodore Stockton arrived at San Pedro on the warship Congress, bringing U.S. forces to over eight hundred men, in addition to the crews remaining on the ships. Stockton prepared to march on Los Angeles, and his men fought several short skirmishes with Mexicans in the vicinity of San Pedro. Stockton, now convinced that he would need a larger force to take Los Angeles, sailed south for San Diego.

In that vicinity, another engagement occurred, the Battle of San Pasqual, a Mexican victory fought on December 6 and 7, 1846, near Escondido in present-day San Diego County.[83] While Stockton was in San Diego preparing his next move, Captain Andrés Pico, in command of about eighty men armed with lances and swords, was dispatched to this area to guard the movements of the enemy. At the same time, United States Army General Stephen Watts Kearny was approaching the same area from New Mexico. Guided by Kit Carson, General Kearny was on his way to Alta California with a contingent of about 140 officers and men, plus civilian camp followers, with orders from President Polk to take command of land operations from the navy. At Carson's advice, he had decided to take with him only a small cavalry force since it was reported that Stockton had occupied the Alta California towns without resistance. Carson had assured Kearny that the Mexicans would not fight.

Shortly after dawn on December 6, Pico's lookouts encountered the U.S. dragoons. Outnumbered, Pico chose to attack, sending forward a small group of vaqueros to draw the Anglos in. As Pico had hoped, Kearny ordered his calvary to attack the group that drew them into a small valley surrounded by low hills. While the dragoons were spread about a mile in pursuit, Pico's lancers hit them before they could use their carbines or their two mountain howitzers. The fighting was short but telling, with lances and swords against heavy cavalry sabers, carbines, and pistols. Stunned, Kearny's troopers entrenched themselves on the side of a hill, surrounded by the Mexicans under Pico, while Kit Carson escaped in the night to seek aid from Stockton in San Diego. The end result of this small quick battle, the bloodiest of the war in Alta California, was twenty-two U.S. casualties, of whom fourteen died; the only Mexican casualty was one wounded. Besides the humiliation of defeat, General Kearny lost his right arm, which had to be amputated due to a lance thrust. Kearny's men were rescued several days later by a force of over two hundred men. The victory of San Pasqual was the high point of the Mexican californio defense.

The invaders, with their superior weapons and numbers, were able to reoccupy the rancherías, except the town of Los Angeles, where two encounters occurred.[84] Against Los Angeles, Stockton concentrated U.S. forces that included additional sailors, Frémont's forces from the north, and two newly arrived regiments. While the californios had been successful in their harassing tactics or in quick, hand-to-hand combat, as at San Pasqual, they could not charge successfully concentrated lines of riflemen or effective artillery. Engagements occurred at San Gabriel River on January 8, 1847, and at La Mesa on January 9, in what is now the City of Industry; both fights ended in stalemates. On January 10, Stockton's forces occupied Los Angeles as Frémont's troops entered the San Fernando Valley, where prominent citizens suspected of anti-United States feelings, such as Pablo de la Guerra, were arrested. Events in California were important to the participants there, but the war was being decided in the interior of Mexico.

On January 13, Andrés Pico and José Antonio Carrillo, acting for the civil and military authority of the Mexican department of Alta California, signed the Treaty of Cahuenga at a ranch house near Cahuenga Pass.[85] The negotiated capitulation did not relinquish Mexican sovereignty over California or end the allegiance of the californios to Mexico. Rather, it was an armistice agreement under which the Mexican inhabitants of Alta California agreed to end armed resistance, submit to occupation, and await the final agreement ending the war between the two nations. Contemporary observers, such as the authors of *Apuntes para la historia de la guerra entre México y los Estado Unidos,* a group of officers and political leaders who were participants in the war, recognized the patriotism displayed by Mexican Californians in these terms:

> This was the last exertion made by the sons of California, for the liberty and independence of their country whose defense will always do them honor, since without supplies, without means or instruction, they rushed into an unequal contest, in which they more than once taught the invaders what a people can do, who fight in defense of their rights.[86]

Thus, not only the declarations but the actions of many californios, as well as those of Tejanos and Nuevo Méxicanos, in the face of foreign aggression, testified to their resolve. The generations that had seen Anglos having to petition while Mexicans held government authority and who resisted them had a certain confidence in dealing with this group that other generations lacked. Their relations with the nomadic Indians, however, were never stable or satisfactory.

Nomadic Indians and the War: The Other Relationship

Mexican frustration in negotiating with nomadic raiders increased their anger toward these Indians and their suspicion of them. Now, as before, Mexican–Indian relations were mixed, characterized as much by cooperation as by hostility. But the violence was most remembered.

Anglo agitation, nomadic Indian economic needs, and pan-Indian relations were substantive aspects of the Mexican War and of its legacy to all of the groups. Mexican settlements were debilitated,[87] and inadequate resources as well as the lacunae in the Mexican Indian policy resulted in the rise of a formidable force of nomadic raiders. Their attacks weakened Mexico's ability to muster its resources to strengthen the frontier; for the nomadic tribes were a significant mobile fighting force, with a wide scope for action in a very large area. These tribes thus diverted Mexican resources as they were marshaled against the Anglo hostilities. The Indian conflict obviously did not decide the issue of the Mexican War; but Apache activity, in particular, had some effect on Mexico's ability to defend itself. It also weakened Mexican settlement vis-à-vis Anglos for the future decades.[88]

In the West, the Arizona–Sonora frontier suffered extremely from nomadic forays.[89] The Santa Cruz Valley, and especially Tucson and Tubac, experienced serious attacks from roving Apache tribes; and as the few troops withdrew to fight North Americans in Chihuahua, raiding increased. Anglo forces took advantage of the situation. After the U.S. occupied New Mexico, Stephen Kearny and his forces persuaded the Apaches and Navajos, some of whom were peaceful at the time, to make an alliance with them. As a result, raids became legitimized campaigns against Mexico's frontier population and enhanced the Anglo position there. United States troops entered the area without experiencing difficulty from Indians, and charted routes toward California. However, as U.S. forces attempted to capture the Sonoran port of Guyamas, Mexicans and local sedentary Indians entered into a union and successfully defended their territory against their common foe. Opatas from Butac, Tepupe, Matape, and Alamos fought with Mexicans against Anglo forces. At first, war operations were somewhat determined by the ability of either side to gain support from the local Indians.

Indians residing along the northeastern frontiers between Mexico and the United States played multiple roles in the Mexican War.[90] They fought with Mexicans against Anglos, and with Anglos against Mexicans, or they were the victims of attacks from combined forces of Mexicans and Anglos. Comanches and Lipan Apaches created difficulties for Mexican and U.S. military operations along the southern Río Grande. As war commenced between the two countries, southern Texas, Nuevo León, and Tamaulipas became areas of dispute and bloodshed, with the Comanches and Lipans launching raids on both

Mexican and Anglo settlements. The Anglos responded by sending commissioners to contact their roving allies, persuading them to remain loyal to the United States. Mexican authorities, in turn, sent agents to the tribes to encourage raids on Anglo settlements. Commissioners sent by the U.S. Congress to Texas promised various bands a liberal supply of presents and protection under the U.S. government. As a result, however, raids increased and all groups blamed each other for the exacerbation of hostilities.

Nomadic Indians undermined Mexican settlements and military operations in Nuevo León and Tamaulipas by attacking muleteers and ranchos.[91] As invading North Americans drew near, Mexican citizens hesitated to leave their homes defenseless against Indian incursions. Local authorities faced the dilemma of choosing between defending homes against the Indians or concentrating their efforts to meet the invading Americans. As is well known, the invading U.S. army committed atrocities that added greatly to the Indian as well as the Mexican heritage of animosities. As the "Yanquis" marched south, they raped women, terrorized both young and old, and executed males. They destroyed churches, wasted crops and animals, and burned structures. When the invading forces pressed further into Mexico, the Anglo Texan frontier became vulnerable, in turn, to devastating Indian raids as well as to incursions by Mexican raiders. The Anglo citizens then called on the Texas Rangers to defend their interests against both Indians and Mexicans.

Indian hostilities in New Mexico created odd configurations that caused alignments of the opposing interests.[92] Navajos, Apaches, and Utes kept Mexican and sedentary Pueblo settlements in a state of constant defense. New Mexico's governor, Manuel Armijo, and the Mexican militia were harassed by Indian incursions as the U.S. forces under Kearny approached. Realizing that many feared Indian raids, Kearny reversed his previous tactics and announced that his policy of conquest would be one of protection from Indian depredations. Therefore, he declared, Mexicans and Pueblos ought not to resist occupation because he was offering to bring the "hostile" Indians under control:

> From the Mexican government you have never received protection. The Apaches and Navajos come down from the mountains and carry off your sheep, and even your women, whenever they please. My government will correct all this. It will keep off the Indians, protect you in your persons and property.[93]

Thus, de facto, Mexicans and Pueblos allied themselves with the Anglos for war against the nomadic tribes in the middle of a major war.

When Kearny prepared a territorial government staffed by civil and military personnel, he appointed aspiring Mexican and Anglo entrepreneurs and ordered a military regiment under Colonel Doniphan to enter into agreements with the "hostiles." Initial agreements with the Utes and the Jicarilla Apaches proved to be feasible, but the Navajos continued to aggravate conditions, with several skirmishes occurring between them and the U.S. forces before negotiations began. Once negotiations had started, the Navajos expressed their confusion over Anglo logic:

> Americans! you have a strange cause of war against the Navajos.
> We have waged war against the New Mexicans for several years.
> We have plundered their villages and killed many of their people,
> and made many prisoners. We had just cause for all this. You have
> lately commenced a war against the same people. . . . You now
> turn upon us for attempting to do what you have done yourselves.
> We cannot see why you have quarrel with us for fighting the New
> Mexicans . . . while you do the same thing.[94]

Eventually a treaty was signed in which peace was to be maintained, while mutual trade was conducted and prisoners were restored.

Relations among the three groups soon deteriorated.[95] The treaty with the Navajos failed because slave raiding was not prohibited, and slavers continued to assure themselves of a labor force. When Colonel Price's regiment was discovered to be weakened by disease, poor equipment, and wasted horses, Navajos moved to retaliate and resumed their raiding ways. The unruly character of the Anglo forces toward Mexicans, the unscrupulous actions by civilian authorities involved in land frauds, and competition between entrepreneurs created a general unrest in the Taos Valley. Guerrilla warfare against the Anglos arose as the Pueblos aided insurgent Mexicans. Utes, Apaches, and Comanches realized the Anglos' vulnerability, and Mexicans encouraged the Utes and Apaches to join them in raiding parties. Comanches, Pawnees, and Arapahos attacked the Santa Fe–Missouri Trail, preventing badly needed supplies from reaching the U.S. army. Meanwhile, Anglos allowed Navajo raids to continue as long as they were directed against the Mexican population. Reportedly, the conditions in 1847 were dismal;[96] but as the Mexican War approached its conclusion, the Indian relations in New Mexico deteriorated further. Mexicans and Pueblos were held in check under military rule, while Navajos and Apaches resumed their raiding. Later, the former pair would be encouraged to volunteer against the latter two. Although a change in governments occurred, conflicts continued, with both the Mexicans and the Indians weakening in comparison with the Anglos and the relations between all of them growing much worse.

The Consequences of the Mexican–American War

The United States military government was imposed first; then, it was followed by civil administration. Despite the traumatic shock of the war and the corresponding transfer of state authority from Mexico to the United States, the communities north of the Bravo faced the situation by taking positive steps. However, the process of displacement and the Anglo subordination of the Mexicano also began. Concomitantly, ethnic and racial attitudes hardened and mutually derogatory stereotypes evolved. The questions surrounding the war's causes and consequences were part of the U.S. legacy for Mexico and for Mexican-Americans.

A deeply compelling aspect of the war, with regard to its motivations and aftermath, is the way in which it cast the die for the future of the United States. Visible then were the tensions, contradictions, economic patterns, and foreign policy as well as the attitudes and values of the majority of the people of the United States.[97] But Mexicans and Mexico became such dramatic issues that more people in the United States were forced to consider them than ever before, or, for some, for the first time. As a result of the war, Mexicans and their territories became part of the United States and joined those groups that had been forcibly incorporated into its sphere. Mexicans in the United States would suffer the legacy of the war as well as express it.

The war was also telling for the future of Mexico.[98] The consequences for Mexico were several. The war was a terrible object lesson about the consequences of weakness and division. On one hand, it concentrated Mexico's territory and people. On the other hand, the historical circumstance that a portion of the nation was to lie outside of the political boundaries was henceforth a reality. Now there was a growing sense of an unjust fate at the hands of others. Xenophobia

became a political attitude that underwent a series of further consequences. The possibility of becoming a significant power had been
abruptly terminated, and Mexico now faced the immediate possibility
of becoming dependent upon the United States. Significantly, Liberals, not Conservatives, were strengthened as the patriotic party.

Though the war is commonly ignored in the United States, it had
had major consequences there, and, in retrospect, appears to have been
a Pandora's box.[99] Through the war, the United States ensured strategically, geographically, and economically its advent as a major power
with all of the concomitant consequences for its institutions and citizens. In the immediate aftermath, internal tensions were exacerbated
to the point that the Civil War became more probable. Moreover, the
war for desired and arguably vital territory was brought about in such a
manner that the victor's rights to it were subject to moral, juridical, and
political questioning or reproach both then and later. As a result of the
war, there was now within the United States a region and a people
distinct not only in their ethnic population and history but in language, customs, cultural practices, and values, and one who has more
in common with Latin America than with the U.S. eastern seaboard.
Yet the war was a material success for the United States, even if it
remained a source of criticism; and such success encouraged subsequent
foreign expeditions that marked its evolution as a nation-state.

Popular opinion in the United States at the time ranged from the
benign to the negative, from the astute to the delusionary. The benign
reasons for why the United States had waged war were numerous and
simplistic, and all were supposedly altruistic. They were commonly
stated in the press of the time, and they would be found in the history
books to follow. People were induced to support the war for various
reasons. Some argued that Mexico would so greatly benefit by a U.S.
military victory that war was warranted for that reason alone. Some
believed that Mexico deserved chastisement for not honoring "valid
American" claims for rejecting "the deal" offered by John Slidell,
President James Polk's emissary, and for "mistreating" U.S. citizens
living in Texas. Others were adamantly convinced that the acquisition
of Mexican territory would be but one step toward fulfilling the "divine" plan that fertile soil and natural resources be placed in the hands
of a "superior" people for its beneficent utilization. Still others proclaimed "outrage" at the Mexican "attack" on U.S. troops on May 9,
1846.

Many among the internal opposition in the United States scoffed at these declamatory reasons, labeling them ex-post-facto rationalizations and justifications for what had been a premeditated plan of territorial aggrandizement. Opponents warned the true motives for the will to war were crasser and less lofty. They pointed to the ambitions of the slaveowners to gain more cotton land and their hopes that more slave states would be carved out of the annexed territory to give the South a stronger voice in the national legislature and economy. President Polk was accused of conspiratorially seeking war for partisan political advantages, one of which was to further the unity and fortunes of the Democratic Party through a military victory. The commercial interests were indicted for coveting the West Coast, particularly the Port of San Francisco, to increase their trade with Asia. The midwestern states, or rather their entrepreneurs, were accused of avaricious land hunger for expansion. As for the Mexican "attack," its truth was exposed: the territory was not in the United States; it was, at best, in dispute; and not only did U.S. troops have no business being there, but they were the ones advancing; and, it was added, they had been so ordered to provoke an incident that would solidify public opinion. Such views may be read in speeches, letters, books, pamphlets, poems, and editorials of the time. In effect, and rather rapidly, major causes and motivations for the war were identified in public discourse.

Today, nearly all historians agree that the United States was clearly the aggressor, and to argue that Mexico was the aggressor is to argue contrary to the facts. Indisputably, the United States was in violation of the ratification of the 1819 treaty. A hundred years ago, Hubert Howe Bancroft called the war "a premeditated and predetermined affair . . . the result of a deliberately calculated scheme of robbery on the part of the superior power." Thus, the significant question today is what interests were involved. There was no one single cause, and this issue alone has created a continuous controversy among many historians. Some major contributing causes were sectional, others national: the slavery interests of the South; the land-expansion interests of the West; the eastern commercial-financial interests; the ideological ambience of Manifest Destiny; and the partisan actions of President Polk.

All interest groups involved dealt with internal differences which were by no means simple. To suggest that a slavocracy existed, which conspired to establish new slave areas, overlooks the absence of unity of purpose and action in the South. Southerners, however, did conspire, and they aided the Anglo immigrants in Texas; few favored outright war, at least publicly, but many did desire the annexation that led to war. Southerners wanted territory, but in preferring land that would be fitted for slavery, such interests contributed to the war. The southern involvement would surface after 1848, in the local politics of the new territories. Interests associated with the West and politicians representing it, such as Andrew Jackson, were interested in territorial acquisition; and many were associated with the Democratic Party. The Democratic platform of 1844 and its candidate James Polk were committed to satisfying the land expectations of their supporters. Banking and trading interests in Boston, Philadelphia, and New York desired ports to trade with Asia, and, to a lesser extent, to enlarge a continental trade that had proved lucrative. Arguably, Mexico was a hindrance to these ends.

Manifest Destiny as a program, a frame of mind emphasizing Anglo Saxon chauvinism, held that the "Americans" were by divine assignment the rightful owners of all North America, even of all of the Western Hemisphere. Furthermore, the indisputable ideals of "freedom" and "democracy" called for extension, and the Anglo Saxons were a chosen people. In effect, some citizens possessed a zealous combination of racial, religious, and chauvinist beliefs, which meant they were ready to sanction government actions that realized these views, regardless of whether they directly benefited personally or not. Manifest Destiny also ensured popular support for the designs of President Polk. Given the fact that much ethnic animosity existed in the United States, conflict between Anglos and Mexicans was sanctioned. Yet the anti-Mexican chauvinist views may have saved Mexico from an attempted total annexation, for more territory would mean more Mexicans.

The individual responsibility of President Polk plays a role in the war. Polk undeniably pushed events; the independence of Texas and its annexation were not enough, for he wanted war. There was more at stake than the Texas issue. The assertion that Polk did not want war is an illogical one, for at every step in the crisis his hand was present. He went out of his way to provoke the Mexicans, while protesting his reluctance for war. Although he was in other matters mediocre, he was a minimally efficient president in wartime, and he presided over a victory. The resentment over the war then and later was, in large part, related to Polk's manipulative actions.

The war, like all U.S. international conflicts, except perhaps for World War II, faced a sizable opposition, and to examine it is to better understand the forces active within the causes. The opposition was of two sorts, often intermixed—those who opposed the war on strictly altruistic grounds, ethical and humanitarian; and those who opposed it for some specific interest, because they viewed the war as actually or potentially endangering a prerogative, privilege, or profit. The opposition was heterogeneous in its class and region; and this fact has encouraged many historians to absolve or castigate completely one group or another. The opposition flowed or ebbed as to the sequences within the conflict and in relation to specific actions or objectives. There was the altruistic opposition, who were not many but included some who were notable. Transcendentalists like Henry David Thoreau and James Russell Lowell opposed the war. Thoreau, who went to jail in opposition to the war, effectively dramatized the issue, although he weakened his protest by leaving jail when somebody else paid his fine. Abolitionists such as William Lloyd Garrison saw the war as unjust, as a war fought for an ignoble purpose, and as a plot to further the slavocracy. The traditionalist Democrats opposed territorial expansion as inevitably corrupting local democracy and representative government. Moreover, there were elected officials, such as former president and Whig congressman John Quincy Adams and Republican congressman Abraham Lincoln, who voiced their qualified opposition. The most principled oppositionists judged an aggressive war as strengthening negative values and features already present within the United States. No one expressed positive expectations for Mexicans to be included within the United States, and, in short, Mexico was not viewed well.

In any case, Mexico was the culprit for many. One school of historians, led by Justin H. Smith, have placed the blame on Mexico and see the conflict as a so-called Mexican war. Their approach is, of course, highly selective, patently absurd, and thoroughly ill grounded in fact and logic. Yet the pattern to the unreasonableness of this approach is clear; quite simply, historical responsibility is denied. Despite the availability of a near-unanimous consensus among professional researchers as to who was responsible for the war, every textbook, to the contrary, adopts to some degree a view which at least partially absolves the United States of the blame. To accept U.S. responsibility for the war would entail a radical critique of U.S. evolution, and this is not the purpose of textbooks, which in all societies disseminate a benign consensus view of national development. Rather than accepting U.S. responsibility, the "war spirit" is identified among a minority of the Mexican public opinion, and indeed some Mexicans were desirous of war. This, however, does not make Mexico responsible for the war, for Mexico did not initiate it. This Mexican "war spirit" came about after two decades of U.S. machinations in the far north, including the annexation of Texas. The determining "war spirit" lay in the United States.

Perhaps what is surprising is the lack of consensus in Mexico for war. Some argue that Mexico brought on the war by refusing to sell its national territory, for the United States then had no alternative but to take it. This is a line that reads, "The U.S. exhausted every peaceful means for . . . ," an argument repeated in other matters, to be sure. An additional argument maintains that Mexico brought on the war by refusing to mediate the Texas issue, and the fact is that it did, unwisely so; however, it refused to agree to recognize the annexation of part of its territory and people by foreigners. But these arguments based on non-negotiation call attention not to the several United States alternatives but to the lack of Mexican alternatives, including the lack of an effective Mexican leadership or policy to deal with United States annexationism.

As the charges were enumerated, Mexico apparently was unjust to Anglos in Tejas; its laws were harsh and arbitrary; and "freedom" was denied. Obviously, the area in question was Mexican territory; second, Anglo immigrants agreed to the laws; third, many of these were Mexican, not U.S., citizens; fourth, local self-government was recognized in Texas, practiced to the extent that it was practiced in other parts of Mexico, and included several Anglos who were both appointed and elected officials. Indeed, there was "freedom" in Tejas, more so than in those United States most of the Anglos came from—the southern states. Mexican aggression that resulted in the allegation of "American blood spilt on American soil" was a demonstrably false argument both then and later. But if ethnically and civically Mexico was correct in stopping a United States patrol, this did not resolve the responsibility of a leadership who had no solution to provocation other than to fall into the provocation and thus enter a war that nearly all foresaw would be lost and who knew it was a war fought for annexation, one in which territory would be taken. But even in understanding that the Anglo charges were transparent, the fact remains that a series of administrations had created a problem but had no means to solve it. Yet this compelling aspect aside, there were Mexican public views and actions of a minority involving economic motivations, political strategies, and foreign policy which contributed to the crisis that led to war.

The internal situation in Mexico was complex, a fact which must be acknowledged and one which also was significant for the society and its later evolution. Examination of Mexican responsibility entails several questions for the Mexican side. Nearly all Mexican historians—and one might add nearly all European ones—see the war, of course, as a result of aggression for a multitude of causes; however, these historians do not absolve Mexicans from responsibility. In fact, in some cases the analysis is unequivocally harsh. It is generally acknowledged, regardless of partisan perspective, that although Mexico does not bear primary responsibility, there were contributing factors from the Mexican side. One party or the other, through its policies, increased the probabilities for the war and its outcome. At the time, the Conservatives blamed the Liberals, and vice versa. As can be imagined, the responsibility for the war was to be a significant political issue during the years after 1848. The partisan responsibility falls evenly. Each party continued its factional disputes and conspiracies through the international difficulties and in the midst of the war. Liberals were questionable in policy before the war, and the conservatives, worse, were traitorous indeed during the war. Liberals promoted ostensibly well-intentioned policies even to the point of disaster. Their devotion to a naive northern colonization policy, except for the Híjar-Padres colony, was disastrous. Oddly, California, a comparatively safer area, followed a more cautious policy, while Tejas, obviously an exposed area, pursued a more adventurous one. Neither party measured what a commitment to centralism or a commitment to federalism in a strictly Mexican situation meant in terms of local governance or in the case of foreigners patently taking over a province. This absence of specificity contributed to the entrepreneurial schemes for profit and lessened the local Mexican resoluteness with which the situation should have been met.

To their credit, the Liberals were the party that prosecuted the war firmly. To their discredit, the Conservatives continued their support of Santa Anna in spite of his obvious inadequacies, and they grossly placed class interests and institutional prerogatives above those of the nation, thus undermining the war and even the negotiations on the treaty. The continued Conservative conspiracies and revolts against the Liberal policymakers during the war were actions that were clearly treasonable. Santa Anna was a bad choice, and he was a known quantity—a mob pleaser gushing phony sincerity and rhetorical appeals for change and for unity, a demagogue with no sense of national responsibility, he was the most influential political leader during the years leading to the war and during it. Conservative to a person, the Mexico City bankers, money lenders, and career military men encouraged the war because the government would be forced to borrow at exorbitant rates and to mortgage property, and they would gain. It cannot be denied, then, that a certain type of individual on the Mexican side urged war to make a profit and that considerable profit was made. Army officers, as part of their class position, saw the possibility or reality of war as an adventure, a way of earning promotions and gaining a profit from war contracts. The lack of Mexican political unity and organization encouraged the United States and ensured the results. Yet in spite of the absence of material resources and a trained army, resistance occurred and certainly a negotiated treaty followed. During the negotiations, a few in the national government of Mexico did consider the Mexicans in the annexed territories.

The Treaty

The Treaty of Guadalupe Hidalgo is one of the harshest treaties between countries of the last two centuries with regard to territorial acquisition.[100] The guarantees for the annexed population and their descendants were minimal and delimited. The most obvious changes between the version agreed to by Mexican negotiators and the one ratified by the U.S. Senate pertain to statehood, the exclusion of the population of Texas from its coverage, and the absence of specific protection for church property. Mexican negotiators sought two important objectives in relation to their citizenship and their social and cultural rights; and clear and specific recognition—in fact, guarantees—of property rights. These objectives were stated in Articles IX and X, but they were not acceptable to the U.S. Senate, which rewrote the concerns into one general statement:

> The Mexicans who, in the territories aforesaid, shall not preserve
> the character of citizens of the Mexican Republic, conformably
> with what is stipulated in the preceding article, shall be incorpo-

rated into the Union of the United States and be admitted, at the proper time (to be judged of by the Congress of the United States) to the enjoyment of all the rights of citizens of the United States according to the principles of the Constitution; and in the meantime shall be maintained and protected in the free enjoyment of their liberty and property, and secured in the free exercise of their religion without restriction.

Though the treaty, contrary to uninformed assertions, does not enumerate extensive and specific protections, it is an important national and international document in itself because it does present specifically basic and recognized general rights for the Mexican population in the United States. The treaty is a basic civil rights statement for Mexican Americans at the time Mexicans received constitutional protections. These rights were secured by a Mexican leadership through negotiations conducted under extremely unfavorable circumstances and despite the changes they witnessed in their proposals. Undoubtedly, the treaty is important as a statement of precedent for Mexicans in the United States; in effect, the one, and as yet only, national public document which addresses them. It was also a statement of precedent for the United States in dealing with ethnic minorities. The treaty, moreover, involved a compromise, with most Mexicans tacitly or explicitly accepting the change in sovereignty. The treaty is one piece in a mosaic, and in each of the many pieces of the mosaic of the 1840s there were nuances for the history of what was now the U.S. Southwest.

Summary

Seemingly, the effort and sacrifices to consolidate the lands north of the Bravo with the interior of Mexico went for naught, for this struggle was negated by annexation as were all of the strategems and experiences of political life during three decades. Yet a relative social, economic, and political consolidation did occur as a result of persons and events, and a political and cultural experience was elaborated which would be transmitted to subsequent generations. Despite assaults, the Mexican communities endured because they were more rooted and tested in 1848 than fifty years earlier and, in fact, they could not be uprooted in the next fifty years, or later.

3
The Consolidation of
North American Domination, 1848–1900

Adjustments: The First Phase,
from 1848 to the 1870s

The period of consolidating Anglo-American domination of the annexed Mexican territories and their peoples was to be a time of continuous transformation, tension, and challenge for the Mexican inhabitants; at the same time, the entire United States was undergoing dramatic conflicts and changes.[1] While these changes occurred unevenly and somewhat unpredictably in the vast region extending from Texas to California and from there to Colorado, overall there was an emerging commonality of form and content in the pattern of domination and subordination that arose between the Anglo-American elite and the Mexican people. The period following the Treaty of Guadalupe Hildalgo was for the Mexican communities one of transition and exhibited both continuities and rudimentary innovations. Accordingly, there developed a subordinate social, economic, and political relationship that has continued to condition the Anglo-American, Mexican American, and Mexican relationship to the present day. While this era witnessed many reverses for Mexicans, it was more than a time of decline; it was also a period in which the Mexican people persisted in maintaining their communities in the face of adversity.

The Treaty of Guadalupe Hidalgo ostensibly guaranteed Mexican people the rights and privileges of full United States citizenship if they decided to remain in their homelands. Although ensured by treaty and the constitution, these economic, cultural, and political rights were not generally respected. The Mexican population of what is now the southwestern United States differed from the Anglo-European immigrant population of the East. The wealth-seeking Anglo-Americans had a different legal system, a different culture, and a different language, and they were ethnically different as well. Anti-Catholic feeling in the United States was prevalent at this time, and Anglo prejudice against darker skinned peoples was increasing. In addition, many Mexicans who were already acquainted with terrorism at the hands of oppressive Anglo marauders now became the victims of harsh economic pillage and exploitation. Although Mexicans were not paragons of virtue, they were indeed the aggrieved party in this case, and they were growing increasingly weaker. Relations between the two cultures were not harmonious.

Anglo newcomers represented an American society in which for the civil and economic sphere, major and local economic elites dominated government electoral politics, and administrative affairs were often corrupt. The notion that government should proactively address, much less ameliorate, inequities was rare in practice for anyone anywhere. In any case, the majority of the people could not vote for one reason or another, and a significant part of the work force was enslaved and had no rights at all. Moreover, across the country there was a great disparity in wealth between the social classes; and indeed, a major civil, governmental, and social crisis would engulf the United States throughout the 1840s and 1850s. To be sure, however, there was some diversity of attitudes among the Anglo elite and worker populations, and these included diverse class interests.

Though continuities existed, politics among Mexicans themselves underwent change and greater diversification and became subject to more, not fewer, pressures.[2] Following the signing of the Treaty of Guadalupe Hidalgo and the annexation of Mexico's northern territories (Alta California, Nuevo México, and Texas), including the Gadsden acquisition involving La Mesilla, which was "purchased" in 1853 to form part of Arizona, the Mexican population in these regions experienced political, economic, and social subordination. Now dominant were the social, political, and economic institutions and relations introduced by the new Anglo-American ruling elite and the populations of settlers. In this economic and political reorganization, no area was exempt, with the specific form and pace of subordination varying according to the economic, geographical, and demographic characteristics of the particular region and locality. The process was also uneven in its effect upon the various social classes within the regional Mexican societies. Often paired yet opposite responses—armed and legal action, resistance and negotiation—were concurrent. Negotiation tended to predominate. Underlying these responses was a general compromise, de facto, of acceptance of United States authority and a commitment to advancing and protecting class and ethnic interests according to U.S. precepts. Nonviolent resistance through the exercise, actual or attempted, of civil rights guaranteed in the Treaty of Guadalupe Hidalgo and negotiation with Anglo elites far and away predominated over armed uprisings, confrontations, riots, and other forms of violence. While there were many instances of violent resistance in the history of Mexicans living in the United States, violence was largely a secondary resort used in self-defense and against specific provocations. Even situations of armed conflict were almost always preceded by attempts at negotiated resolution.

As the Mexicans and Anglos were dealing in varying ways with one another, they both engaged the Indians, who suffered the worst outcome.[3] Indian warfare continued from the 1840s through the 1870s, particularly in the areas of Colorado, New Mexico, Arizona, and Texas, occasionally flaring in California as well as extending across the border. The desire for goods and profit remained at the core of such conflict. Individuals such as Mariano Vallejo, Manuel A. Cháves, Ramon Chacón, Jesús María Elias, and even Juan N. Cortina, who led one of the last major efforts against the Comanches in southern Texas, were prominent in Indian campaigns, which also offered the opportunity for profit. Even after 1848 the major brunt of Navajo, Apache, and Comanche raids were borne by Mexicans, yet as the Cháves and Chacóns reported, trade and close coexistence with Indian groups continued. In any case, the question of the warring nomads and the needs of the agriculturalists for land and water were aspects of local, territorial, and state politics. In a few instances, Mexicans were appointed as Indian agents, for aside from the ability to communicate in Spanish with them there was no remarkable difference between them and Anglo appointees. By 1900 both Mexicans and Indians found themselves in a markedly diminished position vis-à-vis the Anglo society.

The incorporation of Mexicans was a unique step in the construction of the United States in the nineteenth century. In principle at least, a distinct ethnic group and its territory were acknowledged through the special recognition provided by a major international document, the Treaty of Guadalupe Hidalgo.[4] These new citizens— and such they were—possessed their claim to the U.S. Constitution, but this document, unlike others elsewhere, did not sanction ethnic recognition. Undeniably, after 1848, apart from the gradual disavowal of the treaty, most Mexicans as citizens suffered the erosion of their rights, which is to say that their rights had been stronger prior to 1848, which should have been expected, given the motivations for "The War." From the first, and beyond 1848, Mexicans were a disadvantaged population suffering from discrimination and abuse. Contrary to rhetorical claims their rights did not improve under United States rule.

Culture and Identity

The conscious expression of culture and identity acquired an explicit, rather than implicit, importance.[5] Social discrimination, cultural suppression, and economic displacement were interrelated aspects of the general situation, all of which elicited affirmations. As material and political losses occurred, the perception as well as the substance of culture became problematic. Throughout the nineteenth century, the people's sense of identity led them to consider themselves as Mexicans regardless of citizenship or of the boundary line between countries, which at that time was less the barrier that it became later. Efforts were made to maintain the Mexican nationality, identity, and culture, which were strengthened by negative contacts with both prejudiced individual Anglos and U.S. institutions and society. The idea that Mexicans might assimilate into the general Anglo population was not an extensive possibility, except for a tiny sector of the elite; some cultural change, however, did occur. Furthermore, on both the elite and popular levels there continued to be familial and economic contact with Mexico.

Although in Spanish the Mexican people referred to themselves as *mexicanos*, they suffered increasingly from the cultural chauvinism that foreshadowed forced assimilation.[6] The first indication came when a portion of the elite, seeking Anglo acceptance, adopted the euphemistic identity of "Spanish." Particularly in but not limited to New Mexico, some individuals among the native-born people eventually followed the example of the elite and used the term *Spanish* to designate themselves in their dealings with Anglos, such as in the phrase "la raza española." Over time, in effect, a euphemistic and self-deceiving terminology influenced sectors of the Mexican people across the Southwest, creating the ambience that gave rise to subsequent terms like *Hispano, Latin American, Mexican American,* and even *Latino.* Explicitly intended or not, these terms were verbal manipulations serving the dominant power's attempt to divide the Mexican people on the generational, national, regional, and local levels. Despite this trend, and in sometimes in conscious opposition to it, the majority of the people, including those in New Mexico, tenaciously and with great pride retained both the name and the national identity of Mexican. Such was the case with the more recent arrivals as well as many of the oldest settlers' descendants, who refused to deny their historical nationality and heritage in exchange for the cosmetic toleration of a society that had deprived them of the economic, political, civil, and human rights guaranteed by both treaty and common justice. The oppositional trend was not pseudo-hispanicism, but Americanization. But the fact was that these people were not from Mexico as it was now constituted, and except for unnaturalized immigrants, they were not Mexican citizens. What they voiced was a demand for the recognition of ethnic preferences while simultaneously acknowledging the importance of a knowledge of English and a familiarity with U.S. practices.

In general, the Mexicans continued to see themselves, and to be seen, as people of specific regions who retained their social and cultural identity as Mexicans even though they were U.S. citizens. This identity, however, was subject to alterations resulting from social and economic changes in the subregions of the Southwest and along the border, all of which were merely part of U.S. economic relations at midcentury. These relations, in turn, reflected an aggressively expanding capitalism, along with a regional concentration of slavery demarcated by racial lines and embracing a very large work force. Ultimately, the Mexican people were incorporated into the U.S. largely as a subordinate working class labor force concentrated in the annexed territories. As a precondition of economic development, Mexican people had to be subordinated as a group and individuals deprived of the ownership of the means of production, which at that time were primarily agricultural and mineral. But this process was gradual and uneven, particularly in areas such as southern California, northern New Mexico, southern Arizona, and the southern parts of Texas and Colorado, where Mexicans constituted the majority of the population.

Leadership and Change

From the first, Mexicans believed themselves capable of dealing with U.S. political practices and were optimistic about their participation.[7] In areas of Mexican concentration, the elite, primarily a large landowning and merchant group and the most adaptable sector, retained its position of dominance within the mexicano communities. Possessing more education and financial means than the average person, they represented the community to U.S. federal, military, and civil officials of the territorial and state governments, and often to private Anglo American interests as well. In the ideological and political sphere, the Mexican elite shared at least two commitments: one, the devotion to Catholicism, which grew more pronounced perhaps than in earlier periods; and the other, the determination not only to survive but to insist on recognition of both their political and social credentials. They also shared a consciousness of local tradition and identity. Apart from these commitments, and as in the period before the conquest, they came to be characterized both as individuals and as groups, by varying political factions, regional and personal divisions, and motivations and loyalties; but now outsider elements, primarily influential Anglos, were ultimately their audience, and a varying community and regional awareness of general and particular Mexican interests prevailed.

In the initial phase following the U.S. conquest, a diversity of opinion immediately arose as to what attitude mexicanos should take toward the newly introduced Anglo political system; for unless they chose Mexican citizenship and displaced themselves, as a few thousand did, mexicanos became legal citizens of the United States. Some of the landowning class took a position of nonparticipation, while others viewed as questionable certain sectors of the Mexican elite who seemed eager to ingratiate the powerful Anglo leaders. In California, Pío Pico signaled that Juan Bandini, Pedro Carrillo, and Santiago Argüello had been less than resolute during the war, with public opinion condemning Mariano Vallejo in particular. However, many of the elite participated in politics immediately after the treaty, and a small minority had begun to work with the occupiers even before the end of the war. The elite, who constituted the majority of the political integrationists, argued that for the foreseeable future, Mexicans would remain subordinate to the U.S. government—its institutions, laws, and Anglo officials. The participating mexicano políticos included members of the elite who had held official positions under the Mexican state and had fought faithfully for their country during "The War" as long as there was hope that the resistance might succeed; other individuals in this group had been neutral, awaiting the war's outcome. Rather than being landowners exclusively, many of this elite combined a variety of economic activities that emphasized business rather than stock or crop raising. Neither for Mexicans nor for anyone else were the office stipends sufficient for the support of self and family. Expenses incurred in holding an office probably exceeded the official renumeration.

Beginning in the 1850s, the landowning and mercantile elite who participated in the U.S. political process were increasingly joined by small numbers of new merchants and professional men.[8] Particularly noticeable were editors of the new and struggling Spanish-language newspapers that served the community by contributing to the creation of a more informed Mexican public. The motivations of these politicians and their associates varied, ranging from purely personal interests, especially economic, and a quest for local political power and the prestige and status it might confer, to a desire to protect the interests of the Mexican public, the people in general, or in a narrower sense, *la gente decente*, the educated and propertied. Probably, in most cases, motivations were complex and mixed, both in rhetoric and in reality, with those most ingratiating to the representatives of the new order being, understandably, the ones most praised by them. Even the most cynical politicians had to make some show of defending the community, while others, to be "effective," were forced to engage in partisan politics with the usual rewards or disappointments in influence and economic power. The importance of securing and exercising civil rights was understood.

Mexican electoral politics soon resembled U.S. politics, and the understanding became prevalent that such politics followed certain rules and constraints. In general, Mexican political negotiators allied themselves with the parties, cliques, and special interest groups of the Anglo political community, which meant that the initiative was generally Anglo. The Mexicans achieved varying results for themselves and their community. Often, they allied themselves with the Anglo politicians as well as with interests that opposed those Anglos with whom they were in conflict locally. In other cases, local Mexicano cliques in conflict with each other allied themselves with Anglos with the same Mexican opponents. This pragmatic style of politics often led to mixed and shifting ideological and political alliances, as well as to partisan affiliation. Actual or potential shifts underlay electoral campaigns with the varied rhetoric and ideologies of U.S. partisan politics.

The larger and certainly acute sectional crisis in the United States impacted significantly on Mexican politics. On the local level, políticos employed the tactics of strenuously emphasizing registration and voting, and delivering bloc voting—tactics that for decades shaped office holding and political influence. Across the Southwest the major issues revolved around property and language rights, unfair taxation and business practices, local despotism and economic monopoly, the discriminatory administration of justice, statehood or territorial status, location of the capitol, the content of and access to education, religious discrimination, and the turn to an East Coast-centered Catholicism as well as the changeover in clerical personnel. Civil equality and electoral rights were a major concern from the first. The right to vote was not automatically granted or encouraged, but, on the contrary, thwarted.

Even so, certain changes did facilitate politics. As a result of technological innovations, communications among the Mexican people were improved through updated methods of dissemination and of travel and shipping. Literacy was on the increase, and though it was still limited, it nevertheless had an impact. The Spanish-language press often contributed to the development of a more overt Mexican public opinion, which in some cases was encouraged or manipulated by Anglos who found it necessary to gain Mexican support for their projects. On the border or on the Texas and California coasts, the initiation of regular shipping, such as the steam packets from Veracruz to Galveston, and from San Francisco to Acapulco, disseminated newspapers, books, and pamphlets, as well as people, from Mexico.

Newspapers became increasingly important political and civic forums, and though they were established in all parts of the Southwest their existence proved to be discontinuous.[9] During five decades, the best known among the five dozen or more newspapers were: *El Clamor*

Público (1855) and *La Crónica* (1877) in California; *El Bejareño* (1855) and *El Ranchero* (1856) in Texas; the *El Fronterizo* (1878) and *Las Dos Repúblicas* (1877) in Arizona; and *La Voz del Pueblo* (1889) and *La Bandera Americana* (1896) in New Mexico. In general, they served as both sources of income and political vehicles for their owners. Specifically, they reflected a wide range of editorial positions on particular public matters. They were united in rejecting discrimination, encouraging education, calling for greater political participation, and sharing a strong interest on matters or materials related to Mexico. Newspapers echoed the mounting dissonances for Mexicans in areas of public life.

Schools, Church, and Justice

Schools and their advocacy were now persistent in their presence, but schooling practices became contradictory in their effects and the responses they elicited.[10] Given the general endorsement of and even eagerness for education, and the greater availability of public finances as well as civic stability, the need for schools was expected to be filled more satisfactorily than in the past, although they were soon identified as possessing some unwelcome aspects. Wholly Anglo in orientation and staffing, they were discordant to values that Mexicans felt were important—their language, their culture, their history, and even their religion—and thus they weakened rather than strengthened the community. Schools also required higher taxes, but in some cases, the benefits would be greater for Anglos than for Mexicans. Mexicans were inclined to prefer parochial schools, where their culture and language could be better protected without the turmoil of debates, votes, and taxes. Parochial schools depended on family finances and were unable to meet the general need; but the preference persisted, and certain Catholic schools in different parts of the Southwest were recognized as being particularly empathetic toward Mexican youth. Yet even before such recognition, in all parts of the Southwest where their population made it feasible, Mexicans took the initiative, or shared it, in organizing public schools from southern Texas to California and serving on the first school boards as well as presiding over those boards. By the mid-1850s they were also expressing the curricular need for bilingual education and culturally sensitive school personnel. Influence over schools and empathy from school personnel was correlated with political strength and numbers, for without these qualities, schools were discriminatory and schooling became a consistent public issue for Mexican communities across the Southwest.

A more basic and developed institution, the Catholic church, ceased to be wholly Mexican.[11] After Bishop Joseph S. Alemany took over from Bishop García Diego in California, Bishop Jean B. Lamy replaced the Diocese of Durango in New Mexico, and the Texas parishes passed to Anglo-European bishoprics, the Catholic church became increasingly Anglicized in both its practices and its personnel. The Texas church presented a more convoluted question of administration; it had been within the bishopric of Linares (Monterrey, Nuevo León) from 1777 to 1839, when the Vatican created an apostolic prefecture for Texas, which was followed by jurisdiction under Baltimore and later New Orleans. A handful of French and Canadian priests came into southern Texas, a few with marked anti-Mexican attitudes. In Texas and elsewhere, Mexicans came to understand that Anglos were generally Protestant and prejudiced against Catholics— all of which became an issue in public life. However, Anglo Catholics also had prejudices, which were directed at Catholic practices among Mexican people. Mexican priests suddenly were withdrawn—as was Father Gonzáles Rubio in California—or they were removed after long and strong pressure—as in the case of Mexican priests in New Mexico—or not replaced when they died (as in Texas). In May 1852 the Plenary Council of Bishops announced a new effort, a plan to serve as well as integrate immigrant Catholics, including Mexicans. But Irish and Italians were served one way, Mexicans another. The latter were not only treated as foreigners in their native land, but they were orphaned by a major familial institution, the church. Belatedly, as the decades passed the church leaders recognized that the weakening of culture impacted on religious loyalty, a realization the church was to experience again a hundred years later. Even with the concern for the loss of religion, the church was unresponsive. But another institutional complex did pay attention.

The new administration of justice was expected or heralded as a distinct improvement, but not for long:

> The Texas Mexicans enjoyed no greater personal security than
> did their property, and what is remarkable, is that they were

wronged and outraged with impunity, because as far as they were
concerned, justice and oppression were synonymous.[12]

Matters were no better in California, where Mexicans soon found that
the administration of justice was corrupt, lengthy, and prejudicial. A
Mexican was more likely to be accused, more likely to be found guilty,
and more likely to receive a harsher sentence. The so-called race war in
1856 was as savage an episode of ethnic persecution as any in the
history of the Southwest. In Texas, a special police force, the Rangers,
which implicitly were in charge of the supervision of Mexicans, established a horrendous record of atrocities. At a more mundane level,
taxes were now higher and more inflexible in their collection, while
the services provided were rendered prejudicially. But the law and
administration were more than codification and procedures, which
were both ideological expressions and often agents of expropriation and
subordination concerning property and social relations. Justice was
handmaiden to economic ends.

    In the economic sphere, the Mexican people were subject to in-
creasing economic disadvantage and despoilment.[13] Mexican rancheros and large property owners who were relatively successful in
maintaining their economic status often were involved in unequal
partnerships, with a gradually growing tendency of adopting Anglo
commercial business practices. Many of the more marginal property
owners were unable to adapt and rapidly lost their property through
debt, fraud, seizure for nonpayment of taxes, and sometimes through
violent coercion or murder. Numbers of former rancheros, tradesmen,
and artisans were already being forced into the ranks of landless laborers. For the majority of the laboring population, however, the
situation was worse. Employment opportunities gradually were being
restricted. Possibilities existed in occupations, trades, or commerce
where Mexicans did not compete with Anglos. Concurrent with the
spread of Anglo nativism and Know Nothing political activity, Mexicans suffered direct violence for economic entrepreneurship, for the
effort to compete only invited reprisals. Such was the case, for example, with persecution in the gold fields; violence on the range, as in the
Lincoln County wars; and the expropriation of a common resource,
such as the salt beds. Most instructive perhaps was the blatant despoila-
tion by Mexican tradesmen working as freighters. In Texas in the

1850s, Mexican teamsters still handled much of the freighting business from San Antonio to the Texas coast and the Río Bravo because they could freight goods more cheaply and effectively than Anglo wagoners. The Anglos, however, wanted this business; and the result was the infamous "Cart War," with Anglo gunmen murdering scores of Mexican freighters and destroying their cargo. In the end, through terror, Anglos retained the most lucrative part of this business. In the California mining regions, skilled Mexican miners were opposed by Anglos who resented their superior abilities and knowledge.

Violence to Violence

Conflict in everyday life naturally provoked Mexican resistance to Anglo violence.[14] This violence was wreaked upon individuals, families, and entire groups of people, and occurred in several parts of the Southwest; but it was particularly endemic in Texas and California, where there were several instances of group executions. The use of Anglo-oppressor terrorism in the Southwest to ensure Anglo domination was not limited to the Mexican. The nomadic Indians were also subdued during this period, and the sedentary Indians were stripped of previously autonomous traditional rights. Friendly and insurgent Indians were treated alike in a long series of broken treaties, which were a regional variation of the pattern in United States Indian policy. Eventually, a special bureaucracy was established to govern Indians and to administer their property. With the Indians confined to reservations, more Anglos entered the Southwest to take advantage of the increased economic opportunities. Mexican political response to the conquest took a variety of forms: legal, extralegal, violent, nonviolent, and individual, as well as collective, cultural, economic, juridical, and civic.

Following the resistance to Anglo invasion during the war with the United States, and aside from electoral politics, Mexican reaction followed three major forms: social banditry, armed uprising, and clandestine organization. Social banditry was characterized by individuals or groups who were motivated by national feeling and a hatred engendered by the wrongs Anglos had committed against their families, friends, or themselves personally; the social bandit sought personal or group vengeance against the Anglos as a people. Because of severe repression suffered by Mexicans, some rose against immediate and potential Anglo aggression as a legitimate and necessary means of defense. Among major figures in Mexican social banditry during this period were Joaquín Murieta and Tiburcio Vásquez. As Vásquez stated:

> I was born in Monterey County, California at the town of Monterey, August 11, 1835. My parents are both dead. I have three brothers and two sisters. Two of my brothers reside in Monterey County—one unmarried and one married. The other resides in Los Angeles County; he is married. My sisters are both married. One of them lives at San Juan Bautista, Monterey County; the other at the New Idria quicksilver mines.
>
> I was never married, but I have one child in this county a year old. I can read and write, having attended school in Monterey. My parents were people in ordinarily good circumstances; owned a small tract of land and always had enough for their wants.
>
> My career grew out of the circumstances by which I was surrounded as I grew to manhood. I was in the habit of attending balls and parties given by the native Californians, into which the Americans, then beginning to become numerous, would force themselves and shove the native-born men aside, monopolizing the dances and the women. This was about 1852.
>
> A spirit of hatred and revenge took possession of me. I had numerous fights in defense of what I believed to be my rights and those of my countrymen. The officers were continually in pursuit of me. I believed that we were unjustly and wrongfully deprived of the social rights which belonged to us.[15]

In California, Joaquín Murieta, usually identified as a *minero*, represented the initial cohort of the 1850s, and Tiburcio Vásquez, a former small *ranchero*, was the second cohort of the 1870s; both were dispossessed members of the Mexican lower middle class, and both organized guerrilla bands to fight the Anglos. Juan Flores terrorized southern California until he was captured and executed. During the 1870s, a few relatives of elite families such as the Lugos, Carrillos, Sepúlvedas, Castros, and Vallejos also took to banditry. The resentment against the foreigner was strong; however, there is scant evidence in the annals of social banditry of any ideas beyond resentment and the desire for freedom that this may imply. Nonetheless, national consciousness was a part of this resentment. A corrido on Murieta identifies him as *"yo soy ese méxicano de nombre Joaquín Murieta"* who rides against the rich and unjust laws; the corrido also declares *"de México es*

California porque Dios así lo quiso" ("California belongs to Mexico because God wills it"). Similarly, the corrido of Jacinto Trevino, a later figure in border conflict, proudly announces, *"Ah, que Jacinto, tan hombre que no niega ser méxicano"* ("Ah, Jacinto is such a man, he refuses to deny he is Mexican").

A second type of resistance was the armed uprising which, after the initial resistance during the U.S. invasion, appears to have occurred only in Texas with the political activities of Juan N. Cortina during the 1850s, 1860s, and 1870s.[16] Cortina was the son of wealthy rancheros of the northern section of Tamaulipas, south Texas, which was incorporated into Texas after 1848. During the 1850s he organized a political movement based in Cameron County that was designed to guarantee the civil and property rights of mexicanos by force as well as by appeal to the governor of Texas, who at that time was Sam Houston:

> Innocent persons shall not suffer—no. But, if necessary, we will lead a wandering life, awaiting our opportunity to purge society of men so base that they degrade it with their opprobrium. Our families have returned as strangers to their old country to beg for an asylum. Our lands, if they are to be sacrificed to the avaricious covetousness of our enemies, will be rather so on account of our vicissitudes. As to land, Nature will always grant us sufficient to support our frames and we accept the consequences that may arise. Further, *our personal enemies shall not possess our lands until they have fattened [them] with their own gore.*
>
> We cherish the hope, however, that the government, for the sake of its own dignity, and in obsequiousness to justice, will accede to our demand, by prosecuting those men and bringing them to trial, or leave them to become subject to the consequences of our immutable resolve.
>
> Juan Nepomuceno Cortina
> Rancho Del Carmen
> County of Cameron, September 30, 1859[17]

This appeal, although addressed to Houston, was clearly a call for support addressed to the Mexican population of Texas. Initially, Cortina was involved in electoral politics with influence over some fifty votes, a significant block locally, which were delivered to Democrats and in support of family members.

While the context of conflict was the oppression suffered by Mexicans, the immediate gist of the uprising was Cortina's animosity toward the city marshal and his accusations against him of cattle rustling, as well as conflicts with the Benavides and Yturria families and, concurrently, the enmity with Adolphus Glavecke and Charles Stillman. Cortina also resented a law suit concerning his family's clearly known land rights. Supported actively by thousands of local Mexicans, the Cortina movement was characterized not only by some political organization, but by a stated political program. Militia, Texas Rangers, and army units commanded, at one point, by Colonel Robert E. Lee were mobilized. Driven from Texas after fierce fighting, Juan Cortina and perhaps as many as several hundred fighters continued the campaign for the rights of the Mexican people on both sides of the Río Bravo, and he proposed rejoining the Texas side to Mexico. There was an extralegal aspect to his activities, but to many as well as to himself he was the defender of a legitimate order. Eventually, Cortina fought the French imperialists and the Texas Confederates in major battles on both sides of the river, and he was named military governor of Tamaulipas in 1870. In the early 1870s, with some of his friends, he explored the possibility of returning to the U.S. side with legal protection. But, at the time, a period of violence flared again on the border, and Cortina was allegedly supporting Mexicans who in reality were defending themselves. Consequently, many Mexicans died, and the Texas Rangers were reestablished at a strength of six battalions of seventy-five men each, assigned to the area between the Nueces and the Bravo.

Juan Nepomuceno Cortina uniquely combined politics and armed response. He was born into a wealthy family in what is now south Texas and was then a part of Tamaulipas; hence, he had access to the elite circle. After the establishment of Anglo domination, Cortina negotiated with the occupiers. For a while he provided electoral support to local officials, but he ultimately chose to defend the rights of the mexicanos by resisting oppression as well as defending his own property rights and claims to leadership. Of all the resistance figures, Cortina had the most explicit consciousness of fighting foreign domination. He put forth a call to arms in a manifesto that contained ideas on political and economic organization. Obviously, the struggle in south Texas had economic, cultural, and transborder implications. Furthermore, it coincided with the civil wars between liberals and conservatives in Mexico as well as with the sectional crisis in the United States.

Cortina was certainly defending his property interests, a specific land grant; but he was also fighting in defense of other mexicanos on the basis of a political platform. He was able to organize a moderately sized armed force, and in the struggle, Cortina was briefly successful militarily, occupying Brownsville and forcing some Anglo landowners to evacuate; for a while, he held power over a comparatively large area in south Texas. Afterward, Cortina lived in Mexico, serving in the Mexican army as a general and as a military governor of the state of Tamaulipas. Though apparently he was initially a conservative, Cortina became a supporter of the liberal party, the government of President Benito Juárez, and opposed the French intervention. His services were commendable. After the death of President Juárez, he was active in the Sebastián Lerdo–José María Iglesias–Porfirio Díaz dispute in 1876 for the presidency, and he was a competitor in the power struggles of Nuevo León and Tamaulipas, which involved not only political but economic competition, including legal and illegal trade across the border that intensified in the 1870s. Years later, in 1890, he died under house arrest suspected of oppositional intrigue to General Porfirio Díaz, despite the fact that, on occasion, he had actually supported General Díaz. Though possessed of resources and a popular base, Cortina was outflanked by Mexican enemies acting in concert, lost power in the late 1870s, and was indicted by Mexican authorities. The election of Manuel González to the presidency, following Díaz's first term in 1880, may have helped him avoid worse punishment than house arrest. Cortina saw himself as a Mexican and as a citizen of the state of Tamaulipas, and he fought for Mexican land rights and in defense of the Mexican people; perhaps he desired the reestablishment of Mexican sovereignty, but after the 1850s, his focus was primarily Mexico's northern and national politics while members of his family continued to be active in south Texas politics.

Conspiratorial activity was sporadic and reported in different parts of the Southwest. More overt examples included the Taos rebellion in New Mexico and the rumors of several instances in California. Ex-governor Pío Pico was implicated, as was Pablo de la Guerra. In February 1848, Antonio Chávez, Francisco Rico, and Gabriel de la Torre were arrested for conspiracy related to a planned revolt, and their bail was set at five thousand dollars. Supposedly, in the 1851 southern California Indian disturbances, Mexicans, including Antonio Coronel, were implicated in planning a joint effort against U.S. rule. After Cortina's effort in Texas in the 1850s, next in importance were the multiple activities of Catarino E. Garza in the early 1890s, which involved electioneering, newspaper advocacy, incitement to rebellion against the Porfirio Díaz government, and transborder conspiratorial activity.

The Mexican Knot

Throughout this period, Mexicans north of the imposed border continued to maintain their ties, contacts, and mutual influences in many aspects of socioeconomic life with Mexicans south of the border.[18] The most immediate connections were those between families across the Río Bravo, bonds created when north-bank dwellers moved to the south bank. The most salient and organized efforts supported the migration of people to Mexico, accompanied by the provision of special supportive benefits. In August 1848, the administration of President José Joaquín Herrera decreed a program and established a modest budget to facilitate migration; and among the commissioners named was Father Ramón Ortiz, who had ties in New Mexico. Perhaps a thousand or more people moved despite the difficulties imposed by U.S. officials, even though again the treaty stated the contrary. In 1855, under the administration of Ignacio Comonfort, José Islas, a liberal and a comandante of Mazatlán, Mexico, initiated an effort to get California families to migrate to Sonora; and after the Vallejos, Picos, and Alvarados endorsed the move, three hundred left. In 1859 another such effort was organized by Manuel Reyes and Pioquinto Dávila, resulting in the migration of approximately one hundred more people. As late as the 1880s and 1890s efforts were announced that would bring families from New Mexico and California to Chihuahua and Sonora. The more successful colonies were established at La Ascensión, Chihuahua, and Tecate, Baja California.

In the far north Mexicans were increasingly aware of and concerned with the intensifying political conflict in Mexico, first in connection with the partisan Liberal–Conservative struggle, the civil wars of the Reform, and later with the French intervention. The victory at Puebla of Mexican Liberals over the French, the Imperialists, and the Conservatives on May 5, 1862, was widely celebrated; and it was commemorated annually in nearly every Mexican community through the celebration honoring the Cinco de Mayo. This date and September 16 were institutionalized in practice as the major community holidays, and they often elicited considerable participation and pride from local people who organized and staged a parade with floats, costumed Aztec warriors, independence heroes and heroines, bands, delegations of children, and speakers at a formal ceremony.

In some cases, the ties between people along the border were the result of the war, with neighbors of the north bank moving across the river to establish a twin community. Some members of the elite owned property in the northern Mexican states, and conversely, a few mexicanos living in the Mexican states owned property in the United States. Others among the elite had transborder economic ventures. These individuals were vitally affected by and, therefore, interested in the politics of both countries. On the popular level, groups of workers, small peddlers, and entertainers traveled back and forth between parts of both nations. The migration north continued through the change of sovereignty, and in California it accelerated with the 1849 gold strike. Migrants had families in the Mexican republic with whom, in some instances, they maintained varying but important contacts. Literature and news of events in Mexico circulated throughout the southwestern communities. Several important Mexican personages traveled in the Southwest or visited U.S. towns: Benito Juárez, Melchor Ocampo, Guillermo Prieto, Porfirio Díaz, Mariano Escobedo, Vicente Riva Palacio, and Justo Sierra, among others. Prieto commented on his visit with Mexicans in California, and Justo Sierra wrote a book on his journey through parts of the United States.

The Context of Politics:
Domination as Economics and Theft

As the U.S. economy and society grew stronger, the period from the 1850s to the 1900s was for the Mexican a time of social, political, and economic survival, with increasing discrimination and integration in the national economy.[19] These processes were formative in the creation of community during the twentieth century. Major elements of the U.S. western economic empire were consolidated, and included large-scale farming, cattle raising, the railroad transportation system, and industrialized mining, as well as mass labor stratified along national lines. The mexicano participated in, contributed to, and suffered all of these enterprises. Social characteristics associated with economic exploitation and social marginality became evident in the community, and precursory labor and civic organizing also occurred.

In the Southwest there was an ebb and flow of labor, trade, and cultural communication in a dialectical process with U.S. economic expansion and domination, and the continuing movement of people and goods to and from Mexico.[20] Internationally, this period was associated with the transformation of industrial capital into finance capital, with the increasing activities of finance capital, and with the shift of the older, direct-intervention style emphasizing direct occupation to a style that emphasized indirect control through a native elite. The United States emerged as a strong international power and as the foremost capitalist state with respect to gross productivity. Not only was the formerly conquered Mexican territory now economically integrated into the U.S. economy, but U.S. corporations were already penetrating the Canadian and Mexican economies on a major scale. United States capital preceded and followed the expansion of the tracks of the Mexican Central railroad from Mexico City to Juárez–El Paso. United States mining interests, such as Guggenheim copper, not only owned copper mines in Colorado and Arizona, but also in Sonora as well as Chile. United States and other foreign capitalists were welcomed into Mexico by President Porfirio Díaz after the consolidation of his regime, the *porfirato*, with the Mexican government and elite acting as junior partners to foreign corporations. In Mexico the regime of the porfiriato engineered a beginning for industrialization, and Mexico became an integral part of the U.S. economic empire. During the porfiriato, certain ideological developments took place that influenced migration and thinking in the Southwest: on the one hand, the United States was upheld as a model society, authoritarianism and elitism were stressed, and in general, bourgeois social and political values prevailed; on the other hand, in all spheres, Mexican nationalism was interpreted as self-determination involving the class rights of labor and the lower middle class and the means toward achieving an effective electoral democracy.

For the mexicano of the southwestern United States, this period was marked by increasing proletarianization, segregation, and impoverished wages.[21] Increased Anglo settlement made Mexicans the numerical minority in areas where they had been the majority for three decades after the annexation. Increasingly excluded from participation in the "larger" Anglo society, the Mexican people for the most part drew together to form their own communities. Toward the end of this period, the mid-1880s, these communities received the stimulus of increased Mexican labor migration, which, although it was a constant process, occurred in numbers large enough to maintain the population relative to Anglo settlement. Mexican migration predated 1848 and continued immediately after 1848, but it was now seen as a labor-wage rather than frontier process. Except in regions such as New Mexico and south Texas, where a relatively large Mexican majority existed, the Mexican population was economically reduced to particular positions within the stable, temporary, or migratory sector of the labor force. Mexicans were employed in the most dangerous and dirtiest jobs and were paid at a lower rate, the "Mexican rate," than Anglos or Europeans for the same or more difficult work. Employment now became for an increasing number of people marginal and seasonal in its character. Workers were frequently employed in labor "gangs" in, for example, agriculture and the railroad industry. In these and other less desirable occupations, if they were not so already, Mexicans were becoming the majority among those involved in unskilled and semiskilled labor, while European immigrants and native-born Anglos were shifting to more desirable occupations or positions. Aspects of proletarianization thus had political reverberations.

Ultimately, domination was a question not of facility in learning "new" institutions, or even attitudes, but of power—of force, numbers, and wealth. Economic and demographic disparities were important in substantiating domination over the Mexican people.[22] Soon after the war with Mexico, gold was found throughout California, which engendered a great influx of skilled Mexican miners, as well as unskilled Anglos from the eastern United States, who were, of course, more numerous. The discovery of gold and the clamor of the expanding population brought almost immediate statehood to California. The Mexican population, heretofore a majority in California, rapidly became a minority. Anglos in Texas continually extended their area of settlement to secure more land under their control and to ensure the proliferation of slave labor. The Mexican population was able to expand for a short time, then hold its own in southern Arizona; but ultimately the Anglo settlements gained dominance in this region as well. New Mexico was spared major Anglo immigration because it contained no gold or rich agricultural land, only rocky mountains and their valleys. Anglo easterners entered New Mexico slowly; they initially tied themselves to the Mexican merchants of Santa Fe. Although their influence and ultimate economic control took time to develop, these were secured nonetheless. The question of statehood for the new territories depended on Anglo domination and majority.

The process of land loss continued through the nineteenth century.[23] The inclusion of part of the Mexican homeland into the territory of the United States gradually stripped many inhabitants of the land that was their main source of livelihood. Loss of this land affected the entire fabric of the community and the vast majority of the people, whether they were large or small producers; but some land rights survived among both the large and small holders, and regional and local variations also existed. By 1859 Antonio María Pico had a solution:

> It would have been better for the state, and for those newly established in it, if all those titles to lands, the *expedientes* of which were properly registered in the Mexican archives, had been declared valid; if those holders of titles derived from former governments had been declared perpetual owners and presumptive possessors of the lands (in all civilized countries they would have been acknowledged legitimate owners of the land); and if the government, or any private person or official who might have pretensions to the contrary, should have been able to establish his claim only through a regular court of justice, in accordance with customary judicial procedure. Such a course would have increased the fame of the conquerors, won the faith and respect of the conquered, and contributed to the material prosperity of the nation at large.
>
> San Francisco, February 21, 1859.
> Antonio María Pico [and forty-nine others][24]

Though Pico's recommendation was not completely satisfactory, it was preferable to what happened in contrast. In sum, the burden of proof was not on the new claimant. It was on the original possessor, the one who had made it productive, which is the party that traditionally has greater equity. The new claimant should face the costs as well as hostile proceedings. Although the Mexican population was growing and at times experiencing prosperity, those who owned land were unable to retain it because of economic circumstances such as local or national depressions, judicial proceedings, and tax assessments, as well as plainly devious means used to remove it from their ownership. Brutal murder and robbery were used in some cases, while tax fraud was employed in others. Legal battles were waged over many generations. Court costs and lawyer's fees consumed the landowner's wealth; even if he was victorious, then, the Mexican was ruined financially and had to sell his remaining land. At other times, landowners were tricked into signing "voting papers" written in English, which turned out to be bills of sale. Federal laws such as the Donation Act (1854), the Homestead Act (1862), the Timber Culture Law (1873), the Desert Land Act (1877), and the Forest Reserve Act (1891) were used by astute Anglos to enhance their use or possession and to despoil the efforts of others. If all of these methods failed, Anglo claimants resorted to coercion by terror.

The Texas Constitution of 1836 provided "loyal Texans" with land rights that could amount to 4,605 acres; because, ostensibly, Mexicans could be eligible, some applied for and a few even transacted these rights. The constitution, however, also provided for the confiscation of land from those who were not "loyal Texans." Obviously, this provision was directed at Mexicans and encouraged their denunciation by covetous individuals. Though not covered by the treaty, Texas, Spanish, and Mexican authorized titles were eventually recognized in the state when the property was placed in Anglo hands and the new owners or their heirs needed to be assured of valid and historically rooted titles. Congress passed the California Land Act of 1851, providing for a clearly unfair, time-consuming, contradictory, and costly procedure. As in Texas, the Board of Land Commissioners decided on validity of title. Over eight hundred cases were handled, and the average length of litigation was seventeen years. The process initiated in 1854 for Arizona and New Mexico, argued to be an improvement over what had occurred in Texas and California, established that an appointed surveyor general would examine titles and Congress would render judgment. By 1880 there were over 1,000 cases, only 150 of which had been reported to Congress, and this body had acted on half of those. In 1891, Congress established the Court of Private Land Claims for New Mexico, Arizona, and Colorado; its requirements for validation were more exact than even those that had been previously enforced. The court was terminated in 1904, fifty years after Congress had initiated action, and its work was still incomplete. In New Mexico, where landownership was broadest in type and entailed the most people, and land rights was most persistent, 80 percent of the grant claimants lost their land. On the other hand, a foreigner to New Mexico like Thomas B. Catron gained complete ownership of two million acres and shared in another four million.

Mexican farm owners were not lawyers, and they did not have the immediate cash for litigation or to continue paying taxes; and the proceedings were conducted in an alien language. They also lacked significant representation in Washington, in the land courts, or in the Texas courts. Furthermore, as speculators, money lenders, and attorneys profited the most, Mexican landholders were pitted against frustrated, would-be Anglo small holders. In any case, small Anglo family farms did not become the rule in the Southwest. Those who said the courts were benign and that the Mexicans lost through their own doings were arguing, in effect, for those who eventually acquired the land. The colossal land transference and the prejudice that characterized it were undeniable, yet it provided fertile ground for scores of various apologists thereafter. Unlike what was recognized by squatters and other self-proclaimed small farmers who wanted no titles, as well as by the Mexicans who had been driven off the land, the large Anglo interests wanted the titles to be recognized and they sought the Mexicans as workers and even as customers for the products. The issue was settled: Mexicans were removed from the land as owners, but Mexican and Spanish titles were salvaged because without such property conveyance would be made on weaker merits, thus potentially affecting resale profits. Suffice it to say that the Mexican responded by going to court, by drawing up petitions, by lobbying that included delegations to Washington, D.C., and also by revenge. Both as a material right for some as well as a historical grievance stemming from a historical injustice visited upon many, the land issue would be a powerful issue or symbol in twentieth-century politics. In New Mexico it remains a vital issue to the present time.

Dominance of the Anglo elite in the Southwest occurred through various means, and not only by direct repression or by expropriation.[25] Large American and European companies invested massive capital in the economy. They comprised part of the establishment of an economic system that effectively closed the avenues of power to the Mexican people. Also important in strengthening this domination were the railroads and the telegraph. Demographically, the numbers of European immigrants increased at an even higher rate each year, leading to an increase in Anglo-American economic and political influence. Other means of domination were the various anti-labor practices, the usurpation of Mexican skills or knowledge, and general cultural and judicial oppression.

As Anglos and European immigrants entered the newly acquired territories, they drew on existing Mexican knowledge and economic structures of land, livestock raising, legal institutions, ranch management, and trade relations. For example, the gold rush was founded on Mexican mining knowledge. The Anglo immigrants had little mining experience and relied heavily on Mexican and Latin American techniques. Ironically, the state of California and the territories of New Mexico, Arizona, and Colorado were significantly influenced juridically by Mexican law. Mexican mining codes, in particular, were readily adopted as providing a comprehensive legal system that was best suited to the mining industry and related issues. Similarly, Spanish and Mexican water-rights precepts and practices were particularly appropriate given Southwest geography. More critically examined were other portions of Mexican law, especially those providing rights for Indians, Blacks, and women, but in some cases, principles were largely incorporated with modifications in the areas cited above. Anglos adapted, to varying degrees, the music, folklore, languages, and architecture of Mexico, while, at the same time, ridiculing and suppressing Mexicans for practicing the traditions of their culture. In spite of the historical equities and the presence of legal rights, the economic avenues of the Mexican people were gradually suppressed. Mexicans were conscious of what they had contributed to the usurper, and resentment over their dispossession heightened their political activity.

Advocacy as Participation

Among several outstanding advocacy figures, some were involved in the political or legal processes exclusively, while others mixed political activity with business or other activities. Three remarkable individuals, Manuel Antonio Chaves, Rafael Chacón, and José Antonio Martínez,[26] all initiated public service during the time of the Mexican republic.

Chaves was a member of a settler and relatively prosperous family who, in one generation after another, had participated in political life, conducted trade, and raised stock. Chaves traveled on several occasions to the U.S. border and the interior of Mexico, and once to California. His first major experience with the tumult of public life came during the revolt of 1837; he was on the side of dissidents who ousted the governor, José González. After a serious falling out with

Manuel Armijo and a sojourn to the United States, where he learned English, he rejoined the Armijo administration in time to be of value during the events of 1841 and 1846. Initially, he insisted on outright armed resistance to U.S. troops, but reportedly, he became convinced that this action was not likely to be successful ultimately. Though he was suspect because of his past services to the Mexican administration, he took his oath to the United States seriously and sorrowfully witnessed the events of Taos and Mora. After some success in trading and stock raising, he accepted responsibility for forming volunteer militia units, first in the "Indian" campaign of 1855 and later on the Union side in the Civil War, where he achieved the rank of lieutenant colonel. His skills as an organizer and leader were widely recognized, as was his valor and personal honesty. A staunch Republican and aggressive businessman, he avoided elected public office, but his brother, Roman Baca, and his son Amado were prominent in the legislature. His extensive and dedicated service in the militia contributed toward maintaining and advancing his family, to be sure, but Chaves also was a significant bulwark in a semi-independent network of local leaders, mostly Republicans who cooperated in turn with influential Anglos when it was convenient.

Rafael Chacón was also of a prominent and wealthy family, but one more uneven in its fortunes. His early education was at a military school in Chihuahua, and he participated in the events of 1846 when he was a thirteen-year-old cadet. His father, a judge for New Mexico, was also among those who insisted on resistance to the U.S. forces. Chacón, like Chaves, though younger, was initially suspect in the eyes of U.S. authorities. He became, in fact, an efficient officer in the militia and volunteer forces, and his heightened sense of loyalty to the United States led him to make not only a valorous sacrifice, but also to experience financial loss for both him and his family. Even so, he suffered keenly the disrespect shown toward him by fellow Anglo officers, and he stated this in his complaints against discrimination. His business life was a cycle of crisis and prosperity, but in the military he was promoted eventually to major and commander of Fort Stanton. At different times, he served as a Republican in public office, both elective and appointive, in New Mexico and, later, in Colorado. Somewhat unique for their relative military prominence and services, both Chaves and Chacón had a deep sense of civic responsibility, coupled with a marked sense of personal honor, although neither had much empathy for the shabbier side of territorial politics even though they were both involved in them.

Father Antonio José Martínez was born into a well-to-do New Mexican family, educated in Durango, and named curate of Taos.[27] He was clearly influenced by liberal ideas, which comprised the then relatively progressive ideology in Mexico; and he was an energetic worker, introducing the printing press to New Mexico, establishing *El Crepúsculo de la Libertad* (1835), championing education and free schools, and denouncing church fees. He served for a time in the Provincial Assembly and was elected to the Mexican congress. He contributed to the conspiracy of January 1847, which led to the armed revolt in Taos, but he was not arrested. Father Martínez continued as a champion of Mexican rights, working through politics, but he did not enjoy the influence of Father José M. Gallegos or of Monsignor Juan Felipe Ortiz. Martínez continued to be a leader in the Mexican community, in spite of arbitrary and biased opposition to him from the newly installed Bishop J. B. Lamy, from France, who eventually displaced the Mexican priests in New Mexico and ensured Anglo-European control over the church. At bottom were politics, as can be noted in a denunciation over a contested election by an enemy of both Father Gallegos and Father Martínez, who accuses them of interfering by influencing the people:

> Mr. Speaker, . . . I have asserted in my notice, and it is perfectly notorious in the Territory, that the corrupt priests did exert the influence of the church to secure the election of my competitor. . . . But I utterly deny that the Bishop was guilty of any interference whatever, unless that could be called an interference which sought merely to restrain the priesthood from the scandal of an active and zealous participation in the canvas. I myself carried to the bishop a petition signed by several influential and respectable citizens of the sitting Delegate's native county, requesting that the priests who were actively interfering in the election might be forbidden to use the power of the Church for so corrupt a purpose. Not without hesitation and reluctance, the bishop wrote a mild letter to padre Ortiz (the old ex-dean) of San Juan, which letter I also carried to said prelate, advising him to abstain from taking an active part in the contest. The hypocritical padre, while professing obedience to the wish of his superior, utterly disregarded the instruction given. He was a zealous partisan of the sitting Delegate, and made use of all the influence of his position to aid him in the election.[28]

The denouncer's words point that Lamy was intent upon doing what he accused the priests of doing. Martínez remained an important and beloved, though controversial, leader until his death in 1867, at the age of seventy-four.

There were many more local leaders among the small producers and members of the lower middle class. Juan Patrón, teacher, member of the territorial legislature, and one of the rare college graduates among the Mexican people, championed the rights of the Mexican sheepherders and farmers during the Lincoln County wars in New Mexico, but his efforts were ended by his assassination. Francisco P. Ramírez, who oscillated between pro-assimilation and ethnically charged injunctions, adamantly denounced racism, lynching, and other injustices in *El Clamor Público*, the paper he published in Los Angeles between 1855 and 1859.

In those years, *El Clamor Público* was a singular voice for the community, and edited by the twenty-year-old Francisco P. Ramírez:

> El objeto de esta publicación semanal es suministrar lo más pronto posible todas las noticias de algun interes tanto extrangeras [sic] como locales, y al mismo tiempo no es órgano de ningun partido politico ó secta religiosa, usara de sus mejores esfuerzos en favor de las necesidades del pueblo.[29]
> [The purpose of this weekly publication is to provide as quickly as possible all the news of any interest, both foreign and local. At the same time, it is not the organ of any political party or religious sect. It will make use of its greatest efforts in favor of the needs of the people.]

As the first Spanish-language newspaper in Los Angeles, it articulated the views of many Mexicans in the 1850s. It was a notably liberal newspaper for its day. It reported on all national reform movements, as well as know-nothingism, Manifest Destiny, education, and the administration of justice; and most radical for Los Angeles, it concerned itself with African-American rights. The modest-size publication was above all a champion of the Mexican, and had definite overtones of Mexican and Latin American liberalism.

El Clamor Público captured the grievances and distressed ambiences of the Los Angeles community. It gave broad coverage and provided a public forum for views that represented the spectrum of opinion in the community.[30] Ramírez was quite emphatically in favor of rights and against discrimination. He also endeavored to recover a local history that was already beginning to be lost. In particular, El Clamor Público was a public defender speaking out against unfair administration, the manipulation of juries, corrupt practices, and prejudiced application of the law. It also sought to inform and instruct the Mexican people on civics as well as the basics of statute and emigration law. An alleged Anglo friend of Mexicans, Assemblyman Joseph Lancaster Bent accused the paper of "disseminating sentiments of treason and antipathy among the native population." Ramírez loudly and frequently stated that though life had been poorer, matters were a lot better off before 1848, and he used a phrase that would be heard again, this land is our land. On the other hand Ramírez denounced delinquency, Mexican outlaws, and poor public service and urged proficiency in English. The paper had its offices on Aliso Street near the Plaza, which was still the center of the Mexican community. Money problems forced the closing of the newspaper in 1859, and for a time Ramírez lived in Sonora and was appointed state printer. In 1872, Ramírez served again with the newspaper La Crónica, which began publication that year, but he was forced to resign even though the paper continued until 1876. Eventually he left to reside in Baja California.

There were many contradictions surrounding El Clamor Público. It called emphatically for political participation, but expressed doubts about the honesty and effectiveness of politics. Ramírez questioned the practice of straight-ticket voting by Democrats, and he practiced as well as urged voting for a straight Republican ticket. One moment he spoke as a Mexican, another as a Spanish American. He made forthright arguments advocating historical rights and equities for Mexicans, the virtues of culture and its traditions, and political and social assimilation as a means toward lessening discrimination. He felt that Anglos discriminated, but denounced loose practices by youth and preached better behavior among them to make them more acceptable. While he called for due process, he urged the summary execution of "criminals." Though he advised Mexicans to be less concerned with Mexico and to understand that the United States was their country, he covered Mexican liberal news continually and even reprinted the Constitution of 1857, which was dear to Mexican liberals but not an item to be found in many newspapers anywhere else. He denounced U.S. chauvinism and praised the aggressiveness of Jefferson and Frémont. And Ramírez consistently proselytized for electoral participation.

Electoral Politics, 1848–1900

Mexican participation in the electoral politics of the United States dates from the middle of the nineteenth century. Their success was dependent on their absolute and relative numbers in distinct areas, since electoral politics depended on majorities. Moreover, as they quickly found out, Mexican candidates and the issues they espoused had to be acceptable to the Anglo powerholder. If they were not, and the political establishment responded with its most blunt rebuke, the election result would be overturned; such a result occurred in Los Angeles in 1848, and Frederick Law Olmsted believed the same thing would happen in San Antonio if the Mexicans dared to elect their own government. Initially, the major political parties with which Mexican politicians and electorates were identified consisted of the Democratic and Whig parties, and later, the Republican Party. As other political groupings arose in the southwestern territories and states, Mexicans moved among the ranks of many local followings. From the beginning, political viewpoints reflected a broad spectrum and were distributed among liberals, conservatives, independents, pro-assimilationists, and Mexican culturalists. These general tendencies continued to be the major poles of Mexican political identification into the twentieth century.

For nearly two years after the signing of the Treaty of Guadalupe Hidalgo, the annexed region, apart from Texas, was administered by the U.S. military government as unincorporated territories, and thereafter its administration evolved in step with national politics.[31] The acquisition of the new territory created critical political questions for the U.S. Congress that were not easily resolved. The major issues concerned sectional rivalry between the northern and southern United States and the issue of extending slavery to the newly acquired territories. Texas provided for slavery immediately after the overthrow of Mexican rule. Northern congressmen took the position that the territories had been free under Mexican law and should remain so by virtue of guarantees in the Treaty of Guadalupe Hidalgo. Southern congressmen believed that Anglo American settlers should be allowed to organize new slave states among the territories. While a compromise in Congress temporarily banned slavery in the territories annexed from

Mexico (except for Texas), the issue was not finally resolved until the Civil War.

The annexed lands were divided administratively into territories and states.[32] The area popularly known as the beloved "valley," the coastal or southern Río Bravo Valley that was previously part of Tamaulipas, parts of Chihuahua, Coahuila, and all of Tejas proper were incorporated into the slave state of Texas. The eastern half of New Mexico that Texas unwarrantably claimed, and which claim was purchased from the state of Texas by the U.S. government, and the present areas of New Mexico and Arizona (with the exception of La Mesilla), as well as portions of present-day southern Colorado and Nevada were organized into the territory of New Mexico in 1850, with its capital at Santa Fe. Areas northwest of the upper Rio Grande and the present states of Nevada and Utah were organized into the Utah territory in 1850. From 1846 on, Utah had been occupied by tens of thousands of members of the Mormon religious sect, who, as refugees from persecution by other whites, had schemed to seize Mexican territory to found a separate religious state to be called "Deseret." Alta California became the California territory and was governed by military government until 1850, when Anglo-European immigrants, with the participation of some representation from the Mexican population of California, organized a state government and petitioned the U.S. Congress for recognition.

Some of these jurisdictions would undergo considerable geographical changes. Again threatening outright annexation in 1853 through the Gadsden Treaty with the Santa Anna government, the United States purchased the La Mesilla Valley from Mexico. Initially, La Mesilla was joined to the New Mexico territory. In 1861, a section of northern New Mexico was joined to other territory, to form the new territory of Colorado. In 1863, what is now Arizona was separated from New Mexico to form the Arizona territory. In 1863, a section of the Utah territory that would later be part of Wyoming was joined to the Idaho territory. In 1864, the area of Nevada was separated from the Utah territory to form the Nevada territory.

United States territorial governments were under the administration of the federal government. In fact, the territorial system has been characterized by some U.S. historians as the "colonial system" employed by the United States.[33] The governors and administrative and judicial officers of the territories were appointed by the president of the

United States and confirmed by the Congress. The territories were allowed (actually, they were required) to organize territorial legislatures, but these bodies could enact no legislation that the Congress did not authorize or approve. Federal authority was enforced by U.S. marshals and, more significantly, by the presence of the U.S. Army, which constructed ultimately over a hundred installations in the annexed territories. In Utah Mexican influence was slight, and the leaders of the Mormon church especially the "Prophet" Brigham Young in fact ruled the Utah Territory as a Mormon theocracy until after the Civil War when the United States enforced federal law.

Texas

In Texas the electoral situation was more partisan and ethnically complex than in New Mexico, but it experienced less persistent Mexican influences.[34] The immediate future for Mexicans was linked to the recent past. During the "republic," representatives elected as senators were Juan N. Seguín, José F. Ruiz, and José Antonio Navarro; and Rafael de la Garza was elected to the House. This was perhaps the most venal and incompetent government ever to exist on the continent. Anglo sentiments generally held that Mexicans were disloyal and, in any case, not white and thus should not vote, although they were not formally disenfranchised. The capital was placed in Anglo Austin, not in Mexican San Antonio. Upon the annexation of Texas by the United States, one Mexican representative, José Antonio Navarro, attended the 1845 state constitutional convention, and he would be the lone representative at the first legislature. From the Mexican point of view, the major aspects of the state constitution declared that the word *white* was not to be used in the qualifications for voting and noncitizens could vote in certain types of elections; and it also maintained that town and county governments were strong. There was no Mexican participation in the 1875 constitutional convention.

In the 1846 exchange on the rights of Mexicans to the franchise, echoes of similar debates elsewhere as well as three common viewpoints were heard:

> Mr. Rusk: "[H]e hoped the word *white* would be stricken out. If, as decided by the courts of the United States, all others except Africans are white, where is the necessity of retaining it. It will be

the same thing, whether it be stricken out, or remain. But if it remains, it may give rise to misunderstanding and difficulty. Every
gentleman will put his own construction upon the term *white*. It
may be contended that we intend to exclude the race which we
found in possession of the country when we came here. This would
be injurious to those people, to ourselves, and to the magnanimous
character which the Americans have ever possessed."

Mr. Kinney: "[H]e said that from the argument of the gentleman from Brazoria, he was more inclined to believe that it was absolutely necessary that the word *white* should be stricken out. All
must be aware that in closely contested elections every means is
made use of to carry the election on the one side or the other. He
had himself, on such occasions, seen persons known to have been
in the service of the country without ever receiving one dollar of
compensation, refused the privilege of voting. He had known such
men to take the oath of allegiance three times, and the only objection made was that they could not be considered white persons;
they were Mexicans." (Weeks, *Debates,* p. 157)

Then came the rejoinder from opponents to the Mexican vote:

Strike out the term *white,* and what will be the result? Hordes of
Mexican Indians may come in here from the West and may be
more formidable than the enemy you have vanquished. Silently
they will come moving in; they will come back in thousands to
Bexar, in thousands to Goliad, perhaps to Nacogdoches, and what
will be the consequence? Ten, twenty, thirty, forty, fifty thousand
may come in here, and vanquish you at the ballot box though you
are invincible in arms. This is no idle dream; no bugbear; it is the
truth.

Talk not to me of democracy which brings the mean, grovelling
yellow race of Mexico, I say the Indian race of Mexicans, upon an
equality of rights and privileges with the freeborn races of Europe.
The God of nature has made them inferior; he has made the African and the red man inferior to the white. (Weeks, p. 235)

The vote in the convention was carried by Mr. Rusk and Colonel
Kinney, wealthy Democrats who experienced mutually supportive relations with significant numbers of Mexicans. Navarro, a conservative
delegate and an alleged proslavery supporter, reportedly said:

He made no remarks with the idea that this question [white] had
any relation to the Mexican people, for they are unquestionably

entitled to vote. . . . He was as much opposed to giving the right of suffrage to Africans or the descendants of Africans as any other gentleman. He hoped the Convention would be clearly convinced of the propriety and expediency of striking out this word. It is odious, captious and redundant, and many be the means at elections of disqualifying persons who are legal voters, but who perhaps by arbitrary judges may not be considered as white. (Weeks, pp. 268–69)

Anti-Mexican feelings remained prevalent in Anglo public opinion. As Colonel Kinney stated conditionally:

I must say that so far as I am acquainted myself with the people residing in my immediate vicinity, their behavior is such as to warrant the trust and confidence of at least those people who know them. And they maintain, I believe, as good a position in society as the gentleman from Harris does here among us; what his condition may be among his own people, I do not know. It is not without reason that I have taken so much interest in the few poor people who are permitted to stay in the western country. Most of the population, or at least a large proportion of that of the place where I reside, is Mexican. (Weeks, p. 243)

In effect, the franchise for Mexicans in Texas was conditional.

In Texas, imperfect civil rights and discriminatory education as well as social and economic concerns were, from the first, issues. In 1850, however, no Mexicans served in the state legislature, and according to the census, Mexicans were approximately 7 percent (fifteen thousand) of the total population. Numbers favored the approximately twelve hundred to fifteen hundred Mexicans in San Antonio, the one major town where their numbers were significant. There, through the 1840s and 1850s they held local offices as aldermen, as assessors, and, in one case, as state representative. Later, their participation came primarily through support for the Bryan Callahan machine that lasted from the 1850s to 1912. Callahan, whose mother was Mexican, was one of a line of Anglos who used their fluency in Spanish and their cordial relations with Mexicans to espouse sympathetic rhetoric and secure their vote to further their own interests. Prominent accommodationist leaders such as Juan N. Seguín were weakened; and he eventually moved to Tamaulipas where he died with his surviving family maintaining a locally respected position. Though its standing varied, the previous leadership continued as new elements came forth. In the 1850s the wealthier-than-ever José Antonio Navarro was elected to the legislature with his son Angel, Basilio Benavides (1860–61), and, later, T. P. Rodríguez and Santos Benavides. The Menchaca and Ruiz families continued to be prominent. The newspaper editor J. A. Quintero was a respected spokesperson for several years. Leadership persisted, but in addition to their own heritage of rifts from the past, individuals now faced the conflicts and the superimposed pressures of the Civil War and the Confederacy.

Texas was economically and politically a southern state. The decades of the fifties witnessed a remarkable surge in its economy as well as the impact of the North–South tensions. Cotton producers and slave owners were a major part of the state leadership; and the state made distinctions among its U.S.–born Anglo population according to origins, income, and partisan loyalties, as well as among four ethnic groups—Mexicans, Blacks, Germans, and Jews. The overall partisan trend, although it was by no means unanimous, was toward a strong proslavery, prosecessionist position, and Mexican politics were conducted against this backdrop. Mexican efforts were closely linked to the shifting larger assemblage of politics; and their participation, while not easy, did occur, with their voting noticeable in some cases, particularly in the towns of San Antonio, Laredo, and Brownsville and in some south Texas counties. The major newspapers were *El Bejareño* (1855), *El Ranchero* (1856), both located in San Antonio, and *The Ranchero* (1859) of Corpus Christi; and as elsewhere in the Southwest, the Mexican newspapers were strong voices for political participation and integration. Class divisions and color distinctions, while they were as clear as they were elsewhere, were placed in a stronger light because of the Anglos' very pronounced sensitivity toward these factors. Though the populace was often depicted in terms of two poles—a small, Europeanized, pro-Anglo, educated, and wealthy sector and a laboring mass of Indian descent, illiterate and culturally Mexican—the reality was a broad spectrum of culture, levels of education, types of livelihood, and political views. In addition to the prominent pro-Southerners were those who were perceived as being opposed to slavery and as pro-Union, the major questions of the day. Apparently, however, their opinions were shaded rather than stark. Generally, they did not advocate slavery nor favor a government where slave owners would rule absolutely—a stance that set them further apart from many Anglos. However, they judged matters from the viewpoint of their own survival and according to their local conditions. Mexicans in Texas were not about to sacrifice for the threatened Union any more than were Germans, Jews, or most of the small minority of pro-Union Anglos.

One threat, the Know-Nothing party, did arouse Mexican political participants across the spectrum. To combat this threat, they joined with Germans and Jews as well as strengthening their ties with Anglo Democrats who opposed the Know-Nothings for a variety of reasons. The newspapers *El Bejareño* and *El Ranchero* emphatically called for community union and for transcommunity efforts to defeat the Know-Nothings. Somewhat liberal clubs were formed for the 1855 and 1856 elections, which included Mexicans, Germans, and Jews among others in San Antonio. The profit- and nativist-inspired cart war stimulated political activity, while notice of Cortina's reprisals dampened it. More significant for the long run, however, was the fact that the Democrats were split, and within these splits were to be found Mexicans. One point of contention was the gubernatorial candidacy of the repentent flirter with the Know-Nothings, Sam Houston, who drew both strong support and opposition from Mexicans. Generally, San Antonio Mexicans supported him and south Texas Mexicans opposed him; in any case, Houston won. The next major election, the one held in 1860, also split the Mexicans and Democrats along Union and Confederate lines. The older leadership, now without Cortina, followed the wavering politics of Houston until eventually he was forced to retire. The fact was that the surviving conservative Mexican landowners shared many views with prosouthern Anglo landowners; but most Mexicans were not part of that circle. By 1860–61 Mexican politics in Texas were Confederate or subversive—the way of Benavides or that of Cortina—but California politics were not as stark.

California

During 1849, in Alta California—now to be known simply as California—a convention was called to write a constitution and petition Congress for admission as a state.[35] Out of forty-eight delegates, eight were Mexican californios, including Manuel Domínguez, José Antonio Carrillo, Pablo de la Guerra y Noriega, José M. Covarrubias, Mariano Vallejo, Miguel de Pedrorena, Jacinto Ramírez, and Antonio Pico; most of these individuals were active in pre-1846 public life and/or they were from once prominent families. Their participation was commendable, but it required translators. Only Mariano Vallejo and Pablo de la Guerra had some facility with English; and the latter was the most active participant.

The Mexican delegates did not vote as a bloc. By this time a working agreement had been formed between some members of the Mexican and Anglo American elites. Southern California delegates, both Mexican and Anglo, proposed that northern California be made a state and that southern California be designated as a separate territory to be called Colorado. Anglo and Mexican landowners and merchants favored this plan as a means of avoiding the prospect of being outvoted by the 100,000 gold rush immigrants in the north. The proposal, however, was defeated by northern delegates who wanted to tax the lands of southern rancheros, which ultimately would contribute to land sale and subdivision. Optimally californios might prefer the state capital to be located in Monterey or Los Angeles, but Sacramento was chosen, which amounted to another defeat.

The California constitutional convention also debated aspects of Mexican law and policies in Alta California, especially those laws that protected Indians, Blacks, and mestizos. Racially prejudiced Anglo-Americans bitterly resented nonwhites enjoying civil rights and basic legal protections. Indeed, objections were expressed by some Anglo delegates that at least one of the Mexican delegates, former prefect and territorial diputado and prominent ranchero Manuel Domínguez possessed too much Indian blood to be allowed to participate in the convention. To add to the issue, some Mexicans were allied to Anglo Democrats, delegates who had strong views on Black exclusion.

On September 12, 1849, the following debate of consequence occurred in the convention:

> Mr. Noriega desired that it should be perfectly understood in the first place, what is the true signification of the word "white." Many citizens of California have received from nature a very dark skin; nevertheless, there are among them men who have heretofore been allowed to vote, and not only that, but to fill the highest public offices. It would be very unjust to deprive them of the privilege of citizens merely because nature had not made them white. But if by the word "white," it was intended to exclude the African race, then it was correct and satisfactory.
>
> Mr. Botts had no objection to color, except so far as it indicated the inferior races of mankind. He would be perfectly willing

to use any words which would exclude the African and Indian races. It was in this sense the word "white" had been understood and used. His only object was to exclude those objectionable races not objectionable for their color, but for what that color indicates.

Mr. Gilbert hoped the amendment proposed by the gentleman from Monterey (Mr. Botts) would not prevail. He was confident that if the word "white" was introduced, it would produce great difficulty. The treaty has said that Mexican citizens, upon becoming citizens of the United States, shall be entitled to the rights and privileges of American citizens. It does not say whether those citizens are white or black, and we have no right to make the distinction. If they be Mexican citizens, it is sufficient; they are entitled to the rights and privileges of American citizens. No act of this kind could, therefore, have any effect. The treaty is above and superior to it.

Mr. Gwin would like to know from some gentleman acquainted with Mexican law, whether Indians and negroes are entitled to the privileges of citizenship under the Mexican Government.

Mr. Noriega understood the gentleman from Monterey (Mr. Botts) to say that Indians were not allowed to vote according to Mexican law.

Mr. Botts said that, on the contrary, it was because he believed they were, that he had offered the amendment. He wished to exclude them from voting. Mr. Gwin asked the gentleman from Santa Barbara (Mr. Noriega) whether Indians and Africans were entitled to vote according to Mexican law.

Mr. Noriega said that, according to Mexican law, no race of any kind is excluded from voting.

Mr. Gwin wished to know if Indians were considered Mexican citizens? Mr. Noriega said that so far were they considered citizens, that some of the first men in the Republic were of the Indian race.[36]

Eventually, after heated debate de la Guerra and the other Mexican delegates were able to secure agreement that any man who had been considered a Mexican citizen regardless of race would be so considered under the constitution of the state of California. However, those Blacks and Indians who had not been Mexican citizens would be excluded, an act meant to maintain white exclusivity. But the debate underscored the assertion that Mexicans were not white and that an exception was being made, one which presumably could be canceled. The California state constitution, apart from citizenship inclusiveness, also encompassed other notable Mexican influences, including recognition of women's right to community property and a guarantee that all state laws would be printed in the Spanish language. This guarantee of bilingualism in state government was later repealed when a second constitutional convention, which had no Mexican participation, was held in 1879, partly motivated to pass restrictions against Asian immigration to California.

Mexican political stances were initially more mixed than they would be later.[37] In January 1847, Juan Bautista Alvarado declined the invitation to serve as interim governor or as secretary of state. Concurrently, Pío Pico conspired to foment dissent upon his return, but shortly thereafter he ceased his efforts. Attitudes of abstention or of dissidence would occur occasionally, but frustrated participation was more common. Mexicans were disadvantaged politically by the radical and brutal persecution of Anglo immigrants; the special hostility of the area around Sacramento, the state capital; the rapid pace of change and influx of Anglos; the intensity of conflict over land that pitted many Anglo squatters against a few Californios; the North–South split; and their preference for Whigs and Democrats when it was the Republican star that was rising. But more specifically, they were hurt electorally by individual challenges to the franchise, which caused an ever-wider disenfranchisement over a period of time. These hindrances, however, were not as notable as they would become later.

Californio votes were aggressively sought by Whigs, Democrats, and Republicans during the early 1850s and again in the early 1860s. During the 1850s californios held every office except those of governor and lieutenant governor and as many as four seats in the legislature. Though the Whigs were strong for the moment, the Democrats gained at least a plurality of support in Mexican precincts, partly because they stressed their sympathy for Catholic voters. They also understood that in targeting heads of prominent or near prominent families they would probably secure the votes of their kin and those who worked for them. Eventually, many californio leaders allied with Anglo Democrat leaders; however, the prosouthern emphasis and Know-Nothing connections made for uneasy cooperation. When Pablo de la Guerra moved from the Whig to the Democrat party he took votes in the Santa Barbara and Ventura areas with him. Antonio Coronel was both an elected official—superintendent of schools (1852) and mayor of Los Angeles (1853)—as well as chair of the Democratic county committee, and he worked with Judge Benjamin Hayes and Joseph Lancaster Brent. At the same time Ignacio Coronel was county assessor, and Pío Pico and Manuel Requeña sat on the seven-man council. Justice of the peace and election offices were often filled by californios, but supervisorial seats were much less available; only in 1852 were Juan Sepúlveda and Cristóbal Aguilar elected, and both men also served as mayors of Los Angeles. Five years later, three californios served as supervisors for one term. On the board were Julian Chávez, Tomás Sánchez, and Francisco O'Campo—and their number would never be equaled. San Diego politics were less assertive than those in the north. Joaquín Ortega, José Antonio Estudillo, Miguel Pedrorena, and Juan María Marrón held the San Diego posts of mayor, treasurer, and assessor for brief periods. Though a majority of San Diego Mexicans were quickly outregistered by Anglos, and Anglos held nearly all the offices, the most successful local political leader was José Antonio Estudillo, whose family was active in California politics until the first decade of the twentieth century and remained in Baja California politics for a longer time. The relationship with Anglos and the Democratic party was unusually intimate in San Diego.

The first three legislative sessions witnessed the initiative and advocacy of californios. Among those serving were Mariano Vallejo (Sonoma); M. Pacheco (San Luis Obispo); José María Covarrubias, Pablo de la Guerra, and Antonio M. de la Guerra (Santa Barbara); and Andrés Pico and Ignacio del Valle (Los Angeles). In 1851 both Pablo de la Guerra and Vallejo were in the Senate, and the latter was nearly nominated by the Whigs for lieutenant governor. The californios did not increase their number even after the Senate went from eighteen to twenty-five seats and the Assembly from thirty-five to sixty-five. Though they were not successful in moving major legislation, their votes were courted, which gave them some influence. Even U.S. Senate aspirant John C. Frémont sought the vote of Mariano Vallejo, the man he had assaulted and stolen from; but to Salvador Vallejo, Frémont was a thief and a coward. The Californios made their gesture to underscore their legitimacy; and though Mariano Vallejo offered to donate 156 acres for the site of the capital and 350,000 dollars in cash for buildings, he was turned down. If this offer had been realized, it would have contributed modestly as a public reminder of Mexican equities in the state.

Throughout the 1850s Pablo de la Guerra, Andrés Pico, and Ma-

riano Vallejo were the acknowledged spokespersons among the Californios, and tellingly so; even though their names were known and they
were respected, none were able to wield statewide leadership. More
noteworthy, however, was the continuance of the pre-1846 leadership,
although several among them had now dropped from public life. The
popular José Castro, the former governor, migrated to Baja in the
mid-1850s and accepted an appointment as comandante and *subjefe
político*. Juan Alvarado, despite his earlier aggressiveness, had no inclination for public service after 1846. And after participating in the
constitutional convention, José Antonio Carrillo did not act promi-
nently again.

Representing a community in relative decline in relation to the
population, and as part of an elite whose wealthy members were also
disappearing, the californio leadership persisted in the midst of the
tumultuous, corrupt, and erratic sessions that were common in Sacramento. In 1852, Assemblyman José Covarrubias was elected by ac-
clamation at the state convention as delegate to the Democratic national convention in Baltimore. Joaquín Carrillo secured the Second
District Court in Santa Barbara, and Antonio María de la Guerra
pushed through a bill extending the cattle-branding season; but the
1855 legislature did not provide for Spanish translation. Between May
1858 and February 1859, Assemblyman Andrés Pico successfully secured passage of a bill for a referendum to form a southern territory,
"Colorado," extending from San Luis Obispo to the south. Voters
supported the bill, but it died in the assembly. The optimum gambit or
illusion was the continuing effort to divide California into two states,
based on the assumption that a separate southern state would be more
auspicious for Mexican fortunes.

In California three transregional occurrences heightened the political situation. One factor was the rise during the mid-1850s of the
Know-Nothings, who were provocatively named the American Party,
though the Californios referred to them as the "Ignorantes." Their
party platform was a familiar one: they opposed immigration, castigated
Catholicism, denounced foreign influence in education, and called for
the exclusion of foreigners from the militia. In effect, they preached
anti-Mexicanism in California and thereby added to this particular
tradition. Pablo de la Guerra, for one, publicly denounced them. The
Know-Nothings did not do well in southern California's local offices,

but they elected their candidate, J. Neely Johnson, as governor and won several other state offices as well.

The coming of the Civil War and its attendant partisan consequences made political life precarious for some californio políticos. Pablo de la Guerra was suspected of harboring secessionist sympathies because of californio resentment to U.S. rule. With the collapse of the Whigs in the late 1850s, more californios were allied to Anglo Democrats, who were, in turn, divided along what came to be pro-South or pro-Union lines. In general, however, the Democrats were identified as pro-southern, proslavery, and anti-Union. This general association blurred the position of some californios on slavery. Some, such as Mariano Vallejo, Francisco Ramírez, and Romualdo Pacheco, switched to the Republican party. But Pico could easily defeat Ramírez for the assembly in Los Angeles in 1858, and Tomás Sánchez, who would declare for the Confederacy, would win election for sheriff of Los Angeles County in 1859. From another front, californios felt the negative ripples of the anti-Latin American, anti-Mexico thrust voiced by Democrats in Washington and acted upon by, among others, William Walker and Henry A. Crab, who organized filibuster expeditions against Baja California and Sonora. In 1861, Pío Pico and Andrés Pico were pointedly required to define their position vis-à-vis the Union; Andrés stated that he respected "the Constitution and the Union entire." Servulio Varela and Tomás Sánchez opted for the Confederacy, and as a result, Sánchez lost a leg in Confederate service as well as losing local political standing.

The precarious times also allowed for revival. A strong contest between Pablo de la Guerra and District Judge Benjamin Hayes reflected the tensions of the Civil War climate. Previously a Whig and then a Democrat, de la Guerra publicly supported the Union and won; while Mariano Vallejo turned Republican in 1856 and four years later was elected mayor of Sonoma by attracting Anglo votes. Mariano Vallejo traveled east to meet with President Lincoln, supposedly to discuss the land issue. Apparently he spent the time complimenting rather than demanding. In any case, this meeting may have been a first between a Mexican American political leader in the United States and the White House. Andrés Pico, Manuel Requena, José Maracel, and Abel Stearns founded the Lincoln–Johnson Club in Los Angeles. In March 1864 a Unionist junta organized by californios met in Agustín

Olvera's home. After they formed a slate, Olvera was elected county judge, Ignacio del Valle county recorder, and Manuel Garfias county treasurer; and Judge Hayes, who had abandoned the so-called chivalrous Democrats, ran for district attorney and won with Californio support. The Civil War crisis provided a reversal of the decline, for the moment at least. Moreover, the French Intervention in Mexico fomented newspaper discussion, and supportive organizing and local patriotic and benevolent societies increased. Mexicans in California were needed and courted, their own community was in ferment, and the leadership was still energetic.

Antonio Coronel (1817–1894) spanned the major part of the nineteenth century, experiencing a relative success financially and politically in Los Angeles.[38] Son of one of the few Mexican school teachers, he arrived with his father in California with the Padres–Híjar colonists. During the Mexican republic he served as sergeant in the militia, as administrator of the southern missions, and as judge. After 1846 he was elected to several posts including councilman, mayor, county assessor, and state treasurer, his last elected office, in which he served from 1867 to 1871. In 1850 his holdings were estimated at 8,000 dollars and in 1877 at 212,524 dollars. He was among those californios who wrote and lectured on civic matters and regional history, and whose papers survive to some extent. His general civic views were echoes of early Mexican liberalism, idealizing democracy as the highest value but calling for an orderly and exact administration that stressed order. For Coronel, democracy was majority rule, and "tranquility" was not only to be expected but imposed if necessary, for anarchy was the worst possible civic condition, signaling downfall or disintegration. Governance was hierarchical from the local to the national levels, but it must be based on majority rule. Coronel distinguished between the moral sphere of justice, humanitarianism and reason, and the political sphere of acquired rights, which presumed their dispensation and exercise. These were the general views of an individual who was seasoned in politics, aware of the increasing minority status of the people he represented and the persecution they faced because he himself had faced violence in the gold fields. In another period a Mexican leader with numbers on his side might propound such views with a clearer advantage to be gained; Coronel, however, did not circumscribe himself to arguing from a minority position.

Like some other Californios, Coronel felt strongly about the Spanish language. He either did not bother to learn English or refused to use what English he knew; in any case, his disregard for English cost him politically because he was criticized for it. Notably, his arguments for using Spanish in government affairs were not based on sentiment or historical rights, but on effective public service and the economic interests of the state. Having assisted his father in the latter's school from 1846 to 1855, he and others petitioned in 1856 for a bilingual curriculum in the Los Angeles schools; the petition failed, but in 1872 he provided the majority of the funds for the Spanish-language *La Crónica*, which he published for five years. He also directed the Hispano American Society and the 1881 centennial commemoration. Coronel was among those who after some vacillation became a U.S. citizen after 1848. He used the term *Spanish* early as a community referent, yet in the best-known picture of him in his old age, he is reading history next to his Mexican flag and sword.

Throughout the 1850s and 1860s, though their Mexican constituency was only 15 percent of the state population and declining, the Mexican elite in California, in conjunction with Anglo politicians, were able to be elected representatives to the state legislature as well as to local offices. Seats declined, but pockets of strength remained. For two decades Santa Barbara was a Mexican political stronghold in California. Between 1865 and 1870 Mexicans held the offices of mayor, city councilmen, county board of supervisors, and district judge, and they held the majority in the grand jury and on the Democratic county committee. Mexicans retained local power because of an economic base, able leadership, and an organized vote in conjunction with a divided Anglo vote.

Santa Barbara continued to be a Mexican political social milieu. With the admission of California into the United States,[39] the elite Mexican políticos, together with the majority of the Mexican voters in the city, voted Democrat and dominated the political arena. However, the growing Anglo-American population repeatedly attempted to overturn the traditional, long-standing political dominance of the rancheros and the Mexican electorate. And when the Anglos achieved numerical ascendancy they finally were able to break the political hold that Mexican politicians in Santa Barbara had maintained until the early 1870s.

The durability of the Santa Barbara political alliance or system was based primarily on two aspects. One factor involved the electoral

allegiance to the California Mexican elite that was the result of kinship, compadrazgo ties, and employer relationships among the laboring
majority. This alliance survived in the face of Anglo attempts to
weaken the ethnic, social, and religious ties of the Mexican population. The other factor was the conscious effort of the elite políticos and
their Mexican constituency to preserve their society by grasping the
reins of political power, which meant the conscious exclusion of any
meaningful Anglo influence. Even when the balance of voting numbers shifted in favor of the Anglos, the Mexican voting bloc ensured
that their own would be placed in the most important offices (sheriff,
tax collector, judge). Or, as in the late 1860s, the Mexican electorate
formed modest and tenuous alliances with the laborers and small merchants of other ethnic groups in order to offset the voting power of
prejudiced Anglos who were led by their wealthy.

Santa Barbara remained for the longest period of time the stronghold of Mexican political and social influence in southern California.
Senior leadership was exercised by Pablo de la Guerra, Joaquín Carillo,
José María Covarrubias, and Antonio María de la Guerra. Pablo de la
Guerra served as mayor several times and was also district judge. All
together, Pablo de la Guerra served more years in California's elected
public offices than any other Mexican, a record not to be exceeded for
one hundred years. The inevitable increase of the Anglo population
forecast the diminishing significance of local mexicanos. By 1873, even
Mexican bloc voting could not prevent the election of Anglos to key
county and city posts, and Mexican leverage decreased each election
year. Once Anglos were able to gain important county, municipal,
judicial, and law enforcement positions, they actively sought to destroy
the leadership base of the alliance, and once the leadership became
weaker some Anglos sought to limit the rights of Mexican voters. The
concentration of Mexican votes into a single ward or precinct meant
that mexicanos would no longer be able to exert influence on citywide
politics; however, they could elect one representative from their ward
to sit on the council. By the 1880s mexicanos had become politically
constrained, as attested by their reluctance to register; spokespersons
became rare. In the twentieth century, however, they did elect a
Mexican representative each time from a barrio ward.

The political accomplishment of Santa Barbara mexicanos during
the period 1850–70 may be seen as an attempt to preserve a Mexican
political space amid a period of transition throughout the entire state.

This effort was a functional front, based upon traditional and contemporary relationships and values, against the encroachment of Anglos into their community. For the Anglos, the move toward political dominance was concurrent with their attempt to establish economic hegemony over the area's Mexican populace. By controlling politics, Anglos facilitated change in the local and regional economic systems. Next followed the act of dislodging Mexicans from the schools and implanting ethnocentric values in the local society.

A process of Mexican displacement began in many places, although an alliance between the Anglo and Mexican elite continued on the surface. His wealth, education, and past services did not extend the political life of Mariano Vallejo beyond the 1860s, when a Mexican base north of Santa Barbara ceased to exist. Compromise or trade-offs often did not work for the elites, and alliances with Anglos were short-lived and dependent upon the Anglos enjoying the advantage. In California many of the Mexican elite lost their fortunes, while a minority tried to conceal their nationality or were assimilated through intermarriage. This latter route provided familial survival of sorts; for example, eight of Vallejo's children married non-Mexicans. But most Mexican elite were forced eventually into the lower-middle class or the working classes, and many lived to lament their optimism once their country had experienced annexation to the United States. There were also many others who were neither optimistic or pessimistic about what to expect under foreign rule, but who sought to protect their interests and those of their kindred even though office holding continued and the Mexican vote counted for patronage or some special consideration. In sum, the electoral experience of the California elite was generally frustrating in contrast to what occurred in New Mexico.

New Mexico

From the beginning of the occupation in New Mexico, Mexicans were active participants in political issues.[40] Occupation was an immediate issue. Military government in New Mexico was unpopular to many because it limited the expectations for civil and political participation. The supporters of this government were those who profited from it. Postponement of territorial status was due to national north–south issues rather than local circumstance, and, in any case, statehood was preferred. A critical issue was the reduction of the historical area of

New Mexico into several territories and the loss of about a half-million acres to Texas, which at one time had claimed the area. Division reduced the numbers of those who remained in New Mexico and transformed the Mexican population in what were now small minorities in Colorado and Arizona. New Mexicans opposed these fragmentations; among them were some Whigs, more Democrats, and many more Republicans. The issue pitting the military versus the territorial forms of government coalesced some factions. However, the origins of partisan affiliations were a mixture of choices. For example, some who were later staunch Republicans, such as the Vigils, Oteros, and Armijos, were first sympathetic to the Whigs. The Republicans, which included most, though not all, of the elite, were the dominant trend, a trend that continued to the end of the territorial period. Challengers therefore were Democrats, though Republicans had more patronage or benefits to offer since Republicans often predominated in Washington, D.C.

Upon attaining territorial status, New Mexico possessed a relatively large native Mexican population, an economic base for the surviving elite, and a means for delivering the Mexican vote. In major parts of the territory, Mexicans outregistered and outvoted Anglos, which made possible a moderately strong political participation supported by the major parties, who could not dispense with the Mexican vote. Furthermore, an astute and experienced leadership was in place. Tellingly, the elite persisted from the Mexican through the U.S. periods, as individuals or members of families who had held office during the colonial and Mexican periods continued to be prominent through the late nineteenth century. Especially significant was the fact that few of the elite sent its offspring to midwestern and eastern colleges and universities. The Mexican elite thus maintained a tradition, reinforcing the proper educational credentials and possessing the skills, wealth, and local mass support to win political elections. Donaciano Vigil, who had held office previously, was appointed interim territorial secretary, and briefly was interim governor; and after Albino Chacón refused, Antonio José Otero was appointed one of three territorial judges. Later, in 1861, Miguel Antonio Otero, Sr., was appointed secretary of the territory by President Lincoln. Members of the Pino, Chávez, Chaves, Ortiz, Baca, and Armijo families who had sought to resist U.S. forces were active in post-1846 politics. Former resistance leaders Diego

Archuleta and Antonio José Martínez honorably served fourteen years in the Territorial Assembly.

Mexicans held elected and appointed office at several levels throughout the late nineteenth century. Several held judgeships, while others were elected locally to the Territorial Assembly; still others held intermittently, from 1850 to 1911, the office of territorial representative in Congress, as well as the governorship of the territory on two occasions. They also extended their participation across state lines politically and economically, moving primarily into Colorado but into Arizona as well. Participation in the militia and volunteer regiments was important during the Civil War and in Indian campaigns, it became a means of revalidating political credentials with the new order. More substantive, however, was the ability to make profits from the trade with the military and other operations.

Familiar with the law, Donaciano Vigil, if not quite originating precedents, added to the stamp of certain political practices. His appointments by the U.S. military as secretary and interim governor were related to the public opposition to occupation, from which he benefited. He was also adept at telling U.S. authorities what they wanted to hear, which were their own preferences and biases. Vigil also turned his political office to economic advantage. Moreover, he acquired land to sell rather than to keep. In sum, Vigil continued his checkered politics with financial and political success, moving politically to his own advantage during the Mexican republic, as he had done under U.S. rule. To some he was an opportunist and scoundrel, but to others he was a statesman and businessman.

New Mexican politics were a convolution of many different aspects. Apart from frequent participation and electioneering in New Mexico, substantive conflict arose that involved significant numbers, questions of leadership, and political issues—all of which lay outside electoral parameters. Nevertheless, electoral politics were important and visible, requiring interaction across ethnic lines and some degree of interethnic equality, and more so in politics than in economics, in the professions, or in education. Consciously, the political system defended communities and families, resulting in the so-called patrón system, which involved an area's farmers, sheepherders, laborers, its leading family, and secondary families which were often kin, cooperating to maximize the vote for targeted offices and in behalf of agreed-upon individuals. Overall, it was a practical exchange arrangement, but one in which some gained more than others. Because New Mexicans bene-fited from the patrón system, but lost outside of it, maintaining it was a rational choice. Nonetheless, there was opposition to *patrones*. When leadership rivalries occurred, they were exploited by Anglo leaders. In New Mexico, as in the United States as a whole, there were voting blocks and patronage along partisan as well as ethnic and economic lines. The so-called race issue, Mexican versus Anglo, united many Mexican people. Anglos sought to keep the issue quiet, as did their Mexican spokesmen; yet it was acknowledged aggressively or defen-sively, for as Miguel Antonio Otero Sr., noted:

> For many years past there have been two parties in that Territory—one calling itself the Mexican party, and indulging in great hostility against the institutions of these States; the other de-nominated the American party, and looking to annexation as the only security from the perpetual discords and civil wars of Mexico. These visions commenced before the late war between the two countries, and continue to the present day as the fundamental dis-tinction between existing parties. I confess I have always been at-tached to the institutions of this country, and to have been taught from childhood to look to this quarter for the political regeneration of my people. Though of unmixed Spanish descent, I received my education in this country; and I am happy to entertain the thought that I am the first native citizen of that acquired Territory who has come to the Congress of our adopted fatherland, and address it in the language of its laws and its Constitution. And I am proud to know that my own people at home do not consider me the less qualified, on that account, to represent them in this body, what-ever may be the opinion of the sitting delegate. [41]

In this case, the reference was by a Republican *agringado* to a pro-Mexican Democrat, who was also a priest. One cross-cutting aspect was the identification of those who were more pro-Anglo and those more pro-Native, and among these were hispanophiles and *mexicanistas*. Religious bias and political differences were also related to religious differences. As before 1848, priests like Fathers Gallegos, Ortiz, and Martínez continued to participate as leaders. All were Democrats; yet Mexicans did not slight Republican vote allegiance on the basis of Catholicism alone, for being Republican held its own attractions. Because Republicans were the dominant party in New Mexico, dissidents often went over to the Democrats. In any case, Mexicans were members of both parties, and the number of Mexican Protestants increased over time.

One of the early issues calling for reflective response was the threat of annexation by the state of Texas, which was antedated by the initiative of President Taylor to seek statehood for New Mexico concurrently with California. A group known as the Alvarez faction, with which the Santa Fe *New Mexican* newspaper was associated, sought to promote statehood. To thwart the Texas move as well as to initiate statehood proceedings, a convention was called and a constitution drawn up with a strong statement on education. The conflict over state versus territorial status was strong, but the ethnic and partisan lines involved were fluid. Statehood engendered political organizing, and large meetings were held in 1848, 1849, and 1850. Generally, the military authorities were unfavorable to statehood, failing in California, they did prevail in New Mexico. Apart from James S. Calhoun in 1850, Mexicans such as Miguel Antonio Otero, Sr., were leaders in the fight for statehood as well as playing a significant role in arguing for its delay. Hispanos' pro- or anti-statehood position depended on the content of the measure, amounting to a rather judgmental approach. Moreover, Hispanos did not hold a universal position, and nativists often conflicted with assimilationists. The argument that Hispanos preferred statehood because of office possibilities is a partial view, as is the contention that Anglos preferred a territory because of access to appointments. At first, the perceived antislavery sentiment of New Mexico delayed progress toward statehood in Congress. More to the point, ethnicity and religion kept New Mexico from attaining statehood through an act of Congress. Furthermore, most large financial interests opposed statehood because of the likelihood of higher taxes.

The "Omnibus Compromise of 1850" provided territorial status as a national compromise; locally, it limited Hispano rights. The positions of governor, secretary, U.S. district judges, U.S. attorney, surveyor general, and U.S. marshal were appointed by the president, while other appointments were made by the governor. Territorial elections determined the legislature; the upper house, or Territorial Council, numbered thirteen seats, and the Territorial House, or Assembly, twenty-four seats. All laws passed were submitted to Congress for approval. A territorial delegate elected for two years could debate but not vote in Congress, but the influence of the delegate's position was nonetheless considerable, especially if his or her party affiliation coincided with the president's. Budget allocations, laws, regulations, and their application and appointments were at stake. Suffrage was limited to "white" males over twenty-one, who were one-year residents. In practice, Anglos received appointment benefits and Hispanos local voting benefits. There were recurring differences between appointed Anglos and elected Hispanos. New Mexico Hispanos, in effect, had restricted local self-government. However, the Spanish language was used in debate, and materials were published in Spanish. A majority of the elected Mexican members belonged to a circle of some twenty families, but they were divided in their partisan and regional allegiances. According to W. H. H. Davis, these representatives "cut quite a respectable figure and played their part with considerable credit to themselves and their constituents." The condescending Davis could not say the same about the Anglo políticos, who were often rough and corrupt. Under territorial status, appointive power was the source and focus of influence; thus, this political circumstance was reminiscent of early times. The first territorial delegate, Major R. H. Weightman, was elected in 1850 with Hispano support, which was a result of his strong views in favor of statehood. A more popular choice came in 1852, with Father José M. Gallegos, who did not, however, have the confidence of the key elite. This elite elected their own—among them, Miguel A. Otero, Sr., who served from 1855 to 1861; Francisco Perea, from 1863 to 1865; and J. Francisco Chaves, from 1865 to 1871. Of these three, the first benefited most financially and had the most reciprocal ties with Anglo capitalists; the second was a confirmed elitist conservative who disliked Anglo intrusion and development; and the last, charismatic and respected, practiced the most varying politics.

Blocs and lobbying soon solidified. Up to 1864 there was a fairly judicious legislative process; then bribery appeared in 1864, related to the Indian question of Bosque Redondo and the influence of General James H. Carleton. Anglos invariably chaired the party's territorial committees, whether Democrat or Republican, and Mexicans headed county committees. While the interests of prominent families were protected, party strife as well as party loyalty divided the leadership more frequently than ethnic distinctions. Nevertheless, independent leadership and some opposition to these groups were recurrent, and the office of territorial delegate was often a cause of contention. An early chief figure was the priest José M. Gallegos, a Democrat who had a large following and periodically ran for office, often contesting the current status quo, although he too was from an influential family. Colonel J. Francisco Chaves, a Republican, also expressed some political resistance to maneuvers by Anglos within the elite. His father had resented U.S. intrusion and reportedly told his son to prepare to defend his people; he was sent to school in Chihuahua, St. Louis, and New York, and after serving as territorial delegate in 1865 and 1869, he was defeated in 1871. This led to the Mesilla riot, a conflict between Gallegos and Chaves supporters in which nine were killed and fifty injured, mostly Hispanos. For Chaves the "race" issue was clear: positively, it indicated solidarity and equity; negatively, it meant discrimination and unfairness. Often, assertive Mexican Democrats or Republicans were faced with opposition.

A major opponent was Thomas B. Catron, chair of the Republican Territorial Committee, and after the 1860s the major Anglo political figure in New Mexico, one who enjoyed cooperative relations with some Mexicans. Catron became the central figure in the so-called Santa Fe Ring, a network devoted to using politics to make money, and which included the well-connected Republican Stephen Elkins, several governors, and the leading publisher Max Frost. Ring members argued that they promoted economic development, and one focus attempted to control elected and appointed offices to secure contracts, concessions, and property. Because of Washington, and East Coast connections, and a local alliance, the Ring worked with local politics, even though it was corrupt and often brutal. It did not, however, control local Mexican politics, which were established by the late 1860s and continued after the late 1890s when the Ring declined. At one time, Catron was profitably associated with Donaciano Vigil. Both became immense landowners who often manipulated laws, deeds, and tax debts, and in several instances, both appropriated entire land grants. Vigil, in turn, profited politically from friendship with a locally well-known woman, "La Tules."

In New Mexico, Doña Gertrudis Barcelo, or "La Tules," allegedly an influence on Governor Armijo and others, was at least within the information circuit of politics and business, all of which she used to advance herself.[42] Upon their arrival, North Americans took both a moralistic and opportunist attitude toward La Tules: she was scorned, but her money was borrowed and her information deployed. Among

Mexican patriots, she was suspected to have worked against the plot of the revolt against North American occupation in 1846, supported by the opponents of U.S. authority, along with Donaciano Vigil, who was also a major player of events in 1837. Her roles as a known gambler and successful businesswoman was not incompatible with being an influential lady—a combination some North Americans found disconcerting but useful. What made her important was her astuteness, her money, and her contacts. From the first, she and other Mexican women drew attention from Anglo commentators.

Women and Political Socialization

Along with domination, mutual impressions and evolving stereotypes were a part of the milieu impacting on politics and contributing to a certain socialization for generations after 1846.[43] As part of the entire Mexican spectrum, women were notably a focus of this socialization and subject to all of its contradictions and paradoxes. They were upheld as "exceptions"; they were denigrated; they were manipulated and treated like all Mexicans. Anglos pronounced judgment, declaring who was "good" or "bad"—that is, who was serviceable—among women and then between men and women.

As the North Americans had more contact with the Mexicans, their impressions gradually grew more detailed. The first mention of frontier women occurred in the nonfiction of the 1840s that was written by travelers to northern Mexico. Particular attention was given to their manners and dress, and they were viewed as coarse and unfeminine yet, at the same time, as exotic. They were unfavorably compared with the supposedly sedate Anglo women, with Mexican women seeming flamboyant and uninhibited. Their customs of smoking and gambling, traditionally male activities in Anglo society, allegedly appalled provincial Anglo women, though these practices were common in continental Europe. Calvinists, in particular, thought the women were immodest because of their light attire and their predilection for dancing and social festivities. Other Anglo views provided contrasts, focusing favorably on the women's behavior and their appearance in contrast to that of the males. Qualities singled out included Mexican women's strong common sense, their natural sympathy for suffering people, and their social grace and hospitality. Unless they

:nt, Mexican men were the women's opposites. Although
ere was and continued to be a distinction between good
can males and females, and women were somewhat less
than the males, North American hostility extended from
: to all Mexicans. As one writer declared, "They were
of Mexican Government and Catholicism, and they
ans as indolent, bigoted, cheating, dirty, cowardly, and
)ften, North Americans who had the least contact with
)unced them most virulently. Francis Parkman, the his-
urneyed west in 1846 as a young man, was one who
.... oetween the sexes by referring to Mexican women as
"Spanish" and to men as "Mexican." Though this was the extent of the
exemption, it was telling. After the Mexican annexation, the women,
like the men, experienced prejudices from the Anglo Americans; but
there were particular exceptions.

A few women were exceptional for their fortunes and their social
status,[44] which depended generally on some legacy from the pre-1848
period. These women increased their social status when they confirmed
their land, for property allowed both self-reliance and more independence. After 1850 only exceptional women succeeded in securing their
land grants and ultimately a patent from the United States. California's
constitution provided women the right of property, both real and
personal, that was obtained before, during, and after marriage, either
by inheritance or as a gift. Other women elsewhere obtained similar
patents from the U.S. government; and a few of these women also
performed exceptional service. The respected, hardworking Eulalia
Elias ran the first major cattle ranch in Arizona when it was open
frontier; and Rosa Ortiz established and operated a private school for
Mexican children.

Since women could not vote under either the Mexican or U.S.
constitutions, their formal political status did not improve under Anglo
dominance, in contrast with the traditional practices and legal rights
extant in Mexican society. Worse, in addition to gender and class
discrimination, women faced anti-Mexican attitudes, and though they
might be tolerated more than the male, there were accompanying
economic and schooling consequences. To be sure, change occurred in
the economy and property laws, but certain social expectations also
continued.

Intermarriage for advantage was a fact, and since there was a need both to affirm some historical claims and to deny others, status-conscious and prodevelopment writers of the late nineteenth century constructed a mythical view of their times to rationalize some intermarriage and thereby claim Anglo status as "pioneer," thus blurring Mexican claims to historical equities. The romanticizations of an imagined pre-1848 "Spanish society" focused on "history," which, without much difficulty, were claimed by Anglos as their heritage, usually through a woman. This process denied the Mexican pioneers, to be sure, but it also particularly obscured the role of Mexican women as proactive builders of the frontier, as well as their role in resistance to the Europeans. Spanish fantasy history therefore developed because it served prominent Anglos.

The reality of intermarriage entailed several forms of social relations as well as political results.[45] All social relations between Mexicans and Anglos connected class, gender, and nationality. In one extreme, the situation exhibited subjugation through prostitution, and along lines of nationality. Intermarriage often resulted from the availability of wealthy Mexican women and the lack of Anglo women, but intermarriage was disapproved as more Anglo women became available. In the annexation period, marriage between Anglos and Mexicans was based on economic and political advantage: the Mexican family hoped for legal and political protection, with the Anglo receiving wife and property since Mexican daughters could inherit and possessed rights to the family property that were coextensive with those of the male siblings. Concurrent with intermarriage was a tendency among a part of the elite class to negotiate with Anglos for their mutual benefit. Children during the first generation of intermarriage were influenced socially and religiously by Mexican culture, but this legacy was weaker for the second generation.

Even in intermarriage there was still ethnic discrimination, for mixed marriages did not indicate ethnic rapport. Whether the Anglo married for love or security, he only expeditiously accepted his wife's culture, religion, and relatives. Nevertheless, intermarriage occurred between Mexican women and Anglo men; and in the period following 1850, the wealthy woman from a Mexican family who married an Anglo was more likely to see her children become Anglicized rather than grow up as part of the extended Mexican community. The families that resulted from mixed marriages were often exceptions to the proletarianization process experienced by the majority of the community;

they provided some candidates for public life, and if they were light skinned they had an advantage.

Annexation had an impact on women as well as on men, varying according to region and class, with more women becoming a part of the formation and change that underpinned political activity. Manipulation, discrimination, displacement, and their consequences were widespread. Women were citizens but not voters, and therefore considered less important than men. If they were wealthy, they possessed assets that could be used politically, and some, like Estefana Cavazos, mother of Juan Cortina, supported resistance; or they supported the community interests through contributions to electoral or group activities. The extension of the U.S. "frontier" into the Mexican frontier did not mean democracy or equality for women. They were affected pejoratively by an influx of Anglos, as well as by the practices of the new government and the new institutions, all of which weakened Mexican political power and economic strength. Ironically, though the more liberal laws pertinent to women and property in the Southwest were in part due to Mexican influence, both Mexican men and women suffered from discrimination and lost judicial protection. From the outset of Anglo interference, women experienced degradation in status, which affected the political strength of the community.

Disjunctiveness between the previous and the new orders involved women; and the major institution in the private sphere, the nuclear and extended family, was no more immune to public pressure than others.[46] Apart from public interaction and work experience, the home, the family, and only limited schooling socialized Mexicans, providing a personal context to their politics that was in some ways beneficial in maintaining tenuous family collectiveness, while in others it was debilitating. The patriarchal family was upheld, and tradition, legal precedence, and social rituals reinforced marriage for mexicanos, but its economic underpinning was different and gradually adapted. Elite families continued to preside over social life, advocating older values, yet change was self-evident and influenced some women. Young ladies were still courted with music serenades, but many songs, such as "La pasión funesta" and "La sinaloense," told of suffering, abandonment, and violence as the fate of women. Apart from other pressures, Mexican women within the family structure were undercut by legislation that ignored traditional community property practices. Shares in family property had been the mainstay of the propertied Mexican family both economically and politically; court decisions, however, continually undermined women's economic rights. In contrast, though the courts did not provide proactive educational rights to women, some nonetheless acquired an education. Women received their education mostly at home or through religious instructions from the church. A few attained a post-elementary education in the local schools, and an even smaller number went away to school in Mexico. Though they were few in number, educated women had some impact on other women, generally transmitting their knowledge and traditions orally as well as in letters. The need for working women, as well as working men, to be highly literate was judged as unimportant since reading and writing were not considered generally useful to them at the time. Nevertheless, schooling in the late nineteenth century slowly increased. Significantly, Mexican community efforts to found schools—a response to segregation—created openings for women as students and teachers.

But work and its discrimination, rather than private schooling, impacted most women, and its prejudices were a more common experience, an experience which provided a widening avenue for advocacy and eventually for protest. Not surprisingly, Mexican American women were found working in mining camps, where they faced stark reality in a rough environment. During the gold rush, women were scarce and their labor coveted. Intermarriage was only an occasional phenomenon in the camps; most Mexican American males were driven out and the women abused. Nor were women exempt from racist violence. Josefa Segovia, Juanita of Downieville, California, was lynched during the gold rush. She had killed an Anglo named Cannon who made advances toward her that she rejected. She was hung without a fair trial, and in spite of being pregnant; a white woman would not have been executed. Juanita was one more example of the violence that Anglo-Americans exercised on Mexican Americans. Also found guilty and hung was Chipita Rodríguez, alleged to have killed a man named John Savage in Texas.

As the economy changed qualitatively, the situation of women followed these trends. The percentage of Mexican American families headed by women was perhaps one-third. Women gradually managed to enter the wage labor force in spite of handicaps. Many worked in small establishments or as paid servants. In the semiprofessional fields the jobs most likely to be open to women were those of teacher, nurse, and musician. Trades included those of clerk, merchant, restauranteur, peddler, and shopkeeper, and many worked with male relatives. Women skilled laborers were bakers, candymakers, tailors, and hatters. Unskilled women worked as cooks, servants, and laundresses. Even with employment, women's lives were too often circumscribed by hardship, a lack of education, and crisis; nevertheless, they continued to influence the crisis of a changing society and economy.

The National and the International: Civil War in the United States and Foreign Intervention in Mexico

The Civil War not only had an economic and political impact on the Mexican community, but provided a stage for Mexican American politics.[47] Apart from the starkly intransigent position of Union advocates like Francisco Ramírez, the generally pro-Union sentiment varied according to region; that is, most politically active Mexicans were against slavery and for the Union, but they were not overly demonstrative and their sympathy varied—in New Mexico because of anti-Texan feelings, and in Texas or California because of anticonservative Democratic party views or even a perceived linkage between Mexico's liberals and U.S. Republicans. The Civil War provided a stimulus to U.S. industrial development and commercial transactions, and it accentuated the demand for land and natural resources owned by Mexicans. Some Mexicans prospered during the war by selling supplies to one side or to the other, and the war also increased the demand for exploitable labor. Like other peoples in the United States, individual Mexicans fought on both sides during the war. For example, in California Andrés Pico, Romualdo Pacheco, and Salvador Vallejo organized a battalion of California volunteers, the Native cavalry; but the respected Tomás Sánchez and Servulio Varela served the Confederacy. Cortina participated on the Union side, and a rival of the Cortina family, Santos Benavides, fought for the Confederacy as a brigadier; and José Antonio Navarro, a vociferous successionist, had four sons in the Confederate ranks. Manuel Antonio Chaves and Rafael Chacón distinguished themselves in significant Union commands in New Mexico; at the same time, Confederate sympathizers in New Mexico among the Mexicans included Manuel Armijo and Saturnino Barrientos, who were both from politically active families.

In the Southwest, Republican and Democratic party partisanship intensified and Mexicans were caught in the middle. Many had been Democrats, but to be a Democrat now was to be disloyal and associated with the losing party. Many uneasily changed to the Republican Party, but they lost standing with Democratic partisans. Whether some Mexicans favored the Confederacy because of their negative attitudes toward the United States is impossible to know; the general impression is that the community favored the Union, perhaps because of its more liberal character, its perceived support to the Benito Juárez government against the French Intervention, or a combination of both of these aspects. At any rate, a Republican–Democratic division was visible in the Mexican community, as was the influence of events in Mexico.

Dramatic events in Mexico during the 1850s and 1860s impacted on Mexicans in the United States, and their general outlines were debated and elicited responses.[48] In the middle and late 1850s, the ideological struggle between conservatives and liberals peaked with the events leading to the French intervention.[49] The liberals gained political power under President Ignacio Comonfort, who was backed by the caudillo Juan Alvarez; they formulated the Constitution of 1857 and proceeded to legislate reform of the government, the church, and to some extent the national landholding and economic patterns. This effort resulted in a conservative counter coup and a civil war. *La guerra de la reforma* was to last several years, from January 1858 to January 1861, with liberals ultimately victorious under the leadership of Benito Juárez. At this point, conservative exiles and the Catholic church, including the Vatican, started a major diplomatic and propaganda campaign to bring about foreign intervention in Mexico. In 1861 President Juárez, in an effort to restore the nation's economy, suspended payment on the foreign debt, an act that created the pretext for Spanish, British, and French harassments. The French intervened with troops and there ensued a six-year war, "La Intervención francesa," lasting from December 1861 to May 1867. The conservatives were briefly successful in reestablishing a monarchy in Mexico, under the titular rule of an Austrian, Maximilian von Hapsburg, who was supported by France but ultimately defeated by the republican liberals and their "chinaco" forces comprised of scores of border volunteers and the Texas-born Mexican general Ignacio Zaragosa, the distinguished commander at the battle of Puebla on the cinco de mayo 1862.

The intensification of the ideological struggle in Mexico increasingly influenced the consciousness of many political activists of the Mexican communities in the Southwest.[50] The Spanish-language newspapers reported, assessed, and argued the merits of the contending positions in the conflict. On the whole, the majority of the Mexican press supported the liberal cause, which was identified with the national interest of the Mexican nation as opposed to the conservative or foreign interest. The elite as well as other sectors were somewhat conversant with Mexican republican institutions and ideology, including the divisions between the liberals and conservatives. While opinions were strongly influenced by local conditions and by regional factionalism, many Mexicans nevertheless had taken pride in the forms of the republican government, if not its actual substance, and they preferred it over the governance of conservatives and monarchists; but as in Mexico itself, the liberals were viewed as the "patriotic" party. These sympathies and conscious ideological and political agreements became intertwined with both the regional subordination of the Mexicans in the southwestern United States as well as with the general political and ideological situation in the United States generally.

In the United States, a point of political crisis was reached in a continuing conflict concerning the ideological and economic differences separating the southern states from the North and West.[51] With the secession of the southern states from the Union in 1860, the very existence of the United States as a country was at stake, along with the political and economic fate of the Southwest's Mexican, Indian, and Anglo inhabitants. With the secession of the South, the political lines were drawn, often reversing past political fortunes or improving them. The first mexicanos to feel the impact were the partisan allies of Anglos, Mexican políticos who clearly identified with an Anglo political faction. In the U.S. election of 1860, the possibility of secession in the event of Abraham Lincoln's election was advocated publicly. The direct effects of this campaign were limited to those regions that were states and whose inhabitants could vote in the federal election. In southern California the campaign was hard fought, with Mexican políticos serving on all the several sides. In Texas the Mexican situation was even more precarious, especially when it became clear that a large majority of Anglo Texas would go with the South. Many of the small mexicano elite that survived in Texas, such as the Navarro and

Benavides families, continued their pattern of questionable collaboration by taking up the Confederate position. Many mexicanos in Texas
kept their pro-Union or pro-Juárez opinions to themselves, out of fear
of reprisal. This was a time when white Unionists were subject to
violence at the hands of the secessionist majority. In Texas, the political struggle on both sides of the river was interlinked with the Confederates and French, on one side, and Mexican patriots, on the other
side, who, like Juan N. Cortina, were fighting for the Juárez cause and
the defense of the Mexican people in Texas.

As the political crises in Mexico and the United States took the
form of military conflicts, politically conscious mexicanos not only
took political positions, but volunteered and contributed to the defense
of one cause or the other. The specific nature of the choice depended
on the actual conditions existing within the locality. To take a Union
or Juarista stand in Texas often meant to take up a weapon; and while
local factors were not as acute in the other regions, they were nevertheless conflictual. In New Mexico, during 1861, Manuel Chaves, Rafael
Chacón, José Guadalupe Gallegos, and Miguel Pino organized Union
regiments and militia, and these troops were involved in several encounters against Confederates. In 1862, californios Salvador Vallejo
and others organized the Union Native Cavalry Battalion of four
hundred men. At considerable personal and financial risk, the Tucson
merchant Estevan Ochoa refused allegiance to the Confederacy when
he was required to do so by occupying Confederate troops, but he also
stressed his loyalty to the Union. On the Arizona–Mexico border, the
major figures of 1850, Manuel María Gandora, a conservative, and
Ignacio Pesquiera, a liberal, continued their struggle for power in
Sonora; the first sided with the Imperial forces and the other with the
Republicans, but both drew support from Arizona–Sonora elements.

Concurrent with the Civil War activity that affected Mexican
Americans, the government of President Benito Juárez sent Mexican
diplomatic consular personnel and special commissioners to build public support and to recruit arms and men for the French war.[52] In
California, their efforts received sympathetic support among many of
the Mexican people, particularly in the San Francisco and Los Angeles
communities. General Placido Vega, the liberal former governor of
Sinaloa and a field commander, made the most impact among the
mexicanos, while the efforts of other Mexican representatives were
directed mainly toward Anglos and the U.S. public generally. Special

Commissioner Vega arrived in San Francisco in March 1864, and moved swiftly to gain and strengthen the support of both Mexican and Anglo populations for the Mexican cause.

Among the prominent California politicians who cooperated with Plácido Vega and supported his efforts was California Treasurer Romualdo Pacheco, who introduced Vega to state officials, including the California governor. Pacheco contributed financially and actively supported the fund-raising and propaganda activities of the Juaristas, support that was particularly important in offsetting the pro-Imperialists among San Francisco's large and wealthy French community. These French partisans worked actively to influence federal customs officials in seizing arms destined for the Juaristas. Contraband violated U.S. official policy of neutrality in the war in Mexico, or so Edmund Burke, police chief and deputy collector of customs in San Francisco, told the Mexican consul. On a few occasions, however, Pacheco persuaded state officials to protest the seizure of an arms shipment. Also among the more prominent pro-Juarista mexicanos were Mariano Vallejo, whose son Uladislao served as an officer in the Juarista army; Agustín Aliviso; Victor Castro; and Silvio Pacheco. Many of these men contributed substantial sums of money and were directly active in influencing popular opinion.

Spanish-language newspapers were particularly important in informing Mexican public opinion. In San Francisco, two of the major Spanish-language newspapers were pro-Juárez: *El Mundo Nuevo* (1864), edited by the respected liberal José María Vigil, and *La Voz de Méjico* (1864), edited by Pedro Macillas; the third, *Eco del Pacífico* (1852), was owned by a Frenchman, E. Derbes, and was emphatically pro-Imperialist and anti-Juárez. Newspapers and journalists played a role in informing the Spanish-speaking community of the progress of the conflict. They carried advertisements for recruitment of volunteers, and received letters from readers throughout California and as far east as Virginia City, Nevada. Many readers sought information on volunteering, for they wanted to join the Juarista army.

The anti-French effort led to a network of community groups acting in consensus, and perhaps doing so for the first time in the Mexican community. Especially important were the *Juntas Patrióticas*, or Juárez clubs, which were organized by Plácido Vega and his agents throughout California. Active branches of the Juntas Patrióticas existed in San Francisco, Los Angeles, Jackson, San José, Marysville, Vallejo, Sacramento, Martínez, Greenwood, Hornitos, La Plancha, New Almaden, Sonora, San Pablo, Pinole, San Juan Bautista, and West Point, California, and in Virginia City, Nevada; but support came from other areas too. The clubs were active in raising funds, recruiting volunteers, locating arms for purchase, and organizing public meetings and activities in support of the Mexican republic. In addition to the towns, support came from mexicanos in the mining districts, many of whom joined the Mexican clubs. The Juntas Patrióticas worked with the Monroe Doctrine clubs, which organized Anglo supporters of the Mexican cause.

Plácido Vega and the Juntas Patrióticas also encouraged support for California Republican candidates. Mexican Republicans and Mexican patriots worked to bring out the Mexican vote for Lincoln in the election of 1864, because of the U.S. government's continued recognition of the government of Benito Juárez and the alleged identification of the Confederacy with the Imperialist cause. Perhaps some California mexicanos who participated in the Union army believed there was a linkage between the Union and the Juarista cause. Elements of the Native Cavalry Battalion, under the command of Captain José R. Pico, encountered French Imperial troops while pursuing Imperial deserters on the Sonora frontier. The French commander demanded that Pico acknowledge Maximilian's authority. Pico replied that he recognized only President Juárez, whose cause he supported. Some arms were sent from California to the Juarista forces on Mexico's West Coast, and many of these arms were purchased with the contributions of the Mexican people of California. Several scores of mexicanos from California ultimately reached Mexico, along with numbers of Anglo volunteers. However, the U.S. policy of "friendly" neutrality toward the Mexican republican government sometimes took the form of seizing arms shipments to Mexico, as well as seeking a diplomatic advantage over this government.

In Texas, along the border, local fighting broke out between the Confederacy and the Union, with the struggles between the French and the mexicanos closely intertwined.[53] Conditions here were more dangerous because Texas was part of the Confederacy, and large numbers of Confederate troops were stationed directly on the border, at the mouth of the Río Bravo, the location of one of the most important supply lines of the Confederacy. Since the Texas coast was blocked by the Union fleet, the Confederate government exported large quantities of cotton through Tamaulipas, at first with the cooperation of a few well-paid local Mexican officials and later with the help of the occupying French and Mexican Imperialist troops. In those years, Bagdad, the port of Matamoros at the mouth of the Río Bravo, grew into the largest cotton port in the world; and now blockade runners managed to ferry arms and other military supplies to the Texas Confederates as significant quantities of cotton were exported to Europe.

In Tamaulipas and on the Texas side of the river, *chinaco guerrilleros* under the command primarily of Juan N. Cortina, Juarista governor of the state of Tamaulipas, raided both French and Confederate bases as well as destroying materials and supplies. There were, in fact, several Juarista factions besides that of Governor Cortina. One of the most spectacular and important victories by these forces was the capture of Confederate Brownsville and Imperialist Matamoros. In a battle on March 9, Cortina crossed the Río Bravo and helped to drive the cluding many Texas Mexicans, engaged and defeated five thousand Imperial troops near Matamoros, forcing them to retreat to Bagdad. On March 9, Cortina crossed the Rio Bravo and helped to drive the Confederate forces from Brownsville. Here, he, the accused "outlaw," joined in raising the U.S. flag, and the town was offered to the Union commander at Brazos de Santiago on the Texas coast. United States forces were unable to occupy the town permanently because they lacked sufficient manpower. Until the end of the Civil War in 1865, Juarista forces under Cortina cooperated with the blockading Union forces in combating the Confederates, while fighting to drive the Imperialists from Tamaulipas and northeastern Mexico.

Several prominent Mexican families from Laredo allied themselves with the Confederate side and used their resources and prestige to consolidate or regain some of the political and economic ground they had lost to the town's handful of mostly Anglo and European residents. During the five years the war lasted, Laredo's native-born Mexican elites were indeed partly successful in meeting this objective. They, in fact, gained back some of the loss in wealth and political control forfeited to Anglos between 1847 to 1860 by serving simultaneously as Confederate officers and cotton traders. When the South lost the war and the Republican mandate was temporarily established during Reconstruction, the political competition that had existed before the war continued. But, significantly, the Mexicans of the region were not entirely on the side of the Confederacy, for many had fought for the

Union. The Laredo Mexican community, like the Anglo, was divided
on the specific merits of the issues leading to the war as well as those
stemming from it.

After the Civil War

In the aftermath of the Civil War significant changes occurred
throughout the United States.[54] Industry, banks, railroads, and extrac-
tive industries flourished. Potential immigrant wage laborers were allowed to enter in great numbers, adding to the country's ethnic diversity. There ensued a period of Republican dominance, and clearly, the
greatest political influence was centered in the large urban financial–
industrial centers east of the Mississippi. Among the assortment of
national legal adaptations, two created during this major crisis were
particularly important. The passage of the Thirteenth, Fourteenth,
and Fifteenth Amendments were important potential civil guarantees
for everyone who was discriminated against and disenfranchised. The
Homestead Act at last made it possible for nonprivileged persons to
have access to land, thereby strengthening the small-farm sector as a
constituency in some areas. On the other hand, the act had a negative
affect on surviving Mexican and Indian open-range practices, and it
encouraged greater numbers of whites to move west. Indeed, the Civil
War was not fought to extend economic or civil equities, but to
strengthen the Union, that is, the state, and to ensure the priorities of
major financial interests that now largely coalesced around the Republican party and its dual platform—one for large business and another whose rhetoric addressed the concerns of the small property
holder and white-collar professional. As collusion between government and business led to gross incompetence, a broad and significant
reform movement arose during the last fifteen years of the nineteenth
century, which provided a basis for gradual democratization in the
twentieth century.

In the Southwest continuing property loss among mexicanos, as
well as greater difficulties experienced by the elite in accessing the
dominant economy and the independent medium to small producers,
further eroded their social and political position in comparison to
Anglo-Americans. With Anglo-Americans in control of the economy
and its supporting political institutions, the Mexican elite retreated,

and ultimately, the scramble to maintain some sort of socioeconomic standing became harder for them. The rate of decline varied according to the state and its subregions, coinciding with Mexican participation in electoral politics as well as with border conflict involving Mexico. This was a gradual process, particularly where Mexicans constituted a significant population, in areas such as southern California, northern New Mexico, southern Arizona, and parts of southern Texas and southern Colorado. In these regions the mexicano elite retained its position of leadership within the Mexican communities, functioning as community representatives in federal and state affairs as well as in dealings with private Anglo interests.

California

In California decreased participation in formal electoral politics was becoming generalized.[55] In the 1870s, some californios argued that one of them should be on every slate, for to ignore their vote was to invite defeat or worse; this unusually blunt affirmation occurred when their decline was accelerating. During a time of waning influence, Romualdo Pacheco was elected to the office of lieutenant governor, and he was eventually, for a brief time, interim governor. Though he was not nominated to be governor in the next election, Pacheco did serve two terms in Congress. While he had a base of Mexican support, Pacheco was a Republican and not obliged to the Democratic-party circle of californios, but he owed Anglo Republicans for his selection as a candidate.

In Los Angeles, during the early 1870s, the vote was approximately one-fifth. Here, reputedly in early 1873, among 5,600 voters poten-tially approximately 22 percent were Mexican. During 1872, again in Los Angeles, Cristóbal Aguilar was mayor and Ignacio Sepúlveda served as county judge; two Mexicans were on the council, three sat on the city Democratic committee, and four were sent as delegates to the Democratic state convention. In the 1873 election, however, nega-tive campaigning and intimidation lowered the voter turnout. Agui-lar's English was the main issue, and he lost 715 to 358; the next mayor then ended the ordinance that provided for the bilingual printing of laws.

Apparently, some californio políticos did well politically as individ-uals, consistent with their economic and social standing; their assets had to be marshaled to try for office as well as to secure office. Estevan Castro, son of José Castro, was elected constable and a member of the assembly in Monterey; and Martín Aguirre, son of José Antonio, was elected sheriff for Los Angeles in 1885. When Ramón Pico, son of Andrés Pico, ran for state treasurer, he lost but drew favorable comments. Andronico Sepúlveda was elected county treasurer in 1875; Andrés Castillero sat in Congress in 1880; José G. Estudillo served as state treasurer during 1875–80; and Angel G. Escandón was in the assembly between 1869 and 1874. Besides family assets, what was notable was their political centrism.

Three figures stand out, one each from the Sepúlveda, Pacheco, and del Valle families.[56] Born in the 1840s, Ignacio Sepúlveda of Los Angeles was helped by receiving an eastern education. Licensed to practice law, he was elected to the assembly in 1864; then he served as county judge from 1870 to 1873, as district judge from 1874 to 1879, and as superior judge from 1879 to 1884. He left the bench and represented Wells Fargo in Mexico for over twenty years; he also served as *chargé d'affaires* at the embassy. Born in 1831, Romualdo Pacheco was the son of a Mexican army officer from Guadalajara; he was raised in Hawaii, receiving an English-language education. After the Mexican War, he oversaw the family's San Luis Obispo ranch. Pacheco, at age 22, was elected to the assembly in 1853. He was state senator as a Democrat in 1858, and became a Union Democrat in 1862. After a stint in the Union army, he turned Republican, served four years as state treasurer, and helped pass the office to his kin Ramón Pacheco. Married to an Anglo and popular, but with no marked partisan views, he was nominated for lieutenant governor and elected in a Republican sweep in 1871. He served until February 1875, when the governor appointed himself senator; Pacheco became governor in late February and served to December, afterward returning to private life as a stock broker in San Francisco. Between 1878 and 1882, he served two terms in the U.S. Congress as a representative from Santa Clara and later traveled to Texas and Mexico.

Born in the 1850s, Reginaldo del Valle passed the bar in 1877, and oversaw the del Valle properties. He was elected to the assembly in 1880, becoming its presiding officer in 1881. Elected state senator in 1882, he lost a reelection bid, but won in 1884 when he ran for Congress as a Cleveland Democrat against an Anglo. Del Valle was apparently among the first to combine Spanish and English into an effective rhetoric that was applauded by community members. With some exceptions, Anglos spoke English and the older californios spoke Spanish, of course, and a Mexican politician who used both languages on the stump was convincing. On occasion, del Valle appeared with a small entourage, all dressed alike, but it was increasingly clear that he was limited to the Mexican precincts. The last notable state post he held was as chair of the 1888 state Democratic convention, and during the Woodrow Wilson administration he served briefly in Mexico as a presidential envoy. As Coronel was a major Democrat, del Valle was a visible spokesperson; he continued to serve on several public and community boards and committees until his death in 1938, with his daughter following him in her own civic activity.

By the 1880s, del Valle, Sepúlveda, Pacheco, and Coronel were out of public office, though they continued to be active in civic affairs, working with local organizations and organizations related to the church as well as enjoying positions of honorary political influence. Though numbering perhaps twelve thousand in Los Angeles in 1887, Mexicans were now less than 10 percent of the U.S. population. Californios in their decline were often bitter, for they saw their patrimony literally usurped and were themselves treated with increasing condescension. Salvador Vallejo—who never fully reconciled himself to U.S. rule but served in the Union army because he believed the United States was worth preserving as a bulwark against even worse governments—was particularly bitter. His obituary noted that he was "a man of very strong prejudices." A broken Mariano Vallejo, angered by Alfred Robinson's anti-Mexican book *Life in California* (1846), sought to write "a true history of the country." Fire destroyed his five-hundred-page manuscript in 1867, but he began writing it again in 1873. He had tacitly welcomed U.S. occupation because he believed he would benefit, but he had not. When he died in 1890 some were surprised at the news, believing he had long been dead. In sum, californio-expressed bitterness was closer to the truth than the self-serving pieties of the Anglo historians.

New Mexico

New Mexican politics seemed the most active in North America. though the substance of its power was less than the vitality it displayed.[57] The positive enumeration of the participating elite in New

Mexico included nine members who served as territorial delegates to the U.S. Congress; they provided strong representation in both territorial houses, and their strength was also measured by the number of local offices they held and by their significant representation in the eventual statehood constitution. Mexicans expected and demanded the congressional territorial delegate seat, and an event that proved to be particularly irksome to them was the election in 1873 and 1875 of Stephen B. Elkins, a partner to Catron. In the 1880s Francisco Chávez, a militant by comparison to others, was at the center of efforts to thwart the Catron circle's further extension of power. Often opposing Chávez was Amado Chaves, speaker of the legislature in 1884, the first superintendent of schools (1891), and mayor of Santa Fe between 1901 and 1903. In New Mexico, Mexican participation ensured that legislative sessions were held in Spanish and that statehood and educational measures would be blocked or passed. Miguel A. Otero, Jr., served as governor between 1897 and 1906. Eventually, among one hundred delegates to the 1910 state constitutional convention, thirty-five were Mexicans led by Solomón Luna. They obtained equality between Spanish and English and wrote into the state constitution an explicit recognition of the rights granted by the Treaty of Guadalupe Hidalgo. Mexicans were then 60 percent of the population; their representation however, was not equal to their population, and in several instances the Ring's association with local Mexican políticos prevailed over the interests of the common people. Even though some of the elite and the large companies were doing well, the Mexican small farmers were losing their land and enduring increased violence; therefore, benefits to the vast majority of Mexicans from such political participation were modest. The range wars took their toll on Mexican life, and the small landholders lost greatly. The record of lynchings and shootings was nearly comparable to that of Texas or California, and the actions of Thomas B. Catron and others led to open conflict in several instances.

A Mexican American appointment to the governorship was a concession in a time of strife, but the appointment went to one who possessed great wealth and the confidence of the Anglo elite, and whose appointment was lobbied by an eastern banker. Miguel A. Otero, Jr., held the office from 1897 to 1906, and built an influential network, eventually limiting Catron. This Otero promoted statehood and favored stability and negotiation in state politics. His most striking initiative was to propose raising volunteers from the Southwest for action against Spain. But Otero did not greatly or overtly favor Hispanos. Even so, he was accessible to them, mediating small disputes and listening to petitions for pardons. Such attention boosted his moderate popularity without costing him political resources.

Politics often centered on bills for education, the location of the capital, and the election of territorial delegates, often involving near and distant relatives on opposite sides. J. Francisco Chaves, a Republican, was territorial delegate before he served as president of the state Senate six times between 1886 and 1903; and in between, he was appointed superintendent of schools. In 1872, a strong campaign to secure statehood failed; and in 1889, a major effort to provide public finance for parochial and private schools was also frustrated. The Education Law of 1891 was a lightning rod for ethnic apprehension. Anglos and Mexicans each thought the other would control education to its own benefit and the other's detriment. Securing the appointment of Mexicans as superintendents of the schools was an achievement, but again the appointments went to those who had strong working relations with non-Mexicans: first Amado Chaves, then J. Francisco Chaves.

Another major issue was the location of the capital. Democrats and the more independent Mexican leadership favored Santa Fe, while Republicans and Anglos generally favored Albuquerque. To make the initiative favoring Albuquerque less attractive, Francisco Chávez, leading the Democrats, forced passage of a bill for expensive construction at Santa Fe. Chávez secured his majority by one vote, that of a delegate carried to the capital in his sick bed; and when the bill passed, the delegate died. In 1892, when the building burned down, the question of the capitol's relocation reopened, and although Santa Fe retained it, some said threats were involved.

Violence in New Mexico politics had an impact on nearly every social class, but as elsewhere, the poor suffered most. As its most rudimentary level, conflict was ethnic, involving Mexicans, Indians, and whites. But the political and economic violence that affected the majority involved certain groups and their leaders, and the most notorious comprised the antagonists in the Lincoln County wars (1876–78), a conflict which is exemplary of both New Mexican violence and its particular intricacies. These wars may be seen variously as New Mexicans versus outsiders, merchants against bankers, Anglos fighting

Mexicans, outlaws versus law-abiding citizens, sheep herders pitted against cattle raisers, Democrats warring with Republicans, honest leaders combating corrupt bosses, the poor versus the wealthy. All of these factions were involved in a turbulent maze. It was notable politically because it involved a challenge by Democrats to Republicans. One significant figure in the wars was the respected Mexican leader Juan B. Patrón, who was eventually assassinated after much success in defending poorer Mexicans. The wealthy Manuel B. Otero, son of Miguel A. Otero and the son-in-law of Antonio José Luna, was a powerful figure in Valencia before he was killed, in a gun battle over the Estancia Land Grant, by J. G. Whitney, whose brother was a railroad president. Three brothers in a Baca family were accused of the political murder of A. M. Conklin, a newspaper editor, and one was killed, another lynched, and the third fled, or at any rate, he was never heard from again. Democrat leader Francisco Chávez who was accused of plotting against Catron, was killed in 1892; and the respected older J. Francisco Chaves was assassinated in 1904. Luis Antonio Chacón, the son of Rafael Chacón, was murdered in 1898. The home of Amado Chaves was burned in 1890. Although members of the elite obviously felt the violence, they also benefited in some ways; hence, they were sometimes suspected of being instigators, and at other times of being the targets. In the aftermath of the violence and unrest that followed the protest by Mexicans of the loss of their land, Otero's appointment seemed like a kind of concession to the Mexican element; and though he worked with Catron, Otero also somewhat cut him down politically. Campaigns in New Mexico were often tough and close, as well as challenged on a relatively frequent basis.

Elfego Baca, born in Socorro, New Mexico, in 1865, was a controversial figure, sometimes mistakenly identified with resistance.[58] During the late nineteenth century, when Anglos from Texas were gaining control of New Mexican land and government, Baca was being educated in Kansas. His education was exceptional for mexicanos at that time, and the fact that he was bilingual suggests that some assimilation was occurring during this period. When Baca returned to New Mexico at the age of fifteen, he allegedly grew angry with the Anglo Texans' behavior toward his people. Ethnically sensitive as well as individualistic, he became a deputy sheriff and enforced the law in dealing with both whites and Mexicans. The Anglo Texans objected to Baca's treatment and ambushed him in a small adobe house, where he battled eighty men for thirty-six hours before the attackers retreated. After this encounter, his reputation spread and resulted in his election as sheriff. During his heyday, no one doubted that Baca was one of the foremost gunmen of the West. Later, Baca became a lawyer and aligned with conservatives, attending meetings, offering his services, and generally maintaining his visibility in politics. He worked with questionable politicians such as the members of the Santa Fe Ring; he made himself available to support Thomas Catron against Francisco Chávez; and though he involved himself in Mexican border politics, he did not oppose the government. He opposed the Mexican "revolution," however, by supporting the regimes of Porfirio Díaz and Victoriano Huerta. In addition to being a lawyer, Baca was a government marshal, the mayor of Socorro, and a school superintendent; and he held such notable local offices as county clerk and district attorney. And as he strengthened his skills in view of the coming age of industrialization, he also cooperated with owners in harassing Mexican workers who went on strike. Baca became the reflection of a particular ideological milieu, a political operative serving wealthy interests.

The New Mexican elite benefited from the town workers and the rural population, trading their national identification for class status as many Mexicans became "Spanish." Class and ideological differentiation were introduced as regional phenomena. In sum, the elite strengthened their class position, but they did not forego their claim to community political leadership. For example, the merchant Miguel Antonio Otero, Sr., appointed by President Lincoln as territorial secretary, organized a major trading firm, was offered the position of ambassador to Spain, became a beneficiary of the Santa Fe Ring, headed the Maxwell Grant company, served as vice president of the Atchison, Topeka and Santa Fe Railroad, and was president of the San Miguel National Bank, while his son became governor of the state. He referred to himself as "Castilian" and insisted that he represented the "native" New Mexican. His son, Miguel Antonio Otero II, was more likely not a fair representative of the virtues and limits of the elite. Educated at St. Louis University and Notre Dame, and fully bilingual, he had extensive experience in business, law, and politics, and enjoyed contacts with leading Republicans outside New Mexico, including Presidents Harrison and McKinley, and with political figures in Mexico. President McKinley appointed him governor, and Otero's nine-year term was the longest of any territorial governor.

The dominance of J. Francisco Chaves, a Republican, covered several areas—stock-raising, the militia, business, law, and politics. His family had held office during the colonial and Mexican periods, and he was related to the wealthy Pereas. Educated at St. Louis University and fully bilingual, he served in the militia, achieving the rank of lieutenant colonel. First elected to the territorial assembly from Valencia County, Chaves was elected territorial delegate in 1865, 1867, and 1869, and he was defeated in a bitter election by Father José M. Gallegos, a Democrat. Afterward, he served fourteen terms in the territorial assembly. He was assassinated in 1904, while serving as superintendent of public instruction. Merchant and landowner Tranquilino Luna, another Republican, was related to the Oteros, educated at the University of Missouri, served as a delegate in 1880–84, and with his brother Solomón, a graduate of St. Louis University and president of Albuquerque's Bank of Commerce, established an influential electoral network at Valencia that would persist into the twentieth century. Francisco and Pedro Perea twice served as delegates, Francisco in 1863 and Pedro in 1899. Francisco went to St. Louis University, and Pedro to Georgetown University; both were Republicans and wealthy stock-raisers, merchants, and bankers. Isadoro Armijo, a descendant of the Armijo family, graduated from New Mexico College, served as county recorder, presided over the local board of education, attended the constitutional convention, and edited a newspaper.

Though they were challenged by Anglos as well as by other Mexican political leaders, this relatively stable elite was united in wealth and family ties, and often family members move between both political parties, and had contacts outside New Mexico. The elite's spokespersons occasionally engaged in polemics in newspapers like *Las Dos Repúblicas*, *El Defensor del Pueblo*, and *La Voz del Pueblo*; and their descendants would continue to be active in twentieth-century politics.

Colorado and Arizona

In Colorado, a Mexican constituency and an elite would experience a persistent yet varied economic, social, and electoral continuity. Dating from the 1840s,[59] Mexican settlers included members of well-off families, traders and stockmen from native-born New Mexico families, and sheepherders and vaqueros who worked for shares or wages. As a part of the context of the politics preceding the Civil War and the activity of speculators in 1861, Colorado was organized as a territory that included portions of the extensive northlands of New Mexico, principally the San Luis Valley; this annexation meant that Colorado would have a Mexican settler population attached to an Anglo and European immigrant population centered around Denver. In Colorado, there came together the older Mexican farming and ranching economy, the commercial Anglo town, and post-1850 mining enterprises that were, at first, individual and small, devoted to precious metals, and then grew into large corporate enterprises exploiting industrial metals and a diverse immigrant work force including Mexican laborers. Though Anglos were moving in, so were mexicanos coming from New Mexico and points farther south to settle the Pueblo and Trinidad areas. By the mid-1860s, and for several decades thereafter, Mexicans were the majority population in southern Colorado, until large numbers of Anglos and European immigrants arrived and began to buy cattle ranches, and to work in the mines, in lumber, and on the railroads. The contest between landowners and industrial concerns, the competition between Republicans and Democrats, and the relatively late penetration of large non-Mexican immigration into southern Colorado explains, in part, why the small and modest Mexican elite initially was able to utilize effectively its economic power and popular support in gaining political power and office at several government levels in certain areas.

Mexican legislators such as José Urbano Vigil, Felipe Baca, and Casimiro Barela were prominent Colorado políticos and enjoyed some influence. Educated and with some means, they all combined business and ranching with politics. Additionally, the Mexican vote was important to a few Anglo politicians, and this added to the Colorado políticos' influence. Because of anti-Mexican practices, Mexican wage workers needed protection, services, supplies, and loans. To some degree, the elite used mutually supportive practices to maintain support for laborers, and they sought to enlarge their wealth and power in the growing economy, a practice that often involved family or other social ties and was based on a real but uneven exchange: votes and labor in return for jobs and protection from the patrón, who acquired profit, status, and an economic political position. In one case, a propertied Anglo working within the Mexican society became a local leader. These electoral leaders also were able to increase political power and to gain and maintain their offices on the basis of support from Mexican farmers and laborers. In a few noteworthy instances, elite Mexicans went beyond furthering their personal interests and worked to protect their community's general welfare.

Colorado's partisan politics reflected its economic interests and the social origins of its population, which, given the sectional conflict, were contentious and vague. Many Colorado players were also fairly experienced in territorial and state politics elsewhere. The lines of partisanship were unclear because while there were many Democrats, the label was for a while considered best avoided. Although Republicans were present, most voters were often pro-South and anti-Lincoln; however they were interested in Republican planks like "free soil." As a result, the initial elections were waged not between Democrats and Republicans, but between the so-called Union and People's Party, and both included a mix of Democrats and Republicans.

Although the Mexican population generally preferred the Democratic party, there were also Republican affiliates. A Republican like Rafael Chacón, formerly of New Mexico, could receive an appointment from the Democrat's Jesus María García and run for county treasurer (and later, sheriff) and be elected with Democratic support. Jesús Barela, from San Luis, and Victor García, from Pueblo, were elected to the first assembly in 1861, but they moved from the Union to the People's Party, and their participation was dependent on a translator, for they spoke Spanish primarily. A Democrat, John M. Francisco, a Virginian and the representative of the St. Vrain trading firm, based in Santa Fe and one of the major businesses in the territory, claimed to represent the Spanish-speaking community. From 1861 to 1876 and through statehood, Las Animas, Costilla, and Conejos counties had one or more representatives. Although several financial crises affected the Mexican elite, particularly the crash of 1893, their representation endured.

As was the case elsewhere, one of the first issues in Colorado was the location of the capital. Denver eventually was chosen as the site, even though Varelas and García advocated Pueblo. Next came a failed attempt to secure public financial support for Catholic schools. Mexican participation then became more visible and effective with the election in 1871 of the charismatic Casimiro Barela, a Democrat for most of his career. In 1875, President Grant signed the enabling act for Colorado and a constitutional convention was called; and among the delegates was Jesús María García, who remained as secretary of the

Democratic Party in Las Animas County area for more than two decades.

José Urbano Vigil and Casimiro Barela provided two noteworthy examples of Mexican elite participation in Colorado politics. Vigil embodied the elite Mexican who successfully met the needs of his supporters and, in return, could count on their support in his endeavors to gain political power and become a wealthy entrepreneur. A former schoolteacher, he was successful in politics and highly active in business. Vigil served as Las Animas County chairman of the Democratic Party and was a member of the Democratic state central committee. From the 1880s to 1915, when he died, Vigil was active in party politics, publishing, and relations with Mexico, and he was a strong supporter of the La Sociedad de Beneficencia Mutua.

Barela was the best-known and most influential politician in the Colorado Mexican elite.[60] Called "The Perpetual Senator of Colorado," Barela practiced politics that exhibited an ambition for wealth and power concurrent with an interest in protecting the rights of his people. Barela's family left New Mexico during the Taos Revolt of 1848, and settled in southern Colorado. The family quickly reestablished its former economic prominence by engaging in livestock and merchant activities. Barela, after holding a number of important county offices, was elected as a representative to the territorial legislature in 1871. In 1876, he was elected to the Colorado State Senate and held that office for more than forty years, until 1920, a fact which indicates his political strength. He attended two Democratic Party national conventions, and was the consul for both Mexico and Costa Rica in Denver, Colorado. Barela also prospered through his involvement in the new economic order as part owner of the San Luis Valley Railroad and the American Savings Bank of Trinidad, while he continued to expand his interests in more traditional economic activities like cattle and sheep ranching. Socially prominent, he became one of the wealthiest men in the state. One of his three daughters married Eusebio Chacón, the son of Rafael Chacón and a graduate of Notre Dame, who served on the staff of the United States Court of Private Land Claims and became a deputy district attorney for Las Animas County, winning popular respect through his forthright speaking and writing in behalf of the Mexican people. While he was well-connected both nationally and in Mexico, Barela was also acknowledged as one of the wealthiest persons in southern Colorado.

A centrist and pragmatist, Barela was one of the major leaders of the Mexican community. Increasing Anglo discrimination against the Mexican people led Barela to advocate legislation to protect Mexican rights. In so doing, he referred on occasion to the Treaty of Guadalupe Hidalgo. To aid the native population in becoming familiar with the new legal system, Barela succeeded in having the Colorado legislature specify that all laws until 1900 would be published in Spanish, German, and English. Barela blocked a proposal for the state constitution intended to disenfranchise immediately all non-English speakers by delaying its enforcement until 1890; thus did he support the political rights of his people and ensure the preservation of his constituency. Barela also proposed that Mexican children be instructed in their native language of Spanish and learn English as a second language—a proposal that failed. In 1888, Barela succeeded in influencing Colorado to support statehood for the territory of Nuevo México; for he believed that Mexican lives and land-grant rights would be protected more effectively if New Mexico was a state. However, the effort did not prosper until much Mexican land had been lost. Similarly, much Mexican land was lost in Colorado, although Barela did succeed in having Colorado create a land court in 1912 to adjudicate land claims. In 1908, he switched parties rather than lose the influence he had gained. Teodoro Abeyta held local offices in Trinidad between 1885 and 1902, and his brother Vivian was elected in the 1890s as state legislator and county commissioner, as was José R. Aguilar; while J. M. Madrid was state legislator, county superintendent of schools, and as late as 1932, state senator. With a limited base, Mexican political influence surprisingly persisted in Colorado as well as in Arizona.

As part of Sonora until 1856, Mexicans in Arizona often were embattled by Indian pressures and Anglo Texan interlopers as well as by the contest over control of the Sonora governorship.[61] The appropriateness of the Gadsden negotiation aside, the fact that the transfer was negotiated avoided conflicts and recriminations locally. Several propertied families in the Tucson area—the Comaduran, the Aguirre, the Ramírez, the Elias, and the Otero families and others—had exercised leadership during the colonial and Mexican periods, and they would continue to be prominent under United States rule. These families were reinforced by two recent arrivals from La Mesilla and Chihuahua—Estevan Ochoa and Mariano Samaniego, both of them educated in St. Louis and from propertied families.

Economic and social ties to Chihuahua and Sonora and New Mexico remained as important as they had been before 1856. Separated by
decree from the New Mexican population, Mexicans in the Tucson and
Mesilla areas were a majority soon to become a minority. These areas
were overrun by opportunists of every kind, but mostly Democrat and
pro-Southern. The Civil War crisis forced many Mexican Arizonans to
become active opponents to Confederate moves because they ema-
nated from Anglo Texans, and slavery was regarded as a detriment to
their status and economic fortunes. Anti-Mexicanism was associated
with Southerners, particularly Anglo Texans, and these, in turn, were
associated with Democrats.

Partially as a response to Confederate actions that established the
Confederate territory of Arizona, in December 1861 the U.S. Congress
introduced the Arizona Organic Act, passing it in February 1863.
President Lincoln appointed the governor, the secretary, and other
officials, all of whom were Anglos and presumably Republicans. Since
the journey to Arizona was hazardous, the new cabinet was assigned an
escort of New Mexico Volunteers under the command of Colonel
J. Francisco Chaves and Captain Rafael Chacón, both notables in the
public life of New Mexico. Both were at Navajo Springs for the inauguration of the new territory, and in the winter of 1863 and spring of
1864, they were present at the establishment of Fort Whipple, near
Prescott, as the territorial capital. Seemingly, Governor John I. Good-
win, Secretary R. C. McCormick, and Judge J. Q. Allyn were better
disposed toward the local Mexicans than would be the case for later
Arizona state officers, with the exception of Governor Anson P. K.
Safford. In this area, Anglo immigrants had been Southern and Democrat in sympathy, but in the post–Civil War period, Republicans generally received the official appointments.

Since the Gadsden Purchase and the consequent treaty had previously provided the choice of citizenship for Mexicans, the local
Mexican leadership was mobilized from the first.[62] For years, the area
had benefited from the unique leadership of the propertied Teodoro
Ramírez, descendant of a settler family. Estevan Ochoa and Mariano
Samaniego, the prominent leaders for the next two decades moved
from Chihuahua; but the most notable leaders were Ignacio Ortiz and
José M. Martínez, who signed a memorial to Congress for territorial
status. Though Democrats were initially dominant, Republicans soon
eclipsed them. Prominent residents Juan Elias and Pedro Aguirre, as

well as the wealthy and respected Estevan Ochoa, participated, in July and August 1856, in early conventions to organize the territory.

In 1864, among slightly over 1,000 Tucson residents, more than 700 were Mexicans; and of the 250 voters, the majority were Mexicans and Republicans dominated. In the elections of 1864, only two Mexicans ran for legislative office: Jesús María Elias in the assembly, and Francisco S. León for council; and both won convincingly. In 1865, Estevan Ochoa and León won election to the assembly. These representatives voiced several issues: Spanish-language translation of proceedings; access to supplying government purchases; safeguards for property, trade, and business dealings in general; and organization and financial support for public schools. However, when Tucson was incorporated as a city in 1871, the first council and mayor were Anglo, despite the strong presence of Mexicans. Later, in 1875, Estevan Ochoa, a wealthy freighter, was elected as mayor. Mariano Guadalupe Samaniego, a medical doctor, prosperous merchant, and relative newcomer, won election to the assembly and other city and county offices, and was active for some thirty years.

Arizona Mexicans had a particularly effective spokesman and local newspaper. Carlos Velasco, through El Fronterizo (1878), was an outspoken advocate for Mexican representation and electoral participation:

> The raza, because of its respectable numbers in Arizona, could well partake of the greatest amount of guarantees, if they had their just representation in the more important public posts. But in a very injurious manner it seems that, with a few honorable exceptions, the raza has resigned itself to licking the chain which binds it to the controlling powers of those who would take advantage of their ignorance and disunity, those who do not return the service rendered, nor judge them worthy of any kind of consideration.[63]

Although he was a fervent Republican, Velasco supported Mexican Democrats if their election meant increased representation. The newspaper El Fronterizo published perhaps the clearest and strongest advocacy for Mexican electoral and civic rights of any southwestern newspaper in the 1870s. To a lesser degree, this position was echoed by Las Dos Repúblicas, which urged mexicanos to use their political skills and heritage to affirm their rights. However, Mexican prominence in politics was concurrent with Republicans holding the offices of governor and territorial delegate, offices held to the mid-seventies by Stafford and McCormick; thereafter Democrats were winning elections and Mexican participation declined.

The small group of Mexican merchants based in Tucson and Yuma, where the Mexican community was relatively large, played a notable role in early territorial government. But this modest and intense political presence was diminished by the late seventies, roughly concurrent with the arrival of the railroads and due to greater economic activity, larger numbers of Anglos, and harsher attitudes directed toward Mexicans. The elite, however, did not decline, but was superseded by stronger players; they remained competent, civically active, and, in many cases, relatively wealthy.

On a smaller scale, politics in Arizona resembled the political process in other parts of the Southwest. Mexicans had settled the Santa Cruz Valley, which would become the area of the densest continuing Mexican settlement, of which the principal center was Tucson. Mexicans were active in trade, ranching, mining, and freighting. The Mexican political influence was often local rather than statewide, and it was exercised through a merchant elite who were, for the most part, Republicans. State advocacy was aimed at influencing the governor. Mexicans who served in the territorial legislature were instrumental in establishing public education, including the state university. Ochoa and Samaniego were particularly active in improving elementary and university, public and Catholic education, and both were commendable in their civic participation.

Apart from holding seats in the assembly, Mexicans held the mayorships of Yuma and Tucson for a few terms and served in offices such as justice of the peace, trustee, constable, and in addition to county and council seats, they elected one representative to the Constitutional Convention of 1910. The Mexican constituency was made up of merchants, landowners, farmers, farm or ranch hands, and workers from the mines, the smelters, and the railroad. Though Republican preference dominated in the 1860s and 1870s, this consensus deteriorated along with Republicans politics generally, with lesser men who were anti-immigrant and anti-worker serving as leaders. Democrats were somewhat pro-labor but opposed Mexican immigrant workers, while Democratic identification increased with Samaniego's leadership, as did competition between the two parties. However, there was crossover support along ethnic lines and concurrent with notable party participation by a few. The southern Mexican Arizona community was strengthened by the immigration of labor for employment in the mines and on the railroads. These laborers, in turn, made the ties with Sonora stronger, as well as strengthening the impetus toward labor and community organization.

Texas

In Texas, chances for outspoken yet official indigenous political leadership were limited, and politics often were conducted under negative conditions,[64] such as violence, exploitation, and pervasive anti-Mexicanism. Newspapers as distinct in tone and separated by over twenty years as were El Bejareño (in the 1850s) and El Horizonte (in the 1880s) repeatedly raised the myriad issues of discrimination. There were also partisan delimitations. For all practical purposes, there was only one party, the Democrats. San Antonio politics was dominated by Democrats, and one of the dominant figures was Bryan Callahan II, who had a major influence in ensuring that the Mexican vote would be tolerated. Among the prominent and surviving leadership were the veterans José Antonio Navarro and Alejo Ruiz, who joined new figures such as Vicente Martínez, Rafael Yturris, and John Barrera. They comprised probably the most reactionary and sycophantic leadership to be found in the Southwest. They were arch-Confederates voicing the pertinent rhetoric. The one phenomenon that shocked them was the Know-Nothing movement, which they criticized as Catholics, not as Mexicans, although in Texas the Know Nothings were as emphatically anti-Mexican as the Ku Klux Klan. The San Antonio políticos also reacted, in step with other Mexican leaders, when Anglos sought to formally segregate and disenfranchise Mexicans. Yet José Antonio Navarro would argue in favor of the Ku Klux Klan in the years following the war and shortly before his death in 1871.

Two noteworthy political events in San Antonio were created by such reactionary efforts. When the dance floor of San Pedro Park was prohibited to Mexicans in August 1883, a former veteran, Juan Cárdenas, organized a successful public protest. Equally, a strong response was made in the case of Ricardo Rodríguez's denial of naturalization papers because of Indian, that is, not white, ethnicity. Such action, of course, could threaten voting and encourage more segregation. The case was won and underscoring its political implications was the timeliness of A. L. Montalbo's initiative in organizing the protest of the earlier decision.

During the Civil War Mexicans served in a few offices, but these were fewer than previously, and similarly, there were fewer offices following the war. In the 1870s, José Flores served as alderman, Eugene Navarro as city clerk, and José Cassiano as city assessor; the latter's tenure was exceptionally extended, however. Bexar County positions held by Mexicans included those of the justice of the peace, the county tax assessor, the deputy county and district clerks, and the county collector, as well as the two county commissioners, Rafael Quintana and Juan Antonio Chávez. Northeast and southeast of San Antonio were a half-dozen officials in Wilson and Oldham counties. To the south, in 1881–82, Atascosa elected T. P. Rodríguez to the state legislature.

In south Texas, throughout the period from the end of the Civil War to the arrival of the railroads, there was an increasing concentration of wealth favoring the Anglos, but with some persistent Mexican strengths. This uneven shift in wealth was reflected in occupational structure, occupational persistence, mobility, and residential and domestic patterns, and in politics. A significant political phenomenon was the Democratic coalition of Anglos and Mexicans.[65] The political participation of Mexicans deep in south Texas during the second half of the nineteenth and the early twentieth centuries has been characterized generally as "machine politics," an inappropriate term because it suggests a close analogy to the electoral practices of New York and Boston. In south Texas, the dominant party was the Democrats, and mainly they represented the class interests of some Anglo lawyers, the Mexican elite, and the Anglo landowners who had started out as merchants. Their motivations were protection, gain, and patronage.

Throughout the period, in some localities the Democratic Party elected candidates on the strength of the Mexican voting populace who held poll tax receipts. They voted because of intimidation or the need for protection from a few politicians who were expected to ward off the worst aspects of anti-Mexicanism. In many places, however, such practices excluded the majority of the Mexican population. In short, the Democratic party could control selected elections by giving the vote to selected groups of Mexicans who held an allegiance to a local party functionary, who was usually also a Mexican. Though it was noted most often in Cameron County, the practice embraced Hidalgo, Starr, and Duval counties as well.

The key functionary within the party in this regional system was the county Democratic chairman. One such prominent person was James G. Wells, a local attorney for the landed interests, who controlled Brownsville politics for many years. The situation combining local leaders and a dominated vote made for conflict because it excluded some Anglo interests. The particular political environment was rooted in the process of hegemony maintained by Anglo merchants and adventurers ambitious to be landowners as well as those wealthy and influential in state and even national politics. The vulnerability of the Mexican elite and the terrorization of Mexican laborers facilitated the practice. A central fact was the numerical majority of Mexicans, and since the rules of the game called for voters and voting they were necessary. The *American Flag* of Brownsville reported, on August 20, 1856:

> Americans have at times committed offenses which in them have been overlooked, but which, if committed by Mexicans would have been severely punished. But when election time comes, it is wonderful to behold the friendship existing for the Mexican voters, and the protection extended to them, the sympathy which until then had remained latent or concealed, suddenly reveals itself in all its plentitude, and many are astonished not to have found until then the amount of kindly feeling professed towards them by their whilom friends. Promises of all kinds are made to them, but scarcely are the promises made, when they are broken. An hour before the election they are fast friends,—an hour after the election they are a 'crowd of greasers.'[66]

In the 1850s, Stephen Powers organized a coalition of Anglos and Mexicans to organize and direct the vote. Powers and the Democrats were generally stronger in the seesawing competition of the Democratic–Republican rivalries. Upon Powers's death, James B. Wells became the head of the arrangement, which was a frequently shifting coalition and often challenged. Except for state senator generally and federal representative always, Mexicans periodically had access to nearly all other offices. Among Wells's close associates were Santiago A. Brito, sheriff of Cameron County, and Manuel Guerra, head of the Democratic Party in Starr County. In a controversy over whom to support for governor, Brito challenged Wells and was assassinated shortly thereafter, in 1892. Guerra eventually loosened his ties with Wells by making an arrangement with one of Wells's enemies, but not until 1910 did Wells begin to decline. Apart from the better-known and endemic ethnic violence between Mexicans and Anglos, there also existed targeted political violence aimed directly at leaders, their associates, or their kin and across class and ethnic lines.

For several decades, the west Texas area offered a base for political activity because of the Mexican numbers; there was marked continuity of leadership; and for a while one newspaper, *El Valle del Bravo*, voiced defensive sentiments.[67] Mexicans held some city and county positions in El Paso and in neighboring communities, even as a strong Republican–Democratic competition involved Mexicans on both sides. Community sentiment was visible along nativist lines, and the arena produced at least one remarkable figure, Octaviano Larrazolo, as well as one notorious event. The El Paso Salt War of 1877 starkly indicated the dire situation and the spirit of Mexicans, underscored by the basic economic struggle, but also characterized on the surface by spontaneous protest laced with politics. Although salt had been available to the public since colonial times, problems with Anglos over its use began in 1853. In 1868, when Mexican residents cleared a road to the beds, an enterprising businessman named Charles Howard decided to charge a fee for public salt, claiming title that was based on earlier claims and related to San Antonio politician Sam Maverick and state Senator W. W. Mills. Father Antonio Borajo, a local Italian priest who depended on Mexicans, spoke out against Mills and urged support for his opponent, A. J. Fountain, who ran on a promise to make the salt public and won the election. Now Borajo wanted a share of the beds, and he struck an alliance with Cardis, a compatriot Italian who ran for state senator while the two supported Charles Howard, who won election as county judge. Rather than supporting Borajo, however, Howard advanced his own claims through his father-in-law; while Borajo used the pulpit to incite Mexican parishoners. Howard sought out church officials, and the bishop intervened to oust Borajo. When protest continued and two Mexicans were arrested, a group of several hundred released them and held a meeting for free salt. The Mexicans had refused to pay. Instead, they arrested Howard, forcing him to renounce his "claim" and to agree to leave the town. Howard went to the governor, returned with Texas Rangers, and personally shot Cardis.

A Texas Ranger, Major Jones, supported Howard. The Mexicans led by Francisco Barela first arrested, then executed, Howard, and forced the unheard-of surrender of the Rangers. Ranger reinforcements and the army were called; this was not a case of "one riot, one Ranger," and for good measure, thirty gunmen were hired. These forces killed Mexicans and committed rape and other crimes. A congressional investigation and the establishment of Fort Bliss followed. In time, the salt was put on sale again and the Rangers demanded thirty-one thousand dollars from the Mexican government, which had no standing in the affair.

After the Civil War, in the mid-1860s, Reconstruction politics reached the south Texas border.[68] Locally, this meant the weakening of the coalition headed by leading Mexican families and by resident European merchants and professionals who had sided with the Confederacy. In its place, a coalition was strengthened that reflected other leading native-born Mexican families and Anglo interests who had opposed the Confederacy. This changeover was marked in Laredo when the military, headed by General D. C. Buchanan, issued a decree removing the mayor, Agustín Salinas, and two aldermen, Francisco Farias and Gervasio de Leon, from office. However, one Mexican alderman, Cleofas Garza, was included among the Republican appointees; yet after Reconstruction, Agustín Salinas returned as mayor of Laredo in 1881. Between 1865 and 1881, Mexicans were elected as representatives to the City Council and the County Commissioners Court. Santos Benavides, a former Confederate officer, was elected as state representative for several terms in the early 1880s, and a relative, Porfirio Benavides, served as the mayor of Laredo. One notable political event marking an energized contestation occurred in 1886 when the so-called Laredo Election Riot ran its course in the Texas city's streets.

For times past Laredo politics were intense, and in the fall elections of 1884 *El Horizonte* reported what was anything but passive interest:

"La Democracia Triunfante."
La *Sociedad Unión Democrática*, está consiguiendo su fin propuesto, es decir, la estrecha unión del elemento méxico-tejano. Por todo Encinal y Webb se están recogiendo numerosas firmas y de éstas solamente se tienen MAYOR NUMERO QUE LA MITAD DE LOS VOTANTES, es decir, ya para ahora hay mayoría manifiesta.
Aquí en laredo, el número de votantes llega apenas á 1100, segun el resultado arrojado por la pasada elección municipal, y para

ahora la sociedad, en solo dos sesiones, ha reunido 581 *firmas*, es decir, mas de la mitad del número de vontates. No son estos datos elocuentes?—Al fin de estas líneas van las firmas recogidas en la segunda sesión, que son unas 200 y que juntas con las anteriores ya publicadas hacen 581.

La noche del miércoles, los *reformadores* quisieron *establecer competencia* y con una tambora y un clarinete empezaron á meter ruido en los bajos de la Banca, llenaron de asientos la basta sala, donde pueden caber 500 personas, y . . . , qué creen ustedes que resultó? que ni fué nueva gente y algunos de los que habián ido la noche anterior, se pasaron á la Sociedad Democratica, convencidos de que aquella masa popular constituye y representa al pueblo méxico-texano.[69]

Democracy Triumphant

[The Sociedad Unión Democrática is attaining its proposed goal, that is to say, the close union of the Mexico-Texas element. In all, Encinal and Webb have collected many signatures, and from these alone, they have more than half the voters, that is to say, that there is now a clear majority.

Here in Laredo, the number of voters scarcely reaches 1,100, according to the final tally of the votes cast in the last municipal election. For now, the society, in only two sessions, has collected 581 signatures, that is to say, more than half the number of voters. Are these not eloquent facts? At the end of these lines are the signatures collected in the second session, which are some 200, and together with the earlier ones already published, they total 581.

Wednesday night, the reformers tried to establish competition and with a bass drum and a clarinet, began to attract attention on the floor of the Banca. They filled the huge hall with seats where they could fit 500 people. And what do you think happened? It was not new people, and some of those who had come the previous night went over to the Sociedad Democrática, convinced that that popular mass constitutes and represents the Mexican-Texas people.]

Many of the native-born Mexican elites had placed their interests in the Democratic Party and were popularly known as Los Huaraches, or those who represented the common person. Contesting them was the mostly Anglo-European coalition that formed the "Citizens Party" around the time of the arrival of the first railroads in 1881, and assumed a stance of pretended nonpartisanship and reformism, as well as, incidentally, real anti-Mexicanism. The Citizens Party's members were known as Las Botas, those coming from the well-heeled crowd, those who wore the boots. In the spring elections of 1886, the Citizens Party nearly swept both city and county offices by inhibiting the Mexican vote. In taunting mockery, the Citizens Party adherents staged a public funeral for the Democratic Party, the mexicano elites. There followed a free-for-all shootout in downtown Laredo, which left about two dozen dead and twice as many wounded. The election riot was quelled by locally garrisoned federal troops, and days later the Texas Rangers arrived to maintain the "peace." Out of this affair came a coalition called the Independent Club, which would be influential in one form or another until the late 1970s. The mexicano elites were subsumed to play a secondary brokering role in the new political arrangement, but specifics were convoluted because of the shifting of political factions linked to a modest Mexican electorate.

There was also the ongoing electioneering. On December 1, 1893, the *Corpus Christi Caller* described an election, as follows:

> The city immediate to the rear of the crest of the bluff is, in common parlance, called the "Hill," and is dotted with residences [of Mexicans] ranging from those of the descendants of the Cid to the autocratic employees of the Texas-Mexican and San Antonio and Arkansas Pass [railroads]. The Hill is generally the scene of busy excitement, especially during a hotly contested canvass for county or municipal offices, the balance of power being held by the "Mexico-Texano," who knows a good thing when he sees it and doesn't let it get away. The candidates vie with each other in their attention to the wants and comforts of the Hilly suffragan. The tri-colored and star-spangled banner wave side by side; the characters of Washington and Hidalgo are compared midst the laudatory plaudits of the surging masses, and during these political ebullitions the "Mexico-Texano" becomes the recipient of such distinguished consideration at the hands of the candidates that he wishes the canvass would last forever. The constant shout of the suffragans for their prospective favorites make an aching void of prevalent drought, which only can be appeased by recourse to a neighboring saloon, where the *entente* cordial between the candidate and suffragan is cemented by vows of friendship and fealty.

These aspects of an election were part of a specific locality, within a panorama evolving throughout the late nineteenth century.

In the nineteenth-century south Texas towns of Laredo and Brownsville, scenes of spirited contest intersected with the Jim Wells machine of Brownsville. In these places, Mexicans were courted and some used as a voting bloc by Anglos, but others were independent and followed their own leadership. Nonetheless, Anglos made continual efforts to disenfranchise Mexicans through physical intimidation, manipulation of requirements, and, of course, denial on ethnic grounds, which was illegal. However, some Anglo interests were opposed to such disenfranchisement because the vote that remained favored them. To the extent that "vote buying" existed, this practice was initiated by Anglos to secure Anglo votes and was eventually extended to some of the poor Mexicans. Poll tax exclusion (1904) and all-white primaries (1902) were early twentieth-century refinements in Anglo Texas.

Bitterly contested elections represented attempts to gain office by recently arrived midwestern and eastern Anglo farmers and white collar elements who opposed the control exerted by large landholders within the Democratic Party. These insurgent elements sought to gain power by discrediting the Democrats for their ability to negotiate with large groups of Mexican voters through allegedly underhanded methods. Both the political process and the negative view of the Mexican that it fostered were used to disparage Mexicans, although the main conductors and beneficiaries were Anglos. Aspects of the policies continued into the twentieth century as did some players and their descendants.

Transition and Response

From the 1870s to 1900, the United States went through booms and depressions while Mexicans experienced increasing social and political discrimination as well as more economic integration,[70] processes that were formative for the community of the twentieth century. Major elements of the economy in the western United States such as large-scale farming, cattle raising, the railroad transportation system, and industrialized mining, stratified mass labor along national lines; and the mexicano participated in and contributed to all of these enterprises, while suffering, at the same time, social discrimination, cultural suppression, and economic displacement. The proportion of Mexicans to Anglos sharply decreased in parts of the Southwest, and as a rule, barrios and colonias increasingly became culturally, politically,

and economically dominated communities. Social characteristics associated with economic exploitation and educational deprivation were
already present in the community, and labor organizing now appeared
for the first time.

The early organization of the Mexican working class grew out of
specific developments during the late nineteenth century.[71] Because
the exploitation of Mexican workers was indispensable to economic
growth, the number of Mexicans in the labor force was increased by
forceful displacement from the land and from traditional occupations,
and by migration from Mexico. Large-scale capital development required mass labor, which, in turn, encouraged progressive ideas and
trade-union aspirations; and newcomers from Mexico arrived in the
United States with newly developing traditions of labor organizing that
would enhance the political character of the Mexican community.
Intellectual stimulation was provided by the social unrest in Mexico,
and demographic, cultural, and ideological reinforcement from Mexico
would become an important feature of the way in which Mexican
experience was organized in the United States during the late nineteenth and twentieth centuries. And political stimulus was also the
result of ideas and activist efforts that originated in the United States.
In any case, miners, dockworkers, and some craftsmen engaged in
sporadic labor organizing, and conflict surrounding their participation
led to the adoption of various ideologies and the advocacy of numerous
political movements and plans of action, all of which were facilitated
by travel and contacts among workers throughout the Southwest in the
late nineteenth and early twentieth centuries. In this way, some mexicanos became familiar with radical efforts, one of which was strongly
localist as well as influenced by ideas that were current beyond the
locality.

Las Gorras Blancas and
the Partido del Pueblo Unido

By the mid-1880s economic conditions for the Mexican in Nuevo
México had deteriorated considerably. Furthermore, politically targeted violence was becoming a practice on many sides. Through a
variety of legal and illegal means, Mexicans increasingly were losing
their communal and private lands; and large land companies, cattle-

men, and the railroads were stepping up their demands for access to both land and water rights held by Mexicans.

Las Gorras Blancas, or the "White Caps," emerged as a semi-conspiratorial organization dedicated to protecting the mexicano's property, life, and security.[72] Their protest focused particularly on the machinations of the Santa Fe Ring, Thomas B. Catrón and their associates, including Mexicans, with activity centered in San Miguel County. Actually, this element initiated the violence with the confidence that they would not be punished.

Tapping older precedents of justice in New Mexico, and inspired by notions of *hermandad* as well as by previous conspiracies, Las Gorras Blancas was a group willing to use violence, if necessary, to defend Mexican rights against the elite, to prevent the takeover of land by companies, and to fight the railroad's exploitive practices, especially its usurpation of irrigation projects. Las Gorras Blancas members included despoiled landholders, railroad and lumber workers, and local political leaders. To fight both Anglo and Mexican exploiters, they combined armed defense, labor organizing, and electoral activity. Las Gorras Blancas shared its membership with an early dissident electoral party, the Partido del Pueblo Unido (the Partido, or PDP), and both shared participants with the Knights of Labor and the national People's Party; but Las Gorras Blancas and the Partido also included dissidents from both the Democrats and Republicans.

While the Partido was a significant precursor and notably indicative of political needs and shifts, Las Gorras Blancas publicly proclaimed its grievances and demands:

NUESTRA PLATFORMA—

Our purpose is to protect the rights and interests of the people in general and especially those of the helpless classes.

We want the Las Vegas Grant settled to the benefit of all concerned, and this we hold is the entire community within the Grant.

We want no "land grabbers" or obstructionists of any sort to interfere. We will watch them.

We are not down on lawyers as a class, but the usual knavery and unfair treatment of the people must be stopped.

Our judiciary hereafter must understand that we will sustain it only when "Justice" is its watchword.

We are down on race issues, and will watch race agitators.

We favor irrigation enterprises, but will fight any scheme that tends
to monopolize the supply of water sources to the detriment of
residents living on lands watered by the same streams.
The people are suffering from the effects of partisan "bossism" and
these bosses had better quietly hold their peace. The people
have been persecuted and hauled about in every which way to
satisfy their caprices.
We must have a free ballot and fair court and the will of the Majority shall be respected.
We have no grudge against any person in particular, but we are the
enemies of bulldozers and tyrants.
If the old system should continue, death would be a relief to our
suffering. And for our rights our lives are the least we can
pledge.
If the fact that we are law-abiding citizens is questioned, come out
to our houses and see the hunger and desolation we are suffering; and "this" is the result of the deceitful and corrupt methods
of "bossism."

The White Caps, 1,500 Strong and Gaining Daily

In San Miguel County, Republicans were the influential party,
among whom the most influential were perhaps the Romeros, who had
held political offices, including that of territorial delegate, owned
ranching and commercial interests, and generally had swayed the local
vote. Now action was galvanized by the political system's seeming
inability to guarantee the sanctity of the Las Vegas Grant in San Miguel
County from encroachment. The takeover of major parts of the Tierra
Amarilla and Chama land grants caused deep anger, and in 1889 over
fifteen hundred members of Las Gorras took to night riding, destroying
fences, and physically intimidating their enemies—a practice they
continued on an occasional basis for several years. They demanded that
Mexican rights be respected, that encroachment on the Las Vegas grant
cease, and that access to water be maintained for all users; and by 1890,
Las Gorras had succeeded both through violence and its participation
in the Knights of Labor in temporarily slowing major incursions against
the land grants.

To further their goals, Las Gorras members also participated in
rudimentary organized-labor activities. Initially, Las Gorras had used
violence to counter the machinations of the railroads, which flagrantly
violated the common people's water rights, depressed wages to exploi-

tive levels, and sought to initiate disastrous rate competition among Mexican teamsters supplying the railroads with lumber. In 1889, three hundred members of Las Gorras destroyed more than nine thousand railroad ties belonging to the Atchison, Topeka and Santa Fe line. Las Gorras members also responded significantly through their participation in the Knights of Labor; and to the displeasure of the national Knights president, Terence V. Powderly, the Knights assemblies of San Miguel County became the railroads' overtly militant enemies. The Knights tried to alleviate the economic ills caused by the railroads by demanding high wages and high standard freight rates, and locally, the Knights became a public "arm" and proselytizing audience for Las Gorras. Eventually, Las Gorras emphasized electoral politics that were familiar to members and leaders who had been influenced by Juan José Herrera, a major leader acting in conjunctive agreement with Félix Martínez, an influential Democratic investor and publisher.

El Partido del Pueblo was created by a number of complex and often contradictory elements that sought to maximize the power potential in the Las Gorras challenge to established authorities. Ostensibly, the Partido adopted as its platform the issues raised by Las Gorras, especially the issues of land and the common people's mistreatment by dominant political leaders, both Anglo and Mexican. The Partido also somewhat favored anti-monopolist positions. As a reform effort, the Partido advocated anti-Republicanism, because the Republicans were associated with large land and railroad interests, even though Republicans were linked to the PDP; and in this way, the Partido coincided with the Populist Party while it was simultaneously more socially inclusive. The "Partido" was also aligned with Democratic Party elements, to the extent that office-holding Republicans were attacked and weakened. There were legitimate grievances and courageous leaders, as well as a full chessboard of players with diverse and immediate interests that were superimposed on family, local, and partisan ties.

The founders of El Partido del Pueblo constituted a coalition of lower middle-class Mexican Democrats, disgruntled middle-class Mexican Republicans, Anglo lawyers and laborers, and a larger and more resentful Mexican labor membership. Ostensibly, all of these diverse elements agreed on the necessity of displacing the Republican Party from control of the state government. In 1890, El Partido, with the support of disgruntled political leaders, swept all offices in San Miguel County.

While the Partido ran both Anglos and mexicanos for office, the Mexican electorate showed a clear preference for candidates of their own nationality. The Partido had clearly won influence based on the Mexican's desire to settle the land issue through the electoral process; but even though the Partido was conscious of its constituencies' wants and needs, it failed to engage in the kind of politics that would guarantee the return or safeguard of the land grants, much less justice for former grant holders. The influence it gained was not sufficient for such a major task, and it could not solve the conundrum of how the electoral, judicial, or economic rights of the dispossessed could be secured in a legal system that favors corporate capital.

One major reason for the Partido's failure was the Republican Party's intense opposition. During this period, the Alliance League and Los Caballeros de Ley y Orden, counterorganizations opposed to Las Gorras, were initiated; the League was the more overtly and electorally partisan, while the Los Caballeros offered protection and conducted reprisals. The Republicans organized the Sociedad de los Caballeros de Ley y Orden y Protección Mutua to offset the electoral support that the Las Gorras-dominated Knights of Labor had developed for the Partido del Pueblo. The Republicans also organized a newspaper, *El Sol de Mayo* (1891), to counteract the popularity of the Partido's sometimes sympathetic *La Voz del Pueblo* (1889). Between 1891 and 1894, the Partido and the Republicans engaged in fierce verbal battles, competed for new recruits, and sought to discredit and disrupt each other's organization. There were also instances of physical violence: the death of Faustino Ortiz, a Republican ward leader; the attempted assassination of Catron and, in reprisal, the lamentable assassination of Francisco Chaves, an effective and charismatic leader of the insurgent populist Democrats and a public sympathizer of Las Gorras (who, in fact, was suspected of being one of Las Gorras's covert but major leaders).

In 1892, the Partido again won control of San Miguel County, although its support had been cut noticeably by the Republicans and would continue to be diminished. Several circumstances contributed to the Partido's loss of public support: (1) fencing of common land was a less immediate and pressing problem; (2) factional political loyalties had been invigorated by the Partido's efforts to develop solutions for incorporating and registering land titles; and (3) the Mexican-labor majority, who were mostly excluded from leadership and holding office by the Partido's middle-class leaders, reduced their participation as

Republicans and regular Democrats courted the leaders, whose "progressive" rhetoric seemed to grow more distant from the initial issues. Public support also fell off because of factors. When dissident partisan leaders received the recognition and leverage they had sought, they moved away from the Partido. Furthermore, the brief but intense populist militancy became disconcerting to many Partido members, for whom rivalries were best conducted in conventional ways. For Mexicans, the core issues were land, water, and impoverishment, which could not be addressed either fully or effectively through the existing system of electoral politics any more than they could be resolved through the practices of the court system. But in any case, the Democrats made notable gains over the previously dominant Republicans, and the 1890s marked a turning point in New Mexico biparty politics.

By 1894, the Partido had been decimated by factional disputes among its leadership, the adverse economic effects of the Depression of 1893, and increasing factional conflict. Although El Partido del Pueblo essentially had followed traditional mobilizing tactics and had not resolved the crucial issues of the principles of landownership and use, it nevertheless reflected the people's struggles and aspirations. Las Gorras Blancas, the Knights of Labor, and El Partido were all manifestations of the New Mexican's cultural and class consciousness, which was expressed through conserving traditional landownership and usage patterns, as well as through the effective expression of a democratic local sentiment willing to use new modes of politics in addressing labor and reform issues.

Legal authorities were unable to suppress Las Gorras completely. As late as 1903 over three hundred men rode several nights through Anton Chico, destroying Anglo fences on Mexican land. Intermittent violent activity lasted until 1926.

Discrete Community Organizations and Networks

In contrast to these continuous organizational efforts were the more discrete, less flamboyant ones that lay within the sphere of the community.[73] In Nuevo México, the traditionalist, more low-profile Penitentes provided an organization and leadership that maintained religious and cultural rights as well as providing succor. The Penitentes' responsibilities and procedures were clearly defined and its leadership process was stated clearly. Their persistence reflected their base in small villages pervaded by community grants, work practices, and small economic enterprise as well by an explicit sentiment of village and kinship ties that would be the targets of slander and attack by foreign bishops, the rich, and intolerant Protestants. But the Penitentes survived and their organization actually became more extensive and elabrate in the nineteenth and early twentieth centuries. Acequia organizations of local water distribution also strengthened rather than weakened in organization, which now followed written procedures and regularly scheduled meetings.

Interest, occupational, or specialized groups of one kind or another also continued to thrive. Also present, though on an infrequent basis, were Masonic groups in which Mexicans participated; some of these groups, comprised wholly of Mexican members, owed their existence to Mexican Freemasonry, while others, whose membership included only a few, select Mexicans, were a part of U.S. Freemasonry. *Sociedades literarias,* literary and philosophical groups, also were commonly organized with a constitution, bylaws, procedural and membership requirements, and an explicit schedule. There were also music, church, and civic groups, and, importantly, worker associations.

Mutual-aid group organizing would emerge and eventually provide a major organizational pattern.[74] In different parts of the Southwest, there arose mutual-aid groups such as the Club Recíproco of Corpus Christi, Texas, which began as early as 1873, and La Sociedad Hispano Americana de Beneficio Mutuo, of Los Angeles, California, which dated from 1875. These organizations offered modest financial and material support for dues-paying members, particularly at the time of family death or illness, or in some cases, when the head of the family became unemployed. For many groups, organizational objectives became more ambitious. La Sociedad, for example, was incorporated for the purpose of creating a charitable fund and the establishment of a hospital, and announced events organized to raise the needed monies. Furthermore, a petition was circulated and presented to the city council for a Spanish-language school, and other projects to improve the community were encouraged. The preeminent mutual-aid society, and the one that eventually slated a public civil-rights agenda as well as a regional network, was La Alianza Hispano-Americana, founded in Tucson, Arizona, in 1893. In part, La Alianza was a product of the civic activism that had been visible in southern Arizona for several decades, and it included political veterans like Manuel Samaniego, Carlos Velasco, and the younger Ignacio Calvillo. Organized along the lines of a fraternal order, with specific procedures and a constitution, it held regular meetings locally and convened a biannual assembly; and its benefits of several hundred dollars for members were relatively attractive.

Throughout the last half of the nineteenth century, Mexican consuls and, eventually, consulates were incrementally active in the Southwest.[75] Mexican consulates played a modest political role in responding to conflictual relations, seeking to protect the Mexican community in the United States, its own citizens in particular, and encouraging trade with Mexico. The Mexican consul in San Francisco protested the punitive foreign Miners Tax of 1850 as a violation of the Treaty of Guadalupe Hidalgo, and generally sought to protect Mexicans from Anglo violence. As post-1850 persecution of Mexicans continued, the consulates supported the establishment of colonias in Mexico, and lands, funds, and transportation were obtained through them.

From the middle of the nineteenth century until the middle of the twentieth century, the consulates were at the center of the social and cultural activity in the community. Throughout the nineteenth century, the consulates were relatively active on behalf of Mexican civil land-property rights. Though success, or even the possibility of consular action, was uneven, the consulates fomented concern for, and identification with, Mexico through the part they played in the continuing celebration of Cinco de Mayo and the Sixteenth of September commemorations. Consulates, who were members of a local social hierarchy, might reflect or take up community currents or issues, but as officers of a foreign government they could not reduce grievances. They also reacted negatively to groups and individuals who seemed threatening to the Mexican government in office.

Women's Transitions

Class differences continued along with anti-Mexican chauvinism, and both involved women who were being impacted by change.[76] In Southwestern society, with all its modifications and "specialness," the poor, the landless, Indians, *and* women did not generally participate in formal means of leadership. Participation for women was linked strongly to their socioeconomic status and their indirect impact on men. The wealth of an elite family often involved women, even though these women may not have emerged as major public figures, as the men did. In some cases, stricter social rules were increasingly reinforced, rather than lessening with the pervasiveness of Anglo society. Arguably, women lost some of their previous property rights, but the economy either opened or enforced others. Under Anglo Saxon precedent, a wife possessed limited standing. Legally, she could not own property or sign a contract, but over the long term, the imperatives of the electoral system eventually increased women's rights.

A few prominent women were close to politics. [77] The successful del Valle family was headed, for a time, by the matriarch Isabel del Valle. Here was a family which perhaps escaped the California elite's worst ruins. The family fame was used by Helen Hunt Jackson as the basis of her novel *Ramona* (1883), in which the head of the family was described fictionally as a haughty and cruel woman. In actuality, the financially very successful and inventive del Valle family made money in several ways: they increased their wealth by transforming their sheep and cattle farming into intensive farming and advantageously selling parts of their land without it being taken over by Anglos; and they catered to tourists visiting the house of "Ramona," which was owned by the del Valles. The del Valle offspring were educated to enter the professions, and the family successfully maintained their participation in politics and civic affairs well into the twentieth century.

Even more wealthy and influential was Doña Arcadia Bandini (1827–1912), whose life span encompassed the time of the Mexican Republic and the twentieth century. Attractive and reluctant to speak English, she married two influential Anglos: first, Abel Stearns, and later, Colonel Robert Baker; and through philanthropy, she supported many civic projects. Twice a widow and an astute investor, at her death Bandini's wealth was conservatively estimated at eight million dollars, and at real market value it would have been twice that amount, which would have made her the wealthiest woman in California. Arcadia Bandini shared some patterns of elite intermarriage, but not others. She made major donations benefiting the public, among them land for schools, parks, hospitals, and cemeteries. Truly, she enjoyed a position distinctly different from the majority of women.

The development from previous economic modes, which was directed toward industrial capitalism, had an effect on women, with increasing numbers seeking employment outside the home, working as seamstresses, and in textiles, canneries, laundries, and restaurants, as well as in other retail and light manufacturing establishments in both the Southwest and Mexico.[78] As they increased their numbers in the labor force, a few working-class women became familiar with, or engaged in, radical organizing during the late nineteenth century, participating from the beginning in the early anarchist and socialist movements; and even though they were not expected do so, eventually they exerted their leadership. Working women were forced to labor under virtually the same, or worse, conditions as men, and for comparably long hours at lower wages. Thus, women in the Southwest as well as in Mexico emerged as labor dissidents and organizers.

Accompanied by violence between social classes, the increasing proletarianization of Mexicans, and the intensification of an oppression based on ethnic prerogatives certainly made the situation of Southwestern working-class women more harsh; and their chances in life may have been even fewer than those of working women in Mexico. In the struggle against domination, women were too often limited to supporting the activities of men. They certainly played a strong role in the preservation of Mexican culture in the home, but they also contributed by participating in mutual-benefit and cultural societies that would be important in Mexican cultural and political activity. Although women were a part of all mobilizations involving mexicanos, they did not play major public roles. For example, women supporters were included in New Mexico's the militant Gorras Blancas and the Partido del Pueblo Unido of the 1890s.

Activists were the exceptions, even among nonconformist women; but several individuals gained a unique notoriety and reflected the society's currents of discontent and radical participation. Whether Lucy González Parsons, the well-known socialist, working-class activist from Texas who was usually identified as a U.S. Black, was, in fact, of Mexican mulatto descent, given her Spanish-surnamed parents, remains unclear, although she had Southwest experience and contacts and was described by her husband as Spanish and Indian.[79] In any case, she did not stress or claim either ethnicity, and she worked in the Chicago area among European immigrants as well as Mexicans. She gained prominence in the Chicago area as an organizer and activist from her efforts with the Haymarket martyrs in 1886, and for over fifty years she worked indefatigably to build socialist organizations in contentious urban areas.

At the turn of the century, the border was also a particularly intense area. A woman on the border, Teresa Urrea, or "la niña de Cabora," gained fame as a *curandera*, or healer, who made social pronouncements against the discriminatory practices of the Catholic church and the Díaz government and was particularly critical of the treatment of Indians.[80] She was associated with a revolt of Indians and mestizos in two northern Mexico mountain villages, and afterward she was forced to enter the United States, where her popularity increased among the Mexican residents to whom she propounded the opinion that local political rights must be respected, a common belief, but a radical one along the border. Her denunciations transformed her into a symbol of resistance to oppression.

Teresa Urrea's travails possessed several dimensions. Her trade of public healer incorporated, in some ways, the functions of the Indian curandera, but with Christian and communitarian political overtones that were more likely to be effective among rural mestizos. Certainly, she was not Indian in tradition, in dress, or in other features; "la santa de Cabora" became a *symbol* of mountain mestizo discontent in northern Mexico, witnessing local uprisings in 1892 even though her advocacy did not have any explicit progressive character politically. When she was expatriated, she concentrated on the healing of people, but voiced the grievances of workers, mine and track laborers among them. Whether she was an authentic rural charismatic, a nonconformist, another "holy woman," or a "loca," Teresa Urrea suggested an as yet unraveled amalgamation of women's discontent. But she also addressed issues of economic inequities, as well as gender and ethnic discrimination, and clearly, she symbolized a people's discontent.

Elsewhere, the political sphere was witnessing signs of unrest among Mexican women.[81] In central Mexico and along the border, women formed civic groups calling for greater female participation in a reform politics that would blossom in the early twentieth century but whose roots were formed earlier. In Mexico and in the Southwest, modest legal and social improvements for women were gained during the aftermath of each successive progressive period, even though the vote was not granted. Along with increased industrialization came the acknowledgment of the importance of schooling for all classes, women included. The fate of Mexican women in the United States generally paralleled that of their sisters in the south because of the cultural oppression, political subjugation, progressive economic displacement, and proletarianization of the Mexican people, all of which were the results of U.S. economic, cultural, and political hegemony. The tensions between programs of assimilation and of the preservation of national identity were significant factors in Mexican American political life, and were noted most often in disparities in schooling. Ethnic discrimination provided a stimulus for political activity among women, which developed among women teachers and writers along the border at the end of the nineteenth century and early in the twentieth century. Yet as these few sparks flared, the ashes of an updated conservatism were stirred.

To literate women on the border came a reaffirmation of domesticity and familial values from late nineteenth-century England, Europe, and Mexico, and coinciding with the apogee of the upper middle class under the Victoria reign and the Díaz regime.[82] Although this message was for the literate, it was diffused to others as well. The importance of the home, family, and motherhood was propounded extensively, along with reinvigorated notions of propriety that stressed conformity to conservative values. The church was highly active in this movement; but at the same time, the stress on personal cultivation and the domestic arts demanded recognition of the importance of education and protection for women. In the press and at public convocations, the roles and treatment of women, as well as their education, and employment, received some attention, and as modest as this was, it was greater than it had been. Thus, the diffusion of these values had paradoxical conservative and liberal effects, with, for example, the slow diffusion of Protestantism among Mexicans contributing to a greater latitude for women and the possibility of more diverse roles for them in religion. As major components of U.S. capitalism in the Southwest were affirmed and Mexican economic displacement, social discrimination, and cultural suppression took place, women were increasingly exploited and abused in their work and family relations. Paradoxically, industrialization, education, and domesticity were endorsed. At the same time, labor and civic organizing appeared among both women and men.

Again, the International

Two significant international events occurred at the end of the century. One extended the radius of U.S. expansionism into the Carib-

bean and the Pacific, while the other involved interventionism in
Central America.[83] In the press, the threat or actuality of intervention
generally was viewed negatively, and any moves against Mexico were
denounced, as were threats of filibustering or of further annexations.
The 1898 war evoked mixed responses and some convolutions, with
many Mexicans generally sympathetic to Cuban and Puerto Rican
independence and negative toward Spain, but sympathies were mixed
when the United States went to war against Spain. Alberto F. Martínez, a New Mexico schoolteacher, was fired for supporting Spain. At
the same time, protestations of loyalty to the United States were
proclaimed, and there were even a few volunteers. Colorado state
senator Casimiro Barela and New Mexico governor Miguel A. Otero
offered to raise companies for the war effort, and New Mexicans comprised two such companies. Spanish-language newspapers took opposing sides, yet the apprehension over the possibilities of perceptions of
disloyalty was plain. However, more people denounced United States
occupation of foreign territories once the war was seen plainly as the
means toward such an end.

Mexico affairs were more mixed. The coming of the Mexican
Revolution made a notable impact, particularly along the border,
where, as in the past, there were close relations with events in Mexico.[84] Border politics were galvanized as much by grievances on the
United States side as by issues originating from the Mexican side; and
on both sides violence was extensive. After 1898, there were indica-
tions of change in the border Mexicans' view of the Mexican government, ranging from less endorsement to more criticism. The political
relationship between Mexican communities in the United States and
the Porfirio Díaz regime in Mexico, which had succeeded the governments of presidents Juárez and Lerdo de Tejada, gradually grew increasingly important. San Francisco's La Voz del Nuevo Mundo (1878)
supported Díaz in the early 1880s, and Albuquerque's El Defensor del
Pueblo (1891) criticized him to the point of urging violence in the
1900s. At first, Porfirio Díaz had support in his bids for power along
both sides of the border region; later, however, the border became a
refuge for opponents of President Díaz.

Three individuals were particularly prominent.[85] Forced into exile
by the Mexican government, Paulino Martínez, an uncompromising
reform liberal, continued his opposition to the government from San
Antonio, publishing El Monitor Democratico (1888), and from Laredo,

Texas, where he published *La Voz de Juárez* (1889) and *El Chinaco* (1890). He was a constant advocate of political participation while in the United States, and Martínez survived to play a role in the Díaz opposition. Another veteran of politics in Mexico, the idiosyncratic General Ignacio Martínez, exile resident of Brownsville, also published a newspaper critical of Díaz, *El Mundo* (1885), while sporadically planning rebellions involving other Mexican residents of Texas. In 1891, Martínez was shot down by horsemen who fled to Nuevo Laredo. Later, Francisco Ruiz Sandoval recruited fifty men, allegedly for action in Mexico; but when they were denounced to U.S. authorities and Ruiz Sandoval and ten others were arrested, the Laredo jury refused to convict them. Even so, Ruiz was not as well respected as others in his family involved in opposition activities.

Like some others along the border, Catarino E. Garza worked in both Texas and Mexico.[86] Both Garza and his wife were educated and modestly propertied individuals, although some of their relatives were wealthy. In the late 1880s and early 1890s, Catarino Garza of Brownsville and Eagle Pass participated in local electoral politics; published two newspapers, *El Libre Pensador* (1890) and *El Comercio Mexicano* (1888); and criticized the violence, usurpation, and manipulation suffered by Mexican Americans. He particularly denounced the Democrats. During 1888, he confronted a U.S. customs inspector for assassinating two Mexican prisoners. Garza was wounded in the confrontation, and when he recovered his activities became more adamant, with both he and his family members suffering as a result. Garza drew support from small farmers, laborers, and some former Juan Cortina sympathizers on both sides of the border. Many Anglo landowners feared him, and Texas politicians mobilized against him. An outspoken critic of the Díaz regime in his publications, he also tried to organize several revolts along the border, with his major attempt coming in 1892. Briefly successful, Garza was forced back across the border to the United States, where a special force of Rangers as well as an army unit and some volunteers, including Mexicans, were deployed against his raiders. Several men were captured, and Garza, unable to flee into Mexico, eluded capture by traveling to New Orleans and eventually to Central America, where reportedly he was killed while fighting on the Liberal side against Conservative partisans. Garza enjoyed wide local respect on the border, as is evident from the two corridos dedicated to him.

In Texas, sporadic efforts were made to defend Mexican exiles from persecution and extradition. With the tolerance and sometimes active support of the United States, the Mexican government countered its opposition by subsidizing a press favorable to its policies, organizing public support, and increasing its vigilance of radicals. In effect, both sides sought to discredit each other, with one accusing the other of insufficient patriotism. New and traditional opposition was met by both old and new forms of repression—by immigration, for example.

The Coming Growth

The need for labor underscored the value of a Mexican population even as the people were castigated. Immigration was a nineteenth-century phenomenon that had continued through the change in sovereignty. Thousands were reported in California and Texas and in the mining areas of other territories. In the 1900 census, over 100,000 persons were reported to have been born in Mexico, and this was a low figure. Immigration also placed on the table of public-policy discussion pertinent questions concerning a Mexican population within U.S. jurisdiction. The 1882 head tax law and the 1885 contract labor laws were national polity initiatives impacting Mexicans regionally. Also of consequence indirectly were the Chinese Exclusion Act of 1882 and the Gentleman's Agreement of 1907 with Japan. More immediately, however, immigration also affected numbers. In a particularly qualified way, immigrant Mexicans were subject to all other disabilities experienced by resident Mexicans, but, in addition, they were de jure disenfranchised and subject to deportation. The segregation of Mexicans and their primary utility as labor were visible in the location of their residences, the barrios, and the labor camps ubiquitous in the Southwest.

The Bottom Time

Industrialization, urbanization, mass capital, and mass labor evolved on a parallel plane with anti-Mexican chauvinism, discrimination, and disenfranchisement. Since the most significant interests involved in the United States–Mexico War were those of United States businessmen and companies, as well as of adventurous individuals in pursuit of the region's resources and land, interests that continued to be paramount where status meant wealth; for generally, political practices were exclusionary and favored the wealthy.

Capital growth during the last fifty years had taken much and given less to the mexicanos. But such was the game of material progress for those who did not establish the rules. Across the spectrum of local and state politics were a few impermeable varieties that would remain salient for at least several generations: (1) the uniqueness of the mexicano communities as land-rooted, ethnic, and cultural enclaves; (2) the persistence of cultural and political efforts in behalf of their own interests; and (3) the animosity and exploitation they faced—which was striking considering the so-called tolerance for the presence and contribution of those whose suffering received so little notice from interpreters or shapers of the American experiment.

4
A New Century and
New Challenges, 1900–1941

Themes and Conditions

A varied and adamant political discourse reflected the Mexican community's experience of a more complex process of social change as the country expanded, integrated social groups, and changed as a whole.[1] During the first fifty years of the twentieth century, the Mexican community was shaped by three principal processes: increased industrialization, immigration, and urbanization. With progress in these areas came the further development of a transformational and interactive political organization. Since Mexicans provided a basic labor resource of gradually increasing importance in mining, agriculture, and construction, regional labor conflicts increased, with poor wages and work conditions stimulating labor organizing, which became fairly widespread. Simultaneously, larger numbers of migrants arrived from Mexico, and the urban communities took on greater importance.

Mexican communities extended beyond the Southwest: urban affairs and leaders predominated over their rural counterparts, and politics were a mix of the conventional with the radical. Although electoral political activity continued in its late nineteenth-century forms, radical, socialist, and anarcho-communist groups appeared. Thus, political activity, on one hand, concentrated on electoral representation and civic issues, and on the other, attempted to secure a major transformation, through extralegal means if necessary. Most activity, however, was oriented toward the local needs of the communities in the United States, with some activity concerned with events in Mexico.

Intertwined were aspects of immigration, labor exploitation and repression, rural–urban dichotomies, cultural reaffirmation, deculturalization, increased politicalization, labor conflict, intracommunity factionalism, and transborder politics, as well as the quests for educational
emancipation and political equities. Most of these elements were the
continuing development of what had been visible in the late nineteenth century, and were rooted in the economy and in class relations.
These trends were preeminently evident in the five major contemporary problems of the community: political disparateness, ideological
ambiguousness, economic exploitation, social fragmentation, and educational discrimination. Thus, the three areas of contestation would be
the ideological, the political, and the economic.

Though the early 1900s seemed like a nadir, the twentieth century
would confront the Mexican community in the United States with an
accelerating process of social, economic, and political change.[2] In
1900, the status of the Mexican population of the United States was
generally dismal and nowhere more graphic than in the area of political
representation. In California, an occasional Mexican assemblyman
appeared (the last to be elected to office was in 1908, and the last
Mexican state senator served in 1912). Texas was at its lowest point of
mexicano representation, although there were several Mexican local
officials. Southern Colorado and the Tucson and Yuma areas of Arizona
had some elected mexicano representation. The exception to the
accelerating decrease in Mexican representation was the territory of
New Mexico, soon to become a state in 1912, where Nuevo Mexicanos
comprised the majority of the population; yet even here mexicanos
enjoyed less political representation than they had possessed during the
decades following the middle of the nineteenth century. Though mexicanos continued to hold office in some areas, Anglos increasingly controlled economic resources and dominated politically. The decrease in
representation was due both to the growth of systematic discrimination
based on a recognized special relationship between Mexicans and Anglo-Americans, and to the rapid increase in the southwestern Anglo-
American population, which, outside New Mexico, the Rio Grande
Valley, and some border counties, greatly outnumbered Mexicans. In
this period, Anglo and European migrants to the Southwest arrived
with ethnic and cultural biases, and they frequently adopted and
thereby reinforced existing prejudices. Particularly hostile were Anglos

from the South, as well as East European immigrants—Poles, Jews, Slavs, and others—who frequently sought to dominate over Mexicans.

From 1848 to 1900 the Mexican population in the United States grew from 116,000 to 500,000.[3] Massive European immigration in the same period, however, increased the total U.S. population to nearly 100 million. Thus, while Mexican population increased, the percentage of Mexicans in 1900 was claimed to constitute less than 1 percent of the population of the republic. But in the Southwest areas of significant population concentration continued to exist. Mexican population began to increase after 1900 at a much greater absolute rate for several reasons, apart from reproduction: the economic development of the Southwest United States; economic development in Mexico that stimulated labor displacement and migration; the increasing linkage of the economies of the two countries; the population displacements of the Mexican Revolution; and the economic stimulus and labor demands of World War I. By the beginning of the World War II Mexicans numbered over two and a half million.

For the Mexican people of the Southwest, increased economic migration represented a numerical, cultural, and ideological strengthening of the population, as already existing transborder contacts and influences were increased and expanded. Increased migration, combined with the rapidly expanding economy of the Southwest, led to the expansion of large urban concentrations of Mexicans in the Southwest's major cities. Mexican communities were established outside the Southwest in such midwestern centers as Chicago and Kansas City, where colonies of railroad workers provided the nucleus of the developing barrios. Los Angeles and San Antonio, in particular, became the major centers of concentration, with such cities as Denver, San Diego, Houston, Oakland, Phoenix, Tucson, Laredo, and El Paso forming major secondary Mexican cultural and social communities. Each had several social and political organizations, and occasionally a continuing Spanish-language press reflected the political spectrum.

The increase in Mexican population in the United States brought with it social, regional, and class diversity within the Mexican community, and was reflected in greater organizational participation and diversity as well as a continuing discourse on the culture's political identity.[4] *Mexicanidad, hispanicismo,* and *americanización* were not merely known and identifiable tendencies expressed by individuals and meriting some argumentative notions; they became relatively explicit commitments to be defended and argued not only culturally and socially, but also to be manipulated politically. Mexicanidad was obviously the more rooted and widespread tendency, but politically it was the most convoluted. Though it predates 1910, it grew stronger as nationalism was articulated in Mexico. Music, art, poetry, dance, and literature that seemed to be particularly Mexican were viewed as exemplifying mexicanidad. Mexicanidad could entertain strong ethnic *indigenista* and cultural sentiments and loyalties alongside a spectrum of political affiliations, even utopian ones, and yet distinguish all these from formalities of citizenship and preferences in residence, even though at its core was the notion of "us" versus "them." In contrast to the other two tendencies, no one other than Mexicans contributed to mexicanidad. Psychologically and politically, *hispanicismo* and *americanización* were more transparent; however, *hispanofilia*, or love of the "Spanish," was more interesting at the time. On the surface, seemingly, claims of being "Spanish" could be factual or false, and *hispanidad* could be endorsed by those of settler descent or by immigrants. Apart from individuals born in Spain, claims to Spanish ethnicity were and continue to be, for the most part, a social and political ploy introduced by prejudiced Anglos and adopted by mestizos to curry favor. Among nineteenth-century political figures, a few allude to this claim in a way roughly analogous to claims to criollismo in Mexico.

In the twentieth century, the "Spanish" ploy definitely bears upon social and political argumentation and even possesses a literature, even though it was and is an abstraction since there is no materially organic relation linking Spain's ongoing evolution with that of the Southwest. Both Anglos and natives contribute to the "Spanish fantasy"; though it demarcates the native from the Anglo foreigner, it is also frequently anti-Mexican and anti-Indian and invariably a means of disassociation from the Mexican. It is rarely found on the liberal-to-progressive side of the political spectrum, more often forming a part of the conservative-to-reactionary discourse. But substantive or not, the Spanish ploy would recur over the decades; and "americanización," the forced inculcation of alleged "American" culture and status, would not only be continuous, but would comprise a discourse raised by members of the dominant society, particularly and ironically by descendants of eastern European–origin minorities as well as by eventually assimilated perons of Mexican descent. Initially, "Americanization" was targeted mostly at

East European minorities, and, in turn, some educators from these groups became its apostles.

In fact, "Americanization" was aggressively promoted with significant resources, but Mexicans were a relatively late-targeted group. The anti-Mexicanness tendency was both proactive and reactive, and was institutionally supported, particularly by the Protestant churches, the schools, and some Catholic spokespersons. In political discourse, "americanización" was dissonant in two ways. One way was the promulgation of the majority society's obvious ethnic chauvinism; the other way was disfunctional to ethnic mobilization qua ethnicity, which was one of its intentions.

Mexicans suffered assaults with scant major institutional protection raised in their behalf. Though they were mostly Catholic, they were often treated by the church as second-class members. And even though they were primarily workers, the established AFL unions begrudgingly tolerated only a few, who were often in the ranks of those attacking the Mexican presence. Schools offered very little to youth in general, and were mostly hostile to Mexicans. Only occasionally were writers interested in their problems, and the English-language newspapers not only had no Mexican participants, but were a source of sensational negative news about them. Protestant churches were interested only in changing them, and philanthropic institutions cared little for their progress or welfare. Yet mexicano communities developed despite such indifference and hostility. Within the United States generally, Mexicans continued to be socially and politically excluded from the dominant society and its institutions. Nativism and chauvinist antagonisms were especially intense during this period; many Mexicans were subject to terrorism, coercion, and murder in its most brutal form, lynching.

Demographic growth and diversification spurred the growth of cultural and mutual-aid groups, publications, small businesses, and entertainment enterprises. A larger population also stimulated the continuance of class differentiation within the Mexican community and in its relation to U.S. society as a whole. In part, a reaction to this already existing network of organizations, such as the *mutualistas* and the Alianza Hispano-Americano, spread, and new organizations like the Liga Protectora Latina arose. Organization in the defense of the Mexican people regionally increased, and was reflected in groups such as El Congreso Mexicanista in Texas and in the attempts of Mexican organizations to coordinate activities in communities throughout the United

States. Mexican farmers and agricultural workers, particularly in Texas and Nuevo México, were major activists in the populist movement and in the Land Leagues fighting for the rights of the small landowner. Similarly, throughout the first decades of the twentieth century, many unions and workers' groups waged a struggle in defense of the economic rights of Mexican workers. Though they were not the majority, many Mexicans were significant participants in labor struggles in the South and the Midwest regions of the United States, even where they were systematically excluded from leadership or from union membership by exclusionist unions such as the American Federation of Labor. Mexican workers played an important and often leading role, especially in the more militant sectors of the U.S. labor movement such as the Industrial Workers of the World (the IWW). Moreover, community and labor activism occurred within a context of international intensity and a greater access to information.

Spanish-language newspapers were major vehicles of such communication because of the increase in literacy and in both human and material resources for their production.[5] Newspapers ranged in size from small to medium, four to eight pages in length. They depended on their readership and on advertisements for financial survival. They were a middle-class business, and with few exceptions, they were managed and produced by members of this sector. Generally, they supported civic participation and cultural enforcement, while opposing discrimination and intervention in Mexico. Owners of newspapers ranged from business persons to active políticos, and from organizations or groups to self-sacrificing, self-appointed advocates. Within their shared commonalities, the newspapers varied in their editorial positions and the focus of their content. For example, some opposed confrontational tactics, especially by workers, but called for employment fairness; others empathized with one faction or another in local contentions or in Mexico, while still others refrained from overtly partisan positions.

Newspapers were a basic vehicle for political news. *La Crónica* (1910) of Texas and *El Labrador* (1896) of New Mexico stressed regional issues, while *El Heraldo de Mexico* (1915) of Los Angeles emphasized aspects of immigration. Among the scores of newspapers across the Southwest were *Regeneración* (1900), a major ideological newspaper that appeared in Mexico, Texas, and Los Angeles; Laredo's *El Defensor del Obrero* (1905), and Los Angeles's *Revolución* (1908). The more successful informational newspapers were *La Prensa* (1913), in San Antonio, and *La Opinión* (1926), in Los Angeles, both of which covered a range of topics with a special interest in Mexico, while practicing a moderate editorial policy. Both papers were founded by the middle-class immigrant Ignacio E. Lozano, whose descendants continued for the next several decades to make a significant contribution to the institutional resources of the community. Consistently liberal and never radical or reactionary, they defended civil rights and denounced discrimination.

International economic expansion and military conflict affected Mexicans and their condition. On a world scale, the twentieth century was marked by increasing rivalry between great powers, with investments and trade reaching the available geographical limits of expansion. In this context, the U.S. economy outpaced the production of all other industrial nations, particularly in basic industries such as steel, heavy machinery, machine tools, and chemicals, and technologically advanced areas like electricity and petroleum. United States investment in Latin America and the colonial world increased dramatically in oil, copper, iron ore, and rubber.

With the victory in the Spanish American War of 1898, the United States emerged as a leading international and colonial power, directly controlling colonies in the Philippines, Puerto Rico, Guam, the Marianas, Samoa, and Panama. With the outbreak of World War I, the United States took advantage of the conflict to capture many of the international markets of the warring European powers. Even in the midst of an internal rebellion, Mexico continued to be part of the international vortex because it was a leading producer of petroleum in the world and a major supplier to the Allies. As the world war continued, British, French, and German investors were forced to dispose of many of their Mexican and Latin American investments by selling them to U.S. financed firms, and thus contributing to greater U.S. economic hegemony in most of the Western Hemisphere. Mexicans were drafted into the U.S. labor and military mobilization, where they served with distinction on the western front alongside regular troops and British and French colonial subjects. At the same time, United States interference and intervention in Mexico increased as U.S. policymakers attempted to manipulate the 1910–1920 conflict to their own advantage under the guise of "protecting American lives and interests." Anti-Mexican feelings led to intervention at Veracruz and the Punitive

Expedition, and in turn, these incursions were bitterly resented by the Mexican people, in general, and by many Mexicans in the United States, in particular.

The Mexican Magnet

Working-class and lower middle-class ties and interests with Mexico persisted across two broad sectors.[6] Throughout the Mexican communities, from San Francisco to Houston, thousands followed events in Mexico and identified with political issues there. Indeed, relations between Mexican people in the United States and those in Mexico reached a high point that would not be exceeded until late in the twentieth century. These ties were reflected in some of the activities of the hundreds of Mexican societies, mutualistas, and civic, social, and political associations located in the major centers of the Mexican population in the United States, where Mexican heritage and related matters were emphasized.

With a stake in U.S. society generally and with ties to Mexico, large sectors of the Mexican population followed events in Mexico that directly affected the members of their own families living under the Porfirio Díaz regime (1876–1911). Recently arrived immigrants moved among established residents, particularly in labor. Despite the barriers erected by Anglo chauvinism in the ranks of the radical left in the United States, Mexican immigrant workers were to be found in the leading efforts of the labor struggle in several areas of strife; and the syndicalist and socialist movements in the southwestern United States, and wherever conditions permitted, shared in the exercise of local leadership. Radical Mexican workers played an active part in the newly organized Industrial Workers of the World and the Socialist Party. In many instances, militant immigrant Mexican workers gained their experience in trade-union struggle against foreign companies in Mexico, or in the struggle for the organization of Mexican workers in the United States. In other cases of transborder ties, lower middle-class immigrants played a role in the struggle for the democratic, human, and civic rights of the resident Mexican community. Where local conditions permitted, some of these immigrants acted as spokespersons for the local Mexican community. Moreover, the Mexican people in the United States provided a dynamic and broad base for a variety of leaders and propagandists arriving from Mexico.

As in the past, the question of Mexico played a significant part in determining future consequences concerning international relations and domestic U.S. financial interests as well as Mexican relations across the borders.[7] The establishment and consolidation of the Porfirio Díaz regime represented the political hegemony of those sectors of Mexico's ruling elite that favored an economic policy based on foreign investment and maximum benefits to the owners of production. Mexico exported raw materials, and the wealthy realized immense profits from such labor-intensive industries as mining and commercial agriculture. The development of the Mexican economic infrastructure via a partnership between foreign and domestic owners generated changes in most spheres of Mexico's social life, and stimulated the growth of nationalist, electoral, and radical movements. A small but dynamic and expanding industrial proletariat arose, composed of workers involved in the extraction of minerals, light manufacturing, and transportation. The increasing commercialization of agriculture created a new strata of landless workers, many of whom previously had enjoyed some economic independence. Internal conflict in Mexico was imminent, and eventually the economic, social, and political contradictions involved the Mexican wealthy, the middle-class, the workers, and the campesinos in political ferment that lasted for two decades. Members of the Mexican elite, however, found themselves in conflict with the formation of the electoral suffrage, trade-unionist, anarcho-syndicalist, feminist, and, later, socialist movements among sectors of the intellectuals, the lower middle class, the industrial workers, and the agricultural wage laborers.

The Mexican economy increasingly became subject to the effects of cyclical depressions, inflation, and periodic mass unemployment, which, in turn, generated social unrest, while the government attempted to maintain the conditions necessary for the profitable exploitation of labor and the nation's resources. Fluctuating economic conditions and the lack of an electoral democracy contributed to the increasing discontent with the extreme socioeconomic contradictions that distanced foreign capital and the comprador elite from the majority of the people. The small but socially important lower middle class, in resenting the lack of political democracy that kept them from effective participation, organized to change the exploitation, deplorable working conditions, inflation, periodic employment, and hunger from which the vast majority of laboring people suffered. At the same time, divisions were noticeable between the ranks of the elite linked to foreign companies and the small, national free-standing business and manufacturing sectors that complained of increasing competition with foreign capital.

Overt dissatisfaction was reflected in periodic and spontaneous work stoppages, riots, and individual acts of resistance against the government and foreign companies. Ideologically, dissatisfaction was reflected in the emergence of an anti-regime opposition from the ranks of the nation's intellectual bourgeoisie, middle class, and industrial working-class sectors, including women. These struggles took the form of electoral discontent by members of the middle class, student demonstrations, the organization of small circles of workers and intellectuals espousing radical, nationalist, anarchist and syndicalist, and even Indianist ideas. Political clubs were formed that were primarily interested in electoral and legal reform. Political opposition coalesced, evolved, split, and also crossed the border. In 1900, the nucleus of the opposition to the regime had crystalized around the Liberal Clubs organized by Camilo Arriaga, a wealthy engineer and mine owner from San Luis Potosí. The Liberal Clubs reflected an ideologically diverse and oppositionist political spectrum, including elements primarily interested in democratic electoral reform and a policy favoring development for Mexican capital. In contrast, radical oppositionists favored the overthrow of the capitalist state and argued for basic economic and social changes in the interest of the laborers. Soon a split occurred within the regime's opposition movement, and the electoral faction came to be led by Francisco Madero, while another, calling for social economic measures as priorities, was led by Ricardo Flores Magón.

The overall dissatisfaction also generated local leaders who were not associated at first with formal political groups. Ideological opposition to the dictatorship increased in scope and in propagandistic activities. The main body of the liberal movement stepped up its attacks on the regime by using the medium of a radical press, which included newspapers such as *El Hijo del Ahuizote* (1884) and *Regeneración* (1900). Opposition liberals focused on the democratic demand of "no reelection" of the president or of state governors, and they pointed to federal, state, and local elected offices that were monopolized by the ruling elite surrounding the president. The opposition radicals emphasized labor organizing as well as rural movements seeking to oppose and to end large landownership and the power of large companies.

Given their difficulties, both moderate and radical opposition chose, or were forced, to consider forces across the border. Largely under the leadership of the radical opposition, major demonstrations erupted against the abuses of the Díaz regime. The response was a repressive wave of police violence, mass arrests, and suppression of the radical press. Known leaders and militants and scores of others were persecuted or imprisoned along with hundreds of rank-and-file opponents. Many who escaped or who were released were forced into exile in the United States. The Flores Magonista leaders of the radical movement arrived in Texas and met in Laredo on February 5, 1904, to plan the transborder reorganization of their movement and the overthrow of the regime. The southwestern Mexican communities along the border felt the impact of these developments in mining areas, agricultural camps, and towns like Los Angeles. Unlike many revolutionary exiles from Europe, Asia, and Africa, Mexican revolutionaries arriving in the United States found themselves in the midst of a large and growing dynamic sector of their working class, which was fairly receptive to the revolutionary ideas of Mexican radicals and among whom they already had contacts and adherents. The revolutionaries also consciously chose not to retire to the parlor politics or hat-in-hand politics so often common to exiles. They now proceeded to organize a base where circumstances had placed them, in the Mexican communities of the Southwest, where, in fact, one more layer was added to an already active political arena.

Social Classes and Dynamics of the Mexican Community

For Mexicans in the United States, the political relations of the time were affected by incremental changes in class composition and alignments affecting women and men.[8] Ironically, the class most in decline within the U.S. Mexican community was the minuscule bourgeois or capitalist sector, which presumably was the most respected in the larger society. Except for isolated cases of reputedly wealthy individuals, it appears that few Mexicans who were permanent residents of the United States could be considered members of the bourgeoisie as it was generally understood. Certainly, few individuals possessed ownership of the "means of production" or sufficient capital to "reproduce itself" at levels sufficient to be considered other than comfortably wealthy. Among such individuals may have been isolated owners of commercial agricultural lands and mineral resources, and perhaps a few large-scale merchants and professionals who had managed to multiply small amounts of capital with fortuitous investments.

Outside the network of the very wealthy few in New Mexico, there was no politically cohesive and active sector of wealth within the Mexican community in the United States during this period. To the extent that there were individual wealthy Mexicans, some of these persons and their families tended to identify with the wealthy class in Mexico, with the Anglo-American wealthy, or with both. In some cases, especially in border areas like Texas, such people were bicultural and identified with the elites of both nations, and to the extent that they exercised influence within the Mexican community, it was in association with members of the larger sector of wealthy Anglos. Apart from loss of wealth and discrimination, the sparse numbers of wealthy persons of Mexican descent was partially explained by the tendency of those with wealth to assimilate socially and culturally into the Anglo population. In many cases, assimilation had become a precondition of social mobility and the maintenance of status. For all intents and purposes, therefore, some of such individuals abandoned significant connection with the Mexican community and, in effect, became members of the Anglo upper-middle and upper classes. But there were obvious examples of this sector's continuance in Mexican leadership roles according to area and individual means and abilities.

The various sectors of the Mexican middle class were numerically larger than the wealthy and constituted a recognizable strata. Historically, the middle class was an important and influential political sector within the Mexican community in the United States. Such individuals, often through organizations, continued to provide some political, social, and cultural leadership for sectors of the Mexican working class, with their influence ranging from advocacy of virtually complete subordination of the interests of the Mexican community to the outspoken militant defense of Mexican social, cultural, and economic interests. Generally, the type of influence exercised by the middle class as a whole has corresponded with its class interests at a given time and place.

Major variables that condition dynamics within the Mexican petite bourgeoisie have included the degree of their social and economic approximation to the Anglo middle class locally, and opportunities or disadvantages derived from their advantaged position within the Mexican community.

There were two continuing and contradictory trends within the Mexican middle class. On the one hand, its members sought to escape from oppression as members of the Mexican nationality by identifying with or even completely assimilating into the dominant Anglo-American population. On the other hand, they sought economic, social, and political advantages to be gained from their position as the upper strata within the Mexican population. These contrasting tendencies were intermixed in the social practice of middle-class individuals and important in any attempt to analyze their political behavior and influence.

During the 1848–1941 period, when overt anti-Mexican chauvinism was most intense, members of the middle class—composed primarily of small-scale retail merchants, agriculturalists, and ranchers, and a handful of professionals and semiprofessionals such as doctors, pharmacists, public notaries, morticians, and teachers—struggled to maintain themselves as members of a modestly advantaged economic sector. Mexican retail merchants and storekeepers usually were at a disadvantage, however, with Anglo and European immigrant merchants. Mexican merchants had fewer resources to buy wholesale at favorable rates, and their trade was circumscribed by the income of the Mexican worker. Mexican teachers, where they existed, usually taught in segregated Mexican schools and were paid at lower rates than Anglo educators. The Mexican middle sector tended to maintain a moderate civic profile, particularly when called upon by Anglo authorities to act as intermediaries with the community. An exception to this pattern occurred in instances when community survival and basic civil rights were threatened. In cases of unusually severe brutality and injustice, members of the middle class organized defensive activities, which usually took the form of appeals to the "responsible elite" in the dominant Anglo community to use their influence in preventing further outrages and restoring order. Collections were also sometimes taken to aid victims and their families.

In their recognition as the "elite," the "respectable sector" of the Mexican community, members of the middle class also provided social and cultural influence. While economically based in the Mexican

community, some in the middle class sought to copy and cultivate a
Mexican identity and culture that was based on the model of the values
and norms of the upper and middle classes in Mexico. A countertrend
to this social pattern was offered by individuals who, under favorable
circumstances, sought social mobility in the dominant Anglo society.
The price of such mobility at this time, however, usually involved at
least partial denial of Mexican identity, which was accomplished by
clams to "Spanish descent" and mixed European descent and in stren-
uous efforts to assimilate.

There were two intermediate sectors quite distinct and even distant
from one another: farmers and émigrés, who were undergoing changes
of a particular kind beyond those occurring because of industrialization
and urbanization. Throughout the twenties and thirties there survived
thousands of small farmers who combined their production with part-
time work for hire in several of the southwestern states, with the
exception of California. These enclaves of traditional culture and fairly
evenly shared work responsibilities among women and men, the young
and the old, in some cases also represented voter enclaves. These small
producers were increasingly unable to maintain themselves, resulting
in family and gender as well as electoral changes. Some integrated into
the wage-labor sector, while others became part of the lower rungs of
the middle sector, usually through education but sometimes by way of a
small business. Another distinct sector was composed of upper- and
middle-class émigré Mexicans from Mexico, rather than of immigrants
seeking wages. These individuals possessed sufficient economic means
to be temporarily independent of existing economic relations and to be
fairly well-informed on formal culture as well as committed to a political and/or religious conviction. They began arriving prior to 1920 and
continued through the 1920s, and ideologically they represented the
spectrum of Mexico's political and institutional life. They could not be
categorized simplistically as to their political viewpoint or according to
their great wealth. The exiles with most wealth and political standing
went to New York and Paris, not to the Southwest. Some émigrées in
the Southwest returned to Mexico, while others stayed, the overwhelming majority of whom were lower and upper middle class; and
when they merged they became skilled workers or part of the white-
collar sectors. The most frequent situation resulted in a loss of status,
income, and public voice, in contrast to their previous situation in
Mexico. The attitudes they communicated to their children about

being Mexican and about the larger society combined pride with re-sentment. Although they were an aggrieved element and were often involved in a variety of political manifestations, they did provide individuals who became leaders.

During this period, and historically, the most socially important strata of the Mexican people in the United States were the majority, the working people.[9] After the annexation of Mexico's northern prov-inces, Mexican labor provided a gradual but increasingly important sector of the U.S. labor force. After 1848, Mexican labor in Mexico and the United States experienced several major phases of economic and social transformation. These phases coincided with the interna-tionalization of capital and labor, the consolidation of regional into national markets and the international market, and the transition from an agrarian to an industrial economy, from being direct producers to becoming an agrarian labor force and an industrial work force, and from a situation in which few people did more than unskilled industrial work in a few basic activities to one in which more people were involved in a broader range in both skills and industries. In effect, the Mexican labor force in the United States moved from involvement primarily in agriculture and grazing, with a small declining artisan sector, to become a growing urban laborer class involved basically in semiskilled work. This change occurred in concert with the increasing integration of Southwest and Pacific regional economies into the na-tional economy and home market of the United States and the estab-lishment of a capitalist infrastructure and commercial agriculture. This integration, which included Mexican workers and was functionally important, did not result in improved standards, but only intensified already existing practices of repression. This work force, however, was not an undifferentiated mass of unskilled workers: most performed skilled and semiskilled tasks, even though their employers' job classi-fication would seem to have contradicted this fact; and as in the past, but with greater frequency now, they produced individual leaders.

Mexican workers, the largest sector in the community, were se-verely disadvantaged both in their condition and in their organization as workers. Only in a few instances was labor's political mobilization salient beyond that of the community as a whole.[10] During this period, Mexican labor suffered from severe and open chauvinism displayed by both Anglo employers and laborers. In general, Mexican laborers were restricted to employment in the most menial tasks and subjected to

severe working conditions. Where they were employed alongside Anglo and East European workers, they were paid at a lower wage scale,
the "Mexican rate"; and they were usually segregated by occupation or
shift, which was frequently contracted on a temporary or irregular basis
and was supervised by an Anglo foreman.

Employers systematically utilized and promoted national and ethnic
chauvinism to divide the labor force and enforce discipline. As a
consequence, Mexican laborers frequently suffered hostility in the form
of violence from Anglo and European workers. Such was the case in the
developing mining industry, where Mexicans were viewed as taking
"white men's jobs." An 1896 strike at the Old Dominion copper mine
in Globe, Arizona, resulted in its major demand being the exclusion of
Mexican workers.

Unionization alongside Anglo workers was not readily available to
Mexican workers. Yet Mexican workers increased despite such negative
conditions. Concurrently, a relentless change occurred pushed by several factors, including: U.S. investment and production hegemony in
the Mexican economy; the growing interdependence and incorporation of Mexico's labor force as a source of labor supply for the United
States; and a large-scale migration of Mexican workers to the Southwest. Taken together, these forces intensified the transformation of
Mexican labor from one whose workers were employed in small numbers by individual owners to a mass wage-labor force working for large
companies; and at the same time, their local rights grew worse or were
lost. Railroad construction, one aspect of the construction of an economic infrastructure, was a significant force contributing to changes in
the rural economy and the labor force of the U.S. Southwest and
Mexico.

Combined with an increase in the growth of mass industrial labor
and commercialized intensive agriculture, several conditions created
the growth of a vulnerable mobile force of wage laborers. The collective organization of workers was as difficult as the maintenance of their
voting rights, if, that is, they had them. Exploitive working conditions
and anti-Mexican chauvinism gave impetus to the labor struggle and to
organizing against class and ethnic oppression. As participants in the
major union struggles, Mexican workers battled within the labor movement itself for the right to work in the same occupations as Anglos and
European immigrants, and for equal wages, better working conditions,
and the basic right to join labor organizations or to form their associa-

tions. Where they were allowed membership, Mexican workers joined and actively participated in labor organizations. In general, until the founding of the CIO, Mexican workers were able to achieve only limited admission to North American unions, but they still made relatively large-scale mobilizing efforts, with agricultural labor conflict involving the entire family and the major strikes in San Antonio and Los Angeles including women who were part of the majority.

Women occupied a subordinate position in all the different classes and in the constituent families. Their situation was more disadvantaged than that of the males vis-à-vis the larger society. Political changes for women were occurring slowly because of slight increases in access to education, but also, and more importantly, due to their participation in the work force in greater numbers. Under conditions of severe exploitation, the most important political movement for women gave limited support to Mexican women's rights but through it the eventual attainment of suffrage.

Social, Cultural, and Civil Rights Organizations

At the end of the nineteenth and the beginning of the twentieth century, the increasing size and diversity of the Mexican community in the United States, as well as the discrimination it faced and its heritage of organization stimulated the growth of various cultural and civic-type organizations, which were to contribute to organizational germination throughout the following decades.[11] Along the border, Mexican masonic orders dating from the nineteenth century had been involved in the defense of mexicanos and their culture. The Mexican masonic lodges were membership-exclusive organizations composed mainly of small entrepreneurs and middle-class elements. Although, to some extent, the Mexican masonic movement had its origins in anticlericalism and early republicanism, the organizations were culturally nationalistic and mainly interested in charitable and educational work, as well as in defending members' class interests and positions in the Mexican community. The Masons were a contributing influence to the development of other middle-class organizations that shared a common structure, form of selectivity, and ceremonies.

The Orden Caballeros de Honor was established at least by 1892 as a Mexican fraternal lodge whose purpose was philanthropic and cultural and involved both wage earners and lower middle-class activists. Particularly large chapters active in Brownsville, Corpus Christi, and Laredo were keen on structure, with dues and attendance required; their activities drew praise and holding lodge office became a notable honor.

Distinct from all these, and dating from the nineteenth century, *las sociedades patrióticas*, or *juntas patrióticas*, as the cultural associations were generally known, sponsored festivities for Mexican Independence Day, Cinco de Mayo parades, beauty contests, speeches, and debates about general social and political issues. Often, they worked closely with the Mexican consulates, and their cultural character reflected their political and social character. Membership was drawn from the remaining pioneering families, storekeepers, and the slightly more affluent people in the Mexican community, with some participation by women. *Comités cívico-patrióticos*, descendants of these earlier organizations, functioned throughout the twentieth century, and although their memberships and activities overlapped with that of others, there may have been class or status distinctions.

The mutualista societies had a more working-class character than the cultural juntas, and they were also more structured, with such telling names as *La Concordia, Miguel Hidalgo, Sociedad Obreros, Sociedad Juárez, Organización Hispano-Americana, Sociedad Progresista Mexicana, Sociedad Protección Mutua, Union Protectiva de Santa Fe, Sociedad Unión y Fraternidad Mexicana*, and *Sociedad Mutualista Hispano-Azteca*. Their membership was primarily composed of wage workers, some lower middle class elements, and a large number of new immigrants. Services at low cost as well as camaraderie were the principal attraction. For Mexicans, these organizations functioned as local institutions providing funeral and illness benefits, collective support, group defense, and cultural recreational services, and sometimes employment referrals as well. They were planned, organized, and directed by the members themselves, who provided both written constitutions and bylaws, as stated, for example, by the Organización Hispano-Americana:

> El primer objeto de esta sociedad es el ayudarnos mutuamente de
> una manera efectiva en todos los casos necesarios. Es decir en
> todo aquello en que por justicia y humanidad manifestar [sic]
> nuestra filantropía, con liberalidad. [12]
> [The first goal of this society is to help ourselves mutually in an ef-
> fective manner in all necessary instances. That is to say, in every-

thing in which, through justice and humanity, our philanthropy, with generosity, may be shown.]

To achieve the objective of mutual aid officers were assigned duties, and all members had responsibilities. Minutes were kept and attendance stipulated. There were explicit membership requirements, and as was customary among Mexican organizations, a *juramento*, or public oath, was required. Mutualistas varied in their membership, their services, their formal stipulation, and their financial resources as well as in the degree of their overt activities beyond specific death and illness benefits; as a whole, however, they encompassed thousands of members in the Southwest and the Midwest. The single largest network of mutualista local chapters was the Alianza Hispano-Americana, which began in the 1890s in Tucson, Arizona, and encompassed thousands of members, held regular meetings and conventions, and possessed a respectable fund that provided it with resources for its activities. Its significance was recognized:

> It must be confessed that in Arizona our brothers [*nuestros hermanos de raza*] are ahead, inasmuch as they have arrived at the grand conclusion that in union there is strength, and from the societies proceeds the well-being and progress of the people.
>
> The *Sociedad Alianza Hispano-Americana* has branches or lodges in Phoenix, Jerome, Congress, Tempe, Nogales, Yuma, Kofa, Clifton, Morenci, Metcalf, and other places that we do not recall in the territory of Arizona. In New Mexico they have finally been established in Silver City and Hillsboro, and there are hopes that many more might be established in different places.
>
> This institution was established in Tucson, Arizona, in the year 1898 [1894]. The benefits which it offers are enormous, protecting the wife and children with $1,000 in case of the death of the member, and in the case of the death of the wife, $200 for a decent funeral. Besides these benefits, there is weekly help of a doctor, medicine, and cash money.
>
> It is a demonstrated fact that by means of societies our people progress, and the society which concerns us [*La Alianza*] is solidly based with the funds it holds in reserve, and has always met its contractual obligations punctually.
>
> Every two years it has its conventions where all of the delegates of each lodge gather together to elect supreme officials, and to make whatever reforms might be necessary in the bylaws. The next convention will take place in Phoenix, capital of the territory of

Arizona, and it is hoped that a large number of delegates will attend since the Lodge there is making great preparations to worthily
receive all the delegates.

Young people have never had a better opportunity than now to
join a good society such as this. It costs them an extremely low
monthly fee and we hope that all will make a good effort to join, in
order that thus our people may be represented in a society that in
every sense protects the interests of the Hispano Americanos. [13]

Importantly, mutualistas were frequently the focal point in the
barrios for political and social activity, and also they indirectly participated in electoral politics. Some of these organizations' leaders were
wary of direct political activity even though it occurred. When the
community came under pressure, the mutualistas reacted at some levels, seeking support, for example, from the Mexican consulate. Occasionally, mutualistas tried to use the consulate services for lodging
complaints against Anglo authorities, and sought its cooperation in
cultural programs. During the twenties, apprehension surrounded the
"Americanization" movement because it would affect language and
cultural cohesion, and such concern encouraged countersteps to provide youth with cultural instruction.

Generally, mutualistas were not readily disposed to large-scale public protest, perhaps because of the racism and repression they encountered. A vigilante tradition of anti-Mexicanism and persecution were
facts of life for Mexicans, and the more easily such a tradition was
exercised, the more clearly identifiable the group became. More often,
mutualista groups acted to defend the community from direct persecution by complaints and appeals. On other occasions, individual members and local groups contributed to political activity or labor organizing. Through the twentieth century, mutualistas persisted among the
largest community-membership organizations, as radical civil rights
and electoral politics arose.

The First Congress

In reflecting the heightened consciousness of the times, a significant effort to coalesce Texas contemporary political activity and issues
was "El Primer Congreso Mexicanista" of 1911, held in Laredo, Texas,

during the week of September 14 through the 20, the independence holidays:[14]

> La idea de formar un Congreso Mexicanista, es grandiosa en todo concepto, pero más grandioso es plantar la obra: es decir, sembrar el árbol de la fraternidad en los corazones de los mexicanos todos; y mientras este comienza á desarrollarse con bastante lozaniá, el árbol que cobija á los déspotas comienza á carcomerse por los años: así pues, formémos desde luego en nuestro cerebro, en nuestra alma, los beneficios que reportaría la unión del elemento mexicano en el Estado de Texas.
> [The idea of forming a Mexicanist Congress is magnificent in every sense, but even more magnificent is the planting of the work, that is to say, planting the tree of brotherhood in the hearts of all Mexicans. While this begins to develop with much vigor, the tree that protects the despots begins, through the years, to decay. Let us therefore from this moment develop in our minds and in our souls the benefits the union of the Mexican element in the State of Texas would bring.]

A number of incidents from the 1890s through the century's first decade had aroused the Texas Mexican population, including lynchings and the persecution of the Cerda brothers and Gregorio Cortés:

> El Congreso Mexicanista, reunido hoy por elementos nuevos y al parecer heterogéneos y disímbolos, tiene lazos de unión tan estrechos que harán viables sus tendencias humanitarias á pesar de los trabajos disolventes que se le opongan; porque no es una vana presunción de figurar lo que nos convoca en este recinto. Nos traen aquí, las lágrimas.
> [The Mexicanist Congress, reunited today by new elements, seemingly heterogeneous and dissimilar, has ties of union so strong that they will make their humanitarian tendencies live, despite the disuniting work that opposes it, because it is no vain conjecture to imagine what brings us to this place. What brings us here is tears.]

Led by Nicasio Idar, editor of *La Crónica*, the Congreso's purpose was the organizational unification of Mexicans for action against social injustices. Such action was to be premised on a consensus that would arise from addressing the following questions: (1) Mexican civic consciousness, that is, "nationalism" in the community; (2) trade-union organizing; (3) social and education discrimination; (4) the role of the Republic of Mexico's consular offices and relations with consuls; (5) the necessity of community-supported schools to promote Spanish-language and Mexican cultural instruction by Mexican teachers; (6) strategies and tactics to protect Mexican lives and economic interests in Texas; and (7) the importance of women's issues and organizations for improving the situation of "La Raza." In part a civil rights agenda, the program was a combination of questions or themes as well as organizing or advocacy priorities that took into account cultural, economic and political aspects:

> El capital, como los políticos, ven un peligro amenazador para sus intereses cuando se trata, como en el asunto que nos ocupa, de unir al elemento obrero. Urge, pues, unir á la clase obrera y principalmente á los mexicanos que residimos en este país; pero aquí hay otro inconveniente: el méxico texano, tiene mucha razón para desconfiar de los que se dicen ser sus protectores; se han presentado tantos casos donde los políticos, durante las elecciones ofrecen dar á los trabajadores, tierras, protección y garantías, les ponen los ojos azules, tan azules como los de los blancos mientras escalan el puesto, después. . . . después necesitan los pueblos bajarlos de allá porque se hacen insoportables; de aquí que todo el tiempo nos encontremos divididos, y es natural que exista cierta desconfianza contra los que se proponen fraternizarlo. El asunto que nos ocupa en este momento, es encaminado á propagar la unificación del elemento obrero mexicano, hacer ver que unidos todos, cual una sola familia, nos guiemos por el principio de Fraternidad.
>
> [The capital, like the politicians, sees a threatening danger to its interests when it is a matter, as in the subject that occupies of, of uniting the worker element. It urges uniting the working class and principally the Mexicans living in this country. Here, though, there is another troublesome point: the Texas Mexican has much reason to mistrust those who say they are our protectors. So many cases have been presented where during an election the politicians offer to give the workers land, protection, and guarantees. They give them blue eyes, as blue as those of the whites, while they climb to their positions. Afterwards, afterwards, the people bring them down from them because they become unbearable. It is from this that we have forever been divided, and it is natural that a certain lack of confidence exists against those who propose brotherhood. The matter that occupies us at this moment is to put the spread of the unification of the Mexican working element on the right road,

to show that, all united together as only one family, we shall let ourselves be guided by the principle of brotherhood.]

A concluding statement by Father Pedro Grado summed up priorities:

There are two black points that, with a prophetic threat, sprout forth and grow in the pure heaven of our liberty and which day by day, worry all good Mexicans, all true patriots, and all persons who shelter altruism and philanthropy in their souls.

The first of these points concerns the oppression and the abuses that the sons of Uncle Sam commit daily to our countrymen, especially in the State of Texas.

The first point has the following classification: I. Bad application of the law when it deals with Mexicans. II. Unpunished molesting of Mexicans by particular Americans. III. The exclusion of Mexican children from the American schools.

Order demands that the bad application of the law in treating Mexicans be discussed. The disease has its remedy, and it is here that the utility of the Congreso Mexicanista is illustrated, inasmuch as experience teaches us that isolation causes weakness and that weakness produces failure. Reason tells us to make ourselves strong.[15]

The Congreso concluded its work by attempting to form "La Gran Liga Mexicanista," which was envisioned as an organization of organizations, including women's groups. It proposed five objectives, developed a constitution, and installed officers and collected funds. Its motto explicitly conveyed the ethos of the effort, "Por la raza y para la Raza," a motto that would appear again in larger Mexican American efforts. Education and ethnic pride were viewed as a means to strengthen the community; or as Soledad Flores stated:

Patria querida! Tus hijos se instruirán para conservarte, y sus inteligencias iluminadas por altos ideales serán tu salvaguardia. . . . Todavía la sangre fecunda de los niños héroes de Chapultepec dará ánimo a tus pequeños á quienes nosotras, sus madres, educaremos para que no se avergüencen nunca de decir que son mexicanos.

[Beloved homeland! Your children teach themselves to protect you, and their intelligence, illuminated by high ideals, will be your safeguard. The fertile blood of the boy heroes of Chapultepec will continue to inspire your little ones, whom we, their mothers, shall educate, so that they will never be ashamed to say they are Mexicans.]

The Congreso was rooted in the multiple organizational efforts of South Texas and was a result of careful planning and organization. Three to four hundred persons attended—both citizens and noncitizens—representing a spectrum of groups with the discussion in Spanish and exhibiting notable polemic interventions. Lack of resources as well as extremely hostile circumstances precluded longevity for the Congreso. Apart from the Gran Liga, the Congreso generated the Liga Femenil Mexicana, the majority of whose officers were teachers; it was one of several efforts by women.

Women

Mexican women's organizational participation in both Mexico and in the Southwest antedated the twentieth century, and in both places women's political organizing during the first two decades was related to labor and reform advocacy. [16] As the revolution ensued in Mexico, women's groups became a visible phenomenon. Most of the participants, whether in groups in Mexico or in the Southwest, came from the small landholders or the middle class, although some participants were from the wealthy sector. Both moderate and progressive tendencies could be found among women's groups, and were distinguishable very generally as two broad types: those who were reformers in different guises and those who advocated radical change—although in practice some participants were involved in both.

Texas seemed to have a stronger profile of women's activism than other areas, and the number of Mexican schoolteachers and newspapers may have contributed to this constituency. Many of these women were devoted to cultural enrichment, while others were more explicitly political. Hortencia Moncayo and Soledad Flores de Peña were among the women who helped to shape the Primer Congreso Mexicanista's political policies. [17] For example, Hortencia Moncayo insisted on proactive unity:

> ¿porqué no nos unimos en uno solo y organizamos debidamente
> una misma familia y prestamos el apoyo que necesita este Congreso
> Mexicanista, para que nos ayude y nos proteja?
> [Why are we not united as one only and duly organized as one self-
> same family, lending the support this Mexicanist Congress needs so
> that it can help and protect us?]

And Soledad Flores underscored what she and others believed would cement such unity:

> Más para esto, es necesario comprender bien los deberes de cada uno y obrar según ellos, yo, como vosotros creo, que el mejor medio para conseguirio es educar a la mujer, instruirla, darle ánimo á la vez que respetarla.
>
> [But for this, it is necessary to understand well the duties of each person and work according to them. I believe, as you do, that the best means to achieve this is to educate women, instruct them, and give them encouragement, at the same time that you respect them.]

Some women had a critical injunction as to both the personal and political changes that were required.[18] Such was the following statement in *Regeneración*, February 25, 1921, made by "El Grupo Regeneración" in San Antonio, whose officers were Presidenta Teresa Villareal, Secretaria Isidra M. de Ibarra, Vocal Concepción Ibarra, Colectoras Emilia T. de Sánchez, Teresa Villareal, C. Ibarra and Lina Love:

> Es alentado [r] que la mujer se [emancipe] y venga a tomar el puesto que le corresponde al lado de su compañero el hombre, en la grandiosa lucha social que tiende á la liberación de la humanidad. Ya es tiempo de que así sea. La mujer ha estado esclavizada al hombre por muchas centurias debido á la pésima organización social en que ha vivido la humanidad; se la ha enseñado a considerar al hombre como un ser superior; conforme á la ley es una menor de edad sin discernimiento propio y sujeta á la voluntad del padre, esposo o cualesquiera otro macho en la casa; por la Iglesia es más descaradamente considerada como una bazona humana, asqueroza y despreciable, sin mas voluntad que la del hombre de la casa, como por la ley; y en la práctica, en la vida diaria se tropieza a cada paso con los actos salvajes cometidos en las mujeres, que no hablan del todo a favor de la pretendida superioridad del hombre.
>
> Ya es tiempo de que la mujer se independiza y de que el hombre dejando de considerarse el centro del universo, cese de oprimarla y la de en la vida diaria el puesto de compañera que le corresponde. Por propio interés hasta por egoismo debe el ayudar a la mujer a independerse: mientras la mujer sea esclava, el hombre continuará siéndole tanto por influencia del sexto contrario, como por que es axiomático que una esclava amanta hijos esclavos fatalmente.

[It is encouraging that women emancipate themselves and come to take their place at the side of men, their comrades, in the great social struggle that tends toward humanity's liberation. Now is the time that it should be so. Women have been men's slaves for many centuries because of the very worst type of social organization in which humanity has been living. It has taught them to think of men as superior beings. In accord with the law, they are minors without their own sense of judgment and subject to the will of their fathers, spouses, or any other man in the home. More insolently, the church considers them human dirt, loathsome and despicable, with no more will than that of the men of the house, just like the law. In practice, in daily life, at every step one comes up against savage acts committed against women, which does not completely speak in favor of men's supposed superiority.

Now is the time for women to free themselves and for men to stop considering themselves the center of the universe, for them to stop oppressing them and give them in daily life the role of companion that corresponds to them. In their own interest, even for egotism's sake, they owe women help in freeing themselves. As long as women are slaves, men will continue being so, both because of the influence of the opposite sex and because it is axiomatic that a female slave fatally cloaks child slaves.]

Among prominent early twentieth-century women spokespersons was Sara Estela Ramírez, who accomplished much before dying at the age of twenty-nine.[19] Jovita Idar said of her:

. . . siempre estaba pronto para impartirnos del caudal de los vastos conocimientos que atesoraba; soberana de la moral, sus enseñanzas iban impregnadas de inteligencia, ternura y talento.

[She was always ready to give to us from the store of vast knowledge she had accumulated. Queen of what was ethically correct, her teachings were suffused with intelligence, tenderness, and talent.]

Born in Villa de Progreso, Coahuila, she attended the teacher's normal school at Saltillo and lived in Laredo, where she earned her living as a schoolteacher. Ramírez was a strong participant in cultural activity and was herself a romantic poet and newspaper writer. She published in *La Crónica* and *El Demócrata Fronterizo*, and she cofounded the publications *La Corregidora* and *Aurora*; and she was widely respected as a political speaker and organizer in the region. Ramírez stressed political action and organizing workers:

El obrero es el brazo, el corazón del mundo.

Y es á él, luchador incansable y tenaz, a quien está encomen-
dado el porvenir de la humanidad.

Que vosotros, obreros queridos, parte integrante del progreso
humano, celebreis aun, incontables aniversarios, y que con vuestro
ejemplo enseneis a las sociedades a quererse para ser mutualistas, y
a unirse para ser fuertes.

[The worker is the arm and the heart of the world.

It is to him, tireless and tenacious fighter, that the future of humanity is entrusted.

May you, dear workers, integral part of human progress, celebrate yet countless holidays and with your example teach societies
to love in order to be supporters of mutual aid and to unite in order
to be strong.]

A fervent supporter of worker organizing, she believed that mutualism
was a step toward laying the foundation for trade-union organization,
and she worked to support the Sociedad de Obreros and the Laredo
strikes of 1906. At the age of twenty or so, she came into contact with
the Flores Magón group, and by 1904 she was the designated representative and contact person for what would soon be the Partido Liberal
Mexicano (PLM):

Una digna correligionaria que siempre ha colaborado y colabora ac-
tivamente en nuestros trabajos.

[A worthy coreligionist who has always collaborated and actively
collaborates with our work.]

Clearly, her choice and stand was progressive in contrast to other
women activists of her time and later.

Anarchist and socialist activities were important to women's mobilization, as they were for labor or political activity generally.[20] But for
some the ideological was less important than other matters. The liberal
women's club "Leona Vicario" was devoted to educational reform, and
secondarily it supported PLM, as did the Liberal Union of Mexican
Women. Prominent women adherents of PLM do stand out; in addition
to Sara Estela Ramírez, there were María Talavera, Francisca Mendoza,
Modesta Abascal, Ethel Duffy Turner, and, for a while, Andrea and
Teresa Villareal, who were later associated with the periodical *La Mujer
Moderna* (1915–1919?), whose editor was Hermilda Galindo. The
PLM claimed that the oppression of women stemmed from the same
source as for men—primarily, private property and capital, and sec-

ondarily, state and church—and thus had to be combated in multiple ways and on many levels, including personal relations. The PLM called for equality between men and women and struggled against chauvinism, discrimination, or condescension, but it was critical of "feminism" per se, calling it a middle-class phenomenon. The "Grupo Regeneración" of San Antonio was made up of women who emphasized the PLM. As Sara E. Ramírez wrote to Flores Magón, factional discords made an impact:

> I've become sad and weary, Ricardo, of so many personal antagonisms. I tell you frankly, I am disillusioned with everything, absolutely everything . . . I don't want to analyze the causes of your quarrels with Camilito. I believe you both are right and both to blame.

Many women remained loyal to the PLM through its factional splits, even though they caused stress. For example, a March 4, 1912, letter from women adherents Margarita Andejos, Domitila Acuña, Severina Garza, María Cisneros, Concepción Martínez, and Carmen Lujan to Ricardo Flores Magón called for firm measures:

> [somos] trabajadoras emancipadas de las necias preocupaciones que han tenido a la humanidad esclavizada . . . Si los hombres no han abierto los ojos para ver claro, nosotras las mujeres no nos dejamos embabucar por los politicastros. Compañero Magón: duro con el burgés que desea encumbrarse para tenernos a los trabajadores con el mismo yugo que por siglos hemos padecido.
> [We are female workers freed from the stupid preoccupations that have enslaved humanity. If men have not opened their eyes in order to see clearly, we women shall not let ourselves be tricked by petty politicians. Comrade Magón: be hard with the bourgeois who wants to rise in order to keep us workers in the same yoke that we have suffered for centuries.]

Other women abandoned the PLM because it insistently called for revolution and for adherence to the directives of its junta, which made some too uncomfortable.

There were differing tendencies, but there were also ongoing contacts among activists. Women and others in the PLM worked together in La Liga Femenil Mexicanista of the Congreso Mexicanista,[21] and in several other women's efforts which took place in Texas and elsewhere.

In 1914, a women's group may have distributed a manifesto entitled "A los hijos de Cuauhtémoc, Hidalgo, Juárez,"[22] which advocated political insurgency in calling for disavowal of United States authority, armed rebellion, and the secession of the state from the United States. Women contributed to several publications, and at least two publications were established by women. San Antonio and Laredo women were also involved in a 1915 effort to bring peace among the contending factions during the Mexican Revolution through the Junta Femenil Pacifista, presided over by María de Jesús Perez. Others contributed to the founding of a "red cross" organization, La Cruz Blanca, such as Maria Villarreal and Leonor Villegas. Some women, such as Jovita Idar, María Villareal, and Leonor Villegas, supported Venustiano Carranza and his policies through the Club Femenil Constitutionalista. Several of these women from these activities would be active in educational, suffrage, and anti-discrimination efforts through the years.[23]

Women were potent spokespersons for factional moderation as well as advocates for specific rights. Thus, in the first two decades as well as through the thirties, women exhibited progressive to moderate tendencies similar to those in political activism generally. Efforts to secure suffrage were followed, in both the U.S. and Mexico as were feminist activities in Mexico for example, by the 1923 Primer Congreso Feminista de la Liga Panamericana de Mujeres and the biweekly *Mujer* (1927). Women's activities were prominent in Texas, New Mexico, and California. Among those active during the first two decades were some who would continue their activism in labor, the suffrage movement, and civic affairs through the thirties. Anarchist, civil rights, and communist groups provided organizational recognition in particular, though these types of organizations provided a relatively positive contrast with others in regard to women; hence, for the time, progressive women were subordinated in practice. Among women as well as men, a contradictory politics coupled with harsh economic conditions were part of a time of hope and disillusionment.

Statehood for Arizona and New Mexico

The territories of Arizona and New Mexico were admitted in 1922 as states in the Union—the last states from the territory of the Mexican cessation.[24] Territorial status for both had lasted fifty and sixty years, respectively, and places such as Utah and Nevada had been admitted before them. Apprehension was present among the leadership:

> We have clearly seen that a hostile sentiment has unfolded regarding the necessity of having interpreters in our courts and in our conventions, etc. This sentiment has hardened a true antagonism against the Spanish-speaking element. It was so pronounced among the majority [of Congress] that, if it had not been for the fact of the establishment of the Hamilton Law, through which if we accept [statehood] we will have our own government, legislation would have passed to prevent persons who are not able to speak and understand English well from serving on juries. In fact, Senator Spooner from Washington made such a proposition. . . .
>
> The other question of restricting suffrage for those who do not know English, was also much discussed, and this discussion took place in Washington and in the other states, as well as inside our own territory. And do not believe that it will stop at this point. In order to better prove the tendency of the American government toward the establishment of the English language in this country, we will cite the citizenship law that was decreed by the Congress which just adjourned. This prescribed that hereafter no person will be admitted as an American citizen until he knows the English language.
>
> Reflect, fellow citizens, on what this means if we remain longer under the tutelage of Congress. This is not a theory, it is a real and positive fact. For that reason we say that if we decline to accept the liberty of statehood, it is *more than probable* that the next Congress will decree legislation to define the qualifications for suffrage, as well as for the exercise of the duties of jurors and of public employees, based on knowledge of the English language. Cut out this paragraph and keep it well guarded in order that later you can see that the sincere and disinterested friend of the people warned you in proper time, *La Voz del Pueblo.*
>
> There is another probability, and this we wish the Neo-Mexicanos as well as the Arizonenses of Hispanic-American origin would make note of. If we form our own constitutional convention today, we are in numerical condition to see that the fundamental law will be one that does not deny us any of our rights. After being written, the constitution will be submitted to the vote of the people for their ratification or rejection. If it contains something that might be detrimental to our people, we will be able to reject that

clause or articulate while we are yet in numerical condition to do it, and we are able to do it. But if we reject statehood now, and we are admitted in ten or fifteen years, by that time the outside immigration will have drowned us numerically and then [it] will be very late to defend our rights. The constitution is the cement of a government; now is the time to construct that cement. If we do not do it now, perhaps tomorrow will come antagonistic peoples, and then [it] will be very late and we will see ourselves compelled to accept that which is given us, irrespective of our will. [25]

Repeated statehood attempts had been made by residents in both Arizona and New Mexico, and New Mexico Governor Miguel A. Otero, Jr., was an ardent advocate of statehood. Both ethnicity and partisanship were involved, for both territorial areas had heavy Mexican and Indian populations, one-sixth in Arizona and over half in New Mexico.

Republicans worried that Arizona would come under the control of the Democrats, who did not appreciate New Mexico's Republicanism. One characteristic the two populations shared was suspect loyalty; another was the language and culture of mexicanos. Senator Albert J. Beveridge raised these issues in 1902, declaring that the fact that both areas had contributed volunteers to the "glorious" war of 1898 demonstrated their loyalty. To lessen the impact of the admission of two states to the Union, one compromise, which was considered as late as 1906, would be to consolidate both territories into one state. New Mexico, the area with the larger population, favored this idea more than Arizona, but consolidation did not happen. On June 10, 1910, Congress passed an enabling act and constitutional conventions were called for both territories.

The Arizona convention was held at a time when anti-Mexican sentiment had reached a high pitch in a region noted for such hostility. [26] Agitation centered on two efforts—first, the attempt to enforce English language and civic requirements, which would, in effect, disenfranchise many Mexicans; and second, to eliminate "foreigners" from certain categories of employment. Both declarations were passed, but they were stated in such a way that protected native-born Mexicans.

Democrats, who were associated with both efforts, dominated the convention; and Carlos C. Jacome, the merchant from Tucson, was the only Mexican of the Yuma and Tucson leadership to play a role in the proceedings. The convention produced, then, a somewhat liberal document containing provisions for the initiative, referendum and recall, employer liability, and anti-child labor measures as well as placing some limits on corporate practices. And members at least discussed forbidding capital punishment and providing for juvenile delinquency, female suffrage, and other liberal concerns. The clearest measure of direct impact to Mexicans was the vote prohibiting formal segregation. A sigh of great relief came from the Mexican American local elite, who, more than most local elites, clung fervently to the conviction that Arizona, and Tucson in particular, treated Mexicans differently than Texas, California, or even New Mexico.

A threshold electoral-status change occurred once statehood became a reality in New Mexico; and if political relations continued as they had in the past, there was some incremental change.[27] The most significant change lay in the growing numbers of Anglos who eventually reached parity with Mexicans and eventually surpassed them. The thirty-two Mexicans, all Republicans, who served as delegates to the New Mexico constitutional convention attended by a total of one hundred members, were primarily directed by Solomón Luna, with Octaviano Larrazolo important inspirationally on a number of points.

With effective leadership, therefore, Hispanos were able to secure important constitutional provisions. Basic was the guarantee that distinct racial and linguistic groups would have the rights and privileges granted to all other residents. Furthermore, the rights enumerated in the Treaty of Guadalupe Hidalgo were explicitly recognized sixty years after its U.S. federal ratification. Language rights were affirmed in two areas, education and law; teachers were to be proficient in both English and Spanish, and laws were to be published in both languages for the next twenty years. Finally, amendment to the constitution was made difficult, with Hispanos ensuring, in effect, that provisions favoring them could not be easily changed. Amendments would require the approval of three-quarters of the electorate in the state, and two-thirds of those in each county; and the proposed amendment was required to be published in at least one newspaper in each county. One provision not specifically addressed by Hispanos, but one that would have an impact on them, was women's suffrage in school elections. Aside from these provisions, the convention was dominated by Republicans and produced a document favoring the monied interests centered in Santa Fe. Even so, the Mexicans had been recognized as political players, and they had secured a few but very specific guarantees for themselves, which, in itself, was unique for the southwestern states. However, the ethnic identity publicly articulated read "Spanish Americans" rather than "Mexicans."

Indeed, the constitution provided, in effect, a minimum program of safeguards for Mexicans: suffrage, language, schooling, and, implicitly, political representation; there was, as well, in the reference to the Treaty of Guadalupe Hidalgo, a specification of general protections:

Article II.
Sec. 5. *Rights under treaty of Guadalupe Hidalgo preserved.* The rights, privileges and immunities, civil, political and religious, guaranteed to the people of New Mexico by the treaty of Guadalupe Hidalgo shall be preserved inviolate.

Article VII.
Sec. 3. *Religious and racial equality protected, restrictions on amendments.* The right of any citizen of the state to vote, hold office, or sit upon juries, shall never be restricted, abridged or impaired on account of religion, race, language or color, or inability to speak, read or write the English or Spanish languages except as may be otherwise provided in this Constitution; and the provisions of this section and of section one of this article shall never be amended except upon a vote of the people of this state in an election at which at least three-fourths of the electors voting in the whole state, and at least two-thirds of those voting in each county of the state, shall vote for such amendment.

Article XII.
Sec. 8. *Teachers to learn English and Spanish.* The legislature shall provide for the training of teachers in the normal schools or otherwise so that they may become proficient in both the English and Spanish languages, to qualify them to teach Spanish-speaking pupils and students in the public schools and educational institutions of the State, and shall provide proper means and methods to facilitate the teaching of the English language and other branches of learning to such pupils and students.

Sec. 10. *Educational rights of children of Spanish descent.* Children of Spanish descent in the State of New Mexico shall never be denied the right and privilege of admission and attendance in the public schools or other public educational institutions of the State, and they shall never be classed in separate schools, but shall forever

enjoy perfect equality with other children in all public schools and
educational institutions of the State, and the legislature shall provide penalties for the violation of this section. This section shall
never be amended except upon a vote of the people of this State,
in an election at which at least three-fourths of the electors voting
in the whole State and at least twothirds of those voting in each
county in the State shall vote for such amendment. [28]

These were no small legislative accomplishments. Octaviano Larrazolo
was a moving force in making the protections as specific as possible;
hence, he was accused of raising "race feeling." His articulate voice
motivated Mexican delegates, and some Anglo opposition turned into
Anglo support. Fortunately, the convention was held while Mexicans
still possessed a numerical majority in the territory. And because electoral guarantees were granted independently of the ability to read,
speak, or read English, the suffrage obstacles common to Texas and
California were avoided. Spanish was recognized in the courts, on
ballots, and in legislatures.

The Hijos del País Movement

As in other parts of the Southwest, the population of Mexican
descent in New Mexico was experiencing a period of heightened consciousness and mobilization, but all in accordance with New Mexican
ways. Before and after the statehood convention there was apprehension about the possibility that the Mexican population either was or
would become disadvantaged politically. [29] Significantly, a "native son"
movement arose, inspired by the threat to rights expressed in discourse,
in writings, and more intensely in public assembly. The movement,
which was both cultural and political, liberal and conservative, was
partly a response to the relegation of Mexicans to a marginal and
foreign status as voiced by members of the elite as well as by populist
elements; and it emphasized cultural and political rights due to Hispanos as natives with historical claims. As pressure mounted, Hispanos
in state conventions of *both* parties adopted a more adamant posture,
and though both parties were blamed for past underrepresentation, the
Democrats, in particular, came under fire.

A major show of strength occurred in 1916, when Republicans
nominated an Anglo, and Democrats nominated the eventual winner,

Ezequiel Cabeza de Baca, who benefited from the native-son effort. A highly vitriolic campaign ensued, and the native-son press was strongly attacked, *La Voz del Pueblo* (1889) particularly. Upon Baca's death, and the ascendance to office of an Anglo Democrat, the tables turned again.

With both parties employing the same rhetoric, 1918 became the high point of the native-son movement. The demand for half of the positions became a basic practice in rhetoric. Both parties nominated Hispanos—the Republicans, Octaviano Larrazolo, and the Democrats, Félix García. Larrazolo was elected governor and served his term well as a capable liberal, while the more moderate Benigno Hernández was elected to Congress in 1918. Larrazolo strongly supported bilingual education and the concerns of small farmers, but provided little more than token support to industrial workers. Hispano representation declined between 1921 and 1932 as the native-son movement declined, even though some prominent victories were realized.

The state governors Ezequiel Cabeza de Baca and Octaviano A. Larrazolo, who were among the most significant Mexican politicians in New Mexico, were studies in contrast.[30] Cabeza de Baca, a moderate, was the descendant of a prominent family and son of a two-term member of the New Mexico Territorial Assembly, Judge Tomás Cabeza de Baca. In the 1880s, he entered politics as a Democrat and worked under the patronage of important Democratic político and wealthy businessman Félix Martínez, of Las Vegas, New Mexico, and alongside Antonio Lucero. All three men benefited economically and politically from the changes of the 1890s and the Republicans' splits. Cabeza de Baca, who often wrote for Martínez's newspaper, *La Voz del Pueblo*, gained political experience in campaigning for Democrats and in witnessing the activity of the Partido del Pueblo, in which both Democrats and dissident Republicans formed important factions. By 1910, Cabeza de Baca was editor of *La Voz del Pueblo* and chairman of the San Miguel County Democratic Party, and during the debate on the state constitution, he gained wider recognition through a series of articles articulating the particular constitutional interests of the Mexican population. Cabeza de Baca was thus chosen by the Democratic Party as its candidate for lieutenant governor in the first New Mexico state election of 1911; and as the first elected lieutenant governor of the new state, he served from 1912 to 1916. As lieutenant governor, he was credited with supporting bilingual education and the right of women to vote in school elections. In 1916, he was nominated for governor by the Democratic Party, waging a strong and emotional campaign, and the support of many Mexican Republicans helping in electing him as the third Mexican governor of New Mexico after 1848. Unfortunately, Cabeza de Baca died in February 1917, after only forty-seven days in the governor's office.

The native-son movement was associated with Larrazolo's electoral leadership, rhetoric, and maneuvers. He was one of two men born in Mexico to be elected governor of one of the United States.[31] Larrazolo was born in 1859, in the Valle de San Bartolomé, which is now Allende, Chihuahua; his family faced severe economic straits, and he was eventually orphaned on the border. Sponsored by Bishop J. B. Salpointe of Arizona, educated in Catholic schools in New Mexico and Arizona, and at one time considering the priesthood, Larrazolo became an attorney in El Paso, Texas, where he was twice elected district attorney in the early 1890s and served on the school board. Though he refused an offer to serve as counsel for the Santa Fe Railroad, he was active in private as well as in public service. He was a strong advocate of collective civic equities and for Mexican rights. In 1895, Larrazolo moved to Las Vegas, New Mexico, where he became a Democratic political candidate. Emphasizing ethnic representation, he ran for the post of territorial delegate in 1900 as a Democrat, but he lost by over three thousand votes. He ran again as a Democrat in 1906 and 1908, and lost by less than four hundred votes. After losing these three bitter contests, he denounced Democrats for "a decidedly unfriendly feeling and disposition towards the Spanish-American element in New Mexico," and he indicated that the offices of governor, senators, and other high representatives were meant for Anglos, while that of lieutenant governor was reserved for a Mexican. In his campaigns in the northern counties, he stressed the need for representation, but in 1911 he resigned from the Democratic Party because of the alleged lack of equal opportunity for Mexicans in the party—a resignation that may have ended his political career. As a Republican, Larrazolo was defeated for nomination as Superior Court Justice in 1913. However, he now became an important figure in the Republican Party because of his general political skills and his ability as an orator in both English or Spanish. Following his activity at the constitutional convention, he was blamed or credited with fomenting the native-son movement, although he was actually reflecting widespread feeling and was only one of several spokespersons. Historical claims and political rights were intertwined and rooted in the land, Larrazolo argued. Yet paradoxically, at the height of Larrazolo's influence and the impact of the native-son movement, Hispanos gave enthusiastic support to an Anglo from out of state.

In New Mexico, where ethnic consciousness was overt for many players, party divisions, not ethnic ones, were more politically visible, though these were a superimposition on others, including the ethnic.[32] Furthermore, to a limited extent ethnic representational rights were understood as conventions rather than as exceptions. As important as party affiliation was, the state apparatus was based on county organization, which included shifting alliances, some moving across party lines. These alliances, in turn, were controlled by a coterie of individuals representing local areas and, very often, kinship networks; the seniors in an extended family provided the core, one of whom was the spokesperson and granted respect, but was more a first among equals rather than an absolute leader. The spokesperson carried influence to the extent that benefits were produced, and the bargains that sealed the arrangement were temporary. A specific aspect that made the process a viable one was the distribution of places on the ticket and the promises of appointments. Anglos ran against Anglos, natives versus natives, and the distribution of offices was key, with platforms secondary; however, county platforms could be a significant signpost indicating local attitudes. To the coterie, electoral loss or displacement of a senior leader was compensated by some rewards to family members, sometimes by adding them to the state payroll. Favoring senior leadership rather than popular support was the key to admittance into the political arena, where personal contact, demonstrations of commitment, and proper appearances were important. Among New Mexico Hispano voters, a gradual swing to the Democrats was accompanied by more voter independence. In this seemingly liberal move to the Democratic Party, state-funded programs grew more important than liberal rhetoric; and as the decades passed, economic change undermined electoral arrangements to the extent that they were based on stable social networks rooted in traditional rural economies.

One characteristic of politics in New Mexico was the continual presence of Mexicans in office as well as their electoral participation, which was allegedly the result in large measure of a conscious bargain, a "gentlemen's agreement." Ostensibly, this agreement contained two

parts: (1) Anglo and Hispanos did not compete for the same offices; and
(2) certain state offices were the prerogative of Hispano candidates,
with others available for Anglos. Credit for advocating a balance
between the two major groups generally was given to Octaviano Larrazolo, who, it was said, had made this possible because he was a major
leader of the Mexican American people in the state. Yet Larrazolo's
leadership was always contested, and on occasion he was defeated; and
party conventions frequently were marked by intergroup clashes over
Anglo dominance and their tendency, if unchecked, to monopolize
nominations, that is, an alleged failure to observe "the gentlemen's
agreement." From the first, the call for representation was actually a
demand rather than a practice, and Larrazolo represented the aggrieved
political players more than the traditional insiders.

An increase in the Anglo population caused Hispano leaders to
consider the consequences of potentially enlarging the erosion of
power. Assertions to the effect that the Mexican people were "losing
out" politically were premised, in fact, on an existing imbalance. Since
statehood, the number of Mexican American officeholders had declined over the years, except in the lower house, where increases and
decreases alternated. Major offices, both elected and appointed, were
dominated by Anglos, and there was never an equal or proportional
division of political offices. There was a near absence of Mexicans in
the judicial branch of government, as well as in the governor's chair.
Mexicans who held these offices were exceptions. The governorship
continued to be a near monopoly of the Anglo Americans, and no
Hispano governor was elected after 1918 for more than fifty years.
Throughout the 1940s, the lieutenant governorship was more evenly
divided between the two predominant groups, but disparity remained.
Twelve Anglo Americans held the lieutenant governor's office, with
seven Spanish surnames appearing on the official record, and two
offices were held nearly exclusively by members of each major group.
Mexican Americans, including women, secured the office of secretary
of state, while Anglos held the post of state treasurer; and the auditor's office was often held by a Hispano. In general, state elective posts
were held by Anglos more often than not, and among major state
appointive offices Anglos were in the overwhelming majority. The
Anglo–Hispano disbalance, first evident after 1848, remained relatively unchanged throughout the twentieth century.

The ethnic distribution of legislative and county offices was more mixed than statewide offices. Anglo Americans were in the majority in the state Senate, and they came to have a bare majority in the House of Representatives. However, upward and downward trends occurred in Hispano representation in both houses. Anglos in county offices became a decided majority in the total seats held, while Hispanos were a majority in only a few counties; and some counties never elected a Mexican. However, Hispano participation in select northern counties was persistent. Mexicans were never elected in Anglo counties, but Anglos were elected in Mexican counties. Mexicans were indeed underrepresented in New Mexico, though they had significant numbers and were the majority population in the state until the thirties. There were also areas in which the voting participation of Hispanos was comparatively high. With some exceptions, Mexican candidates who challenged Anglos in tightly contested elections went down to defeat, and strongly supported Anglo candidates could capture whatever positions were targeted, including secretary of state and auditor, both of which were considered Hispano posts. In effect, to win Mexican candidates had to be unusually astute and have wide and unshakable support.

Texas

Perhaps the most diverse political context in the Southwest was Texas,[33] which reflected a growing population, both Anglo and Mexican; the overlays of immigration; and the relative diversity of the economy in some areas and the proximity to the border, where a relatively developed region existed simultaneously with turmoil in Mexico. There was no overall consensus established, and any local arrangements were continually challenged; the only stability was provided by the momentary acquiescence of Mexicans after a particularly brutal period of suppression in a given locality. Certainly, Mexican politics in Texas were not limited to electoral matters, which, in any case, were unusually convoluted compared to other parts of the Southwest; and they were, of course, shaped by a consensual reality unique to Texans. There was no doubt that the electoral participation allowed was permitted at the behest of Anglos; that is, even the bargaining that was possible through votes was a dispensation that could and was taken away. Furthermore, there was a clear understanding that Mexicans were not able to influence state policy, much less the federal; and county and city government were the imposed limits. Mexicans had the possibility of the vote when they were present in significant numbers and when it was to the interest of a section of the Anglo elite for them to vote. This possibility for local influence was enhanced markedly when there was still considerable Mexican landownership. Texas politics, shaped and fashioned by Anglos for Anglos, were nearly always corrupt and often brutal, and were not so much taught to Mexicans as imposed upon them. The only acceptable Mexican electoral leadership was that which, to a large extent, endorsed Anglo practices.

Texas Mexican electoral politics were an imitation of Anglo politics, if not their complete mirror image; and the image existed in the shadow of force and favoritism. Anglo marauding, followed by military occupation and Anglo control of the Austin statehouse, occasioned the need for some protection beyond the Mexicans' own numbers and their outmatched arms. Protection was dependent, of course, on an exchange of some kind, and the protectors were more likely to have both influence and resources. Most often, they were major merchants, the post-1848 major Anglo landowners, or the enterprising lawyer and all-purpose business agent. The more approachable were those who enjoyed some Mexican tie, familial or business, and were conversant in Spanish. Though class diversity existed within the community, by 1900 the majority of the Mexican population were laborers, or town, ranch, or farm hands; they were uniquely dependent upon their employers for sheer survival. Anglo immigration into Texas from other states continued through 1900; and these immigrants were even more anti-Mexican than previous Anglos. They understood that their economic horizons and political equities were limited by the entrenched Anglo elite and Mexicans, and they preferred not only to disenfranchise, but to remove Mexicans.

For some time, politics among Anglos were, to some extent, competitions for power among elite cliques, the older versus the newer. Reconstruction policies had allowed some dual party presence, and indeed a Democratic–Republican competition was present intermittently. The difference between parties was slight, but Texas had been mostly Confederate in sympathy and the partisan beneficiaries were conservative Democrats, who eventually became dominant. The Democratic primary was the important election, and it detracted from the latitude that existed for the Mexican, emphasizing adhesion to an outstanding local individual; and nearly all such individuals were Democrats. However, the primary occurred at the time when an aspiring candidate needed Mexicans most, and for some years Mexicans could vote in the party primary without citizenship. Anglo elites sought to control and organize the electorate as a whole, in addition to the Mexican subelectorate. The assignment for the latter was usually a local Mexican whose family had some standing, and who had sufficient education or experience to serve as a competent liaison. At the initiation of this arrangement, wherever it occurred, the Mexican leadership experienced some initiative and leverage; as the arrangement became stable, they grew increasingly dependent, and rather than negotiating, they became subordinates. In some cases, the Anglo "boss" dealt directly with the Mexican electorate, with no need of an intermediary. There were also instances of Mexican leaders with property and education in areas where Mexicans were a majority; these individuals retained some landownership and thus had significant local influence, such as that enjoyed by the Guerra and Canales families. Electoral arrangements were aided by the fact that how an individual voted could be known; but ultimately, the key ingredient was violence. When an option existed, some of the Mexican electorate could choose between the more accommodating Anglo elite or the more callous ones who espoused both reformism and anti-Mexicanism. Yet, in contrast to the trapped Mexican electorate, there were politically mobile sectors drawn from the pockets of nonagricultural wage workers; members of the lower middle class who participated in the more dissident efforts; or the small agricultural producers who either rose in armed revenge or joined benevolent organizations that stressed individual enhancement through mutual practices and began to propagate the belief of collective benefits through stable, delimited permanent organization.

A local arrangement in Texas involved a dominant figure and several major supporters and actors who endeavored to control and direct both county and city government.[34] Their presupposition was based on resources, skills, and standing; and contributions to and from constituents were combined with their influence over public employment, ranging from significant appointments to day laborers, to cleaning or repairing streets. Also significant was access to the courts, the governor's office, the state legislature, the federal government, and Congress. Neither the predominant figure nor his immediate circle were absolute, nor did their influence go unchallenged, but was continually confronted by "boss rule." In effect, local control represented shifting memberships and alliances with as many defections as there were, and charades between "ins" versus "outs" were replayed constantly. Graft and corruption were a part of local politics, as were loyalty and some vision of governance; in any case, both virtues and faults were shared by Republicans and Democrats, Anglos and Mexicans. With the onset of an ostensible movement of reformers—that is, "liberals" or "progressives"—the same tactics were practiced, but, if anything, "reformers" appeared even more prejudiced than those they sought to "reform." Texas was thus a patch quilt of local political relations that more or less followed county lines, but also fluctuated according to color schemes determined by conflicts between the urban and the rural, farmers opposed to ranchers, and Mexicans against Anglos.

Mexican electoral politics were particularly important in the towns of San Antonio, El Paso, Corpus Christi, Laredo, and Brownsville, and, in particular, the south Texas counties of Webb, Cameron, Hidalgo, Starr, and Duval. Mexicans may not have been in a position to initiate major policy, but their potential threat did cause the enactment of significant policies such as, first, the institution of the poll tax; second, the all-white primary; third, the enactment of laws pertinent to language and assistance at polls; fourth, the movement to subdivide counties; fifth, the institutionalization of segregation in schooling and residence for Mexicans; and sixth, the belated and brave, but defeated effort to limit the size and scope of Ranger activity, not because of their violent behavior, but due to their brazen intrusion in electoral politics. All of these policies were a response to the Mexican presence, their economic role, and their electoral participation. Regulations could be applied to contain the more controllable sectors of the Mexican migrant laborers and ranch hands and to limit the less controllable vote. The "race issue"—agitation against Mexicans—was exploited by all of the significant Anglo political sectors: Democrats, Republicans, progressives, and, to a lesser degree, even a few retrograde socialists, and even at the very times when the Mexican vote was sought. Furthermore, to the extent that an element of protection was involved in the electoral arrangement, it was striking that during moments of violent persecution, the alleged protectors did not protect, and they not only tolerated the violence; they protected the perpetrators of violence against Mexicans.

However the mix and contradictions of the arrangements changed, the partially Mexican-based Anglo leadership persisted from the nineteenth century to the 1960s, involving not only minor and middle-level officials, but figures of national importance like John Nance Gardner and Lyndon Baines Johnson. Such persistence, like other examples of political endurance, was a reflection of the satisfaction of constituent needs, and however idiosyncratic or opportunistic individual actions or the advocacy of issues may have been, they were consistent in furthering profit margins and political self-advancement. Because of the international, situational context of south Texas, customs authority and patronage intersected partisan activity, but because these resources were under federal jurisdiction, the party that held the White House could tilt county and city politics, as well as, to a lesser extent, the constitution of other federal offices.

Apart expecting support for their business transactions, the powers in control were concerned about, for example, the security of land titles now in the majority in Anglo hands; but in some areas, Mexican landholding persisted nevertheless; hence, there arose support for efforts toward making title securance convenient, such as recognizing entitlement by the Mexican Republic, even until 1848 in the Nueces strip; by notice of possession or by notice of allocation in a Mexican record, and also by equity to rights of possession. Taxes were a major and continuing concern; any likelihood of raising taxes engendered political energy, but the different sectors expressed somewhat different fears concerning taxes and all feared partisan or ethnically biased collection of taxes. Security in a violent land was desired by every sector, with each sector blaming a different form of insecurity and with violence further complicated by the border's proximity. Development was expected, and politics was expected to facilitate transportation, irrigation, finance, and an acquiescent and cheap labor force. An increasing concern for efficient government services, with regard to the administration of city, town, and county, also focused on the judiciary, law enforcement, and, most of all, electoral practices. In spite of the need to ameliorate actions, the reformers were no different than the stalwarts, and in any case, reform usually meant increased subjugation and discriminatory treatment.

Lastly, a deeply felt concern for schooling bore upon political patronage and Mexicans' access to teaching and it also strengthened a trend toward instituting a system of Mexican schools, not separate and equal but explicitly inferior. School reform by Anglos and for Anglos meant inferior education, and even no schooling, for Mexicans, a policy that provided an answer to several concerns pertinent to Anglo politics and economics. Prohibition, as espoused by middle-class Anglos with anti-Mexican feelings, repeatedly raised the political temperature, providing another rhetorical whip with which to castigate the Mexican community. There were Mexican Americans who were sympathetic to banning liquor, while other Mexicans benefited from its transport and sale before and after the issue was temporarily settled locally by the federal amendment; a few of these tradesmen realized modest fortunes that were parlayed into more legitimate investments as well as political influence.

Similarly, women's suffrage caused repeated controversies, with conservative Democrats rising in opposition, while other sectors generally supported suffrage provided that it was limited to Anglo women. However, distrust arose concerning the possible consequences of Mexican women voting, especially since this would increase the number of Mexican voters. Presumably, the Mexican community would oppose it, but in fact, Mexicans understood that the women's vote would be as fraught with travail as suffrage for the men. Among a range of viewpoints, the single elected Mexican official who could vote on the matter in the legislature, José T. Canales, was a steadfast proponent of extending the suffrage.

Local Mexican political leaders dealt with these issues vis-à-vis their own constituency as well as the Anglo leadership and political sectors. Both Republican and "Independent" voters generally shared the position of conservative Democrats because it suited their interests. But to survive, they needed to have respectability and to be accepted; and for them, as for others of their kind elsewhere, Anglo powerholders made it all possible. Mexican leaders were stronger than those in California, but weaker than those in New Mexico. The electoral leadership maintained elected positions through the first half of the twentieth century as city councilmen, constables, tax collectors, hide inspectors, justices of the peace, county commissioners, treasurers, and public attorneys, and several scores of patronage positions were also filled. The leadership did not put themselves forth as champion reformers or defenders at large, but within their limited purview their administration was ethnically more evenhanded. They opposed existing discrimination and any threat of its spread, and they were staunch defenders of, first, their own economic interests, and second, the Mexican vote; and both of these items obviously pertained to their own standing. If they broke ranks with the more powerful Anglos politicians, they, as well as their kin, suffered political, economic and physical reprisals, including murder. Despite periodic Republican insurgencies and even the florescence of an Independent effort, the Democratic Party increased its hegemony, and its hold on the Mexican electorate became even more pronounced through the New Deal. In tempo with this trend and resulting from this practice was the mystique of loyalty to the party, irrespective of issues and ethnic disparities, because the party was a vehicle of power, not a debating forum, and anyone who disagreed did not belong in politics. Inherent to such pervasiveness and loyalty was the submergence of beliefs on issues in order to achieve a livable compromise; the subjects of and the identities of the parties to such compromise were continually shifting matters.

Two figures particularly salient in electoral politics were Manuel Guerra of Starr County and José T. Canales of Cameron County, both of whom were descendants of settler families.[35] The conservative Manuel Guerra's political advance beyond a secondary role was partially made possible by the interethnic and partisan strife at Rio Grande City surrounding Catarino E. Garza and his followers as well as the Republican–Democrat rivalry. He was an educated, bilingual, and moderately wealthy merchant and landowner who secured the confidence of Jim Wells, a major political patron. In 1894, Guerra consolidated Democratic control in Starr County politics, in partnership with Sheriff W. W. Shely, and after Shely's demise he retained major control until his own death in 1915, whereupon his influence was continued by his son. In 1906, while he held a seat on the county commissioner's court and his brother Jacobo Guerra was county treasurer, he brazenly sought to make his cousin, Deodoro Guerra, sheriff and his son, H. P. Guerra, tax collector. Opposition within the Democratic ranks was led by a disgruntled aspirant, Gregorio Duffy, who went over to the Republicans. The Guerras won the struggle, but several murders surrounded this victory. Legal charges followed, but the Guerras emerged unscathed. As problems with dissident Democrats and Republicans mounted, Guerra moved to loosen his ties with conservative Democrat Jim Wells and a key local ally, County Judge John R. Monroe. For the county elections of 1910, he proposed a fusion ticket with nothing less than his own rivals, and worse, the enemies of his patron. Though this startling proposition failed to settle the problem of allocation of offices, Guerra then ran his own slate on the basis of his Mexican electorate. After winning the primary, Guerra was willing to compromise with his former allies, and next, he endorsed the division of Starr County, a proposal then gaining strength and pushed by Republicans, reformers, and Anglo farmers, and one which he had fiercely opposed previously because he believed it diminished the county. The division essentially created an Anglo county while maintaining a Mexican county and the Guerras. And if the Guerras were generally conventional in daily practice, they were daring in a few stratagems.

José T. Canales, the most prominent Mexican local elected official, was orthodox in his values and refused to conform on selected issues; yet his general position was conservative, and he certainly benefited from existing political practices, but what he resented acutely was discrimination.[36] Wealthy and educated as an attorney, possessing a strong interest in local history, and supported by Jim Wells, Canales followed a conservative Democratic line on most issues. To reassure his Anglo allies, he voiced the stock Texas Anglo mythology of the Alamo and "Texas Republic," and he was elected to the state legislature from 1905 to 1909. In 1910, he shifted to endorse the Independents; and while supporting prohibition sentiment, he ran for county judge in Cameron. Next, he focused on the office of superintendent of schools, which he won as a regular Democrat; and in this role, he vigorously supported improved teaching and larger resources for rural schools while he endorsed the curtailment of Spanish and later called for a ban on the teaching of German. During the turmoil of 1915–1916, Canales formed a volunteer force to assist the U.S. Army in operating on the border, while at the same time denouncing blatant anti-Mexican brutalities—the lone political figure to speak out with determination. Shifting once again, and now working in conjunction with Jim Wells, he was again elected to the state legislature. Upon being seated, he soon departed from the Democratic line and supported prohibition measures and women's suffrage, as well as measures that would restrict Mexican voting, such as restrictions on language tolerance and assistance in voting. He also broke party ranks and voted for nine of twenty-two articles for the impeachment of Democratic Governor James Ferguson.

Perhaps sensing an opening when the Rangers irritated Democratic conservatives by their hostile intervention in electoral politics, Canales called for an investigation of the Rangers based on the charges that he listed. He proposed a bill to reduce their number, budget, and scope, and to provide for local control and the bonding of officers. If he thought allies or reformers would come to his support, he was mistaken. For a Mexican to denounce the Rangers in the Texas legislature and publicly campaign against them constituted an intolerable audacity. If he thought his position as a legislator and his status as a wealthy man would protect him, he was also mistaken. Already known as a critic, but prior to the proposal of the bill, he and his relatives were threatened by a Ranger captain and a Ranger officer. What may have saved Canales was a witness to the threat and the fact that Canales publicized the threat, beginning with letters to the governor and adjutant general. Canales was immediately tossed into a multicornered controversy involving the governor, Democratic insurgents, the Rangers, and Democratic regulars. Up to 1919, his trajectory of moving back and forth from conservative to reform positions may have been due to his assessment of the more varied liberal and independent electorate he found in Brownsville, confidence in his own credentials, and a belief that he should be able to transcend the confines which were the rule for Mexican elected officials and to speak to the issues and develop a base of *both* Mexicans and Anglos. In any case, the proposed bill and its debilitating amendments were referred to committee, and an investigatory hearing was held in part because Canales's nineteen charges forced Ranger supporters to seek, rather than deny, a hearing. Needless to say, the Ranger record presented was a listing of incident upon incident of intimidation, unwarranted searches and seizures, killings, beatings, manslaughtering, venality, blatant partisanship, and so forth—a unique record for a U.S. police force. Canales was attacked politically, and even in a closing instance of the process, the chair of the committee threatened to hit him. The report of the legislature exonerated the Rangers, but one conciliatory note was offered: a willingness to consider reduction of the force. Though the matter was a foregone conclusion, Canales, in a provocative act with no chance of success, now moved to reject the report, and he was overwhelmingly defeated, 87 to 10; and the revised bill on the Rangers, which actually strengthened them, passed 95 to 5.

In the same session, votes were held on prohibition, restrictions in voting, and women's suffrage. The last two impacted on the Mexican vote, diminishing its importance in one way by limiting it, and in another way by increasing the Anglo vote. Furthermore, the turmoil of past years and the displacement of Mexicans, as well as the use of the Rangers by the governor's office independently of the local political leadership, also affected the vote. Worse was the rise of Ku Klux Klan membership in Texas; anti-Catholic and anti-Mexican, the Klan won in several places and even carried Cameron County.

Mexican response over the years would be more salient through labor and civic organizing, which some electoral leaders like J. T. Canales supported. Canales continued erratically in politics, though he was not elected in the thirties; and now he quarreled with the Guerras as both he and they had quarreled with others. Both families, however, did share a dislike of radicals.

The PLM

In contrast to, but occurring simultaneously with, the participation of Mexicans in electoral political parties, advocacy groups, and cultural social-service activities were the radical actions of Mexicans during the first two decades of the century. The rise of the Partido Liberal Mexicano (PLM), led by Ricardo Flores Magón, represents an innovation in the political history of the Mexican people in the United States and in Mexico.[37] The PLM was an international, revolutionary, ideological, and clandestine party that fought for the destruction of the porfiriato in Mexico and capitalism in general.

The PLM had a base of operations and support in the Southwest. Many in the U.S. Mexican community participated in the organization, supporting the PLM in all of its activities. The widespread and diverse areas of radical activity ranged from forming local PLM chapters, organizing newspapers, and conducting propaganda and defense work, to raising funds and securing supplies and weapons for revolutionary participation in armed action against both Mexican and U.S. forces—activities that attested to the solidarity and extensive support of the PLM in the Mexican community in the United States. The PLM, however, suffered from the limitations of its anarcho-communist ideology, its inability to stabilize its membership base, its factionalism, and, of course, its intense persecution. The PLM's influence in Mexico and in the United States was visible throughout the 1930s, even though the organization had disbanded by 1920. The PLM, in particular, had a definite socioeconomic base of aggrieved members in different strata, but it was only one of several groups that reflected discontent.

Under the leadership of Ricardo Flores Magón, the PLM was the ideological vanguard of the radical movement among Mexicans, even when it was isolated by the right wing in the political, organizational, and military spheres. While adopting an uncompromising anarchist-communist ideology whose goal was clearly the overthrow of capitalism and the capitalist state in Mexico, the PLM acknowledged the need to struggle for democratic demands and to develop a broad democratic movement among the laboring people not as an end in itself but as the basis of organization in moving ultimately toward a revolutionary victory.

The PLM's strategy for organization involved the creation of a major propaganda apparatus to reach the opposition as well as the laboring people. Central to this strategy was the reestablishment of *Regeneración*, previously located at Mexico City, in the United States. Integral to the effectiveness of the publication was the organization of a clandestine network to disseminate *Regeneración*, pamphlets, and other propaganda throughout Mexico and within the Mexican population in the United States. In 1910–11, distribution exceeded twenty thousand copies, and despite police vigilance, the newspapers were smuggled to many regions of the republic. PLM militants and sympathizers among the railroad workers were able to distribute the paper to the major centers of population via the rail lines, where copies could be redistributed to other nuclei. Also crucial to this strategy was the establishment of a network of local newspapers in Mexican communities throughout the United States, as well as the clandestine publication of materials in Mexico. Within two years a network of local PLM and allied newspapers was established that widely disseminated information throughout the United States and Mexico. These newspapers rapidly became local organizing vehicles for the PLM, reporting the progress of the struggle in Mexico and championing the struggle of the Mexican people against ethnic oppression in the United States.

The party was organized under the central leadership of the junta in exile and operated through local chapters in both the United States and Mexico. Financially, the party depended on contributions, membership dues, and the sale of *Regeneración.* Organizational activity centered around the ongoing struggle against the regime, and in local struggles in both the United States and Mexico. The central focus of party activity was on propaganda for workers and the support of labor organizing waged on both sides of the border, and which served, of course, as preparation for armed struggle. Major organizing drives were conducted in 1906, 1908, and 1910, when the PLM message was reaching thousands of Mexicans throughout Mexico and the United States. Although the Partido focused on the industrial worker, its influence was also widely felt among the most advanced sectors of the *campesinos,* the rural petite bourgeoisie, and particularly among progressive intellectuals.

The PLM's constituency and its partisans among the Mexican people fell into two groups. First was a broad audience of sympathizers composed primarily of artisans, industrial workers, and laborers in both Mexico and the United States. This sector rapidly expanded with the increasing dissemination of *Regeneración* and the rest of the party press, forming the basis for recruitment and the organization of new branches of the party and sympathizing affiliated groups. Second was the local leadership core of district organizers, chapter officers, and journalists operating within the United States in conditions of semi-legality and under constant threat of suppression.

The PLM's major constituencies among mexicanos in the United States were strongest in three major areas: (1) along the Texas border; (2) among the mining areas of Nuevo México, Arizona, and El Paso; and (3) among the large expanding urban and semiurban Mexican population of Los Angeles. The specific emphasis and character of PLM organizing in these and other areas reflected their own social, economic, and demographic conditions.

Significant to the radical movement generally and to the influence of PLM, in particular among mexicanos across the border, was the issuing of the PLM "Program of 1906" in the February 20, 1906, issue of *Regeneración.* Months in advance, the public had been asked to contribute suggestions for the formulation of the program. On both sides of the border, this drive stimulated the ideological development, interest, and contributions of thousands of Mexican workers and many intellectuals. The program stressed the potential harmony of all national sectors and appealed to the working people, in particular, to the anti-Díaz opposition. The program incorporated many democratic demands, a number of which had revolutionary socioeconomic ramifications; it was composed of eight major sections: (1) constitutional reforms; (2) improvement and development of education; (3) foreign relations; (4) restrictions on abuses by the Catholic clergy; (5) capital and labor; (6) land; (7) taxes; and (8) general points. One clause referred to the right of Mexicans in the United States to be eligible for land allotments, and among the more radical points were those calling for an eight-hour workday, minimum wages, the prohibition of child labor, the confiscation of uncultivated lands to be distributed to the landless, protection of the Indian, and the establishment of unity with Latin American countries. The PLM "Program of 1906" would exert continuing influence throughout the rebellion in Mexico, and much of it was incorporated into the Constitution of 1917. Moreover, its general democratic aspirations were translatable into a United States context for Mexicans. The program would become a vehicle for organization and for the ideological education of potential supporters.

Four major trends were championed by the party. First, there was a strong emphasis, albeit qualified, on the role of the woman in the struggle and in women's rights. This emphasis was reflected in the key roles played by many Mexican women in the party and in affiliated organizations. Second, the party worked with the advanced sectors of the socialist and syndicalist movements in the United States. Several Anglo militants from the Socialist Party, and the IWW in particular, played a major role in supporting the Mexican radical struggle. The PLM consistently supported the struggle of U.S. workers in general, and maintained an active support for international radical movements. It advocated the need for a worldwide revolution, including the United States as well as Mexico. Third, relations between labor and trade unionists were urged. Fourth, a cultural program concurrent with the political was developed that focused rudimentarily on schooling, literature, drama, songs, and art.

The major focus of PLM was directed toward the industrial worker, and PLM militants were among the leaders and most advanced sectors of the rank and file of the trade-union movement in the United States and Mexico. The last trial in federal court and the conviction of Flores Magón were based on charges pertinent to the United States for actions allegedly directed at the U.S. government. On November 27, 1913, *La*

Prensa had identified Flores Magón: "He is in large part responsible for the spread of Socialism among Mexicans in the United States." *La Prensa's* twenty-fifth-year anniversary issue featured a photograph of Flores Magón, "Uno de los más famosos periodistas mexicanos" (one of the best known Mexican journalists). Adherents of the PLM continued to propagate their ideals through the years of Flores Magón's imprisonment, and after his death in 1922 they constituted the "Grupo Cultural Ricardo Flores Magón," which focused on disseminating his ideas. As individuals, those in the PLM continued to be active in labor efforts both in Mexico and the United States.

The PLM represented a continuing tradition of ideological, political, and organizational relations between mexicanos on both sides of the border. In many respects, the broad influence of the party as well as its leadership in struggles throughout the "Southwest" and Mexico, its broad base of sympathizers, and its network of branches throughout the Southwest represented a high tide of radical organizational success. The PLM—despite its ultimate failure to prevent the capture of the insurgency movement by liberal reformers during the rebellion in Mexico, or to consolidate the advance sector of the Mexican American community into a coalition with anarchist and socialist groups in the United States—reflected the reality and vitality of radical organization among the Mexican people across the border. The PLM's experience, its successes and failures, represented an instructive guide, symbol, and challenge for sympathizers as well as critics.

During the times of the PLM, several radical Mexicans carried out activities with other organizations like the Socialist Party (SP) and the Industrial Workers of the World (IWW).[38] Much of the activity centered on organizing workers in the cities and on farms, and sharecroppers and tenant farmers in the rural areas. There was Mexican participation in the Socialist Party and the IWW in areas where Mexicans lived and worked, from the Canadian to the Mexican borders, and participation increased where local organizations proved to be both empathetic and effective. J. A. Hernández and F. A. Hernández were tireless organizers in Texas, and whatever ideological differences existed between them, some Mexicans, whether in the Socialist Party, the IWW, or the PLM, expressed their class consciousness and leftist ideological preferences. Among these currents were elements that would contribute to Mexican leftist politics during the twenties and thirties.

Border Violence and Insurgency

Because of actions originating both in the United States and in Mexico, the border was an area of conflict. From 1910 to 1917 the main activity along the border for many Mexico-born radicals in the United States centered around the Mexican Revolution.[39] Throughout the period, Mexicans supported and fought alongside the various Mexico-centered groups, and the result was consular reaction, further complicating the internal politics of the community. The United States served as a base of operations for the different factions during the revolution, and Mexicans suffered suppression by U.S. police agencies. Even more notable in this period was the repression and harassment resulting from the selective enforcement of the Neutrality Acts; the landing of troops in Veracruz and Tampico in 1914; the reaction to Francisco Villa's raid on Columbus, New Mexico; and the U.S. punitive expedition into Mexico—and all of these events elicited responses in the Mexican community. During these years there was not only civil war between mexicanos in Mexico, but also conflict between Mexico and the United States.

The Plan de San Diego and the surrounding activity in 1915–17 reflected historical sentiments and international conflict as well as local economic and cultural conflict that were the result of displacement and persecution.[40] Tapping various participatory elements and motivations, the Plan and allied actions involved armed conflict by Mexicans in south Texas against U.S. authorities and Anglo ranchers and merchants. In a subsequent mobilization of an estimated several thousand U.S. troops and several companies of Texas Rangers to quell the rebellion, hundreds of Mexicans were killed and reportedly thousands driven from their lands and homes.

In January of 1915, one Basilio Ramos was captured and taken to Brownsville, Texas. Among his personal papers was found the Plan de San Diego, which, he allegedly testified, had been transmitted to him by a friend while in jail in Monterrey, Mexico. He was accused of conspiracy against the U.S. government, but later the case was dismissed and with it the Plan—despite actions and rumors along the border. In effect, during 1914–15, Mexicans, citizens both of the United States and of Mexico, were involved in an attempt to implement a manifesto of liberation they named the Plan de San Diego. The

Plan called for a general uprising on February 20, 1915, in which the
Mexican people of the Southwest would reconquer territories lost in
1836 and 1848.

> On the 20th day of February 1915, at two o'clock in the morn-
> ing, we will arise in arms against the Government and country of
> the United States of North America. ONE FOR ALL AND ALL
> FOR ONE, proclaiming the liberty of the individuals of the black
> race and its independence of Yankee tyranny which has held us in
> iniquitious slavery since remote times; and at the same time and in
> the same manner we will proclaim the independence and segrega-
> tion of the States bordering upon the Mexican nation, which are:
> TEXAS, NEW MEXICO, ARIZONA, COLORADO, AND UP-
> PER CALIFORNIA, OF WHICH states the Republic of MEXICO
> was robbed in a most perfidious manner by North American impe-
> rialism.

Importantly, clauses in the Plan were addressed to the Black, the
Indian, and the Asian, and provisions were made for their freedom and
autonomy. Under a junta organization, an interim republic was to be
established with perhaps an eventual reannexation to Mexico, if desired; and Anglo and Mexican opponents would be dealt with harshly.

This Plan, so alarming to the Anglo Texans, can best be understood
in the light of historic, economic, and social conditions of the Mexicans in the Southwest; the repression the Mexican people suffered, the
aspirations they held, and the prejudice, brutality, and fear they experienced from the Anglo populace. In an atmosphere of distrust, hysteria,
and violence, the Plan de San Diego mirrored some of the Mexican
hopes and galvanized the worst of Anglo fears. Thus, the actions taken
in the name of the Plan, and the reactions to it, must be seen in the
light of Mexican agitation, Anglo fear, and a long history of violent
conflict between the two peoples. Doubts concerning the authorship of
the Plan notwithstanding, military actions did occur that were alleged
to be related to the Plan's proposals. Later, after the capture of Ramos
and the seizure of his documents, a junta was organized in Laredo
according to the framework outlined in the Plan, and this activity
seems to have enjoyed both urban and rural support as insurgent leaders
like Aniceto Pizana and Luis de la Rosa, Mexicans who were native to
Texas, directed armed organized bands of from twenty-five to one
hundred men in a series of actions in the Lower Rio Grande Valley. By
July 1915 the irredentist movement had begun to attract widespread

attention as raids and encounters became a daily occurrence. From reports given at the time, these well-organized groups, often averaging fifty men, raided, destroyed bridges, and engaged in numerous encounters with Texas Rangers, various posses, and the U.S. Army. Reportedly, the flag of the Plan de San Diego flew as a number of Anglos were killed, in executions which were apparently targeted in advance.

The rural struggle of the Mexicans also concurred with activity in urban areas. On August 30, in San Antonio, Texas, twenty-eight men were arrested following a riot between Mexicans and the police, apparently set off by the Mexicans shouting that the time had come to rise up against the Anglo. Identified as adherents of the Plan de San Diego, they were accused of treason; reportedly, there was widespread fear of a Mexican uprising in the area. There were also numerous actions throughout the Southwest at the time, and although there is no conclusive evidence that they were connected to the Plan, these actions may have been set into motion by those with convictions that inspired the Plan de San Diego. The irredentist movement seems to have been spreading and gaining in size and momentum, and additional revisions of the Plan were circulating that were much more radical ideologically.

Although Anglos at first disregarded the Plan de San Diego, they became more and more alarmed as the raids in the Lower Rio Grande Valley increased. As usual in the Southwest, Anglo apprehension and self-interest was manifested by brutal vigilante action and economic reprisals, with some taking advantage of unsettled conditions to turn a profit. Of course, then, as later, peace officers suspended the laws where Mexicans were concerned, and joined and often led in hunting down Mexicans who were allegedly raiders. As the major participants in these actions, the Texas Rangers were considered unsavory even by the military, who worried that the prestige of the army might be tarnished by association. General Frederick Funston, commander of the army in that area, pointed out the difficulty of cooperating with "peace officers who are such scoundrels," and refused to "tolerate such malicious deviltry and so flagrant an attempt to make matters worse."

The Rangers, in fact, were a major cause of the border trouble. Four years later, Representative José T. Canales of Brownsville charged the Rangers with shooting Mexicans in jail without trials, and said that "the Rangers had been the cause of most of the border trouble, because the families of the victims of the Rangers' lawlessness turned to banditry to avenge their relatives." During these vigilante actions, many

Mexicans were killed and lynched as their homes were burned, arms seized, and the people forcibly removed. Out of fear and because of forced migrations, over half of the valley's population left, and the economy of the area was severely damaged. Such severe repression existed until October 1915, when patrols on both sides of the border increased and the raids declined, even though generalized repression continued throughout the years that followed.

Much doubt and conjecture still surrounds the Plan de San Diego in all its aspects, not least of which is the fact that the Plan's authorship remains in question. Some feel that Venustiano Carranza sponsored the Plan as part of a series of actions designed to gain diplomatic recognition of the United States; if so, it seems odd that this man who was perhaps the most cautious among Mexico's major leaders, would risk incurring the reprisal of a U.S. government that had invaded Mexico often and currently held an area of Veracruz. In any case, Carranzista adherents were involved, as well as Villistas, Magonistas, and former followers of Catarino E. Garza. It has also been suggested that German agents devised the Plan in an effort to draw the attention of the United States away from Europe. Others hint that a prominent Anglo Texan may have encouraged the Plan to further personal economic and political interests. Another possibility holds that the Plan was a device used by either Mexican or U.S. groups to elicit further United States intervention in Mexico. Or the Plan may have been a hoax, either after the fact or concurrent with spontaneous raiding. There is, however, a possibility that the Plan de San Diego was what it purported itself to be, a *plan* by Mexicans in Texas to have the Southwest reclaimed by its rightful heirs and to have the oppressed people living within its border liberated by an armed vanguard that saw itself as a legitimate force sanctioned by history and its norms of justice.

In the Plan de San Diego itself, a number of points tend to indicate Mexican American authorship. The Plan made a historic claim to the Southwest as a unity, and it was stipulated that the area would become an independent republic; yet reannexation with Mexico might occur, *if expedient*, which seems to indicate that the claim was being made for and by the Southwest as an entity that was not viewed as being an intrinsic part of either the United States or Mexico. Another important aspect of the Plan was the emphasis on other oppressed groups in the area: Blacks, Indians, and Asians. It would seem that the concern expressed for these peoples would more likely arise from persons that had suffered the same experiences rather than from ones that had not. Clauses calling for punishment of oppressors and traitors, harsh as they may seem, can best be understood in view of the brutal ethnic relations between Anglos and Mexicans, and the bitter feeling of the latter toward members of their own community who collaborated with Anglo civilians, politicians, and peace officers. Furthermore, the Plan was neither more nor less than an articulation of a point of view and a tradition common to a particular border area. Most likely, then, the Plan de San Diego was a militant response and reaction within a particular set of historical circumstances, to which others responded in more conventional ways.

The Exercise of Civil Rights

Advocacy of electoral and civil rights was reinforced by oppression along the Texas border, the heightened repression of Mexican radicals during World War I, and the increase of reactionary middle-class Anglo chauvinism.[41] As radical activity waned, the concern of the Mexican lower middle class in the United States intensified, for repression had heightened class and ideological distinctions within the Mexican community, and the small but active political sector of the Mexican middle class was strengthened by the resurgence of middle-class exiles from Mexico. There were also more workers, for whom the middle class now functioned as political brokers.

The native-born middle class was significantly aided by various new arrivals. In addition to workers and defeated revolutionaries, exiles came from Mexico, some of whom were professionals who had served in the governments of presidents from Díaz to Carranza. They too sought to form groups, establish newspapers, and influence people. Radical advocates, on the other hand, experienced hard times. In the aftermath of World War I, with the triumph of the Bolsheviks in Russia and corporate fear of the radical movements in Mexico, political repression in the United States, exercised through the Department of Justice, expanded into a heightened harassment of radicals. Thus, many Mexican radicals were deported or imprisoned for long periods; Ricardo Flores Magón died under questionable circumstances while in prison, and his colleague Libardo Rivera said he was murdered.

The years between 1920 and 1941 were marked by increasing

tensions, by ferment, and occasionally by public strife.[42] This period was also characterized by increasing contrasts between Mexican electoral politics and civic organization in the United States. Although the 1920s generally have been characterized as an era of prosperity in U.S. history, many sectors of the Mexican population witnessed continual infringements upon their civil rights and abrupt as well as slight increase and decrease in their economic and social position, even though numbers maintained an absolute increase. Unsurprisingly, at the same time the degree of Mexican political activism rose, too. The crucial variable, however, was not simply the size of population; the focus was local conditions: economic strength, enfranchisement of Mexican voters, and effective mobilization of voters in support of the concerns of the various sectors of the Mexican community. Several aspects increasingly contributed to the unevenness of Mexican political potential: the exclusion of the large number of noncitizen immigrants from voting; elections at large, which impeded a minority representative from being elected, or the practice of "gerrymandering" or dividing Mexican voters among several districts to prevent a majority from prevailing in any one district; the "poll tax," a tax to vote that was charged in states such as Texas and tended to exclude Mexicans and persons of low income; literacy requirements, which provided only for English-language literacy and excluded not only English illiterates but also potential voters who were literate in Spanish or in other languages. Furthermore, these measures were frequently applied in a discriminatory manner. For example, non–English-fluent European immigrants might be permitted to vote without challenge, while even Mexicans known to be U.S. citizens by birth were indeed challenged. Moreover, representation by Anglo elected officials was consistently inadequate for Mexican voters.

In the early twentieth century, as in the nineteenth century, Mexican voters in all areas were distributed among both major parties, and the meaning of Democrat and Republican was often ambiguous or varied according to time and place.[43] The dominant party was the Republican, stressing a platform of past successes, patriotism, and civic fairness—a basic message which did have appeal. Even though it was vague, it was more effective than any message the Democrats could muster. Republican popularity persisted in Colorado, New Mexico, and Arizona; while Mexicans in California and Texas moved overwhelmingly into the Democratic Party, or they were already there, in one place because of overall state partisan control, and in the other because the Democrats were believed to be more hospitable to them as Catholics and as workers.

By 1920 there were three states where Mexicans had notable political representation, and two states where they had little. There were only a few elected officials in Arizona, and these held minor offices, except for Perfecto M. Elias, a Tucson city councilman. However, there were significant organizational efforts and identifiable voter turnouts, as well as examples of some excellent leadership. In California, which in the mid-1920s surpassed Texas as the state with the largest Mexican population, there was not a single Mexican state legislator or federal representative between 1913 and 1963, and only a handful of local officials were Mexican, none of whom saw themselves as representing the Mexican people. Members of the Estudillo family and Reginaldo del Valle were perhaps the only ones able to claim some continuous representational leadership. In 1910, a notable following developed around Job Harriman, who ran unsuccessfully for mayor of Los Angeles on the Socialist ticket. Sporadic efforts in organizing the vote included the formation of the Federation of Spanish Speaking Voters. Political activism was generally limited to newspaper polemics and to the activities of local membership organizations. Colorado's representation never exceeded the three state senators elected in 1926 and a handful of state representatives whose influence in state politics was only modest; however, this representation was continuous through 1952 and it was based on four counties with a significant Mexican presence, and limited though it was, it was greater than what was available in California. In south Texas, José T. Canales, related to the Cortina family, had served in the legislature from 1909 to 1911, and from 1917 to 1919; after him the only state representative of Mexican descent was Augustine Celaya, also from Cameron County; however, Mexicans did hold local offices in the region through World War II. Only in New Mexico—until the late 1930s the only state with a Mexican majority population—were Mexicans politically potent, enjoying significant representation at several levels of government. Yet even in New Mexico, there was some erosion of the basis for Mexican political power as Anglo American population increased; this was especially the case in southeastern New Mexico, known as "little Texas," where Anglo immigration from Texas created a majority Anglo population with strong anti-Mexican prejudices.

In New Mexico alone, Mexican politicians exercised some policy and decision-making power.[44] Thus, Mexican political leaders secured the state's recognition of Spanish as an official language in education and in state government. New Mexican political elites, however, did not form a unified partisan political bloc. Mexican politicians were represented in both the Republican and Democratic parties and among other minor political groups that arose occasionally. Benigno Hernández was elected to the sixty-fourth (1915–16) and sixty-sixth (1919–20) U.S. Congress, and he was followed by Nestor Montoya in the sixty-seventh (1921–22); there were also the major figures of de Baca and Larrazolo. Consistent in his support for Mexican political representation, Octaviano Larrazolo had broken ranks with the Republican Party to support Ezequiel C. de Baca for governor in 1916.[45] After Cabeza de Baca's death, Larrazolo was nominated by the Republican Party as their candidate for governor, and he was elected and served from 1918 to 1919. While governor of New Mexico, he supported a state income tax, the state assumption of federal lands, and women's voting rights enumerated in the Nineteenth Amendment to the U.S. Constitution. After losing some political standing because he was perceived as too liberal and pro-Hispano, he returned to private life; but he was said to have been considered by President Harding for appointment as governor of Puerto Rico. Once again a major figure in 1927 and 1928, Larrazolo served two terms in the New Mexico House of Representatives. Upon the death of Andrews A. Jones in 1928, he was nominated by the Republican Party for U.S. senator, was elected, and served a partial term from 1928 to 1930; thus, he became the first senator of Mexican descent. Larrazolo is said to have made his nomination contingent upon continued Republican Party agreement to reserve half of the nominations for office for Spanish-surnamed New Mexicans; this became a consistent call, but the extent to which it was considered was a matter of party pragmatism. While he was only at the beginning of his Washington career, Larrazolo became seriously ill and returned to New Mexico, where he died in early 1930.

While both Ezequiel Cabeza de Baca and Octaviano A. Larrazolo supported important Mexican interests during their careers, each was part of a broader political network that included both Anglo American and Mexican elites. Both men were thoroughly committed to the electoral political system of the United States as well as to free-enterprise economics. From their perspective, Mexican political activities would best be directed toward broadening participation in both the existing political and economic arenas. The complexity of New Mexican political life and the numbers of individuals involved on the local, state, and federal levels exceeded what was then common in other states.

Bronson Cutting, a wealthy Harvard alumnus, was a master of manipulation, first sharing, then acquiring Larrazolo's following.[46] From 1912, as leader of the progressive Republicans he voiced tacit support for Hispano equities; his major office was U.S. senator, which he secured in 1928, and he was supported by the American Legion, which had a significant Hispano membership. Cutting developed a notable personal following with a combination of money, a congratulatory press, fluency in Spanish, and patronage. He actively cultivated certain Hispanos, visited communities, frequented weddings and funerals, and even attended Penitente ceremonies. Cutting's public courtship was something of a new twist for an Anglo politician, and it isolated some Hispanos while embittering some Anglos. But Cutting achieved directly what other Anglos had failed to realize, a Hispano electoral base. He bridged ethnic polarization but did not end it; and in a way he established, for other Anglo liberals who followed him, support from the Hispano voters not only in holding office but also in gaining individual prominence. Upon his death in 1935, he was followed by another twentieth-century model, the prominent liberal-conservative "national Hispanic," Dennis Chávez. Chávez waged a hard campaign against Cutting in 1934, and was seated in the Senate; he was a strong advocate for the state of New Mexico and served until 1962.

In 1922, the Democratic Chávez was elected to the New Mexico House after having entered politics as an aide and interpreter to A. A. Jones during the latter's 1916 campaign for the Senate and later working on the Senate staff.[47] In 1930, he was elected to the U.S. House of Representatives and served four terms. He sponsored bills for Pueblo Indian land claims, for moratorium on farm debts, and for farm-credit legislation. In 1934, in a sharply disputed election for the U.S. Senate against Bronson Cutting, Chávez lost by 1,261 votes. However, upon Cutting's death, Chávez was appointed to the Senate as a Democrat. He was a generally consistent New Dealer on social legislation and favored a strong military. By knitting together both the constituency and the methods of Larrazolo and Cutting, and above all, by being a strong state representative in Congress, Chávez became the major Mexican leader in New Mexico. Also adopting the then-popular New

Deal was another Democrat, Joseph Montoya, who served an apprenticeship in the state legislature and was also elected eventually to
represent New Mexico in the U.S. Congress.

Women's Suffrage

Mexican women activists in the Southwest, particularly in New
Mexico, were involved in the vigorous effort to secure the vote for
women in the United States. It was assumed that Mexican males would
not support suffrage for women, but in fact, as in the Anglo community, a diversity of opinion reached across party lines, and in counties in
Texas, New Mexico, and Colorado, there was significant male support
for women's suffrage. Canales, Larrazolo, and Solomon Luna favored
suffrage, and they were eventually joined by Benigno Hernández and a
few other male elected officials as well as by some of the Spanish-
language press like *La Prensa.*

An active suffrage organizer became the first woman of Mexican
descent to run for a congressional seat in the United States. This was
Adelina Otero-Warren, the niece of Solomon Luna, the prominent
Republican politician known as the "Boss" of Valencia County and a
major figure in the state's constitutional convention.[48] Adelina Otero-
Warren, a young widow, well educated, bilingual, and wealthy, and
already a notable figure in her circle, was recruited by middle-class
Republican women suffragettes to campaign among Spanish-speaking
women and the Mexican community in support of the Nineteenth
Amendment to the U.S. Constitution. She, Aurora Lucero, daughter
of the secretary of state, and some two dozen educated Hispano women
from the middle class or above were active in the suffrage effort.
Adelina Otero had several concerns. Proud and conversant with politics, she believed that women must participate electorally, and she also
believed that the terrain of the Hispano elite should be maintained. For
her, improving and extending education was a means of defending the
community; and she was also among tthose who argued that the traditional farming and craft economy needed to be consciously preserved.

A Republican, Otero-Warren combined constituencies to advance
women's electoral rights and their access to office. Supported by Alice
Paul, New Mexico organizer of the Congressional Union, one of the
several women's suffrage organizations, Otero was elected in September

(handwritten margin notes: "New Mex" "+ politics (356-358)")

lew Mexico state president of the Congressional Union,
comprised primarily of Anglo-American women. In 1917,
cancy occurred, her ability as well as her Otero family con-
-her father, Manuel B. Otero, succeeded Solomon Luna as
:al boss of Valencia County—led to her appointment as
ident of schools of Santa Fe County, and in the next elec-
defeated a male challenger. Concurrently, Otero-Warren
n acknowledged leader in securing New Mexico's ratifica-
e Nineteenth Amendment. She was instrumental in defeat-
uffragette male Anglo Republicans who sought to defeat the
ent while shifting blame to allegedly conservative Mexican
male voters. She successfully lobbied Hispano male officeholders, and
in the process she reportedly became the first woman to enter a state
Republican political caucus. On February 19, 1920, New Mexico
became the thirty-second state to ratify the amendment, with some
Mexican political leaders playing a laudable role in the victory. Soon,
calls were being made addressed to Mexican women voters:

> Mañana es el día la elección. Es un día de mucha importancia
> para las señoras de Santa Fe. Esta es nuestra primera participación en
> una que no sea solamente elección para escuelas, y las señoras se si-
> enten algo tímidas acerca de ejercer sus privilegios; miedosas de dar
> un golpe recio con una nueva arma. Pero no debemos tener miedo de
> pegar con todas nuestras fuerzas en defensa de nuestros hogares. . . .
>
> Para asegurar el depositar sus votos, todas las señoras deben vis-
> itar los lugares de votación al abrirse las casillas electorales a las
> nueve de la mañana, y deben votar antes que los hombres salgan de
> sus trabajos, cuando la mucha gente hará que sea difícil que se
> pueda votar, especialmente en los Precintos 3 y 4. Debería saber
> bien como va a votar para que cuando llegue a las casillas elec-
> torales no se pierda el tiempo ni haya demoras al votar, a fin de que
> cada uno de los votantes pueda tener tiempo de votar.
>
> Con toda confianza dejamos la cuestión en manos de las señoras
> votantes de Santa Fe.
>
> [Tomorrow is election day. It is a very important day for the
> women of Santa Fe. This is our first participation in one that is not
> just an election for schools, and women feel somewhat timid about
> exercising their rights, fearful of striking a harsh blow with a new
> weapon. We should not, however, be afraid of hitting with all our
> strength in the defense of our hearths and homes. . . .
>
> In order to ensure being able to vote, every woman should visit

the polling places when the voting booths open at nine in the morning and vote before men leave their workplaces, when many people will find it difficult to be able to vote, especially in precincts 3 and 4. She should know precisely how she is going to vote so that when she arrives at the voting booth, she neither wastes time nor causes delays while voting, so that every one of the voters can have time to vote.

With every confidence, we leave the question in the hands of the women voters of Santa Fe.]

And soon women in New Mexico had established a relatively high rate of voter participation.

In the fall of 1922, Adeline Otero-Warren was nominated by the Republican Party for the U.S. House of Representatives from New Mexico; unfortunately for her candidacy, 1922 was a year of heavy Democratic victories in New Mexico, including the election of a Democratic governor. Although Otero-Warren lost to her male Democratic opponent, she set a precedent in becoming the first Mexican woman to run for the U.S. Congress, and she carried four of the five Hispano counties, losing in the Anglo counties. In the election, however, a Hispano Democratic woman won the office of secretary of state, and an Anglo woman Democrat was elected as state superintendent of public instruction. A noted hispanophile, Otero-Warren's earlier election as superintendent of schools of Santa Fe County and her role in securing New Mexico's ratification of the Nineteenth Amendment were clearly significant accomplishments in the political history of Mexican women in the United States, and they broke electoral ground for all women.

In 1923, Soledad C. Chacón became the first Mexican woman to win a state office when she was elected as New Mexico's secretary of state, and in the 1930s she was followed by Marguerite Baca and Elizabeth González. Eventually, P. Saiz and E. Gallegos were elected to the House. Like Concha Ortiz y Pino, who had been an influential member of the House in the thirties, these women were connected to the elite, yet were also proponents of social-reform legislation.

Repression and Cultural Aggression

Internationally and domestically, though it was not without recessions, the post–World War I U.S. economy and society continued to expand at an unprecedented rate and to suffer greater problems both internally and in foreign relations. The inextricable linkage between the national and the international provided particular twists for Mexicans.[49] Contrary to isolationist rhetoric, the United States in reality was diplomatically and militarily active on a world scale, and particularly in the Americas, where resources were used systematically to support the interests of U.S. business expansion and economic penetration throughout the world.

Investment and intervention in Mexico, Latin America, and the colonial world reached new heights as Wall Street replaced London and Paris as the major money market of the world. In Mexico, despite the provisions of the Constitution of 1917, U.S. and British corporations continued to influence the Mexican economy, and in attempting to manipulate the Mexican political process, they distorted it, causing an impact across the border. United States diplomacy was particularly active in thwarting the nationalist impulse, and in the aftermath of the Mexican Revolution, the U.S. State Department continued to engage in an ongoing diplomatic battle with the administrations of Alvaro Obregón and Plutarco Elias Calles. When the United States sent marines to support the right-wing coup in Nicaragua and to fight the revolutionary Augusto Sandino and his forces, it sought to weaken sympathy for Nicaragua among Mexicans. During these years, U.S. propaganda, generated by conservative business interests in league with Porfirista, Huertista, and reactionary Catholic exiles from Mexico, depicted the Mexican regimes as radically oriented while simultaneously attempting to destabilize the country. While carrying on a progressive foreign policy of nonintervention and limited internal reforms, the Mexican government, in reality, was steadily moving toward neoconservatism, with a new bureaucracy formed from the right wing of the revolution. Groups both for and against the government sought audiences in the United States in their attempts to affect the Mexican American public's perception of Mexico.

Domestically, the 1920s were a period of continuing social and cultural animosities in the United States; the rapid transition from a small-town, semi-rural culture to a predominantly urban existence resulted in many strains and antagonisms.[50] One contributor in this respect was the growth of nativist movements, such as the Ku Klux Klan, which articulated North American cultural and racial chauvinism. As in the nineteenth century, the Klan concentrated in the

Southwest on Mexicans, since Blacks were numerically few except in east Texas. But there were other nativist groups within the U.S. intellectual and cultural elite. A biased ideological-sociological view of the Mexican, rooted in nineteenth-century chauvinist writings, was defined during these years, and "eugenics" grew as a "respected science" at major U.S. universities. Purporting to be professionals practitioners of a science of "race" and "racial differences," eugenicists claimed to demonstrate the biological and genetic inferiority of such peoples as Blacks and Mexicans, and they published their "data" and interpretation in academic publications and popular periodicals. Throughout this period, eugenicists functioned as "intellectual" proponents of racism, exclusionism, and forced "Americanization."

In the "booming" twenties, as Mexican migration to the far north continued in accordance with the steadily increasing demand by business for more exploitable Mexican labor, the number of voices raised in concern and protest also grew.[51] These were neither European (of course) nor Black nor Asian; many were Mestizo and Mexican Indian and opponents to their presence echoed the past in their dissenting views. Their attention increased as Mexican urban centers in the United States grew in size and in the development of their internal social, cultural, and organizational life. The Mexican people were increasingly subjected to a particular type of cultural aggression, through the advent of the mass media and compulsory education, which increasingly penetrated the home and family, the targets of the so-called Americanization effort. For some proponents, this effort was considered to be benign, fostering "integration" and its presumed benefits. For many others, "Americanization" meant the weakening of Mexican culture, identity, and language in order to facilitate political domination and economic exploitation. Uprooted, uneducated immigrants were targeted, particularly the women among them. Educators and religious functionaries were at the forefront of this assault, and it was amply supported by liberals and reformers.

The Mexican child enrolled in schools (segregated or desegregated) was subjected to a racial and cultural barrage deprecating the Mexican culture, race, nationality, and language, all of which were branded as inferior and backward. The speaking of the Spanish language on school grounds was prohibited, and those caught doing so were severely punished. In contrast, the alleged superiority of the United States and Anglo American culture was promoted and impressed upon the minds of the Mexican children. This chauvinist consensus view of U.S. history stressed its evolution and promoted its institutions as a paragon of virtues, and therefore, by direct or indirect comparison, degraded history of other peoples. Children were told to aspire to, and model themselves after, North Americans and to accept the "benefits" of U.S. society, even at the cost of being relegated to a secondary status, which Mexicans should be "grateful to receive." In reality, of course, discrimination continued, and integration remained a facade.

Mexicans were not viewed with the same tolerance granted to eastern or southern Europeans. Some Mexicans were alleged to possess traits that were relatively positive—stamina and patience, for example—while others were cheerful and, above all, cooperative. Among the youth, "potential leaders" were those who were particularly ingratiating and gave evidence of their "initiative" by criticizing Mexican individuals or aspects of their own culture. The "sullen Mexican" in school or in the workplace was trouble, and recalled an analogy with the Mexican *bandido* image of times past. In church, at school, and on the job, Mexicans were disciplined to accept their subordinate place in society, to refrain from the practice of Mexican culture, and to forego the assertion of political, educational, labor, and cultural rights. This direct process of dogmatic "Americanization" and cultural aggression was reinforced by anti-Mexicanism through radio and films.

Cultural aggression also meant attacking Mexico, the Mexican government, and Mexican historical development—all of which were depicted as socialistic or nondemocratic, with liberals branding them as fanatical and the religious calling them godless. For the Catholic population, Mexico's reform effort was depicted as an atheistic movement attacking God and his representative government on earth, the United States, and promoting socialist propaganda; for others, the Catholic church was deemed to be both anti-Christian and anti-modern. Since the target populations were generally laborers or those who would soon be laborers, and they might come in contact with "foreign" ideologies, "Americanization" actively propagandized against socialism and unionism, both of which were "un-American." Thus, many Mexican children were indoctrinated with feelings of self-hatred and ethnic and cultural inferiority, as well as consciously depoliticized; and the tremendous psychological effects of this inculcation would continue throughout the twentieth century. In fact, the most sinister impact affected the youth and, in particular, the youth who found favor.

Continuing and New Organizations

Though electoral leadership in some areas continued to exercise modest or significant political influence, other organizational forms increased among mexicanos and provided them with advocacy and the enlargement of the space previously limited by political exclusion. Since the late nineteenth century mutualistas and Masonic groups had been continuing influences.[52] In effect, attempts were made to combine the benefits offered by mutualista groups, the social solidarity of lodges, and the protection from public abuses and the advocacy for basic rights promised by political groups.

One group with a particularly large membership and range of activity was the Alianza Hispano-Americana, founded in 1894 and based in Tucson, Arizona. Like other groups, it provided benefits and activities. Moreover, it was animated by the intention of enhancing its public standing and that of its leadership to give voice to its advocacy on behalf of Mexicans and to enhance the social and political standing of the community. During the first half of the twentieth century, the Alianza was the best-funded, best established, and most aggressive of all mutualista organizations. Like others, its membership was composed of skilled and semi-skilled workers, some small producers, and a leadership drawn from middle-class merchants and professionals. In many cases, participation was transmitted from generation to generation in the same family, and members were noted for their organizational pride and loyalty. Though it included immigrants, it was not an immigrant organization. Nevertheless, the Spanish language and the Mexican symbology and organizational mystique were very much a part of the Alianza. It combined in its stresses and strengths culturalist and integrationist thrusts.

In 1940, the Alianza had nearly eighteen thousand enrolled and dues-paying members as well as many others who were either supporters or not fully enrolled currently. Its membership expanded between 1920 and 1940, and particularly during the late thirties; it was concentrated in Arizona, Texas, and other states, especially in California, where half of its membership resided. In time, the Alianza placed even greater stress on civil-rights equities and members' fulfillment of their civic responsibilities. After World War II the organization faced serious financial problems, and this factor eroded its growth, which in turn hindered its ability to adapt or to recruit new members in the face of ongoing societal and governmental changes. Much reduced, a core of the organization survived, but whether it was small or large, the Alianza made significant contributions.

Influenced by preexisting efforts in the area, La Liga Protectora Latina developed in Phoenix, Arizona, in 1914, and continued through the 1920s.[53] It was a response to the pervasive degradation and disparagement felt by Mexicans, particularly those in the lower middle class. Especially aggravating were the inferior schooling and levels of education, discrimination in arrests and sentences, and the exploitive conditions faced by Mexican labor. Initially, organizers sought the sympathy of Governor George Hunt. The very particular threat posed by the Democrat-sponsored Claypool–Kinney Bill, which sought to limit "alien" employment, increased the numbers, visibility, and activity of the Liga; and this threat encouraged them to look to Republicans. Thus, La Liga's concerns were cultural, and status as well as economic equities, for its members were both laborers and nonlaborers, for whom basic benefits were important. From the first La Liga included women participants. Notable spokespersons were Pedro M. Salinas, Ignacio Espinosa, Pedro G. de la Loma, Jesús Melendez, and Amado Cota Robles—all educated, and most of them lower middle-class immigrants with experience in the local politics of Arizona or Mexico. Innovatively, they elaborated *planes* (plans) pertinent to their main concerns: benefits, civil rights, and education. In Arizona, the Liga sought to counter the Democratic, anti-Mexican bias by supporting and petitioning the Republicans, and addressing Republican governor Thomas Campbell directly. They also implemented their concerns for education by establishing a program of night classes with attention to English, while providing instruction in Spanish on a range of subjects, including history. Other aspects of their origins and their agenda included the notion of a protective group which would be more active than the Alianza Hispano-Americana, and one that was energized by the competing efforts of different Mexican factions; and in this context was the radical anti-capital, anti-state message of the PLM and the IWW. The Liga leadership was moderate, but strongly pro-Mexican. Its civic stance supported Carranza, Wilson, and the World War I effort, and it cautioned against radicalism; it dealt with both U.S. and Mexican authorities, forwarding complaints or recommendations.

Labor protection efforts were part of a dilemma faced by others, before and after the Liga. Mexican laborers raised demands, but to some members unions were discriminatory. The Liga was obviously not workplace-centered but community-based, but it provided a civic organization available to speak for Mexican workers. Understandably, it insisted on being the only voice if it were asked to speak on behalf of laborers. In these circumstances, the union present was not one that _La Liga_ believed was fair, given their own practices. This tension between an ethnic organization and a discriminatory union could not be resolved until national changes introduced union-enabling legislation and changes occurred in the unions; both kinds of changes took place during the Franklin Roosevelt administration. But the Liga's position was premised on the common belief that Mexicans should be represented by Mexican organizations under Mexican leadership. Their slogan was "uno para todos, todos para uno" (one for all, all for one).

For approximately seven years, the Liga increased its membership to nearly five thousand, distributed in over thirty "lodges" located principally in Arizona, California, New Mexico, and Texas. Based on dues, membership provided employment and financial assistance, and in 1919 an informational publication, _La Justicia,_ was conceived and distributed to its widespread members. Regular conventions were held for several years, with the Liga advocating legislative remedies for education, bilingual curriculum, and teachers; efforts to increase naturalization and voting, fair treatment and wages for workers, and the defense of accused or sentenced mexicanos. Leadership struggles and faulty finances, however, weakened their momentum.

The decline of the Liga was related to two common circumstances. Activity required resources, and resources were available only from those who received services and the membership in general; and nowhere else were there sources of support. The fact of fees and the raising of fees were internal issues of conflict, and priorities and organizational vision also led to the alienation of members. The initial leadership believed in addressing government, electoral parties, general community enhancement, and interethnic relations more than the membership. The members, in turn, were more interested in specific services and internally oriented organizational programs than the leadership. Struggles between competing leaders thus grew bitter. Apparently combining benefits with advocacy proved to be an uneasy alliance because neither leadership nor membership agreed on the balance between them. Though individual chapters survived longer than the central structure, the Liga, after a remarkable start, began to decline midway through the 1920s and disappeared by the late 1930s.

As the twenties and thirties passed, regional organization of the entrepreneurial and professional sectors developed from roots in the past, and on the basis of already understood ideological tenets that would bridge constraints. Politics and ideology divided those who generally advocated the exercise of political and civil rights within the existing political system from those favoring political advocacy through alternative politics; and a second division was between socialists and all others. In certain areas, increasing fragmentation took place in rural communities and social dissonance increased among urban ones, but the cities were understood to be more important. In both rural and urban areas, however, the twenties and thirties were marked by discrimination in the spheres of socioeconomic life. There was no absolute divorce between moderates and radicals, nor a disavowal of urban from rural concerns; what emerged was a gradually understood distinction as to focus and means.

La Orden, the Knights, and the LULAC

Social and economic conditions were worst in Texas, and were suffered by large concentrations of Mexicans, yet there existed a small and politically active professional and merchant sector in south Texas and San Antonio, as well as a pronounced heritage of activism there. In Texas, two key organizations developed: La Orden de Hijos de America and the League of Latin American Citizens. Members of La Gran Liga Mexicanista were influential in founding "La Orden," or, in English, "The Order of Sons of America." As had happened before and would happen again, former activists from one organization were influential in organizing a succeeding organization.

La Orden was founded in San Antonio in 1921, and by 1928 it had seven chapters. There were elements of the Masonic tradition in its attention to ritual and hierarchy. Significantly, its membership was limited to citizens of the United States; unnaturalized immigrants were excluded, and it accepted only those who endorsed the existing political system and were willing to set aside partisanship. Thus, the divisions between Mexicans who were U.S. citizens and those who were not, and between those who were ideologically moderate and those who were not, were underscored as participatory requirements. La Orden's purpose was to achieve full civil rights for the Mexican. Accordingly, the organization focused on increasing voter registration and jury-service inclusion. Obstacles to registration and service were specific grievances, and La Orden sought to correct them. It was moderately successful in its objectives, but some of the members felt that the Orden was too moderate and too narrow in its membership horizon; and in any case, organizational divisions existed. The San Antonio chapter ceded and became the Order of the Knights of America. On August 24, 1927, an additional group in Harlingen, Texas, declared itself the League of Latin American Citizens. Given the difficult times and the similarities between the elements composing these groups, and in spite of the friction, an effort at unification was attempted, with a meeting called for February 17, 1929, at Corpus Christi.

In an atmosphere of repression, membership in a civil-rights-advocacy organization was proposed to advance the rights and interests of mexicanos in specific ways; hence the creation of the League of United Latin American Citizens (LULAC).[54] The League's basic idea was that if mexicanos displayed accouterments of the dominant society, that is, visibly became "americanos," and stressed gratitude and loyalty, they would become acceptable to the Anglo population and would no longer face discrimination and supremacism, and hence would possess rights. Thus, assimilationism as an ideological and organizational tenet appeared among sectors of the Mexican people.

This conscious pro-assimilationist tendency developed into a major ideological current among a sector of the people of Mexican descent. It embraced not only the advocacy of accommodation to capitalism, consumer society, and U.S. foreign policy, but also a commitment to the political status quo while demanding admittance for Mexicans, that is, for those among them who would agree to the status quo. All this was premised on the eventual assimilation of the Mexican people on the basis of egalitarian pluralism. The seemingly logical combination of these elements gave this tendency an ideological coherence. Individually, anyone would fit a variety of political affiliations; for example, some sectors of the left were also assimilationist, but they were insistent on radical change and voiced harsh criticism.

Because the society was deeply anti-Mexican, arguably there existed an obligation to defend the interests of the Mexican community in fighting segregation and overt discrimination through avenues that were tolerated and sanctioned by the society. In the early phases of the pro-assimilation tendency, assimilationism could be viewed as an attempt to ward off the worst aspects of oppression, although it also tried to obtain a privileged status for individuals representing the Mexican community. Arguably assimiliationists offered a sensible and qualified leadership for both the dominant institutions of the larger society and the Mexican community. Inherent here was the belief that civil rights would be granted by appeals of the enlightened members of the community to the dominant leadership, which was also believed to be enlightened. There were partially contrasting mobilizations, however, occurring at the same time.

In the economic sphere, Mexican workers, while they were a mainstay of the economy, were under constant attack from both employers and exclusionist unions, who, in adopting nativist and eugenicist rhetoric, called for the exclusion of Mexican labor from the United States through a restrictive immigration policy and the deportation of Mexican people. Accordingly, Mexican unions were organized to defend the economic interests of Mexican workers. In some cases they engaged in direct militant protest at the workplace and relied on force stressing worker rights as well as human rights. In contrast, the LULACs believed in appeal.

Under Alonso Perales, one of the important Mexican civic leaders and middle-class ideologues, members of La Orden de Hijos de America, La Orden Caballeros de America, and the League of Latin American Citizens, as well as other activist but moderate elements, formed in 1929 the League of United Latin American Citizens (LULAC),[55] which would eventually become one of the largest membership groups, and one that emphatically upheld organization:

> We Latin-Americans must organize. We must get out of the rut and forge ahead. Let us catch up with and keep abreast of our hard-driving fellow-citizens of Anglo-Saxon extraction. To accomplish this, no man should be allowed to stand in our way. No man is big enough to block our progress. A fraction is not larger than the whole. For the sake of posterity and the good name of our people, let us get together, my friends, and begin to solve our great problems. We can only do it through a well disciplined, solid, powerful organization.[56]

Through Perales's reflections and their articulation in meetings and organizational documents, the LULACs developed the so-called Mexican-American set of precepts that entailed their promises, strategies, and tactics socially, culturally, and politically. An often quoted—and often with negative intent—aim was "to develop within the members of our race the best, purest and most perfect type of a true and loyal citizen of the United States of America." More organizationally telling, however, were twenty-four other aims and purposes that, in effect, announced to the public an organizational reason which could not be challenged by the mythical canon of the society.

The initial LULAC agenda was as self-conscious and reflective as any other, and certainly more so than most. Yet LULAC read the lessons of the past differently, believing, in effect, that the best way for the Mexican community to progress was to demonstrate its willingness to integrate politically and to announce this repeatedly in public. Concomitantly, the best tactic for defending the community was for a small, well-educated group to act in its defense through legal channels. LULAC argued for the classification of Mexicans as white, and for restricting immigration to the extent of supporting deportations— supporting the first to avoid established and accepted segregational practices, and endorsing the other for two reasons, to establish a floor for integrational progress and to eliminate the hardships of immigrants. Contrary to the allegations of a few simple status-seeking spokespersons, class and cultural aspects were mixed, and the majority of the members were wage earners and evidently practiced Mexican culture. Though middle-class elements were a minority, this group saw itself as the one to lead working-class Mexicans toward these goals. In effect, a consciously moderate sector of the middle class was assuming a self-proclaimed and articulated position of leadership, and rationalizing its interests and identity as those best for the community, even if they contradicted more conflictual stands occurring in some areas of the community life. But there was also a lengthier list of aims, priorities, and objectives than those espoused by the often quoted leadership, and this list represented commonly acknowledged priorities by community activists. In retrospect, it was psychologically interesting how the LULAC formative statement was disparaged by academics while they and other members of the post-sixties middle class had so obviously emulated and practiced it in private and public life. As for other threshold accomplishments, LULAC's achievement lay in synthesizing available forms, notions, and practices as well as encompassing experienced leadership—in some cases, activists of twenty years standing.

Though there were often differences among the leadership, it was capable and counted several outstanding individuals. Among them was a steadfast activist, María L. Hernández, an immigrant whose activities promoting civic organization were to span six decades.

The LULACs not only explicitly believed the Mexican community's problems could be resolved within the existing practices of the United States system, but also propagated this belief as a premise to be accepted as a position distinctly opposed to those who believed that it was a system to be challenged. Though they rejected the label *political*, they were, in practice, a political organization representing the class interests of the leadership. The denial was an understandable political ploy. Initially, the LULACs did not press for the full political participation of the Mexican community, but focused on the use of the legal system against overt discrimination directed against Mexicans. Importantly, LULAC also provided for women's participation as "auxiliaries," and though this was a far cry from the "equality" upheld by PLM, they did encourage such participation. As can be noted by the action of other contemporary groups, their argument that integrationist politics was the only politics possible within the milieu in which they operated was an argument not endorsed unanimously. In any case, the organization multiplied into several chapters, and their membership increased in the thirties; and for many years the LULACs consistently defended Mexican civil rights. An early legal effort was the 1930 Salvatierra anti-segregation case, which succeeded in ending the practice of labeling certain schools as "Mexican"; but the verdict was precursory since nothing changed but the public designation. Nonetheless, the case demonstrated LULAC's resolve to go to court for civil rights. During the thirties and forties it evolved as a moderate and successful organization, but one that contained a spectrum of views and whose members revealed a variety of backgrounds. There were several serious internal disputes, but they did not break up the organization. LULAC was an organization of Mexicans for Mexican rights and, in specific ways, one that brought about specific changes in the system through much effort and courage.

The rise of such an organization in the late twenties may be seen as a response to the intensification of repression against the Mexican communities in the United States. This repression developed an overwhelming nativist and quasi-fascist character and, in part, can be seen as one of several logical sequences of the earlier "Americanization" movement. The aim of this repression was to increase anti-Mexican feelings during a period of extreme economic hardship for many in the United States. By scapegoating Mexicans and others, the sources of economic inequalities, and especially of Anglo middle-class frustration, were shifted away from the crisis of the capitalist economy onto a segment of the working class and an ethnic community. Although a variant of this ideological assault had existed since the late nineteenth century, these nativist and racist formulations were particularly propagated in the twenties and thirties when quasi-fascist organizations arose in many parts of the country. Intellectual justifications also were used to call for the deportation of Mexicans, and for the removal or obliteration of their communities, if necessary, to placate public discontent. As an assault bent upon dividing the general U.S. working sector, anti-Mexican ideology found fertile ground in the minds of an economically threatened white-collar group and the unpoliticized white working class; and it was readily received by these sectors, especially by the rightist American Federation of Labor. However, there were progressives who opposed these reactionary attacks and acted to oppose them. But chauvinism and hostility also contributed to the interest in electoral activity in Mexico, which was viewed as a source of hope and of interest in a rhetoric of assertion rather than in one of sufferance.

The Vasconcelos Mobilization of 1928–1929

During the late 1920s and later, José Vasconcelos, a prominent educator in Mexico, influenced Mexicans in the United States through his political activities, particularly in his campaign for the presidency of Mexico and in his writings.[57] However his politics may be judged, Vasconcelos was a uniquely energetic, well-educated, and politically experienced individual with major talents as an ideologue, administrator, writer, and speaker. Among the major contributing circumstances to the Vasconcelos phenomenon were: (1) a widespread disillusionment with the political process in Mexico, but also a time of grievance for Mexicans in the United States; (2) the belief that the "revolutionary" government was closed and not electorally democratic, which was viewed by some as a violation of constitutional principles. At this point, Vasconcelos increased his political activities in what would become a dissident campaign for the presidency, which was not only a contest between him and his opponent but a challenge to the leadership consensus that evolved in Mexico during the conflict between 1910 and 1920, as well as a forum for disseminating a particular set of ideas pertinent to politics and history. Vasconcelos brought to his exile campaign the assets of his schooling, his residence on the border, and his knowledge of English.

While in the United States, Vasconcelos gained stature as perhaps the most prominent voice on the Mexican question. In his rhetoric, Vasconcelos raised several points that would draw a positive response from a variety of sectors. Passing over his own participation, he criticized Mexico's administrators for their authoritarian style of leadership; and in pointing to the prominence of the military in government, he advocated a regime with a democratic, "honest," and civilian leadership. Vasconcelos suggested constitutional reform: he wanted a less radically liberal, more moderate constitution. Pointedly, he underscored support for the Catholic church at a time when the Mexican government was again in conflict with it. Vasconcelos criticized the government for the violence employed to suppress the revolt, but he did not mention the violence of *cristeros*, right-wing pro-Church rebels, against those, particularly teachers, who did not share their views. Moreover, as recurrent themes he emphasized arch-Hispanicism, and arch-Catholicism, appealing to mythical "traditional" Mexican values, which were allegedly based on the intertwining of the Spanish heritage with the foundational role of the church in Mexican life. As a result of this rhetoric, he enjoyed the support of the Catholic church, critics of the revolution, immigrant cristero sympathizers, foreign companies, and others among the alienated and the aggrieved who questioned change and preferred disruption while ostensibly proposing a return to an idealized past. Also Vasconcelos did not remind audiences that he had voiced at one time elitist disparagements of border Mexicans and that while he held influence he had ignored appeals for combating discrimination.

Contradictory as it was, the Vasconcelos campaign was a continuation of the process of inter-Mexican contacts across the border. The Vasconcelos campaign reflected and incorporated into its program points, themes, and nuances to which some people across the border could respond. Vasconcelos's extended public speaking included both Anglo college audiences and audiences in the Mexican communities throughout the United States. His emphasis shifted from attacking the deficiencies of a regime of military políticos to advocating the necessity for a charismatic civilian leader and administrative reforms. At the same time, Vasconcelos sought to curry favor with Mexican exiles and immigrants of varying class backgrounds. He referred to the delays and incompleteness in social reform and the lack of economic equities. He urged the necessity of highly skilled conservative exiles who would benefit the country by their return and who should be guaranteed liberty of religion, the right to property, and the opportunity to work. Addressing Mexicans in the United States, and knowing his audience, Vasconcelos condemned widespread discrimination. In particular, he denounced the anti-Mexican immigration "Box Law" and the exclusivist unions that supported its passage. He pointed to the widely perceived hypocrisy of the U.S. trade-union movement, with its emphasis on economic demands and chauvinist practices. Vasconcelos also denounced violence and the lynchings of Mexicans, especially by the Ku Klux Klan, to whom he compared the exclusionist unions. Vasconcelos emphasized the strong national identity of the Mexican people and the need to consciously strengthen the cultural basis of the community. He advocated the establishment of Mexican schools and other cultural institutions that were to be funded by the government of Mexico throughout Mexican communities in the United States.

Vasconcelos's clubs were organized throughout many, if not most, of the major centers of Mexican population in the United States. Some of these were later represented in a convention held in Mexico City. Aspects of the platform appealing to or directly concerning Mexicans north of the boundary included the following: (1) increased consular protection; (2) patriotic and Spanish-language educational programs; (3) repatriation to irrigated, that is, developed, agricultural centers in Mexico; (4) demands for equal economic treatment and working conditions for Mexican workers in the United States; (5) protection for Mexican women; and (6) Mexican government intervention in behalf of immigrants. Vasconcelos, who had spent time as a child on the border and had seen discrimination firsthand, was aware of the possibilities of Mexicans within the United States in creating a political base for activity in Mexico. Nevertheless, the Vasconcelos effort was not well organized, for Vasconcelos himself was not an organizer and he did not have capable associates who were. Clearly, discontent was present and he aroused enthusiasm, but the force was not made substantively effective and it eventually dissipated.

The relative influence and following of the Vasconcelos movement north of the Río Bravo can be attributed to the popularly emphasized radical aspects of the Vasconcelos platform and rhetoric. His "Revolucionismo" called for the defense of the political and economic rights and the national identity of Mexicans within the United States. Vasconcelos's image of legitimacy and respectability, and his renown as an educational reformer and internationally respected intellectual, certainly contributed to his attractiveness. Importantly, he was one of the few Mexicans acknowledged by sectors of the U.S. intellectual elite, and therefore his image and achievements helped to counter the supremacist stereotype of Mexicans as a biologically inferior race, which was then prevalent in its most developed form in the United States. In this context, but beyond it in scope, was the Vasconcelos popular diffusion of betrayal as an explanation for a misdirection in Mexican history, which was concurrent with the promise of a great future and the utopian vision of "La Raza Cósmica," the ideal people whose miscegenated origins gave it unmatched strength and whose historical experience endowed it with unsurpassed virtue; these were repeated points of departure for political discourse, even if they were not read in their original exposition. More, immediately, they offered a counter-view to the one propagated by "Americanization" efforts. "La Raza Cósmica" was a magnetic phrase appealing to a tortured history and a future utopia, eulogizing the strengths of miscegenation. The Vasconcelos project took some traditional liberal notions, added to them a conservative canon and gave them a culturally biological twist. Though defeated in the elections of 1929, Vasconcelos continued to be active in conservative circles and to have contacts with Mexicans in the United States. In any case, the ultimate results of the campaign and its impact on supporters of the Vasconcelos movement may have been depoliticization, in view of subsequent developments that included Vasconcelos's electoral defeat and later openly reactionary views. Certainly, the decades between the wars were conductive not only to disillusionment, but, more importantly, to strife.

Repression and Response: The Depression

With the onset of the depression in 1929–30, Mexican workers and their families were subjected to increasing hardship.[58] Mexicans,

Blacks, Asians, and Native Americans, of course, were the first to feel
the effects of the economic collapse as wages dropped and even menial
labor jobs were difficult to obtain. Furthermore, white fascist groups,
such as the Silver Shirts in California, proliferated, targeting minorities and supporting conservative politicians and policies.

Nativism and chauvinism were strengthened in the thirties as business interests financed campaigns to divert the anger of the unemployed and often hungry Anglo worker from the shortcomings of the
economic system to blame the even more severely affected Mexican.
This campaign called for the mass deportation of Mexicans from the
United States and established the ideological foundation for the forced
repatriation to Mexico of nearly a million Mexicans, some born in the
United States. A policy was enacted and enforced, but there was also a
community response of defense and succor for these workers. In addition, thousands were coerced by methods of intimidation into leaving
"voluntarily." Although efforts to segregate Mexican school children
continued, they were nevertheless contested; and in two noteworthy
instances, members of the community effectively questioned segregation. In 1930, M. C. Gonzales and J. T. Canales supported successfully
the LULAC suit of Jesús Salvatierra to enjoin the segregation of Mexican children at Del Rio, Texas. Though the verdict was limited to an
agreement that segregation on the basis of Mexican descent was not
legal, and not much else resulted, it did set an early precedent. During
the same year, at Lemon Grove, California, the parents of Mexican
schoolchildren, with the support of the Mexican council and Anglo
liberals, also won a suit against segregation based on Mexican descent.
Schooling remained an often pejorative experience, but efforts to
improve schooling rather than discourage it increased.

Overall, with the impact of unemployment and world crises, the
radicalization that occurred throughout the United States, and specifically among Mexicans, was related to conditions, to advocacy, and to
communications. In the midst of great labor strife reminiscent of earlier
periods, mexicanos during the 1930s were often among the leading
participants in many of the major strikes of this period throughout
the western United States. Significantly for future political resources,
Mexicans gained some entry- and middle-level leadership positions in
established industrial unions. Contemporary political organizations
emerged and spread, some of which were partly inspired by efforts
elsewhere. For example, in California in the 1930s, the Mexican

American Movement, an organization of students, was established; and in 1938, El Congreso de Pueblos de Habla Española (the Congress of Spanish-Speaking People of the United States) held a national conference in Los Angeles.

Mexicans were active participants in the major progressive and radical organizations within the United States, particularly in the Communist Party, and their contribution to its organization of workers reached significant proportions. There was also some contact with activists and members of the Mexican Communist Party. Probably a larger sector in the community reflected a general skepticism, based on the actual experiences of the people, about the political process in the United States. However, the electorate, as a rule, tended to favor those political groups identified with the interests of labor and the disadvantaged. Among those who identified with the U.S. political process, there was strong support for President Roosevelt, the Democratic Party, and New Deal rhetoric. Equally, political organizational influences from Mexico had an impact throughout the thirties, with both progressive tendencies stemming from the Lázaro Cárdenas administration in Mexico (1934–1940) and from the conservatives, whose extremist elements emulated fascist movements then current in Europe, the United States, and elsewhere.

Community information by improved newspapers and a new medium, radio, added to heretofore uneven weeklies and leaflets, and rallies and assemblies. Though moderate in editorial stance, the major daily newspapers, *La Prensa* (1913), of San Antonio, and *La Opinión* (1926), experienced a dramatic surge in readership. These papers maintained quality and diversity in their published items and provided graphic coverage of major events, including world news. There were many writers among the exiles, and immigrants increased the readership; there was much activity to report and interpret. Too often, the tone was one of seeking or establishing status as was common to the middle class at any time. Nevertheless, political events, strikes, and court and police malpractice were reported, and readers were informed. With the advent of radio, programs that interspersed music, information on community events, and job information, as well as issues of unfairness, were available in many areas. Much of this print and audio journalism implicitly upheld mexicanidad in a time of trouble. And troubles there were aplenty. In effect, following the stock market crash of 1929, the Mexican people, both south and north of the Río Bravo, suffered the political effects of the great depression throughout the 1930s; and this suffering brought forth once more progressive and reactionary trends, with some of them again stemming from Mexico.

Right and Left in Mexico

In Mexico, the economic repercussions of the world economic collapse sharpened the already great contradictions in the economic, social, and political spheres of life, and all these fissures had an impact across the border.[59] In particular, the contradictions between the goals of the Mexican Revolution, as embodied in the Constitution of 1917, and the subsequent rightward movement of specific Mexican sectors following the insurgency approached a more critical point. Nonetheless significant was the counterpush to the left within the Mexican government, which was due largely to progressive elements within the administration taking advantage of broad popular support to reinitiate the process of social and economic reform. This process can also be viewed as a compromise within the governmental elite between progressive forces, as personified by President Lázaro Cárdenas, and the more farsighted and pragmatic sector of the bureaucracy which, given the economic and political situation, realized that concessions had to be made if the ruling group was to remain in power. At the same time, sectors of the "new" financial and business elite, as well as elements of the petite bourgeoisie and particularly the landholding sector, countered this progressive trend, which they feared, if it were allowed to continue, could lead to even more basic social, economic, and political change. With financial backing from business elements and disaffected militarists, counterrevolutionary right-wing organizations, which had contacts with reactionary circles in the United States, were set up to counteract the left and progressive sectors. Among these organizations were groups like the "Gold Shirts," modeled on and influenced by the Spanish fascist Falange, and the largest one, the Unión Nacional Sinarquista (UNS). Organized along conventional fascist lines, they called rhetorically for "social justice for all classes," and through demagoguery they sought to organize disaffected sectors of the middle class and rural dwellers. The rise of such organizations owed much to European influences on right wing groups in the United States.

Founded at a conference in León, Guanajuato on November 1,

1937, the Unión Nacional Sinarquista (UNS) portrayed itself as the most militant exponent of a ridiculous chauvinism masquerading as "patriotism."[60] It embraced a program that would have turned Mexico into a fascist state, along the lines of Franco's Spain and Mussolini's Italy. Some of the leaders were devoted to "Hispanidad" as advocated by Spanish fascists. Among other points, the Sinarquista program called for (1) order and production; (2) an authoritarian state; (3) national greatness; (4) the curtailment of social, political, and cultural dissidence; (5) Roman Catholicism as the official national religion; (6) education under the joint auspices of the state and church; (7) the promotion of capital; and (8) the subordination of unions and labor questions to management- and government-appointed councils. They were virulently anti-socialist and anti-trade union. Among the rhetorical points intended to gain popular appeal were (1) the opposition to U.S. influence and Protestant missionaries; (2) the reclamation and restoration of territories lost to the United States; and (3) the defense of Mexicans in the United States. From the first they had specific international and organizational objectives. Supporters argued the UNS was a Christian social movement; critics saw it as a menace to liberal constitutional government in both Mexico and the United States. The UNS's anti-United States rhetoric found support among some Mexicans in the U.S., especially those who were conservative but nationalistic and resisting assimilation.

Soon after the founding of the Unión Nacional Sinarquista in 1937, agents moved to establish it among the Mexican people north of the U.S. boundary by emphasizing the discrimination they faced.[61] Given the widespread fascist propaganda, sinarquismo north of the boundary drew its major support from and exerted a notable influence on the sectors of the Mexican people most influenced and organized by antisocialist elements: out-of-power politicians, exile conservatives, sectors of the Catholic church, and probably elements of the small, marginal petite bourgeoisie, or those embracing such an ideological orientation. Among these contributing sectors women were notable adherents and sympathizers. The first regional sinarquista group north of the border was organized in Los Angeles, California, in November 1937, shortly after their organization in Mexico. Roughly five years later, by 1942, the sinarquistas claimed a modest total of two thousand members in the United States. According to the U.S. Department of Justice, sinarquistas allegedly were organized in fifty branches centered mainly in California and Texas, but including a major branch in Chicago, Illinois, and scattered groups in other states, particularly in the Southwest. Branches were located in Pacoima, San Fernando, San Bernardino, La Verne, Ontario, Watts, Belvedere, El Monte, Oxnard, Pomona, and Azusa, in Southern California; and El Paso, McAllen, Mission, and Laredo, in Texas. Sinarquismo promoted a reactionary version of Mexican pseudo-patriotism through exploitation of the issue of discrimination and rhetorical demands for the rights of the Mexican people, while, in effect, seeking to advance sectors of the elite. Their activity primarily took the forms of rallies and forums, and attacking those they considered "communists."

The sinarquista movement across the border and in Mexico was seemingly well organized and structured hierarchically, and was commanded directly by a semi-clandestine senior political directive of the movement in Mexico, which included both public and non-public leadership. In the prewar period, efforts often centered around the organizing of large regional or community-wide events, incorporating religious, social, and cultural activities where sinarquista speakers presented their program to relatively large audiences, including women and youth, and often employed such propaganda as films on fascist activities abroad and in Mexico. The sinarquista movement also had a fairly developed press with an apparently wide circulation. The major organs of the Unión were its weekly newspaper, *El Sinarquista* (1938), and a monthly magazine, *Orden* (1942). By the early forties, thousands of copies of these publications were being circulated to Mexican communities throughout the United States. With the beginning of World War II, the sinarquistas were required to register with the U.S. Department of Justice under the "Foreign Agents Registration Act," and they came under the surveillance of the FBI. As a consequence, this movement, like others, curtailed most of its public activities, and members joined ostensibly nonfascist, conservative groups.

The sinarquista movement in the United States apparently received financial support from right-wing corporate and Anglo Catholic organizations, and possibly other white supremacist groups. Presumably conservative organizations, as well as some major U.S. financial interests, would have benefited from the anti-progressive, anti-labor ideology of sinarquista fascism counteracting the influence of progressive, leftist organizations and militant unionism in the Mexican communities and among Mexican workers. Moreover, influencing the government in Mexico to move in a conservative direction was a continuing goal of right-wing groups in the United States. United States business interests were hardly subtle in buying bureaucratic opportunities in Mexico and in financing right-wing opposition movements. Sinarquistas could not speak directly to the issues of electoral empowerment, labor organizing, and police brutality. They could and did speak to historical injustices. Though sinarquismo employed the rhetoric of Mexican chauvinism, it represented for the Mexican people an end that entirely contradicted their actual interests as a nationality composed primarily of working people. While in the immediate period sinarquismo assertively proclaimed its defense of the rights of the Mexican nationality against discrimination and oppression and, in certain instances, took an active role, at least propagandistically, in the long run the sinarquista movement was allied with, and received financial and propagandistic support from, historical exploiters and was supported by mistaken values. Furthermore, the agitation of support was again intended to increase the leaders' leverage in relation to policies and positions in the Mexican government. This opposition to a sitting government in Mexico City was involved in an interrelationship of a particular kind; as the government moved so did the opposition, and vice versa. The results were more activity in the Southwest.

During the 1920s and 1930s, more than before, the Mexican government tolerated and encouraged more social and organizational proactive efforts. The administrations of Obregón-Calles (1920–1924 and 1924–1928) and Cárdenas (1934–1940) were generally sympathetic to Mexican residents in the United States and to Mexican workers in particular, often taking specific steps to provide aid and assistance to Mexicans abroad through giving orders to consulates or by providing resources. If a consul acted negatively, it was due less to standing government policy and was more the result of personal bias. The contribution of the consul to a community-organization role must be viewed through specific situations. Often, consulates were quite active in cultural, political, and labor situations, and their advice and leadership, for better or worse, were consistently sought. Their role and function had been stabilized and restabilized after the erratic interim of the years of conflict between 1910 and 1920. By 1930, Mexico had over fifty consular agencies in the United States. With the assistance of "*abogados consultores*" and "*comisiones honoríficas,*" they were quite active and generally enjoyed respect and support. Although by regulation and the Havana Convention of 1928, they were empowered to intervene only on behalf of Mexican citizens, citizenship by consanguinity, or *jus sanguinis,* had been argued and recognized for the protection of foreign-born Mexicans. Mexican consular officials became involved in strikes, sometimes favoring the owners and at other times the workers.

During the thirties, Mexican government officials and elected congressmen and senators, as well as artists and writers, visited southwestern communities. There was considerable written material and poster art sent across the border. In the thirties, in a concerted effort, consular officials organized and reorganized elements and activities that revolved around their offices, thus increasing these resources in the community; for example, through merchant groups, charity drives, literary and educational programs, the Sixteenth of September and Fifth of May celebrations, and so forth. Consular staff occasionally became involved in labor questions and at this time there was considerable labor activity. Major trade union organizations in Mexico sent representatives and materials to Mexican communities in the Southwest and Midwest.

In addition to progressive labor and political influences, cultural maintenance continued, and influences stemmed from Mexico. Moreover, the deportation drives and several cases of flagrant injustice to Mexican individuals kept sensitivities alive, as did cultural programs and visits by Mexican artists and intellectuals. These years witnessed a further elaboration and formalization of the celebration of the Sixteenth of September and the participation in it by the Mexican government. Significantly, Mexican film comedies, songs, novels, and plays featuring political and class themes were widely disseminated. In turn, Mexico-based periodicals, records, and entertainers, and Mexico's film industry dramatically increased their United States sales; and magazines and radio were important in communicating political information. Many Mexican Americans accepted as a fact of life the community's interest in Mexico, and some believed that there would be equal interest displayed by Mexico, other than by relatives, some government functionaries, and a few unionists, artists, and entertainers, but such was not the case. In the United States, however, the interaction had clear organizational, ideological, and cultural impact.

Progressive Labor and Youth Organizing

Spontaneous and organized labor activity linked Mexicans together in the United States throughout the twentieth century, creating solidarity among field workers, miners, railroad workers, and others.[62] Much of this activity was related to U.S. labor, as well as inspired by several groups from Mexico. Like previous efforts, the activities of the early Confederación Regional Obrera Mexicana, and later the Confederación de Trabajadores de México, affected the United States.

Efforts to organize workers occurred in all southwestern states. In California, Mexican workers took the initiative to organize themselves at a meeting of a federation of Mexican societies held in Los Angeles in November 1927. This led to the formation of the Confederación de Uniones Obreras Mexicanas (CUOM), an effort influenced structurally and ideologically by the Confederación Regional Obrera Mexicana. A general CUOM convention was called in May 1928, and was attended by twenty-one unions representing both agricultural and industrial workers. Emilio Mújica, a fraternal representative from CROM, attended and remained in Los Angeles to aid in organizing Mexican unions there. By 1933 the confederation had some ten locals remaining, mostly agricultural; and generally it stimulated unionism among Mexican workers at a propitious time.

Regardless of how they began, the labor organizations of the 1930s were the result of a political response which was closer to large numbers of people and more militant than the middle-class organizations. With remarkable tenacity, labor unions made a political impact, and their activities or influence were not limited to strikes. With roots in the early 1900s, large, militant efforts had been carried on through the twenties by Mexican labor in mining, agriculture, and manufacturing, and these efforts increased in the thirties. Community organizations often became involved in strikes, and labor organizing took place across the Southwest, emphasizing trade-union issues as well as community rights in general. A particularly intense wave of strikes occurred in agriculture, as well as in mining and the garment industry. The twenties and thirties produced several outstanding labor leaders: Jesús Pallares, in New Mexico; Guillermo Velarde, in California; C. N. Idar, in Texas, Colorado, and Arizona; Juan Peña and Emma Tenayuca, in Texas. Much of the organizing among Mexicans was done by radical

Mexicans and Anglo organizers rather than by trade-union staff; and owners, government officials, and journalists debated the threatening potential of labor activity organized by Mexicans.

In this activity, two remarkably charismatic women leaders contributed significantly to communitywide activities. Emma Tenayuca, of Texas, and Josefina Fierro, of California, were aggressive, articulate, well read, and experienced in leadership and in populist organizing. They were both forthrightly committed to radical reforms and intensely associated with activities of the Communist Party and labor and civil rights efforts in the Mexican community.

An increase in labor activity and organizing efforts also led to intensified organizational efforts along different political lines. In 1935 the rise of the Congress of Industrial Organizations (CIO) led to further organizing efforts among Mexican industrial and urban workers, both immigrant and native born. In October 1935, the Convención Constitutiva pro Derechos Mexicanos de Texas was held. Trade unionists, socialists, unemployed workers, and mutualista delegates attended the convention to issue progressive political and economic resolutions. One resolution called for the right of self-determination by the Mexican people of south Texas.

A potentially farsighted attempt was made to organize a range of Mexican organizations across the Southwest, which linked other Spanish-speaking organizations in the Midwest, East, and Southeast into a congress.[63] It also involved non-Mexican and non-Latino groups and individuals in key roles. Several strands had led to this effort: one involved the recurrent aspiration of creating a major Mexican convocation of local leaders and organizations to discuss and articulate a program for the community as a whole; and another focused on the effort to enroll Mexicans, particularly to draw upon their organizing momentum as a constituency on behalf of the priorities of the Communist Party of the United States of America (CPUSA), whose vitality was similar to organizational efforts among Blacks.

A frequently acknowledged impetus for organizing lay in the conditions of life for Mexicans in the Southwest. More particular were several galvanizing circumstances. The strongest one was the continually impeded effort to unionize workers, on the one hand, and the highly visible and massive deportations, on the other. Another circumstance was the chronically unfair treatment of Mexicans by police and the courts, several instances of which had aroused public indignation during the twenties and thirties. Concern for the quality of schooling and discriminatory practices had repeatedly been expressed for generations, and now small groups of young people were raising the issue in behalf of other youth. Similarly, questions of housing, health, and nutrition had been raised, and protests were mounted over the availability of food. Community groups also stressed the discouragement of citizenship and the need to increase naturalization. Among a few, the belief had been voiced that broadcasting cultural understanding and a knowledge of Latin American history, art, and society would improve relations between the dominant class and minority groups. Events in Europe, Latin America, and Mexico during the late thirties received constant attention in newspapers and spurred interest in foreign relations. A specific conference concept stemmed from an idea voiced by a local of the United Cannery, Agricultural, Packing, and Allied Workers of America (UCAPAWA), in this case a Texas organization.

In effect, the congress represented a synthesis and a turning point. An initial organizing group for a "Mexican congress" was led by, among others, Josefina Fierro of California, members of the Arizona Correa family, and Professors George I. Sánchez and Arthur L. Campa of New Mexico. Their efforts were followed with interest by a few elected and organizational officials. A conference was initially called to form the "Congreso Hispano Americano" at Albuquerque, New Mexico, in March 1939, but this effort was aborted in the course of a preliminary meeting in Albuquerque. There were differences among sponsors, between moderates and progressives, and between those who primarily wanted a Mexican conclave and those who wished to include others, while some would not support a mixed convention or one visibly led by non-Mexicans. Luisa Moreno, a Guatemalan immigrant who had access to some resources, took over a major part of the organizing effort, increasing the influence of the UCAPAWA leadership, Donald Henderson and Leo Gallagher. Initially, the Congreso was meant to involve primarily Mexican people from Texas, New Mexico, Colorado, and California, but this plan was later expanded to include other peoples. At first, Mexican representatives presumed that a platform for united action would arise from sharing experiences and from local organizational priorities; but this plan was replaced by a prepared proposal to guide action on a national scale, and in concert with a multi-group coalition; advocate economic improvement; aid trade-union organizing; and improve relations between minorities and Anglos, an effort which referred to a mass campaign against "racism" by primarily addressing Black–white relations and anti-Semitism. Though it was more developed because it covered more of the region and was ideologically attuned to Mexican needs and issues as well as general ones, the Congreso echoed the Congreso Mexicanista of 1911 only partly, and from the first there was organizational and issue ambiguity. Though many organizations were listed, most of them were only endorsements rather than allegiances to a project, and in its factional disputes, local support from New Mexico and Texas was lost in some measure, and thus regional, organizational, and experienced leadership was weakened. The Congreso's name was translated into English as the Congress of Mexican and Spanish-Speaking People, and later changed to the National Congress of Spanish-Speaking People. Tellingly, the name was changed from a nationality designation to a language designation because Anglos and Jews were more comfortable with such a change, and then the language was changed from Spanish to English.

Eventually, the major conference was held at Los Angeles on April 28, 29, and 30, 1939. At least 126 delegates attended, with Mexican organizations in attendance, dominating the organizations and California with the most. Significantly, there was representation from unions in Mexico and support from the Mexican consul. There were delegates with experience in trade-union organizing, as well as those with mutualista and masonry backgrounds. Some had previous contact with PLM efforts, others had experience with revolutionary factions in Mexico, and several were from families who were in the United States before 1900. Actual representation by non-Mexican Latinos was sparse, though these few claimed to represent many. Ed Quevedo was elected president, and Josefina Fierro executive secretary; Quevedo was involved in "popular front" activity sponsored by the Communist Party. At the Congress several committees were established, which were chaired by non-Mexicans, even though Mexicans at the convention were as informed or more informed on the subject of the committee as the appointed chair. Overall, this organization was indeed progressive in its public stance, articulating demands and combining strong union representation with proactive lower middle-class leadership, and with native-born individuals and immigrants, Mexicans and non-Mexicans united on an impressively broad agenda of issues.

The Congreso synthesized many issues of concern to past as well as contemporary efforts, but it also echoed CPUSA precepts for the Black community and clichés of the Anglo and Jewish left intelligentsia. On occasion, in stating a problem the language of the proceedings was almost eloquent in the Spanish version, and the English suffered by comparison. And the solutions that followed were quite conventional. For example, the solutions offered to civil rights and discrimination problems were public education and civic participation. The Congreso sought to strengthen unionizing efforts among the Mexican sector of workers, particularly in agriculture, but with a clear affirmation of the primacy of orthodox trade-union organizing. It called for an end to police abuses, job discrimination, and segregated housing, but it provided for no action against discriminatorily elected officials, employers, or owners. It weakly referred to foreign affairs, and those were primarily European, not Latin American, except for an uncritical view of the "Good Neighbor" policy, in reference to Mexico in particular; and it was weak because progressives were tentative on foreign issues, given the shifts in Soviet foreign policy. The strongest statements were made on health and education because here there was a greater consensus on these; that is, no one was threatened.

The Congreso also called for intensive voter registration, support for progressive candidates, and, in general, the right to political, social, and economic rights. The resolutions were reasonably stated in both Spanish and English, in fact better than was to be expected from an intense conference. Resolutions lacked specific resolve because specific actions were not detailed, with many of them were derived from other platforms and available at the start of the congress. Those on trade unionism did not address discrimination within specific unions, nor the importance of large urban industrial organizing by Mexicans. The rights of political representation for Mexicans or by Mexicans was unclear, and Democrat official districting and voter requirements went unchallenged. Immigration rights or abuses were addressed in political and religious, but not economic, terms. In sum, discrimination was indeed stressed, but not empowerment or cultural rights in relation to nationality equities, which were themes common to Mexican conferences; and between the first and second conferences momentous events occurred in Europe.

The statement produced at the second conference, soon held, and commendably so, on December 9 and 10, 1939, was available only in English and was much shorter and more generalized, suggesting ambiguity and a lack of result. Seemingly the issuers purposely avoided specifics until international politics cleared. In any case, Josefina Fierro ran the activities of the Congress and raised the money for them.

In sum, the Congress proclaimed a broad effort and set major objectives. Results were quite modest, with few major actions or results following. Organizational work, apart from declarations, was uneven. Local committees were to carry forth the program, but at most some meetings were held. Initially, there was response, but either it was not answered or it dissipated; and there was not much reported activity, other than in Los Angeles. In Los Angeles, the Congress claimed several thousand "members," though there was no membership in the formal sense or as practiced by existing Mexican organizations; for if there had been, its development would have been different. But there was activity in Los Angeles, particularly by Josefina Fierro, Ed Quevedo, and Frank López, who were awarded some minor advising roles by local officials. Representatives of the Congress spoke to issues and registered voters, and Quevedo ran for the California assembly and the Los Angeles city council. There was, however, a precedent-setting rally at Sacramento, with hundreds of supporters and an address by the governor. The demise of the Congress in Los Angeles and its failure to surface elsewhere contrasted with the claims made for it concerning the enthusiasm it aroused and its thousands of supporters.

There was apprehension among members over the large role played by non-Mexicans, usually adherents of the Communist Party, and concern that they, in turn, were less interested in promoting civil rights protest in behalf of Mexicans than other issues that were viewed as the priority. However, factionalism and inefficiency, as well as disinterest, meant that the Congress eventually dwindled to become only a mailing address common to a number of "progressive" groups. Since the first proceedings were a synthesis of current issues and solutions, they became part of the programmatic heritage, and even though an organization might decline, individuals continued. Many participants in the Congress would be active in several efforts for the next thirty years, as were the critics of the Congress. Although the efforts were modest, the Congress provided a program, an intended national structure, public advocacy, and protest actions.

In the aftermath of the Congress, there was visible a slightly greater interest in the "Mexican problem" than had been previously compelled by demographics, age distribution, and the coming of war. Liberals were in the forefront, and a basic realization was the growth of the

Mexican community, one with a disparate status and a growing young population. To address this fact were some standard things and some that were novel: one would create a greater awareness of the "problem," while another would enhance self-improvement by those approved to be enlightened within the community; still another focused on tentative and publicly funded programs intended to upgrade skills that were related to youth.

The Mexican American Movement

A significant liberal effort of the 1930s was the Mexican American Movement (MAM).[64] With the support of Protestant church affiliates and the YMCA, MAM was organized in 1932 by several dozen high school and college Mexican youths in the Los Angeles area, as part of a broader concern by its sponsors, among whom were proponents of "Americanization," Protestant proselytizing, and anti-socialism. In MAM discourse, deculturalization and the internalization of stereotypes were evident, as well as a naiveté about Mexican formal culture, history, and organizational activity. They held up as a model idealized Anglo Saxon, not merely American, ways of thinking and acting, integrated with the undeniable fact of their Mexican descent. They also put themselves forth as a model; and among the leading figures in this respect were Paul Coronel, Felix Gutiérrez, Stephen Reyes, Juan Acevedo, Manuel Ceja, Arthur Casas, Angelo Cano, Mary Escudero, Mary Anne Chavolla, Rebecca Muñoz, and others. Initially, MAM was overwhelmingly male, but over time, women members increased. Many members became conscientious teachers, social workers, middle-level administrators, or business persons, but none emerged as a major political figure. Nevertheless, several members participated in community civic organizations while continuing to support the organization of their youth.

The MAM leadership expressed their views through their publication, *The Mexican Voice*, the voice of the "modern" Mexican, as they saw it. As for other Mexicans who might not share their beliefs, they said: *"Don't believe them. They don't want you to progress. They are greedy and jealous, because you have a better chance. They want you to be like them—easy-going, time-wasting Mexicans—fellows who drag down our name."*[65] Strong on sports, they had this inspirational

message: "We Mexicans are *as good athletes as any other race!* Let's follow
the examples of these champions of our race! . . . You can do all these
things all of these fellows have done. All you need is encouragement . . ."[66] Direct action was seldom advocated, and when it occurred
it was speculative:

> the only thing to do is to elevate ourselves, to command respect by
> becoming educated . . . I wonder what we could do though. For
> example, let us take San Fernando. There are about 5,000 of Mexi-
> can descent in this town of about 9,000 people. More than half are
> paisanos. Yet in one of the theatres of this town, those of Mexican
> descent must sit up in the balcony, and in this theatre the balcony
> was packed while on the main floor only a few attended. What
> would happen to this theatre's business if all of Mexican descent
> decided not to attend unless allowed the privilege of sitting any-
> where?[67]

They felt that with education, discrimination would disappear. The
editor, Félix Gutiérrez, wrote in 1938: "When a Mexican is "up there"
on the same level with others, he is taken for what he is worth—his
ability—not for his nationality."[68] Their notions of cultural pride
would have drawn derision in Mexican newspapers. At one point, in
mid-1938, Manuel Ceja wrote: "A Mexican must be a Mexican. His
heritage of rich Aztec and Spanish blood has provided him with characteristics born of a high cultural civilization. When this rich background has been tempered with the fires of the Anglo-Saxon understanding and enlightenment, you will have something which will be
the envy of all."[69] At this point, they were more European than Indian.
In reaction to ethnic arguments against the Mexican community, these
young men retaliated with racial arguments, saying, "We're of the same
white race that segregates us." Apparently, they had no other arguments as a result of their "Americanization." Through the reach of *The
Mexican Voice,* they actively sought to expound their "Americanism,"
thinking they could salvage a rhetorical Mexican heritage: "Best of all,
let us be Americans of Mexican descent!"[70] What was striking in their
commentary was the absence not only of acknowledgment of Mexican
organizational heritage, but of the reality of the thirties, as well as their
partial resonance with the LULACs.

　　Their imitative and derivative set of beliefs focused principally
on two growing concerns, education and youth problems, and their slogan was "Progress through Education." More precisely, MAM's pro-

gram was individual and community self-improvement through education, and the enhancement of the Mexican's self-image by developing
"proper" habits of dress, study, and discipline. MAM also was involved
in addressing juvenile delinquency, by denouncing it as counterproductive to individual and community progress. Among some of the *Voice's*
articles were vivid testimonies of the anguish, confusion, and im-
itativeness caused by cultural aggression, but also testimony indicating
an evolution, albeit a slow one. Their principal activities were their
general convention and their publication, interspersed with modest
recreational and educational efforts. Because many of the members
joined the armed forces during World War II, MAM went into decline,
but it reorganized and survived into the fifties, dwindling then in the
sixties.

On December 18, 1945, when the MAM was incorporated as a
distinct group from the YMCA, their principles and objectives were
more clearly formulated:

1. The Movement is a politically non-partisan, non-profit,
non-sectarian organization.

2. The chief purpose of the Mexican-American Movement is to
improve conditions among the Mexican-American and Mexican
people living in the United States.

3. The goal of the Movement, which is the betterment of our
people, can be achieved through a process of education.

4. The endeavor is to promote a mutual understanding and better cooperation between the Mexican-Americans and other Americans. The aim is to base all endeavors on cooperation, sympathy,
and encouragement.

5. The members of the M.A.M. believing in American institutions and in the democratic way of life, have confidence that by
raising the social level of Mexican-American people and improving
their living conditions they are helping to improve America. [71]

This organization was a precursor to later student-based efforts in the
1960s in its commitment to a programmatic set of goals focused on
youth and active on their behalf. Conventions continued to be held
sporadically, and Edward Roybal, an organizational leader and elected
official, spoke at one of them. MAM's last effort in 1965 was to
facilitate fifty college scholarships, and presumably some recipients
became student activists. Over time, MAM did not remain a youth
group, but evolved into a group focused on education and consisting

mostly of the original members, who were now youth centered. MAM was not remarkable for its composition—there were more students, and more of them were organized, and there were more student groups in other states—nor for its anxious status seeking, or its somewhat average writings. They were a particular group of Mexicans organized for a specific purpose. What was notable was their commitment over two decades to concerted activism in behalf of youth, and their rudimentary understanding and commitment to the need to consciously develop the young and youth leadership, both of which were understood to be resources. In short, MAM represented a growing interest in youth—some of it positive, some of it negative.

During subsequent years the young received increasingly positive attention, from organizations like the "Coordinating Council for Latin American Youth" in 1942, which was a federation of smaller youth or youth-focused organizations in the Los Angeles area. With the coming of World War II, youth community activity added to its concerns the international European and Pacific arenas and the war effort, and certainly the young responded. Unorthodox youth activity remained, however, and the good intentions of liberals inside and outside the community were shocked by a much older pattern, the persecution of Mexicans, which was now focused on the young.

During the early forties, as some positive changes occurred, anti-Mexican activities continued that were reminiscent of the attacks during other decades, and these involved the district attorney and police agencies more in step with old policies than with new ones. Two examples of anti-Mexican and, in effect, "fascist" attacks on the Mexican community were the Sleepy Lagoon case in 1941 and the at-large "racist" attacks on the Mexican community, both of which occurred in Los Angeles and during a war effort against fascism, one of whose main features was "racism"; both targeted the young, but more significantly, both became symbols for the future.

The Sleepy Lagoon case involved twenty-two Mexican youth-gang members who were arrested and charged falsely with criminal conspiracy in the death of José Díaz. [72] The newspapers and the police incited anti-Mexican sentiment by publicly presenting the case in all its lurid details and depicting Mexicans as inherently criminal and violent. Although evidence was lacking, the youths were convicted on charges ranging from assault to first-degree murder. At the initiative of Josefina Fierro, progressives and Anglo liberals joined Mexican labor and com-

munity representatives in forming the Sleepy Lagoon Defense Committee. Although the committee was harassed by the police and red-
baited by the press and the state legislature, it was successful in having
the convictions overturned and the youths set free in 1944. As the
Sleepy Lagoon case proceeded, the police and press intensified their
attacks on the Mexican community in east Los Angeles.

In many of the urban centers of California, attacks on Mexican
youth increased during the early forties, and culminated in the infamous Zoot Suit riots in the summer of 1943.[73] These riots consisted of
systematic attacks on Mexican youth who favored using "drapes" or
"zoot suits." The most publicized attacks were carried out by soldiers
and sailors on leave and supported by the Los Angeles police. Anglo
armed-forces personnel rioted, and Mexicans became their victims.
Once again, the newspapers and police played an important role in sin-
gling out Mexican youths for cultural and ethnic attacks. Again, Mexican labor and organizational representatives joined with Anglo liberals
and progressives to protest. The Mexican government intervened diplomatically to protest these anti-Mexican attacks, though the majority
of those who suffered were not Mexican citizens. Others joined the
protest and many were influential in having authorities end the attacks
and even offer some vague apologies.

Both the Sleepy Lagoon case and the Zoot Suit riots indicate that
the Mexican community continued as a regional target for chauvinism
at a time when a national hysteria was focusing on the "foreign enemy."
However, the community and civil-rights supporters, as well as other
allies, responded to challenge these persecutions effectively. The Communist Party (USA) was among the few groups condemning these
attacks on the Mexican community, and though its ostensible purpose
was not liberal, but radical, it helped to stimulate liberal interest in
response to its efforts in organizing among the Mexican people.

The Liberals and the Left

A Mexican left continued throughout the thirties and forties to
draw from diverse past and present leftist currents; in particular, however, it was strengthened by invigorated Communist Party activities, to
some extent, by those in Mexico, but obviously by programs of the
Communist Party of the USA. The role of the USA Communist Party

within the Mexican organizations enhanced the activism in the community, even though its numbers remained modest, and the failings the party exhibited with this community were in step with its organizational failings and its ideological weakness as a national "revolutionary" organization in comparison to communist parties elsewhere.[74] Contrary to the consternation often aroused by the name, the organization emphasized liberal reforms, but gave some attention to direct protest. Mexicans were not a part of the national leadership, nor were they a major priority. Although the party partially provided progressive ideas, leadership, and organization, and called for the defense of all minorities, it placed modest importance on the organization of Mexicans.

For a while, there were two youth party–sponsored groups: the Nueva Vida Club and the No Pasarán chapter of the Young Communist League and the Workers Alliance campaign included Mexican organizers and rank-and-file members. Support for increased numbers of Mexican organizers never followed through on a continuing and consistent basis, nor were adequate ideological materials developed; nor were appropriate cadre training, or culturally sensitive ways and means for outreach and organizing programmatically considered. Other deficiencies resulted from neglecting to incorporate Mexican cultural symbols and activities and the use of Spanish in meetings. Worst was the ethnic discrimination within the organization, as the party upheld European minorities and practiced condescension toward colored peoples. Some of these failings were not significant in contrast to liberal organizations, but they were notable given the fact that the Communist Party was supposedly a much more conscious and purposive organization.

The Communist Party of the USA interacted with the Mexican community through its energetic labor activity since the 1920s and into the mid-1930s. Equally energetic was the "Popular Front" strategy, which sought to unite all liberal and progressive elements into a united bloc to stop the spread of fascism. Communist Party advocacy would call for "red" revolutionary and independent unions and denounce all elements to the right of it, and later it would call for all labor efforts to be within the AFL or the CIO and to cooperate with and support liberals. The party followed the imperatives set in motion by European events, and it was concerned with the defense of Russia. Initially, the European war was seen as a fight against fascism; then, after the Soviet–

German peace pact, it was viewed as an imperialist-inspired war and then again as a struggle against fascism. On the domestic scene, the party priority, for the most part, was supportive of the war effort, as evidenced by the support of the no-strike pledge within industry; thus, the encouragement of ethnic protest was not urgent. Other priorities included denouncing fascist groups and non-Communist Party leftist groups. However, party activities in the Mexican community continued although they were minimal. As a whole, the party supported civil-rights activities, and the protection of the rights of the foreign-born. It protested police brutality, and advocated the elimination of discrimination against Mexicans. In the Southwest, it aggressively combated sinarquista influence among Mexicans.

Importantly, one major statement was produced from the party ranks. "The Mexican Question in the Southwest" (1939), by Emma Tenayuca and Homer Brooks, which was inspired more by Stalin's dogma than Leninist analysis, stressed the distinctive commonality of the Mexican people in the Southwest because of class and cultural oppression. Though they comprised a "people," they were not sufficiently distinct to warrant the tactical and organizational recognition identified for Blacks, who were viewed as a "nation" because of what the authors judged as an insufficient economic or territorial base. Mexicans were part of the larger working class, and their political and class needs were best served by their integration into organizations such as the Communist Party and labor unions. Thus, organizationally there was no consideration of the people's acknowledged distinctiveness. Worst, there was no reflection upon how organizationally absurd it was that an "outsider" party was attempting to lead the Mexican community. The Communist Party, an organization overwhelmingly composed of non-Mexicans, would not recognize either the independence or the equality of Mexicans organizationally. In effect, the party never resolved its position or practice on the Mexican "national question" in the United States, which for a Marxist party meant that its actions would be surrounded by ambiguity.

Party leaders were frequently insensitive, even arrogant, and occasionally exploitive, but generally, they were obedient to the interests of the U.S.S.R., whose priorities were counterproductive to the U.S. party's own development. An operative assumption was that Mexicans had nothing of value to contribute politically, organizationally, or ideologically. Some of the party's males even revived the frontier dichotomy between bad Mexican men and good Mexican women, and they liked the women. The Communist Party of the USA attracted some Mexicans, but kept few of them. Apart from some endemic deficiencies, there were particularly aggravating points that caused confusion and alienation. After the Hitler–Stalin Pact was signed, some Mexicans went over to the Socialists, and the repetitious idealiza-tion of Russia was not only boring, but unconvincing as a motivation for organized activity. Glib, English-speaking party members could out-debate a sinarquista rival who was limited to Spanish, but they could not elicit the fervent resonances that some party members could arouse among some Mexicans in Mexico. The party's last viable and visible supporting effort occurred in the Mexican community in 1948, and the party would not be as visible again until the late 1960s and early 1970s.

Nevertheless, the record of progressive efforts in the Mexican com-munity during the thirties and forties was part of a commendable record of party-inspired or -supported activity, and a profile of militant Mexi-can leadership was, in part, a profile of Mexican party members and sympathizers. The Communist Party's Committee for the Defense of the Foreign Born performed valuable, courageous work in defending the rights of Mexican workers and radicals throughout the fifties, when party members were uniquely persecuted, resulting in the publication of several strong statements of abuses suffered by Mexicans. One fea-ture of party tactics in the Mexican community was its organizing flexibility, with the party working through its own groups as well as through others, and as occasion required, establishing or abolishing special efforts and working inside and outside electoral politics. Much remains unknown about the party's activities or internal debates, or, of course, its membership, which may have numbered approximately five hundred Mexicans. In the late thirties, Emma Tenayuca may have been persecuted and run out of San Antonio, and terrorized to drive her from activism, but her efforts and those of other members eventually added to political progress.

World War II: Needs, Transition, Programs, and Politics, 1941–1945

During the 1940 presidential campaign, Mexican activists, includ-ing many World War I veterans led by Professor George I. Sánchez and

Cleofas Calleros, as well as Senator Dennis Chavez, sought to interest President Roosevelt in their problems. Some verbal assurances were made, and Professor Sánchez received several modest appointments. Perhaps more telling was the interest voiced by Eleanor Roosevelt in an episode which apparently was not a formal organizational effort, but occurred in isolation and was one example of Mexican advocacy at the U.S. national level. Eventually some consequences followed. Moreover there was discussion of a White House–sponsored informational conference on Mexican Americans, which would focus attention on youth and education.

Mexicans came to be positively needed, recruited, and viewed in qualitative and quantitative terms as the crisis unfolded. They were affected vitally when, in the late 1930s and early 1940s, the world was again threatened with impending war and then engaged in the actual war between the major fascist states—Nazi Germany, Fascist Italy, and imperialist Japan—and the Western "democratic" states—represented preeminently by Great Britain, France, and the United States. The national government needed support, workers, and soldiers. Involved in the threatened conflict were progressive forces, at that time specifically represented by the Soviet Union, and socialist and communist parties and their sympathizers. One priority was to denounce fascism and promote peace, while another focused on recruiting sympathizers; and Mexicans had demonstrated that they could organize.

The great conflict itself was immediately preceded by the aggressive actions of Japan in Asia, Italy in Ethiopia, and Germany in Central Europe, and, above all, by the Spanish Civil War of 1936–1939, which had an impact on Mexicans in Mexico and the United States. During the Spanish Civil War, progressive and revolutionary elements, comprising Spain's legitimate Republican government, were pitted against Spanish fascism, which was actively supported by the German and Italian fascist states. In contrast, the world communist and progressive movements gave support to the Republic, with arms sent by a few progressive governments, such as that of President Lázaro Cárdenas in Mexico. Mexicanos from both sides of the border, who were considered worthy participants in progressive causes, were among the volunteers of the international brigades fighting in the ranks of Republican Spain.

While the United States vascillated about entering the conflict, the government and corporations took advantage of the situation faced by major rivals by increasing production and sales abroad, and strengthening defenses. The U.S. government, however, fully feared the fascist threat to its sphere of influence, particularly the threat of Japanese expansion in the Pacific. When the Philippines were attacked, many of the U.S. servicemen were observed to be Mexican Americans from New Mexico. The Roosevelt administration and the Democratic national leadership sought to ensure consensus at home and with their allies abroad. Though fascist tendencies in the United States paralleled New Deal reforms, the attack of the Axis powers upon the United States and Russia impacted internal politics in the community and those of the country as a whole. Overt fascist activity was ostracized and leftists were more tolerated, left activity centered on war aims, rather than mass protest or organizing; and the left-right debate was relatively muted until the late forties.

War meant that the United States needed Mexican American men and women as soldiers and workers, and it needed Mexico's resources and workers, but not its trade unions, of course. Negative propaganda waned a little and U.S. needs provided the Mexican people with some leverage. In a few instances, members of the Mexican government articulated equities for Mexicans in the United States and discrimination against Mexicans in Texas decreased slightly. War underscored the need for production, and this, in turn, led to a concern for work-force adequacy and satisfaction, all of which added to the impetus for New Deal labor legislation and partially led to the then unique experience of government as a benign intervenor.

Crisis called for attention to questions of labor and ethnic and cultural differences. As a part of the war mobilization, the federal government established the Fair Employment Practices Committee (FEPC) and the Coordinator of Inter-American Affairs (CIAA), agencies that in part ostensibly sought innovative policies designed to reduce employment and social discrimination in the Mexican minority.[75] Through these agencies, there was now a means for paying positive attention to grievances voiced for generations—economic and social discrimination, and the precedent of Mexicans being invited to legitimate, formal tables of discussion with the private and public leaders of the majority society. These agencies presaged minority agencies developed in later decades.

Thus, the stage of "discussion" of the problem began. Created by presidential order in 1941, the FEPC was intended to thwart discrimination in employment. Although most efforts were devoted to investigating complaints by Blacks, Western regional offices paid some attention to cases initiated by Mexicans. A major supporter of the FEPC in Congress during the war years was the Mexican spokesman from New Mexico, Senator Dennis Chávez. He introduced several bills to give the FEPC legislative sanction, for White House support for such legislation was not forthcoming during wartime. As the only Mexican American in the U.S. Senate, Chávez was in a unique position to act under relatively favorable circumstances on two issues of traditional concern; publicly, he urged his supporters to speak out against discrimination and to support both FEPC and CIAA efforts. The Mexican American population, however, in direct contrast to Blacks, did not immediately reach out to utilize the help of the FEPC. There was little relevant publicity and few staff members, and Mexicans did not readily turn to a government office. Encouraged by Senator Chávez, Director Harry Kingman appointed a special agent for Mexican Americans in Los Angeles to publicize the work of the commission and to facilitate the use of its offices. Veteran activist Ignacio L. López, the special examiner, found resources to be inadequate and discrimination widespread; but however limited in results, he persisted in his efforts. Eventually appointed as the regional director for the Rocky Mountain and Southwest region was Dr. Carlos E. Castañeda, a Texas Mexican and a distinguished educator, who sought a wide range of cases. Although discrimination against Mexican Americans existed everywhere, the Tenth Regional Office of the FEPC (Region 10) received more complaints from Texas, Arizona, and New Mexico; thus, despite limited resources, FEPC provided a significant initiative.

The CIAA focused more inclusively on Mexican Americans than the FEPC, and proposed a wide range of activities throughout the West; its aims were domestic and international, and clearly political in behalf of overarching U.S. interests. Headed by Nelson Rockefeller, this agency was ostensibly designed to demonstrate the Good Neighbor policy of the Roosevelt administration. Strengthening the ties between the United States and Latin America was important, and Latin Americans within the United States were seen as a bridge to more cordial relations with Latin America; toward that end, then, the CIAA sponsored programs that anticipated some federal policies toward Latinos during Lyndon B. Johnson's Great Society era. In their entirety, CIAA wartime activities constituted the most salient federal effort to deal with Latino questions up to that time. CIAA official Joseph E. Weckler

analyzed the major goals of these programs and found them to be social
and educational, and emphasizing skill enhancement:

> If the Spanish-speaking people in this country are given the proper
> training and opportunities, they will be able to aid considerably the
> war production. To achieve this end considerable social rehabilita-
> tion needs to be done in many sections of the country. It will also
> be necessary to break down, so far as possible, Anglo prejudices
> against resident Latin Americans which have done so much to pre-
> vent them from securing training or jobs. This discrimination is
> also directly injurious to our relations with the other Americas,
> particularly Mexico. [76]

The CIAA attempted to stimulate benign cultural awareness through a
variety of modest programs, including print materials, radio, and film.
By 1943 Rockefeller had envisioned inter-American activities both
domestically and abroad. Materials for teachers concerning the Latin
heritage of the Americas were developed, and the teaching of Spanish
in the United States was encouraged. In Texas a statewide program in
training teachers for Spanish-speaking communities was promoted,
while Claremont College in California instituted a workshop to train
community leaders. In Denver, Salt Lake City, and Los Angeles, the
CIAA also sponsored small inter-American centers, which involved
community, business, and educational leaders in activities relating
to Latin American culture in both the United States and in Latin
America.

The CIAA's programs among Spanish-speaking Mexicans in the
United States, particularly in Texas, New Mexico, Arizona, and California, were developed out of the concern that problems arising
from discrimination could stimulate movements among Mexicans that
would hinder the war effort and, perhaps, weaken hemispheric solidarity. The CIAA made small grants to universities and chambers of
commerce in the Southwest to ameliorate discrimination and to improve teaching among Spanish-speaking minorities. Of the CIAA's
several conferences on the condition of Mexican Americans in the
Southwest, one of the most important was held in Washington in July
1943, and was attended by various government officials, agency field
representatives, and educators.

Significantly, in economic terms the war meant that the United

States faced labor needs, for industry was again in full production. The Bracero agreement was another major economic and demographic result of the war; under this program, hundreds of thousands of Mexican workers were sent to work in the United States, and some in time brought their families north. The Bracero labor program had several consequences, and one was the intended result of ensuring greater access and control over the agricultural labor force and, in addition, reducing the probability of labor organizing in the fields. In effect, for decades this program intersected with the organizing of Mexicans in the labor sector where numerically they were strongest. Other consequences, however, were less visible. Local Anglo elites did not need to exert as much effort in institutional control over Mexican American and Mexican workers who were legal residents in rural areas, and finally many of these were driven to the cities. The war also made it possible for some Mexican workers to enter occupations that had been previously closed to them. Furthermore, thousands of Mexican women entered the labor market in semi-skilled and skilled occupations that had been previously closed to women, in general, and to Mexican and non-white women, in particular. The war also promoted cultural regimentation in the interest of the war effort; although in theory it was carried out under the guise of pluralism, in practice it usually resembled the old, forced "Americanization" of the past, now dressed in patriotic war garb.

Surprising to some, the government became a military recruiter, an employer of Mexicans, and a reluctant promoter of limited civil rights. The entrance of hundreds of thousands of Mexican young men into the armed forces, many from south of the Río Bravo, had an even stronger impact on the Mexican community as a whole. Thousands of mexicanos fought against the Axis powers on every Allied front, where they would win a large portion of the decorations for heroism. With many men at the front, however, the Mexican community's resulting loss of manpower affected its social relations. Nevertheless, even in the U.S. military, which supposedly was fighting for democracy, Mexican troops faced many problems engendered by chauvinism and racism. Initially, segregated Mexican units were organized, although mexicanos were given the "choice" of belonging to either an integrated or an all-Mexican unit. But segregated units were not found workable or useful; integrated ones were better, and servicemen and their relatives might be voters. In any case military service was an important shared experience for perhaps 300,000 Mexican Americans, a remarkable number given the size of the community at the time.

For mexicanos north of the border, World War II in many respects marked a transition. One immediate consequence of the war was to heighten some organizational activities and to reduce others; for example, the LULACs were greatly strengthened as a result of their efforts in behalf of the war effort, while a decline occurred in labor and civil rights organizing, which had grown stronger toward the end of the thirties. Many activists went directly into the armed forces as volunteers, and their absence was felt. The efforts of civilian organizers in the Mexican community were devoted to combating fascism and promoting the war effort or civilian defense. At the end of the war, Mexicans returned home with new hope and aspirations and expecting a change in their status. Some changes did take place. The G.I. Bill, which provided benefits for veterans, did provide some job opportunities, access to selected educational institutions, and home loans.

The Vote

Unevenly and modestly, but slowly and surely, the Mexican vote counted. Electorally, since the turn of the century and earlier, the proactive facilitation of Mexican voting rights, other than by their own efforts, had been nil. The panorama of voting was mixed, but it was slightly more benign than troubled. By and large, there continued to be no encouragement of the vote outside those areas where it had persisted historically, in parts of southern Colorado, northern New Mexico, southern Arizona, and south Texas; and in these areas, the permitted voting was in tempo with that of larger interests and forces. In other situations, Mexicans continued to be barred from voting through direct intimidation, bureaucratic impediments, or social humiliation. In many areas, for example in what is now the largest urban concentration, Los Angeles, there was no compelling direct reason to vote, and federal, state, county, and city officeholders referred to Mexicans primarily as migrant labor or delinquents. Furthermore, candidates, from those for president on down, were not compellingly attractive, although significant exceptions did quicken interest—for example, on a national level, Franklin Delano Roosevelt's 1932 campaign; and in California, Upton Sinclair's unsuccessful campaign of 1933 and the successful one by Gulvert Olson for the governor's office in 1938. Maury Maverick campaigns for Congress and for mayor in San Antonio witnessed strong efforts by both him and his opponents to mobilize the Mexican vote; the fact that there were Mexicans actively working for, as well as against, the Maverick candidacy underscored their need.

Overall, there were two significant developments in relation to the franchise. In one case, Mexicans, both women and men, continued to vote in slightly increasing numbers, depending on the candidates or the issues, and at equal, lower, or even higher rates than other groups locally across the southwestern states. The other development, impelled by the depression and the economic measures of the Roosevelt administration, resulted in the ever greater numbers voting for Democratic candidates. Prior to the thirties, outside Texas the vote was divided between the two parties, and in some districts of New Mexico the majority vote occasionally went to the Republican ticket. After the 1932 election, the Democrats possessed a relatively vast coalition, in which Mexicans were numerically a modest part. Mexican Americans were shifting to the Democratic Party as a response to the Democrats' more effective articulation in addressing the problems of industrialization; the Republicans were viewed as offering neither inspiration nor programs. In any case, the vote was very much on the agenda in statement after statement issued by Mexican Americans. That the vote had, and would mean, less than what they needed was not of their doing, but the result of the ways and means of U.S. politics.

There were also elements of leadership related to this party alignment, which, though some roots lay in the past, was much influenced by the events and efforts of the thirties and early forties. Many of the organizational and elected officials of the following decades were included among the participants. In New Mexico, these future leaders were already in office: Antonio Fernández, a former state legislator and eventually a congressman; Tibo Chávez, a state legislator; Dennis Chávez, a senator; and José Montoya, a state legislator, congressman, and senator. Each man shared a willingness to advance not only his own constituents' interests, but a civil-rights agenda that would embrace education, jobs, language protections, and voting for those beyond their constituencies.

The Continuing Summary

Numerically, the first fifty years of the twentieth century experienced assaults more negative in their impact than any in the nineteenth century. Mexicans were not only persecuted, but slaughtered; they suffered large-scale removal and deportation; their laboring masses were subjected to massive exploitation; and two of the few assets they enjoyed, their cultural life and identity, were perversely undermined, if not destroyed. Yet during those years of great changes for the United States as a whole and to some extent for the community as well, and even though there were inadequate resources for the tasks at hand, in one part of the country or another organizational responses occurred and, in a few cases, continued as long-term group enhancements.

Conclusion

Social Change

A span of several hundred years allows us to see Mexican Americans evolving as a group through a succession of contacts, conflicts, interferences, resolutions, and fusions. Mexicans have undergone a few instances of relatively harmonious contact as well as intense assaults and even removal, prolonged conditions of despoilment and exploitation, and over time later florescence and resurgence. Clearly, Mexicans developed their own historical tradition and one that was integral to the history of the United States; the first can be noted by conceptualizing patterns of facts and events, while the second is readily claimed at one level, but more elusive at another. To be integral is not only a matter of social presence and contribution, but also the result of formative contribution. In addition to numbers, resources, and labor, Mexicans provided the United States with cultural and political innovation, contributing not only to its diversity, but to its cultural creativeness and vitality. Because of the Mexican people, the United States is a richer country economically, socially, and civically, and importantly, they contributed to the nation's egalitarianism. The specificity of the record allows for particular generalizations on their historical evolution, some comments in conclusion on social change, the record, diversity, ethnicity, governance, leadership, gender, ethnic relations, ideology, repression, and politics and class.

For Mexican Americans, as for others, social change as it has been observed involves both objective and subjective causes and results over time as well as internally and externally. In the Southwest economic impulses and necessities, as well as gender, familial, and cultural ones, recurrently took shape in Mexican political expressions. Economic adaptations or innovations require changes in work relations, and in all societies of some complexity these factors are related to authority; and in both areas, there is a continual process of formation and displacement. Though the dance occurs in the community, the rhythm of major economic and transformational change is struck somewhere outside the community itself. Change is more perceivable at the level of politics, while changes in work relations are more difficult; and changes in gender, familial, and cultural dimensions occur far more slowly and require a longer time to appreciate.

In the record, the causes and impact of threshold stages in the evolution of the political relationships obviously lie in the interaction of major external and internal changes. Agitational ideas and agitators, if they maintained consistency with their agitation, were not tolerated for long. More structural innovations, however, did compel change. Not surprisingly, the more spectacular ethnic confrontations occurred in periods of transition and crisis, whether economic or political, domestic and/or international, and concurrent with some modest economic or ideological change in some Mexican sector. And these confrontations were followed by some readjustments. World War I and World War II, which occurred during years of obvious impact for everyone, coincided roughly with changes in internal political and group perceptions.

The facts of social survival and political persistence are compelling ones. Between the 1845 and 1945, when the majority of the U.S. ethnic groups, primarily eastern and southern Europeans, were being incorporated, Mexicans went through a negative, primarily contrasting process in which their segregation and exclusion as a group increased. Politically, socially, and economically, they were more penalized, and in the 1930s, unlike the 1840s, this became more critical because of their relatively small numbers in relation to the U.S. population as a whole. The conditions, and the memories of, such disparate treatment greatly enhanced their probable advantage in ethnic persistence over many other groups. Moreover, continued immigration provided them with an ability to maintain themselves numerically in relation to the other older groups. During the first decades of the twentieth century, the trend toward numerical and relative diminution was reversed, and only gradually did numbers come to make a difference. Mexicans also improved their political, educational, and economic resources gradually.

For Mexican Americans, social survival and political persistence are results of being both a "charter" and an immigrant community. Economic utility is combined with synthesizing experiences, which, in turn, overcome generalized suppression by consciously organized and varied responses. In effect, politics as a game for resources among Indians, criollos, and mestizos—as Mexicans—has been continuous; politics as a struggle for survival and politics as persistence dates from the 1840s.

Diversity and Heterogenity

From the history examined here, several conclusions are warranted that explain aspects of diversity, which is itself an aspect of class stratification and the uneven possession of resources by individuals within the community, across time as well as throughout social and economic changes and major currents of ideological influences. The cultural and ideological process of the group is both protean in expression and rife with paradox and irony.

The synthesis of the Indian and the European and its concurrent pathologies were continuous. After U.S. annexation and consequent despoilment, the assets of Mexicans became their labor power and their ethnic distinctiveness, and perversely so for both the ruled and the ruler. One consequence was the denigration of Mexican culture by the dominant society and its transmittal to members of the Mexican community. Thus, some Mexicans sought to distance themselves from their community, parroting debasement and seeking individually to emulate the dominators. As a strategy in ethnic relations qua ethnicity, this practice was not only self-annihilating, but it failed to achieve fully the desired effects. One effect, however, was to heighten ethnic awareness by other members of the group and to encourage a consciously ethnic cultural revitalization, which, in turn, strengthened ethnic political efforts. As this happened, candidates for leadership among the more ethnically concerned gained an advantage. While living within their own families and community, and after enduring and surviving the often alienating and annihilating dominant schooling, they were conversant with their own cultural resources, had their own cultural refuge, and could deal somewhat effectively within the dominant society.

Ethnicity and the Record

In the United States, most ethnicities in the late twentieth-century are expressed by the occasional, conscious maintenance of some cultural artifacts. In the case of the Mexican, ethnicity is an organic construct of dynamically interacting elements with material and emotional content. Acculturation brought ethnicity into being, and acculturation maintains it. It is descent, recognized and perceived by others, for sure, but only in relation to a particular space, a geography, and authentic cultural artifacts; moreover, its being is part of a social universe, a strong sense of being a part of it as a matter of life itself. Not all persons of Mexican parentage share these qualities; however, in contrast to those who are disaffected, there are others for whom these qualities move them to a conscious participation in the institutions of the community, thereby contributing to the advancement of ethnicity.

Overall, the record has much to teach students of ethnicity. In the critical political history of ethnocultural communities, what must be established first is a record—the nexus of data, scale, and a usable past, some systematic understanding with the means pertinent to a real and living society, rather than an abstraction of one. The Mexican American community represents a unique case of ethnicity within the United States.

The Mexican American community is particularly attractive to study because its roots coincide with the rise of the modern world in the 1600s. Equally of interest is its domicile within a major and changing state power, which is a complex society of unusual class, ethnic, and regional diversity. It is a specific case of the ethnic linked with the primordial and the historical coupled to evolving definitional contents and boundaries, all of which are connected to economic and political constraints and potentials. The community is salient for its physical substance, its means and form of communication, and its consciously shared origins and history. Moreover, in having existed beyond the cult of a shared religious commonality for much of its history, it is itself a secular cult, and includes a sense of social nationality, even though it is under assault, to be sure.

The study of ethnicity, assuming that it is appropriately grounded in an economic context and observed over a significant period of time, ought not to focus on conflict or cultural content qua conflict and its attributes, but should focus on its persistence in evolving. A political focus is particularly enlightening because political activity presumes consciousness, choice, and concurrence, shared by a number of actors sufficient to create collective action. Comparative studies of minorities, if humanistically intended, are welcome, but conventional comparisons of differences and similarities do not greatly contribute to new knowledge or to new survival strategies for members of the group; they are inherently reductionist and serve primarily the curiosity of outsider academics.

The foundations for the United States of the twenty-first century and its ongoing definition lie in the twentieth century, and Mexican Americans are an integral part of this definition. Perhaps by the end of the twenty-first century, the East Coast beginnings of the seventeenth and eighteenth centuries conventionally claimed for the United States will be deemed a kind of prehistory for an integral history dating from the twentieth century; but whether it is dated from the seventeenth or the twentieth centuries, this chronology of development is shared by Mexicans.

Governance

For centuries there has existed an orderly structure of governance involving law and authority. Most relevant is the local organization and that which lies within the boundaries of a subregion. Continually, there has also been a ranking order of offices, with the local the most immediately important. Yet the experience with governance has varied, and government has not been remarkably efficient or pervasive among Mexicans.

Mexicans in the Southwest evolved from being the denizens of the frontier of a larger society to become this society's subordinate minority. Central and local government has been perceived as a focus of resentment, a provider of services and protections, or a goal to be obtained. As practitioners of governance, Mexicans have not been better or worse than others, but the negative and positive qualities of central government have had a centripetal influence.

Certainly, there are historical reasons for Mexicans to be leery of government, as well as evidence that in some specific circumstances they provided a challenge to government. More striking is the fairly continuous expectation that government should provide for the general welfare, combined with the practical awareness that it provides for a select number. Ideas about governance have frequently been tempered by forces of liberal or conservative inclination in vogue at a particular time. There have been radical leaders with radical organizations at times, but no radical has been elected or allowed to be elected to office.

Gender

As the Mexican society formed over the centuries, there was continuity and change for women in the areas encompassing the woman's role in the economy, in religion, and in the family. When the European truncated the autochthonous development of Mesoamerica, an emerging synthesis with a particular history of gender construction, the years that followed created a social synthesis from an amalgam of ethnic groups, economic practices, and local cultures, but also one with specific gender roles, class differences, and ethnic differences. Politics and economics combined to perpetuate and initiate the transformation of women's roles, and in contradiction, they redefined the place of women in the political arena and, of course, in the family and society. Politically, what is readily apparent is that women's articulation is the result of time, depth, and diversity, and that innovative efforts better provide for their participation. What is also visible is the slow pace of change in gender relations.

Leadership Role and Status

From the first, the presence of organized property holding, government, the military, and religion made for a range of leadership, status, and discrete functions. Increasing economic and social development provided a continually broader spectrum; leadership assignments, role latitude, and accrued status were located in class distinctions, and often related to the family.

Periodically, a new elite and a new variation of leadership arises in relation to economic and social changes as well as being impacted to some extent by a dramatic event, but the new arrives with some relations of continuity to the old. The United States–Mexico War and the treaty, an event and an instrument, created a condition of similarity across classes and functions—the status of being Mexican and a concomitant, discrete treatment which varied according to class and the usefulness of the individual, but was invariably pejorative. Significantly impacting politics and society after the 1836–1848 period was the fact that a "foreign" player could allocate leadership roles and status in relation to its interest. Diverse at settlement, leadership, role and status became more complicated over time, rather than diminishing.

Ethnic Relations

Mexicans have experienced a series of ethnic relations. Despite an obscure record of ethnic relations, the epic conflicts, such as Native American relations with the Europeans, would provide both inspiration and lessons. Native American relations with the Mexican, or mestizo, varied; through the nineteenth century, however, a synthesis was in process. Yet both groups were dominated by a third, the "Anglo." The Native American was socially segregated, and was made dependent on the government, while the Mexican was neither. In repeated instances, and in localities across the Southwest, efforts were made to segregate Mexicans, but, of course, they resisted.

To complicate matters, Mexicans were forced to deal with and suffer from a range of ethnic groups, in addition to the "Anglo." In some cases, European immigrant ethnics used their white skin as leverage to maximize their gains at the expense of Mexicans, and Mexicans were not noticeably effective in dealing with the mainstream elements of these groups. Seemingly, Mexican radicals could work with other ethnic radicals, but a dominant–subordinate relation was present nonetheless, and disparate ethnic relations were reinforced by work arrangements. A conflictual or demeaning system of interethnic relations, whatever its overall negative content, was not stable or homogeneous across the Southwest, for, like other systems, it went through readjustments, which, in turn, improved societal conditions.

Ideology

The articulation of demands, or the proposal of programs, occurs first in class terms, secondarily in institutional and ethnic terms. Ideas rationalize interests in behalf of pragmatic gains, and utopian nuances comprise a response to conditions of oppression for all sectors, attempting to achieve a class benefit for some, while addressing everyone in language appealing to general, idealized values or commonly understood needs. Middle-class spokesmen have been the most articulate, although demands from the laboring sector are commonly heard at different times. Labor programs date from the nineteenth century, and not surprisingly, they are more consistently found among labor organizations.

To be Mexican in the United States meant that one was of Mexican parentage and possessed a cultural and social allegiance which was at variance with the orthodox allegiance of the country; and this amounted to life under assault, not because of some unresolvable conflict but because of prejudice. To the extent that Mexicans across the Southwest experienced the effects of prejudice, their consciousness of their own condition and the way they were treated remained sharply clear. Mexicans who did not accept or did not recognize this prejudicial boundary—and in generation after generation there were some—were viewed as delusionary. In contrast, those who sought to make a distinction between themselves and others—in effect, between "good" and "bad" Mexicans, or those who were "cooperative" versus those who were "sullen"—were viewed with contempt by other Mexicans. In any case, ironically discrimination and relative separateness strengthened views upholding positively the quality of being Mexican, and as mentioned, Mexican distinctiveness.

Designations or names and cultural symbols were obviously of major importance, and were stressed positively by pro-Mexican Mexicans, almost in tempo with the negative attacks from outsiders. It was also important that they remember they were natives, that the Southwest was their homeland, and that, in effect, they were charter settlers. In fact, in considering themselves as insiders, they implicitly stigmatized the dominant class as foreign intruders. Making the "Anglo" an adversary gave the group a common focus, but the group also needed allies, and because the group was also divided the "Anglo" did not always turn out to be *the* enemy.

Force and Repression

Coercion was present in the formation of the society from the first, but it actually increased after the 1836–1848 period. Force was a means to intimidate the Mexican population as a whole, but of particular importance in maintaining subordination was labor repression. Subjugating Mexican labor had value in relation to the maximization of profit, but it was also a way of inhibiting the political expression of the most numerous sector of the Mexican people; and it also provided a way of limiting the political strength of the other sectors. Labor repression was often the result of stark force, produced through abysmal wages, laws, and courts, and even through labor leadership.

In this context, views or perceptions were not the main stuff of ethnicity or interethnic relations; the gist was power underscored by force. To be sure, power is a social relationship that is often accepted by all of the parties involved; but even though a discussion could be waged on economic versus political distinctions, it was clear that, finally, Mexicans were living under the rule through force. Through World War II, however, the rule for coping with challenges from Mexican labor was force. Based on force the political system was established, from which followed the allocation of resources and the implantation of social and institutional practices. Force was not a one-time or one-generational occurrence for Mexicans, nor was it limited to one instrument. It was not superseded by institutional arrangements and ideological inculcations, but remained concurrent with both of these instruments. This fact can be so clearly documented that "Chicano history" can become a year-by-year litany of instances of force.

It may be argued, from another perspective, that force was necessary for the oppressor to ensure submission and, therefore, order. For, however important force may be, power is enhanced ultimately by control and the allocation of resources, including employment allocations, which, in turn, have to do with the more ideological instruments of norms, educational institutions, and channels of communication. Obviously, Mexicans were restrained not only economically but also institutionally, as well as in the area of communications. That norms and values were imposed and accepted is evident in a number of ways, and starkly so in instances where Mexicans were permitted representation in their own behalf or to administer the affairs of other Mexicans.

In short, Mexicans, though not unanimously, often did relegate themselves to their assigned places within the established order. Interestingly, this accommodation, when it occurred, never served as an inducement for the dominant group to increase Mexican representational and executive opportunities. Nor was it an incentive for universally reducing social distances, for reducing the competitive advantage of chauvinism, or for extending the range of occupational possibilities. Conflict, in some instances, did provide such an incentive, and frequently resulted in a change for the worse.

Politics and Class

Politics both affects, and is the effect of, the social order and the specific class formations and factions of Mexican society; and under annexation, the ethnic requirements of survival and recognition intrude upon class articulations. Class maintenance for the upper, middle, and skilled sectors was inhibited by the conditions of unfair competition; for there was no lack of will to compete, nor was there a lack of ability or response to innovation.

Consciousness of the need for change motivated efforts toward organization. Mexicans established their organizations on their own and in their own ways, drawing from their own organizational heritage. Internal movements invariably drew internal reaction, for factions in the community have always been as diverse as its social spectrum internally with leaders competing against one another. To the extent that a group's membership and leadership were drawn from its more successful members, the more likely was that these would favor the dominant arrangement, even though they insisted on adjustments to the benefit of others. Radical efforts, then, did challenge existing arrangements, and professed to speak in behalf of the larger constituency. For the most part, however, efforts remained within the accepted legal framework, and radical efforts therefore were severely disadvantaged.

Over a broad period of change, radicalism and accommodation blend interactively. At a distance from immediate events, reformers may be viewed as conservatives in two situations—when they were traditionalists within the community, seeking cultural maintenance, and when they seek inclusion for all Mexicans into the dominant society's system. However, given anti-Mexican attitudes and practices, the assertion of cultural rights and civil equities concurrently was, and is, a radical act. Change happened paradoxically, the result of both conservative and innovative impulses. What changes occurred were incremental, but space and recognition were preserved and occasionally extended. Successful articulation or advocacy was not the result of the acts of individual leaders, but of organizations in continuously sustaining a program of change. The hundred years from 1845 to 1945 made possible and legitimized the option of aggressive and militant politics because acquiescent means and overly slow incremental gains ultimately proved to be so disappointing.

Given the needs and results of the late twentieth century, two tacit public agreements of some impact were made in the United States for members of the Mexican American ethnic group. Constitutional protections and the condemnation of discrimination were the rule of public life for all residents within the country's borders. Somewhat later, being ethnic was publicly sanctioned and was to be publicly tolerated. Although neither subordination, discrimination, nor exploitation faded for colored minorities, there were dispensations, and these applied to Mexican Americans. In scope and breadth, Mexican Americans were moving toward an unprecedented engagement with the larger society. As an ethnic group, they had arrived at the gates of benign public recognition and institutional access, and this had become possible because they had endured and persisted in the face of suppression and discrimination. Equally important, however, was the fact that the larger society was in need and in crisis. World War II proved to be a threshold, but a half-century later, the ethnic issues of that day remain with us. While history informs us, it does not resolve issues of equitable empowerment; only living human beings acting in concert can do that.

Notes

Introduction

1. There are several general histories on Mexican Americans: Rodolfo Acuña, *Occupied America: A History of Chicanos* (New York: Harper and Row, 1988); Carey McWilliams, *North from Mexico: The Spanish-Speaking People of the United States* (New York: Greenwood Press, 1968); Matt S. Meier and Feliciano Rivera, *The Chicanos: A History of Mexican-Americans* (New York: Hill and Wang, 1972); James Diego Vigil, *From Indians to Chicanos: A Sociocultural History* (St. Louis: C. V. Mosby Company, 1980); and Julian Samora and Patricia Vandel Simon, *A History of the Mexican-American People* (Notre Dame: University of Notre Dame Press, 1977). For a discussion of the historiography, see Juan G.-Quiñones, "Toward a Perspective on Chicano History," *Aztlán* 2, no. 1 (Fall 1971); Juan G.-Quiñones and Luis L. Arroyo, "On the State of Chicano History: Observations on Its Development, Interpretations and Theory, 1970–1974," *The Western Historical Quarterly* 7, no. 2 (April 1976); Albert M. Camarillo, "The 'New' Chicano History: Historiography of Chicanos in the 1970s," in Isidro D. Ortiz, ed., *Chicanos and the Social Sciences: A Decade of Research and Development, 1970–1980* (Santa Barbara: Center for Chicano Studies, University of California, 1983); and Alex M. Saragoza, "The Significance of Recent Chicano-related Historical Writings: An Appraisal," *Ethnic Affairs*, no. 1 (Fall 1987). Linking periods that are often viewed as disparate, a historiographical critique which forcefully and persuasively presents "the perspectives and insights now offered by recent research compel historians to reevaluate Spain's experience in North America and to integrate it into United States history," is Gerald E. Payo and Gilberto M. Hinojosa, "Spanish Texas and Borderlands Historiography in Transition: Implications in United States History," *Journal of American History* 75 (September 1988).

2. See this author's comments on politics in general, in the first chapter of Juan Gómez-Quiñones, *Chicano Politics: Reality and Promise 1940–1990* (Albuquerque: University of New Mexico Press, 1990). On the political experience and various views of it, there are several texts available: F. Chris García, ed., *La Causa Política: A Chicano Politics Reader* (Notre Dame: University of Notre Dame Press, 1974); Carlos Muñoz, "The State of the Art in the Study of Chicano Politics," in Ortiz, *Chicanos and the Social Sciences*. A recent book of readings is F. Chris García, ed., *Latinos and the Political System* (Notre Dame: University of Notre Dame Press, 1988). For an introduction to how Mexican American politics may be reviewed, see F. Chris García and Rudolfo de la Garza, *The Chicano Political Experience: Three Perspectives* (North Scituate: Duxbury Press, 1977). For a systems approach to politics generally, see David Easton, *A Systems Analysis of Political Life* (New York: John C. Wiley and Sons, 1965). For critiques of contemporary political history writing, see: Lawrence Stone, "The Revival of Narrative: Reflections on a New Old History," *Past and Present* (November 1979); and Philip Abrams, "History, Sociology, Historical Sociology," ibid. (May 1980). For comment on Stone's essay, see E. J. Hobsbawm, "The Revival of Narrative: Some Comments," ibid. (February 1980).

3. For an overview of the Mexican American population, see Leo Grebler, et al., *The Mexican American People, The Nation's Second Largest Minority* (New York: Free Press, 1970); and Joan Moore and Harry Pachon, *Hispanics in the United States* (Englewood Cliffs: Prentice Hall, 1985). For an examination of post–World War II politics, see Gómez-Quiñones, *Chicano Politics*.

4. Among the many definitional statements on ethnic groups are the following. According to R. A. Schermerhorn, an ethnic group may be considered as "a collectivity within a larger society [with a] real or putative common ancestry, memories of a shared historical past, and a cultural focus on one or more symbolic elements defined as the epitome of their peoplehood" (Richard A. Schermerhorn, *Comparative Ethnic Relations: A Framework for Theory and Research* [New York: Random House, 1970]). According to F. Barth, however, "Ethnic groups are largely biologically self-perpetuating, share fundamental cultural values, realized in overt unity in cultural forms, make up a field of communication and interaction, and has [have] a membership which identifies itself, and is identified by others, as constituting a category distinguishable from other categories of the same order" (Frederick Barth, *Ethnic Groups and Boundaries* [Boston: Little, Brown and Company, 1969]). Milton Gordon defines ethnicity as "peoplehood," which is either primordially given or optionally cultivated. A basic statement on ethnicity in the United States may be found in Milton M. Gordon, *Assimilation in American Life: The Role of Race, Religion, and National Origins* (Oxford: Oxford University Press, 1964); this work is often a point of departure for those studying the "integration" and "assimilation" of Mexican Americans. Also seminal is the work of Robert E.

Park, *Race and Culture* (Glencoe: University of Illinois Press, 1953). A useful examination of ethnicity is Joe R. Feagin, *Racial and Ethnic Relations* (Englewood Cliffs: Prentice Hall, 1978). In contrast to conventional views, there is Ronald Takaki, *From Different Shores: Perspectives on Race and Ethnicity in America* (Oxford: Oxford University Press, 1987). An attempt at a comprehensive statement on ethnic groups in the United States and the "new" ethnic history is Stephen Thernstrom, et al., eds., *Harvard Encyclopedia of American Ethnic Groups* (Cambridge: Harvard University Press, 1980).

5. See Manning Nash, *The Cauldron of Ethnicity in the Modern World* (Chicago: University of Chicago Press, 1989); Harold R. Isaacs, *Idols of the Tribe: Group Identity and Political Change* (New York: Harper and Row, 1975); John Higham, "Current Trends in the Study of Ethnicity in the United States," *Journal of American Ethnic History* 2 (Fall 1982); see also Rudolph J. Vecoli, "Return to the Melting Pot: Ethnicity in the United States in the Eighties," in ibid. 5 (Fall 1985); R. J. Vecoli, "Ethnicity: A Neglected Dimension of American History," in Herbert J. Bass, ed., *The State of American History* (Chicago: Quadrangle Books, 1970); Oscar Handlin, *The Uprooted: The Epic Story of the Great Migrations that Made the American People* (Boston: Atlantic-Little Brown, 1951); and John Higham, "Integrating America: The Problem of Assimilation in the Nineteenth Century," *Journal of American Ethnic History* 1 (Fall 1981). For an example of the "new" ethnic history, see Deborah Dash Moore, *At Home in America: Second Generation New York Jews* (New York: Columbia University Press, 1981). On the post–World War II debate on ethnic comparisons, see Samuel Koenig, "Second and Third Generation Americans," in Francis James Brown and Joseph S. Roucek, eds., *One America: The History, Contributions and Present Problems of Our Racial and National Minorities* (New York: Prentice Hall, 1952); Nathan Glazer and Daniel P. Moynihan, *Beyond the Melting Pot: The Negroes, Puerto Ricans, Jews, Italians and Irish of New York City* (Cambridge: M.I.T. Press, 1973); Stephen Steinberg, *The Ethnic Myth: Race, Ethnicity, and Class in America* (Boston: Beacon Press, 1981); Milton Gordon, *Assimilation in American Life;* Michael Novak, *The Rise of the Unmeltable Ethnics* (New York: Macmillan, 1972). See also R. J. Vecoli, "European Americans: From Immigrants to Ethnics," in William H. Cartwright and Richard L. Watson, eds., *The Reinterpretation of American History and Culture* (Washington, D.C.: National Council for Social Studies, 1973); Olivier Zunz, "American History and the Changing Meaning of Assimilation," *Journal of American Ethnic History* 4 (Spring 1985). For comments on ethnic political history, see John Higham, ed., *Ethnic Leadership in America* (Baltimore and London: Johns Hopkins University Press, 1978). For the arrival of ethnic groups, see Sallie Te Selle, ed., *The Rediscovery of Ethnicity: Its Implications for Culture and Politics in America* (New York: Harper and Row, 1973).

6. For a discussion, see Tamotsu Shibutani and Kian M. Kwan, *Ethnic Stratification: A Comparative Approach* (New York: Macmillan 1965). On learning politics see, David Sears, "Political Socialization," in Fred Greenstein and Nelson Polsby, eds. *The Handbook of Political Science* (Reading: MA: Addison-Wesley, 1975).

7. See David J. Weber, "'Scarce More than Apes': Historical Roots of Anglo-American Stereotypes of Mexicans," in David J. Weber, ed., *New Spain's Far Northern Frontier: Essays on Spain in the American West 1540–1821* (Albuquerque: University of New Mexico Press, 1979). In depreciating reality in favor of pejorative myth, the interpretive work by Bernardo de Voto, *The Year of Decision, 1846* (Boston: Houghton Mifflin, 1943), is not that far from the novel by Helen Hunt Jackson, *Ramona* (Boston: Roberts Brothers, 1884).

Chapter 1

1. For a survey of the political sphere within Mexican history, see Daniel Cosío Villegas, *Historia general de México*, vols. 1 and 2 (4 vols., México, D.F.: El Colegio de México, 1976); and the classic Justo Sierra, *Evolución política del pueblo méxicano*, vol. 12, *Obras completas del Maestro Justo Sierra* (14 vols., México, D.F.: Universidad Autonoma de México, 1948). For a discussion of national formation and some observation on a political tradition, see Eric F. Wolf, "The Mexican Bajío in the Eighteenth Century: An Analysis of Cultural Integration," in *Synoptic Studies of Mexican Culture* (New Orleans: Middle American Research Institute, Tulane University, 1977); and James Lockhart, *Provinces of Early Mexico* (Los Angeles: Latin American Center, University of California, Los Angeles, 1976).

2. For discussion of European economic and social development, see John H. Parry, *The Age of Reconnaissance* (Cleveland: World Publishing, 1963); and Immanuel Wallerstein, *The Modern World System* (New York: Academic Press, 1974). For Castile, see Jaime Vicens Vives, *An Economic History of Spain* (Princeton: Princeton University Press, 1967); and John H. Elliot, *Imperial Spain, 1469–1716* (New York: St. Martin's Press, 1962).

3. For resistance, see María Elena Galaviz de Capdevielle, *Rebeliones indígenas en el norte del reino de la Nueva España, XVI–XVII* (México, D.F.: Editorial Campesina, 1967); María Teresa Huerta Preciado, *Rebeliones indígenas en el noroeste de México en la época colonial* (México, D.F.: Instituto Nacional de Antropología e Historia, 1966); G. Ivanov, "Sublevaciones populares mexicanas de la segunda mitad del siglo XVII," *Punto Crítico*, no. 1 (February 1965); and William B. Taylor, *Drinking, Homicide and Rebellion in Colonial Mexican Villages* (Stanford: Stanford University Press, 1979).

4. For the Mexica, see Manuel M. Moreno, *La organización política y social*

de los aztecas (México, D.F.: Instituto Nacional de Antropología e Historia, 1962); Gonzalo Aguirre Beltrán, *Formas de gobierno indígena* (México, D.F.: Universidad Nacional Autónoma de México, 1953); Robert C. Padden, *The Hummingbird and the Hawk* (Columbus: Ohio State University Press, 1967); and Charles Gibson, *The Aztecs under Spanish Rule* (Palo Alto: Stanford University Press, 1967). For other groups, see Carlos Besauri, *La población indígena de México,* 3 vols. (México, D.F.: Secretaría de Educación Pública, 1940); and Frederick W. Hodge, *Handbook of American Indians North of Mexico,* 2 vols. (Washington, D.C.: Bureau of American Ethnology, Bulletin 30, 1907–1910); and for intragroup distinctions see Mercedes Olivera, *Pillis y macehuales, Las formaciones sociales y los modos de producción de Tecali del siglo XII al XVI* (México, D.F.: Ediciones de la Casa Chata, 1978); and Iris Blanco, "El sexo y su condicionamiento cultural en el mundo prehispánico," in Adelaida R. del Castillo, ed., *Between Borders: Essays on Mexican/Chicana History* (Encino: Floricanto, 1990). See also Iris Blanco, "Participación de las mujeres en la sociedad pre-Hispánica," in R. Sánchez, et al., eds., *Essays on La Mujer* (Los Angeles: CSRC, UCLA, 1977); and "La mujer en los albores de la conquista de México," *Aztlán* 11 (Fall 1982); Eric Wolf, *Sons of the Shaking Earth* (Chicago: University of Chicago Press, 1959), pp. 220–23 and passim; Jacques Soustelle, *The Daily Life of the Aztecs* (New York: Macmillan, 1968), pp. 88 and 183; José Limón, "La llorona, The Third Legend of Greater Mexico: Cultural Symbols, Women, and the Political Unconscious," in Castillo, *Between Borders;* and Adelaida del Castillo, "Malintzin Tenepal: A Preliminary Look into a New Perspective," *Encuentro Femenil* 1 (1974).

5. For general studies on the colonial period, see Wigberto Jiménez Moreno and Luis González, "Historiografía prehispánica y colonial de México," in *Enciclopedia de México,* vol. 6 (1972), pp. 1074–1111. For a review of the colonial society and economy, see A. Rene Barbosa-Ramírez, *La estructura económica de la Nueva España* (México, D.F.: Siglo Veintiuno, 1971); and Sergio Bagu, "La economía de la sociedad colonial," *Pensamiento Crítico,* no. 27 (April 1969). For political governance, see José Miranda, *Las ideas y las instituciones políticas mexicanas, Primera parte, 1521–1820* (México, D.F.: Universidad Nacional Autónoma de México, 1952); Bradley Benedict, "El estado en México en la época de los Hapsburgs," *Historia Mexicana* 23 (1974); and Roger B. Merriman, *The Rise of the Spanish Empire in the Old World and the New,* 4 vols. (New York: Cooper Square Publishers, 1962); J. I. Israel, *Race, Class and Politics in Colonial Mexico: 1600–1670,* (London: Oxford University Press, 1979). For Spanish women, see María T. Casal Villafane, "La mujer española en la conquista de América," *Cuaderno Hispano Americano,* 59, (1964). For a provocative overview of "woman's place" in colonial society, see Elsa Malvido, "El uso del cuerpo femenino en la época colonial mexicana a través de los estudios de demografía histórica," in Castillo, *Between Borders.* On the

church, see Peggy K. Liss, *Mexico under Spain, 1521–1556: Society and the Origins of Nationality* (Chicago: University of Chicago Press, 1975); Jacques Lafaye, *Quetzalcoatl and Guadalupe: The Formation of Mexican National Consciousness, 1531–1813* (Chicago: University of Chicago, 1974); and Mariano Cuevas, *Historia de la Iglesia en México,* 5 vols. (Tlapan and El Paso, 1921–1928).

6. Consult Gloria Grajales, *Nacionalismo incipiente en los historiadores coloniales* (México, D.F.: Universidad Nacional Autónoma de México, 1961). For insight into the broader context, see Liss, *Mexico under Spain, 1521–1556.*

7. Francisco de la Maza, "Los evangelistas de Guadalupe y el nacionalismo mexicano," *Cuadernos Americanos* 48 (November–December 1949), pp. 163–188; Jacques Lafaye, *Quetzalcoatl and Guadalupe;* and Robert Richard, *The Spiritual Conquest of Mexico* (Berkeley and Los Angeles: University of California Press, 1966), pp. 188–91. See also Eric F. Wolf, "The Virgin of Guadalupe: A Mexican National Symbol," *Journal of American Folklore* 71 (1958); and Bernardo Bergoend, *La nacionalidad mexicana y la Virgen de Guadalupe* (México, D.F.: Editorial Jus, 1968).

8. Angel María Garibay K., "Los historiadores de México antiguo en el virreinato de la Nueva España," *Cuadernos Americanos* 23 (1964), pp. 128–47. For a review of the historiography, see Jiménez Moreno and González, "Historiografía prehispánica."

9. On the north, see Enrique Florescano, "Colonización, ocupación del suelo y la 'frontera' en el norte de nueva España, 1521–1750," in Alvaro Jara, ed., *Tierras nuevas* (México, D.F.: El Colegio de México, 1973); James Lockhart, *Provinces of Early Mexico* (Los Angeles: Latin American Center, University of California, Los Angeles, 1976); Leopoldo Martínez Caraza, *El norte bárbaro de México* (México, D.F.: Panorama Editorial, 1983); Robert C. West, *The Mining Community in Northern New Spain: The Parral Mining District* (Berkeley and Los Angeles: University of California Press, 1949); Wolf, "Mexican Bajío in the Eighteenth Century"; P. J. Bakewell, *Silver Mining and Society in Colonial Mexico: Zacatecas, 1546–1700* (Oxford: Cambridge University Press, 1971); Phillip W. Powell, *Soldiers, Indians and Silver: The Northward Advance of New Spain, 1550–1600* (Berkeley: University of California, 1969); and John Francis Bannon, *The Spanish Borderlands Frontier, 1513–1821* (Albuquerque: University of New Mexico Press, 1979). On aspects of mestizaje, see Marc Simmons, "Tlascalans in the Spanish Borderlands," *New Mexico Historical Review* 39 (April 1964); and Philip W. Powell, "Caldera of New Spain: Frontier Justice and Mestizo Symbol," *The Americas* 17 (April 1961). For expansion in the Southwest in relation to broader geographical advances, see Abraham P. Nasatir, *Borderland in Retreat: From Spanish Louisiana to the Far Southwest* (Albuquerque: University of New Mexico, 1976).

10. For basic chronology, see Hubert Howe Bancroft, *History of Arizona*

and New Mexico, 1530–1888 (San Francisco: The History Company, 1889); Hubert Howe Bancroft, *History of the North Mexican States and Texas, 1531–1883,* 2 vols. (San Francisco: A. L. Bancroft and Company, 1889); Herbert Eugene Bolton, *Texas in the Middle Eighteenth Century* (Austin: University of Texas Press, 1970); and Hubert Howe Bancroft, *History of California, Vol. 1: 1542–1800* (San Francisco: The History Company, 1884).

11. For expansion, see Bannon, *Spanish Borderlands Frontier.* For firsthand experiences of frontier activity, see Antonine Tibesar, ed., *Writings of Junípero Serra* (Washington, D.C.: Academy of Franciscan History, 1955); and Herbert E. Bolton, ed., *Kino's Historical Memoir of Pimería Alta, 1683–1711,* 2 vols. (Cleveland: The Arthur H. Clark Company, 1919). For aspects of society, economy, and culture, see Oakah L. Jones, *Los Paisanos* (Norman: University of Oklahoma Press, 1979); Frances Leon Swadesh, *Los Primeros Pobladores* (Notre Dame: University of Notre Dame Press, 1974); and Juan Gómez-Quiñones, *Development of the Mexican Working Class North of the Rio Bravo: Work and Culture among Laborers and Artisans, 1600–1900* (Los Angeles: Chicano Studies Research Center, University of California, Los Angeles, 1977).

12. See Philip Wayne Powell, *Mexico's Miguel Caldera: The Taming of America's First Frontier, 1548–1597* (Tucson: University of Arizona Press, 1977); the quote from the Caldera statement is in the appendix, pp. 275–76. See also by Powell, *Soldiers, Indians and Silver;* and *War and Peace on the Mexican Frontier: A Documentary Record, Vol. 1, Crescendo of the Chichimeca War, 1551–1585* (Madrid: J. P. Turanzas, 1971). On how the Chichimeca experience was crucial to later developments, see Primo Feliciano Velásquez, *Colección de documentos para la historia de San Luis Potosí* (San Luis Potosí: P. F. Velasquez, 1897–99); and Eugenio de Hoyo, *Historia del Nuevo Reino de León, 1577–1723* (Monterrey, N.L.: Instituto Tecnológico y de Estudios Superiores, 1972), as interpreted by Powell:

> The events of this war and the manner of its ending shaped subsequent Spanish-Mexican advance into the heart of the continent. Experience of nomadic Indian ways of life and fighting, often gained at terrifying cost in lives and scars and goods, called forth presidio and mission as frontier institutions. This war also fashioned the first of that distinctly American breed, the frontier rider (Spanish, Indian, Negro, and mixed) who was simultaneously master of Indian fighting, stock herding, and of the hardy horseflesh that enabled his life. This north Mexican horseman still pounds leather.
>
> This man on horseback was but one of many types—Spanish or mestizo miners, missionaries and other religious, traders, innkeepers, prospectors, wagoners, soldiers; Indian colonists, laborers, merchants, miners; free and slave Negroes and mulattoes—who formed this frontier people. These were the men and women (and children) who, with the coming of the

Chichimeca Peace of the 1590s, made feasible the advance to New Mexico; then bred the frontier colonists of Chihuahua, Coahuila, Nuevo Leon, Sonora, and finally dared the plains, mountains, and deserts of Texas, Arizona, and Upper California.

In this half-century of silver strikes, of blood-spilling war, of the unusual way in which the Chichimeca Peace was made, and of formation of this frontier society, one man stands out as unique and as prototype; in much an unusual fashioner of frontier ways and destinies, but also an excellent image of precisely what he was creating. He was Miguel Caldera, the first important historical personage to be born in the North American wilderness, coming to life in the Zacatecas country at the time of the first great strikes.

Miguel Caldera's father was one of the Spanish explorers who discovered northern silver; his mother was of the primitive Chichimecas. Miguel rose to fame as a solder in war against his mother's people. Then, as captain and frontier chief justice, he shaped a humane and intelligent peace which joined Chichimecas with the more civilized Spanish, Indian, Negro, and mixed-blood home builders on this frontier.

Miguel Caldera was the first of the continent's notable mixed-blood frontiersmen. He played the key role in bringing peace to a land of war—of torture, scalping, murder, burning, and slavery—where it was said that loss of life and property ran much higher than in the Cortes Conquest. Miguel discovered one of the richest of the silver lodes and founded one of Mexico's most important cities. Despite his humble mestizo origins, he came close to magnate status in his native land. (*Mexico's Miguel Caldera,* pp. ix–x)

13. For institutions, see Gilbert R. Cruz, "Spanish Town Patterns in the Borderlands: Municipal Origins in Texas and the Southwest," (Ph.D. diss., St. Louis University, 1974); France Scholes, "Civil Government and Society in New Mexico in the Seventeenth Century," *New Mexico Historical Review* 10 (April 1935); and Mattie Alice Austin, "The Municipal Government of San Fernando de Bexar, 1730–1800," *The Quarterly* 8 (April 1905). For a basic, though by now dated, treatment of the origins and development of the *encomienda* system, see Lesley Byrd Simpson, *The Encomienda in New Spain* (Berkeley: University of California Press, 1966). For other institutions, see: Sandra L. Meyers, *The Ranch in Spanish Texas* (El Paso: Texas Western Press, 1969); Nora Ramírez, "The Vaquero and Ranching in the Southwestern United States, 1600–1870" (Ph.D. diss., Indiana University, 1978); Jack Jackson, *Los Mesteños: Spanish Ranching in Texas, 1721–1821* (College Station, Tex.: Texas A&M University Press, 1986); J. Lloyd Mecham, "The Real de Minas as a Political Institution," *Hispanic American Historical Review* 8 (February 1927); Herbert Eugene Bolton, "The Mission as a Frontier Institution in the Spanish American Colonies," *American Historical Review* 22 (1917); Odie B. Faulk, "The Presidio: Fortress or Farce?" *The Journal of the*

West 8 (January 1969); and Sidney B. Brinckerhoff and Odie B. Faulk, *Lancers for the King* (Phoenix: Arizona Historical Foundation, 1965). On land and water distribution, see Victor Westphall, *Mercedes Reales: Hispanic Land Grants in the Upper Rio Grande Region* (Albuquerque: University of New Mexico, 1983). On Indian relations, see Galaviz de Capdevielle, *Rebeliones indígenas en el norte del reino;* Preciado, *Rebeliones indígenas en el noreste de México;* Edward Dozier, *The Pueblo Indians of North America* (New York: Holt, Rinehart and Winston, 1970); Francisco R. Almada, "Los Apaches," *Boletín de la Sociedad Chihuahuense de Estudios Históricos,* 2 (1939); Roxanne Dunbar Ortiz, "The Roots of Pueblo Indian Land Tenure and Spanish Colonization," *The Journal of Ethnic Studies* 5 (Winter 1978); Edward H. Spicer, *Cycles of Conquest: The Impact of Spain, Mexico and the United States on the Indians of the Southwest, 1533–1960* (Tucson: University of Arizona Press, 1962); and Elizabeth A. H. John, *Storms Brewed in Other Men's Worlds: The Confrontation of Indians, Spanish and French in the Southwest, 1540–1795* (College Station: Texas A&M University Press, 1975). The encomienda, as an economic institution in New Mexico, proved to be unsatisfactory because the Indians rejected it, and it tended to monopolize the diminishing supply of indigenous labor, reducing revenues to the crown and limiting the opportunities of new settlers. For a survey see Ralph H. Vigil, "Colonial Institutions," in Ellwyn R. Stoddard et al. *Borderlands Sourcebook: A Guide to the Literature on Northern Mexico and the American Southwest* (Norman: University of Oklahoma Press, 1983).

14. "Complaints of the Town Council of Santa Fe Against the Missionaries (October 1638)," in Charles W. Hackett, ed., *Historical Documents Relating to New Mexico, Nueva Vizcaya and Approaches Thereto to 1772,* vol. 1, 1923; vol. 2, 1926; vol. 3, 1931, collected by Adolf and Fanny R. Bandelier (Washington, D.C.: Carnegie Institute).

15. "Report Made by Reverend Father Fray Carlos Delgado, March 17, 1750" in Hackett, *Historical Documents,* vol. 3, pp. 425–30.

16. On political relations, see: Herbert E. Bolton, ed., *Font's Complete Diary* (Berkeley: University of California Press, 1933); Hubert Howe Bancroft, *History of California,* Vol. 1; Herbert E. Bolton, *The Spanish Borderlands: A Chronicle of Old Florida and the Southwest* (New Haven: Yale University Press, 1921); Francisco R. Almada, "La Comandancia general de provincias internas," *Boletín de la Sociedad Chihuahuense de Estudios Históricos* 1 (1938); Bolton, *Texas in the Middle Eighteenth Century;* Marc Simmons, *Spanish Government in New Mexico* (Albuquerque: University of New Mexico Press, 1969).

17. The quote is from Hackett, *Historical Documents,* vol. 1, pp. 101–3; see also the informative S. M. Horvath, "The Social and Political Organization of the Genizaros of Plaza de Nuestra Señora de los Dolores de Belen, New Mexico" (Ph.D. diss., Brown University, 1979).

18. New Mexico has the most extensive documentation available, despite the fact that calamities have diminished the total records. For printed documents, see Hackett, *Historical Documents;* H. Bailey Carroll and J. Villasana Haggard, trans. and eds., *Three New Mexico Chronicles* (Albuquerque: Quivira Society, 1942); Eleanor B. Adams, ed., "Bishop Tamaron's Visitation of New Mexico, 1760," *Publications in the History of the Historical Society of New Mexico* (February 1954); George P. Hammond and Agapito Rey, eds., *Don Juan de Oñate, Colonizer of New Mexico, 1595–1628* (Albuquerque: University of New Mexico Press, 1953); and J. Manuel Espinosa, ed. and trans., *First Expedition of Vargas into New Mexico, 1692* (Albuquerque: University of New Mexico Press, 1940).

19. Luis de Velasco, "Oñate's Appointment as Governor of New Mexico," *New Mexico Historical Review* 13 (July 1938), pp. 246–48.

20. "Complaints of the Town Council of Santa Fe . . . ," in Hackett, *Historical Documents,* vol. 3, pp. 66–74.

21. For the standard treatment of the Pueblo revolt of 1681, see chapter 2 of Charles W. Hackett and C. C. Shelby, *Revolt of the Pueblo Indians of New Mexico and Otermin's Attempted Reconquest, 1680–1682,* Coronado Historical Series, vols. 8 and 9 (Albuquerque: University of New Mexico Press, 1942). For a revised interpretation, see Dunbar Ortiz, "Roots of Pueblo Indian Land Tenure," pp. 33–53. For an examination of repressed sexuality as a part of the context, see Ramon A. Gutiérrez, *When Jesus Came, the Corn Mothers Went Away: Marriage, Sexuality, and Power in New Mexico, 1500–1846* (Stanford: Stanford University Press, 1991).

22. From "Letter from the Governor and Captain-General Don Antonio de Otermin . . . ," in Hackett, *Historical Documents,* vol. 3, pp. 327–35.

23. Ibid. See comments in Hackett, *Historical Documents,* Vol. I, pp. 130 and 299.

24. "Report Made by Reverend Father Fray Carlos Delgado . . . ," in Hackett, *Historical Documents.*

25. See Frank W. Blackmar, *Spanish Institutions of the Southwest* (Baltimore: Johns Hopkins University Press, 1891); Rose Hollenbaugh Avina, *Spanish and Mexican Land Grants in California* (New York: Arno Press, 1976); Marc Simmons, "Settlement Patterns and Village Plans in Colonial New Mexico," *Journal of the West* 8 (January 1968); W. A. Kelcher, "Law of the New Mexico Land Grant," *The New Mexico Historical Review* 4 (October 1929); and Frankie McCarty, *Land Grant Problems in New Mexico* (Albuquerque: Albuquerque *Journal,* 1969).

26. Glen E. Leonard, *The Role of the Land Grant in the Social Process of a Spanish American Village in New Mexico* (Albuquerque: Calvin Horn, 1970), pp. 167–70.

27. The terms *rancho* (singular) and *ranchos* (plural) had several denota-

tions, and could refer variously to a farm, a ranch, or a mobile camp, including a herd of cattle and attendant vaqueros with their families. These terms were often used interchangeably, as in "los ranchos de Albuquerque," which were described as *plazas* in the 1790 census. Occasionally, the term *plaza* referred to a concentrated village whose houses were grouped wall to wall around a central plaza and forming a defensive perimeter against attack. *Ranchos*, in the plural as opposed to *rancho*, referred to a group of farm houses in close proximity. See Horvath, "Social and Political Organization of the Genizaros"; and Antonio Rios Bustamante, "New Mexico in the Eighteenth Century: Life, Labor and Trade in la Villa de San Felipe de Albuquerque, 1706–1790," *Aztlán* 7 (Fall 1976).

28. Within a given perspective, considerable political data on Nuevo México, Texas, and the northern Mexican states is to be found in Hubert Howe Bancroft's *History of Arizona and New Mexico*, and in his *History of the North Mexican States and Texas*. Though not empathetic to the society, these works are informative because Bancroft collected an immense amount of documentation; the documentation is available in the Bancroft Library at the University of California at Berkeley, and his works follow those documents and secondary materials closely. The most detailed account available of the politics of any of the northern provinces or departments is to be found in Bancroft's *History of California*, in which he, according to his own interpretation, chronologizes year by year, and seemingly issue by issue, the politics of the province and those of many of the various pueblos. For example, Bancroft had the entire archives of the Department of Alta California copied for his collection.

29. Informative recent reinterpretation of Indian relations will be found in Dunbar Ortiz, "Roots of Pueblo Indian Land Tenure"; Charles R. Cutler, *The Protector de Indios in Colonial New Mexico, 1659–1821* (Albuquerque: University of New Mexico Press, 1986); and John, *Storms Brewed in Other Men's Worlds*. Earlier treatments are Spicer, *Cycles of Conquest*; Oakah L. Jones, *Pueblo Warriors and Spanish Conquest* (Norman: University of Oklahoma Press, 1966); and Joseph F. Park, "Spanish Indian Policy in Northern Mexico, 1765–1810," *Arizona and the West* 4 (Winter 1962). See also the informative works of Alfred B. Thomas: *After Coronado: Spanish Exploration Northeast of New Mexico, 1696–1727* (Norman: University of Oklahoma Press, 1935); *Forgotten Frontiers: A Study of the Spanish Indian Policy of Don Juan Bautista de Anza, Governor of New Mexico, 1777–1787* (Norman: University of Oklahoma Press, 1932); and *The Plains Indians and New Mexico, 1751–1778* (Albuquerque: University of New Mexico Press, 1940).

30. See *Reglamentos, reglas, y regulaciones de la acequia del llano* (n.d., facsimile); Marc Simmons, "Spanish Irrigation Practices in New Mexico," *New Mexico Historical Review* 47 (April 1972); Wells A. Hutchins, "The

Community Acequia: Its Origins and Development," *Southwestern Historical Quarterly* 31 (1927–1928); Fray Angélico Chávez, "Early Settlements in the Mora Valley," *El Palacio* (November 1955); Eleanor B. Adams, "The Chapel and Cofradia of Our Lady of Light in Santa Fe," *New Mexico Historical Review* 22 (October 1947); Paul Kutsche and Dennis Gallegos, "Community Functions of the Cofradiá de Nuestro Padre Jesus Nazareno," *Colorado Studies* 15 (1979); and the excellent book by Thomas J. Steele and Rowena A. Rivera, *Penitente Self-Government Brotherhoods and Councils, 1797–1947* (Santa Fe: Ancient City Press, 1985).

31. Quote is from Don Pedro Bautista Pino, in Benjamin M. Read, *Illustrated History of New Mexico* (Santa Fe: New Mexico Printing Co., 1912), p. 356.

32. On early Arizona, there is Bolton, *Kino's Historical Memoir*; Juan M. Mange, *Unknown Arizona and Sonora, 1693–1721* (Tucson: Arizona Silhouettes, 1954); and Ray H. Mattison, "Early Spanish and Mexican Settlements in Arizona," *New Mexico Historical Review* 21 (October 1946); and James E. Officer, *Hispanic Arizona, 1536–1856* (Tucson: University of Arizona Press, 1987); Henry F. Dobyns, *Spanish Colonial Tucson: A Demographic History* (Tucson: University of Arizona Press, 1976); Yjunio Aguirre, "Echoes of the Conquistadores: Stock Raising in Spanish Mexican Times," *Journal of Arizona History* 16 (Autumn 1975); Sidney R. de Long, *The History of Arizona from the Earliest Times Known to the People of Europe to 1903* (San Francisco: The Whitaker and Ray Co., 1905); and Jay J. Wagner, *Early Arizona: Prehistory to Civil War* (Tucson: University of Arizona Press, 1975).

33. For Texas conditions, see Fray Francisco Celiz, *Diary of the Alarcón Expedition into Texas, 1718–1719*, 2 vols., trans. F. L. Hoffman (Los Angeles: The Quivira Society, 1935); Fray Juan Agustín de Morfi, *History of Texas, 1673–1779*, trans. and ed. Carlos E. Castañeda (Albuquerque: The Quivira Society, 1935); and Ernest Wallace and David M. Vigness, eds., *Documents of Texas History* (Austin: The Steck Company, 1960). Major published accounts of the province of Tejas during the colonial period include: Lino Gómez Candeo, *Primeras exploraciones y poblamiento de Texas, 1686–1694*; Vito Alessio Robles, *Coahuila y Texas en la época colonial* (México, D.F.: Editorial Cultura, 1938); Carlos E. Castañeda, *Our Catholic Heritage in Texas*, 7 vols. (Austin: Von Boeckmann-Jones Company, 1936–1950; repr., New York: Arno Press, 1976); Bolton, *Texas in the Middle Eighteenth Century*; Gerald Ashford, *Spanish Texas: Yesterday and Today* (Austin: Jenkins, 1971); James McCorkle, Jr., "Los Adaes and the Borderlands Origins of East Texas," *East Texas Historical Journal* 11 (1984); Odie B. Faulk, *The Last Years of Spanish Texas, 1778–1821* (The Hague: Mouton and Co., 1964). Also, see Jones, *Los Paisanos*, chapter 2, "Texas"; and J. Villasana Haggard, "Spain's Indian Policy in Texas," *Southwestern Historical Quarterly* 46 (July 1942). To date, the most

complete discussion of the historical boundaries of Tejas is José Antonio Pichardo, *Pichardo's Treatise on the Limits of Louisiana and Texas*, 2 vols., trans. Charles Wilson Hackett (Austin: University of Texas Press, 1931–1932). For a critical examination of the literature on colonial Tejas, see Gerald E. Poyo and Gilberto M. Hinojosa, "Spanish Texas and Borderlands Historiography in Transition: Implications for United States History," *The Journal of American History* 75 (September 1988).

34. Father Damián Mazanet wrote to Carlos Sigüenza y Góngora about the expedition of 1689:

> 1.—El año de 1685 y 1686 . . . al señor Marqués de San Miguel de Aguayo, el cual era actual gobernador del Nuevo Reino de León, para que despachase una compañía de soldados de a caballo por las costas del Mar del Norte, que está adelante de Tempico hacia el Río Bravo, y de la Magdalena, y dicho gobernador envió cincuenta hombres, y por cabo de ellos al capitán Alonso de León. Dicho cabo con sus soldados llegaron a la costa del mar, y siguiendo la costa pasaron el Río Bravo con harto trabajo. Este rió es el mismo del Paso del Nuevo México, y los indios, a este mismo rió, le dan diferentes nombres; porque unos le llaman Río Bravo, Río Grande y Río Turbio. Este río, en el Nuevo México, nunca se supo su origen, lo más que llegaron a alcanzar fue que salía de la Gran Quivira. Esto decían los indios que de la tierra adentro venían al Nuevo México.

The observant priest had identified a major economic and social lifeline of the region, and one which was to have recurring historical significance. The quotation is from "Carta de Fray Damián Mazanet a Sigüenza y Góngora" (1690), in Gómez Candeo, *Primeras exploraciones*, p. 6.

35. The quote is from "Carta del Padre Damián Mazanet al Virrey sobre la situación en San Francisco de los Tejas (1692)," in Gómez Canedo, *Primeras exploraciones*, p. 265. For difficult conditions a hundred years later, see Marilyn McAdams Sibley, ed., "Across Texas in 1767: The Travels of Captain Pages," *Southwestern Historical Quarterly* 71 (April 1967).

36. See Castañeda, *Our Catholic Heritage in Texas*, vol. 4, pp. 296–343; Bolton, *Texas in the Middle Eighteenth Century*, pp. 113–19 and 389–446; Myl C. King, "Captain Antonio Gil y Barbo, The Founder of Modern Nacogdoches, 1729–1809" (Master's thesis, Stephen F. Austin University, 1949); and James Christopher Harrison, "The Failure of Spain in East Texas: The Occupation and Abandonment of Nacogdoches, 1779–1821" (Ph.D. diss., University of Nebraska, 1980).

37. See J. Autry Dabbs, ed. and trans., "The Texas Missions in 1785," *Mid America* 22 (January 1940); and Alicia Vidaurreta Tjarks, "Comparative Demographic Analysis of Texas, 1777–1793," in Weber, *New Spain's Far Northern Frontier*.

38. For the lower Rio Grande, see Lawrence H. Hill, *José de Escandón and*

the Founding of Nuevo Santander (Columbus: Ohio State University Press, 1926); Florence J. Scott, "Spanish Colonization of the Lower Rio Grande, 1747–1767," in Thomas E. Cotner and Carlos E. Castañeda, eds., *Essays in Mexican History* (Austin: Institute of Latin American Studies, University of Texas, 1958); and Rogelia O. García, *Dolores, Revilla, and Laredo: Three Sisters Settlements* (Waco: Texian Press, 1970).

39. Weber, *New Spain's Far Northern Frontier*, p. 158; Bolton, *Texas in the Middle Eighteenth Century*, pp. 387–446.

40. For the San Antonio area, see Morfi, *History of Texas*; Antonio Bonilla, "Brief Compendium of the Events which Have Occurred in the Province of Texas from Its Conquest, or Reduction to the Present [1772]," trans. Elizabeth H. West, *Texas State Historical Quarterly* 7 (July 1907); Lota M. Spell, "The Grant and First Survey of the City of San Antonio," *Southwestern Historical Quarterly* 66 (July 1967); Bolton, *Texas in the Middle Eighteenth Century*; and Jesús F. de la Teja, "Land and Society in Eighteenth Century San Antonio de Bexar: A Community on New Spain's Northern Frontier" (Ph.D. diss., University of Texas, Austin, 1988); and Esther MacMillan, "The Cabildo and the People, 1731–1784" in *San Antonio in the Eighteenth Century* (San Antonio: San Antonio Bicentennial Heritage Committee, 1976). See also Frederick Charles Chabot, *With the Makers of San Antonio: Genealogies of the Early Latin, Anglo American and German Families* (San Antonio: Artes Gráficas, 1937).

41. See Nicolás de Lafora, *Relación del viaje que hizo a los Presidios Internos* (México, D.F.: Editorial P. Robledo, 1939).

42. See discussions of early Spanish considerations for the Alta California colonization in Henry J. Bruman and Clement W. Meighan, *Early California: Perception and Reality* (William Andrews Clark Memorial Library, Los Angeles: University of California, 1981). For information regarding the Manila trade between Mexico and the Philippines, the basic source remains the classic by William Lyle Schurz, *The Manila Galleon* (New York: E. P. Dutton, 1939). For perceptions of California, see Lesley Byrd Simpson, ed., *The Letters of José Senan, O.F.M.*, trans. Paul D. Nathan (Ventura County: Historical Society, 1962); Pedro Fages, *A Historical, Political and Natural Description of California*, trans. H. I. Ernestly (Berkeley: University of California Press, 1937); and Charles E. Chapman, *History of California: The Spanish Period* (New York: Macmillan, 1921). Spaniards and their Mexican subjects visited the seacoast of Alta California in 1542. Interest in locating a safe harbor for the Manila galleons from the Philippines led to several exploratory expeditions along the Pacific Coast.

43. For the colonization, see Herbert E. Bolton, ed., *Fray Juan Crespi: Missionary Explorer on the Pacific, 1769–1774*, trans. Herbert E. Bolton (Berkeley: University of California Press, 1927); Miguel Constanso, *The Constanso Narra-*

tive of the Portola Expedition, trans. Ray Brandes (Newhall: Hogarth Press, 1970); Herbert E. Bolton, ed., Anza's California Expeditions, 5 vols. (Berkeley: University of California Press, 1936); Pedro Font, Diary of the Anza Expedition of 1775–1776, H. E. Bolton, ed. (Berkeley: University of California Press, 1933); and Charles E. Chapman, The Founding of Spanish California: The Northwestward Expansion of New Spain, 1687–1783 (New York: Macmillan, 1916). For materials on California, I am indebted to Professor A. Rios Bustamante. For a revisionist view of social, economic, and political evolution of northern California, see Jack D. Forbes, "Hispano-Mexican Pioneers of the San Francisco Bay Region: An Analysis of Racial Origins," Aztlán 14 (Spring 1983); and Helen Lara-Cea, "Notes on the Use of Parish Registers in the Reconstruction of Chicana History in California Prior to 1850," in Castillo, Between Borders. On southern California, see Antonio Rios Bustamante, "Los Angeles Pueblo and Region, 1781–1850: Continuity and Adaptation on the North Mexican Periphery" (Ph.D. diss., University of California, Los Angeles, 1985). Visitador General Gálvez's plans for the occupation of Alta California, supported by his friend, Viceroy Teodoro de Croix, were approved by the Spanish king in 1768, when the Spanish ambassador to Russia reported that the Russians were planning to occupy the area around Monterey Bay in California. See Alfred B. Thomas, Teodoro de Croix and the Northern Frontier of New Spain, 1776–1783 (Norman: University of Oklahoma Press, 1941); and Herbert I. Priestley, José de Gálvez, Visitor-General of New Spain 1765–1771 (Berkeley: University of California Press, 1916).

44. For conditions, see Fray Juan Crespi: Missionary Explorer on the Pacific Coast, 1769–1774; Constanso, Constanso Narrative; Fray Francisco Palou, Historical Memoirs of New California, ed. Herbert E. Bolton (Berkeley: University of California Press, 1926); Chapman, History of California, pp. 216–31. See also Robert F. Heizer, ed., The Indians of Los Angeles County: Hugo Reid's Letters of 1852 (Los Angeles: Southwest Museum, 1968), pp. 75–76.

45. For early California society, see Nellie Van de Grift Sánchez, Spanish Arcadia (1929); New York: Arno Press, 1976); and Ruth Staff, "Settlement in Alta California before 1800" (Master's thesis, University of California, Berkeley, 1931). For early families, see Marie E. Northrop, Spanish-Mexican Families of Early California, 1769–1850, vol. 1 (New Orleans: Polyanthos, 1976); and for a family which rose to prominence, the Vallejos, see Charles Howard Shinn, "Pioneer Spanish Families in California," The Century Magazine 41 (January 1891).

46. For governance, see Bancroft, History of California, vol. 1; Theodore Grivas, "Alcalde Rule: The Nature of Local Government in Spanish and Mexican California," California Historical Society Quarterly 4 (March 1961); and Francis F. Guest, "Municipal Government in Spanish California," California Historical Society Quarterly 46 (December 1967). Edwin A. Beilharz,

Felipe de Neve: First Governor of California (San Francisco: California Historical Society, 1971); Lindley Bynum, "Governor Felipe de Neve—Chronological Note," *Southern California Quarterly,* part 1, vol. 15 (September 1931); Lindley Bynum, "Four Reports by Neve, 1777–1779," *Southern California Quarterly,* part 1, vol. 15 (September 1931); Thomas Workman Temple, II, "Se Fundaron un Pueblo de Españoles—The Founding of Los Angeles," *Southern California Quarterly,* part 1, vol. 15 (September 1931); see, in particular, "Reglamento," in Beilharz, *Felipe de Neve,* pp. 85–96; and *Regulations for Governing the Province of California,* trans. John Everett Johnson (San Francisco: Grabhorn Press, 1929).

47. Simpson, *Letters of José Senan,* pp. 1–9.

48. William Mason, "The Garrisons of San Diego Presidio, 1769–1794," *Journal of San Diego History* 24 (Fall 1978); Leon G. Campbell, "The First Californios: Presidial Society in Spanish California, 1769–1822," *Journal of the West* 11 (October 1972); Howard J. Nelson, "The Two Pueblos of Los Angeles: Agricultural Village and Embryo Town," *Southern California Quarterly* 59 (Spring 1977); J. Gregg Layne, *Annals of Los Angeles* (San Francisco: California Historical Society, 1935); Harry Kelesey, "A New Look at the Founding of Old Los Angeles," *California History* 55 (Winter 1976); and Mary E. Northrup, ed., "Los Angeles, in 1816," *Southern California Quarterly* 43 (June 1961).

49. For a discussion of missionary, military, and settler conflicts in reference to the West Coast, see Stuart F. Voss, "Mission Society: Inclination to Permanency, 1530–1700," in his *On the Periphery of Nineteenth Century Mexico: Sonora and Sinaloa, 1810–1877* (Tucson: University of Arizona Press, 1982), pp. 9–24.

50. William Mason, "Indian–Mexican Cultural Exchange in the Los Angeles Area, 1781–1834," *Aztlán* 15 (Spring 1984); William D. Estrada, "Indian Resistance and Accommodation in the California Missions and Mexican Society, 1769 to 1848: A Case Study of Mission San Gabriel Archangel and El Pueblo de Los Angeles" (unpublished paper, Los Angeles: University of California, 1980); Maynard Geiger, O.F.M., "Mission San Gabriel in 1814," *Southern California Quarterly* 53 (Summer 1971); Maynard Geiger, O.F.M., and Clement W. Meighan, eds., *As the Padres Saw Them: California Indian Life and Customs as Reported by the Franciscan Missionaries, 1813–1815* (Santa Barbara: Santa Barbara Mission Archive Library, 1976).

51. Sherburne F. Cook's studies of the California mission Indian population indicate considerable Mexican Indian intermarriage and contact. See Cook, *The Population of the California Indians, 1769–1970* (Berkeley: University of California Press, 1976), chapter 5, "Degree of Blood," pp. 161–64.

52. Thomas Workman Temple, II, "Toypurina the Witch and the Indian Uprising at San Gabriel," *The Masterkey* 32 (July–August 1969), pp. 136–52.

Also, see W. D. Estrada, "Indian Resistance and Accommodation"; Bancroft, *History of California,* vol. 2, p. 92.

53. See David Hornbeck, "Land Tenure and Rancho Expansion in Alta California, 1784–1846," *Journal of Historical Cartography* 4, no. 4 (1978); William Wilcox Robinson, *Land in California* (Berkeley: University of California Press, 1948); Ruth M. McGinty, "Spanish and Mexican Ranchos in the San Francisco Bay Area," (Master's thesis, University of California, Berkeley, 1921); Robert G. Cowan, *Ranchos of California* (Fresno: Academy Library Guild, 1956); Myrtle Garrison, *Romance and History of California Ranchos* (San Francisco: Harr Wagner Publishing Company, 1935); and William W. Robinson, *Ranchos Become Cities* (Pasadena: San Pasqual Press, 1939). As explained by A. Rios Bustamante, "Los Angeles Pueblo and Region" in "New Mexico in the Eighteenth Century," a hacienda, by regional standards extensive, was an economically diversified estate, usually combining agriculture, grazing, and other production, and for major commercial sale, employing a sizeable labor force. Only a few such enterprises would be found in the far north. A pragmatic definition of the hacienda and its relative relationship to the rancho is given in Eric Van Young, *Hacienda and Market in Eighteenth Century Mexico: The Rural Economy of the Guadalajara Region, 1675–1820* (Berkeley: University of California Press, 1981), pp. 107–13. Variables identified by Van Young include capital, labor, land, markets, technology, and social sanctions. Assertions on the hacienda and rancho in Alta California and in other far north Mexican contexts arises from observations on alleged size and the residence of kin and laborers, although other variables were minor. The term *hacienda,* when used by one contemporary Mexican in the context of Alta California, applied to the missions. For example, Governor José Figueroa, writing to the central government in 1833, referred to the missions as "valuable hacienda." Alan C. Hutchinson, *Frontier Settlement in Mexican California* (New Haven: Yale University Press, 1969), pp. 216–20; and Alan C. Hutchinson, trans., *A Manifesto to the Mexican Republic* (Berkeley: University of California Press, 1978), p. 6. Prior to 1848, only three California rancheros had large holdings, and Don Pío Pico, Don José de la Guerra y Noriega, and Don Mariano Guadalupe Vallejo were all quite active politically. During the seventies, considerable revisionist scholarship on estates evolved. Additional information on the Mexican haciendas and their various types and relationship to other types of landholdings may be found in the following sources: Kenneth Duncan, et al., eds., *Land and Labour in Latin America* (Cambridge: Harvard University Press, 1977); Enrique Florescano, ed., *Haciendas, latifundios y plantaciones en America Latina* (México, D.F.: Siglo Veintiuno, 1975); Enrique Semo, ed., *Siete ensayos sobre la hacienda mexicana, 1780–1880* (México, D.F.: Instituto Nacional de Antropologiá e Historia, 1977); Jan Bazant, ed., *Cinco haciendas mexicanas* (México, D.F.: El Colegio de México, 1975); Franz J.

Schryer, *The Rancheros of Pisaflores* (Toronto: University of Toronto Press, 1980); and David Brading, *Haciendas and Ranchos in the Mexican Bajío* (Cambridge: Harvard University Press, 1978).

54. For the last years of colonial control, see Chapman, *History of California*. For events elsewhere, see Philip C. Brooks, *Diplomacy and the Borderlands: The Adams–Onís Treaty of 1819* (Berkeley: University of California Press, 1939); Odie B. Faulk, *The Last Years of Spanish Texas, 1778–1821* (The Hague: Mouton and Co., 1964); and Sidney B. Brinkerhoff, "The Last Years of Spanish Arizona, 1786–1821," *Arizona and the West* 9 (Spring 1967).

55. For an informative firsthand account of conditions during the last quarter of the eighteenth century, see the valuable Francisco Atanasio Dominguez, *The Missions of New Mexico, 1776: A Description*, ed. and trans. Eleanor B. Adams and Angélico Chávez (Albuquerque: University of New Mexico Press, 1956); and Janie L. Aragon, "The People of Santa Fe in the 1790s," *Aztlán* 7 (1976). On transitions generally, see Bannon, *Spanish Borderlands Frontier*, chapter 12; Swadesh, *Los Primeros Pobladores*, pp. 51–52. For changes generally in the Bourbon period, see Enrique Florescano, *La época de las reformas borbónicas y el desarrollo económico, 1750–1808* (México, D.F.: Instituto Nacional de Antropología e Historia, 1974); and Eduardo Arcila Farias, *Reformas económicas del siglo XVIII en el reinado de Carlos IV*, 2 vols. (México, D.F.: Sep-Setentas, 1974).

56. The quote is from Nettie Lee Benson, ed., "Report that Dr. Miguel Ramos de Arizpe . . . Presents to the August Congress . . ." (1812; repr., Austin: University of Texas Press, 1950), pp. 16–17.

57. Susan Dakin, *Rose or Rose Thorn? Three Women of Spanish California* (Berkeley: Friends of the Bancroft Library, 1963); and Sánchez, *Spanish Arcadia*, pp. 10–17.

58. For relatively greater latitude, see Swadesh, *Los Primeros Pobladores*, chapters 1 and 2; Jones, *Los Paisanos*, chapter 11; and Salome Hernández, "Nuevo Mexicanos as Refugees and Reconquest Settlers, 1680–1696," in Joan M. Jensen, et al., *New Mexico Women* (Albuquerque: University of New Mexico Press, 1986). See also Frederic J. Athearn, "Life and Society in Eighteenth Century New Mexico" (Ph.D. diss., University of Texas at Austin, 1974). The term *chicana* was perhaps applied to the women of the migratory camps of northern Mexico.

59. On women and the family, see Hubert H. Bancroft, *California Pastoral*, Chapter X. Gloria E. Miranda, "Gente de Razón Marriage Patterns in Spanish and Mexican California: A Case Study of Santa Barbara and Los Angeles," *Southern California Quarterly*, 63 (Spring 1981); Antonia Castañeda, "Presidarias y Pobladores: Spanish Mexican Women in Frontier Monterey, Alta California, 1770–1821" (Ph.D. diss., Stanford University, 1990). Though there was concern for education, formal schooling was the exception, when it

existed it meant learning from a priest or soldier. Most often, children learned by watching their parents and performing tasks. For an informative presentation on education, see Bernardo Phillip Gallegos, *Literacy, Education, and Society in Colonial New Mexico, 1692–1821* (University of New Mexico Press 1992).

60. On the courts, see Gutiérrez, *When Jesus Came*; and also Angelina Veyna, "Women in Early New Mexico: A Preliminary View," in Teresa Cordova et al., *Chicana Voices: Intersection of Class, Race, and Gender* (Austin: CMAS Publications, 1986).

61. For early Anglo intervention, see Zebulon Montgomery Pike, *The Journal of Zebulon Montgomery Pike* (Norman: University of Oklahoma Press, 1966); W. Eugene Hollon, *The Southwest: Old and New* (Lincoln: University of Nebraska Press, 1961); J. Leitch Wright, *Anglo-Spanish Rivalry in North America* (Athens: University of Georgia Press, 1971); Cesar Sepúlveda, *Tres ensayos sobre la frontera septentrional de la Nueva España* (México, D.F.: Editorial Porrua, 1977); and Roy F. Nichols, *Advance Agents of American Destiny* (Philadelphia: University of Pennsylvania Press, 1956), and Richard A. Bartlett, *The New Country: A Social History of the American Frontier, 1796–1890* (London: Oxford University Press, 1974). For the role of Spain in the United States independence movement, see Juan F. Yela Utrilla, *España ante la independencia de los Estados Unidos*, 2 vols. (Lerida: 1922) and Melvin B. Glascock, "New Spain and the War for America, 1779–1783" (Ph.D. diss., Louisiana State University, 1969). Thousands of men and hundreds of thousand *pesos fuertes* and material, including *mantas* drawn from Mexico, were used. Gálvez and New Spain did more for independence than other foreign figures or allies, and with little recognition. Mexican funds (one thousand silver pesos) even went to the construction of the first Catholic church in New York, St. Peters. For another point of view, see Robert H. Thonhoff, *The Texas Connection with the American Revolution* (Burnett, Texas, 1981). I am indebted to Professor Juan Bruce Navoa for insights on Cromwell, Mather, and Jefferson. For Anglo-American attitudes, see Reginald Horsman, *Race and Manifest Destiny: The Origins of American Racial Anglo Saxonism* (Cambridge: Harvard University Press, 1981).

62. From Nicolás de Lafora, *Relación del viaje que hizo a los Presidios internos . . .* (México, D.F.: Robredo, 1939), p. 33. For reorganization, see Bernardo de Gálvez, *Instructions for Governing the Interior Provinces of New Spain 1786*, ed. Donald E. Worcester (Berkeley: University of California Press, 1951); and Fernando Ocaranza, *Crónica de las Provincias Internas* (México, D.F.: 1939); see also María del Carmen Velasquez, *Establecimiento y pérdida del Septentrion de Nueva España* (México, D.F.: El Colegio de México, 1974), pp. 167–215. At a time when the residents of the colony of New Spain were desperate for monies, defense and other resources, soldiers and a veritable

treasure were spent on the independence of the thirteen colonies. See also James Lewis "New Spain During the American Revolution, 1779–1783: A Viceroyalty at War" (Ph.D. diss., Duke University, Durham, 1975).

63. Margarita Nolasco Armas, "Continuidad y cambio sociocultural en el norte de Mexico," *America Indígena* 31 (1971); see David J. Weber, *El México perdido: Ensayos sobre el antiguo norte de México, 1540–1821* (México, D.F.: Sep-Setentas, 1976), this historian of U.S. West, writing on the national aspect of the formative frontier process states: hasta que esa zona cayó en posesión de los Estados Unidos, su historia fue desde luego, parte de la historia de Mexico." (p. 5) He adds, "Es la Mexicanidad del sudoeste lo que contribuye a darle un caracter distintivo a la región dentro del ambiente norte americano." (p. 7) Weber concludes by observing: "para 1821, año en que España perdió su soberania sobre México, se había desarrollado en el antiguo norte una cultura distintiva con variantes regionales en California, Arizona, Nuevo México y Texas. Española en su origen pero alterada por hallarse expuesta a los mexicanos y a los indios del septentrión y templada por la geografía y el aislamiento, esta sociedad de frontera se habia hecho verdaderamente mexicana." (p. 32)

64. See Bernabé Navarro, *La introducción de la filosofia moderna en México* (México, D.F.: El Colegio de México, 1948). See also comments in Samuel Ramos, *Historia de la filosofia en México* (México, D.F.: Imprenta Universitaria, 1943), p. 86; and Xavier Tavera Alfaro, *El nacionalismo en la prensa mexicana del siglo XVIII* (México, D.F.: Club de Periodistas de México, 1963). For intellectual intolerance, see Pablo González Casanova, *La literatura perseguida en la crisis de la colonia* (México, D.F.: El Colegio de México, 1958). For a study which stresses orthodoxy, see David Mayagoitia, *Ambiente filosófico de la Nueva España*, (México, D.F.: Editorial Jus, 1945). For the diffusion and objection to new intellectual currents, see Dorothy Tanck Estrada, *La educación ilustrada, 1786–1836* (México, D.F.: El Colegio de México, 1977); and Pablo González Casanova, *El misioneismo y la modernidad cristiana en el siglo XVIII* (México, D.F.: El Colegio de México, 1948); Monelisa Lina Pérez Marchand, *Dos etapas ideológicas del siglo XVIII en México* (México, D.F.: El Colegio de México, 1948). For the activities of the Inquisition in censoring subversive ideas in the far north, see Richard E. Greenleaf, "The Inquisition in Eighteenth Century New Mexico," *New Mexico Historical Review* 60 (January 1985). Among the Jesuits and their students were Francisco Clavijero, Francisco Javier Alegre, Diego José Abad, Agustín Castro, Raymundo Cardan, Julián Parreno, Andrés de Guevara y Basoazabal, Ignacio Bartolache, Beneto Díaz de Gamarra y Davalos, and Miguel Hidalgo.

65. See Luis Villoro, *El proceso ideológico de la revolución de independencia* (México, D.F.: Universidad Nacional Autónoma de México, 1967); and Javier Ocampo, *Las ideas de un día: El pueblo mexicano ante la consumación de su*

independencia (México, D.F.: El Colegio de México, 1969); Francisco López Cámara, *La genesis de la conciencia liberal en México* (México, D.F.: El Colegio de México, 1954); and Bernabé B. Navarro, *Cultura mexicana moderna en el siglo XVIII* (México, D.F.: Universidad Nacional Autónoma de México, 1964). On Servando Teresa y Mier, see John V. Lombardi, *The Political Ideology of Fray Servando Teresa de Mier, Propagandist for Independence* (Cuernavaca: Centro Intercultural de Documentación, 1968); and Jesús Silva Herzog, "Fray Servando Teresa de Mier," *Cuadernos Americanos*, número 154 (1967), 162–69. For Carlos M. Bustamante, see his *Cuadro histórico de la revolución de la America mexicana*, 6 vols. (México, D.F.: 1823–32); and Juan A. Ortega y Medina, "El historiador Don Carlos María de Bustamante ante la conciencia histórica mexicana," *Anuario de Historia*, vol. 3 (1966), pp. 11–58.

66. For the social context and early efforts, see Enrique Florescano, *Nueva España, 1764–1817* (México, D.F.: Sep-Setentas, 1973); and Antonio Pompa y Pompa, *Origenes de la independencia mexicana* (Guadalajara: 1970). On Hidalgo, see Luis Castillo León, *Hidalgo: La vida del héroe*, 2 vols. (México, D.F.: 1948–49). For Morelos, see Ernesto Lemoine Villicana, *Morelos: Su vida revolucionaria a traves de sus escritos y de otros testimonios de la época* (México, D.F.: 1965). For documents of the independence movement, see Ernesto de la Torre Villar, et al., *Historia documental de México*, vol. 2 (México, D.F.: Universidad Nacional Autónoma de México, 1964), pp. 16–154.

67. Ernesto de la Torre Villar, ed., *La Constitución de Apatzingan y los creadores del estado mexicano* (México, D.F.: Universidad Nacional Autónoma de México, 1964); and Catalina Sierra, *El nacimiento de México* (México, D.F.: Universidad Nacional Autónoma de México, 1960); and Luis Chávez Orozco, *Historia de México (1808–1836)* (México, D.F.: Editorial Patria, 1947).

68. For the impact of the independence insurgency, see Laureano Calvo Berber, *Nociones de historia de Sonora* (México, D.F.: Manuel Porrua, 1958), pp. 127–32; Eduardo W. Villa, *Historia del Estado de Sonora* (Hermosillo: Editorial Sonora, 1951), pp. 153–59; Officer, *Hispanic Arizona*, pp. 84–96.

69. Don Pío Pico, *Historical Narrative*, trans. Arthur P. Botello (Glendale: Arthur H. Clark Company, 1983), pp. 22–23, in an interview with Henry D. Barrows, 1881.

70. For the independence movement in Chihuahua, see "Conspiración de Trespalacios 1814," *Boletín de la Sociedad Chihuahuense de Estudios Históricos*, vol. 7 (Septiembre–Octubre 1950); and for reference to a conspiracy in New Mexico, see William Watts Hart Davis, *El Gringo or New Mexico and Its People* (Lincoln: University of Nebraska Press, 1982), p. 83. For the sermon of Father Martínez, see Antonio M. Stevens Arroyo, *Prophets Denied Honor* (Maryknoll: Orbis Books, 1980), pp. 85–87.

71. In Read, *Illustrated History of New Mexico*, pp. 258–59; see also Nettie

Lee Benson, ed., *Mexico and the Spanish Cortés, 1810–1822* (Austin: University of Texas Press, 1966).

72. See Elizabeth H. West, ed., "Diary of José Bernardo Gutiérrez de Lara," *American Historical Review* 34 (Oct. 1928–Jan. 1929); Castañeda, *Our Catholic Heritage in Texas, 1519–1936,* vol. 6, *Transition Period: The Fight for Freedom, 1810–1836* (New York: Arno Press, 1976), pp. 1–3. For a brief biography of Gutiérrez de Lara, see Rie Jarrat, *Gutiérrez de Lara, Mexican-Texan* (Austin: Creole-Texana, 1949). For the last years of Spanish authority in Texas, and for a detailed narrative of its politics and governor from the point of view of his office, see Felix Díaz Almaraz, *The Tragic Cavalier: Governor Manuel Salcedo of Texas, 1808–1813* (Austin: University of Texas Press, 1971); and the informative collection of letters, Virginia H. Taylor, trans. and ed., *The Letters of Antonio Martínez: Last Spanish Governor of Texas, 1817–1822* (Austin: Texas State Library, 1957); see also David Vigness, *The Revolutionary Decades: The Saga of Texas, 1810–1836* (Austin: Steck-Vaughn, 1965).

73. Bancroft, *History of the North Mexican States and Texas,* vol. 2, 1531–1883 (San Francisco: A. L. Bancroft and Company, 1889), pp. 17–19; and Carlos E. Castañeda, *Our Catholic Heritage in Texas,* vol. 6, pp. 7–23; see also Frederick C. Chabot, *Texas in 1811: The Las Casas and Sambrano Revolutions* (San Antonio: Yanaguana Society, 1941).

74. For the quote, see "The Governing Junta of Texas and Its President Juan Manuel Sambrano to the Commandant General," *Yanaguana Publications* 6 (San Antonio, 1941), pp. 112–14; see also J. Villasana Hagard, "The Counter Revolution at Béxar, 1811," *Southwestern Historical Quarterly* 43 (October 1939).

75. Bancroft, *History of the North Mexican States and Texas,* vol. 2, pp. 19–20. Carlos E. Castañeda, *Our Catholic Heritage in Texas,* vol. 6, pp. 57–60; Jarrat, *Gutiérrez de Lara.* See, in contrast, Walter F. McCaleb, "The First Period of the Gutiérrez-Magee Expedition," *Texas State Historical Quarterly* 4 (January 1901); and Harry McCarry Henderson, "The Magee-Gutiérrez Expedition," *Southwestern Historical Quarterly* 55 (July 1951).

76. Carlos E. Castañeda, *Our Catholic Heritage in Texas,* vol. 6, pp. 63–65.

77. Carlos E. Castañeda, *Our Catholic Heritage in Texas,* vol. 6, p. 77. Castañeda cites as source a letter from Captain Bustamante to M. Salcedo, Camargo, June 7, 1812, in the Bexar Archives; see also Greenleaf, "Inquisition," for the possibility of unorthodox ideas circulating in New Mexico and Tejas; and Odie B. Faulk, "The Penetration of Foreigners and Foreign Ideas into Spanish East Texas, 1793–1810," *East Texas Historical Journal* 2 (October 1964).

78. Hubert Howe Bancroft, *History of the North Mexican States and Texas,* vol. 2, p. 26; for contrast, see Henry P. Walker, "William McLane's Narrative

of the Magee-Gutiérrez Expedition," *Southwestern Historical Quarterly* 66 (October 1962–January 1963).

79. Hubert Howe Bancroft, *History of the North Mexican States and Texas*, vol. 2, p. 31; see Ted Schwarz, *The Forgotten Battlefield of the First Texas Revolution, The Battle of Medina, August 18, 1813* (Austin: Eakin Press, 1985).

80. For early independence, see Sierra, *El nacimiento de México*, and Ocampo, *Las ideas de un día*; Romeo Flores Caballero, *Counterrevolution: The Role of the Spaniards in the Independence of Mexico, 1804–38* (Lincoln: University of Nebraska Press, 1974); Stanley C. Green, *The Mexican Republic: The First Decade, 1823–1832* (Pittsburgh: The University of Pittsburgh Press); and Barbara Tenenbaum, *The Politics of Penury: Debts and Taxes in Mexico, 1821–1856* (Albuquerque: University of New Mexico Press, 1986).

81. See Jesús Reyes Heroles, *El Liberalismo Mexicano*, 3 vols. (México, D.F.: Universidad Nacional Autónoma de México, 1957); Gaston García Cantú, ed., *El pensamiento de la reacción mexicana: Historia documental, 1810–1962* (México, D.F.: El Colegio de México, 1954); and Charles Hale, *Mexican Liberalism in the Age of Mora 1821–1853* (New Haven: Yale University Press, 1968). The Laws of 1833 and the Constitution of 1857 represented high marks in Liberal political action. Because the Liberals' political and social formulation more closely fitted popular aspirations, and because their tenacity in foreign conflicts gave them a special sanction, they clearly eclipsed the Conservative element by 1867.

Mexico existed as an independent state, and the development of the nation and of the Mexican nationality continued, with and as a result of tremendous challenges. After a brief period of constitutional monarchial rule under Iturbide ended, precedents of major significance ensued. Events of the twenty years since the turn of the century were major influences as were the experiences of the Spanish Cortes of 1810–1814 and 1820–1822, and the Spanish Constitution of 1812. At the November 1823 convention a consensus adhered to "sovereignty" residing in the "people" who constituted a "nation." Of at least four views on where the locus of the exercise of sovereignty was to be, the general conviction was that implicitly the nation precedes sovereignty. Miguel Ramos Arizpe, the major drafter of the document, convinced others that sovereignty may be shared by local and federal government. A republican form of government was established by the constitution of 1824 and Guadalupe Victoria was the first president elected. Within an organized federal pattern and specified civil rights, the constitution provided for separation of executive, legislative, and judiciary powers; a bicameral federal congress; state governments with respective legislatures; and territorial procedures and an electoral system to provide the franchise to persons meeting property qualifications established by the state legislatures. The executive was to be elected by the state legislatures for a period of four years. Again a special state-church relation was recognized exempting the clergy and military from civil courts, *fueros*, and were subject only to their own procedures. The immediate problem was the insufficiency of government revenues. Loans were one recourse and from this ensued the mistaken precedent of a government dependent on borrowing.

There are facsimilie editions of *Actas constitucionales mexicanas, 1821–1824* 9 vols. (Mexico, D.F.: 1980); the debates of the second Constituent Congress under the title *Crónicas del Acta Constitutiva* (Mexico, D.F.: 1974); and *Crónicas de la Constitución Federal de 1824* (Mexico, D.F.: 1974). José Barragán Barragán published two monographs on the events and ideas of 1824, *Introducción al federalismo* (Mexico, D.F.: 1978), and *El juicio de responsabilidad en la Constitución de 1824* (Mexico, D.F.: 1978). See also Nettie Lee Benson, *Mexico and the Spanish Cortes, 1810–1822* (Austin: University of Texas Press, 1966); Nettie Lee Benson, *La Diputación Provincial y el federalismo mexicano* (Mexico, D.F.: 1955); and James Q. Dealey, "The Spanish Sources of the Mexican Constitution of 1824," *The Quarterly of the Texas State Historical Association*, vol. III (January 1900).

Chapter 2

1. For significant statements and documents for the period that were pertinent to all of Mexico at the time, see Ernesto de la Torre Villar, et al., eds., *Historia documental de México* vol. 2 (México, D.F.: Universidad Nacional Autónoma de México, 1964), pp. 16–236. See also Stanley G. Green, *The Mexican Republic: The First Decade, 1823–1832* (Pittsburgh: University of Pittsburgh Press, 1987). For circumstances at the time of independence, and for an extensive studious survey of the far north during the period of Mexican sovereignty, see David J. Weber, *The Mexican Frontier, 1821–1846: The American Southwest under Mexico* (Albuquerque: University of New Mexico Press, 1982). The Arno Press has made available a valuable collection of imprints from the Mexican period; see David J. Weber, ed., *Northern Mexico on the Eve of the United States Invasion: Rare Imprints Concerning California, Arizona, New Mexico and Texas* (New York: Arno Press, 1976). The works of Hubert Howe Bancroft continues to have informational value for the period. For legislative enactments, see Manuel Dublan and José M. Lozano, comps., *Legislación mexicana: O colección completa de las disposiciones legislativas expedidas desde la independencia de la República*, 5 vols. (México, D.F.: Imprenta del Comercio, 1876–1904).

2. There are several key works for each of the major regions which, when examined together, can provide a preliminary overall view of political events

in the far north. In the case of Alta California, the major published source is Hubert Howe Bancroft, *History of California*, 7 vols. (San Francisco: The History Company, 1888). In Spanish, there is Alfonso Trueba, *California, Tierra Perdida*, 2 vols. (México, D.F.: Jus, 1958). The late Pablo L. Martínez, historian of Baja California, began but did not finish a history of Alta California. The unfinished work was published after his death as Pablo L. Martínez, *Historia de la Alta California, 1542–1945* (México, D.F.: Editorial Baja California, 1970). This work, however, emphasizes the colonial period, for which it is a convenient reference. Basic published sources for the political history of Nuevo México include Benjamin M. Read, *Historia ilustrada de Nuevo México* (Santa Fe: New Mexican Printing, 1912), available in English translation, and Ralph Emerson Twitchell, *The Leading Facts of New Mexican History*, 5 vols. (Cedar Rapids: Torch Press, 1911; repr., 2 vols., Albuquerque: Horn and Wallace, Publishers, 1963). Twitchell's work, a lengthy chronicle of New Mexican history from original settlement to the 1900s, is based on the archives of New Mexico. A companion work is Ralph Emerson Twitchell, *The Spanish Archives of New Mexico*, 2 vols. (Cedar Rapids: Torch Press, 1914; repr., 2 vols., New York: Arno Press, 1976). This is a compilation of document references from the Spanish and the Mexican territorial archives, and the U.S. territorial archives of New Mexico, which includes translations of selected Spanish language documents. Twitchell's extensive volumes can be supplemented by Lansing B. Bloom, "New Mexico under the Mexican Administration, 1821–1846," *Old Santa Fe*, vols. 1–2 (July 1913–April 1915). For Texas, there is Vito Alessio Robles, *Coahuila y Texas, desde la consumación de la independencia, hasta el Tratado de Paz de Guadalupe Hidalgo*, 2 vols. (México, D.F.: 1945). Less informative for the period, but nonetheless useful, are the volumes of Carlos E. Castañeda. More informative is Andrew A. Tijerina, "Tejanos and Texas: The Native Mexicans of Texas, 1820–1850" (Ph.D. diss., University of Texas at Austin, 1977).

3. Economic and demographic growth is evident in Nettie Lee Benson, ed. and trans., *Report that Dr. Miguel Ramos de Arizpe . . . Presents to the August Congress on the Natural, Political, and Civil Condition of the Provinces of Coahuila, Nuevo Leon, Nuevo Santander, and Texas . . .* (Austin: University of Texas Press, 1950); and Pedro Bautista Pino, *Exposición sucinta y sencilla de la Provincia del Nuevo México: Hecha por su Diputado en Cortés . . .* (Cádiz: 1812), facsimile in H. Bailey Carroll and J. Villasana Haggard, eds. and trans., *Three New Mexico Chronicles* (Albuquerque: Quivara Society, 1942). Tadeo Ortiz de Ayala, who was to travel extensively, provided a general view at the time of Mexican independence in his *Resumen de la estadística del imperio mexicano, 1822*, ed. Tarsicio García Díaz (1st ed., 1822; repr., México, D.F.: 1968). For California, see also Francisco Castillo Negrete, *Informe y propuestas que hace al Supremo Gobierno para la prosperidad y seguridad de la Alta California, su Comi-*

sionado . . . (México, D.F.: 1944); and Manuel Castanares, *Colección de documentos relativos al departamento de Californias* (México: 1845), facsimile in Weber, *Northern Mexico.* Published descriptions of New Mexico by Mexicans include the following: Manuel de Jesús Rada, *Proposición hecha al Soberano Congreso General de la Nación por el diputado del territorio de Nuevo México* (México: 1829), facsimile in Weber, *Northern Mexico;* Antonio Barreiro, *Ojeada sobre Nuevo México* (Puebla: 1832), an English version of which is in Carroll and Haggard, *Three New Mexico Chronicles.* Barreiro, an attorney from Chihuahua who lived in New Mexico, augmented Pino's 1812 *Exposición.* Barreiro's work, in turn, was annotated and reprinted by José Agustín de Escudero (another Chihuahua attorney, who had traveled through New Mexico), as *Noticias historicas y estadisticas de la antigua provincia del Nuevo México* . . . (México: 1849), also translated by Carroll and Haggard. Escudero's *Noticias estadísticas del estado de Chihuahua* (México: 1834) is informative for New Mexico as well as Chihuahua, and his *Noticias estadisticas de Sonora y Sinaloa* (México: 1840) includes information on what is today southern Arizona. See also Ignacio Zúñiga's *Rápida ojeada al estado de Sonora* (México: 1835), facsimile in Weber, *Northern Mexico.* See, too, José Francisco Velasco, *Noticias estadísticas del estado de Sonora* (México: 1850). Both make references to California. For Texas, accounts by two Mexican officials who came north are informative: José María Sánchez, "A Trip to Texas in 1828," trans. Carlos E. Castañeda, *Southwestern Historical Quarterly* 29 (April 1926), pp. 249–88; and Juan N. Almonte, *Noticias estadísticas sobre Tejas* (México: 1835), trans. Carlos E. Castañeda as "Statistical Report on Texas, 1835," *Southwestern Historical Quarterly* 28 (January 1925), pp. 177–220. A facsimile of the 1835 imprint is in Weber, *Northern Mexico.*

4. See *Colección de leyes fundamentales: Que han regido en la República Mexicana, y de planes que han tenido el mismo caracter, desde el año de 1821, hasta el de 1856* (México, D.F.: Imprenta I. Cumplido, 1856), pp. 117, 132, and 171; and Manuel Dublan and José M. Lozano, comps., *Legislación mexicana,* vol. 1, pp. 694–97 and 710–37. On Tejas, see the volumes of Vito Alessio Robles, *Coahuila y Texas desde la consumación de la independencia hasta el Tratado de Paz de Guadalupe Hidalgo* (México, D.F.: 1945); and Carlos E. Castañeda, *Our Catholic Heritage in Texas, 1519–1936,* Vol. 6, *Transition Period: The Fight for Freedom, 1810–1836* (Austin: Von Boeckmann-Jones Company, Publishers, 1950; repr., New York: Arno Press, 1976). While there is a large literature concerning Tejas, it focuses upon the military events of the insurrection, or solely upon the political activities of the Anglo colonists, which are treated in a highly subjective manner. The political activities of Mexican Tejanos and their relations with the Anglo American colonists are much less explored.

5. See Carlos Bosch García, *Problemas diplomáticos del México independiente*

(México, D.F.: El Colegio de México, 1947); Romeo Flores Caballero, *La contrarevolución en la independencia* (México, D.F.: El Colegio de México, 1969). For some discussion of the significance and effects of U.S. economic extension in the far north, see María del Carmen Velázquez, *Establecimiento y pérdida del Septentrión de Nueva España* (México, D.F.: El Colegio de México, 1974); and Weber, *Mexican Frontier*, pp. 122–46.

6. See Adele Ogden, *The California Sea Otter Trade, 1748–1848* (Berkeley: University of California Press, 1941); and Ogden, "Hides and Tallow: Mc-Cullough, Hartnell and Company, 1822–1828," *California History* 8 (December 1929). Ogden's work contains considerable sociopolitical comment as well as economic information; see also the prejudiced Alfred Robinson, *Life in California* (Oakland: Biobooks, 1947, first printed in 1846); and Jessie Davies Francis, *An Economic and Social History of Mexican California, 1822–1846* (New York: Arno Press, 1976).

7. Max L. Moorhead, *New Mexico's Royal Road: Trade and Travel on the Chihuahua Trail* (Norman: University of Oklahoma Press, 1958); and David A. Sandoval, "Trade and 'Manito' Society in New Mexico" (Ph.D. diss., University of Utah, 1978).

8. Informative published sources for U.S. expansionism and the acquisition of Louisiana and Texas include: Phillip Coolidge Brooks, *Diplomacy and the Borderlands: The Adams-Onís Treaty of 1819*, University of California Publications in History, Vol. 24 (Berkeley: University of California Press, 1939); Thomas Maitland Marshall, *A History of the Western Boundary of the Louisiana Purchase, 1819–1941* (Berkeley: University of California Press, 1914); José Antonio Pichardo, *Pichardo's Treatise on the Limits of Louisiana and Texas*, trans. Charles Wilson Hackett, 2 vols. (Austin: University of Texas Press, 1931–1932); William C. Brinkley, *The Expansionist Movement in Texas, 1836–1850* (Berkeley: University of California Press, 1925); Robert V. Remini, *Andrew Jackson and the Course of American Empire, 1767–1821* (New York: Harper and Row, 1977); Frank Lawrence Owsley, Jr., *The Struggle for the Gulf: The Role of the Gulf States in the War of 1812* (Gainesville: University of Florida Press, 1977); Don E. Fehrenbacher, *The Era of Expansion, 1800–1848* (New York: John Wiley and Sons, 1969); Cesar Sepúlveda, *La frontera norte de México: Historia, conflictos, 1762–1983* (México, D.F.: Porrua, 1983); Ray Allen Billington, *Westward Expansion: A History of the American Frontier*, 4th ed. (New York: Macmillan, 1974); Ray Allen Billington, *The Far Western Frontier, 1830–1860* (New York: Harper and Row, 1956); Ferol Egan, *Frémont, Explorer for a Restless Nation: A New and Full Biography of John Charles Frémont, Spearhead of Manifest Destiny* (New York: Doubleday, 1977).

9. See Frederick Merk, *Manifest Destiny and Mission in American History* (New York: Alfred A. Knopf, 1963); Albert K. Weinberg, *Manifest Destiny: A Study of Nationalist Expansionism in American History* (Chicago: Quadrangle

Books, 1963); Gene M. Brack, *Mexico Views Manifest Destiny, 1821–1846: An Essay on the Origins of the Mexican War* (Albuquerque: University of New Mexico, 1975); David J. Weber, "'Scarce More than Apes': Historical Roots of Anglo-American Stereotypes of Mexicans," in David J. Weber, ed., *New Spain's Far Northern Frontier: Essays on Spain in the American West* (Albuquerque: University of New Mexico Press, 1979); Reginald Horsman, *La raza y el destino manifiesto* (México, D.F.: Fondo de Cultura Económica, 1985); and Norman A. Graebner, *Empire on the Pacific: A Study in American Continental Expansion* (New York: Ronald Press, 1955).

10. For political events, see José M. Tornel y Mendeval, *Breve reseña histórica de los acontecimientos mas notables de la nación mexicana desde el año de 1821 hasta nuestros días* (México, D.F.: Cumplido, 1852); Francisco de Paula Arrangoiz y Berzabal, *Mejico desde 1808 hasta 1867*, 4 vols. (Madrid: A. Pérez Dubrull, 1871–1872); and Luis Chávez Orozco, *Historia de México (1808–1836)* (México, D.F.: Editorial Patria, 1947). For background, see Catalina Sierra, *El nacimiento de México* (México, D.F.: Universidad Nacional Autónoma de México, 1960).

11. For legislative action, see Manuel Dublan and José M. Lozano, comps., *Legislación mexicana*, vols. 1–3; see also Edmundo O'Gorman, *Historia de las divisiones territoriales de México* (México, D.F.: Porrua, 1968); and Javier Ocampo, *Las ideas de un día el pueblo méxicano ante la consumación de su independencia* (México, D.F.: El Colegio de México, 1969). On the Mexican state between 1820 and 1854, see Stanley C. Green, *The Mexican Republic: The First Decade, 1823–1832* (Pittsburgh: University of Pittsburgh Press, 1987); and Michael P. Costeloe, *La primera república federal de México, 1824–1835* (México, D.F.: Fondo de Cultura Económica, 1975). For events in the far northern states, see Woodrow James Hansen, *The Search for Authority in California* (Oakland: Biobooks, 1960); and David J. Weber, chapter 1, "Viva La Independencia," in Weber, *Mexican Frontier.*

12. On liberalism and conservatism, see Jesús Reyes Heroles, *El liberalismo mexicano*, 3 vols. (México, D.F.: Universidad Nacional Autónoma de México, 1957); and Charles Hale, *Mexican Liberalism in the Age of Mora, 1821–1853* (New Haven: Yale University Press, 1968). For background as to origins, see Francisco López Cámara, *La génesis de la conciencia liberal en México* (México, D.F.: El Colegio de México, 1954).

13. Bancroft, *History of California, 1542–1890*, vol. 2, 1801–1824, pp. 194–219, 392–93, and 484; and Alfonso Trueba, *California, Tierra Perdida*, 2 vols. (México, D.F.: Editorial Jus, 1958). See also George Tays, "Revolutionary California" (Ph.D. diss., University of California, Los Angeles, 1932); Leonard Pitt, *The Decline of the Californios: A Social History of the Spanish Speaking Californians, 1846–1890* (Berkeley: University of California Press, 1966), chapter 1, "Halcyon Days: Mexican California, 1826–1845";

Hansen, *Search for Authority in California*; George L. Harding, *Don Agustín V. Zamarano* (Los Angeles: The Zamarano Club, 1934); Pío de Jesús Pico, *Narración Histórica*, trans. Arthur P. Botello, as *Don Pío Pico's Historical Narrative* (Glendale: Arthur H. Clark Company, 1973); George Tays, ed. and trans., "Pío Pico's Correspondence with the Mexican Government, 1846–1848," *California Historical Society Quarterly* 15 (November 1931); and Antonio Rios Bustamante, "Los Angeles, Pueblo and Region, 1781–1850: Continuity and Adaptation on the North Mexican Periphery" (Ph.D. diss., University of California, Los Angeles, 1985), which provides a critical, revised view of Los Angeles's early development. For the only biography, though incomplete, of a leading church figure and a few eschewed commentaries on church-related politics, see Francis J. Weber, *Francisco García Diego: California's Transition Bishop* (Los Angeles: Dawson's Book Shop, 1972). I am indebted to A. Rios Bustamante for materials on California.

14. Bancroft, *History of California*, vol. 2, pp. 451–452 and 457–469, and vol. 3, pp. 37–38.

15. David Hornbeck, "Land Tenure and Rancho Expansion in Alta California, 1784–1846," *Journal of Historical Cartography* 4 (1978); Rose Avina, *Spanish and Mexican Land Grants in California* (New York: Arno Press, 1976); and W. W. Robinson, *Land in California*, chapters 4 and 6 (Berkeley: University of California Press, 1949).

16. See Bancroft, *History of California*, vol. 2, chapters 13 and 19; and vol. 3, chapters 5 and 13; see also Jessie Davies Francis, "An Economic and Social History of Mexican California, 1822–1846" (Ph.D. diss., University of California, Berkeley, 1936).

17. Bancroft, *History of California*, vol. 2, p. 559; vol. 3, pp. 252–55 and 633–37; Vol. 4, p. 553. For realignments according to shifts in Mexico City, see Vol. 3, pp. 181–239 and 414–607; and George Tays, "Revolutionary California." A detailed secondary treatment of the political history of Mexican Alta California, Tays's work sought to evaluate the significance of periodic "revolutions" to the political process in Mexican California. His pious conclusion was that these movements were counterproductive and a waste of limited resources. For names, appointments, and capsule biographies of these officeholders, see Bancroft, "California Pioneer Register," *History of California*, vols. 2–5.

18. Bancroft, *History of California*, vol. 3, pp. 8–10, 301–38; see also Rios Bustamante, "Los Angeles, 1781–1850."

19. For the legislative action pertinent to California, see Dublan Lozano, *Legislación mexicana*, vol. 2, pp. 546–49. Significant published sources concerning the land grants and secularization of the missions in Alta California include: José Figueroa, *Manifesto a la república mexicana*, ed. and trans. C. Alan Hutchinson, with facsimile of original Spanish, as *A Manifesto to the*

Mexican Republic (Berkeley: University of California Press, 1978); Robinson, Land in California; Robert H. Becker, Diseños of California Ranchos: Maps of Thirty-seven Land Grants, 1822–1846 (San Francisco: Book Club of California, 1964); Robert H. Becker, Designs of the Land Diseños of California Ranchos (San Francisco: Book Club of California, 1969); C. Alan Hutchinson, Frontier Settlement in Mexican California (New Haven: Yale University Press, 1969); Bancroft, History of California, vol. 3, pp. 301–38 and 339–62, chapters 9, "Missions and Secularization, 1831–1833" and 12, "Mission and Indian Affairs"; Warren A. Beck and Ynez D. Haase, Historical Atlas of California (Norman: University of Oklahoma Press, 1975); and Manuel P. Servin, "The Secularization of the California Missions: A Reappraisal," Southern California Quarterly 47 (June 1965). An important but polemical source is Zephyrin Englehardt, The Missions and Missionaries of California, 4 vols. (San Francisco: James H. Barry Company, 1915).

20. Bancroft, History of California, vol. 3, pp. 181–215.

21. Ibid., pp. 636–637.

22. C. Alan Hutchinson, "General José Figueroa's Career in Mexico, 1792–1832," New Mexico Historical Review 48 (October 1973).

23. Hutchinson, Frontier Settlement in Mexican California.

24. Figueroa, Manifesto; for the quotes, see the closing section, pp. 95–97.

25. See Lic. D. José Agustín de Escudero, ed., "Noticias historicas y estadísticas del Nuevo México, presentadas por su diputado en Cortés D. Pedro Bautista Pino, en Cadiz el año de 1812. Adicionadas por el Lic. D. Antonio Barreiro en 1839 y ultimamente anotadas por el Lic. D. José Agustín de Escudero, para la Comisión de Estadística Militar de la República Mexicana," in Enrique Florescano y Isabel Gil Sánchez, eds., Descripciones económicas regionales de Nueva España: Provincias del Norte, 1790–1814 (México, D.F.: Secretaría de Educación Pública/Instituto Nacional de Antropología e Historia, 1976), pp. 201–318, particularly 263–72; see also Bloom, "New Mexico," pp. 28–30.

26. Read, Illustrated History, pp. 361–93; Marc Simmons, Spanish Government in New Mexico (Albuquerque: University of New Mexico Press, 1968), pp. 8–24; and for a brief summary of developments in governance see Lansing B. Bloom, "Beginnings of Representative Government in New Mexico," New Mexico Historical Review 21 (April 1946).

27. David J. Weber, "An Unforgettable Day: Facundo Melgares on Independence," New Mexico Historical Review 48 (January 1973), pp. 27–44.

28. Lansing B. Bloom, "New Mexico" pp. 166–75; Read, Illustrated History, pp. 361–65. Apparently, procedures followed the stipulations of 1812 and 1820. For conditions in Santa Fe, see Charlotte Marie Nelson Parraga, "Santa Fe de Nuevo México: A Study of a Frontier City based on an Anno-

tated Translation of Selected Documents (1825–1832) from the Mexican Archives" (Ph.D. diss., Ball State University, 1976).

29. Weber, *Mexican Frontier*, pp. 19–20 and 25; Twitchell, *Leading Facts*, vol. 2, pp. 1–2. For the activity of the vicar, see Connie Cortazar, "The Santa Visita of Agustín Fernández de San Vicente to New Mexico," *New Mexico Historical Review* 59 (January 1984).

30. Marc Simmons, *Albuquerque: A Narrative History* (Albuquerque: University of New Mexico Press, 1982), pp. 132–42.

31. Ibid. See also Moorhead, *New Mexico's Royal Road;* and Weber, *Mexican Frontier*, pp. 122–46. See also Alex David Sandoval, "Trade and the 'Manito' Society in New Mexico"; and, in contrast, Robert Luther Duffus, *The Santa Fe Trail* (London: Longmans, Green and Company, 1930).

32. Daniel Tyler, "New Mexico in the 1820's: The First Administration of Manuel Armijo," (Ph.D. diss., University of New Mexico, Albuquerque, 1970).

33. For a view of circumstances and problems, see Father Martínez's statement in David J. Weber, ed., "El Gobierno Territorial de Nuevo México—La Exposición del Padre Martínez de 1831," *Historia Mexicana* 25 (Octubre–Diciembre 1975); Janet Lecompte, *Rebellion in Río Arriba, 1837* (Albuquerque: University of New Mexico Press, 1985), pp. 9–11; also Twitchell, *Leading Facts*, pp. 27–50; Bloom, "New Mexico" pp. 348–51; and Philip Reno, "Rebellion in New Mexico—1837," *New Mexico Historical Review* 40 (July 1965).

34. Martin González de la Vara, "La política del federalismo en Nuevo México," *Historia Mexicana* 36 (Julio–Septiembre 1986); Daniel Tyler, "New Mexico in the 1820's," pp. 38–42; and Weber, *Mexican Frontier*, p. 28.

35. Castañeda, *Our Catholic Heritage in Texas*, vol. 6, pp. 1–174, 186–222; Charles A. Bacarisse, "The Union of Coahuila and Texas," *Southwestern Historical Quarterly* 61 (January 1958); Hubert Howe Bancroft, *History of the North Mexican States and Texas*, 2 vols. (San Francisco: A. L. Bancroft, 1884–1889), vol. 2 1801–1889; and Margaret Swett Henson, "Hispanic Texas, 1519–1836," in Donald W. Whisenhunt, ed., *Texas: A Sesquicentennial Celebration* (Austin: Eakin Press, 1984); see also Jesús de la Tejada and John Wheat, "Bexar: Profile of a Tejano Community, 1820–1832," *Southwestern Historical Quarterly* 89 (July 1985).

36. Castañeda, *Our Catholic Heritage in Texas*, vol. 6, pp. 90, 193, 196, and 222–23; and Nettie Lee Benson, "La elección de José Miguel Ramos Arizpe a las Cortés de Cádiz in 1810," *Historia Mexicana* 33 (Abril–Junio 1984).

37. Charles A. Bacarisse, "Union of Coahuila and Texas"; and Castañeda, *Our Catholic Heritage in Texas*, vol. 6, pp. 223–24.

38. Castañeda, *Our Catholic Heritage in Texas*, vol. 6, pp. 191–93. On

Anglos, Texas, and S. Austin, see Eugene C. Barker, *Mexico and Texas, 1821–1835* (New York: Russell and Russell, 1965); and Eugene C. Barker, *Life of Stephen F. Austin* (Nashville and Dallas: Cokesburg Press, 1925); and Gerald Ashford, "Jacksonian Liberalism and Spanish Law in Early Texas," *Southwestern Historical Quarterly* 57 (July 1953).

In 1820, Moses Austin, an Anglo merchant from Philadelphia with U.S. citizenship and a resident of Louisiana, as well as a one-time Spanish subject, had petitioned the Spanish authorities in Mexico City for a large grant of land in Tejas, in return for which he promised to bring loyal colonists. Austin secured a grant from the viceroy of Nueva España, but died on his return to the United States. The colonization project was continued by his son, Stephen Austin, who journeyed to Texas and Mexico to have the grant confirmed by the Spanish authorities. In August of 1821, Austin, presumably a Spanish citizen, secured recognition of his concession from the last Spanish governor of Texas, and made preparations for occupation of the land. Upon Mexican independence in 1821, Mexican authorities refused to recognize the validity of the royal grant made to Austin. Journeying to Mexico City in April 1822, Austin, a shrewd businessman and politician, found that a committee on colonization had been established to formulate legislation for a settlement policy. By changing citizenship and lobbying the members of the committee, Austin astutely worked for a favorable decision on his claims. On January 4, 1823, the Junta Instituyente passed a colonization law establishing the *empresario* system. Under the provisions, empresarios were to receive three haciendas and two labores of land for every two hundred settlers they introduced to Texas. A hacienda consisted of 25,000 square *varas* or 22,195 acres; while a labor was equal to 1,000 square *varas*, or 887.8 acres. On April 11, 1823, the Mexican Congress passed a special act approving the Austin grant, which was the first of many empresario grants to foreigners in Texas. This program was a major cause of the subsequent loss of the area to the United States.

39. Charles H. Harris, *A Mexican Family Empire: The Latifundio of the Sánchez Navarro Family, 1765–1867* (Austin: University of Texas Press, 1975), pp. 271–306.

40. For Anglo incursions and conflicts, see Castañeda, *Our Catholic Heritage in Texas*, vol. 6, pp. 160–62; and T. R. Fehrenbach, *Lone Star: A History of Texas and Texans* (New York: Macmillan, 1968), pp. 110–51; and the informative chronology in Gaston García Cantú, *Las invasiones norteamericanas en México* (México, D.F.: ERA, 1971), pp. 125–62.

41. Castañeda, *Our Catholic Heritage in Texas*, vol. 6, pp. 199–201 and 202–34; Fehrenbach, *Lone Star*, pp. 132–51; and Weber, *Mexican Frontier*, pp. 158–78.

42. Castañeda, *Our Catholic Heritage in Texas*, vol. 6, pp. 205–12, 213–

14, and 235–36; and Allaine Howren, "Causes and Origins of the Decree of April 6, 1830," *Southwestern Historical Quarterly* 16 (April 1913). See also Weber, *Mexican Frontier*, pp. 166–78.

43. This first quote from Mier y Terán is in Mier y Terán to Guadalupe Victoria, Nacogdoches, June 30, 1828, found in Howren, "Causes and Origins," pp. 395–98. The second quote is in Ohland Morton, *Teran and Texas: A Chapter in Texas–Mexican Relations* (Austin: Texas State Historical Association, 1948), pp. 99–101; for another inspection report a few years later, see Helen Willits Harris, "Almonte's Inspection of Texas in 1834," *Southwestern Historical Quarterly* 41 (January 1938).

44. See Juan Nepomuceno Seguín, *The Personal Memoirs of John N. Seguin, From the Year 1834 in the Retreat of General Woll from the City of San Antonio, 1842* (San Antonio: Ledger Book and Job Office, 1858).

45. Carlos E. Castañeda, *Our Catholic Heritage in Texas*, vol. 6, pp. 206–10; Bancroft, *History of the North Mexican States and Texas*, vol. 2, pp. 115–215.

46. For events between 1832 and 1835, see Castañeda, *Our Catholic Heritage in Texas*, vol. 6, pp. 251–86; Fehrenbach, *Lone Star*, pp. 174–89.

47. David J. Weber, ed., *Troubles in Texas, 1832: A Tejano Viewpoint from San Antonio with a Translation and a Facsimile*, trans. Conchita Hassell Winn and David J. Weber, of *Representación Dirijida por el Ilustre Ayuntamiento de la Ciudad de Bexar al Honorable Congeso del Estado* (Brazoria: D. W. Anthony, 1833; Dallas: Southern Methodist University Press, 1983). For an examination of sentiments see James Ernest Crisp "Anglo-Texan Attitudes Toward the Mexican, 1821–1845" (Ph.D. diss., Yale University Press, New Haven, 1976).

48. For a critical view of the campaign from the Mexican side, see Enrique de la Peña, *With Santa Anna in Texas: A Personal Narrative of the Revolution*, trans. and ed. Carmen Perry (College Station: Texas A&M University Press, 1975); and Vicente Filosola, *Memorias para la historia de la guerra de Tejas*, 2 vols. (repr., México, D.F.: Editoria Nacional, 1968); see also Castañeda, *Our Catholic Heritage in Texas*, vol. 6, pp. 258–306. For a critical view of both sides see Jeff Long, *Duel of Eagles: The Mexican and U.S. Fight for the Alamo* (New York: Morrow, 1990).

49. For impressions of several individuals, see Carlos E. Castañeda, ed., *The Mexican Side of Texas Revolution* (New York: Arno Press, 1976). This work contains translations of the accounts published by the Mexican military commanders of the 1836 military campaign, including one by Antonio López de Santa Anna. See also Castañeda, *Our Catholic Heritage in Texas*, vol. 6, pp. 271–306.

50. Seguín, *Personal Memoirs*; David J. Weber, ed., *Foreigners in Their Native Land, Historical Roots of the Mexican American* (Albuquerque: The University of New Mexico Press, 1973), pp. 92–93; and see, for others like him, Joseph Martin Dawson, *José Antonio Navarro: Co-Creator of Texas* (Waco:

Baylor University Press, 1969); Raymond Estep, "Lorenzo de Zavala and the Texas Revolution," *Southwestern Historical Quarterly* 57 (January 1954); and Rubén Rendon Lozano, *Viva Tejas: The Story of the Mexican-born Patriots of the Republic* (San Antonio and Houston: Southern Literary Institute, 1936); and Cecil Robinson, "Flag of Illusion: The Texas Revolution Viewed as a Conflict of Cultures," *American West* 5 (May 1968). For changes and adaption among Mexicans, see Tijerina, "Tejanos and Texas." For details of continuing conflict, see John Milton Nance, *After San Jacinto: The Texas Mexican Frontier 1836–1841* (Austin: University of Texas Press, 1963); and John Milton Nance, *Attack and Counterattack: The Texas Mexican Frontier, 1842* (Austin: University of Texas, 1964); Noel M. Loomis, *The Texan–Santa Fe Pioneers* (Norman: University of Oklahoma Press, 1958); the excellent Josefina Z. Vásquez, "La supuesta República del Río Grande," *Historia Mexicana* 36 (1986); David M. Vigness, "The Republic of the Rio Grande: An Example of Separatism in North Mexico" (Ph.D. diss., University of Texas, Austin, 1951); and Jerry Don Thompson, *The Republic of the Rio Grande* (Laredo: Laredo Junior College, 1985). For events in San Antonio, see Ray F. Broussard, *San Antonio during the Texas Republic: A City in Transition* (El Paso: Texas Western Press, 1967); and for aspects of the literature on events, see Arnoldo De León, "Tejanos and the Texas War for Independence: Historiography's Judgement," *New Mexico Historical Review* 61 (April 1986). For impact on Mexico see Manuel Urlsina, "The Impact of the Texas Revolution on the Government, Politics, and Society of Mexico, 1836–1846" (Ph.D. diss., University of Texas, Austin, 1976).

51. *Colección de leyes fundamentales*, p. 132; and Dublan and Lozano, *Legislación mexicana*, vol. 3, pp. 230–54.

52. For an overview of views on the Indian question, see Moisés González Navarro, "Institutiones indígenas en México independiente," in *Métodos y resultados de la política indigenista en México* (México, D.F.: 1954); Paul H. Ezell, "Indians under the Law: Mexico 1821–1847," *América indígena* 15 (July 1955); and Carlos J. Sierra, *Los indios de la frontera* (México, D.F.: Ediciones de la Muralla, 1980). For New Mexico, see the following by Antonio José Martínez, "Exposición que el presbítero," "Cura de Taos de Nuevo México . . . ," and "Proponiendo la civilización de las naciones bárbaras . . . ," in Weber, *Northern Mexico*; and the overview in Roxanne Dunbar, "Land Tenure in Northern New Mexico: An Historical Perspective," (Ph.D. diss., UCLA, 1974). Dunbar traces the succession of historical processes in New Mexico land-tenure development and the rise of an entrepreneurial class within the context of mestizo–Indian relations. For developments in Texas, see Frank D. Reeve, "The Apache Indians in Texas," *The Southwestern Historical Quarterly* 50 (October 1946); and LeRoy P. Graf, "Colonizing Projects in Texas South of

the Nueces, 1820–1845," *The Southwestern Historical Quarterly* 50 (April 1947). For trade impact, see Sister Mary Loyola, "The American Occupation of New Mexico, 1821–1852," *New Mexico Historical Review* 14 (January, April, and July 1939), pp. 34–75, 143–99, and 230–86, respectively. Sister Mary Loyola, in the January issue, discusses the importance of the Santa Fe trade and the consequences of its disruption on the economy of the Navajos, Apaches, Utes, Kiowas, and Comanches. See also Max L. Moorhead, "The Significance of the Santa Fe Trade," in Richard N. Ellis, ed., *New Mexico, Past and Present* (Albuquerque: University of New Mexico Press, 1971), pp. 104–13; and Ralph A. Smith, "Indians in American–Mexican Relations before the War of 1846," *Hispanic American Historical Review* 43 (February 1963); and David J. Weber, "American Westward Expansion and the Breakdown of Relations between Pobladores and 'Indios Bárbaros' on Mexico's Far Northern Frontier, 1821–1846," *New Mexico Historical Review* 56 (July 1981). For California, see George Harwood Philips, *Chiefs and Challengers: Indian Resistance and Cooperation in Southern California* (Berkeley: University of California Press, 1975); and Doug Monroy, *Thrown Among Strangers: The Making of Mexican Culture in Frontier California* (Berkeley: University of California Press, 1990). For an overview of the Southwest, see Edward H. Spicer, *Cycles of Conquest: The Impact of Spain, Mexico and the United States on the Indians of the Southwest, 1533–1960* (Tucson: University of Arizona, 1962). I thank Mike Fraga for insight and information on Indian relations.

53. D. W. Meining, *Three People in Geographical Change, 1800–1970* (Oxford: Oxford University Press, 1971), p. 40. For Apaches, see John Upton Terrel, *Apache Chronicle* (New York: World Publishing, 1972).

54. William M. Malloy, et al., eds., *Treaties, Conventions, International Acts, Protocols and Agreements between the United States of America and Other Powers, 1776–1909* (Washington: U.S. Government Printing Office, 1910), vol. 1, pp. 1095–96.

55. See José Francisco Ruiz, *Report on the Indian Tribes of Texas in 1828* (New Haven: Yale University Press, 1972); David M. Vigness, "Indian Raids in the Lower Rio Grande, 1836–1837," *Southwest Historical Quarterly* 59 (July 1955); Isidro Vizcaya Canales, *La invasión de los indios bárbaros al noreste de México* (Monterrey: Instituto Tecnológico y de Estudios Superiores, 1968); and Ralph A. Smith, "Indians in American Mexican Relations before the War of 1846," *Hispanic American Historical Review* 43 (February 1963).

56. Graf, "Colonizing Projects in Texas," p. 447; Reeve, "Apache Indians in Texas," pp. 200–204; Robert A. Trennert, *Alternative to Extinction* (Philadelphia: Temple University, 1975), pp. 61–63; Spicer, *Cycles of Conquest*, pp. 39–40 and 245; and Smith, "Indians in American–Mexican Relations," pp. 42–54.

57. For figures on depredation, see Spicer, *Cycles of Conquest*, p. 240 and 244–45. For a brief list of Indian hostilities in the area during the Mexican period, see Hubert H. Bancroft, *History of Arizona and New Mexico, 1530–1888* (San Francisco: The History Company, 1889), pp. 315–16; for aspects of conflict, see Sister Mary Loyola, "American Occupation of New Mexico," pp. 34–75; Alvin R. Sunrise, "The Indian Slave Trade in New Mexico, 1846–1861," *The Indian Historian* 6, (Fall 1973), pp. 20–22; Frank McNitt, *Navajo Wars: Military Campaigns, Slave Raids, and Reprisals* (reprint, Albuquerque: University of New Mexico, 1990), chapter 4; Edward H. Spicer, *Cycles of Conquest*, pp. 214–15 and 244–45. According to Spicer:

> The raiding which they carried on against the Pueblo and Mexican villages was not a widely organized activity and rarely involved more than a few such groups on any occasion. The making of a raid depended on the food needs of the various communities. The objectives were food, material goods, and captives to sell or use as slaves. The killing of Pueblos or Mexicans, except in some instances of revenge, was entirely incidental to acquiring goods and animals. (p. 215).

58. On Yaquis and Yuman, see Bancroft, *History of Arizona and New Mexico*, pp. 399–407; Spicer, *Cycles of Conquest*, pp. 240–41; also, see Spicer, *Cycles of Conquest*, chapters 2, 3, and 5; Jack D. Forbes, "Nationalism, Tribalism, and Self-determination: Yuman–Mexican Relations, 1821–1848," *The Indian Historian* 6 (Spring 1973), p. 21; and Robert A. Hackenburg, *Aboriginal Land Use and Occupancy of the Papago Indians* (New York: Garland Publishing, 1974, initially published by the Indian Claims Commission, 1964); for the spread of activities, see the narrative and quoted documents, Bloom, "New Mexico" pp. 348–368; and Twitchell, *Leading Facts*, vol. 2, pp. 69–82.

59. Lecompte, *Rebellion in Rio Arriba;* see also Bloom, "New Mexico," part 2, *Old Santa Fe* 2 (July 1914), pp. 3–46; Phillip Reno, "Rebellion in New Mexico"; and Read, *Illustrated History*, pp. 370–93.

60. For this statement on education, see Twitchell, *Leading Facts*, vol. 2, pp. 57–59.

61. The Plan de Tomé is in Read, *Illustrated History*, pp. 378–80.

62. The *décima* on events is in Rafael Chacón, *Legacy of Honor: The Life of Rafael Chacón, A Nineteenth-Century New Mexican*, ed. Jacqueline Dorgan Meketa (Albuquerque: University of New Mexico Press, 1986), appendix 1, pp. 343–44; also, see Fray Angélico Chávez, "José Gonzales: Genizaro Governor," *New Mexico Historical Review* 30 (July 1955).

63. Janet Lecompte, "Manuel Armijo's Family History," *New Mexico Historical Review* 48 (July 1973); Lecompte, *Rebellion in Rio Arriba*, pp. 59–63, 61, 79, and 89; Bloom, "New Mexico" pp. 123–60. which reports on Armijo's actions.

64. The *décima* on Cook is in Chacón, *Legacy of Honor* appendix 1, p. 341.

65. Bloom, "New Mexico," pp. 351–80. See also the documents in E. Bennett Burton, "The Taos Rebellion," *Old Santa Fe* (1913–1914), pp. 175–200; Arnold L. Rodríguez, "New Mexico in Transition," *New Mexico Historical Review* (July 1949).

66. For reports on and consequences of this subject, see Bancroft, *History of California*, vol. 3, pp. 420 and 521; for turnovers in administration see pp. 414–77 and 636–37. See also Trueba, *California, Tierra Perdida*, vol. 2, pp. 87–139. For Indian conflicts, see Marian Lydia Lathrop, "Mariano Guadalupe Vallejo, Defender of the Northern Frontier of California" (Ph.D. diss., University of California, Berkeley, 1921); and Marian Lydia Lathrop, "The Indian Campaigns of General M. G. Vallejo," *Quarterly of the Society of California Pioneers* 9 (September 1932).

67. Bancroft, *History of California*, vol. 3, pp. 545–78; 636–37.

68. Ibid., vol. 4, pp. 281–97, 298–329, 401–20, 455–517.

69. See Nellie Van de Grift Sánchez, *Spanish Arcadia* (San Francisco: Powell Publishing, 1929), pp. 99–101. A notable event of 1842 was the latest discovery of gold by a vaquero named Francisco López in Placeritas Canyon, near the San Fernando Valley. While tracking stray cattle, López had stopped to pick a wild onion, only to discover a small nugget of gold caught in the onion's roots. Though the amount of gold was limited, the find briefly attracted several hundred men from as far away as Sonora and New Mexico. In 1845, one visitor to the area observed about 30 *gambusinos* (prospectors), mainly New Mexicans, working the area and sifting small findings. This discovery preceded that by John Marshall at Sutter's Mill in Sonoma in 1848, but was itself preceded by other minor discoveries along the Alta California coast, all of which failed to attract much attention because of the limited quantity of the precious metal.

70. Bancroft, *History of California*, vol. 4, pp. 513–45.

71. Pitt, *Decline of the Californios*, pp. 23, 27–30, 43, 46, and 278.

72. For documents, reports, and correspondence, see Carlos E. Cortés, ed., *The United States Conquest of California* (New York: Arno Press, 1976); Ralph E. Twitchell, *The History of the Military Occupation of the Territory of New Mexico from 1846 to 1851* (Denver: Smith-Brooks Company, 1909); and Phillip St. George Cooke, *The Conquest of New Mexico and California* (New York: G. P. Putnam and Sons, 1978).

73. Bloom, "New Mexico," pp. 366–71, 371–80; Burton, "Taos Rebellion," pp. 175–200; and Angela Moyano, "La Resistencia en Nuevo México," *Aztlán* 15 (Fall 1984).

74. For events, see Bancroft, *History of California*, vol. 5; and Trueba, *California, Tierra Perdida*, vol. 2, for a caustic and fervid summary of events, pp. 138–96.

75. Bancroft, *History of California*, vol. 5, pp. 101–90. For U.S. actions,

452 Notes to pages 172–75

see Neal Harlow, *California Conquered: War and Peace on the Pacific, 1846–1850* (Berkeley: University of California Press, 1982).

76. Tays, "Pío Pico's Correspondence," *California Historical Quarterly* 13 (June 1934). For concurrent U.S. actions, see Bancroft, *History of California*, vol. 5, pp. 267–68, 275–79, and 281–82.

77. "Pronunciamiento de Varela y otros Californios contra los Americanos, 24 de Set. 1846," manuscript, Bancroft Library, Berkeley, University of California. For the quote, see Bancroft, *History of California*, vol. 5, p. 310, and for the actions of Captain Archibald Gillespie, see ibid., pp. 305–6. After intimidating *angelinos*, Stockton left a well-armed garrison of fifty U.S. marines, under Captain Archibald Gillespie, to occupy Los Angeles. At about the same time, other naval and marine units were occupying Santa Barbara and San Diego. Gillespie and his men mistreated some of the people of Los Angeles and placed several citizens under arrest.

78. Informative accounts and assessments published in English of Mexican resistance in Alta California are the following: Pico, *Don Pío Pico's Historical Narrative*; Benjamin D. Wilson, "The Narrative of Benjamin D. Wilson," in Robert Glass Cleland, ed., *California Pathfinders* (Los Angeles: Powell Publishing Company, 1929), pp. 371–416; José del Carmen Lugo, "Life of a Rancher," *Southern California Quarterly* 32 (September 1950); Tays, "Pío Pico's Correspondence," *California Historical Quarterly* 13 (June 1934); Tays, "Revolutionary California," Bancroft, *History of California*, vol. 5; Arthur Woodward, *Lances at San Pasqual* (San Francisco: California Historical Society, 1948); Harlow, *California Conquered*; Karl Jack Bauer, *The Mexican War, 1846–1848* (New York: Macmillan, 1974), chapters 9 and 10, pp. 146–200; Dorothy F. Regency, *The Battle of Santa Clara* (San José: Smith and McKay Printing Company, 1978).

79. Jose del Carmen Lugo, "Vida de un Ranchero," manuscript 34, Bancroft Library, Berkeley: University of California; also, see Bancroft, *History of California*, vol. 5, pp. 311–15.

80. For these incidents, see Bancroft, *History of California*, vol. 5, p. 318.

81. Bancroft, *History of California*, vol. 5, pp. 253–312.

82. José Antonio Carrillo, "Acción de San Pedro contra los Americanos, 8 de. Oct. 1846," manuscript. Bancroft stated that an official Mexican report of the October 6, 1946, battle was printed in the Sonoran periodical *El Sonorense*, 8 de enero de 1847. Mexican authorities were informed by occasional couriers on developments in Alta California. Antonio F. Coronel mentions acting as an official commissioner to the authorities in Sonora, but he turned back because his route was intersected by U.S. troops from New Mexico. Antonio F. Coronel, "Cosas de California," manuscript, Bancroft Library, University of California, Berkeley. See Bancroft, *History of California*, vol. 5, pp. 319–20; also Bauer, *Mexican War*, pp. 185–86; and Benjamin D. Wilson,

"Observations of Early Days," manuscript, pp. 85–88, Bancroft Library, University of California, Berkeley. Wilson provides accounts of several encounters as viewed from the californio side. Wilson was the husband of Ramona Yorba and a grandfather of General George Patton. See also Bancroft, *History of California*, vol. 5, pp. 322–25. To mislead the North Americans, Carrillo adopted the tactics of "displaying his men on the march along the hills in such a way that each man could be several times counted. He also caused large droves of riderless horses to raise clouds of dust in the distance." The tactics may have been a success, for in early November, U.S. forces were reconcentrated.

83. Andrés Pico, 6 de Dec., manuscript, Janssens, Documents Manuscript, pp. 45–56, Bancroft Library, University of California, Berkeley; Coronel, "Cosas de California," pp. 115–19; Narcisco Botello, "Anales del sur de la California," manuscript, pp. 154–56, Bancroft Library, University of California, Berkeley. See also Bancroft, *History of California*, vol. 5, pp. 334–54. Kearney later claimed victory on the basis that he had remained in possession of the field of battle. This rationalization, however, was unconvincing as it was known that his men were surrounded and did not move until the arrival of the reinforcements.

84. Bancroft, *History of California*, vol. 5, pp. 385–86 and 385–92. In each encounter, about five hundred californios faced a larger number of troops under Stockton. The californios charged, but stopped their charges prior to coming within range of the Anglo American weaponry. The Mexican lancers had no weapons with sufficient range to avoid a massacre.

85. Coronel, "Cosas de California," pp. 120–23; Botello, "Anales del sur," pp. 156–57; and also, see Bancroft, *History of California*, vol. 5, pp. 392–99, 404–7.

86. Ramón Alcaraz, et al., *Apuntes para la historia de la guerra entre México y los Estados Unidos* (México: Tipografiá de Manuel Payno, Hijo, 1848), p. 361. For a judgemental view of resistance activists in Texas read R. W. Johannsen, *To the Halls of the Montezumas* (Oxford: Oxford University Press, 1985), p. 24.

87. On Indian relations involved in the war, see Smith, "Indians in American–Mexican Relations" and "The Scalp Hunter in Chihuahua," *New Mexico Historical Review* (April 1965); Weber, "American Western Expansion"; and Ward Alan Minge, "Frontier Problems in New Mexico Preceding the Mexican War, 1840–1846," *New Mexico Historical Review* 51 (April 1976).

88. On Apaches, see Donald E. Worcester, "Apaches in the History of the Southwest," *New Mexico Historical Review* 50 (January 1975); Reeve, "Apache Indians in Texas"; Trennert, *Alternative to Extinction*, pp. 63–68. For earlier relations, see Max L. Moorhead, *The Apache Frontier, 1769–1791* (Norman: University of Oklahoma, 1968).

89. On Arizona's Sonora area, see Bernard L. Fontana, *The Papago Tribe of Arizona, United States of America* (New York: Garland Publishing, 1974;

initially published by the Indian Claims Commission, n.d.), p. 27; Hackenburg, *Aboriginal Land Use and Company;* and Bancroft, *History of Arizona and New Mexico,* pp. 474–75.

90. On the Texas border, see Trennert, *Alternative to Extinction,* p. 68. As he comments:

> Because the War Department could not maintain sufficient force on the Texas frontier during the Mexican War, Texans wanted the Rangers subsidized by the federal government and sent after the Indians. This proposal coincided with the desire to eliminate Mexican nationals from Texas soil. Mexican agents were generally believed to be among the tribes encouraging depredations and spreading stories that Texans intended to steal tribal lands and exterminate the Indians. Texans thus saw a chance of killing two birds with one stone—the Rangers promised to stop Indian depredations and limit the activities of Mexicans.

91. As described by David A. Cossío,

> Al mismo tiempo que Mejia se preparaba de la mejor manera posible para defender la ciudad de Monterrey contra el ataque de los invasores norteamericanos, los indios bárbaros, aprovechandose de la intranquilidad y desorientación reinantes, atacaban á hacendados y arrieros, siempre que hallaban ocasión, aumentando las preocupaciones del gobierno. La leva se . . . poniá trabas constantes para conseguir elementos, viendose en los pueblos del Departamento comunmente imposibilitados los habitantes de venir á Monterrey á tomar las armas contra los invasores por tener que abandonar a sus familias, sin defensa alguna sus hogares, expuestos á las incursiones de los bárbaros y a los desmanes de la soldadesca invasora. (*Historia de Nuevo León* [Monterrey: Consejo de Educación Pública, 1928], pp. 166–67)

92. Bancroft, *History of Arizona and New Mexico,* pp. 414–17; McNitt, *Navajo Wars,* pp. 90–97; Sister Mary Loyola, "American Occupation of New Mexico," pp. 143–45; Spicer, *Cycles of Conquest,* pp. 214 and 245; Ward Alan Minge, "Frontier Problems in New Mexico"; and Daniel Tyler, "Mexican Indian Policy in New Mexico," *New Mexico Historical Review* 55 (April 1980).

93. Kearney's statement is reprinted in Trennert, *Alternative to Extinction,* p. 97; repr. in Averam B. Bender, *A Study of the Mescalero Apache Indians, 1846–1880* (New York: Garland Publishing, 1974), p. 9. Reportedly one Mescalero leader declared to Kearny:

> "You have taken New Mexico and will soon take California, go then, and take Chihuahua, Durango, and Sonora. We will help you . . . (the) Mexicans are rascals; we hate and will kill them all." (Bender, *Study,* p. 9)

94. Bancroft, *History of Arizona and New Mexico,* p. 422; and McNitt, *Navajo Wars,* p. 118.

95. Bender, *Study,* pp. 13–14; Trennert, *Alternative to Extinction,* pp. 99–102; McNitt, *Navajo Wars,* pp. 102–3 and 118; Bancroft, *History of Arizona*

and New Mexico, p. 422; Joseph P. Peters, ed., *Indian Battles and Skirmishes on the American Frontier, 1790–1898* (Washington, D.C.: Historical Section, Army War College, 1925), p. 33 of appended compilation; McNitt, *Navajo Wars*, pp. 102–3 and 119–20; Sunrise, "Indian Slave Trade," pp. 20–22; see also Lynn Robin Bailey, *Indian Slave Trade in the Southwest* (Los Angeles: Western Lore Press, 1966). Spicer, *Cycles of Conquest*, p. 216; Ralph E. Twitchell, "Conquest of New Mexico," in Ellis, *New Mexico*, pp. 114–21; and Bancroft, *History of Arizona and New Mexico*, pp. 474–75.

96. Bancroft, *History of Arizona and New Mexico*, pp. 438–39; and Spicer, *Cycles of Conquest*, p. 245. For an assertion in reference to U.S. vulnerability, see Trennert, *Alternative to Extinction*, pp. 104–5:

> At Santa Fe and in the settlements generally for six months after the revolt, the state of affairs was far from satisfactory, worse in every respect than before. For a time, indeed, a greater degree of vigilance and discipline was observed; but the former, with its accompaniments of severe punishments, habitual distrust, and oppressive regulations, rapidly destroyed the confidence and friendliness before shown by large portions of the native population; while the latter soon became relaxed, and the soldiers more turbulent and unmanageable than ever. The New Mexicans were regarded as at heart deadly foes, and were treated accordingly. Sickness continued its ravages; supplies were still obtained with difficulty; the Indians constantly attacked the caravans on the plains; Navajo raids on the settlements never ceased, there being some reason to believe that they were not discouraged by the Americans so long as directed against the natives; and the situation was still further complicated by disagreements between military and civil authorities, and by serious dissensions among military officers, there being much dissatisfaction with Colonel Price's management.

97. For an analysis of the opinion expressed on the war and its relation to later U.S. history, see Robert W. Johannsen, *To the Halls of the Montezumas: The Mexican War in the American Imagination* (New York: Oxford University Press, 1985). For an excellent examination as to the significance of the war in Mexican political discourse, see the lead article in Josefina Vásquez, *Mexicanos y norteamericanos ante la guerra del '47* (México, D.F.: Sep/Setentas, 1972); Jesús Velasco Márquez, *La Guerra del 47 y la opinión pública, 1845–1848* (México, D.F.: Sep/Setentas, 1975); and Charles A. Hale, "La guerra con Estados Unidos y la crisis del pensamiento mexicano," *Secuencia* vol. 16 (1990).

98. On the U.S.–Mexico war origins, process, and results, see from the Mexican side the direct observations: Carlos María de Bustamante, *Historia de la invasión de los anglo-americanos* (México, D.F.: Secretaría de Educación Pública, 1949); José María Roa Barcena, *Recuerdos de la invasión norte americana (1846–1848)*, (México, D.F.: Editorial Porrua, 1947), pp. 25–37; Al-

caraz, *Apuntes;* and Albert C. Ramsey, ed. and trans., *The Other Side, or Notes for the History of the War between Mexico and the United States* (repr., New York: Burt Franklin, 1970). For an excellent critical account of Slidell's mission, see Dennis Eugene Berge, "Mexican Response to United States Expansion, 1841–1848" (Ph.D. diss., University of California, 1965).

99. For the U.S. side, see J. D. Richardson, *A Compilation of the Messages and Papers of the Presidents,* 10 vols. (Washington, D.C., 1905), vol. 4, pp. 428–42; Winfield Scott, *Memoirs of Lieut.-General Scott,* vol. 2 (New York: Sheldon, 1864); Samuel E. Chamberlain, *My Confessions* (New York: Harper and Row, 1956); Abiel Abbott Livermore, *The War with Mexico Reviewed* (Boston: American Peace Society, 1850); John Y. Simon, ed., *The Papers of Ulysses S. Grant,* vol. 1 (London, England, and Amsterdam: Feffer and Simons, 1967); William Starr Meyers, ed., *The Mexican War Diary of General B. Clellan,* vol. 1 (Princeton: Princeton University Press, 1917); and Grady McWhiney and Sue McWhiney, eds., *To Mexico with Taylor and Scott, 1845–1847* (Waltham, Mass.: Praisell, 1969). For interpretive narratives, see Glenn W. Price, *Origins of the War with Mexico: The Polk–Stockton Intrigue* (Austin: University of Texas Press, 1967). Also, see Norman E. Tutorow, *Texas Annexation and the Mexican War* (Palo Alto: Chadwick House, 1978); Robert Self Henry, *The Story of the Mexican War* (New York: Ungar, 1950); John D. P. Fuller, *The Movement for the Acquisition of All Mexico* (New York: DaCapo Press, 1969); and Gene M. Brack, *Mexico Views Manifest Destiny, 1821–1846: An Essay on the Origins of the Mexican War* (Albuquerque: University of New Mexico Press, 1975).

100. Antonio de La Peña y Reyes, ed., *Algunos documentos sobre el Tratado de Guadalupe y la situación de México durante la invasión americana* (México, D.F.: Secretaría de Relaciones Exteriores, 1930); Dublan and Lozano, *Legislación mexicana,* vol. 5, pp. 367–80; and Telefect Foundation, eds., *El Tratado de Guadalupe Hidalgo 1848: The Treaty of Guadalupe Hidalgo 1848* (Sacramento: Telefact Foundation, in cooperation with the California State Department of Education, 1968). This is a facsimile reproduction of the Mexican Instrument of Ratification and Related Documents. For insight on Mexican negotiation, see Rosa Rojas Garcidueñas, "Don José Bernardo Couto: Jurista, diplomático y Escritor, con un Apendice que contiene cuatro obras de J. B. Couto: La Exposición de Motivos del Tratado de 1848 con los Estados Unidos . . ." (México, D.F.: Universidad Veracruzana-México, 1964), in Bill Tate, ed., *Guadalupe Hidalgo Treaty of Peace 1848 and the Gadsden Treaty with Mexico 1853* (Truchas, N.M.: Tate Gallery Publication, 1967). For a summary and analysis of the congressional debate on the treaty, see Philip Anthony Hernández, "The Other North Americans: The American Image of Mexico and Mexicans, 1550–1850" (Ph.D. diss., University of California, Berkeley, 1974). Thoughtfully, the Tate Gallery publication includes an extract from the

constitution of the state of New Mexico, which declares that "the rights, privileges and immunities, civil, political and religious guaranteed to the people of New Mexico, by the Treaty of Guadalupe Hidalgo shall be preserved inviolate" (article 2, section 5, *New Mexico Statutes*, vol. 1). For a fine detailed examination of the treaty and its consequences, see Richard Griswold del Castillo, *The Treaty of Guadalupe Hidalgo: A Legacy of Conflict* (Norman: University of Oklahoma Press, 1990).

Chapter 3

1. For a collection of U.S. reports, documents, correspondence, and other material that provide views of the circumstances and events concerning occupation, see United States, Zachary Taylor President, *Executive Document no. 17 of the United States Congress, First Session* (1850) (New York: Arno Press, 1976); United States Senate, 56th Cong., 1st sess., no. 42, "Report on the Insurrection against the Military Government in New Mexico in 1847," Donaciano Vigil, Santa Fe, June 25, 1847; Philip St. George Cooke, *The Conquest of New Mexico and California* (New York: Arno Press, 1976); John C. Rayburn and Virginia K. Rayburn, eds., *Century of Conflict* (Waco: Texian Press, 1966); Juan Nepomuceno Seguín, *Personal Memoirs of John N. Seguin, from the year 1834 to the Retreat of General Woll* (San Antonio: 1858); Rafael Chacón, *Legacy of Honor, The Life of Rafael Chacón, A Nineteenth-Century New Mexican*, ed., Jacqueline D. Meketa (Albuquerque: University of New Mexico Press, 1986); Miguel Antonio Otero, *My Life on the Frontier*, vols. 1– 3, (1864–1906; repr., New York: Arno Press, 1974); Ralph Emerson Twitchell, *The History of the Military Occupation of the Territory of New Mexico from 1846 to 1851 by the Government of the United States* (Chicago: Rio Grande Press, 1963); George Griggs, *History of the Mesilla Valley or the Gadsden Purchase* (Las Cruces: Ronson Printers, 1924); Theodore Grivas, *Military Government in California, 1846–1850* (Glendale: Arthur R. Clark, 1963); Benjamin M. Read, *Illustrated History of New Mexico* (repr. of the 1912 ed., New York: Arno Press, 1976); and Leroy P. Graf, "The Economic History of the Lower Rio Grande Valley 1820–1875" (Ph.D. diss., Harvard University, 1942). For a general history of the Southwest between 1846 and 1900, see Howard Roberts Lamar, *The Far Southwest, 1846–1912: A Territorial History* (New York: Norton, 1970); and for a range of documentary statements, see David J. Weber, *Foreigners in Their Native Land: Historical Roots of the Mexican Americans* (Albuquerque: University of New Mexico Press, 1973), chapters 4 and 5. On electoral participation for three states, see Fernando V. Padilla and Carlos B. Ramírez, "Patterns of Chicano Representation in California, Colorado and Nuevo México," *Aztlán: Chicano Journal of the Social Sciences and the*

Arts 5, (Spring and Fall 1974); José Martí, Latin American writer and radical activist, commented critically on U.S. politics as he judged them, in the 1880s; see José Martí, *Political Parties and Elections in the United States*, ed. Philip S. Foner, trans. Elinor Randall (Philadelphia: Temple University Press, 1989). For a more contrasting view of events than the one presented here, see Rodman W. Paul, "The Spanish-Americans in the Southwest, 1848–1900," in John J. Clark, ed., *The Frontier Challenge: Responses to the Transmississippi West* (Lawrence: University of Kansas Press, 1971). For a thoughtful overview of selected figures and events using the judgmental criteria of "accommodation," see Manuel G. Gonzáles, *The Hispanic Elite of the Southwest* (El Paso: University of Texas at El Paso, 1989); and for territorial politics, see Lamar, *Far Southwest*. For autobiographical materials consult Genaro M. Padilla, "The Recovery of Chicano Nineteenth-Century Autobiography," *American Quarterly* 40 (September 1988).

2. For an examination of the context and patterns of nineteenth-century Mexican resistance and negotiation, see Gilberto López y Rivas, *La guerra del '47 y la resistencia popular a la ocupación* (México, D.F.: Editorial Nuestro Tiempo, 1976); Robert J. Rosenbaum, *Mexicano Resistance in the Southwest: The Sacred Right of Self-Preservation* (Austin: University of Texas Press, 1981); and Rodolfo Acuña, *Occupied America: A History of Chicanos* (New York: Harper and Row, 1988), pp. 3–117. For the literature on violence, see Richard Maxwell Brown, "Historiography of Violence in the American West," in Michael P. Malone, ed., *Historians and the American West* (Lincoln: University of Nebraska Press, 1983).

3. On relations of mexicanos with nomads, see David J. Weber, "American Western Expansion and the Breakdown of Relations between Pobladores and Indios Barbaros on New Mexico's Far Northern Frontier, 1821–1846," *New Mexico Historical Review* 56 (July 1981). For general Indian relations and policy, see Charles L. Kenner, *A History of New Mexico–Plains Indian Relations* (Norman: University of Oklahoma Press, 1969); and Reginald Horsman, *Expansionism and American Indian Policy* (East Lansing: Michigan State University Press, 1967); and Robert M. Utley, *The Indian Frontier of the American West, 1846–1890* (Albuquerque: University of New Mexico Press, 1984); David J. Weber, *Arms, Indians and the Mismanagement of Indian Affairs: Donaciano Vigil, 1846* (El Paso: Texas Western Press, 1986); see also James L. Raives, *Indians in California: The Changing Image* (Norman: University of Oklahoma Press, 1984); Albert Hurtado, *Indian Survival on the California Borderland Frontier* (New Haven: Yale University Press, 1988). For specific instances, see Rafael Chacón, *Legacy of Honor;* and Marc Simmons, *The Little Lion of the Southwest: A Life of Manuel Antonio Chávez* (Chicago: Sage/Swallow, 1973). In Chacón's recollections, there is a continuity, but one within a new institutional framework; for example, socially:

> The Pueblo Indians celebrated the feast of whichever saint their pueblo was named for, such as San Juan, San Francisco, San Felipe, Santa Clara, etc. They invited the Mexican people and had great feasts with clean and well-prepared food. The Indians danced in their customary paint and feathers, and their dances were very clever and entertaining, and they also had foot races. Each of the pueblos had a *casa plazuela de posada*, which they called La Comunidad [community hall]. In this house the guests lodged themselves without asking permission, and the Indians brought them firewood and gave pasture for the animals without demanding any payment. The Mexicans were called neighbors by the Indians. Those they knew well they called *compadres*, and these were invited to their homes and treated comfortably with much affection and friendliness. (p. 79)

Politically, there were a few occasions such as the following:

> This second term as magistrate was served during 1869–1870. On New Year's Day of 1870, I had the opportunity, in this humble post, to participate in an ancient custom that was celebrated from the time of the Spanish, and this was the investiture of the officers of the pueblo of Picuris with their symbols of authority. That day a commission of the Indians from that pueblo came so that I, as precinct Justice of the Peace, could swear in the new officials of the Indian community, who had been named according to their customs. These were the governor, lieutenant governor or war captain, two *caciques*, and the *alcalde* of the pueblo. All of them had their staffs adorned with ribbons, perhaps from the colonial times, demonstrating the authority that each one exercised. As this was, for me, a new and unknown thing, I told them that I had to practice the ceremony, and they told me that I should swear them into their respective offices in the way that had been observed by tradition. I agreed to go with them, and at the community house of the pueblo, in the presence of other Indians and the Mexicans who resided at the pueblo, I gave them the oath to observe the laws and the Constitution of the United States and to promise loyalty to the government and to administer the laws according to their custom. Afterward, I began to hand over their staffs, using the following words more or less: "This rod is the insignia of the authority conferred upon you and gives you the right to administer justice without partiality, fraud, or favor, with said authority conforming with your laws and customs. If you work well God will reward you." Immediately, they all embraced me and shook hands, very pleased and admiring, saying that never, according to them, had they seen this ceremony conducted in such a lovely manner and that in their hearts the memory would remain engraved with gratitude for me as long as I lived. In proof of this they established the custom of coming to my house on fiesta days with the dance of the *Matachines*, and they were welcomed in my house and given gifts. (pp. 313–14)

One study that looks at both Mexican and Indian political participation in the post-1848 period is Richard N. Ellis, "Hispanic Americans and Indians in New Mexico State Politics," *New Mexico Historical Review* 57 (January 1982); see also Hurtado, *Indian Survival on the California Frontier.*

4. On the treaty, see Antonio de la Peña y Reyes, ed., *Algunos documentos sobre el Tratado de Guadalupe Hidalgo* (México, D.F.: Porrua, 1971); Richard Griswold del Castillo, *The Treaty of Guadalupe Hidalgo: A Legacy of Conflict* (Norman: University of Oklahoma Press, 1990); and Fernando Chacón Gómez, "The Intended and Actual Effects of Article VIII of the Treaty of Guadalupe Hidalgo: Mexican Treaty Rights under International and Domestic Law" (Ph.D. diss., University of Michigan, 1977).

5. For observations or recollections of cultural life, see Nellie Van de Grift Sánchez, *Spanish Arcadia* (Los Angeles: Powell, 1929); Aurora Lucero White, *Los Hispanos* (Denver: Sage, 1947); Francisca López de Belderrain, "The Awakening of Paredon Blanco under a California Sun," *Historical Society of Southern California Annual*, vol. 14 (1928); Guadalupe Vallejo, "Ranch and Mission Days in Alta California," *The Century Magazine* 41 (December 1890); Jovita González, "Social Life in Cameron, Starr and Zapata Counties" (Master's thesis, University of Texas, 1930); Fabiola Cabeza de Baca, *We Fed Them Cactus* (Albuquerque: University of New Mexico Press, 1954); Emilia Schunior Ramírez, *Ranch Life in Hidalgo County after 1850* (Edinburg: New Santander, 1971); and Raquel Rubio Goldsmith, "Hispanics in Arizona and Their Experiences with the Humanities," in F. Arturo Rosales, et al., *Hispanics and the Humanities* (Tempe: Center for Latin American Studies, Arizona State University, 1963). For interpretive comments on identity, society, and culture, see Arnoldo de León, *The Tejano Community, 1836–1900* (Albuquerque: University of New Mexico Press, 1982), chapter 9, "Culture and Community"; Richard Griswold del Castillo, *The Los Angeles Barrio, 1850–1890* (Berkeley: University of California Press, 1979), chapter.4, "An Emerging Ethnic Consciousness." See also Américo Paredes, "The Folk Base of Chicano Culture," in Joseph Sommers and Tomás Ybarra-Frausto, eds., *Modern Chicano Writers, A Collection of Critical Essays* (Englewood Cliffs, N.J.: Prentice Hall, 1979).

6. See the discussion of this and the emergent "Hispanophile thesis" in relation to folklore and culture, in Paredes, "Folk Base of Chicano Literature"; and see also the arguments of Arthur L. Campa, in *Hispanic Folklore Studies of Arthur L. Campa* (New York: Arno Press, 1976). For a discussion of the political significance and origins of the euphemistic use of the terms *Hispano, Spanish,* and *Spanish American* in the Southwestern United States, see James Blaut and Antonio Rios Bustamante, "Commentary on Nostrand's 'Hispanos' and Their 'Homeland,'" *Annals of the Association of American Geographers* 74 (March 1984). See also Richard L. Nostrand, "The Hispano Homeland in 1900," *Annals of the Association of American Geographers* 70 (1980). One concise explanation of the origins of use of the term *Spanish American* in New Mexico is given by E. B. Fincher, *Spanish Americans as a Political Factor in New Mexico, 1912–1950* (New York: Arno Press, 1974), p. xiv:

One indication of the status of the Hispanic-American of New Mexico is the evolution of popular terminology. Until recent years, the Spanish-speaking New Mexican usually referred to himself as a "Mexican" and was given that cognomen by his Anglo-American neighbor. . . .

In the last 20 years, however, the Hispanic-American people have come to resent the word "Mexican" when applied to them. Newcomers to the state, particularly Texans who have settled in the eastern section, have used "Mexican" in a derogatory sense to the point that Hispanic-Americans throughout the state have become highly sensitive to the word. That explains why the terms "Spanish-speaking," Spanish-American," "Latin-American," "Ibero-American," and "Hispanic-American" have developed in recent years as descriptive of persons of Spanish or Mexican descent.

For a discussion of the development of a similar phenomena, the "Spanish myth" in California, see Antonio Rios Bustamante, "Introduction" and "Bibliographic Essay" in Rios Bustamente, "Los Angeles, Pueblo and Region, 1781–1850: Continuity and Adaptation to the North Mexican Periphery" (Ph.D. diss., UCLA, Los Angeles, 1985). Rios Bustamante also examines related historiographic misuse of the terms *californio* and *gente de razón* by some historians and other social scientists.

7. Providing available insight on the politics of the time are the extant newspaper, personal recollections, and memoirs; the first two are informative and diverse, while the last is unfortunately few. Blue books or rosters of state officials are also available. For a secondary examination of political relations and negotiation in particular regions, see Arnoldo de León, *The Tejano Community, 1836–1900* (Albuquerque: University of New Mexico Press, 1982); Arnoldo de León, *They Called Them Greasers: Anglo Attitudes toward Mexicans in Texas, 1821–1900* (Austin: University of Texas Press, 1983); David Montejano, *Anglos and Mexicans in the Making of Texas, 1846–1986* (Austin: University of Texas Press, 1987); Leonard Pitt, *The Decline of the Californios: A Social History of the Spanish-Speaking Californians, 1846–1890* (Berkeley: University of California Press, 1966); Joseph Cassidy "The Life and Times of Pablo de la Guerra" (Ph.D. diss., University of California, Santa Barbara, 1977); Alvin R. Sunseri, *Seeds of Discord: New Mexico in the Aftermath of the American Conquest, 1846–1861* (Chicago: Nelson and Hall, 1979); and Robert J. Rosenbaum, *Mexican Resistance in the Southwest*; Bancroft, *History of Arizona and New Mexico, 1530–1880* (Albuquerque: Horn and Wallace, 1962); and Jay J. Waggoner, *Arizona Territory, 1863–1912: A Political History* (Tucson: University of Arizona Press, 1970); and Thomas E. Sheridan, *Los Tucsonenses: The Mexican Community in Tucson, 1854–1941* (Tucson: The University of Arizona Press, 1986).

8. For the published narrative literature, see Arnoldo de León, chapter 2, "Politics and Tejanos," in León, *Tejano Community*; Leonard Pitt, chapter 8,

"Serapes and Split Breeches in Politics," chapter 14, "Upheavals—Political and Natural, 1860–1864," chapter 15, "The Second Generation, 1865–1890," in Pitt, Decline of the Californios; Castillo, chapter 4, "An Emerging Ethnic Consciousness," and chapter 5, "Isolation: Geographic, Political, Spiritual," in Castillo, Los Angeles Barrio; Robert W. Larson, New Mexico's Quest for Statehood, 1846–1912 (Albuquerque: University of New Mexico Press, 1968); Alvin R. Sunseri, chapter 9, "The Mexican Americans as Politicians," in Sunseri, Seeds of Discord; Tobias Durán, "We Come as Friends: The Social and Historical Context of Nineteenth Century New Mexico" (Working Paper no. 106, Southwest Hispanic Research Institute, University of New Mexico, Summer 1984); Manuel P. Servín, "The Role of Mexican Americans in the Development of Early Arizona," in Servín, ed., An Awakening Minority: The Mexican American, 2d ed. (Beverly Hills: Glencoe Press, 1974).

9. For a listing of newspapers according to state, town, and date, see the basic and seminal La Prensa, "Importante contribución histórica de 'La Prensa'" (San Antonio, Texas: La Prensa, 13 de febrero, 1938, tercera sección); and Herminio Ríos and Lupe Castillo, "Toward a True Chicano Bibliography," part 1, El Grito, vol. 3, no. 4 (Summer 1970); and Ríos and Castillo, "Toward a True Chicano Bibliography—Part Two," El Grito 5, no. 4 (Summer 1972). For a tentative exploration of the history of Spanish-language newspapers in the United States, see Félix Gutíerrez, special editor, "Spanish Language Media Issue," Journalism History 4 (Summer 1977); and, in particular, Félix Gutíerrez, "Spanish Language Media in America: Background, Resources, History," Journalism History 4 (Summer 1977). For specific regional and case studies of particular periodicals, see Porter A. Stratton, The Territorial Press of New Mexico, 1834–1912 (Albuquerque: University of New Mexico Press, 1969); Leonard Pitt, chapter 11, "El Clamor Público: Sentiments of Treason"; and chapter 9, "Culture and Community," in León, Tejano Community; and Castillo, chapter 4, "An Emerging Ethnic Consciousness," in Castillo, Los Angeles Barrio. For an analysis of a contributor, see Francisco A. Lomeli, "Eusebio Chacón: A Literary Portrait of 19th Century New Mexico" (Albuquerque: Southwest Hispanic Research Institute, University of New Mexico, 1987, Working Paper no. 113). For an overview of literacy in one state, see B. P. Gallegos and Z. Maggart, "The History of Literacy in New Mexico" (in three parts), New Mexico Journal of Reading 7 (1986 and 1987); and for a city, see Richard Griswold del Castillo, "Literacy in San Antonio, Texas, 1850–1860," Latin American Research Review 15 (1980).

10. For comments on nineteenth-century schooling, see Guadalupe San Miguel, Let Them All Take Heed (Austin: University of Texas Press, 1987), pp. 1–25; Read, Illustrated History, pp. 533–63; and Pitt, Decline of the Californios, pp. 224–28, and 295; see also Benjamin Read, A History of Education in New Mexico (Santa Fe: New Mexican Printing Co., 1911); Myra E. Jenkins,

"Early Education in New Mexico," *National Education Association—New Mexico School Review* 53 (Midwinter 1977); and J. Atkins, "Who Will Educate: The Schooling Question in Territorial New Mexico, 1846–1911" (Ph.D. diss., University of New Mexico, 1982).

11. On Mexicans and the Catholic church during the nineteenth century, see: José Roberto Juárez, "La Iglesia Católica y El Chicano en Sud Texas, 1836–1911," *Aztlán* 4 (Fall 1983); John Bernard McGloin, S.J., "The California Catholic Church in Transition, 1846–1880," *California Historical Society Quarterly* 42 (March 1963); Paul Horgan, *Lamy of Santa Fe: His Life and Times* (New York: Farrar, Straus and Giroux, 1975); Carlos E. Castañeda, *Our Catholic Heritage in Texas*, vol. 7 (Austin: Von Boeckmann Jones, 1936–1958); and Antonio M. Stevens Arroyo, ed., *Prophets Denied Honor* (Maryknoll: Orbis Books, 1980), pp. 77–87. For a biography of the earliest Mexican bishop in the Southwest, see Frances J. Weber, *Francisco García Diego: California's Transition Bishop* (Los Angeles: Dawson's Book Shop, 1971). On anti-Catholicism see Ray Allen Billington, *The Protestant Crusade, 1800–1869: A Study in the Origins of American Nativism* (New York: Macmillan Company, 1938) and also see Alvin Packer Stauffer, "AntiCatholicism in American Politics 1865–1900" (Ph.D. diss., Harvard University, 1933).

12. On the administration of justice, see *Report of the Mexican Commission on the Northern Frontier Question* (1875); Edward Joseph Escobar, "Chicano Protest and the Law: Law Enforcement Responses to Chicano Activism in Los Angeles, 1850–1936" (Ph.D. diss., University of California, Riverside, 1983); and Julian Samora, et al., *Gunpowder Justice* (Notre Dame: University of Notre Dame Press, 1979). For the evolution of law and its relation to social interests, see Henry Steele Commager, *The American Mind: An Interpretation of American Thought and Character since the 1880s* (New Haven: Yale University Press, 1950), chapter 27, "The Evolution of American Law." For a more general exposition on the relation between law and dominant social thought, see Robert Mangaheira Unger, *Law in Modern Society: Toward a Criticism of Social Theory* (New York: Free Press, 1976). *El Clamor Público* (February 21, 1857) reported a California incident:

In a few words, a company (all Americans), its captain Sanford, headed toward the Mission of San Gabriel. All the Mexican residents in that place were arrested and treated with unequalled brutality. Two of these unfortunates had been arrested at the entrance of the Mission. They had to submit to an interrogation of the most provocative sort. Intimidated by the threats, and impelled by the instinct of self preservation, they began to run, especially when they saw the captain draw his pistol. But, ay! at the first movement that they made, a general volley followed. One fell wounded from various shots. The other was able to reach a lake or marsh. He abandoned his horse and concealed himself in the rushes. Vain efforts.

The American band arrived, set fire to the marsh, and very soon, among the general cries of gaiety, they discovered the head of the unfortunate above the flames. A second volley and all was done.—I deceive myself. It was not finished so quickly. The body, loaded over a horse, was transported to the Mission in the midst of cries and shouts of joy and gaiety. Here, overtaken by horror, thought stops because it is impossible to find expressions to describe the scene which took place and was related to me by many witnesses worthy of trust. The body was thrown to the ground in the midst of the mob. One being, with a human face, stepped forward with a knife in his hand. . . . With one hand he took the head of the dead man by its long hair, separated it from the body, flung it a short distance and stuck his dagger in the heart of the cadaver. Afterward, returning to the head, he made it roll with his foot into the middle of his band and the rabble, amidst the cries and the hurrahs of the greater number. . . . Is it not horrible? But wait, we have not yet seen all. Another band arrived from another place with two Californios. They had been arrested as suspects, one of them going in search of some oxen, the other to his daily work. They were conducted into the middle of the mob. The cries of "To death! To death!" were heard from all sides. The cutter of heads entered his house, coming out with some ropes, and the two unfortunates were hanged—despite the protests of their countrymen and their families. Once hangèd from the tree, the ropes broke and the hapless ones were finished being murdered by shots or knife thrusts. The cutter of heads was fatigued, or his knife did not now cut! Perhaps you will believe that this very cruel person was an Indian from the mountains, one of those barbarians who lives far from all civilization in the Sierra Nevada! Wrong. That barbarian, that mutilator of cadavers, is the Justice of the Peace of San Gabriel! . . . He is a citizen of the United States, an American of pure blood. . . .

Afterwards, two Mexicans were found hanging from a tree, and near there another with two bullets in the head.

On the road from Tejon another company had encountered two poor peddlers (always Mexicans) who were arrested and hanged as suspects.

For instance, in Texas read J. Frank Dobie, *A Vaquero of the Brush Country* (Austin: University of Texas Press, 1981), p. 62. Benjamin A. Botkin reports, in *A Treasury of American Folklore* (New York: Crown, 1944), that in the alleged decision by Judge Roy Bean against Carlos Robles and that of "hanging" Judge Parker against José Gonzáles, the colorful and blatantly hostile language communicates the acknowledged gusto in hanging Mexicans (pp. 136 and 148).

13. On economic discrimination, see Richard Morefield, "The Mexican Adaptation in American California, 1846–1875" (Master's thesis, University of California, Berkeley, 1955); David Montejano, *Anglos and Mexicans;* Rodolfo Acuña, "Freedom in a Cage: The Subjugation of the Chicano in the United States," in William H. Cartwright and Richard L. Watson, Jr., eds., *The Reinterpretation of American History and Culture* (Washington, D.C.: Na-

tional Council for the Social Sciences, 1974); Castillo, chapter 2, "Exclusion from a Developing Economy," in *Los Angeles Barrio;* and Ellen Schneider and Paul H. Carlson, "Gunnysackers, Carreteros and Teamsters: The South Texas Cart Wars of 1857," *The Journal of South Texas* 1 (Spring 1988). See also Richard Griswold del Castillo, "Tucsonenses and Angelenos: A Socio-Economic Study of Two Mexican American Barrios, 1860–1880," *Journal of the West* 24 (1985); and Albert Camarillo, *Chicanos in a Changing Society: From Mexican Pueblos to American Barrios in Santa Barbara and Southern California, 1848–1930* (Cambridge: Harvard University Press, 1979).

14. Comments on bandits often were made in *El Clamor Público* (1855–1859). For overviews, see Carlos Cortés, "El bandolerismo social chicano," in David Maciel, ed., *Aztlán: historia del pueblo Chicano* (México, D.F.: Sep-Setentas, 1975); Diego Vigil, *Early Chicano Guerrilla Fighters* (Upland, Calif.: 1974); and Pedro G. Castillo and Albert Camarillo, eds., *Furia y Muerte: Los Bandidos Chicanos* (Los Angeles: Chicano Studies Research Center/University of California, Los Angeles, 1973). See also for the Southwest, Rosenbaum, chapter 4, "Social Bandits and Community Upheavals," in *Mexican Resistance in the Southwest;* Joseph Henry Jackson, *Bad Company: The Story of California's Legendary and Actual Stage Robbers, Bandits, Highwaymen and Outlaws from the Fifties to the Eighties* (New York: Harcourt Brace, 1949); and for comparative discussion, see Eric J. Hobsbawn, *Bandits* (London: Weidenfeld and Nicolson, 1969).

For specific figures, see Robert Greenwood, *The California Outlaw: Tiburcio Vasquez* (Los Gatos: Talisman Press, 1966); Leonard Pitt, chapter 4, "The Head Pickled in Whiskey," *Decline of the Californios,* particularly pp. 162–66, 169–73, 178, and 181–94; Ruben E. López, "The Legend of Tiburcio Vasquez," *Pacific Historian* 15 (Summer 1951); and the classic literary romanticization published in 1854 by Yellow Bird (John Rollin Ridge), *The Life and Adventures of Joaquin Murieta: The Celebrated California Bandit* (San Francisco: 1854; repr., Norman: University of Oklahoma Press, 1982); and Richard G. Mitchell, "Joaquin Murieta: A Study of Social Conditions in California" (Master's thesis, University of California, Berkeley, 1927). Of special interest are recent titles: the massive and detailed investigation by the enthusiast Frank Latta, *Joaquin Murrieta and His Horse Gangs* (Santa Cruz: Bear State Library, 1980); and the unique and revisionist works by Manuel Rojas, *Joaquín Murrieta, "El Patrio"* (Mexicali: 1986), and Celso Aguirre Bernal, *Joaquín Murrieta* (Mexico, D.F.: 1985).

For examples of songs recalling resistance figures, see: "Corrido de Joaquín Murrieta" and "Corrido de Jacinto Trevino," in Antonia Castañeda Shular, Tomas Ybarra-Frausto, Joseph Sommers, eds., *Literatura Chicana, Texto y Contexto: Chicano Literature, Text and Context* (Englewood Cliffs: Prentice Hall, 1972), pp. 65–66 and 67–68, respectively: and Américo Paredes, *A*

Texas Mexican Cancionero: Folksongs of the Lower Border (Urbana: University of Illinois Press, 1976), pp. 46–71. For the classic examination of the *corrido* in the United States, see Américo Paredes, *With His Pistol in His Hand: A Border Ballad and Its Hero* (Austin: University of Texas Press, 1958).

15. For the Tiburcio Vasquez quote, see *Los Angeles Star* (May 16, 1874), and for his activities, see Ernest R. May, "Tiburcio Vasquez," *Historical Society of Southern California Quarterly* 24 (1974).

16. On Cortina and his activities, see *Report of the Mexican Commission on the Border Question*, (New York: 1875); and José T. Canales, *Juan Cortina Presents His Motion for a New Trial* (San Antonio: Artes Gráficas, 1951), pp. 107–9. For the context in Mexico, see Daniel Cosío Villegas, *Historia moderna de México, El Porfiriato, La vida política interior, primera parte* (9 vols., México, D.F.: Hermes, 1957–1972), pp. 575–797; and for a poor but available biography, see Charles W. Goldfinch, *Juan N. Cortina, 1824–1892: A Reappraisal* (Chicago: Charles W. Goldfinch, 1949). For some still useful contextual information, see J. Fred Rippy, "Border Troubles along the Rio Grande, 1848–1860," *Southwestern Historical Quarterly* 22 (1919–1920); and for a recent reassessment, see James Ridley Douglas, "Juan Cortina: El Caudillo de la Frontera" (Master's thesis, University of Texas at Austin, 1987). See also Michael Gordan Webster, "Texan Manifest Destiny and the Mexican Border Conflict, 1865–1900" (Ph.D. diss., Indiana University, 1972).

17. Cortina's quote is from U.S. Congress, House, *Difficulties on the Southern Frontier*, 36th Cong., 1st sess., 1860, H. Exec. Doc. 52, pp. 70–82.

18. For Mexico ties, the contemporary press reflects news items, communiqués, and commentary on politics and literature, and the records of Mexican government offices as well as U.S. border consular offices document this interaction. See Juan Gómez-Quiñones, "Notes on the Interpretation of the Relations between the Mexican Community in the United States and Mexico," in Carlos Vasquez and Manuel García y Griego, eds., *Mexican–U.S. Relations: Conflict and Convergence* (Los Angeles: Chicano Studies Research Center, University of California, Los Angeles, 1983); and Robert Ryal Miller, "Arms across the Border: United States Aid to Juárez during the French Intervention in Mexico," *Transactions of the American Philosophical Society*, new series, vol. 63 (part 6, 1973). Also, see Pitt, *Decline of the Californios*, chapter 14, "Upheavals—Political and Natural, 1860–1864"; and Castillo, *Los Angeles Barrio*, pp. 135 and 151.

19. For U.S. economic expansion, see Lamar, *Far Southwest*; Robert V. Hine, *The American West: An Interpretive History* (New York: Little, Brown, 1973), pp. 112–89; and William Appelman Williams, *The Roots of the Modern American Empire* (New York: Random House, 1969).

20. For the Mexican economy and its increasing foreign participation, see Diego G. López Rosado, chapter 4, "Período independiente, 1881 a 1910," in

Diego G. López Rosado, *Historia y pensamiento económico de México* (México, D.F.: Instituto de Investigaciones Económicas, Universidad Nacional Autónoma de México, 1968); John M. Hart, *Revolutionary Mexico: The Coming and Process of the Mexican Revolution* (Berkeley: University of California Press, 1987) part I; and James D. Cockcroft, *Mexico: Class Formation, Capital Accumulation, and the State* (New York: Monthly Review Press, 1983), chapter 3, "Dictatorship and Revolution, 1880–1920." For estimates of the amount of U.S. and other foreign capital investments in Mexico, see Mira Wilkins, *The Emergence of Multinational Enterprise*, vol. 1, *American Business Abroad from the Colonial Era to 1914* (Cambridge: Harvard University Press, 1970), pp. 128–130; and Mira Wilkins, *The Maturing of Multinational Enterprise*, vol. 2, *American Business Abroad from 1914 to 1970* (Cambridge: Harvard University Press, 1974), pp. 55, 114, and 225–29. See also Lawrence A. Cardoso, chapter 1, "Porfirian Mexico: The Background of Massive Immigration," in Lawrence A. Cardoso, *Mexican Immigration to the United States, 1897–1931* (Tucson: University of Arizona Press, 1980).

21. For proletarianization, see Juan Gómez-Quiñones, *Development of the Mexican Working Class North of the Río Bravo: Work and Culture among Laborers and Artisans, 1600–1960* (Los Angeles: Chicano Studies Research Center, University of California, Los Angeles, 1982); Arnoldo de León and Kenneth L. Stewart, "A Tale of Three Cities: A Comparative Analysis of the Socio-Economic Conditions of Mexican-Americans in Los Angeles, Tucson and San Antonio, 1850–1900," *Journal of the West* 24 (1985); and Richard Romo, "The Urbanization of Southwestern Chicanos in the Early Twentieth Century," *New Scholar* 6 (1977). For economic and demographic disparities, see Mario Barrera, *Race and Class in the Southwest: A Theory of Inequality* (Notre Dame: University of Notre Dame, 1979), chapter 2, "The Nineteenth Century"; and Richard Nostrand, "The Hispano Homeland in 1900," *Annals of the Association of American Geographers* 70 (1980).

22. On population figures, see Oscar J. Martínez, "On the Size of the Chicano Population: New Estimates, 1850–1900," *Aztlán: International Journal of Chicano Studies Research* 6 (Spring 1975); and Roberto M. Villareal, "Model for Estimating the Spanish Surname Population of Texas, 1850–1930" (unpublished research note, University of Texas, 1973). The commonly cited low figures were estimates stated in a military report provided by a person not particularly knowledgeable about the Southwest and reported by Carey McWilliams without source, in his classic *North From Mexico* and repeated ever since. Several scholars have suspected the figure to be unreasonably low. For low figures, see Rodman W. Paul, "The Spanish-Americans in the Southwest, 1848–1900."

See, for economic impoverishment, Acuña, "Freedom in a Cage"; see also the preface by Rodolfo Acuña, in his *Occupied America*. For a sociological approach to the extension of Anglo American domination, see Barrera, *Race and Class in the Southwest*. For the premises of political chauvinism, see Reginald Horsman, *Race and Manifest Destiny: The Origins of American Racial Anglo-Saxonism* (Cambridge: Harvard University Press, 1981), chapters 11 and 12, pp. 204–48; for nativism, see John Higham, *Strangers in the Land: Patterns of American Nativism, 1860–1925* (New York: Atheneum, 1977).

23. On the land question, see Victor Westphall, *The Public Domain in New Mexico, 1854–1891* (Albuquerque: University of New Mexico Press, 1965); Herbert O. Brayer, *William Blackmore: The Spanish-Mexican Land Grants of New Mexico and Colorado, 1863–1878*, 2 vols. (Denver: Bradford-Robinson, 1949); Bruce T. Ellis, "Fraud without Scandal: The Roque Locato Grant and Gaspar Ortiz y Alarid," *New Mexico Historical Review* 57 (January 1982); Victor Westphall, "Fraud and Implications of Fraud in the Land Grants of New Mexico," *New Mexico Historical Review* 49 (July 1974); Paul W. Gates, "Adjudication of Spanish-Mexican Land Claims in California," *The Huntington Library Quarterly* 21 (May 1958); and Florence J. Scott, *Royal Land Grants North of the Rio Grande, 1777–1821* (Rio Grande City: La Retama Press, 1969); for New Mexico overview, see Roxanne Dunbar Ortiz, *Roots of Resistance and Tenure in New Mexico, 1680–1980* (Los Angeles: CSRC and AISC, UCLA, 1980), chapters 5 and 6; and William P. deBuys, *Enchantment and Exploitation: The Life and Hard Times of a New Mexico Mountain Range* (Albuquerque: University of New Mexico Press, 1985).

24. For Pico's quote and context, see Robert Glass Cleland, *Cattle on a Thousand Hills: Southern California, 1850–80* (San Marino: Henry E. Huntington Library, 1951), pp. 238–43.

25. On domination, see Acuña, "Freedom in a Cage"; Barrera, *Race and Class in the Southwest* and Montejano, *Anglos and Mexicans*. For a summary discussion of the influence of Mexican law in the Southwest, see Manuel Ruiz, *The Mexican Legal Heritage in the Southwest* (Los Angeles: 1972); and James M. Murphy, *The Spanish Legal Heritage in Arizona* (Tucson: Arizona Pioneer's Historical Society, 1966).

26. See Simmons, *Little Lion of the Southwest*, and Chacón, *Legacy of Honor*. The latter left some sharp observations on his encounters with discrimination. Chacón records the treatment encountered while in the service:

> At the table when we were seated at the meal, Damours would begin to talk against the Mexicans, Don Julián Solis who was the second lieutenant, would contradict him even as far as saying to him that he was a disgrace to our people, that after the hunger of adventurers such as he was taken away, they repaid us with bad talk about ourselves and our customs. I always remained in silence in order to see where this was going to end up, and this silence Damours perhaps interpreted as approval of what he was saying.

It was the duty of the first lieutenant to teach military drill to the soldiers, and when walking in this duty Damours would prick the soldier's thighs with his sword because they were not marching well. To others he put a stick on their neck in order to make them straighten up, and he always mistreated and insulted the Mexicans. I, who was very impetuous in my youth, repressed my anger all that I could, in order to see if he would correct his ways, until one day when he told the soldiers that he should be the captain because the one they now had was no good and that it was up to them to see that he was elected if they wished. Since most of the soldiers were my cousins, friends, and comrades, they came later and told me what he had said. The next time when he began with his jokes once again at the table, I said, "Until now I have suffered and allowed you to talk of my race, but from now and henceforth I will not allow you to return to denigrating them in my presence." He replied that I did not have the right to keep him from speaking, which I knew to be true. I repeated that in my presence he was not to do it any more, and that if he would try to do it he should know that I would stand behind my word. He was frightened and used arrogant language. Then I seized some loose boards that were there and broke them into two or three pieces. He attempted to draw out his sword but I did not give him time to use it, but I began to hit him with the boards with much force and I broke five more sticks. Then, seeing me infuriated, he fled outside, dragging his sword, and ran over into the middle of a group of officers, and I went after him until I arrived at where the officers were. (p. 131)

27. On Father Martínez, see Pedro Sánchez, *Memorias sobre la vida del Presbítero Don Antonio José Martínez*, original Spanish text with English trans. Ray John de Aragon (Santa Fe: Lightning Tree, 1978); Fray Angélico Chávez, *But Time and Chance: The Story of Padre Martínez of Taos, 1793–1867* (Santa Fe: Sunstone Press, 1981); E. K. Francis, "Padre Martínez: A New Mexican Myth," *New Mexico Historical Review* 31 (October 1956); and Ray John de Aragon, *Padre Martínez and Bishop Lamy* (Las Vegas: Pan American Publishing, 1978); Stevens Arroyo, *Prophets Denied Honor,* pp. 77–87; and Juan Romero, *Reluctant Dawn* (San Antonio: Mexican American Cultural Center, 1976). A man of notable skills in argument, Father Martínez's reputation was blatantly slandered, as were other Mexicans of the time, by the prejudiced and condescending Willa Cather, who was as ignorant of New Mexicans as she was troubled in her personal life. Juan Romero provides excerpts from Father Martínez on a few of the salient issues with the racist Lamy, whom he addressed directly; for example, on tithing:

Its total payment as you demand under most severe penalties is in violation of the rights of this my people among whom I first saw the light of day. . . . I beg Your Excellency to respect my viewpoint for what I am about to say. . . . The diocesan statues invite the faithful to enter into mercantile agreements making the parish priests appear like hucksters or traders. They also make the sacraments, masses, and other spiritual gifts as so much merchandise in a warehouse by order of Your Excellency. . . . Compare this way of acting with the account of Simon Magus in the Acts of the Apostiles.

On the removal of the Mexican priests:

Is it that you wish to treat me the way you treated and injured other priests who because of their candor suffered all exactly the same way I do? What you did to Father Manuel Gallegos, the pastor of San Felipe, the church in Albuquerque, who because he had made a trip to Mexico in 1852 with due letters from the Vicar General returned to find himself suspended, his books and property thrown out of his rectory, and Father José Prospecto Machebeuf ensconced in his place. You did the same with the Vicar Forane, Father Juan Felipe Ortiz, the next year without canonical regard, dividing his parish, taking his rectory away from him, and finally suspending him.

On his excommunication:

Please do not destroy the peace and repose of my home, nor would I wish you to distress my faithful parishioners who come to me in their needs. The obligation to help them is imposed on me by reason of the Catholic religion I profess as by my position as their pastor. I recognize the duties which my conscience unfolds to me, as well as the help and consolation I have in canon law and in our liberal republican American government in which I believe so confidently. These I feel will not allow the machinations of others to trouble me. . . . I am yours with due regard to the protests I have made to you and I offer you my esteem and good will.

Lamy did not have the ability or the integrity to answer these arguments; his actions, not Martínez's, were in violation of canon law, and these violations were due to prejudice, politics, and finances. For a contrast to the negative views of Father Martínez, see E. A. Mares, _Padre Martínez: New Perspectives from Taos_ (Taos: Millicent Rogers Museum, 1988), and _I Returned and Saw under the Sun_ (Albuquerque: University of New Mexico Press, 1989).

28. On Miguel Antonio Otero condemning Father Gallegos, see Horgan, _Lamy of Santa Fe_, pp. 234–35.

29. _El Clamor Público_ (1855–1859); see also William B. Rice, _The Los Angeles Star, 1851–1864_ (Berkeley: University of California Press, 1951).

30. _El Clamor Público_ (June 19, 1855), vol. 1, no. 1.

31. See Jack Picson Eblen, _The First and Second United States Empires_ (Pittsburgh: University of Pittsburgh Press, 1968); Earl S. Pomeroy, _The Territories of the United States, 1861–1890: Studies in Colonial Administration_ (Philadelphia: University of Pennsylvania, 1947); and Lamar, _Far Southwest_.

32. For a discussion of the changing boundaries of the territories, see D. W. Meinig, _Southwest: Three Peoples in Geographical Change, 1600–1970_ (New

York: Oxford University Press, 1971), pp. 17–26; and see also the maps in Meinig on the boundaries of the territories annexed from Mexico.

33. For an examination of the United States territorial system as a form of colonialism, see Eblen, *First and Second United States Empires;* and Pomeroy, *Territories of the United States.*

34. For post 1836 Texas–Mexican politics, see Seguín, *Personal Memoirs;* Antonio Menchaca, *Memoirs* (San Antonio: Yanaguana Society, 1937); José M. Rodríguez, *Memoirs of Early Texas* (San Antonio: Standard Printing Co., 1961); and though it is disappointing, there is also José Antonio Navarro, *Apuntes históricos interesantes de San Antonio de Béxar* (San Antonio: 1969); and Jacob de Cordova, *Texas: Her Resources and Her Public Men* (Philadelphia: E. Crozet, 1858). For earlier context, see Ray F. Broussard, *San Antonio during the Texas Republic: A City in Transition* (El Paso: Texas Western Press, 1967); see also John Denny Riley, "Santos Benavides: His Influence on the Lower Rio Grande, 1823–1891" (Ph.D. diss., Texas Christian University, 1976); Joseph Martin Dawson, *José Antonio Navarro, Co-creator of Texas* (Waco: Baylor University Press, 1969); and Thomas Lloyd Miller, "José Antonio Navarro, 1795–1871," *Journal of Mexican American History* 2 (Spring 1972). For views of the opposition to Mexican voting, see William F. Weeks, *Debates of the Texas Convention* (Houston: J. W. Cruger, 1846); and for electoral rules, see Dora Ryan, "The Election Laws of Texas, 1827–1875" (Master's thesis, University of Texas, Austin, 1922). For elected state representatives, see *Members of the Legislature of the State of Texas* (Austin: State of Texas, 1939); and Ralph A. Wooster, "Membership in Early Texas Legislatures, 1850–1860," *Southwestern Historical Quarterly* 69 (October 1965). For observations on society and politics, see Frederick Law Olmsted, *A Journey through Texas; or, A Saddle-Trip on the Southwestern Frontier* (New York: Dix, Edwards and Co., 1857); John C. Riley and Virginia Kemp, eds., *Century of Conflict, 1821–1913;* Sister Paul of the Cross McGrath, *Political Nativism in Texas, 1825–1860* (Washington, D.C.: Catholic University of America, 1930); and Caroline Remy, "Hispanic Mexican San Antonio: 1836–1861," *Southern Historical Quarterly* 71 (April 1969). For demographics, see Terry G. Jordan, "Population Origins in Texas, 1850," *Geographical Review* Vol. 59 (January 1969); and for a review of Tejas Mexican political participation, see León, *Tejano Community,* chapter 2. See also Andrew A. Tijerina, "Tejanos and Texas; The Native Mexicans of Texas, 1820–1850" (Ph.D. dissertation, University of Texas, 1977); Gilberto M. Hinojosa, *A Borderlands Town in Transition: Laredo, Texas, 1755–1870* (College Station, Texas: Texas A&M University, 1983); and Arnoldo de León and Kenneth L. Stewart, "Lost Dreams and Found Fortunes: Mexican and Anglo Immigrants in South Texas, 1850–1900," *Western Historical Quarterly* 14 (July 1983).

35. J. Ross Browne, *Report of the Debates in the Convention of California on the Formation of the State Constitution in September and October, 1849* (Washington, D.C.: John T. Tower, 1850). A Spanish edition of the debates is also available as J. Ross Browne, *Relación de los debates de la convención de California* (New York: S. W. Benedict, 1851). See also Donald E. Hargis, "Native Californians in the Constitutional Convention of 1849," *Historical Society of Southern California Quarterly* 36 (March 1954). For judgmental comments on californio ways and politics, see Benjamin Hayes, *Pioneer Notes from the Diaries of Benjamin Hayes, 1849–1875* (Los Angeles: Marjorie Tisdale Wolcott, 1929); Josiah Royce, *California from the Conquest in 1846 to the Second Vigilante Committee* (Boston: Houghton Mifflin 1886); Horace Bell, *On the Old West Coast* (New York: Morrow, 1930); Stephen Clark Foster, *El Quachero: How I Want to Help Make the Constitution of California*, in Carlos E. Cortés, ed., *California after the U.S. Conquest* (New York: Arno, 1976); William H. Ellison, ed., " 'Recollections of Historical Events in California, 1843–1878' of William A. Streeter," *California Historical Society Quarterly* 18 (March, June, and September 1939); and Joseph Lancaster Brent, *The Lugo Case: A Personal Reminiscence* (New Orleans: Search and Pfaff, 1926). For Los Angeles officials, see "Chronological Record of Los Angeles City Officials, 1850–1938" (typescript, Los Angeles: Municipal Reference Library, City Hall, 1938).

36. Browne, *Report of the Debates*, p. 63; see also Pitt, *Decline of the Californios*, pp. 40–48; and Robert F. Heizer and Alan J. Almquist, *The Other Californians: Prejudice and Discrimination under Spain, Mexico and the United States to 1920* (Berkeley: University of California Press, 1971), pp. 92–119.

37. For California politics in the 1860s, see Fernando Y. Padilla and Carlos B. Ramírez, "Patterns of Chicano Representation in California, Colorado and Nuevo México," *Aztlán* (1974), pp. 191–96; see also Pitt, *Decline of the Californios*, chapters 8, 12, and 14. For an introduction to the diversity of californio views and situations, see Harry Clark, "Their Pride, Their Manners and Their Voices: Sources of the Traditional Portrait of the Early Californians," *California Historical Quarterly* 53 (Spring 1974); see also Madie Brown Emparan, *The Vallejos of California* (San Francisco: University of San Francisco, Gleason Library, 1968); and George Tays, "Mariano Guadalupe Vallejo and Sonoma—A Biography and a History," *California Historical Quarterly* 16 (1937); and Joseph E. Cassidy, "Life and Times of Pablo de la Guerra, 1819–1874" (Ph.D. diss., University of California, Santa Barbara, 1977). See also Mario T. García, "The Californios of San Diego and the Politics of Accommodation," *Aztlán* 6 (Spring 1975); and Charles Hughes, "The Decline of the Californios: The Case of San Diego, 1846–1856," *The Journal of San Diego History* 21 (Summer 1975).

38. For Antonio Coronel, see the appendix of Richard Morefield, "The Mexican Adaptation in American California, 1846–1875."

39. For Santa Barbara, see Pitt, *Decline of the Californios,* chapters 9 and 15; and Albert Camarillo, *Chicanos in a Changing Society,* chapters 4 and 5.

40. On politics in New Mexico, see Chacón, *Legacy of Honor;* Read, *Illustrated History,* chapter 12; Otero, *My Life on the Frontier,* vol. 1, chapters 1 and 23; Twitchell, *History;* Durán, "We Come as Friends"; W. G. Ritch, *New Mexico Blue Book 1882* (Albuquerque: University of New Mexico Press, 1968); Padilla and Ramírez, "Patterns of Chicano Representation," pp. 210–28; William A. Kelleher, *Turmoil in New Mexico, 1846–1848* (Albuquerque: University of New Mexico Press, 1952); Sister Mary Loyola, *The American Occupation of New Mexico, 1821–1852* (Albuquerque: Historical Society of New Mexico, University of New Mexico Press, 1939); Arnold L. Rodríguez, "New Mexico in Transition," *New Mexico Historical Review* 34 (July 1949); and David Weber, *Foreigners in Their Native Land,* pp. 143–44 and 210–28. For perspective, see Jack E. Holmes, *Politics in New Mexico* (Albuquerque: University of New Mexico Press, 1967), chapter 2. See also F. Stanley [Stanley Francis Louis Crocchiola], *Giant in Lilliput: The Story of Donaciano Vigil* (Pampa, Tex: Pampa Print Shop, 1963); and Philip J. Rasch, "The People of the Territory of New Mexico vs. the Santa Fe Ring," *New Mexico Historical Review* 47 (April 1972).

41. On Miguel Antonio Otero's quote, see Horgan, *Lamy of Santa Fe,* pp. 234–35.

42. On Doña Gertrudis, see Angélico Chávez, "Doña Tules: Her Fame and Her Funeral," *El Palacio* 57 (August 1950); and Janet Lecompte, "La Tules and the Americans," *Arizona and the West* 20 (Autumn 1978). After marriage to Manuel Antonio Cisneros and his subsequent leavetaking of her, she kept her property and exerted her rights to make contracts and to litigate. This economically independent woman was equally independent socially. La Tules was literate, which was exceptional for a woman in her time and place. She aided Armijo on several occasions, particularly during the events of 1837. A survivor, La Tules seems to exemplify the latitude of frontier life; her personal life was exceptional, and the tolerance she received seems to indicate that some of her liberties could be attributed to accepted exceptions to the role of women in Mexican society. She was not exceptional in her middle ground ethnically or economically.

43. On stereotypes and economics, see Antonia I. Castañeda, "The Political Economy of Nineteenth Century Stereotypes of California," in A. R. del Castillo, *Between Borders: Essays on Mexican/Chicana History* (Encino: Floricanto, 1990). On stereotypes generally, see Cecil Robinson, *With the Ears of Strangers* (Tucson: University of Arizona Press, 1963); and for stereotypes and mythmaking, see Michael P. Malone, ed., *Historians and the American West* (Lincoln: University of Nebraska, 1983). See also Weber, *Foreigners in Their Native Land,* pp. 52–61.

44. On women and intermarriage, see Darlis A. Miller, "Cross-Cultural Marriages in the Southwest: The New Mexico Experience, 1848–1900," *New Mexico Historical Review* 57 (October 1982); Rebecca M. Craver, "The Impact of Intimacy: Mexican–Anglo Intermarriage in New Mexico, 1821–1846" (El Paso: Texas Western Press, 1982); and Jane Dysart, "Mexican Women in San Antonio, 1830–1860: The Assimilation Process," *Western Historical Quarterly* 76 (October 1976).

45. According to J. N. Bowman, among propertied California women were: María Romana de la Luz Carrillo de Wilson: patent for 48,837.27 acres

Josefa Soto de Stokes	"	" 37,637	"
María Antonieta de Castro	"	" 30,593.95	"
Martina Castro	"	" 32,702.41	"
María del Rosario Estudillo	"	" 48,847.28	"
Vicenta Sepúlveda	"	" 17,774.19	"

(Bowman, "Prominent Women in Provincial California," *Historical Society of California Quarterly* 37 [June 1957].)

46. For data and the examination of women's economic position, see Richard Griswold del Castillo, *La Familia: Chicano Families in the Urban Southwest, 1848 to the Present* (Notre Dame: University of Notre Dame, 1984), pp. 10–92. He reports some women were self-supporting, while others were supported by offspring and relatives. Common-law marriages increased (by 7 percent) and perhaps circumvented the controls of the extended family. An 1862 California civil code made free unions valid, but local tradition had tolerated them before that. Women married later in 1880 than in 1844. In some areas, public education was opened to women, and some used the opportunity. While the U.S. national birth rate fell 14 percent after 1850, the mexicana rate fell at least that much. See also Castillo, "Only for My Family: Historical Dimensions of Chicano Family Solidarity—The Case of San Antonio in 1860," *Aztlán,* 16 (1985); and Deena J. González, "The Widowed Women of Santa Fe: Assessments in the Lifes of an Unmarried Population, 1850–1880" in E. C. DuBois, et al., *Unequal Sisters* (New York: Routledge, 1990).

47. On the Civil War and Mexican participation, see Chacón, *Legacy of Honor* and Simmons, *Little Lion of the Southwest;* see also Jerry Don Thompson, "Mexican Americans in the Civil War: The Battle of Valverde," *Texana* 10 (1972); Darlis A. Miller, "Hispanos and the Civil War: A Reconsideration," *New Mexico Historical Review* 54 (April 1979); Robert W. Delaney, "Matamoros, Port for Texas during the Civil War," *Southwestern Historical Quarterly* 58 (1955); Curtis R. Tyler, *Santiago Vidaurri and the Southern Confederacy* (Austin: State Historical Association, 1973); Betty Gay Hunter Ash, "The Mexican Texans in the Civil War" (Master's thesis, East Texas State University, 1972); Riley, "Santos Benavides"; and Walter L. Buenger, *Secession and*

the Union in Texas (Austin: University of Texas Press, 1984), chapter 5, "Orthodoxy and Ethnicity."

48. On Mexico from the 1850s to 1910, see Daniel Cosío Villegas, et al., *Historia moderna de México: La república restaurada*, 3 vols. (México, D.F.: Hermes, 1955–1957); and Daniel Cosío Villegas, *Historia moderna de México: El porfiriato*, 9 vols. (México, D.F.: Hermes, 1957–1972). As a result of a number of major difficulties, of which defeat in 1848 was not the least, political and ideological struggle between conservatives and liberals in Mexico during the 1850s began to intensify and polarize around the continuing political, economic, and social conditions of the country. In a general sense, the two major ideological tendencies became more defined. The conservatives expressed the view that the Mexican people were as yet incapable of solving their problems alone or of successfully governing their country, and they contended that Independence was actually a cause of Mexico's problems. They believed the majority of the mestizo and Indian population had to be socially and culturally tutored, and should be excluded from political power. They also concluded that to advance, Mexico must reestablish a monarchy headed by a European prince, preferably a member of the Spanish royal family. They argued that European immigration would be an element capable of regenerating and developing the country as in the days of the viceroyalty. This position came to be strongly supported by sectors of the landholding elite, and particularly by the leading economic corporation of the nation, the Catholic church, whose hierarchy still was composed largely of European Spaniards or criollo Mexicans. Indeed, the Vatican itself would have a major role in "solving Mexico's problems." The Liberal Party held, however, that for the nation to develop, it must modernize its political, social, and economic institutions by means of a strong democratic and liberal republican government. For the liberals, the problem was not independence or republican institutions, but the lack of these; or rather, the problem was the retention of colonial institutional forms and values. The solution had to be political, and the legal reform designed that would bring Mexico through development and into the nineteenth century.

49. On the anticonservative, anti-French struggle, see Arturo Arnaiz y Freg and Claude Bataillon, eds., *La intervención francesca y el imperio de Maxmiliano cien años despues, 1862–1962* (México, D.F.: Asociación Mexicana de Historiadores, 1965); Ralph Roeder, *Juárez and His Mexico*, 2 vols. (New York: Viking Press, 1947), vol. 2; and Moisés González Navarro, *La Reforma y el Imperio* (México, D.F.: Sep Setentas, 1972). For consequences on the border there is Mario Cerutti y Miguel González Quiroga, "Guerra y comercio en torno al Río Bravo (1855–1867), Linea fronteriza, espacio económico común," *Historia Mexicana* Vol. 40 (Octobre–Diciembre, 1990).

50. See Gómez-Quiñones, "Notes on the Interpretation of the Relations" and Robert Ryal Miller, "Arms across the Border."

51. The Civil War in the Southwest has not received extensive monographic treatment, except for Texas. For information on strategy and campaigns in New Mexico and Arizona, see Ray C. Colton, *Civil War in the Western Territories* (Norman: University of Oklahoma, 1959); Martin Hall Hardwick, *The Confederate Army of New Mexico* (Austin: University of Texas Press, 1978); Oscar Lewis, *The War in the Far West, 1861–1865* (New York: Doubleday, 1961); Arthur A. Wright, *The Civil War in the South West* (Denver: Big Mountain Press, 1964); and Aurora Hunt, *The Army of the Pacific: Its Operations in California, Texas, Arizona, New Mexico, Utah, Nevada, Oregon, Washington, Plains Region Mexico, etc., 1960–1866* (Glendale: A. H. Clark Co., 1951).

52. See Plácido Vega, *Da cuenta al gobierno de la República* (Tepic: 1867); Miller, "Arms across the Border"; and Robert Ryal Miller, "Plácido Vega: A Mexican Secret Agent in the United States," *The Americas* 19 (1962); Pitt, *Decline of the Californios*, pp. 242–44; David M. Potter, *The Impending Crisis, 1848–1861* (New York: Harper and Row, 1976), chapters 4 and 5, pp. 63–120; and Robert W. Frazer, "Matías Romero and the French Intervention in Mexico" (Ph.D. diss., University of California, Los Angeles, 1941). For views see Jay M. Maisel, "The Origins and Development of Mexican Antipathy Toward the South, 1821–67" (Ph.D. diss., University of Texas, Austin, 1955).

53. For Mexican Confederate participation, see Jerry Don Thompson, *Vaqueros in Blue and Gray* (Austin: Presidial Press, 1976); Gilberto Miguel Hinojosa, *A Borderlands Town in Transition: Laredo, 1755–1890* (College Station: Texas A&M University Press, 1983), pp. 77, 82–86; Pitt, *Decline of the Californios*, pp. 230–33; Betty Gay Hunter Ash, "Mexican Texans"; and Riley, "Santos Benavides."

54. On the post–Civil War period, see Alwyn Barr, *Reconstruction to Reform: Texas Politics, 1876–1906* (Austin: University of Texas Press, 1971); and Peter Camejo, *Racism, Revolution, Reaction, 1861–1877: The Rise and Fall of Radical Reconstruction* (New York: Monad Press, 1976).

55. On California politics, see Padilla and Ramírez, "Patterns of Chicano Representation," pp. 191–95; and Weber, *Foreigners in Their Native Land*, pp. 148–49 and 209–11.

56. For Reginald del Valle, see Wallace E. Smith, *This Land Was Ours: The Del Valles and Camulos*, Grant W. Heil, ed. (Ventura: Ventura County Historical Society, 1977); and Richard Griswold del Castillo, "The Del Valle Family and the Fantasy Heritage," *California History* 59 (Spring 1980).

57. On New Mexico society, politics, and political events, see Otero, *My Life on the Frontier*, vols. 2–3; Chacón, *Legacy of Honor*; Cabeza de Baca, *We*

Fed them Cactus; Read, *Illustrated History of New Mexico,* pp. 453–532; Durán, "We Come as Friends," and Francisco Chávez, "Thomas Benton Catron and Organized Political Violence," *New Mexico Historical Review* 59 (July 1984); Padilla and Ramírez, "Patterns of Chicano Representation," pp. 210–17; Bancroft, *History of Arizona and New Mexico;* and Robert W. Larson, *New Mexico's Quest for Statehood, 1846–1912* (Albuquerque: University of New Mexico Press, 1968); and Holmes, *Politics in New Mexico;* John O. Baxter, "Salvador Armijo: Citizen of Albuquerque, 1829–1879," *New Mexico Historical Review* 53 (July 1978).

58. See Kyle S. Crichton, *Law and Order, Ltd.* (Santa Fe: New Mexico Publishing Co., 1978), which is a biography written with Baca's cooperation.

59. On Colorado, see *House Journal of the First Legislative Assembly of the Territory of Colorado* (Denver: 1861); and *The House and Council Journals of the Legislative Assembly of the Territory of Colorado* (Denver, 1862 et. seq.); Frank Hall, *History of the State of Colorado,* 4 vols. (Chicago: 1889); Robert G. Athearn, *High Country Empire: The High Plains and Rockies* (Lincoln: University of Nebraska Press, 1965); and William B. Taylor and Elliot West, "Patron Leadership at the Crossroads in the Late Nineteenth Century," *Pacific Historical Review* 42 (August 1973); and Padilla and Ramírez, "Patterns of Chicano Representation," pp. 206–10. Felipe Baca would have a descendant, Polly Baca Barraga, who, a hundred years later, would also win elected office in Colorado.

60. On C. Barela, see José Emilio Fernández, *Cuarenta años de legislador: Biografía del Senador Casimiro Barela* (Trinidad: 1911); Ray Burrola, "Casimiro Barela: A Case Study of Chicano Political History in Colorado," in Reynaldo Flores Macias, ed., *Perspectivas en Chicano Studies* (Los Angeles: National Association of Chicano Social Science, Chicano Studies Center, University of California, Los Angeles, 1977).

61. On Arizona politics in general, see Waggoner, *Arizona Territory,* and B. Sacks, "The Creation of Arizona Territory," *Arizona and the West* 5 (Spring 1963). For a general social history, see Thomas E. Sheridan, *Los Tucsonenses: The Mexican Community in Tucson, 1854–1941* (Tucson: University of Arizona Press, 1986); and James E. Officer, *Hispanic Arizona, 1536 and 1856* (Tucson: University of Arizona Press, 1984).

62. On local Mexican politics and society in Arizona, see Hilario Gallego, "Reminiscences of an Arizona Pioneer," *Arizona Historial Review* 6 (January 1935); Frank C. Lockwood, *Life and Old Tucson, 1854–1864, As Remembered by the Little Maid Atancia Santa Cruz* (Los Angeles: Ward Ritchie, 1943); Sheridan, *Los Tucsonenses;* Manuel P. Servín, "The Role of Mexican-Americans in the Development of Early Arizona," in Servín, ed., *An Awakening Minority;* Salome Hernández, "They Also Voted: Mexican Americans of Tucson, 1863–1880" (unpublished paper, n.d.); George Griggs, *History of the Mesilla Valley*

(Las Cruces, N.M.: Bronson Printing Co., 1930); James E. Officer, "Historical Factors in Interethnic Relations in the Community of Tucson," *Arizoniana* 1 (Fall 1960); James E. Officer and Henry F. Dobyns, "Teodoro Ramírez, Early Citizen of Tucson," *Journal of Arizona History* 25 (Autumn 1984); Marcy Gail Goldstein, "Americanization and Mexicanization: The Mexican Elite and Anglo-Americans in the Gadsden Purchase Lands, 1853–1880," (Ph.D. diss., Case Western Reserve University, 1977); Thomas E. Sheridan, "Peacock in the Parlor: Frontier Tucson's Mexican Elite," *Journal of Arizona History* 25 (Autumn 1984); Jay J. Waggoner, *Arizona Territory;* Margret Kathleen Purcell, "Life and Times in Tucson before 1880" (Master's thesis, University of Arizona, 1969); and Henry Pickering Walker, "Freighting from Guaymas to Tucson, 1850–1880," *Western Historical Quarterly* 1 (July 1970).

63. For the C. Velasco quote, see *El Fronterizo* (Tucson), November 18, 1880. On Velasco, see Manuel G. Gonzales, "Carlos I. Velasco," *Journal of Arizona History* 25 (Autumn 1984).

64. On Texas, see the following firsthand but disappointing accounts: Seguín, *Personal Memoirs;* Menchaca, *Memoirs;* Rodríguez, *Memoirs of Early Texas;* and Navarro, *Apuntes históricos interesantes.* See also Frank Cushman Pierce, *A Brief History of the Lower Rio Grande* (Menasha, Wisc.: George Bantu Publishing Co., 1917); and W. H. Chatfield, *The Twin Cities of the Border* (New Orleans: E. P. Brandao, 1893). For interpretation of the background, see Paul Schuster Taylor, *An American–Mexican Frontier: Nueces County, Texas* (Chapel Hill: University of North Carolina Press, 1934), pp. 3–40; and Paul Horgan, *Great River: The Rio Grande in North American History,* vol. 1, New York: Rinehart & Co., 1954 pp. 298–345; see also Roberto R. Calderón, "The Mexican Electorate and Politics in South Texas, 1865 to 1881: Laredo Webb County Texas" (paper presented at the 16th National Association for Chicano Studies Conference, Boulder, Colorado, April 14–16, 1988); Montejano, *Anglos and Mexicans,* chapter 6, "The Politics of Reconstruction"; Paredes, *With a Pistol in His Hand,* chapter 1; Barr, *Reconstruction to Reform;* and Jack C. Vowell, "Politics at El Paso: 1850–1920" (Master's thesis, Texas Western College, 1952). For an overall view that has the tone of the times, see Oran M. Roberts, "The Political, Legislative, and Judicial History of Texas for Its Fifty Years of Statehood, 1845–1895," in Dudley G. Wooten, ed., *A Comprehensive History of Texas* (Dallas: William G. Scariff, 1898).

65. On the Brownsville phenomena, see Evan Anders, *Boss Rule in South Texas: The Progressive Era* (Austin: University of Texas, 1979), pp. 26–64.

66. *The American Flag* (Brownsville), August 20, 1856.

67. On West Texas, see U.S. Congress, *El Paso: Troubles in Texas,* 45th Cong., 2d sess., House Executive Doc., no. 93, ser. 1809; C. L. Sonnichsen, *The El Paso Salt War, 1877* (El Paso: C. Hertzog, 1961); and the series by Leon

Metz in the *El Paso Times*, February 17 and March 10 and 17, 1974. On west Texas politics, see William W. Mills, *Forty Years at El Paso, 1858–1898* (El Paso; C. Herzog, 1962); and Vowell, "Politics at El Paso." For development of the area, see Russel A. White, "El Paso del Norte: The Geography of an Area through 1906" (Ph.D. diss., Columbia University, 1968); see also Mary Romero, "El Paso Salt War: Mob Action or Political Struggle," *Aztlán* 16 (1985).

68. On post–Civil War politics for south Texas, see Calderón, "Mexican Electorate"; Montejano, *Anglos and Mexicans*, part 1, and Anders, *Boss Rule*, chapter 1. On the Laredo riots, see Seb. S. Wilcox, "The Laredo City Election and Riot of April 1886," *Southwestern Historical Quarterly* 45 (July 1941) and Jerry D. Thompson, *Warm Weather and Bad Whiskey: The 1886 Laredo Election Riot* (El Paso: Texas Western Press, 1991). For the attempts at disenfranchisement, see Dale S. McLemore, "The Origins of Mexican American Subordination in Texas," *Social Science Quarterly* 53 (March 1973); and Arnoldo de León, *Rev. Ricardo Rodríguez: An Attempt at Chicano Disenfranchisement in San Antonio, 1896–1897* (San Antonio: Caravel Press, 1979).

69. *El Horizonte*, October 11, 1884; on Laredo, see Calderón, "Mexican Electorate."

70. On late nineteenth-century U.S. social and economic-related changes, see Lamar, *Far Southwest*; and Robert H. Wiebe, *The Search for Order, 1877–1920* (New York: Hill and Wang, 1967).

71. On pre-1900 labor and a few instances of labor organizing, see Juan Gómez-Quiñones, *Development of the Mexican Working Class*; see also Robert W. Larson, *Populism: A Study of Radical Protest in a Western Territory* (Boulder: Colorado Associated University Press, 1974); and Robert E. Zeigler, "The Cowboy Strike of 1883: Its Causes and Meanings," *West Texas Historical Association Yearbook*, vol. 47 (1971). For labor immigration, see Arthur F. Corwin, "Early Mexican Labor Migration: A Frontier Sketch, 1848–1900," in A. F. Corwin, ed., *Immigrants and Immigrants: Perspectives on Mexican Labor Migration to the United States* (Westport: Greenwood Press, 1978).

72. On Las Gorras Blancas and Partido del Pueblo, see Cabeza de Baca, *We Fed Them Cactus*, 89–92; Otero, *My Life on the Frontier*, vol. 2, pp. 248–55; Rosenbaum, *Mexicano Resistance in the Southwest*; Andrew B. Schlesinger, "Las Gorras Blancas, 1889–1891," *Journal of Mexican American History* 1 (Spring 1971); Robert W. Larson, "The White Caps of New Mexico: A Study of Ethnic Militancy in the Southwest," *Pacific Historical Review* 44 (May 1975); and Robert W. Larson, "The Knights of Labor and Native Protest in New Mexico" in Robert Kern, ed., *Labor in New Mexico: Unions, Strikes and Social History since 1881* (Albuquerque: University of New Mexico Press, 1983). The platform quote is from the *Las Vegas Daily Optic*, March 12, 1890.

73. For the several organizational types, see the following. On the Penitentes, see Thomas J. Steele and Rowena A. Rivera, *Penitente Self-Govern-*

ment, Brotherhoods and Councils, 1797–1947 (Santa Fe: Ancient City Press, 1985); and Cabeza de Baca, *We Fed Them Cactus,* pp. 55–56. For the conventional views, see Alexander M. Darley, *The Passionists of the Southwest, or the Holy Brotherhood* (Pueblo, Colorado: 1893); Alice Corbin Henderson, *Brothers of Light: The Penitentes of the Southwest* (New York: Harcourt Brace, 1937); Dorothy Woodward, "The Penitentes of New Mexico" (Ph.D. diss., Yale University, 1935); and Holmes, *Politics in New Mexico,* pp. 33–49. On acequias, see W. Kroenig, "El Condado de Mora," *La Revista Católica* (1885); and Fray Angélico Chávez, "Early Settlements in the Mora Valley," *El Palacio* (November 1955). For masonry, see José María Mates, *Historia de la masonería en México desde 1806 hasta 1884* (México, D.F.: 1884); Joseph W. Hale, "Masonry in the Early Days of Texas," *Southwestern Historical Quarterly* 49 (January 1946); and James D. Caster, *Masonry in Texas: Background History and Influence to 1846* (Waco: Committee on Masonic Education and Service for the Grand Lodge of Texas, 195). For the Constitution and organizational activities of a literary society, see "La Sociedad Social, Literaria y de Devates de Agua Negra, Nuevo México," *De Colores* 1 (Summer 1974).

74. On late nineteenth-century mutualistas, see José Amaro Hernández, *Mutual Aid for Survival: The Case of the Mexican American* (Malabar: Krieger, 1983); James D. McBride, "The Liga Protectora Latina: A Mexican American Benevolent Society in Arizona," *Journal of the West* (October 1975); and on the Alianza, see Kaye Lynn Briegel, "Alianza Hispano-Americana, 1894–1965: A Mexican American Fraternal Insurance Society" (Ph.D. diss., University of Southern California, 1974); and Gonzáles, "Carlos I. Velasco."

75. Consular materials are available at the Secretaría de Relaciones Exteriores, and the U.S. departments of State and Justice on microfilm. For their structure and duties see Secretaria de Relaciones Exteriores, *Guía Diplomática y Consular,* (México, D.F.: Francisco Díaz de León, 1902). On consulates, see Juan Gómez-Quiñones, "Piedras contra la Luna, México en Aztlán y Aztlán en México: Chicano Mexican Relations and the Mexican Consulates, 1900–1920," in James W. Wilkie, et al., eds., *Contemporary Mexico: Papers of the IV International Congress of Mexican History* (Berkeley: University of California Press, 1976). See also Mario T. García, "Porfirian Diplomacy and the Administration of Justice in Texas, 1877–1910," *Aztlán* 16 (1985).

76. On women, see Castillo, *Los Angeles Barrio,* pp. 65–74; J. N. Bowman, "Prominent Women in Provincial California," *Historical Society of California Quarterly* 37 (June 1957), p. 153; Donald P. Hargis, "Women's Rights: California 1949," *Southern California Quarterly* 37 (December 1955), p. 320; and Manuel Ruiz, *Mexican American Legal Heritage in the Southwest* (Los Angeles: 1972), pp. 31–33.

77. See Castillo, "Del Valle Family," p. 7; Barbara Marinacci, "Doña Arcadia, Santa Monica's Godmother," *Previews* (1985); George Fitzpatrick,

"Doña Margarita: Symbol of Life Style Now Gone," *Albuquerque Journal*, November 14, 1976, section A; and Sandra L. Stephens, "Women of the Amador Family," in Joan M. Jensen and Darlis A. Miller, eds., *New Mexico Women: Intercultural Perspectives* (Albuquerque: University of New Mexico Press, 1986). One of the granddaughters of Doña Isabel was at the San Francisco United Nations Organizing Conference in 1946.

    78. On economic changes for Southwest women, see Castillo, *La Familia;* and Kenneth L. Stewart and Arnoldo de León, "Work Force Participation among Mexican Immigrant Women in Texas, 1900," *The Border Lands Journal* 9 (Spring 1986). For changes in Mexico, see *La mujer y el movimiento obrero mexicano en el Siglo XIX* (México, D.F.: Centro de Estudios Históricos del Movimiento Obrero Mexicano, 1975); Margaret Towners, "Monopoly Capitalism and Women's Work during the Porfiriato," in *Women in Latin America: An Anthology from Latin American Perspectives* (Riverside: Latin American Perspectives, 1979); and Vivian M. Vallens, *Working Women in Mexico during the Porfiriato, 1880–1910* (San Francisco: R&E Research Associates, 1978). Social expectations were evident in, for example, one of the concessions from one of the first successful modern strikes in Mexico 1868: the workday for women was reduced to twelve hours per day, in contrast to fifteen hours for men, so that women could attend to their household duties.

    In the labor movement of Mexico during the late 1870s and early 1880s, several women became prominent. In 1879, Carmen Huerta, the earliest-known major female labor leader, was elected as president of the "Gran Círculo de Obreros de Mexico," which claimed eight thousand members. With the decline of real wages and increased repression, women's roles in labor leadership grew uneven. Even among progressives engaged in protest, the appeals to women were most often for them to help men, to agitate, support and nurture men in their struggle for the coming revolution; woman's duty was to be the auxiliary, not the frontline activist. Significantly, however, the early socialist and anarchist understood and deplored the "ancient misfortune of woman." In Central Mexico itself, women's fight for their own rights as women gained visibility and strength with the rise of radical liberalism, anarchism, and socialism during the course of the late nineteenth century. In a few instances, political violence was asserted as a means of moving toward equality. Apart from direct organizing activities, women occasionally were contributors to the radical press of the day, which provided a partial forum for their political views. Eventually, members of La Sociedad Artística Industrial called for equal rights for women, and this issue was debated intensely at the Congreso General Obrero de México in March 1876. See John Hart, "Working Class Women in the 19th Century in Mexico," in M. Mora and A. R. del Castillo, eds., *Mexican Women in the United States: Struggles Past and Present* (Los Angeles: Chicano Studies Research Center, University of California, Los

Angeles, 1980), p. 152. See also Armando List Arzubides, *Apuntes sobre la prehistoria de la revolución* (México, D.F.: 1958). For a quote suggesting a militant viewpoint, see R. R. Baños, *Virginidad y machismo en México* (México, D.F.: DIDA, 1973):

> La violencia revolucionaria es el único vehículo y su enmarcamiento histórico la única jornada definida, en que la mujer adquiere igualdad con el hombre y la hace valedera en todas sus actitudes. (p. 57)

79. On Lucy Gonzales, see Lucy E. Parsons, *Life of Albert Parsons* (Chicago: 1889); and Gonzales's own "Cause of Sex Slavery," *Firebrand* 1 (January 27, 1895); for a fervent view of Lucy Gonzales as a United States Black, see Carolyn Ashbaugh, *Lucy Parsons: American Revolutionary* (Chicago: C. Kerr, 1976).

80. Richard and Gloria Rodríguez, "Teresa Urrea: Her Life as It Affected the Mexican–U.S. Frontier," *El Grito* 5 (Summer 1972), p. 61. See also Mario Gill, "La santa de Cabora," *Historia mexicana* 6 (1957); and David López Plimbert, "Tomochic" (Master's thesis, Universidad Nacional Autónoma de México, México, D.F., 1963). For an outstanding figure active at the turn of the century, see Emilio Zamora, "Sara Estela Ramírez: Una Rosa Roja en el Movimiento," in Mora and Castillo, eds., *Mexican Women in the United States*.

81. For comments on changes, see Carmon Ramos Escandón, "Señoritas porfirianas: Mujer e ideología en el México progresista, 1880–1910," and Jean Pierre Bastian, "Modelos de mujer protestante: Ideología religiosa y educación femenina, 1880–1910," in Carmen Ramos Escandón, ed., *Presencia y transparencia: La mujer en la historia de México* (México, D.F.: El Colegío de México, 1987); and Moíses Gonzáles Navarro, "Educación y trabajo en el porfiriato," *Historia mexicana* 6 (1957); and Gómez-Quiñones, "Notes."

82. See issues of *Las Dos Repúblicas* in the 1870s, *El Fronterizo* in the 1880s, or *La Fe Católica* in the 1890s. See also Julia Tuñon Pablos, *Mujeres en México* (México, D.F.: Planeta, 1987), "La mujer mexicana en el siglo XIX," pp. 83–129; and Francoise Carner, "Estereotipos femeninos en el siglo XIX" in Escandón, *Presencia y transparencia*.

83. On the 1898 conflicts, see David Healy, *U.S. Expansion: Imperialist Urge in the 1890s* (Madison: University of Wisconsin Press, 1970); and H. Wayne Morgan, *America's Road to Empire: The War with Spain and Overseas Expansion* (New York: Wiley, 1965).

84. On the prior border conflict, see *Report of the Mexican Commission on the Northern Question* (New York: 1875). For border dissent, see Cosío Villegas, *Historia moderna de México: El porfiriato*, vol. 1, pp. 322–26; and for discussion of Mexico's politics, see Cosío Villegas, ibid., *La vida política interior*, 2 vols. On transborder interaction, see Gómez-Quiñones, "Piedras contra la Luna," pp. 497–500; and Enrique Cortés, "Chicano Colonies in

Mexico," *Aztlán* 10 (Fall 1979). On border military action, see Robert D. Gregg, *The Influence of Border Troubles on Relations between the United States and Mexico, 1876–1910* (Baltimore: Johns Hopkins Press, 1967); and Clarence C. Clenden, *Blood on the Border: The United States Army and the Mexican Irregulars* (New York: Macmillan, 1969).

85. For Ignacio Martínez, see *El Tiempo*, February 5, 1891; for Pauliso Martínez, *Diario del Hogar*, April 14, 1898; for Francisco Ruiz Sandoval, see Daniel Cosío Villegas, *Historia moderna de México, El Porfiriato, La vida política exterior*, vol. 2, pp. 323–24.

86. On Catarino E. Garza, see his *La era de Tuxtepec en Mexico o sea Rusia en América* (San José: 1894); Matías Romero, "Garza Raid and Its Lessons," *North American Review* 155 (July 1892); and *El Siglo XIX*, February 17, 1892. See also J. C. Valadés, "Revolución fallida en 1891," *La Prensa*, August 10, 1941 and Gilbert M. Cuthbertson, "Catarino E. Garza and the Garza War," *Texana* 12, no. 4 (n.d.).

Chapter 4

1. Newspaper sources for the first half of the twentieth century are *El Demócrata Fronterizo* (1905–1910), *La Crónica* (1910–1914), *Regeneración* (1904–1918), *La Vanguardia* (1921), *La Prensa* (1913–1940), and *La Opinión* (1926–1940); there are hundreds of community-organizing efforts reported in these pages as well as extensive social and labor information. For views on the press see interviews in "Journalism and Leadership," in Manuel Gamio, *The Mexican Immigrant: His Life Story* (New York: Dover Publications, 1971). Apart from primary materials, sensitive insight into the Mexican community is found in the works of Américo Paredes, starting with *With His Pistol in His Hand: A Border Ballad and Its Hero* (Austin: University of Texas Press, 1958). On U.S. economic and social transformation, before and after 1900, see Robert H. Walker, *Life in the Age of Enterprise, 1865–1900* (New York: Capricorn Books, 1971); John W. Dodds, *Life in Twentieth Century America* (New York: Capricorn Books, 1973); and Julius W. Pratt, *Challenge and Rejection, 1900–1921* (New York: Macmillan, 1967).

2. Recently now published as books, dissertations on studies of the urban community at the turn of the century provide insights into aspects of economic changes, but do not substantively address any understanding of political activity. See Ricardo Romo, *East Los Angeles: History of a Barrio* (Austin: University of Texas Press, 1983); and Mario García, *Desert Immigrants: The Mexicans of El Paso, 1880–1920* (New Haven: Yale University Press, 1981). For direct, informative insight as to how Mexicans consciously dealt with aspects of urban change, see Stanley A. West, "The Mexican Aztec Society: A

Mexican Voluntary Association in Diachronic Perspective" (Ph.D. diss., Syracuse University, 1973). For a general view of the urbanization experience, see Ricardo Romo, "The Urbanization of Southwestern Chicanos in the Early Twentieth Century," *New Scholar* 6 (1977). For the Midwest, see Louise Año Nuevo Kerr, "The Chicano Experience in Chicago, 1920–1970" (Ph.D. diss., University of Illinois at Chicago Circle, 1976); Gilbert Cardenas, "Who Are the Midwestern Chicanos?: Implications for Chicano Studies," *Aztlán* 7 (Summer 1976); Francisco Arturo Rosales, "The Regional Origins of Mexicano Immigrants to Chicago during the 1920s," *Aztlán* 7 (Summer 1976); and Richard Parra, Victor Rios, and Armando Gutiérrez, "Chicano Organizations in the Midwest: Past, Present, and Possibilities," *Aztlán* 7 (Summer 1976). Further information on Mexicans in the midwestern United States may be found in Stanley A. West and June Macklin, eds., *The Chicano Experience* (Boulder: Westview Press, 1979).

3. As more studies become available and more sources are examined, it is clearer that the Mexican population was significantly underestimated by the secondary literature of the twentieth century, as well as in nineteenth-century U.S. census reports and other enumerations. For population, see Oscar J. Martínez, "On the Size of the Chicano Population, New Estimates 1850–1900," *Aztlán: International Journal of Chicano Studies Research* 6, no. 1 (Spring 1975); see also Richard Nostrand, "The Hispano Homeland in 1900," *Annals of the Association of American Geographers*, vol. 70 (1980). On World War I Mexican participation, see J. Luz Sáenz, *El Mexico-Americano en la Guerra Mundial* (San Antonio: Artes Gráficas, 1933).

4. Mexicanidad is clearly evident in a range of statements, in folk material, and in newspaper items. Americanización is articulated in institutional programmatic statements, in the writings of social workers or teachers, and in some political statements. The Spanish ploy can be found in the writings of Helen Hunt Jackson, Charles F. Lummis, Bret Harte, Oliver La Farge, Hubert Howe Bancroft, and Herbert E. Bolton, among Anglos; and among Mexicans or Mexican-related individuals, Miguel Antonio Otero, Guadalupe Vallejo, Benjamin Read, Aurelio Espinosa, Nancy González, Adelina Otero, and Fray Angélico Chávez. As is well known, the "Spanish" debate was continued during the post–World War II period. Some glimpses into the ways in which individuals observed and reacted to these identifications can be gleaned from Manuel Gamio, *The Life Story of the Mexican Immigrant: Autobiographic Documents* (Chicago: University of Chicago Press, 1931). For insightful observations by a folklorist working in the first half of the century, see Arthur L. Campa, *Hispanic Folklore Studies of Arthur L. Campa* (New York: Arno Press, 1976). Dr. Américo Paredes, with fine scholarship and wry humor, also explores these identities.

At the turn of the century, persons of Mexican descent in the United

States referred to themselves generally as Mexicans, though terms such as *Latin American, Spanish American,* and *Hispano* were also used, and infrequently, *Mexican American.* Mexican Americans, or long-term Mexican residents of the Southwest, were known by their regional names, such as Tejano, Californio, Hispano (for Nuevo Mexicano) or simply as Mexicanos, as other long-term Mexican residents and upper- and middle-class Mexicans. The term *Chicano,* as in "Chicano Studies" or "Chicano History," is a contemporary designation for persons of Mexican nationality, culture, and/or ancestry, which was not used in the nineteenth century or in the first half of the twentieth century as a general and frequent public term of group identity for Mexicans in the United States. Nevertheless, the term was in use. In some examples of usage during the first half of the twentieth century, the term *Chicano* was a designation for working-class males, including immigrants, and was employed as a diminutive in reference to children. This usage is found in the studies of Dr. Manuel Gamio, which were conducted at this time, or it was recalled later from direct experience, as in the case of Dr. Ernesto Galarza. See also Paul Schuster Taylor, *An American-Mexican Frontier, Nueces County, Texas* (New York: Russell and Russell, 1934), pp. 241–49. For sensitive and substantive analysis, see José E. Limón, "The Folk Performance of 'Chicano' and the Cultural Limits of Political Ideology," in Richard Bauman and Roger D. Abrahams, eds., *And Other Neighborly Names: Social Process and Cultural Image in Texas Folklore* (Austin: University of Texas, 1981). See also George J. Sánchez, "Becoming Mexican American: Ethnicity and Acculturation in Chicano Los Angeles, 1900–1943" (Ph.D. diss., Stanford University, 1989).

5. For the range and merits of newspapers, see the several articles in *Journalism History* 4 (Summer 1977), special issue on "Spanish Language Media"; and for an analysis of the major newspaper, see Onofre di Stefano, "Venimos a Luchar: A Brief History of *La Prensa's* Founding," *Aztlán* 16 (1985); and Francine Medieros, "*La Opinión,* A Mexican Exile Newspaper: A Content Analysis of Its First Years, 1926–1929," *Aztlán* 11 (Spring 1980).

6. For direct insight on immigrants and immigration at the time, see Manuel Gamio, *Mexican Immigration to the United States* (New York: Arno Press, 1930); and Enrique Santibañes, *Ensayo Acerca de la Inmigración Mexicana en los Estados Unidos* (San Antonio: Clegg Co., 1930). For overall interpretation, see Jorge Bustamante, "The Historical Context of Undocumented Mexican Immigration to the United States"; and Juan Gómez-Quiñones, "Mexican Immigration to the United States and the Internationalization of Labor, 1848–1980," both in Antonio Rios Bustamante, ed., *Mexican Immigrant Workers in the United States* (Los Angeles: Chicano Studies Research Center Publications, University of California, Los Angeles, 1981). For a book-length treatment, see Lawrence Cardoso, *Mexican Emigration to the*

United States, 1897–1951: Social Economic Patterns (Tucson: University of Arizona Press, 1980).

7. On transborder ties, material was drawn from the Archivo Secretaría de Relaciones Exteriores and Centro de Estudios de Historia, Archivo Venustiano Carranza. See Juan Gómez-Quiñones, "Notes on an Interpretation of the Relations between the Mexican Community in the United States and Mexico," in Carlos Vasquez and Manuel García y Griego, eds., Mexican–U.S. Relations: Conflict and Convergence (Los Angeles: Chicano Studies Research Center, University of California, Los Angeles, 1983); Juan Gómez-Quiñones, "Relaciones chicano mexicanas y los consulados mexicanos, 1900–1920," Controversia 1 (May–July 1977) and William D. Raat, Revoltosos: Mexico's Rebels in the United States, 1903–1923 (College Station: Texas A&M Press, 1981). On Mexico at the time, see Daniel Cosío Villlegas, et al., Historia Moderna de México: El porfiriato, 9 vols. (México, D.F.: Editorial Hermes, 1957–1972); and Juan Gómez-Quiñones, "Political Discourse, Policy and Dissidence, Nationalism and the Crisis of 1910, Its Antecedents and Its Aftermath," unpublished manuscript based on extensive primary sources.

8. Newspapers, particularly Regeneración and La Prensa, are informative on class perceptions and characteristics. For a general discussion of the historical profile of social classes and socioeconomic stratification in the Mexican community in the United States, see Antonio Rios Bustamante, "Las clases sociales mexicanas en Estados Unidos," Historia y Sociedad, no. 20 (1978); see also Mario Barrera, Race and Class in the Southwest: A Theory of Racial Inequality (Notre Dame: University of Notre Dame Press, 1979). For a particular examination of late nineteenth-century occupational distribution, see Chester Alwyn Barr, "Occupational and Geographic Mobility in San Antonio, 1870–1900," Social Science Quarterly 51 (September 1970); and for the same data at the turn of the century, see Victor C. Clark, Mexican Labor in the United States (Washington, D.C.: Government Printing Office, 1908). For comments on classes in New Mexico, see Caroline Zeleny, Relations between the Spanish Americans and Anglo Americans in New Mexico (New York: Arno Press, 1974), pp. 308–16; and Ernest B. Fincher, Spanish Americans as a Political Factor in New Mexico, 1912–1950 (New York: Arno Press, 1974), pp. 34–79. For classes in Texas, see Taylor, American-Mexican Frontier, pp. 173–90, 241–49.

9. For a view of workers and their conditions at the time, see John William Knox, "The Economic Status of the Mexican Immigrant" (Master's thesis, University of Texas at Austin, 1927); Vernon Monroe McCombs, From over the Border: A Study of the Mexicans in the United States (New York: Council of Women for Home Missions, 1925); and The Survey 66 (May 1, 1931), a special number on Mexicans. For narrative and interpretation, see Juan Gómez-Quiñones, Development of the Mexican Working Class North of the Río Bravo: Work and Culture among Laborers and Artisans, 1600–1900 (Los Angeles:

Chicano Studies Research Center, University of California, Los Angeles, 1982), and "The First Steps: Chicano Labor Conflict and Organizing, 1900–1920," *Aztlán* 3 (Spring 1972).

10. On labor distribution and organizing, see David Maciel, *Al norte del Río Bravo: Pasado inmediato: 1930–1981*, tomo 17, *La clase obrera en la historia de México* (Instituto de Investigaciones Sociales, México, D.F.: Siglo Veintiuno, 1981); Mark Reisler, *By the Sweat of Their Brow: Mexican Immigrant Labor in the United States, 1900–1940* (Westport: Greenwood Press, 1976); and Juan Gómez-Quiñones and Luis L. Arroyó, eds., *Orígenes del movimiento obrero chicano* (México, D.F.: Ediciones Era, 1978). See also Andrés Jiménez Montoya, "Political Domination in the Labor Market: Racial Division in the Arizona Copper Industry" (Berkeley: Institute for the Study of Social Change, University of California, 1977).

11. As an example of mutualista constitutions and bylaws, see *Constitución y leyes de la organización Hispano-Americana de Mutua Protección* (New Mexico: 1920). On masonry among Mexicans, see José María Mateos, *Historia de la masonería en México desde 1806 hasta 1884* (México, D.F.: 1884). For references to the activities of *La Orden Caballeros de Honor*, see *La Crónica*, December 3, 1910, and January 12, 1912. On early twentieth-century organizations, see Miguel David Tirado, "Mexican American Community Political Organization: The Key to Chicano Political Power," *Aztlán* 1 (Spring 1970); José Amaro Hernández, *Mutual Aid for Survival: The Case of the Mexican American* (Malabar Krieger, 1939); Julie Leininger Pycior, "La Raza Organizes: Mexican American Life in San Antonio as Reflected in Mutualista Activities" (Ph.D. diss., University of Notre Dame, 1979); Kaye Briegel, "Alianza Hispano-Americana, 1894–1965: A Mexican American Fraternal Insurance Society" (Ph.D. diss., University of Southern California, 1974); and Maurilio Vigil, "Ethnic Organizations among Mexican Americans of New Mexico: A Political Perspective" (Ph.D. diss., University of New Mexico, Albuquerque, 1974).

12. *Constitución y leyes*, p. 2.

13. *El Labrador*, March 20, 1904, as quoted in David J. Weber, *Foreigners in Their Native Land* (Albuquerque: University of New Mexico Press, 1973), pp. 252–53.

14. See *La Crónica* (1910–11) for the coverage of the Congress, and for interpretive narrative see José E. Limón, "El Primer Congreso Mexicanista de 1911: A Precursor to Contemporary Chicanismo," *Aztlán* 5 (Spring and Fall 1974); and José E. Limón, "El Primer Congreso Mexicanista de 1911: A Note on Research in Progress," *Aztlán* 3 (Spring 1972). Professor Limón includes several speeches from the Congress in the appendix to his 1974 article on it. The three quotes are drawn from this appendix; the first quote is from J. M. Mora, p. 108; the second is from Telesporo Macias, p. 115; and the third is from J. M. Mora, p. 107.

15. Weber, *Foreigners in Their Native Land*, pp. 248–51. The quote from Soledad Flores de Peña is from J. Limón, "El Primer Congreso" appendix, p. 112.

16. See Juan Gómez-Quiñones, *Sembradores: Ricardo Flores Magón y el Partido Liberal Mexicano: A Eulogy and Critique* (Los Angeles: Chicano Studies Research Center, University of California, Los Angeles, 1973); and Gómez-Quiñones, "Piedras contra la Luna, Mexico en Aztlán, Aztlán en Mexico: Chicano–Mexican Relations and the Mexican Consulates, 1900–1920," in James W. Wilkie, et al., eds., *Contemporary Mexico*, Papers of the IV International Congress of Mexican History (Berkeley México, D.F.: University of California Press, El Colegio de México, 1976); and Emilio Zamora, "Sara Estela Ramírez: Una Rosa Roja en el Movimiento," in Magdalena Mora and Adelaida R. del Castillo, eds., *Mexican Women in the United States: Struggles Past and Present* (Los Angeles: Chicano Studies Research Center, University of California, Los Angeles, 1980), pp. 163–69; and Emilio Zamora, "Chicano Socialist Activity in Texas, 1900–1920," *Aztlán* 6 (Summer 1975), p. 226.

17. The quotes are H. Moncayo from J. Limón, El Primer Congreso, p. 113, appendix.

18. T. Villareal, et al., in J. Gómez-Quiñones, *Sembradores*, pp. 76–77.

19. E. Zamora, "Una Rosa Roja"; the quotes are from pp. 164 and 168, and from J. Gómez-Quiñones, *Sembradores*, p. 97.

20. For references to this women's activity, see *Regeneración*, April 15, 1916, and March 25, 1916, for the group's "Luz y Vida" and "Praxedis G. Guerrero," respectively. Juan Gómez-Quiñones, *Las ideas políticas de Ricardo Flores Magón* (México, D.F.: ERA, 1977), p. 56; and Emma M. Pérez, "A la Mujer: A Critique of the Partido Liberal Mexicano's Gender Ideology on Women" in A. Del Castillo, ed., *Between Borders*. On the development of anarchism among Mexicans, including participation of women, see John Hart, *Anarchism and the Mexican Working Class, 1860–1931* (Austin: University of Texas, 1978). The quote from Sara E. Ramírez is in E. Zamora, "Una Rosa Roja," p. 165, and the one from Margarita Andejos, et al., in J. Gómez-Quiñones, *Sembradores*, p. 82.

21. For statements on La Liga Femenil, see *La Crónica*, October 19 and December 7, 1911; and José E. Limón, "El Primer Congreso Mexicanista de 1911: A Precursor," p. 45.

22. Manifesto (photocopy); see also Gómez-Quiñones, "Piedras contra la Luna."

23. Correspondence, Leonor Villegas de Magnon to Venustiano Carranza, May 12, 1915; and Jovita Idar, et al. to María de Jesús Perez, May 11, 1915 (photostatic copy); and Juan Gómez-Quiñones, "Piedras contra la Luna," p. 517.

24. On statehood as seen at the time, see Waldemar Westergard, "Thomas

R. Bard and the Arizona–New Mexico Controversy," *Annual Publications of the Historical Society of Southern California*, vol. 11 (Los Angeles: 1919); and L. Bradford Prince, *New Mexico's Struggle for Statehood: Sixty Years of Effort to Obtain Self-Government* (Santa Fe: 1910).

25. *La Voz del Pueblo* (1906), as quoted in Weber, *Foreigners in Their Native Land*, pp. 245–46.

26. See Con Cronin, ed., *Journal of the Constitutional Convention of Arizona* (Phoenix: n.p., 1925); and Donald Robinson Van Petten, *The Constitution and Government of Arizona* (Phoenix: Sun Country, Press, 1952). For the social history of Arizona, see Thomas E. Sheridan, *Los Tucsonenses: The Mexican Community in Tucson, 1854–1941* (Tucson: University of Arizona Press, 1986).

27. *Proceedings of the Constitutional Convention of the Proposed State of New Mexico* (Albuquerque: Press of the Morning Journal, 1910); and Reuben W. Heflin, "The New Mexico Constitutional Convention," *New Mexico Historical Review* 21 (January 1946).

28. *Constitutions of the United States: National and State* (New York), vol. 2, pp. 25–26.

29. On turn-of-the-century New Mexico politics, see Miguel A. Otero, *My Nine Years as Governor of the Territory of New Mexico, 1897–1906* (Albuquerque: University of New Mexico Press, 1940); and Benjamin Read, *Illustrated History of New Mexico* (Santa Fe: New Mexican Printing Company, 1912), pp. 595–644.

30. See Fincher, *Spanish Americans;* and Zeleny, *Relations.*

31. On Larrazolo, see Alfred C. Cordova and Charles B. Judah, *Octaviano Larrazolo: A Political Portrait* (Albuquerque: Department of Government, Division of Research, 1952); and Paul Walter, "Octaviano Larrazolo," *New Mexico Historical Review* vol. 7 (April 1932).

32. See works by Fincher, *Spanish Americans;* Zeleny, *Relations;* and Jack Holmes, *Politics in New Mexico* (Albuquerque: University of New Mexico Press, 1967), chapters 1, 2, 5, and 6; as well as Warren E. Beck, *New Mexico: A History of Four Centuries* (Norman: University of Oklahoma Press, 1962), pp. 226–41 and 296–315. For figures on voting and ethnic descent of persons, see *New Mexico Blue Book 1915* (Santa Fe: Office of Secretary of State).

33. On Texas politics, see *El Demócrata Fronterizo* and *La Prensa;* José Tomás Canales, "Personal Recollections" (unpublished manuscript, Brownsville, Texas, April 28, 1945); and David Montejano, *Anglos and Mexicans in the Making of Texas, 1836–1986* (Austin: University of Texas Press, 1987). For the context at the turn of the century, see Américo Paredes, *With a Pistol in His Hand* (Austin: University of Texas Press, 1958), chapter 1; and Randal Lionel Waller, "The Callaghan Machine and San Antonio Politics, 1885–1912" (Master's thesis, Texas Tech University, Lubbock, 1973).

34. Evan Anders, _Boss Rule in South Texas: The Progressive Era_ (Austin: University of Texas Press, 1982); Emilio Zamora, _El movimiento obrero mexicano en el sur de Texas, 1900–1920_ (México, D.F.: Secretaría de Educación Pública, 1986).

35. See Anders, _Boss Rule;_ Montejano, _Anglos and Mexicans;_ and Don M. Coerver and Linda B. Hall, _Texas and the Mexican Revolution: A Study in State and National Border Policy, 1910–1920_ (San Antonio: Trinity University Press, 1984).

36. See Canales, "Personal Recollections"; and Taylor, _American-Mexican Frontier._ For a report on J. T. Canales's presentation on the Rangers, see _La Prensa,_ February 11, 1919. For his view on historical events, see José T. Canales, _Bits of Texas History in the Melting Pot of America_ (San Antonio: Artes Gráficas, vol. 1, 1950; vol. 2, 1957).

37. For materials on the PLM, information was drawn from _Regeneración_ and Bancroft Library, University of California, Berkeley, Silvestre Terrazas Collection; National Archives, Washington, D.C., Department of Justice, Record Group 60; National Archives, Washington, D.C., Department of State, Record Group 59; Secretaría de Relaciones Exteriores, Archivo, México, D.F., Asunto: Flores Magón, etc. Colocación L-E-918-954, 36 tomos; and Sterling Library, Yale University, New Haven, Harry Weinberger Collection, as well as interviews with Nicolás T. Bernal (México, D.F.), 1966; José Muñoz Cota (México, D.F.), 1966; and Ethel Duffy Turner (Cuernavaca), 1966. See Gómez-Quiñones, _Sembradores;_ Salvador Hernández, "El Magonismo, 1901/1922: Breve historia de una pasión libertaria," _Memoria, Boletín del CEMOS,_ vol. 1, no. 2 (Junio-Julio 1983) and Javier Torres Pares, _La revolución sin fronteras_ (México D.F.: UNAM, 1990). Also see Arnaldo Córdova, _La ideología de la revolución mexicana, La formación del nuevo régimen_ (México, D.F.: ERA, 1973); and James D. Cockcroft, _Intellectual Precursors of the Mexican Revolution, 1900–1913_ (Austin: University of Texas Press, 1968). As to the actions and views of conservative exiles, see Antimaco Sax, _Los mexicanos en el destierro_ (San Antonio: International Printers, 1916).

38. See Zamora, _El movimento obrero mexicano._ For Southwest radical activity, see James R. Green, _Grass Roots Socialism: Radical Movements in the Southwest, 1895–1943_ (Baton Rouge: Louisiana State University Press, 1978).

39. Juan Gómez-Quiñones, "Piedras contra la Luna," pp. 505–9; Raat, _Revoltosos;_ Walter Prescott Webb, _The Texas Rangers: A Century of Frontier Defense_ (New York: Houghton Mifflin Co., 1935), chapter 21; Charles C. Cumberland, "Border Raids in the Lower Rio Grande Valley, 1915," _Southwestern Historical Quarterly_ 57 (January 1954); and Lyle C. Brown, _Los liberales mexicanos y su lucha en contra la dictadura de Porfirio Díaz, 1900–1906_ (México, D.F.: Mexico City College, 1956).

40. On the plan and concurrent activity, see Senate, Committee on Foreign Relations, Investigation of Mexican Affairs, Senate Document 285, 66th Cong., 2d sess. (Washington, D.C.: Government Printing Office, 1919–1920), vol. 1 and 2. Because of Senator Fall's bias, his Senate testimony emphasizes the negative against Mexico's revolutionary factions. There were two perhaps three versions of the *plan*, and one Spanish version is available. For contemporary coverage, see *La Prensa*, September 9 and 10, 1915; *Corpus Christi Caller*, July–October 1915; *The New York Times*, July–October 1915; and for observations on incidents and individual participants, see Ignacio Muñoz, *La verdad sobre los gringos* (México, D.F.: Ediciones Populares, 1927), pp. 75–131. The events surrounding the Plan of San Diego and conflicts in south Texas during the period of the Mexican Revolution have undergone scrutiny and clarification. For summary information regarding concurrent events and the Plan, see Juan Gómez-Quiñones, "Research Notes on the Twentieth Century: Plan de San Diego Reviewed," *Aztlán* 1 (Spring 1970); see also Friedrich Katz, *The Secret War in Mexico: Europe, the United States and the Mexican Revolution* (Chicago: University of Chicago Press, 1981), pp. 339–44; Douglas W. Richmond, "La Guerra de Texas se Renova: Mexican Insurrection and Carrancista Ambitions, 1900–1920," *Aztlán* 11 (1980); James A. Sandos, "The Plan of San Diego: War and Diplomacy on the Texas Border, 1915–1916," *Arizona and the West* 14 (Spring 1972); and Charles H. Harris and Louis R. Sadler, "The Plan of San Diego–United States War Crises of 1916: A Reexamination," *Hispanic American Historical Review* 58 (1978). Raat, *Revoltosos;* for a fine summary analysis, see Emilio Zamora, "The Chicano Origin and Development of the San Diego Revolt" (paper presented at the 2d annual conference of the Chicano Social Science Association, Austin, Texas, 1973). For a strong argument stressing the role of the adherents of Venustiano Carranza, see Rodolfo Rocha, "The Influence of the Mexican Revolution on the Texas Border, 1910–1916" (Ph.D. diss., Texas Tech University, 1981); and Coerver and Hall, *Texas and the Mexican Revolution.*

41. For repression and difficulties for immigrants and minorities, see Robert K. Murray, *Red Scare: A Study in National Hysteria* (Minneapolis: University of Minnesota Press, 1955); Sidney Lens, *The Labor Wars* (New York: Doubleday, 1974), pp. 256–82. A very benign view of the times and minority relations is Richard Weiss, "Ethnicity and Reform," *Journal of American History* 66 (1979).

42. See *La Prensa* and *La Opinión*, the works of Manuel Gamio; and Victor Nelson Cisneros, "La Clase Trabajadora en Texas," *Aztlán* 6 (Summer 1975); Roberto A. Cuellar, "A Social and Political History of the Mexican American Population of Texas, 1929–1963" (San Francisco: R&E Research Associates, 1974); and O. Douglas Weeks, "The Texas-Mexican and the Politics of South Texas," *American Political Science Review* 24 (August 1930). See also Edgar

Greer Sheldon, Jr., "Political Conditions among Texas Mexicans along the Rio Grande" (Master's thesis, University of Texas, Austin, 1946); Doug Monroy, "Mexicans in Los Angeles, 1930–1941: An Ethnic Group in Relation to Class Forces" (Ph.D. diss., University of California, Los Angeles, 1978); and Richard A. Garcia, *Rise of the Mexican American Middle Class: San Antonio, 1929–1941* (College Station: Texas A & M University, 1991).

43. For elected officials and other data, see *California Blue Book* (Sacramento: State Printing Office, various dates); particularly *California Blue Book (1911)*, comp. Frank C. Jordan (Secretary of State) (Sacramento: Superintendent of State Printing, 1913), p. 472; Colorado Department of State, *Abstract of Votes cast . . .* (Denver: State Printing Office, various dates); *Legislative Blue Book of Arizona* (n.p., several dates); and Fernando C. Padilla and Carlos B. Ramírez, "Patterns of Chicano Representation in California, Colorado, and Nuevo México," *Aztlán* 5 (Spring–Fall 1974), pp. 191–95. For Texas, see Canales, "Personal Recollections"; Anders, *Boss Rule*, pp. 245–47; and Frank L. Madla, Jr., "The Political Impact of Latin Americans and Negroes in Texas Politics" (Master's thesis, St. Mary's University, San Antonio, Texas, 1964). For Texas state-elected representatives, see *Members of the Legislature of the State of Texas from 1846 to 1939* (Austin: State of Texas, 1939).

44. The volumes of Otero provide direct observations on the content of New Mexico politics of the time, particularly volume 3; for his administration see Ronald J. McNeely, "The Otero Administration, 1897–1906" (Master's Thesis, Eastern New Mexico University, 1978); for his career see "Introduction" by Cynthia Secor-Welsh to Otero, *My Life on the Frontier, 1864–1882* (reprint, Albuquerque: University of New Mexico Press, 1987). See also for New Mexico Jack Holmes, *Politics in New Mexico*, pp. 61–109; Fincher, *Spanish Americans;* Nancie L. González, *The Spanish-Americans of New Mexico* (Albuquerque: University of New Mexico Press, 1967), pp. 49–50, 158, and 209; and Zeleny, *Relations.* For elected officials, see *New Mexico Blue Book* (Santa Fe: New Mexico State Printing Office, various dates). See also Maurilio Vigil, *Los Patrones: Profiles of Hispanic Political Leaders in New Mexico History* (Washington, D.C.: University Press of America, 1980).

45. On Baca, see Read, *Illustrated History*, pp. 608, 629, 630, and 638; Zelemy, *Relations*, pp. 216–25; and Beck, *New Mexico*, p. 305. For Larrazolo, see Cordova and Judah, *Octaviano Larrazolo;* Fincher, *Spanish Americans*, pp. 140 and 245; Paul A. F. Walter, "Octaviano Ambrosio Larrazolo," *New Mexico Historical Review* 7 (April 1932), pp. 102–3; L. B. Bloom, "Octaviano Ambrosio Larrazolo," *Dictionary of American Biography, A History*, vol. 6 (New York: Scribner, 1961), pp. 7–9; and Beck, *New Mexico*, pp. 296–315.

46. On Bronson Cutting, see Patricia Cadigan Armstrong, *A Portrait of Bronson Cutting through His Papers, 1910–1927* (Albuquerque: Division of

Government Research, Department of Government, University of New Mexico, 1959).

47. On Dennis Chávez, see: Senator Dennis Chávez, "The Good Neighbor Policy and the Present Administration," in Alonso Perales, ed., *Are We Good Neighbors?* (San Antonio: Artes Gráficas, 1948); and Fincher, *Spanish Americans*, pp. 103–5 and 149–53.

48. For the views of Adelina Otero, see "My People," *Survey Graphic* 66 (May 1, 1931) and *Old Spain in Our Southwest* (New York: Harcourt Brace, and Co., 1936). For her activities, see also Joan M. Jensen, "'Disenfranchisement Is a Disgrace!': Women and Politics in New Mexico, 1900–1940," in Joan M. Jensen and Darlis A. Miller, eds., *New Mexico Women: Intercultural Perspectives* (Albuquerque: University of New Mexico, 1986), where the leaflet "A Las Señoras de Santa Fe" is found on pp. 318–19. See also Antonio Rios Bustamante, "Adelina Otero-Warren: Women's Rights in New Mexico," *Americas 2001* 1 (October–November 1988). For change affecting women in New Mexico see Sarah Deutsch, *No Separate Refuge: Culture, Class, and Gender on an Anglo Hispanic Frontier in the American Southwest, 1880–1940* (Oxford: Oxford University Press, 1987) and Suzanne Forest, *The Preservation of the Village: New Mexico's Hispanics and the New Deal* (Albuquerque: University of New Mexico Press, 1989).

49. On the economy of the twenties, see William E. Leuchtenburg, *The Perils of Prosperity, 1914–1932* (Chicago: University of Chicago Press, 1958); John Kenneth Galbraith, *The Great Crash, 1929* (Boston: Houghton-Mifflin, 1955); and Edward Robb Ellis, *A Nation in Torment: The Great American Depression, 1929–1939* (New York: Capricorn Books, 1971).

50. On nativism, see John Higham, *Strangers in the Land* (New Brunswick: Rutgers University Press, 1955); and Arnold S. Rice, *The Ku Klux Klan in American Politics* (Washington, D.C.: Public Affairs Press, 1962).

51. For these views, see Emory S. Bogardus, *The Mexicans in the United States* (Los Angeles: University of Southern California Press, 1934). For views at the time on Americanization, see Emory S. Bogardus, *The Essentials of Americanization* (Los Angeles: University of Southern California Press, 1919); Merton E. Hilton, *The Development of an Americanization Program* (Ontario, California, 1928); *The Problem of Democracy*, Fourteenth Annual Proceedings of the American Sociological Society, vol. 14 (Chicago: University of Chicago Press, 1920); and Alfred White, "The Apperceptive Mass of Foreigners as Applied to Americanization, the Mexican Group" (Ph.D. diss., University of California at Berkeley, 1927). White, a teacher, had this view:

> The Mestizo thinks he has a race which partakes of the intelligence of the Spaniard and the endurance of the Indian, but the truth seems to be nearer the opposite, that he partakes of the bad qualities of both races . . .

> Because of this they seem to have failed entirely to meet the standard of the white man and are drifting back to the old Indian tribal life. . . . The Mexican has long been known as a quitter due to his inability to pull himself out of a hole. (pp. 11–12)

and this objective:

> The only way to change the mode of living is to teach them to save for phonographs or sewing machines (two things they all desire and which are foremost in their wants) after that get them to wear more clothes, to sleep in beds, sit on chairs, eat from plates and use forks. Whether this can improve the Indian is a question. (p. 54)

For observations on acculturation and change in religious affiliation see Delbert L. Gibson, "Protestantism in Latin American Acculturation" (Ph.D. diss., University of Texas, 1959). For census information and some interpretation on changes among Mexicans see Wilson T. Longmore and Homer Hitt, "A Demographic Analysis of First and Second Generation Mexican Population of the United States, 1930" *Southwestern Social Science Quarterly* 24 (September 1943).

52. On this and related activity, see Julie Lenninger Pycior, "La Raza Organizes: Mexican American Life in San Antonio, 1915–1930, as Reflected in Mutualist Activities" (Ph.D. diss., University of Notre Dame, 1979). For the Alianza, see Tomás Serrano Cabo, *Crónicas Alianza Hispano-Americana* (Las Cruces: La Estrella y Las Cruces Citizen, 1929); Jose Amaro Hernández, *Mutual Aid for Survival*, pp. 63–67; and Kay Briegel, "Alianza Hispano-Americana 1894–1965: A Mexican-American Fraternal Insurance Society" (Ph.D. diss., University of Southern California, 1974).

53. On early activity of the *Liga*, there is Teodoro Olea to Venustiano Carranza, Marzo 16, 1916 (xerox), which includes a leaflet dated April 23, 1916, describing activities signed by Pedro M. Salinas. For a review, see James D. McBride, "The Liga Protectora Latina: A Mexican American Benevolent Society in Arizona," *Journal of the West* 14 (October 1975). For some comment on conditions in Arizona, see *La Prensa*, February 17, 1917; and Anne Pace, "Mexican Refugees in Arizona, 1910–1911," *Arizona and the West* 16 (Spring 1974); and Sheridan, *Los Tucsonenses*.

54. See Alonso S. Perales, "El verdadero origen de la Liga de Ciudadanos Unidos Latino Americanos," in *En defensa de mi raza* (San Antonio: Artes Gráficas, 1931), vol. 1, pp. 101–5; LULAC, *Regulations and By-Laws* (Brownsville, Texas: 1933); Douglas Weeks, "The League of Latin American Citizens: A Texas Mexican Civic Association," *The Southwestern Political and Social Science Quarterly* 10 (December 1929). Weeks includes documents, as does Taylor, *American-Mexican Frontier*, pp. 243–44; see also James R. Lawrence, "A Study of the Latin American Problem and the Growth of the LULAC

Organization" (Master's thesis, Texas A & I University, Kingsville, Texas, 1966); Cynthia Orozco, "Mexican and Mexican American Conflict at the Harlingen Convention of 1927: The Genesis of LULAC" (unpublished paper, n.d.); Miguel David Tirado, "Mexican American Community Political Organization: The Key to Chicano Political Power," *Aztlán* 1 (Spring 1970), pp. 56–59; and Edward D. Garza, *LULAC: League of United Latin American Citizens* (San Francisco: R and E Research Associates, 1972). See also Mario Garcia, *Mexican American Leadership: Ideology and Identity, 1930–1960* (New Haven: Yale University Press, 1989).

55. Ibid. See also Perales, *En defensa de mi raza*, vol. 1; and "El Mexico Americano y la politica del sur de Texas" (San Antonio: 1931). Also, see "A History of LULAC, Part I," *LULAC News*, vol. 36 (1974); and Maurilio Vigil, *Chicano Politics* (Washington, D.C.: University Press of America, 1978), pp. 123–28.

56. Perales, *En Defensa de mi raza*, p. 110.

57. For Vasconcelos's views, see José Vasconcelos, *Obras completas* (México, D.F.: Libreros Mexicanos, 1957–61), vol. 1–4. For critical studies, see John Skirius, *José Vasconcelos y la cruzada de 1929* (México, D.F.: Siglo Veintiuno, 1978); John Skirius, "Vasconcelos and México de afuera," *Aztlán* 7 (Fall 1976); and Nicandro F. Juárez, "José Vasconcelos and La Raza Cósmica," *Aztlán* 3 (Spring 1972). For examples of the uncritical popular view on Vasconcelos, see Mario T. García, "Jose Vasconcelos y la Raza," *El Grito* 2 (Summer 1969); and John H. Haddox, *Vasconcelos of Mexico: Philosopher and Prophet* (Austin: University of Texas Press, 1967).

Vasconcelos had served in Alvaro Obregón's cabinet (1921–23) as Secretary of Education, but for several reasons he exiled himself in the United States, because, among other contributing conditions, he held that there was a widespread perception of government social-reform programs as inadequate in meeting the economic and social needs of the people; and there was popular support for dissidence, such as the ongoing Cristero Catholic rebellion; the suppressed de La Huerta revolt of 1923, which had galvanized former Villistas; the suppressed anti-reelection uprising of General Serrano in 1928, which offered hope to electoral reformers. In addition, he pointed to the national political crisis caused by the assassination of General Obregón on July 17, 1928, and the large number of immigrants and exiles who looked to return to Mexico.

Vasconcelos was both protean and paradoxical. Since the 1900s Vasconcelos had been in and out of politics, often switching camps as well as claiming to be disdainful of politics. Though he served as an obregonista cabinet minister, he participated in the organization of an opposition group. After running unsuccessfully for the governorship of Oaxaca, he left Mexico and went into exile. Then and afterward, he stressed an electoral reformism. In the

United States, he was a professor at the University of Chicago, and later, living in Los Angeles, he earned his living as a professional lecturer. He cultivated relations with both the Mexican community and conservative Anglo politicians and business persons. At this time, allegedly he met Herbert Hoover and other conservatives identified with business-related foreign-policy interests. Vasconcelos appealed to many wealthy Mexican exiles, among whom were some associated with many different political views, including ex-porfiristas, ex-carranzistas, and ex-de la huertistas. Some of the more prominent, including the future Gold Shirt leader General Nicolás Rodríguez, were reported to have met with Vasconcelos privately in Los Angeles, in October 1928, adopting a program emphasizing two among several concerns: (1) the elimination of the Calles–Obregón clique, either by defeat in the election or by military revolt in the case of fraudulent election; and (2) the defense of "religious liberty," that is, Catholicism, which ensured the support of the exiled Mexican Catholic hierarchy. In practice, Vasconcelos's opposition coincided with the interests of several who sought to weaken, displace, or bargain with the government in Mexico City. Though he signaled the shortcomings of the administrations, he did not publicize that the Catholic institution refused to adhere to basic elements of the constitution, endeavored to participate in politics, retained property ownership, and maintained de facto a separate parochial educational system under the guise of private schooling, while covertly encouraging rebellion in manipulating agrarian unrest, which resulted in the Cristero revolt.

The political and ideological position and the actual objectives of Vasconcelos and his major supporters were diverse and contradictory. They maintained a basically unprincipled alliance, with the primary objective of obtaining political leverage over the government in Mexico. Ousting the Obregón-Calles clique, if necessary by revolt in the event of an electoral defeat of Vasconcelos, was unlikely, and was so understood. While appealing for mass support of an ostensibly popular program, the Vasconcelos campaign contained strong conservative aspects even in its platform, endorsing church prerogatives and foreign business interests. In particular, Vasconcelos was committed to ending several of the progressive foreign-relations and foreign business policies of the post-1910 governments. These aspects, as well as Vasconcelos' own subsequent move further to the right, underscored conservatism. In 1929 Vasconcelos received the nomination of the National Anti-Reelectionist Party. Pascual Ortiz Rubio of the Partido Nacional Revolucionario won the election by a wide margin, or so it was reported. In any case, Vasconcelos returned to Mexico, with the government's tolerance, and continued to write, adding to his particular ideological contribution.

58. On the depression years, see the contemporary observations of Frederick Lewis Allen, *Since Yesterday: The Nineteen Thirties in America, 1929–1939*

(New York: Bantam, 1965; first published 1940); and for a narrative summary of the period between wars, see David A. Shannon, *Between the Wars: America, 1919–1941* (Boston: Houghton Mifflin, 1965). On U.S. changes and continuities domestically and internationally, see George E. Mowry, *The Urban Nation, 1920–1960* (New York: Hill and Wang, 1965); and Selig Adler, *The Uncertain Giant, 1921–1941: American Foreign Policy between the Wars* (New York: Collier Books, 1965). For the major policy outreach to Mexicans, see Mercedes Carreras de Velasco, *Los mexicanos que devolvió la crisis 1929–1932* (México, D.F.: Secretaría de Relaciones Exteriores, 1974); and Abraham Hoffman, *Unwanted Mexican Americans in the Great Depression* (Tucson: University of Arizona Press, 1974).

59. On Mexico, see Arnaldo Córdova, *La política de masas del cardenismo* (México, D.F.: ERA, 1974); and Nora Hamilton, *The Limits of State Autonomy: Post-Revolutionary Mexico* (Princeton: Princeton University Press, 1982). For impact, see the consul recollections in "Difícilmente cambiaría mi vida por otra," interview with R. de la Colina, in *La Opinión*, April 25, 1987; and Francisco Balderrama, *In Defense of La Raza: The Los Angeles Mexican Consulate and the Mexican Community 1929–1936* (Tucson: University of Arizona Press, 1982); and also Carlos Zazueta "Mexican Political Actors in the United States and Mexico: Historical and Political Contexts of a Dialogued Renewed" in Vasquez and García eds., *Mexican-U.S. Relations.*

60. For sinarquismo in Mexico, see the recollections of Salvador Abescal, *Mis recuerdos: Sinarquismo y Colonial María Auxiladora* (México, D.F.: 1942); and the studies by Mario Gil, *Sinarquismo, su origen, su esencia, su misión* (México, D.F.: Ed. del CDR, 1941); Jean Meyer, *El sinarquismo: Un fascismo mexicano?, 1937–1947* (México, D.F.: Editorial Joaquín Mortiz, 1979); and Leonor Ludlow Wiechers, "Orígenes sociales, políticas e internacionales del sinarquismo" (Tesis de Licenciatura, Universidad Nacional Autónoma de México, 1972). See also Hugh Campbell, "The Radical Right in Mexico, 1929–1949" (Ph.D. diss., UCLA, 1968), pp. 224–30; Juan Ignacio Padilla, *Sinarquismo contra-revolución* (México, D.F.: Editorial Polis, 1948); Kenneth Praeger, "Sinarquismo: The Politics of Frustration and Despair" (Ph.D. diss., Indiana University, 1975); and David J. Williams, "Sinarquismo and the Southwest" (Master's thesis, Texas Christian University, Fort Worth, 1950).

During the Spanish Civil War, the Mexican right and the sinarquistas fomented support for fascists in Europe and opposed the legitimate republican government of Spain, which was actively supported by the then-progressive Mexican government of Lazaro Cárdenas and by labor and other progressive sectors. They were actively pro-German, and apart from those committed to a fascist program, they appealed to those who were pro-German because of antipathy to the United States and England. In the Americas, they sought to link up with other fascist groups. With the onset of World War II, the sinarquistas acted as the pro-Axis sector in Mexico, actively opposing Mexican support for the Allies on the basis that this was a war that would benefit only England and the United States. They opposed the conscription of Mexicans into the U.S. armed forces, the participation of Mexican troops on the Allied front, and the export of Mexican labor to aid the U.S. war effort. Through their actions, large numbers of Mexicans demonstrated against these efforts.

A convoluted aspect of the extent of support that sinarquismo may have received from conservative U.S. sources is reflected in the subsequent investigation by the California state legislature of its supposed role in the infamous "Zoot Suit Riots" of 1942. While much was made at first in California and, in particular, in the Los Angeles press of the supposed "fascist Sinarquista" influence on the Mexican community and Mexican youth in "instigating" the "riots," the investigating committee rapidly shifted its focus from the sinarquistas to alleged "left wing subversive elements" in the Mexican community. Thus, the sinarquistas were effectively set aside, despite their anti-Allied propaganda, in favor of anticommunism, at a time when the communists were the foremost supporters of the antifascist aspect of the war effort.

61. On sinarquista activity in the United States, see Enrique Prado, "Sinarquismo in the United States," *New Republic* 109 (July 26, 1943), pp. 97–102; Felix Díaz Escobar, "The Spread of Sinarquismo," *Nation* (April 1943); Alcuín Heibel, *Leaders in Mexican Economic and Social Reforms Explain Sinarchism* (Mt. San Angel, Oregon, 1943); and Heinz H. F. Eulau, "Sinarquismo in the United States," *Inter-American Monthly* 8 (March–August 1944). Several newspapers and magazines published reports on the UNS and there are records of their activity in Mexico and the United States.

62. On labor, see Juan Gómez-Quiñones, "Neither Defeated nor Victorious" (unpublished manuscript, 1980); and Victor Nelson Cisneros, "La Clase Trabajadora en Tejas, 1920–1940," *Aztlán* 6 (Summer 1975).

63. Some materials on the effort are in the Ernesto Galarza Collection, Special Collections, Stanford University; and in the Carey McWilliams Papers, Special Collections, University Research Library, UCLA. For contemporary observation, see *La Opinión*, February 26, March 5, 12, and 19, and April 27–30, 1939; John Bright, "Las Mañanitas, A New Awakening," *Black and White* (June 1939). See also Josefina Fierro de Bright, "American-Mexican and New Deal," *Pic* (August 1942) and Gracia Molina de Pick, "The Emergence of Chicano Leadership: 1930–1950," *Caminos* (August 1983). See also Beatrice Griffith, *American Me* (Boston: Houghton Mifflin, 1948), pp. 241–42; John H. Burma, *Spanish Speaking Groups in the United States* (Durham: Duke University Press, 1954), pp. 102–3; Rodolfo Acuña, *Occupied America: A History of Chicanos*, 2d ed. (New York: Harper and Row, 1981), pp. 317–19; and Albert Camar.llo, "The Development of a Pan-Hispanic Civil Rights

Movement: The 1939 Congress of Spanish Speaking People" (paper presented at the Organization of American Historians, April 1986); and García, *Mexican American*. Veteran activist Humberto Corona has provided interviews to historians relating events he was informed on and/or participated in from the thirties through the eighties. For a published recollection mentioning the congress, see Jesús Mena, "Testimonio de Bert Corona: Struggle is the Ultimate Teacher," in *2001 Homenaje a la Cuidad de Los Angeles* (Los Angeles: Latino Writers Association, 1982).

64. *The Mexican Voice*, July 1938–Summer 1944; *Mexican American Forward*, October–May 1947; and Virginia Tonkin, "The First Steps of the Chicano Student Movement" (unpublished paper, UCLA, 1975). On "Y" priorities, see Galem M. Fisher, *Public Affairs and the YMCA: 1844–1944* (New York: Association Press, 1948), p. 89; and Charles Howard Hopkins, *History of the YMCA in North America* (New York: Association Press, 1951). For views at the time of Mexican youth and the population as a problem, see Paul S. Taylor, et al., *The Mexican Immigrant and the Problem of Crime and Criminal Justice*, in *Report on Crime and the Foreign Born* (Washington, D.C.: National Commission on Law Observance and Enforcement 1931); and Citizen's Committee for the Defense of Mexican-American Youth, *The Sleepy Lagoon Case* (Los Angeles: Citizen's Committee for the Defense of Mexican American Youth, 1942). For an extensive statement by a MAM participant, see Ignacio Reyes, "A Survey of the Problems Involved in the Americanization of the Mexican-American" (Master's thesis, University of Southern California, Los Angeles, 1957). There are a few materials on MAM in the Ernesto Galarza Collection; one is an excellent pamphlet surveying its goals and activity. The 1944 and 1950 conference programs are also included in the collection.

65. *The Mexican Voice*, vol. 1, no. 2, July 1938, unnumbered page.

66. Ibid.

67. *The Mexican Voice*, vol. 1, no. 6, Christmas 1938, pp. 14–15.

68. *The Mexican Voice*, vol. 1, no. 4, p. 5.

69. *The Mexican Voice*, vol. 1, no. 3, August 1938, p. 9.

70. *The Mexican Voice*, vol. 1, no. 4, September 1938, p. 5.

71. *Handbook of the Mexican-American Movement Incorporated* (mimeo, ca. 1946).

72. For a report filed to the grand jury, which provides a view of the negative stereotype held by some police and public employees, see Lieutenant Ed Duran Ayres, Los Angeles County Grand Jury, *Minutes*, 1942, and other material in Sleepy Lagoon Defense Committee, file, Special Collection Research Library, UCLA, *Los Angeles Times*, August 1942. See the contemporary summary of events by Guy Endore, *The Sleepy Lagoon Mystery* (Los Angeles: Sleepy Lagoon Defense Committee, 1944); and the social views

expressed in Emory Bogardus, "Gangs of Mexican American Youth," *Sociology and Social Research* 23 (September–October 1943). See also Mario T. García, "Americans All: The Mexican American Generation and the Politics of Wartime Los Angeles, 1941–45," *Social Science Quarterly* 65 (June 1984).

73. For an insightful report at the time, which predated later interpretive insights, see Chester B. Himes, "Zoot Riots Are Race Riots," *Crisis* 50 (July 1943). For a psychohistorical interpretation, see Mauricio Mazon, *The Zoot-Suit Riots: The Psychology of Symbolic Annihilation* (Austin: University of Texas Press, 1984). For the narrative, see Solomon James Jones, "The Government Riots of Los Angeles, June 1943" (Master's thesis, University of California, Los Angeles, 1969).

74. Information is derived from a collection of material, provided by Antonio Rios Bustamante, from Dorothy Rae Healey; for a party-related statement, see Emma Tenayuca and Homer Brooks, "The Mexican Question in the Southwest," *The Communist* 18 (May 1939); see also the recollections of Dorothy Rae Healey, *Dorothy Healey Remembers* (Oxford: Oxford University Press, 1990); and for interpretive analysis, see Douglas Monroy, "Anarquismo y Comunismo: Mexican Radicalism and the Communist Party in Los Angeles during the 1930s," *Labor History* 24, no. 1 (Winter 1983). See also Acuña, *Occupied America*, pp. 161–62, 211–12, 218, 220–37. For interest and incidents underscoring party concern, see Isabel González, *Stepchildren of a Nation: The Status of Mexican Americans* (New York: American Committee for Protection of Foreign Born, 1947); Patricia Morgan, *Shame of a Nation: A Documented Story of Police State Terror against Mexican Americans in the USA* (Los Angeles: Los Angeles Committee for Protection of the Foreign Born, 1954); and Mark A. Chamberlin, et al., *Our Badge of Infamy* (Los Angeles: American Committee for Protection of the Foreign Born, 1959).

75. On the FEPC and CIAA, see the following contemporary references: Carlos E. Castañeda, "Statement on Discrimination Against Mexicans in Employment," in Perales, *Are We Good Neighbors?* pp. 59–63; Carlos E. Castañeda, Testimony, Subcommittee of the Committee on Education and Labor, U.S. Congress, Senate, 79th Cong., 1st sess., March 12, 13, and 14, 1945, pp. 131–35; Coke R. Stevenson and Ezequiel Padilla, *The Good Neighbor Policy and Mexicans in Texas* (México, D.F.: Department of State for Foreign Affairs, 1943); and Pauline Kibbe, *Latin Americans in Texas* (Albuquerque: University of New Mexico Press, 1946), pp. 157–66. For research and interpretation focused on Mexicans, see Emilio Zamora, "The Failed Promise of Employment Opportunity during the War for the Mexican in the Texas Gulf Coast Oil Industry" (*Southwestern Historical Quarterly* 95 January 1992); and the fine book by Gerald D. Nash, *The American West Transformed: The Impact of the Second World War* (Bloomington: Indiana University Press, 1985), pp. 107–27.

One of the major Mexican American FEPC cases was that of W. H. Ural, who charged that although he had been a laborer with the Santa Fe Railroad in Albuquerque for twenty-five years, he had never received a promotion because he was a Mexican American. The complaints that were noted revealed some discriminatory patterns. One examiner, E. G. Trimble, gathered evidence in 1943 of discrimination against Mexican Americans in El Paso, Texas, who worked in the copper industry. Most were employees of the Phelps-Dodge Corporation and Nevada Consolidated Company (a subsidiary of Kennecott Copper Company). Though one-third of the fifteen thousand workers in the copper mines of New Mexico, Arizona, and Nevada were Mexican American, Indian, or Black, the complainants to the FEPC from the copper industry were consistently Mexican Americans. The complaints revealed a standard pattern: they received lower wage rates than whites for similar work, and were not advanced as rapidly. Most complained that they were relegated to the lowest job category, that of ordinary laborer. Trimble concluded, as did other observers, that a general pattern of discrimination against Mexicans existed in the copper industry of the Southwest, that they were excluded from better paying jobs on purely ethnic grounds, and that the industry had been characterized by segregation during the previous half-century. Naively, the FEPC believed that public hearings to expose these practices would suffice to end them, since the fear of publicity would induce most employers to abandon their discriminatory policies. Publicity of discrimination did not end it, and in any case, the hearings were not held because they were alleged to be counterproductive to the war effort; that is, they were dubbed "anti-American."

76. Quoted in Nash, *American West Transformed*, p. 124; see U.S., President's Committee on Fair Employment Practices, *Final Report* (Washington, D.C.: 1946); Louis C. Kesselman, *The Social Politics of FEPC* (Chapel Hill: University of North Carolina Press, 1948); James A. Nuechterlein, "The Politics of Civil Rights: The FEPC, 1941–1946," *Prologue* 10 (Fall 1978), pp. 170–91; Louis Ruchames, *Race, Jobs, and Politics: The Story of FEPC* (New York: Columbia University Press, 1953); Clete Daniel, *Chicano Workers and the Politics of Fairness: The FEPC in the Southwest, 1941–1945* (Austin: University of Texas Press, 1991).

A Selected Bibliography of Books, Reports, Pamphlets, and Anthologies on the Political History of Mexicans North of the Bravo, 1600s–1940s

General

Acuña, Rodolfo. *Occupied America: A History of Chicanos.* San Francisco: Harper and Row, 1987.

Aztlan. Special Issue on Politics, Vol. 5 (1974).

Barrera, Mario. *Race and Class in the Southwest: A Theory of Racial Inequality.* Notre Dame: University of Notre Dame Press, 1979.

Barron, Milton L. *American Minorities.* New York: Alfred A. Knopf, 1957.

Blalock, Hubert J. *Toward a Theory of Minority Group Relations.* New York: Wiley, 1967.

Blauner, Robert. *Racial Oppression in America.* New York: Harper and Row, 1972.

Browning, Rufus P., et al, eds. *Racial Politics in American Cities.* White Plains, New York: Longman, 1990.

Dahl, Robert. *Pluralist Democracy in the United States.* Chicago: Rand McNally, 1961.

Domhoff, William G. *Who Rules America?* Englewood Cliffs, N.J.: Prentice-Hall, 1967.

Domhoff, William G. *The Higher Circles.* New York: Vintage, 1970.

Dye, Thomas R. and L. Harmon Zeigler. *The Irony of Democracy.* North Sictuate, Mass.: Duxbury Press, 1973.

Easton, David. *A Systems Analysis of Political Life.* New York: John Wiley & Sons, 1965.

Eisinger, Paul K. *Patterns of Interracial Politics.* New York: Academic Press, 1976.

Elazar, Daniel J. *American Federalism: A View from the States.* New York: Harper & Row, 1984.

Elkin, Stephen L. *City and Regime in the American Republic*. Chicago: University of Chicago Press, 1987.

Enloe, Cynthia. *Ethnic Conflict and Political Development*. Boston: Little, Brown & Co., 1972.

Flanigan, William H. *Political Behavior of the American Electorate*. Boston: Allyn and Bacon, 1972.

Fuchs, Lawrence. *American Ethnic Politics*. New York: Harper & Row, 1968.

Grebler, Leo, et al. *The Mexican American People*. New York: The Free Press, 1970.

Handlin, Oscar. *Race and Nationality in American Life*. Garden City: Doubleday and Company, 1957.

Held, David, ed. *Political Theory Today*. Stanford: Stanford University Press, 1991.

Higham, John, ed. *Ethnic Leadership in America*. Baltimore: The Johns Hopkins University Press, 1978.

Hill, Paul T. *A Theory of Political Coalitions in Simple and Policymaking Situations*. Beverly Hills: Sage Publications, 1973.

Holloway, Harry with John George. *Public Opinion Coalitions, Elites and Masses*. New York: St. Martin's Press, 1986.

Hrebenar, Ronald J. and Clive S. Thomas, eds. *Interest Group Politics in the American West*. Salt Lake City: University of Utah Press, 1987.

Litt, Edgar. *Ethnic Politics in America*. Illinois: Scott, Foresman and Co., 1970.

Lopez y Rivas, Gilberto. *Los chicanos: Una minoría nacional explotada*. México, D.F.: Editorial Nuestro Tiempo, 1879.

Masuoka, Jitsuichi. *Race Relations: Problems and Theory*. Chapel Hill: University of North Carolina Press, 1961.

McWilliams, Carey. *North From Mexico: The Spanish Speaking People of the United States*. Boston: J.B. Lippincott Company, 1949.

Milbraith, Lester and M.L. Goel. *Political Participation*. Chicago: Rand McNally, 1977.

Mirande, Alfredo. *The Chicano Experience: An Alternative Perspective*. South Bend, Notre Dame University, 1985.

Murgia, Edward. *Assimilation, Colonialism and the Mexican American People*. Austin: University of Texas, 1975.

Novack, Michael. *The Rise of the Unmeltable Ethnics*. New York: Macmillan, 1971.

Piñon, Fernando. *Of Myths and Realities: Dynamics of Ethnic Politics*. New York: Vintage Press, 1978.

Piven, F. Fox and Richard A. Cloward. *The New Class War*. New York: Pantheon Books, 1982.

Piven, F. Fox and Richard A. Cloward. *Poor People's Movements: Why They Succeed, and How They Fail*. New York: Vintage Books, 1979.

Reich, Michael. *Racial Inequality.* Princeton: Princeton University Press, 1981.
Shibutani, Tamotsu and Kian Kwan. *Ethnic Stratification, A Comparative Approach.* New York: Macmillan, 1965.
Simpson, George Eaton and J.M. Yinger. *Racial and Cultural Minorities: An Analysis of Prejudice and Discrimination.* New York: Harper & Row, 1965.
Skerry, Peter. *Mexican Americans: The Ambivalent Minority.* New York: Free Press, 1993.
Sowell, Thomas. *Ethnic America.* New York: Basic Books, 1981.
Sowell, Thomas. *Race and Economics.* New York: David McKay Co., 1975.
Suttles, Gerald. *The Social Construction of Communities.* Chicago: University of Chicago, 1979.
Szymanski, Albert. *Class Structure: A Critical Perspective.* New York: Praeger Perspectives, 1983.
Thernstrom, Abigail. *Whose Votes Count? Affirmative Action and Minority Voting Rights.* Cambridge, Mass.: Harvard University Press, 1987.
Verba, Sidney and Norman Nye. *Participation in America.* Evanston: Harper and Row, 1972.
Wilson, W.M. *The Truly Disadvantaged.* Chicago: University of Chicago Press, 1987.
Wolfinger, Raymond and Steven J. Rosenstone. *Who Votes.* New Haven: Yale University Press, 1980.
Zieger, Robert H. *American Workers, American Unions.* Baltimore: Johns Hopkins University Press, 1986.

Colonial, 1600–1800

Adams, Eleanor B., ed. *Bishop Tamaron's Visitation of New Mexico, 1760.* Albuquerque: Historical Society of New Mexico, 1954.
Alessio Robles, Vito. *Coahuila y Texas en la época colonial.* 2 vols., Mexico, D.F.: 1938.
Alessio Robles, Vito. *Francisco de Urdiñola y el norte de la Nueva Éspaña.* Mexico, D.F.: 1931.
Almaraz, Félix D. *Tragic Cavalier: Governor Manuel Salcedo of Texas, 1808–1813.* Austin: University of Texas Press, 1971.
Almaraz, Felix D. *Crossroad of Empire: The Church and State on the Rio Grande Frontier of Coahuila and Texas, 1700–1821.* San Antonio: University of Texas, Center for Anthropological Research, 1979.
Anna, Timothy E. *The Fall of the Royal Government in Mexico City.* Lincoln: University of Nebraska, 1978.
Bailey, Jessie B. *Diego de Vargas and the Reconquest of New Mexico.* Albuquerque: University of New Mexico Press, 1940.

Bailey, Lynn Robin. *Indian Slave Trade in the Southwest.* Los Angeles: Westernlore Press, 1966.

Bannon, John Francis. *The Spanish Borderlands Frontier 1513–1821.* New York: Holt, Rinehart and Winston, 1970.

Bannon, John Francis. ed. *Bolton and the Spanish Borderlands.* Norman: University of Oklahoma Press, 1964.

Barreira, Antonio. *Ojeada sobre Nuevo México, que da una idea de sus producciones naturales, y de algunas otras cosas que se consideran oportunas para mejorar su estado e ir proporcionando su futura felicidad.* Puebla: Imprenta del ciudadano José María Campos, 1832.

Beers, Henry Putney. *Spanish and Mexican Records of the American Southwest.* Tucson: University of Arizona Press, 1979.

Beilharz, Edwin A. *Felipe de Neve, First Governor of California.* San Francisco: California Historical Society, 1971.

Blackmar, Frank W. *Spanish Institutions in the Southwest.* Baltimore: Johns Hopkins University, 1891.

Bobb, Bernard E. *The Viceregency of Antonio Maria Bucareli in New Spain, 1771–1779.* Austin: The University of Texas Press, 1962.

Bolton, Herbert E. *Texas in the Middle Eighteenth Century.* Berkeley: University of California Press, 1915.

Brayer, Herbert O. *Pueblo Indian Land Grants of the "Rio Abajo", New Mexico.* Albuquerque: University of New Mexico Press, 1939.

Brinckerhoff, Sidney B. and Odie B. Faulk. *Lancers for the King: A Study of the Frontier Military System of Northern New Spain, with a Translation of the Royal Regulations of 1772.* Phoenix: Arizona Historical Foundation, 1965.

Burkholder, Mark A. and D.S. Chandler. *From Impotence to Authority: The Spanish Crown and the American Audiences, 1687–1808.* Columbia: The University of Missouri Press, 1977.

Carter, Hodding. *Doomed Road of Empire: The Spanish Trail of Conquest.* New York: McGraw-Hill, 1963.

Chabot, Frederick C., ed. *Texas in 1811: The Las Casas and Sambrano Revolutions.* San Antonio: Yanaguana Society, 1941.

Chapman, Charles Edward. *The Founding of Spanish California.* New York: Macmillan Company, 1916.

Chapman, Charles Edward. *A History of California: The Spanish Period.* New York: The Macmillan Company, 1921.

Chavez Orozco, Luis. *Las instituciones democráticas de los indígenas mexicanos en la época colonial.* Mexico, D.F.: Instituto Indigenista Interamericano, 1943.

Cook, Sherburne F. and Woodrow Borah. *The Conflict Between the California Indians and White Civilization.* Berkeley: University of California Press, 1976.

Cutter, Charles R. *The Protector de Indios in Colonial New Mexico 1659–1821.* Albuquerque: University of New Mexico Press, 1986.

Dakin, Susanna B. *Rose or Thorn?: Three Women of Spanish California.* Berkeley: Friends of the Bancroft Library, 1963.

De Thomás, Francisco. *Historia popular de Nuevo México desde su descubrimiento hasta la actualidad.* New York: American Book Company, 1896.

Dobyns, Henry E. *Spanish Colonial Tucson: A Demographic History.* Tucson: University of Arizona Press, 1976.

Domínguez, Fray Francisco Atanasio. *The Missions of New Mexico, 1776.* Translated by Eleanor B. Adams and Fray Angélico Chávez. Albuquerque: University of New Mexico Press, 1956.

Englehardt, Fr. Zephryin. *The Missions and Missionaries of California.* 4 vols. San Francisco: The James H. Barry Company, 1915.

Fages, Pedro. *A Historical, Political and Natural Description of California.* Berkeley: University of California Press, 1937.

Farriss, Nancy M. *Crown and Clergy in Colonial Mexico, 1759–1821.* London: The University of London Press, 1968.

Faulk, Odie B. *The Last Years of Spanish Texas, 1778–1821.* The Hague: Mouton, 1964.

Faulk, Odie B. *A Successful Failure: The Saga of Texas, 1519–1810.* Austin: Steck-Vaughan, 1965.

Fireman, Janet. *The Spanish Royal Corps of Engineers in the Western Borderlands, 1764–1815: Instrument of Bourbon Reform.* Glendale: Arthur H. Clark Company, 1977.

Fisher, Lillian Estelle. *Viceregal Administration in the Spanish American Colonies.* Berkeley: University of California Press, 1926.

Forbes, Jack D. *Aztecas del Norte: The Chicanos of Aztlán.* Greenwich: Fawcett Publications, 1973.

Forbes, Jack D. *Apache, Navaho, and Spaniard.* Norman: University of Oklahoma Press, 1960.

Forbes, Jack D. *Warriors of the Colorado: The Yumas of the Quechan Nation and their Neighbors.* Norman: University of Oklahoma Press, 1965.

Garcia, Rogelio O. *Dolores, Revilla, and Laredo, Three Sister Settlements.* Waco, Tex.: Texian Press, 1970.

Garrett, Julie Kathryn. *Green Flag Over Texas: A Story of the Last Years of Spain in Texas.* New York: The Cordova Press, Inc., 1939.

Geiger, Maynard J. *The Life and Times of Fray Junipero Serra, O.F.M.* 2 vols. Washington, D.C., Academy of American Franciscan History, 1965.

Geiger, Maynard J. and Clement W. Meighan, eds. *As the Padres Saw Them: California Indian Life and Customs as Reported by the Francisco Missionaries, 1813–1815.* Santa Barbara: Arthur H. Clark Company, 1976.

Gerhard, Peter. *The Northern Frontier of New Spain.* Princeton: Princeton University Press, 1982.

Gomez-Quiñones, Juan. *Development of the Mexican Working Class North of the Rio Bravo: Work and Culture Among Laborers and Artisans, 1600–1900.* Los Angeles: Chicano Studies Research Center, UCLA, 1982.

Gonzalez-Flores, Enrique and Almada, Francisco R., eds. *Informe de Hugo O'Conor sobre el estado de las provinces Internas del Norte 1771–1776.* Mexico, D.F.: Editorial Cultura, 1952.

Guest, Francis F. *Fermin Francisco de Lasuen (1736–1803): A Biography.* Washington, D.C.: Academy of American Franciscan History, 1973.

Gutierrez, Ramon. *When Jesus Came the Corn Mothers Went Away: Marriage, Sexuality and Power in New Mexico, 1500–1846.* Stanford: Stanford University Press, 1990.

Hackett, Charles W., ed. *Historical Documents Relating to New Mexico, Nueva Vizcaya and Approaches Thereto, to 1773.* Vols. 1–3. Washington, D.C.: Carnegie Institute, 1923–1937.

Hackett, Charles W., ed. *Revolt of the Pueblo Indians of New Mexico and Otermin's Attempted Reconquest, 1680–1682.* Albuquerque: University of New Mexico Press, 1942.

Hackett, Charles W. and Rey Agapito, eds. *Don Juan de Oñate, Colonizer of New Mexico, 1555–1628.* Albuquerque: University of New Mexico Press, 1953.

Harvey, H.R., ed. *Land and Politics in the Valley of Mexico.* Albuquerque: University of New Mexico Press, 1991.

Hateber, Mattie A. *The Opening of Texas to Foreign Settlement, 1801–1821.* Austin: University of Texas Press, 1927.

Hedrick, Basil C., et al., eds. *The North Mexican Frontier: Readings in Archaeology, Ethnohistory, and Ethnography.* Carbondale: Southern Illinois University Press, 1971.

Hedrick, Basil C., et al., eds. *The MesoAmerican Southwest.* Carbondale: Southern Illinois University Press, 1974.

Hill, Lawrence F. *José de Escandon and the Founding of New Santander: A Study in Spanish Colonization.* Columbus: Ohio State University Press, 1926.

Hughes, Anne E. *The Beginnings of Spanish Settlement in The El Paso District.* Berkeley: University of California Press, 1914.

Ives, Ronald L. *José Velasquez: Saga of a Borderland Soldier.* Tucson: Southwestern Mission Research Center, 1984.

John, Elizabeth A.H. *Storms Brewed in Other Men's Worlds: The Confrontation of Indians, Spanish and French in the Southwest, 1540–1795.* College Station: Texas A & M University Press, 1975.

Jones, Oakah L. *Pueblo Warriors and Spanish Conquest.* Norman: University of Oklahoma Press, 1966.

Jones, Oakah L. *The Spanish Borderlands: A First Reader.* Los Angeles: Lorrin L. Morrison, 1974.

Jones, Oakah L. *Los Paisanos: Spanish Settlers on the Northern Frontier of New Spain.* Norman: University of Oklahoma Press, 1979.

Kessel, John L. *Friars, Soldiers and Reformers: Hispanic Arizona and the Sonora Mission Frontier 1767–1856.* Tucson: University of Arizona Press, 1976.

Kessel, John L. and Rick Hendricks, eds. *By Force of Arms: The Journals of don Diego de Vargas, New Mexico, 1691–1693.* Albuquerque: University of New Mexico Press, 1992.

Mather, Christine, ed. *Colonial Frontiers: Art and Life in Spanish New Mexico.* Santa Fe: Ancient City Press, 1983.

Mecham, J. Lloyd. *Francisco de Ibarra and Nueva Vizcaya.* Durham: Duke University Press, 1972.

Miranda, José. *Las ideas y las instituciones políticas mexicanas, Parte 1: 1521–1820.* México, D.F.: Universidad Nacional Autónoma de Mexico, 1952.

Moorehead, Max L. *The Apache Frontier: Jacobo Ugarte and Spanish-Indian Relations in Northern New Spain, 1769–1791.* Norman: University of Oklahoma Press, 1968.

Moorehead, Max L. *The Presidio: Bastion of the Spanish Borderlands.* Norman: University of Oklahoma Press, 1975.

Morfi, Juan A. *History of Texas 1673–1779.* (Carlos Castañeda trans. and ed.) 2 vols. Albuquerque: The Quivara Society, 1935.

Navarro García, Luis. *Don José de Galvez y la Comandancia General de las Provincias Internas del Norte de Nueva España.* Sevilla: Escuela de Estudios Hispano-Americanos, 1964.

Navarro García, Luis. *Las provincias internas en el siglo XIX.* Sevilla: Escuela de Estudios Hispano-Americanos, 1965.

Olmstead, Virginia L., trans. and ed. *Spanish and Mexican Censuses of New Mexico, 1750–1830.* Albuquerque: The New Mexico Genealogical Society, Inc., 1981.

Oritz, Roxanne, Dunbar. *Roots of Resistance: Land Tenure in New Mexico, 1680–1980.* Los Angeles: Chicano Studies Research Center and American Indian Studies Center, UCLA, 1980.

Parry, John H. *The Audiencia of New Galicia in the Sixteenth Century: A Study of Spanish Colonial Government.* Cambridge: Cambridge University Press, 1948.

Pino, Pedro B. *Exposición sucinta y sencilla de la provincia del Nuevo México.* H. Bailey Carroll and J. Villsana Haggard, eds. Albuquerque: Quivira Society, 1942.

Polzer, Charles. *Rules and Precepts of the Jesuit Missions of Northwestern New Spain.* Tucson: University of Arizona Press, 1981.

Porras Muños, Guillermo. *Iglesia y estado en Nueva Vizcaya (1562–1821).* Mexico, D.F.: Universidad Nacional Autonoma de Mexico, 1980.

Porrúa Turanzas, José, ed. *Documentos para la historia eclesiástica y civil de la Provincia de Texas o Nuevas Philipinas, 1720–1779.* Madrid: Ediciones José Porrúa Turanzas, 1961.

Powell, Philip Wayne. *Mexico's Miguel Caldera: The Taming of America's First Frontier, 1548–1597.* Tucson: University of Arizona Press, 1977.

Powell, Philip Wayne. *Soldiers, Indians and Silver: The Northward Advance of New Spain, 1550–1600.* Berkeley: University of California Press, 1952.

Payo, Gerald E. and Gilberto M. Hinojosa, eds. *Tejano Origins in Eighteenth Century San Antonio.* Austin: University of Texas Press, 1991.

Prince, L. Bradford. *Historical Sketches of New Mexico from the Earliest Records to the American Occupation.* New York: Leggat Brothers, 1883.

Pristley, Herbert I. *José de Galvez, Visitor-General of New Spain, 1765–1771.* Berkeley: University of California Press, 1916.

Ramos, Arizpe, Miguel. *Report . . . on the Natural Political and Civic Condition of the Provinces of Coahuila, Nuevo León, Nuevo Santander and Texas.* Edited by Nettie Lee Benson. Austin: University of Texas Press, 1950.

Ribes Iborra, Vicente. *Ambiciones estadounidenses sobre la provincia novohispana de Texas.* Mexico, D.F.: Universidad Nacional Aútonoma de México, 1982.

Richman, Irving Berdine. *California Under Spain and Mexico, 1535–1847.* Boston: Houghton Mifflin Co., 1911.

Rubio Mañe, Ignacio. *Introducción al estudio de los virreyes de Nueva España, 1535–1746.* Mexico, D.F.: Fondo de Cultura Económica, 1982.

Sanchez, Nelli Van de Grift. *Spanish Arcadia.* New York: Arno Press, 1976.

Scholes, Frances V. *Church and State in New Mexico, 1610–1650.* Albuquerque: University of New Mexico Press, 1937.

Scholes, Frances V. *Troublous Times in New Mexico 1610–1650.* Albuquerque: University of New Mexico Press, 1942.

Schutz, John. *Spain's Colonial Outpost in California.* San Francisco: Boyd and Fraser, 1985.

Scott, Florence Johnson. *Royal Land Grants North of the Rio Grande, 1777–1821.* Rio Grande City: La Retama Press, 1969.

Scott, Florence Johnson. *Historical Heritage of the Lower Rio Grande Valley.* San Antonio: The Naylor Co., 1937.

Seed, Patricia. *To Love, Honor and Obey in Colonial Mexico. Conflict Over Marriage Choice, 1574–1821.* Stanford: Stanford University Press, 1988.

Simmons, Marc. *Spanish Government in New Mexico.* Albuquerque: University of New Mexico Press, 1968.

Simpson, Lesley Byrd. *Studies in the Administration of Indians of New Spain.* 4 vols. Berkeley: University of California Press, 1966.

Simpson, Lesley Byrd. *The Law of Burgos, 1512–1513: Royal Ordinances for the Good Government and Treatment of the Indians.* San Francisco: John Howell, 1960.

Swadish, Francis L. *Los Primeros Pobladores: Hispanic Americans of the Ute Frontier.* South Bend: University of Notre Dame Press, 1974.

Thomas, Alfred B., ed. *Forgotten Frontiers: A Study of the Spanish Indian Policy of Don Juan Bautista de Anza, Governor of New Mexico, 1777–1787, from the Original Documents in the Archives of Spain, Mexico and New Mexico.* Albuquerque: University of New Mexico Press, 1940; or Norman: University of Oklahoma Press, 1932.

Thomas, Alfred B., ed. *Teodoro de Croix and the Northern Frontier of New Spain, 1776–1783.* Norman: University of Oklahoma Press, 1941.

Twitchell, Ralph Emerson. *The Leading Facts of New Mexican History.* Vol. 1. Cedar Rapids: Torch Press, 1911.

Twitchell, Ralph Emerson. *Old Santa Fe, The Story of New Mexico's Ancient Capital.* Chicago: Rio Grande Press, 1963.

Weber, David, ed. *Foreigners in their Native Land: Historical Roots of the Mexican Americans.* Albuquerque: University of New Mexico Press, 1973.

Wolf, Eric. *Sons of the Shaking Earth: The People of Mexico and Guatemala— Their Land, History and Culture.* Chicago: University of Chicago Press, 1962.

Worcester, Donald E., ed. *Instructions for Governing the Interior Provinces of New Spain, 1786, by Bernardo de Gálvez.* Berkeley: The Quivira Society, 1951.

Independence and Mexican Period, 1800–1848

Alessio Robles, Vito. *Coahuila y Texas desde la consumación de la Independencia hasta el tratado de paz de Guadalupe Hidalgo.* 2 vols. Mexico, D.F.: 1945–1946.

Almaguer, Tómas. *Interpreting Chicano History: The World System Approach to 19th Century California.* Berkeley: Institute for the Study of Social Change, University of California, 1977.

Aviña, Rose Hollenbaugh. *Spanish and Mexican Land Grants in California.* New York: Arno Press, 1976.

Barker, Eugene C. *The Life of Stephen F. Austin: Founder of Texas, 1793–1836.* Austin: University of Texas Press, 1949.

Barker, Eugene C. *Mexico and Texas, 1821–1835.* New York: Russell, 1963.

Benson, Nettie L., ed. *Mexico and the Spanish Cortes, 1810–1822.* Austin: University of Texas, 1966.

Benson, Nettie Lee. *La diputación provincial y el federalismo mexicano.* México: El Colegio de México, 1955.

Berninger, Dieter George. *La inmigración en Mexico 1821–1857*. Mexico, D.F.: 1974.

Bosch Garcia, Carlos. *Historia de las relaciones entre México y los Estados Unidos, 1819–1948*. Mexico, D.F.: Universidad Nacional Autonoma de Mexico, 1961.

Brack, Gene M. *Mexico Views Manifest Destiny, 1821–1846: An Essay on the Origins of the Mexican War*. Albuquerque: University of New Mexico Press, 1975.

Brooks, Phillip Collidge. *Diplomacy and the Borderlands: The Adams-Onís Treaty of 1819*. University of California Publications in History, Vol. 24. Berkeley: University of California Press, 1939.

Bustamante, Carlos Maria de. *Apuntes para la historia del gobierno del General D. Antonio López de Santa-Anna, desde principios de Octubre de 1841, en que fué depuesto del mando por uniforme voluntad de la Nación, escrita por el autor del cuadro histórico de la revolución mexicana*. México, D.F.: Impr. de José María Lara, 1845.

Bustamante, Carlos Maria de. *Diario histórico de México*. Mexico, D.F.: J. Ortega, 1896.

Bustamante, Carlos María de. *El gobierno mexicano durante el segundo período de la administración del Exmo. Señor Presidente D. Anastacio Bustamante hasta la entrega del mando al Exmo. Señor Presidente Interino D. Antonio López Santa-Anna, y continuación del cuadro histórico de la revolución mexicana*. tomo 11. México, D.F.: Imprenta de José María Lara, 1842.

Carrera Stampa, Manuel. *Los gremios mexicanos*. Mexico, D.F.: 1954.

Carrillo, Carlos Antonio. *Exposition Addressed to the Chamber of the Deputies of the Congress of the Union by Señor Don Carlos Antonio Carrillo, Deputy for Alta California Concerning the Regulation and Administration of the Pious Fund*. San Francisco: John Henry Nash, 1938.

Carroll, H. Bailey and J. Villasana Haggard, eds. *Three New Mexico Chronicles: The Exposition of Don Pedro Bautista Pino, 1812; The Ojeada of Licenciado Antonio Barreira, 1832: and the additions by Don José Agustín de Escudero, 1849*. Albuquerque: The Quivira Society, 1942. Reprinted by Arno Press, New York, 1967.

Castañeda, Carlos E. *The Mexican Side of the Texas Revolution*. Dallas: P.L. Turner, 1928.

Castañeda, Carlos E. *Our Catholic Heritage in Texas*. 7 vols. New York: Arno Press, 1976.

Castañeda, Carlos E., ed. *The Indians of Southern California in 1852*. San Francisco: The Henry E. Huntington Library, 1952.

Castañeda, Carlos E., ed. *The Early Sentiment for the Annexation of California, An Account of the Growth of American Interest in California from 1835 to 1846*. Austin: Texas State Historical Association, 1915.

Cortes, Carlos, E., ed. *Mexican California*. New York: Arno Press, 1976.

Costeloe, Michael P. *La primera república federal de México, 1824–1835: Un estudio de los partidos políticos en el México independiente*. México, D.F.: Fondo de Cultura Económica, 1975.

Covian Martinez, Vidal. *Don José Bernardo Maximiliano Gutierrez de Lara*. Ciudad Victoria Tamaulipas: Ediciones Siglo VV, 1967.

Cowan, Robert G. *Ranchos of California: A List of Spanish Concessions 1775–1822 and Mexican Grants 1822–1846*. Fresno: Academy Library Guild, 1956.

Dana, Richard Henry. *Two Years Before the Mast: A Personal Narrative of Life at Sea*. New York: Harper & Brothers, 1840. 2 vols. Reprint. Los Angeles: Ward Ritchie Press, 1964.

Diputación territorial de Alta California. *Reglamento provisional para el gobierno interior de la Ecma. Diputación territorial de la Alta California*. Monterey: Imprenta De A.V. Zamorano y Ca., 1834.

Eldredge, Zoeth Skinner. *History of California*. 5 vols. New York: The Century History Company, 1915.

Falconer, Thomas. *Letters and Notes on the Texas-Santa Fe Expedition, 1841–1842*. Chicago: Rio Grande Press, 1963.

Falconer, Thomas and Joseph A. Stout, Jr. eds. *The Mexican War: Changing Interpretations*. Chicago: The Swallow Press, 1973.

Figueroa, General José. *Manifesto to the Mexican Republic*. [1835] Berkeley: University of California Press, 1978. Ed.: C. Alan Hutchinson.

Filisola, Vicente. *Memorias para la historia de la guerra de Tejas*. 2 vols. México, D.F..: Editorial Nacional, 1968.

Francis, Jessie Davies. *An Economic and Social History of Mexican California, 1822–1846*. New York: Arno Press, 1976.

Fuller, John. *The Movement for the Acquisition of All Mexico, 1846–1848*. New York: Da Capo Press, 1969.

Gamas Torruco, Jose. *El federalismo mexicano*. Mexico, D.F.: 1975.

García, Genaro, ed. *Historia de Nuevo León: Con noticias sobre Coahuila, Texas, y Nuevo México*. México, D.F.: Porrúa, 1975.

García Cantu, Gaston. *Las invasiones norteamericanas en Mexico*. Mexico, D.F.: ERA, 1971.

Geary, Gerald J. *Secularization of the California Missions, 1810–1846*. Washington, D.C.: Catholic University of America, 1934.

Gregg, Josiah. *Commerce of the Prairies*. Norman: University of Oklahoma Press, 1954.

Green, Stanley C. *The Mexican Republic; the First Decade: 1823–1832*. Pittsburgh: University of Pittsburgh Press, 1987.

Griffin, Charles. *The United States and the Disruption of the Spanish Empire, 1810–1822*. New York: Columbia University Press, 1937.

Guerra, Ramiro. *La expansión territorial de los Estados Unidos*. La Habana: Editorial de Ciencias Sociales, 1975.

Guerra Ord, Angustias de la. *Occurrences in Hispanic California*. Washington, D.C.: Academy of Franciscan History, 1956.

Hale, Charles A. *Mexican Liberalism in the Age of Mora, 1821–1853*. New Haven: Yale University Press, 1968.

Hammett, A.B.J. *The Empresario Don Martin de León, The Richest Man in Texas*. Waco, Tex.: Texian Press, 1973.

Hammill, Hugh M. *The Hidalgo Revolt: Prelude to Mexican Independence*. Gainesville: University of Florida, 1966.

Harding, George L. *Don Agustin V. Zamorano*. Los Angeles: The Zamorano Club, 1934.

Hinojosa, Gilberto Miguel. *A Borderlands Town in Transition: Laredo, 1755–1870*. College Station: Texas A & M University Press, 1983.

Hutchinson, C. Alan. *The Mexican Government and the Mission Indians of Upper California, 1821–1835*. Washington: Academy of American Franciscan History, 1965.

Hutchinson, C. Alan. *Frontier Settlement in Mexican California: The Hijar-Padres Colony and Its Origins, 1769–1835*. New Haven: Yale University Press, 1969.

Jarratt, Rie. *Gutierrez de Lara: Mexican Texan; The Story of a Creole Hero*. Austin: Creole Texana, 1949.

Kenner, Charles A. *A History of New Mexican-Plains Indian Relations*. Norman: University of Oklahoma Press, 1969.

Lecompte, Janet. *Rebellion in Rio Arriba*. Albuquerque: University of New Mexico Press, 1985.

Lederer, Lillian Charlotte. *A Study of Anglo-American Settlers in Los Angeles County Previous to the Admission of California to the Union*. San Francisco: R & E Research Associates, 1974.

Lowrie, Samuel H. *Culture Conflict in Texas, 1821–1835*. New York: Columbia University Press, 1932.

Macias, Anna. *Genesis del gobierno constitucional en México, 1808–1820*. Mexico D.F.: 1973.

Mares, José Fuentes. *Santa Ana: Aurora y ocaso de un comediante*. Mexico, D.F.: Jus, 1959.

Mateos, José María. *Historia de la masonería en Méjico desde 1806 hasta 1884*. México, D.F.: 1884.

McKittrick, Myrtle M. *Vallejo: Son of California*. Portland: Binfords & Mort, 1944.

Meketa, Jacqueline Dorgan, ed. *Legacy of Honor, The Life of Rafael Chacon, A Nineteenth-Century New Mexican*. Albuquerque: University of New Mexico Press, 1986.

Monroy, Doug. *Thrown Among Strangers: The Making of Mexican Culture in Frontier California.* Berkeley: University of California, 1990.

Morehead, Max L. *Mexico's Royal Road. Trade and Travel on the Chihuahua Trail.* Norman: University of Oklahoma Press, 1958.

Morton, Holand. *Teran and Texas: A Chapter in Texas-Mexican Relations.* Austin: The University of Texas Press, 1948.

Northrop, Marie E. *Spanish-Mexican Families of Early California: 1769–1860.* Vol. 1. New Orleans: Polyanthos, 1976.

Ocampo, Javier. *Las ideas de un dia: El pueblo mexicano ante la consumación de su independencia.* Mexico, D.F.: Editorial Cultura, 1952.

Officer, James E. *Hispanic Arizona, 1536–1856.* Tucson: University of Arizona Press, 1989.

Ord, Angustias de la Guerra. *Occurrences in Hispanic California.* Washington, D.C.: Academy of American Franciscan History, 1956.

Pichardo, José Antonio. *Pichardo's Treatise on the Limits of Louisiana and Texas.* 2 vols. Translated by Charles Wilson Hackett. Austin: University of Texas Press, 1931–1932.

Pico, Pío. *Don Pío Pico's Historical Narrative.* [1877] Glendale: H. Clark Co., 1973. Editors: Martin Cole and Henry Welcome.

Ramirez, Jose Fernando. *Mexico During the War With the United States.* Columbia: University of Missouri, 1970.

Read, Benjamin Maurice. *Historia ilustrada de Nuevo México.* Santa Fe: Compania Impresora del Nuevo Mexico, 1911.

Read, Benjamin Maurice. *Illustrated History of New Mexico.* New York: Arno Press, 1976.

Rhoades, Elizabeth R. *Foreigners in Southern California During the Mexican Period.* San Francisco: R & E Research Associates, 1971.

Rios-Bustamante, Antonio. *Mexican Los Angeles: A Narrative and Pictorial History.* Encino, Ca.: Floricanto Press, 1991.

Sanchez Lamego, Miguel A. *Sitio y tomo del Alamo, 1836.* Mexico, D.F.: Editorial Militor Mexicana, 1966.

Seguin, Juan Nepomuceno. *Personal Memoirs of John N. Seguin. From the Year 1834 to the Retreat of General Woll from the City of San Antonio 1842.* San Antonio: 1858.

Sierra, Catalina. *El nacimento de México.* Mexico, D.F.: Universidad Nacional Autonoma de Mexico, 1960.

Smith, Wallace E. *This Land Was Ours: The Del Valles and Camulos.* Ventura, Calif.: Ventura County Historical Society, 1978.

Spicer, Edward H. *Cycles of Conquest: The Impact of Spain, Mexico, and the United States on the Indians of the Southwest.* Norman: University of Oklahoma Press, 1960.

Teja Zabre, Alfonso. *Lecciones de California*. México, D.F.: Universidad Nacional Autónoma de México, 1962.

Tenas Ramírez, Felipe, compiler. *Leyes fundamentales de México, 1808–1957*. México, D.F.: Editorial Porrúa, S.A., 1956–1957.

Timmons, Wilbert H. *Tadeo Ortiz: Mexican Colonizer and Reformer*. El Paso: The University of Texas, 1974.

Tolbert, Frank X. *The Day of San Jacinto*. New York: McGraw-Hill, 1959.

Trueba, Alfonso. *California: Tierra Perdida*. 2 vols. México, D.F.: Jus, 1958.

Valadez, Jose C. *Santa Ana y la guerra de Texas*. Mexico, D.F.: Imprenta Mundial, 1936.

Vazquez, Josefina (de Knauth). *Mexicanos y norteamericanos ante La Guerra del 47*. Mexico, D.F.: Sep-Setentas, 1972.

Vazquez, Josefina (de Knauth) . . *Establecimiento y pérdida del septentrion de Nueva España*. México, D.F.: El Colegio de México, 1974.

Weber, David J. *The Taos Trappers: The Fur Trade in the Far Southwest, 1540–1846*. Norman: University of Oklahoma Press, 1971.

Weber, David J. *The Mexican Frontier, 1821–1846: The American Southwest Under Mexico*. Albuquerque: University of New Mexico Press, 1982.

Weber, David J., ed. *Troubles in Texas, 1832: A Tejano Viewpoint from San Antonio with a Translation and Facsimile*. Dallas: Degolyer Library of Southern Methodist University, 1983.

Woodward, Arthur. *Lances at San Pasqual*. San Francisco: California Historical Society, 1948.

Wright, Doris Marion. *A Yankee in Mexican California: Abel Stearns, 1798–1848*. Santa Barbara: Wallace Hebberd, 1977.

Zalce y Rodriguez, Luis. *Apuntes para la historia de la masonería en México*. 2 vols. México, D.F.: 1950.

Aggression and Annexation, 1840–1900

Aguirre, Bernal Celso. *Joaquin Murrieta: Raiz y razon del movimiento chicano*. Mexico, D.F.: n.p., 1985.

Arnold, Elliot. *The Time of the Gringo*. New York: Knopf, 1953.

Ashbaugh, Carolyn. *Lucy Parsons: American Revolutionary*. Chicago: C.H. Kerr, 1976.

Bartlett, John R. *Personal Narrative of Exploration and Incidents in Texas, New Mexico, California, Sonora and Chihuahua*. 2 vols. Glorieta, New Mexico: Rio Grande Press, 1965.

Barr, Alwyn. *Reconstruction to Reform: Texas Politics, 1876–1906*. Austin, University of Texas Press, 1971.

Beckett, V.B. *Baca's Battle: Elfego Baca's Epic Gunfight at 'Frisco Plaza, N.M.*,

1884, As Reported at the Time, Together with Baca's Own Final Account of the Battle. Houston: Stagecoach Press, 1962.

Beers, George A. *Vásquez: or the Hunted Bandit of the San Joaquin.* New York: R.M. Dewitt, 1875.

Bell, Horace. *Reminiscences of a Ranger.* Santa Barbara: Wallace Hebberd, 1927.

Bell, Horace. *On the Old West Coast: Being Further Reminiscences of a Ranger.* New York: William Morrow, 1930. Reprint, New York: Arno Press, 1976.

Benson, Thomas Hart. *Thirty Years' Views; or, a History of the Working of the American Government from 1820 to 1850.* 2 vols. New York: D. Appleton and Co., 1854. Reprinted by Greenwood Press, New York, 1968.

Billington, Ray Allen. *The Protestant Crusade, 1800–1860: A Study of the Origins of American Nativism.* New York: Macmillan, 1938.

Billington, Ray Allen. *Westward Expansion: A History of the American Frontier.* New York: Macmillan, 1949.

Billington, Ray Allen. *The Far Western Frontier, 1830–1860.* New York: Harper and Row, 1956.

Billington, R. and A. Camarillo. *The American Southwest.* Los Angeles: Clark Memorial Library, UCLA, 1979.

Binkley, William C. *The Expansionist Movement in Texas, 1836–1850.* Berkeley: University of California Press, 1925.

Blanchard, Sarah Eliot. *Memories of a Child's Early California Days.* Los Angeles: Ward Ritchie Press, 1961.

Bliss, Charles R. *New Mexico.* Boston: Frank Wood, Printer, 1879.

Bliss, Charles R. *William Blackmore: A Case Study in the Economic Development of the West.* 2 vols. Denver: Bradford-Robinson, 1949.

Bradfute, Richard Wells. *The Court of Private Land Claims.* Albuquerque: University of New Mexico Press, 1975.

Brown, Richard Maxwell. *Strain of Violence: Historical Studies of American Violence and Vigilantism.* New York: Oxford University Press, 1975.

Browne, J. Ross, ed. *Report of the Debates in the Convention of California on the Formation of the State in September and October, 1949.* New York: John T. Towers, 1850.

Camarillo, Albert. *Chicanos in a Changing Society: From Mexican Pueblos to American Barrios in Santa Barbara and Southern California 1848–1930.* Cambridge: Harvard University Press, 1979.

Canales, José T. *Juan N. Cortina, Bandit or Patriot?* San Antonio: Artes Gráficas, 1951.

Castillo, Pedro and Alberto Camarillo. *Furia y Muerte: Los Bandidos Chicanos.* Los Angeles: Chicano Studies Center, UCLA, 1973.

Caughey, John W. *Hubert Howe Bancroft, Historian of the West.* Berkeley: University of California Press, 1946.

Caughey, John W. Gold is the Cornerstone. Berkeley: University of California Press, 1948.

Caughey, John W. Their Majesties the Mob. Chicago: University of Chicago Press, 1960.

Chavez, Angélico, Fray. But Time and Change: The Story of Padre Martínez of Taos, 1793–1867. Santa Fe: The Sunstone Press, 1981.

Cleland, Robert Glass. The Cattle on a Thousand Hills: Southern California, 1850–80. San Marino: The Henry E. Huntington Library, 1941.

Cleland, Robert Glass. From Wilderness to Empire. New York: Alfred A. Knopf, 1944.

Clendenen, Clarence E. Blood on the Border: The United States Army and the Mexican Irregulars. New York: Macmillan Co., 1969.

Colton, Walter. Three Years in California. Stanford, Cal.: Stanford University Press, 1949.

Conmy, Peter T. Romualdo Pacheco, Distinguished Californian of the Mexican and American Periods. San Francisco: Grand Parlor, Native Sons of the Golden West, 1957.

Cooke, Philip St. George. The Conquest of New Mexico and California. New York: Arno Press, 1976.

Cortes, Carlos, ed. The United States Conquest of California. New York: Arno Press, 1976.

Cruz, Gilberto R. and Marta Cruz. A Century of Service: The History of the Catholic Church in the Lower Rio Grande Valley. Harlingen: United Printers and Publishers, Inc., 1979.

DaCamara, Kathleen. Laredo on the Rio Grande. San Antonio: Naylor Company, 1949.

Dahrendorf, Alexander M. The Passionists of the Southwest: Or the Holy Brotherhood. Glorieta, N.M.: Rio Grande Press, 1968.

Dahrendorf, Alexander M., et al. The Penitentes of New Mexico. New York: Arno Press, 1974.

Dale, Edward Everett. The Indians of the Southwest, A Century of Development Under the United States. Norman: University of Oklahoma Press, 1949.

Davis, William Heath. Seventy-Five Years in California: A History of Events and Life in California. San Francisco: J. Howell, 1929.

Davis, William Watts Hart. El Gringo: or New Mexico and Her People. Santa Fe: Rydal Press, 1939.

Davis, Winfield J. History of Political Conventions in California, 1849–1882. Sacramento: California State Library, 1893.

Dawson, Joseph Martin. Jose Antonio Navarro: Co-creator of Texas. Waco, Tex.: Baylor University Press, 1969.

De León, Arnoldo. Apuntes Tejanos: An Index of Items Related to Mexican Americans in Nineteenth Century Texas. 2 vols. Sponsored by the Texas

State Historical Association. Ann Arbor, Mich.: Monograph Publishing, University Microfilms International, 1978–79.

De León, Arnoldo. *The Tejano Community, 1836–1900*. Albuquerque: University of New Mexico Press, 1982.

De León, Arnoldo. *They Called Them Greasers: Anglo Attitudes Toward Mexicans in Texas, 1821–1900*. Austin: University of Texas Press, 1984.

De León, Arnoldo. *In Re Ricardo Rodriguez: An Attempt at Chicano Disenfranchisement in San Antonio, Texas 1896–1897*. San Antonio: Caravel Press, 1979 or 1978.

De León, Arnoldo. *A Social History of Mexican Americans in Nineteenth Century Duval County*. San Diego, Tex.: County Commissioners' Court, 1978.

De León, Arnoldo. *San Angeleños: Mexican Americans in San Angelo, Texas*. San Angelo: Fort Concho Museum Press, 1985.

De León, Arnoldo and Kenneth L. Stewart. *Tejanos and the Numbers Game, A Socio-Historical Interpretation from the Federal Censuses, 1850–1900*. Albuquerque: University of New Mexico Press, 1989.

De Onis, Jose, ed. *The Hispanic Contribution to the State of Colorado*. Boulder: Westview Press, 1976.

Deutsch, Sara. *No Separate Refuge. Culture, Class, and Gender on an Anglo-Hispanic Frontier in the American Southwest, 1880–1940*. New York: Oxford University Press, 1987.

Dumke, Glenn. *The Boom of the Eighties in Southern California*. San Marino, Cal.: Huntington Library, 1944.

Duran, Tobias. *We Come as Friends: The Social and Historical Context of Nineteenth Century New Mexico*. Albuquerque: University of New Mexico, SHRI, 1984.

Ellison, William Henry. *A Self-Governing Dominion: California, 1849–1860*. Berkeley: University of California Press, 1950.

Fernández, José Emilio. *Cuarenta años de legislador: Biografía del Senador Casimiro Barela*. New York: Arno Press, 1976.

Fulton, Maurice G. *History of the Lincoln County War*. Edited by Robert N. Mullin. Tucson: University of Arizona Press, 1968.

Galvin, John, ed. *The Coming of Justice to California*. San Francisco: John Howell Books, 1963.

Ganaway, Loomis Morton. *New Mexico and the Sectional Controversy*. Albuquerque: University of New Mexico Press, 1944.

Garber, Paul Neff. *The Gadsden Treaty*. Philadelphia: Press of the University of Pennsylvania, 1924.

Gates, Paul W., ed. *California Ranchos and Farms, 1846–1862*. Madison, Wis.: State Historical Society, 1967.

Garza, Catarino E. *La era de Tuxtepec en México o sea Rusia en América*. San Jose.-Costa Rica: 1894.

Goldfinch, Charles. *Juan A. Cortina, 1842–1892: A Reappraisal.* Brownsville: Bishop's Print Shop, 1957.

Goldfinch, Charles and J.T. Canales. *Juan N. Cortina: Two Interpretations.* New York: Arno Press, 1974.

Gonzales, Michael G. *The Hispanic Elite of the Southwest.* El Paso: Texas Western Press, 1989.

Goodman, C.L. *The Establishment of State Government in California, 1846–1850.* New York: Macmillan, 1914.

Goss, Helen Rocco. *The California White Cap Murders: An Episode in Vigilantism.* Santa Barbara: Lawton and Alfred Kennedy, 1969.

Gregg, Andrew K. *New Mexico in the Nineteenth Century: A Pictorial History.* Albuquerque: University of New Mexico Press, 1968.

Gregg, R.D. *The Influence of Border Troubles on Relations Between the United States and Mexico, 1876–1910.* Baltimore: Johns Hopkins University, 1967.

Griggs, George. *History of Mesilla Valley or the Gadsen Purchase.* Mesilla, New Mexico: p.p. 1930.

Griswold del Castillo, Richard. *The Los Angeles Barrio, 1850–1890: A Social History.* Berkeley and Los Angeles: University of California Press, 1979.

Griswold del Castillo, Richard. *The Treaty of Guadalupe Hidalgo, A Legacy of Conflict.* Norman: University of Oklahoma Press, 1990.

Grivas, Theodore. *Military Governments in California, with a Chapter on Their Prior Use in Louisiana, Florida and New Mexico.* Glendale, Cal.: Arthur H. Clarke Co., 1963.

Guinn, James M. *A History of California and an Extended History of Los Angeles and Environs.* 2 vols. Los Angeles: Cole-Holmquist Press, 1915.

Hammond, George P. *The Treaty of Guadalupe Hidalgo, 1848.* Berkeley: Friends of the Bancroft Library, 1949.

Harlow, Neal. *California Conquered: War and Peace on the Pacific, 1846–1850.* Berkeley: University of California Press, 1982.

Hart, John M. *Los anarquistas y la clase obrera mexicana, 1860–1931.* Mexico, D.F.: Siglo Veintiuno, 1980.

Hayes, Benjamin. *Pioneer Notes from the Diaries of Judge Benjamin Hayes, 1849–1875.* New York: Arno Press, 1976.

Heizer, Robert F. and Alan J. Almquist. *The Other Californians: Prejudice and Discrimination Under Spain, Mexico and the United States to 1920.* Los Angeles: University of California Press, 1971.

Hollon, W. Eugene. *Frontier Violence: Another Look.* New York: Oxford University Press, 1974.

Horn, Calvin. *New Mexico's Troubled Years: The Story of the Early Territorial Governors.* Albuquerque: Horn and Wallace, 1963.

Horgan, Paul. *The Centuries of Santa Fe.* New York: E.P. Dutton and Company, 1956.

Horgan, Paul. *Lamy of Santa Fe.* New York: Farrar, Straus and Giroux, 1975.

Horsman, Reginald. *Expansion and American Indian Policy, 1783–1812.* East Lansing: Michigan State University Press, 1967.

Howe, Charles E.B. *Joaquin Murieta de Castillo.* San Francisco: Commercial Book and Job Steam Printing Establishment, 1858.

Johannsen, Robert W. *To the Halls of the Montezumas.* New York: Oxford University Press, 1985.

Keleher, William A. *Turmoil in New Mexico, 1846–1868.* Santa Fe: Rydal Press, 1952.

Keleher, William A. *The Fabulous Frontier: Twelve New Mexico Items.* Albuquerque: University of New Mexico Press, 1962.

Keleher, William A. *The Maxwell Land Grant: A New Mexico item.* Santa Fe: Rydal Press, 1942.

Keleher, William A. *Violence in Lincoln County, 1869–1881.* Albuquerque: University of New Mexico Press, 1952.

Kilgore, D.E. *A Ranger Legacy: 150 Years of Service to Texas.* Austin: Madrona Press, 1973.

Lamar, Howard R. *The Far Southwest, 1846–1912: A Territorial History.* New Haven: Yale University Press, 1966.

Larson, Robert W. *New Mexico Populism: A Study of Radical Protest in a Western Territory.* Boulder: Colorado Associated University Press, 1974.

Larson, Robert W. *New Mexico's Quest for Statehood.* Albuquerque: University of New Mexico Press, 1968.

Long, Jeff. *Duel of Eagles: The Mexican and U.S. Fight for the Alamo.* New York: William Morrow, 1990.

Loomis, Noel M. *The Texas-Santa Fe Pioneers.* Norman: University of Oklahoma Press, 1958.

Loosley, Allyn Campbell. *Foreign Born Population of California, 1848–1920.* San Francisco: R. & E. Research Associates, 1971.

López y Rivas, Gilberto. *La guerra del 47 y la resistencia popular a la ocupación.* México, D.F.: Editorial Nuestro Tiempo, 1976.

Lord, Walter. *A Time to Stand.* New York: Harper and Row, 1961.

Loyola, Mary. *The American Occupation of New Mexico 1821–1852.* New York: Arno Press, 1976.

McCall, George. *New Mexico in 1850.* Norman: University of Oklahoma Press, 1968.

Mares, E.A. et al. *Padre Martinez: New Perspectives from Taos.* Santa Fe: Millicent Rogers Museum, 1988.

Medina Castro, Manuel. *El gran despojo: Texas, Nuevo Mexico, California.* Mexico, D.F.: Editorial Diogenes, 1971.

Meinig, D.W. *Imperial Texas: An Interpretive Essay in Cultural Geography.* Austin: University of Texas Press, 1969.

Meketa, J. Dorgan, ed. *Legacy of Honor: The Life of Rafael Chacon, A Nineteenth Century New Mexican*. Albuquerque: University of New Mexico, 1986.

Menchaca, Antonio. *Memoirs*. San Antonio: Yanaguana Society Publications, 1937.

Merk, Frederick. *Manifest Destiny and Mission in American History*. New York: Vintage Books, 1963.

Mexico. Comision Pesquisidora de la Frontera del Norte. *Report of the Mexican Commission on the Northern Frontier Question*. New York, 1875.

Montejano, David. *Anglos and Mexicans in the Making of Texas, 1836–1986*. Austin: University of Texas Press, 1987.

Morefield, Richard. *The Mexican Adaptation in American California, 1846–1875*. San Francisco: R & E Associates, 1971.

Mowry, Sylvester. *Memoir of the Proposed Territory of Arizona*. Washington: H. Polkinhorn printer, 1857.

Nance, Joseph Milton. *After San Jacinto: The Texas-Mexican Frontier, 1836–1841*. Austin: University of Texas Press, 1963.

Nance, Joseph Milton. *Attack and Counterattack: The Texas-Mexican Frontier, 1842*. Austin: University of Texas Press, 1964.

Nostrand, Richard L. *Los chicanos: Geografía histórica regional*. Mexico, D.F.: Sep Setentas, 1976.

Otero, Miguel Antonio. *My Life on the Frontier. Vol. 1: 1864–1882, Incidents and Characters of the Period When Kansas, Colorado, and New Mexico Were Passing Through the Last of Their Wild and Romantic Years*. New York: Press of the Pioneers, 1935.

Otero, Miguel Antonio. *My Life on the Frontier. Vol. 2: 1882–1897, Death Knell of a Territory and Birth of a State*. Foreword by George P. Hammond. Albuquerque: University of New Mexico Press, 1939.

Otero, Miguel Antonio. *My Nine Years as Governor of the Territory of New Mexico, 1897–1906*. Foreword by Marion Dargan. Albuquerque: University of New Mexico Press, 1940.

Paz, Ireneo. *Joaquin Murieta: His Exploits in the State of California*. Chicago: 1937.

Pearson, Jim B. *The Maxwell Land Grant*. Norman: University of Oklahoma Press, 1961.

Peña y Reyes, Antonio. *Algunos documentos sobre el tratado de Guadalupe y la situación de México durante la invasión americana*. México, D.F.: Secretaría de Relaciones Exteriores, 1930.

Pierce, Frank C. *A Brief History of the Lower Rio Grande Valley*. Menasha, Wis.: George Banta Publishing Company, 1917.

Pitt, Leonard. *The Decline of the Californios: A Social History of the Spanish-Speaking Californios, 1846–1890*. Berkeley: University of California Press, 1966.

Pomeroy, Earl S. *The Territories and the United States, 1861–1890: Studies in Colonial Administration.* Philadelphia: University of Pennsylvania Press, 1947.

Price, Glenn W. *Origins of the War with Mexico: The Polk-Stockton Intrigue.* Austin: University of Texas, 1967.

Quaife, Milo M., ed. *The Diary of James K. Polk: During His Presidency, 1845–1849.* Chicago: A.C. McClury and Co., 1910.

Rambo, Ralph. *Traling the California Bandit Tiburcio Vásquez.* San Jose: Rosicrucian Press, 1968.

Rayburn, John C. and Virginia Kemp Rayburn, eds. *Century of Conflict, 1821–1913.* New York: Arno Press, 1976.

Rendón Lozano, Ruben. *Viva Tejas: The Story of the Native Mexican Born Patriots of the Republic of Texas.* San Antonio and Houston: Southern Literary Institute, 1936.

Richardson, Rupert N. *The Comanche Barrier to South Plains Settlement.* Glendale: Arthur H. Clark, 1933.

Richardson, Rupert N. *The Frontier of Northwest Texas, 1846–1876: Advance and Defense by the Pioneer Settlers of the Cross Timers and Prairies.* Glendale: Arthur H. Clark Company, 1963.

Ridge, John R. *The Life and Times of Joaquin Murieta.* Norman: University of Oklahoma, 1955.

Roa Barcena, Jose M. *Recuerdos de la invasion norteamericana, 1846–1848.* Mexico, D.F.: Editorial Porrua, 1947.

Rodriguez, Jose Maria. *Memoirs of Early Texas.* San Antonio: Standard Printing Co., 1913.

Rojas, Manuel. *Joaquin Murrieta, "El Patrio."* Mexicali: Gobierno del Estado de Baja California, 1986.

Rosenbaum, Robert J. *Mexicano Resistence in the Southwest: "The Sacred Right of Self-Preservation."* Austin: University of Texas Press, 1981.

Royce, Josiah. *California From the Conquest in 1846 to the Second Vigilance Committee in San Francisco: A Study of American Character.* New York: Alfred A. Knopf, 1948.

Ruiz, Manuel. *Mexican American Legal Heritage in the Southwest.* Los Angeles: n.p., 1972.

Samora, Julian, et al. *Gunpower Justice: A Reassessment of the Texas Rangers.* South Bend: University of Notre Dame Press, 1979.

Sawyer, Eugene T. *The Life and Career of Tiburcio Vásquez.* Oakland: Biobooks, 1944.

Schwartz, Rosalie. *Across the Rio to Freedom: U.S. Negroes in Mexico.* El Paso: University of Texas, 1975.

Schroeder, John H. *Mr. Polk's War: American Opposition and Dissent, 1846–1848.* Madison: University of Wisconsin Press, 1973.

Sheridan, Thomas E. *Los Tucsonenses, The Mexican Community in Tucson, 1854–1941.* Tucson: University of Arizona Press, 1986.

Simmons, Marc. *The Little Lion of the Southwest: A Life of Manuel Antonio Chávez.* Chicago: Swallow Press, 1973.

Smylie, Vernon. *A Noose for Chipita.* Corpus Christi: New Syndicate Press, 1970.

Sonnichsen, Charles L. *The El Paso Salt War, 1877.* El Paso: Texas Western Press, 1961.

Soto, Antonio R. *Chicano Reaction to Social Change in Northern California, 1848–1908.* San Jose: Spartan Bookstore, 1978.

Stambaugh, J. Lee and Lillian J. Stambaugh. *The Lower Rio Grande Valley of Texas.* San Antonio: The Naylor Co., 1954.

Stanley, F. (Stanley F.L. Crocchiola). *Giant in Lilliput: The Story of Donaciano Vigil.* Pampa, Tex.: Pampa Print Shop, 1963.

Stanley, F. (Stanley F.L. Crocchiola). *The Grant That Maxwell Bought.* Denver: World Press, 1952.

Stanley, F. (Stanley F.L. Crocchiola). *The Private War of Ike Stockton.* Denver: World Press, 1959.

Stanley, F. (Stanley F.L. Crocchiola). *The Civil War in New Mexico.* Denver: World Press, 1960.

Stephenson, Nathaniel W. *Texas and the Mexican War: A Chronicle of the Winning of the Southwest.* New Haven: Yale University Press, 1931.

Stratton, Porter. *The Territorial Press of New Mexico, 1834–1912.* Albuquerque: University of New Mexico Press, 1969.

Sunseri, Alvin R. *Seeds of Discord: New Mexico in the Aftermath of the American Conquest, 1846–1861.* Chicago: Nelson-Hall, 1979.

Taylor, Morris F. *O.P. McMains and the Maxwell Land Grant Conflict.* Tucson: University of Arizona Press, 1979.

Thompson, Jerry Don. *Vaqueros in Blue and Gray.* Austin: Presidial Press, 1974.

Thompson, Jerry Don. *Warm Weather and Bad Whiskey: The 1886 Laredo Election Riot.* El Paso: Texas Western Press, 1991.

Thompson Fr. Joseph A., O.F.M. *El Gran Capitan: José De La Guerra. A Historical Biographical Study.* Los Angeles: Cabrera And Sons, 1961.

Tijerina, Andrés. *The History of Mexican Americans in Lubbock County.* Lubbock: Texas Tech University, 1977.

El Tratado de Guadalupe Hidalgo, 1848/Treaty of Guadalupe Hidalgo, 1848: A Facsimile Reproduction of the Mexican Instrument of Ratification and Related Documents. Sacramento: Telefact Foundation with California State Department of Education, 1968.

Twitchell, Ralph Emerson. *The History of the Military Occupation of the Territory of New Mexico.* New York: Arno Press, 1976.

Tyler, Ronnie C. *Santiago Vidaurri and the Southern Confederacy.* Austin: Texas State Historical Association, 1974.

Vigil, Diego. *Early Chicano Guerilla Fighters.* n.p.: 1975.

Vigil, Maurillio. *Los Patrones, Profiles of Hispanic Political Leaders.* Washington, D.C.: University Press of America, 1980.

Vignes, David M. *The Revolutionary Decades.* Austin: University of Texas, 1965.

Wagoner, Jáy J. *Arizona Territory, 1863–1912: A Political History.* Tucson: University of Arizona Press, 1970.

Wagoner, Jáy J. *Early Arizona: Prehistory to Civil War.* Tucson: University of Arizona, 1975.

Webb, Walter Prescott. *The Great Plains.* New York: Grosset and Dunlap, 1931. Reprint, Austin: University of Texas Press, 1964.

Webb, Walter Prescott. *The Texas Rangers: A Century of Frontier Defense.* Cambridge: Houghton Mifflin Co., 1935. Reprint, Austin: University of Texas Press, 1965.

Weinberg, Albert K. *Manifest Destiny: A Study of Nationalist Expansionism in American History.* Chicago: Quadrangle Books, 1963.

Westphall, Victor. *The Public Domain in New Mexico, 1854–1891.* Albuquerque: University of New Mexico Press, 1965.

Westphall, Victor. *Thomas Benton Catron and His Era.* Tucson: University of Arizona Press, 1973.

Wiebe, Robert H. *The Opening of American Society: From the Adoption of the Constitution to the Eve of Disunion.* New York: Alfred A. Knopf, 1984.

Early 20th Century, 1900–1940

Anders, Evan. *Boss Rule in South Texas: The Progressive Era.* Austin: University of Texas Press, 1987.

Balderrama, Francisco E. *In Defense of La Raza: The Los Angeles Mexican Consulate and the Mexican Community, 1929 to 1936.* Tucson: University of Arizona Press, 1982.

Bogardus, Emory S. *Essentials of Americanization.* Los Angeles: University of Southern California Press, 1923.

Bogardus, Emory S. *The Mexican in the United States.* Los Angeles: University of Southern California, 1943.

Breckenridge, R. Douglas and Francisco O. García-Treto. *Iglesia Presbyteriana: A History of Presbyterians and Mexican Americans of the Southwest.* San Antonio: Trinity University Press, 1974.

Broadbent, Elizabeth. *The Distribution of Mexican Populations in the United States (1941).* San Francisco: R. & E. Research Associates, 1972.

Córdova, Alfred C. and Charles B. Judah. *Octaviano Larrazolo: A Political Portrait.* Albuquerque: Division of Research, Department of Government, University of New Mexico, 1954.

Cortés, Carlos E., ed. *Church Views of the Mexican American.* New York: Arno Press, 1974.

Cortés, Carlos E., ed. *Education and the Mexican American.* New York: Arno Press, 1974.

Cortés, Carlos E., ed. *Hispano Culture of New Mexico.* New York: Arno Press, 1976.

Cortés, Carlos E., ed. *Perspectives on Mexican-American Life.* New York: Arno Press, 1974.

Cortés, Carlos E., ed. *The New Mexican Hispano.* New York: Arno Press, 1974.

Crawford, Stanley. *Mayordomo: Chronicle of an Acequia in Northern New Mexico.* Albuquerque: University of New Mexico Press, 1988.

De León, Arnoldo. *Ethnicity in the Sunbelt: A History of Mexican Americans in Houston.* Houston: Mexican American Studies, University of Houston, 1989.

Espinosa, Gilberto, Tibo J. Chaves, and Carter M. Ward. *El Rio Abajo.* Belen, N.M.: Pampa Print Shop. n.d.

Fincher, E. B. *Spanish-Americans as a Political Factor in New Mexico, 1912–1950.* New York: Arno Press, 1974.

Foley, Douglas E., et al. *From Peones to Politicos: Ethnic Relations in a South Texas Town 1900–1977.* Austin: Center for Mexican American Studies, 1977.

Galarza, Ernesto. *Barrio Boy.* South Bend, Ind.: University of Notre Dame Press, 1975.

Gamio, Manuel. *Forjando patria (Pro nacionalismo).* [1916] Mexico, D.F.: Libreria de Porrua, 1960.

Gamio, Manuel. *The Mexican Immigrant: His Life Story.* Chicago: University of Chicago Press, 1930.

Gamio, Manuel. *The Life Story of the Mexican Immigrant: Autobiographic Documents Collected by Manuel Gamio.* Chicago: University of Chicago Press, 1931.

Garcia, Juan R., et al, eds. "Mexicans in the Midwest," *Perspectives in Mexican American Studies.* Vol. 2, 1989.

García, Mario T. *Desert Immigrants: The Mexicans of El Paso, 1880–1920.* New Haven: Yale University Press, 1981.

García, Mario T. *Mexican Americans, Leadership, Ideology and Identity, 1930–1960.* New Haven:Yale University Press, 1989.

Garza, Edward D. *LULAC: League of United Latin American Citizens.* San Francisco: R & E Research Associates, 1972.

Getty, Harry T. *Mexican Society in the Community of Tucson, Arizona.* Tucson: Arizona State Museum Library, University of Arizona, 1949.

Gill, Mario. *Sinarquismo: Su origin, su essencia, su mision.* Mexico, D.F.: Ediciones Club del Libro Mexico, 1944.

Gomez-Quiñones, Juan. *Sembradores, Ricardo Flores Magón y el Partido Liberal Mexicano: A Eulogy and Critique.* Aztlán Publications, Monograph no. 5. Los Angeles: Aztlán Publications, Chicano Studies Center, University of California, 1976.

Hernández, José Amaro. *Mutual Aid for Survival: The Case of the Mexican American.* Melbourne, Fla.: Krieger Publishing Company, Inc., 2nd ed., 1983.

Hidalgo, Ernesto. *Protección del Mexicano en los Estados Unidos.* Mexico, D.F.: Ministerio de Relaciones Exteriores, 1940.

Hoffman, Abraham. *Unwanted Mexican Americans in the Great Depression: Repatriation Pressures, 1929–1939.* Tucson: University of Arizona Press, 1974.

Holmes, Jack E. *Politics in New Mexico.* Albuquerque: The University of New Mexico Press, 1967.

Johansen, Sigurd. *Rural Social Organization in a Spanish-American Culture Area.* Albuquerque: University of New Mexico Press, 1948.

Jones, Anita. *Conditions Surrounding Mexicans in Chicago.* San Francisco: R. & E. Research Associates, 1971.

Jones, Robert C. and Louis R. Wilson. *The Mexican in Chicago.* Chicago: Comity Commission of the Chicago Church Federation, 1931.

Lemert, Edwin M. *Administration of Justice to Minority Groups in Los Angeles County.* Berkeley: University of California Press, 1948.

Lopez, Jose Timoteo. *La historia de la Sociedad Proteccion Mutua de Trabajadores Unidos.* New York: Comet Press, 1958.

Lloyd, Jane Dole and Elena Azaola. *La formación y actividades políticas del Partido Líberal Mexicano en 1905–1906.* México, D.F.: Secretaria de Educacion Publica, 1979.

Lowitt, Richard. *Bronson M. Cutting: Progressive Politician.* Albuquerque: University of New Mexico Press, 1992.

Macias, Anna. *Against All Odds: The Feminist Movement in Mexico to 1940.* Westport: Greenwood Press, 1982.

MacLean, Robert M. *The Northern Mexican.* New York: Home Missions Council, 1930.

Marquez, Benjamin. *LULAC, The Evolution of a Mexican American Organization.* Austin: University of Texas Press, 1993.

Martin, Roscoe. *The Peoples Party in Texas: A Study in Third Party Politics.* Austin: University of Texas, 1933.

Montejano, David. *Race, Labor Repression, and Capitalist Agriculture Notes* from South Texas, 1920–1930. Berkeley: University of California Institute for the Study of Social Change, Working Paper Series no. 102, 1977.

Montiel, Olvera J., ed. Year Book of the Latin American Population of Texas. Mexico, D.F.: n.p., 1939.

Muñoz, Ignacio. La verdad sobre los gringos. Mexico, D.F.: Ediciones Populares, 1927.

Paredes, Americo. "With His Pistol in His Hand": A Border Ballad and Its Hero. Austin: University of Texas Press, 1958.

Perales, Alonso S. El Mexicano Americano y la politica del sur de Texas. San Antonio: [s.n.], 1931.

Perales, Alonso S. En Defensa de Mi Raza. San Antonio: Artes Graficas, 1937.

Raat, W. Dirk. Revoltosos: Mexico's Rebels in the United States, 1903–1923. College Station: Texas A & M University Press, 1981.

Reisler, Mark. By the Sweat of Their Brow: Mexican Immigrant Labor in the United States, 1900–1940. Westport: Greenwood Press, 1976.

Romo, Ricardo. East Los Angeles History of a Barrio. Austin: University of Texas, 1983.

Sanchez, George I. Forgotten People: A Study of New Mexicans. Albuquerque: University of New Mexico Press, 1940.

Sandos, James A. Rebellion in the Borderlands: Anarchism and the Plan of San Diego, 1904–1923. Norman: University of Oklahoma Press, 1992.

Santivañez, Enrique. Ensayo acerca de la immigracion mexicana a Estados Unidos. San Antonio: The Clegg Co., 1930.

Sickels, Alice L. and Henry L. Sickels. The Mexican National Community in St. Paul in February 1935. St. Paul: International Institute, 1935.

Sloss-Vento, Adela. Alonso S. Perales: His Struggle for the Rights of Mexican-Americans. San Antonio: Artes Graficas, 1977.

Stowell, Jay, S. A Study of Mexicans and Spanish Americans in the United States. New York: Home Missions Council, 1920.

Taylor, Paul. An American-Mexican Frontier: Neuces County, Texas. Chapel Hill: The University of North Carolina Press, 1934.

Torres Pares, Javier. La revolución sin frontera. El partido Liberal Mexicano y las relaciones entre el movimiento obrero de Mexico y el de Estados Unidos, 1900–1923. Mexico, D.F.: Universidad Nacional Autónoma de México, 1990.

Valdes, Daniel T. A Political History of New Mexico. n.p., 1971.

Valdes, Daniel T. The Spanish Speaking People of the Southwest. Denver: Works Progress Administration Program of Education and Recreation of the Colorado State Department of Education, 1938.

Weigle, Marta. Brothers of Light, Brothers of Blood: The Penitentes of the Southwest. Albuquerque: University of New Mexico Press, 1976.

Zamora, Emilio. The World of the Mexican Worker in Texas. College Station: Texas A & M University Press, 1993.

Zeleny, Carolyn. *Relations Between The Spanish Americans and Anglo-Americans in New Mexico.* New York: Arno Press, 1974.

Mid-Twentieth Century, 1940s–1960s

Acuña, Rodolfo. *A Community Under Siege: A Chronicle of Chicanos East of the Los Angeles River, 1945–1975.* Los Angeles: Chicano Studies Research Center, UCLA, 1984.

Allsup, Carl. *The American G.I. Forum: Origins and Evolution.* Austin: Center for Mexican American Studies, University of Texas, 1982.

Carter, Thomas P. *Mexican Americans in School: A History of Educational Neglect.* New York: College Entrance Examinations Board, 1970.

Colorado Commission on Spanish-Surnamed Citizens. *The Status of Spanish-Surnamed Citizens in Colorado. Report to the General Assembly.* Greeley: Colorado, 1967.

Cooke, W. Henry. *People of the Southwest: Patterns of Freedom and Prejudice.* New York: Anti-Defamation League of the B'nai B'rith, 1951.

Coordinator of Inter-American Affairs. *Spanish Speaking Americans in the War: The Southwest.* Washington, D.C.: Coordinator of Inter-American Affairs and Office of War Information, 1943.

Cortés, Carlos E., ed. *The Mexican American and the Law.* New York: Arno Press, 1974.

Cuellar, Robert A. *A Social and Political History of the Mexican American Population of Texas, 1929–1963.* San Francisco: R & E Research Associates, 1974.

D'Antonio, William and William Form. *Influentials in Two Borders Cities: A Study in Community Decision-Making.* South Bend: University of Notre Dame Press, 1965.

Del Castillo, Adelaida R. ed. *Between Borders, Essays on Mexicana/Chicana History.* Encino: Floricanto, 1990.

Department of Defense. *Hispanics in America's Defense.* Washington, D.C.: Office of the Deputy Assistant Secretary of Defense and Safety Policy, the Pentagon, n.d.

Edmondson, Munro S. *Los Manitos: A Study of Institutional Values.* New Orleans: Tulane University Press, Middle American Research Institute, 1957.

Galarza, Ernesto. *Merchants of Labor: The Mexican Bracero Story, An Account of the Managed Migration of Mexican Farm Workers in California, 1942–1960.* Charlotte and Santa Barbara: McNally and Loftin, 1964.

Galarza, Ernesto. *Farm Workers and Agribusiness in California, 1947–1960.* South Bend, Ind.: Notre Dame University Press, 1977.

Galarza, Ernesto. *Spiders in the House and Workers in the Field.* Notre Dame: University of Notre Dame Press, 1970.

Garcia, Juán Romón. *Operation Wetback: The Mass Deportation of Mexican Undocumented Workers in 1954.* Westport: Greenwood Press, 1980.

Garcia, Mario. *Mexican Americans: Leadership, Ideology and Identity, 1930–1960.* New Haven: Yale University Press, 1989.

Gonzalez, Isabel. *Stepchildren of a Nation: The Status of Mexican-Americans.* New York: American Committee for Protection of Foreign Born, 1947.

Grebler, Leo, Joan W. Moore, and Ralph C. Guzmán. *The Mexican-American People: The Nation's Second Largest Minority.* New York: Macmillan Co., Free Press, 1970.

Griffith, Beatrice. *American Me.* Boston: Houghton Mifflin Co., 1948.

Guzman, Ralph. *The Political Socialization of The Mexican-American People.* New York: Arno Press, 1976.

Holmes, Jack E. *Politics in New Mexico.* Albuquerque: University of New Mexico Press, 1967.

Jones, Robert C. *Mexican War Workers in the United States: The Mexico–United States Manpower Recruiting Program, 1942–1944.* Washington, D.C.: Pan American Union, 1945.

Kibbe, Pauline R. *Latin Americans in Texas.* Albuquerque: University of New Mexico Press, 1946.

Kingrea, Nellie W. *History of the First Ten Years of the Texas Good Neighbor Commission.* Fort Worth: Texas Christian University Press, 1954.

Land, John Hart. *Voluntary Associations Among Mexican Americans in San Antonio.* New York: Arno Press, 1976.

League of United Latin American Citizens. *LULAC in Action: A Report on the "Little School of the 400."* n.p.: 1960.

Lopez, Lino M., ed. *Colorado Latin American Personalities.* Denver: A.M. Pinter, 1959.

Madsen, William. *Mexican-Americans of South Texas.* New York: Holt Rinehart & Winston, 1964.

Mazon, Mauricio. *The Zoot-Suite Riots: The Psychology of Symbolic Annihilation.* Austin: University of Texas, 1984.

Minnesota. Governor's Human Rights Commission. *The Mexican in Minnesota: A Report to Governor C. Elmer Anderson by the Governor's Interracial Council.* St. Paul: Governor's Human Rights Commission, 1953. Reprint, San Francisco: R & E Research Associates, 1979.

Moore, Joan W. and Frank Mittlelbach. *Residential Segregation in the Urban Southwest.* Los Angeles: Mexican American Study Project, University of California, 1966.

Morgan, Patricia. *Shame of a Nation, A Documented Story of a Police State Terror*

Against Mexican Americans in the U.S.A. Los Angeles: CPFB (Committee for Protection of Foreign Born), 1954.

Morin, Raúl. *Among the Valiant: Mexican-Americans in WW II and Korea.* Alhambra, Cal.: Borden Publishing Co., 1966.

Ortega, Joaquín. *New Mexico's Opportunity: A Message to My Fellow New Mexicans.* Albuquerque: University of New Mexico Press, 1942.

Perales, Alonso S. *Are We Good Neighbors?* San Antonio: Artes Graficas, 1948.

Ramos, Henry A. *A People Forgotten, A Dream Pursued: The History of the American G.I. Forum 1948–1972.* Henry A.J. Ramos. [s.i.]: The Forum, 1983.

Roeder, Sandra. *A Study of the Situation of Mexican Americans in the Southwest.* Washington, D.C.: Community Relations Service, U.S. Department of Justice, 1967.

Rose, Arnold M., el. *Race Prejudice and Discrimination.* New York: Alfred A. Knopf, 1951.

Ross, Fred W. *Community Organization in Mexican-American Communities.* Los Angeles: American Council on Race Relations, 1947.

Ross, Fred W. *Get Out If You Can, The Saga of Sal si Puedes.* San Francisco: California Federation for Civic Unity, 1953.

Samora, Julian, ed. *La Raza: Forgotten Americans.* South Bend: University of Notre Dame Press, 1966.

Samora, Julian and Richard A. Lamanna. *Mexican Americans in a Midwest Metropolis: A Study of East Chicago.* Los Angeles: University of California. Mexican-American Project, 1967.

San Miguel, Guadalupe. *"Let All of Them Take Heed," Mexican Americans and the Campaign for Educational Equality.* Austin: University of Texas Press, 1987.

Sandoval, Moises. *Our Legacy: The First Fifty years.* Washington, D.C.: LULAC, 1979.

Shelton, Edgar Green. *Political Conditions Among Texas Mexicans Along the Rio Grande.* San Francisco: R & E Research Associates, 1974.

Simmons, Ozzie. *Anglo Americans and Mexican Americans in South Texas.* New York: Arno Press, 1974.

Tuck, Ruth D. *Not with the Fist: Mexican-Americans in a Southwest City.* New York: Harcourt, Brace & Co., 1946.

Tyandsen, Carl. *Education for Citizens, A Foundation Experience.* Santa Cruz: Foundation Inc., n.d.

Valdes y Tapia, Daniel. *Hispanics and American Politics: A Sociological Analysis and Description of the Political Role, Status, and Voting Behavior of Americans with Spanish Names.* New York: Arno Press, 1976.

Wiley, Tom. *Public School Education in New Mexico.* Albuquerque: University of New Mexico Press, 1965.

Woods, Francis Jerome. *Mexican Ethnic Leadership in San Antonio, Texas.* Washington, D.C.: The Catholic University Press, 1949.

Zelney, Carolyn. *Relations Between the Spanish Americans and Anglo Americans in New Mexico. A Study of the Conflict in a Dual Ethnic Situation.* New York: Arno Press, 1974.

Index